THE RECEPTION OF
THE CHURCH FATHERS
IN THE WEST

THE RECEPTION OF THE CHURCH FATHERS IN THE WEST

From the Carolingians to the Maurists

EDITED BY

IRENA BACKUS

VOLUME ONE

BRILL ACADEMIC PUBLISHERS, INC.
BOSTON • LEIDEN
2001

Library of Congress Cataloging-in-Publication Data

The reception of the church fathers in the West: from the Carolingians to the Maurists/edited by Irena Backus.
    p. cm.
   Originally published: Leiden: E.J. Brill, 1997.
   Includes bibliographical references and index.
   ISBN 0–391–04120–7
    1. Fathers of the church—Study and teaching—History. I. Backus,
Irena Dorota, 1950–

BR60 .R43 2001
270.1'07—dc21

2001043488

ISBN 0–391–04120–7

PRINTED IN THE UNITED STATES OF AMERICA

CONTENTS

Volume One

The Preface ix
The Editor's Introduction xi
List of Contributors xxv

PART ONE
PATRISTIC SOURCES AND THEIR USES UNTIL *CA*. 1200

1. The Texture of Tradition. The Role of the Church Fathers
in Carolingian Theology
  Willemien OTTEN 3

2. The Reception of the Church Fathers in Canon Law
  Jean WERCKMEISTER 51

3. The Church Fathers and the *Glossa ordinaria*
  E. Ann MATTER 83

4. The Church Fathers and the *Sentences* of Peter Lombard
  Jacques-Guy BOUGEROL 113

5. *Sic et non*: Patristic Authority between Refusal and
Acceptance: Anselm of Canterbury, Peter Abelard and
Bernard of Clairvaux
  Burcht PRANGER 165

PART TWO
PATRISTIC SOURCES AND THEIR USES IN THE LATER MIDDLE AGES

6. Robert Grosseteste and the Church Fathers
  Neil LEWIS 197

7. The Patristic sources of the *Legenda aurea*.
A Research Report
  Barbara FLEITH 231

8. The Church Fathers and *auctoritates* in Scholastic
Theology to Bonaventure
    Jacques-Guy BOUGEROL 289

9. Thomas Aquinas and the Fathers of the Church
    Leo J. ELDERS 337

10. The Reception of Augustine in the Later Middle Ages
    Eric Leland SAAK 367

11. *Memores pristinae perfectionis.* The Importance of the Church
Fathers for *Devotio moderna*
    Nikolaus STAUBACH 405

Volume Two

PART THREE

RENAISSANCE, REFORMATION, COUNTER-REFORMATION

12. Italian Renaissance Learning and the Church Fathers
    Charles STINGER 473

13. Gratian's *Decretum* as a source of Patristic Knowledge in
the Italian Renaissance. The example of Timoteo Maffei's *In
sanctam rusticitatem* (1454)
    David RUTHERFORD 511

14. Erasmus and the Church Fathers
    Jan DEN BOEFT 537

15. Martin Luther and the Church Fathers
    Manfred SCHULZE 573

16. Ulrich Zwingli, Martin Bucer and the Church Fathers
    Irena BACKUS 627

17. John Calvin and the Church Fathers
    Johannes VAN OORT 661

18. The Fathers in Counter-Reformation Theology in the
Pre-Tridentine Period
    Ralph KEEN 701

19. The Authority attributed to the Early Church in the
Centuries of Magdeburg and in the *Ecclesiastical Annals* of
Caesar Baronius
  Enrico NORELLI 745

20. English Translations of the Latin Fathers, 1517–1611
  Mark VESSEY 775

PART FOUR
SEVENTEENTH AND EARLY EIGHTEENTH CENTURY

21. The Fathers in Calvinist Orthodoxy: Patristic Scholarship
  Irena BACKUS 839

22. The Fathers in Calvinist Orthodoxy: Systematic Theology
  E.P. MEIJERING 867

23. The Society of Jesus and the Church Fathers in the
Sixteenth and Seventeenth Century
  Dominique BERTRAND 889

24. The Fathers in Seventeenth Century Roman
Catholic Theology
  Jean-Louis QUANTIN 951

25. The Fathers in Seventeenth Century Anglican Theology
  Jean-Louis QUANTIN 987

26. The Benedictines of the Congregation of St. Maur and
the Church Fathers
  Daniel-Odon HUREL 1009

Indexes 1039
  Subject Index 1041
  Index of Ancient Authors 1048
  Index of Modern Authors 1071

PREFACE

The present volume would never have seen the light of day without the commitment of several individuals and institutions. My warmest thanks go first and foremost to the contributors (all eminent specialists in the field) for the worthwhile effort they put into their essays. Thanks also to the translators, Antoinina Bevan, David Gathercole, Ivan Duric, Pascale Renaud, Liam McCarney and James Greig, all of whom showed a truly selfless devotion to the task and who put up patiently with the various suggestions made by the editor. I should also like to express my gratitude to the many colleagues (some of whom have preferred to remain anonymous) who advised me over the years. Particular thanks go to Heiko Oberman (University of Arizona), Lesley Smith (Linacre College, Oxford), Michel Grandjean and Silke Cornu (University of Geneva), Alfred Schindler (University of Zurich) and Pierre Petitmengin (École Normale Supérieure, Paris). Among the institutions that made this work possible I should like to thank the Institut d'histoire de la Réformation in Geneva for providing the academic and administrative infrastructure as well as the Theology Faculty of that same university for providing moral support when it was needed. Thanks are also due to the Fonds national suisse de la recherche scientifique. The publishers E.J. Brill who commissioned the work were ever present and helpful, in the persons of Julian Deahl and Gera van Bedaf. The Herzog-August-Bibliothek Wolfenbüttel graciously gave me permission to use some of my own material for chapter twenty one. Apart from assuming much of the translation work Antoinina Bevan was a scrupulous assistant editor, attentive to every detail. And finally a word of thanks to my husband, Guy Backus who, although neither a patristician nor a historian himself, has helped me in more ways than I would care to mention.

Irena Backus
Institut d'histoire de la Réformation
Université de Genève
August 1996

THE EDITOR'S INTRODUCTION

The present volume is intended to open up a field of studies rather than close it, and that means opening up gaps and new approaches while giving, in synoptic form, information on what has already been accomplished. The work as it stands serves as a guide to the most important developments in the history of the reception of the Church Fathers in the West from the Carolingians to the Benedictines of the Congregation of St. Maur. As is suggested by the title, particular emphasis is placed on the history of patristic scholarship (which, unlike classical scholarship, has tended to be neglected by historians). However, theological questions are by no means left aside: patristic scholarship has in all cases been placed in its doctrinal and cultural context. Moreover, all contributions address themselves, in so far as possible and relevant, to the questions of what is meant by "the Fathers" in the given socio-cultural and doctrinal context; how the authority of the Fathers is measured against that of the Scripture; types and amount of patristic material available, problems of attribution and mis-attribution; uses of the Fathers in Theological innovation and in conservation of tradition or traditions; overtly tendentious or polemical uses of patristic literature, be it institutional (e.g. Conciliar Decrees) or individual (writings of a particular Father, e.g. Basil of Caesarea).

Each article provides a comprehensive bibliography of primary and secondary literature. The bibliographies are intended not merely as reference to material mentioned in the footnotes but as suggestions for further reading. The work can thus be useful to postgraduate students and more advanced scholars in the fields of patristics, history of theology, intellectual history, medieval and Renaissance studies, and seventeenth and eighteenth century history.

The volume comprises twenty six chapters. In the chapter devoted to the Carolingians Willemien Otten notes that the Carolingian period is most often seen by historians as a beginning from scratch in terms of Christian thought. Despite Carolingian claims to universality, theologians of that period show stunning ignorance of certain patristic authors but Otten argues that it is a tribute to Carolingian culture that the meagre quantity of patristic sources was far outweighed by the theological quality of uses that they were put to.

There is no doubt that alongside the Vulgate, the Church Fathers occupy a central place in Carolingian culture and that the period "inaugurates a viable mediaeval tradition built on a relatively coherent patristic foundation." Two particularly probing examples of this are the *Libri Carolini* or the *Caroline Books* (increasingly attributed by modern research to Théodulf of Orléans) and the *Corpus* of John Scot Eriugena (or Erigena). The *Libri Carolini*, Otten shows, represent a divided West as their radical rejection of Eastern adoration of images (against the decree of the second Council of Nicaea, 787) is at odds with the work's professed obedience to Rome. However, the *Libri Carolini*, in attacking iconoclasm on the one hand and adoration of images on the other hand, consider their primary task as that of unifying the Church by appealing to a certain "wholeness" of tradition. In doing so they inevitably compress the very Fathers they appeal to into an indiscriminate force, while never considering patristic authority as being on par with Scriptural authority. An *ordo testimoniorum* (hierarchy of witnesses) is thus established. John Scot Erigena's contribution to the theology of the period was in a large measure due to his knowledge of Greek which enabled him to translate into Latin notably Pseudo-Dionysius, Maximus the Confessor and Gregory of Nyssa. While admitting that Scripture only reveals the true nature of God, Erigena saw total continuity between the Scripture and the Fathers. Moreover, unlike Alcuin and Théodulf, Erigena attempted to harmonise the Eastern and the Western Fathers and thus established a connexion between Pseudo-Dionysius and Augustine which was to become crucial in the twelfth century European intellectual renaissance.

In the chapter on the Reception of the Church Fathers in Canon Law Jean Werckmeister notes some of the methodological problems inherent to the topic, not the least of those being the existence of not one but several canon laws given that each Church possessed its own legislature. Most of the paper is devoted to Western Canon Law and in particular to the *Decree of Gratian*. Several significant points are to be noted here. Firstly, generally speaking it should always be borne in mind that the Fathers had direct influence on ecclesiastical legislation in that most of them were bishops and therefore legislators. Patristic literature entered Western Canon law during the eighth century and left it as early as the thirteenth century. The Fathers thus received were received essentially as commentators of the Scripture. However, the *antiquity* of particular authors or Conciliar decrees was of no particular interest to Gratian and his predecessors. Throughout the Middle Ages the Fathers were *auctoritates* on which the Church founded its doctrine or its law regardless of the time in which they wrote. This a-historical method partly explains the other title of *Decree of Gratian: Concordantia discordantium canonum* (harmony of conflicting canons or norms). Be that as it may, the substantial increase of the presence of patristic Biblical Commentaries and other works in mediaeval canonical collections (1200 in the *Decree of Gratian*) meant that those collections in general and the *Decree* in particular became a source of patristic texts not only for canonists but also for theologians for generations to come.

Alongside the *Decree of Gratian*, the two most significant and influential monuments of twelfth century patristic learning are the *Glossa ordinaria* in the realm of Biblical exegesis and the *Sentences* of Peter Lombard which combine exegesis and systematic theology (our distinction between exegesis and systematic theology here is naturally anachronistic and should therefore be considered as no more than a heuristic device).

In the chapter devoted to the *Glossa ordinaria* E. Ann Matter shows carefully what conclusions can already be drawn about its patristic sources and how much work still remains to be done. It is by now an established fact that the *Glossa* is a twelfth-century compilation, combining interlinear and marginal glosses or notes on every book of the Bible. The exact relationship between the marginal and the interlinear glosses has yet to be analysed in detail but it can be said that the *Glossa* is a particularly good example of what Matter calls mediaeval intertextuality, "the conscious borrowing and rearticulating of old material in a new form." The glosses on each book or collection of books of the Bible had an independent development and thus draw on different sources from earlier centuries of Christian Biblical Learning. Patristic sources for Old Testament books have hitherto been better studied. Among patristic Biblical commentators *sensu stricto* Jerome, Origen and Augustine are particularly well represented. Strong presence of Carolingian authors, e.g. Hrabanus Maurus, is also to be noted particularly in some of the New Testament books. The *Glossa* presented the Fathers in a new guise and also in a convenient form (excerpts intermingled with the Biblical text itself). Like the *Decree of Gratian* it was to serve as a source of exegetical excerpts from the writings of the Fathers for generations to come.

In the chapter on Peter Lombard, Jacques-Guy Bougerol shows why the *magister Sententiarum* occupies a unique position in nascent

THE EDITOR'S INTRODUCTION

Scholasticism. With his *Sententiae* he assembled a *summa* or a hand-book of the theology common to his time. Furthermore, in his *Commentary on the Psalms* and in his *Gloss on the Pauline Epistles* he clarified (in a similar way to the *Glossa ordinaria*) the Scriptural text by placing round it excerpts from patristic commentaries. Long extracts from Lombard's own *Glosses* on the Scripture were often inserted in the *Sentences* not merely to quote the Fathers but to expound theological matters. All in all, the *Sentences* can be seen as an exposition of a measured theology, embedded in a collection of patristic excerpts suitable for clarifying matters of faith and dogma. There is an absence of metaphysics exemplified by the fact that when treating of the doctrine of Trinity Lombard contented himself with searching no further than Augustine via Florus of Lyon. As in the *Glossa*, the *auctoritates* in Lombard's *Sentences* are inextricably interwoven with the text and doctrine itself. The *Sentences* was the standard text for theology students up until Luther's era and beyond. Moreover, it was to join the *Glossa ordinaria* and the *Decree of Gratian* as sourcebook of patristic quotations until well into the sixteenth century.

However, it would be an error to see all mediaeval theology as entirely overshadowed by nascent scholasticism and its way of excerpting from the Fathers as *auctoritates*. Burcht Pranger's article devoted to Anselm of Canterbury, Abelard and Bernard of Clairvaux is a salutary reminder of this. Monastic theologians of the twelfth century were more prepared than the canonists to leave contradictions unresolved or even to reject authorities point-blank. However, argues Pranger, this is no reason why Anselm or Bernard should be called Fathers. To do so is to impose upon them the conflicts of contemporary theology. The fact remains that all three, Anselm, Abelard and Bernard, saw themselves in direct continuity with the Early Church. For this reason the Church Fathers (used more widely by Bernard than by Anselm) are rarely named. Moreover, Anselm's claim to argue *sola ratione* (by reason alone) as Anselm did, or *non per usum sed per ingenium* (not from tradition but by one's own powers of invention) as was Abelard's way shows that they saw themselves in an unbroken line of Christian theologians. Similarly, it is shown, Bernard's flair for imitating the Bible and Origen is rooted in the same vision. The common factor to Anselm's, Abelard's and Bernard's reading of the Fathers is a delicate balance between self-confidence and a sense of authority of thinkers whom they see as their direct predecessors.

Even in the thirteenth century, the scholastic method of reading the Fathers did not find universal following as is shown by Neil Lewis's chapter on Robert Grosseteste, who eschewed dialectical methods such as the *questio*, popular in his time. Grosseteste, according to Lewis, mirrors a growing desire of this day to return to the complete texts of the Fathers and to place less reliance on *florilegia* where the Greek Fathers were only poorly represented. He tried, unsuccessfully, to reconcile the Eastern and the Western Church on the *Filioque* question by linguistic investigation. His considerable Greek learning comes through not only in his Biblical commentaries but also in his translations into Latin of several Greek Fathers including John of Damascus, Ignatius, Pseudo-Dionysius and Maximus the Confessor's *scholia* on Pseudo-Dionysius. He also wrote important commentaries on the latter. Grosseteste, according to Lewis, helped spur a growing interest in the Fathers in thirteenth century England but there is little evidence of any extensive influence on his contemporaries or on future generations. He did not, argues Lewis, revolutionise the approach to the Fathers current in his day.

Barbara Fleith's article on the extremely popular work of piety, the *Legenda aurea* (*ca.* 1260) shows that most of the work on ways in which patristic literature was brought to ordinary people still remains to be done. On the evidence available so far, we can affirm that Jacobus de Voragine worked chiefly from "second-hand" patristic sources, notably the *Vitae Patrum*, often *via* the standard mediaeval encyclopaedias such as the *Speculum* of Vincent of Beauvais or via other legendaries. The *Liber pontificalis* also provided a valuable source.

With Jacques-Guy Bougerol's contribution on the "Fathers in Scholastic Theology to Bonaventure" we return to the reception of the Fathers in the thirteenth century university (i.e. scholastic) circles. Bougerol stresses Bonaventure's capacities for unifying his *auctoritates* so as to arrive at supreme simplicity and clarity in his own thought. Among other authors discussed in the article is Philip Chancellor, his *Summa de bono* and the use made in it of Pseudo-Dionysius. Philip cites the Fathers abundantly both from such works as he had read himself (e.g. John of Damascus' *De fide orthodoxa*, available in Burgundio of Pisa's Latin translation from the twelfth century) and from *Glosses*. Bougerol also notes that it was Alexander of Hales who was the first to introduce Anselm of Canterbury among the *auctoritates* on the same terms as the Church Fathers in the modern sense of the term. As for Bonaventure, there is no doubt, according to Bougerol, that the

Franciscan had received from his masters (especially Alexander of Hales) an Aristotelian Augustinism which he made his own in that he remained faithful to the Augustinian doctrine of illumination. Greek influences (notably Gregory of Nazianzus and John of Damascus) are perceptible in Bonaventure's doctrine of the Trinity. He also shows great attachment to Pseudo-Dionysius' scheme of hierarchy. Medieval sources, e.g. the Victorine school, are treated by Bonaventure on par with patristic sources.

According to Leo J. Elders, a point of special interest when we come to consider Aquinas' reception of the Fathers is the way in which he tried to bridge the gap between the pastoral teaching of the Fathers and the scientific, scholastic theology of his time. Aquinas, true to his scholastic training, does not use the term *patres ecclesiae* preferring *sancti doctores*, a concept which includes more recent *auctoritates*. A consensus of *auctoritates* does not create absolute doctrinal certitude; only the Church in a Council can interpret the Scripture and evaluate patristic and all other human teaching (which is always subjugated to the authority of the Scripture). Exact sources for Thomas' knowledge of the Church Fathers cannot be established until the Leonine edition has been completed. However, Thomas' interest in the Greek Fathers is fairly well documented, despite his lack of knowledge of Greek. He was in fact the first Latin theologian to quote *verbatim* from the *Acts* of the first five Oecumenical Councils, which he apparently discovered in a Latin translation in the 1260s in Monte Cassino. He was also familiar with Burgundio's translations of John of Damascus and Chrysostom. He obtained, as is shown by Elders, an ever increasing number of translations of the Greek Fathers while working on his *Catena aurea in quatuor Euangelia* (chains of excerpts from Patristic Commentaries on the four Gospels). Among the Western Fathers, it was naturally Augustine who was Aquinas' guiding spirit, notably in the *Summa theologiae*.

Very little work has been done on the reception of the Fathers in late mediaeval scholasticism. It is astonishing to note that to this day there is no definitive study of Duns Scotus' or William of Ockham's use of Augustine, let alone the Greek Fathers. Eric Saak's contribution on the "Reception of Augustine in the Later Middle Ages" shows very clearly that such studies as exist on the Fathers in the Later Middle Ages tend to focus on Augustine. Moreover, argues Saak, the attempt to chart the theology of late mediaeval Augustinism has centred around the examination of *Sentences Commentaries* of the

THE EDITOR'S INTRODUCTION

Augustinian *magistri*. Saak's contribution to the present volume shows that there was also a renaissance of Augustine scholarship outside of the fourteenth century *university* framework, thanks to the efforts of friars like Bartholomeus de Urbino and his *Milleloquium Sancti Augustini* (1345). Studies of the reception of Augustine for that period must thus be extended beyond University circles and indeed beyond members of the Order of Augustinian hermits. More generally, studies of the reception of the Fathers by the late mediaeval schoolmen and the possible influences of Conciliarism still remain to be investigated.

Better known, as is shown by the contribution of Nikolaus Staubach, is the reception of the Church Fathers by the *Devotio moderna*. The Fathers (or more accurately, some Fathers) did form a part of the *devoti*'s programme for spiritual reform. Like the scholastics, the *devoti* did not distinguish between writers of Christian Antiquity and more recent *auctoritates*; on Grote's inspiration they took as prescribed reading those sacred authors whose writings could amend morals. Although a systematic reconstruction of the libraries of the *devoti* is not possible in the present state of research, we know that particular attention was paid to the four doctors of the Church (Augustine, Gregory the Great, Jerome and Ambrose). Excerpts and translations from those and other sacred authors were all done with a view to increasing the purity of heart and raising the level of spiritual exercises and meditation. Making of suitable excerpts thus became a major occupation. Among works of patristic parentage translated into the vernacular we might note Augustine, *Vitae patrum*, Gregory the Great and Cassian (two middle Dutch translations of *Collationes patrum*). What made perfect sense in Grote's time became frozen into a pattern of "spiritual scholasticism" by the time of Erasmus. It was probably his early encounter with the "moralising" Augustine of the *devoti* that, according to Staubach, explains Erasmus' relative dislike for the Bishop of Hippo. Erasmus' attitude to the Fathers forced the *devoti* of his period to establish a hierarchy of texts: neither a radical return to the origins nor indiscriminate reception of the continuous tradition was to be determinative for the study of *libri sacri*.

Charles Stinger shows that Italian Renaissance learning saw Patristic authors no longer as (excerpted) *auctoritates* but as *fontes*, individual sources of experiences or interpretations whose meaning and significance needed to be historically assessed. Some humanists did not see Christianity as providing all the answers to moral and personal problems. Greek and Latin classics also provided some civic models. The

Italian humanists' revival of patristic studies should be seen as part of a larger effort to appropriate the wisdom of the ancient world. However, this did not mean that standard mediaeval collections of patristic excerpts disappeared from Italian humanist libraries. David Rutherford's contribution shows how many Italian humanists who were also clerics found that collections such as the *Decree of Gratian* could support their commitment to *studia humanitatis*—thus safeguarding themselves against accusations of excessive hankerings after Pagan culture and education.

Jan den Boeft demonstrates that Erasmus' fundamental contribution to modern patristic studies was also in continuity with his love of the classics. However, unlike many Italian humanists, Erasmus, while considering classical authors as indispensable, thought their usefulness limited in all respects. He considered the Fathers (as individual authors) of incalculable value in the interpretation of Scripture and found that they embodied precisely what was needed for the renewal of true Christianity. He edited a restricted canon of patristic authors, mainly of the third and fourth century. Erasmus' contribution should not be judged by the standards of contemporary textual criticism, although he did indeed make some stunning blunders such as confusing Arnobius the Elder and Arnobius the Younger. All in all, he found that the writers of Christian Antiquity embodied a more peaceful and less cut and dried doctrinal climate. He was also interested in their personal and churchmanlike qualities. Den Boeft also draws our attention to Erasmus' two great patristic loves: Jerome for his qualities as Biblical scholar and philologist and Origen for his literary and exegetical gifts.

With the Italian humanism and finally with Erasmus, the Fathers came to assume a new status, more akin to that of our own time. Moreover, a greater quantity of complete patristic texts was made available. What impact did that have on the Reformation and the ensuing confessional split? And indeed, what impact did the religious upheavals of the sixteenth century have on the reception of the Fathers? Several of the contributions tackle those very questions, directly or indirectly.

In a very comprehensive essay Manfred Schulze shows how Luther urged in a variety of ways and over a period of years that the authority of the Scripture was superior to any patristic consensus. "Even if Augustine and all the Fathers were to see in Peter the Rock of the Church, I will nevertheless oppose them, supported by the authority of Paul and therefore by divine law," Luther was reported to have stated. The German reformer did not believe that the Fathers illuminated the obscurity of the Scripture. On the contrary, "Christians had to judge the Fathers' books in the clear light of Scripture." Luther was not literary historian in the sense that Erasmus was. Patristics (a science invented by Erasmus, one might say) did not interest him, nor did he produce any editions of the Church Fathers. However, Schulze argues that Luther rendered an inestimable scholarly service to the Church, to theology and to historiography: he freed the Fathers from tradition and showed that they too could be mistaken.

The editor of the present volume argues that Zwingli, because of his humanist education, had a much greater and a much more scholarly interest in the Fathers than Luther. This is shown by his still extant personal library. The Fathers that Zwingli read as a young man, prior to his becoming a reformer, shaped his theology in such a way as to allow him to establish a hierarchy of sacred texts with the Scripture at the top broadening out into a pyramid of patristic evidence, indispensable in its turn for construction of a Biblical theology. This did not stop Zwingli from demarkating himself sharply from patristic theology on several matters e.g. saint worship, an issue on which he frankly accused Jerome of falsifying the Bible. However, in general Zwingli found it important to harmonise his own reading of the Scripture with some orthodox representative(s) of the Early Church. It is also to be noted that for both Zwingli and Bucer the *Decree of Gratian* still provided an excellent source of patristic quotations. Among other salient features of *Bucer's* use of patristic literature, his direct application of the Fathers' teachings to practical theology, a tendency to select the doctrines that confirm his own, the crucial role played by the Fathers in his Biblical Commentaries all deserve a special mention. Still to be investigated is the respective role of the Fathers in Bucer's Old Testament and New Testament Commentaries, the nature of his "Augustinianism," his sensitivity to the difference between Greek and Latin Fathers and his interest in the ancient *Histories* of the Church. Zwingli and Bucer share an "implicit normativity" approach in their dealings with patristic writings (which they distinguish sharply from mediaeval authors). However, no attempt is made by either to create a *consensus patrum*. Indeed patristic writings be it of institutional or individual nature are used to overthrow the Roman Catholic *consensus*.

Johannes van Oort provides us with a survey of the main patristic data in Calvin's work starting with 1532 (Commentary on Seneca's *De clementia*) and ending with the 1559 edition of the *Institutes*. Van Oort then goes on to discuss the most important (for Western Christianity) patristic authors and ecclesiastical documents explicitly cited by Calvin. Apart from Augustine, the Church Father who particularly influenced Calvin was Cyprian, and more especially Cyprian's ecclesiology. Our attention is also drawn to Calvin's well-known dislike of Origen and to his liking for Irenaeus. The Genevan reformer found the Cappadocians quite foreign to his way of thinking but had great admiration (in common with all reformers) for the exegetical and homiletical qualities of Chrysostom. Cyril of Alexandria is cited in a Trinitarian and Christological context. With a few exceptions, post 500 A.D. patristic writers are only rarely cited by Calvin. Less interested in Church history than Bucer (although capable of analysing it with some finesse when it suited him), Calvin read widely in such editions of the Fathers as were available to him, while also (like Zwingli and Bucer) relying on the *Decree of Gratian* and Lombard's *Sentences* as sources of patristic material. Calvins' use of the Fathers was primarily polemical: they were meant to support his own teaching against Lutheran and Roman Catholic opponents and were a mere accessory to the Bible.

What of the position of the Roman Catholic Church in the pre-Tridentine period? Ralph Keen argues that, confronted with the Reformation, the need to prove a positive relationship between the Roman Church and the patristic tradition was as difficult as it was urgent. Keen then examines the work of chief Roman Catholic controversialists and their attempts to show that tradition was being understood incorrectly by the reformers. The Roman position as it emerged during the first years of conflict was to see tradition as a whole situated within the Roman Catholic Church, the sole heir and bearer of that tradition. The Romanists adopted the hermeneutic of *consensus patrum* in response to the reformers' isolating and privileging of particular authors and institutional texts.

Enrico Norelli's contribution concentrates on the way in which the two great post-Tridentine Church Histories (the Protestant *Centuries of Magdeburg* and the Roman Catholic response, Baronius' *Annals*) consider the authority of the General Council taking the first Council of Nicaea as an example. The Centuriators insist on the fact that the Council was convoked by the Emperor Constantine and not by Sylvester the bishop of Rome. Baronius for his part stresses that the

Council was convoked by the Roman pontiff. Furthermore, the Centuriators agree that what confers authority on Conciliar decrees is their approval by all bishops while Baronius naturally argues that the Council's decisions are in all cases to be validated by the Roman pontiff. Both sides, argues Norelli, use ecclesiastical history for apologetic ends.

Mark Vessey's systematic enquiry into the question of English translations of the Latin Fathers for the period 1517–1611 takes patristic literature out of the sphere of learned theology and shows how a limited sample of it reached somewhat wider audience in England. (Similar studies might usefully be done for other countries). Vessey shows that behind the conceit of the Fathers being made to "speak in English" there lay a variety of appropriation, mechanical and social, as well as religious and linguistic. He distinguishes several "modes" of patristic translation: "existential" (mainly works of piety destined for both religious and lay people); "dogmatic" (authority of the Fathers has been claimed by another party and must be wrested back; "epideictic" or rhetorical). The article includes a list of the Latin Fathers translated into English during that period. Cyprian, Augustine and Vincent of Lérin's *Commonitorium* seem to have been the most popular. It is also interesting to note that most of the translations date from the *latter* half of the sixteenth century.

Alongside the development of the apologetic approach to the Fathers which reached its culmination with the *Centuries of Magdeburg* and Baronius' *Annals*, a new, more critical, attitude to patristic texts was beginning to emerge. Patristic scholars, whether Protestant or Roman Catholic, increasingly sought to recover the better text "freed from accretions and corruptions" as Thomas James put it in 1611. This critical attitude did not necessarily coexist with a more ecumenical Theology. The real corruptions found by Thomas James in patristic texts were invariably of "Popish" origin. In the contributions on Calvinist orthodoxy the editor of the present volume and E.P. Meijering deal respectively with patristic scholarship and systematic theology. While my own examination of the patristic manuals of Scultetus and Rivet shows that in the case of Basil of Caesarea the beginnings of the new critical approach were sometimes actively thwarted by polemical concerns, E.P. Meijering shows that systematic Calvinist theologians were more speculative than Calvin and less fundamentalistically Biblical, notably in matters to do with the Trinity. This attitude caused them to view the Fathers with approval; this was particularly true of the post 500 A.D. Fathers (ignored by Calvin) who were found to furnish much valuable material against the Socinians. These aporias in the Calvinist reception of the Fathers could be usefully investigated further.

Dominique Bertrand provides prosopographies of the major Jesuit editors of patristic works or works to do with the Early Church. Up until around 1625, he argues, two powerful concerns helped turn the Jesuits in the direction of the Fathers: firstly, their spirituality felt the need of patristic rejuvenation and secondly, they needed materials for religious controversy. This latter need (also felt by the Orthodox Calvinists) spurred the Jesuits of the seventeenth century (Torres, Schott, Fronto Ducaeus, Sirmond) to produce not critically oriented patristic manuals but extremely important patristic editions and to come to the forefront of patristic scholarship so that their editions (e.g. Fronto Ducaeus' Basil or Chrysostom) were also used as works of reference by the enemy camp, i.e. by Calvinist scholars such as André Rivet. However, as is shown by Bertrand, by the eighteenth century Jesuits had lost mastery of the great collections of patristic works, with the sole exception of hagiography as witnessed by the work of the Bollandists.

What of the Anglican Church in the same period? According to Jean-Louis Quantin, the status of the Fathers in seventeenth and early eighteenth century Anglican Theology reflected the somewhat ambiguous position of the Church of England. Originally a Protestant church, it became increasingly preoccupied with suppression of Dissent, especially after 1640 and this led to a growing stress being placed on the Fathers (somewhat at the expense of the Scripture) and on historical reasoning. Conservative theological principles turned out to be beneficial for patristic scholarship. Interestingly enough, the main Anglican patristic editions of the seventeenth and early eighteenth century tend to be of the Apostolic Fathers, the notable exception being Henry Savile's edition of Chrysostom.

In his second contribution Jean-Louis Quantin considers what he finds to be a paradoxical role played by the Fathers in seventeenth century Roman Catholic Theology, particularly in France. As the century progressed, historical theology and patristic scholarship increasingly threatened to curb the authority of the Church and its freedom to define and decide. While Rome invoked authority, infallibility and promises, Jansenists and Gallicans invoked facts, texts and documentary evidence. We might note that a similar aporia is perceptible in Calvinist Orthodoxy of the period, with quite often one and the same theologian invoking the Scripture and/or historical evidence according to the context in which he finds himself (polemical, didactic or learned). The enquiry could usefully be extended to Lutheran orthodoxy.

The volume ends with Daniel-Odon Hurel's contribution on the Benedictine monks of the Congregation of St. Maur (or the Maurists). The Congregation was founded in 1621 to represent in France the reform initiated in the abbey of Saint-Vanne in 1600. From 1672 onwards the Maurists devoted themselves largely to historical and literary works and many of their productions in the field of patristics are monuments of scholarship. Among their members were J. Mabillon, B. de Montfaucon, R. Massuet, C. de la Rue, L. d'Achéry, F. Aubert and many others whose names are familiar to all patristic students and who marked the beginning of the modern era in patristic scholarship, without necessarily ironing out the theological aporias and differences some of which remain a feature of patristic studies to this very day.

I. Backus

LIST OF CONTRIBUTORS

Irena Backus is Titular Professor at the University of Geneva (Institut d'histoire de la Réformation), and a specialist in the reception of the Church Fathers and the New Testament Apocrypha in the fifteenth and sixteenth centuries. She has also worked on the history of Biblical exegesis in the sixteenth century and (as a sideline) on Guillaume Postel and demonic possession in sixteenth century France. Her most recent publications include:

- *The Disputations of Baden (1526) and Berne (1528): Neutralizing the Early Church*, Princeton, N.J., 1993 (Studies in Reformed Theology and History, 1:1).
- *La patristique et les guerres de religion en France. Etude de l'activité littéraire de Jacques de Billy (1535–81) O.S.B. d'après le MS. Sens 167 et les sources imprimées*, Paris, Institut d'Etudes Augustiniennes, 1993.
- *Le miracle de Laon: le déraisonnable, le raisonnable, l'apocalyptique et le politique dans les récits du miracle de Laon (1566–78)*, Paris, Vrin (collection: De Pétrarque à Descartes, no. 58), 1994.
- "Guillaume Postel, Théodore Bibliander et le 'Protévangile de Jacques'. Introduction historique, édition et traduction française du MS. Londres, BL, Sloane 1411, 260r.–267v.", in: *Apocrypha* 6 (1995), 7–65.

Dominique Bertrand, S.J., has been Director of the Institut des Sources Chrétiennes in Lyon since February 1984. He is a specialist in the history of spirituality and of spiritual theology and has published a thesis on the politics of St. Ignatius Loyola in the light of his correspondence and a study of the constitutions of the Society of Jesus (*Un corps pour l'Esprit*). He has followed this with editions of Hilary of Poitiers (*On the Trinity*) and of Bernard of Clairvaux (Complete Works) in the series *Sources Chrétiennes*.

Jacques Guy Bougerol is a Franciscan, Emeritus Professor of the Franciscan University in Rome, and a specialist in the works of Saint Bonaventure (especially his sermons). His most recent publications include an edition of the *Summa de Anima* of John of La Rochelle (Paris, 1995).

J. den Boeft is Professor of Latin at the Vrije Universiteit in Amsterdam and a specialist in the literature of the fourth century. With some colleagues he is engaged in writing commentaries on Ammianus Marcellinus' *Res Gestae*, the most recent of which deals with book 22.

Leo J. Elders is Professor at the Institute of Philosophy at Rolduc, the Netherlands, and at the F.L.P.C. in Paris. He specialises in the study of the thought of Thomas Aquinas. His most recent publications include books on the metaphysics and the philosophy of nature of Aquinas.

Barbara Fleith is "chargée de cours" at the University of Geneva and a specialist in Medieval hagiographical literature. Her most recent publications address problems in the tradition of the Latin *Legenda Aurea*.

Daniel-Odon Hurel is a Researcher (CNRS-URA 1274, Rouen) at the University of Rouen, France, and a specialist in monastic history (the Congregation of Saint-Maur, 17th–18th c.). He was awarded a doctorate for a thesis on the "Voyage littéraire" of dom Martène and dom Durand (1717 and 1724) and is preparing an edition of the correspondence of dom Jean Mabillon.

Ralph Keen is Assistant Professor of Religion at the University of Iowa, specializing in late-Medieval and Reformation theology. His edition of *Philippicae I–VII* by Johannes Cochlaeus was published by De Graaf Publishers in 1995.

Neil Lewis is Assistant Professor of Philosophy at Georgetown University in Washington DC. He specializes in early 13th-century philosophy. His recent publications include "The First Recension of Robert Grosseteste's *De libero arbitrio*", in *Medieval Studies*, 53 (1991).

E. Ann Matter is the R. Jean Brownlee Term Professor of Religious Studies at the University of Pennsylvania. She is a specialist in the intertwined traditions of Medieval spirituality and Biblical interpretation, and has a strong interest in the history of women. Her publications include the critical edition of *Paschasii Radberti De partu Virginis*, Corpus Christianorum, Series Latina, continuatio medievalis 56C (Turnhout, Belgium, 1985), *The Voice of My Beloved: The Song of Songs in the Western Christian Middle Ages* (Philadelphia, 1990) and (edited with John Coakley) *Creative Women in Medieval and Early Modern Italy: A Religious and Artistic Renaissance* (Philadelphia, 1994).

E.P. Meijering is Reader in Patristic Literature at the University of Leiden and a specialist in the Fathers and their "Nachleben". His publications include *Reformierte Scholastik und patristische Theologie* (De Graaf, Nieuwkoop, 1991), *Von den Kirchenvätern zu Karl Barth* (Gieben, Amsterdam, 1993), *Die Geschichte der christlichen Theologie im Urteil J.L. von Mosheims* (Gieben, Amsterdam, 1995).

Enrico Norelli is Professor of Christian Apocryphal Literature at the University of Geneva, specialising in the history of the interpretation of the Bible, Gnosis and Marcionism. His recent publications include: *A Diogneto*, Milan 1991; *L'ascensione di Isaia. Un apocrifo al crocevia dei cristianesimi*, Bologna 1994; *Storia della letteratura cristiana antica greca e latina*, 2 vols. (Brescia 1995–1996) [with C. Moreschini]; *Ascensio Isaiae*, 2 vols., (Turnhout 1995).

Willemien Otten is Assistant Professor of History of Christian Life and Thought in the Theology Department at Boston College and a specialist in the history and theology of the Middle Ages. Her most recent publications include:—"Nature and Scripture: Demise of a Medieval Analogy" in: *Harvard Theological Review* 88 (1995), 257–284;— (co-edited with B. McGinn), *Eriugena: East and West*. Papers of the Eighth International Symposium of the Society for the Promotion of Eriugenian Studies, 18–20 October, 1991 (Notre Dame: University of Notre Dame Press, 1994);—"Eriugena's *Periphyseon*: a Carolingian Contribution to the Theological Tradition", in: *Eriugena. East and West*, 69–93.

Burcht Pranger is Professor of the History of Christianity at the University of Amsterdam. His recent publications include: *Bernard of Clairvaux and the Shape of Monastic Thought*, (Brill, Leiden 1994).

Jean-Louis Quantin is Lecturer at the University of Versailles, France, and a specialist in early modern English and French religious history. His Sorbonne dissertation (defended in 1994 and to be published at the *Institut d'Etudes Augustiniennes*, Paris) deals with the use of the Fathers in France, in the 17th century.

David Rutherford is Assistant Professor at Central Michigan University and a specialist in Italian Renaissance History. His most recent publications include, "Antonio da Rho on Patristic Authority: the status of Lactantius".

E.L. Saak holds a postdoctoral position in the Netherlands Research School for Medieval Studies, and is attached to the Rijksuniversiteit Groningen. Dr. Saak is a specialist in late Medieval religious thought and culture, focusing especially on the Augustinian Tradition. His monograph, *Religio Augustini. Jordan of Quedlinburg and the Creation of a Religious Ideology in the Later Middle Ages* is to be published by E.J. Brill.

Manfred Schulze is Professor of Church History at the Divinity School Wuppertal-Barmen and a specialist in late Medieval and Reformation history. His most recent publications include a history of the political psychology and reform programs of the German princes at the end of the 15th century.

Nikolaus Staubach is Professor at the University of Münster and a specialist in early Medieval history (kingship, political theory, historiography) and late Medieval religious reforms (*Devotio moderna*). His most recent publications include *Rex christianus. Hofkultur und Herrschaftspropaganda im Reich Karls des Kahlen*, 2 vols., vol. 1: in print, vol. 2: Köln 1993; "Pragmatische Schriftlichkeit im Bereich der Devotio moderna", in: *Frühmittelalterliche Studien* 25 (1991), 418–461; "Christiana tempora. Augustin und das Ende der alten Geschichte in der Weltchronik Frechulfs von Lisieux", *ibidem* 29 (1995), 167–205.

Charles L. Stinger is Professor of History at the University at Buffalo, State University of New York. He is a specialist in the history of Italian humanism and is the author of *The Renaissance in Rome*, (Bloomington, Indiana University Press, 1985).

Johannes van Oort, Dr. Theol. (1986) is Associate Professor of Church History at the University of Utrecht. He has published extensively on Patristics (Augustine in particular), on Manichaeism and on John Calvin.

Mark Vessey is Associate Professor of English at the University of British Columbia and a specialist in the Latin Christian literature of Late Antiquity and its reception in early modern Europe. He is currently working on a study of the fortune of Augustine's *City of God* in the English Renaissance.

Jean Werckmeister (1947) teaches Canon Law at the University of Strasbourg (France) and is chief editor of the *Revue de Droit Canonique*. His most recent publications include: *Petit Dictionnaire de Droit Canonique* (Paris, Cerf, 1994); *Le Prologue d'Yves de Chartres* (Paris, Cerf, 1996).

PART ONE

PATRISTIC SOURCES AND THEIR USES
UNTIL *CA.* 1200

THE TEXTURE OF TRADITION: THE ROLE OF THE CHURCH FATHERS IN CAROLINGIAN THEOLOGY

Willemien Otten

I. *The Church Fathers and the Carolingian Renaissance: An Introduction*

Historical research has traditionally labelled the Carolingian period as a renaissance. I want to take as my starting-point for this essay the ambiguity inherent in the term "renaissance," a term that at once points to a bygone past and looks ahead to a new beginning. The past to which the Carolingian renaissance refers can be seen as the age of the Fathers: the early Christian period in which the Latin Fathers Ambrose, Jerome and Augustine, and their Greek counterparts Athanasius and Gregory of Nyssa lived. The Carolingian period, separated from the age of the Fathers by the so-called Dark Ages, may well be the first to see a genuine, systematic flourishing of intellectual activity since the patristic era. This flourishing appears to be propelled by an awareness, perhaps illusory, of intrinsic ties with earlier periods of great bloom. Here the Carolingians refer not only to the realm of theology with its heritage of the great Christian councils and the tradition of the Fathers, but also to that of philosophy and the arts, stretching back to the Academy of Plato.[1] In modelling itself after a great past, the Carolingian era appears to postulate the continuity of the ideals which it sets forth while claiming their universal truth. Given the integrated nature of Carolingian learning, where Scripture and the arts form a marriage of sorts,[2] it is no surprise that these claims of continuity and universality are equally manifest in the way in which the Carolingian West marshals the support of the Church Fathers.

The repeated articulation of continuity seems to have reinforced the nascent Carolingian identity by distinguishing, and gradually

---

[1] In a famous letter Alcuin celebrates the new and better Athens established in Francia, where the sevenfold gift of the Holy Spirit enriches the seven traditional Platonic disciplines. See Alcuin, Epistle 170, MGH Epp. 4:279.

[2] In a letter to Irish monks Alcuin sees the knowledge of secular disciplines as a foundation to help young people climb up to the apex of evangelical perfection. See Alcuin, Epistle 280, MGH Epp. 4:437.

distancing, the West from the Greek East. The naturalness with which the *Libri Carolini* accuse the East, which could boast a continuous link to its patristic past, of distorting the heritage of the Fathers indicates a change of perspective by which the West emerges as the torchbearer of the tradition. From here on the Greeks are seen as deviant on major theological and ecclesio-political issues, notwithstanding the fact that the Second Nicene synod against which the *Libri Carolini* so vehemently react had met with the approval of pope Hadrian. The Carolingian period thus builds on the division of Christianity between a Greek East and a Latin West even though a formal schism does not occur.

It is especially remarkable to see the Carolingian claim of universality arise in view of the rather scanty evidence on which it rests. The lack of correspondence between the universal nature of the Carolingian claims and their meager evidentiary support testifies to another characteristic: the enormous confidence with which many Carolingian attempts at theological reasoning were carried out. Though later generations would refine or abolish the Carolingian arguments, replacing them with a more reliable methodology as in the scholastic era, the confidence with which the Carolingian period underscored certain fundamental Christian tenets was instrumental in gaining their widespread acceptance.

Confidence, especially when not altogether warranted, is not without its setbacks. Accompanying the confidence of the Carolingian era, expressed most poignantly in its self-understanding as representing a universal Christendom, one finds a stunning ignorance of certain important patristic authors. The *Libri Carolini* (*LC*) dismiss the testimony of the Cappadocian Church Father Gregory of Nyssa simply because his writings are unknown to them, and therefore considered irrelevant.[3] On the other hand, when knowledge of patristic sources can be demonstrated, this does not yet guarantee that the ideas contained in them are absorbed or incorporated. More than half a century after the composition of the *LC*, Johannes Scottus Eriugena translated Gregory of Nyssa's early work *De hominis opificio* and quoted more than 25 percent of it in his *Periphyseon*. As Édouard Jeauneau has pointed out, however, it is not Gregory of Nyssa, but Dionysius the Areopagite who is the most influential theologian for

---

[3] See *LC* II ch. 17.

Eriugena, with Maximus the Confessor as a close second.[4] Rather than evaluate Carolingian culture according to its erudite preservation of the past, therefore, it is better to judge it on its own terms, since knowledge of patristic sources measures the depth of its theology inadequately. It is a tribute to the remarkable vitality of Carolingian culture that quantity and quality do not always correspond.

This conclusion can lead us to a further one. Among his contemporaries, Eriugena stands out because of his familiarity with the Greek tradition. It is generally assumed that Eriugena displays more theological profundity than other Carolingian authors due to his wider command of sources. Although this judgment is not unfair, it is somewhat misleading in that it creates the impression that Eriugena, in contrast to the rest of the Carolingian tradition, not only understands the theological traditions of East and West but faithfully integrates them. Such a conclusion does not take into account, however, that Eriugena's own confidence in integrating the traditions of East and West was, at least in part, based on a similar ignorance, which in his case is hidden beneath the flair of genius. Although Eriugena does not flaunt his ignorance, as the author of the *LC* did, he does intimate that his confidence is not altogether merited. An example is his dedicatory letter to Charles the Bald which accompanies his translation of the oeuvre of Dionysius the Areopagite. In this letter he appears to downplay his own translation by encouraging others to check it against the original.[5] His remark is usually seen as a topical display of modesty, which highlights his achievement and bolsters his reputation as an intellectual genius. Yet recent scholarship has established that knowledge of Greek in northern France was rather more widespread than hitherto assumed,[6] which makes his exhortation more than a formality by increasing the likelihood that he may have collaborated with a group of competent scholars. This interpretation becomes even more plausible when one realizes that Eriugena's translations contain indeed many mistakes.[7] Thus even his extraordinary

---

[4] See Jeauneau 1983: 143–149.

[5] *PL* 122, 1032C: Ubi valde pertimesco, ne forte culpam infidi interpretis incurram. At si aut superflua quaedam superadjecta esse, aut de integritate graecae constructionis quaedam deesse arbitratus fuerit, recurrat ad codicem graecum, unde ego interpretatus sum; ibi fortassis inveniet, itane est necne.

[6] On Eriugena's contact with scholarly circles in northern France, see O'Meara 1988: 6–15, 198–212. On the Irish colony in Laon, see Contreni 1978: 81–94.

[7] See below: Eriugena as Translator.

ingenuity in interpreting patristic source-material in such a manner
so as to forge an effective alliance between East and West cannot
disguise the fact that he and his contemporaries lacked adequate
intellectual resources.

This shared paucity of intellectual resources is finally what makes
the Carolingian period a real beginning for Christianity, a beginning totally unlike its actual historical origin. When Christianity first
entered the arena of cultural debate with the generation of second
century apologists such as Justin Martyr, it freely borrowed from an
existing framework of current philosophies, such as Stoicism and
Middle Platonism. As its basic beliefs solidified through internal and
external controversies, Christianity gained strength and was able to
hold its ground in the discussion with rival intellectual movements.
By the time of Augustine it had fused with intellectual Neoplatonism
to such an extent that any retro-active distinction between "Christian" and "Neoplatonic" elements can only be artificial. Having grown
into its own, Christianity had now become the dominant religious
and intellectual movement in the Roman Empire. Well aware of this,
Augustine did not hesitate to criticize and even condemn other intellectual positions. In his *De doctrina christiana* he downplayed the significance of classical authors like Cicero for the Christian preacher, despite
the fact that they had been largely responsible for setting him on the
intellectual journey which culminated in his embrace of Christianity.
Similarly, in his *De civitate dei* he brushed off the importance of the
Roman Empire for the Christian religion, although it is to the Roman
Empire that Christianity owed much of its success. Once Christianity had become established, it seems the impression of dependence
on other, i.e., non-Christian, sources needed to be avoided.

This movement to emancipate Christianity from non-Christian
sources continued in the period between Augustine and Gregory the
Great, which Robert Markus has fittingly termed the "End of Ancient Christianity."[8] Due rather more to unfortunate circumstances
than to willful intent, it seems that when the Roman Empire subsequently disintegrated, the riches of classical education were gradually
depleted, surviving marginally in Ireland and Visigothic Spain. In
reflecting a monastic as well as melancholy strife for human salvation, the writings of Gregory the Great provide eminent testimony to

---

[8] See Markus 1991.

the dire circumstances Christianity came to experience. After these so-called Dark Ages, the Carolingian period witnesses what is virtually a new beginning for Christianity, thus warranting the term "renaissance." Perhaps one does better, however, to call it a beginning from scratch. The scratch here may echo the sound of the monk's stylus on the vellum as he transcribed the text of the Vulgate, the book which in the absence of many classical sources traditionally used for didactic purposes would become the multi-layered source of Carolingian civilization. Ideals of education and salvation could go together for most Carolingian thinkers, as the Bible was the manual for grammar as well as revelation. This both increased and decreased its authority, for much as the Bible was the repository containing the Word of God and providing the hope for humanity's restoration, it was also itself in need of urgent repair. Both Alcuin and Theodulf did much to improve the text of the Vulgate and further its standardization and promulgation.[9] In a related development, the study of Scripture merged with the vestiges of classical techniques, making the distinction between "sacred" and "profane" a rather moot point in the Carolingian era.

What happened to the Vulgate is not unlike what happened to the Church Fathers, as the same arguments suffice to demonstrate their crucial place in Carolingian culture. With many classical sources present only indirectly through their vestiges in patristic texts, the Church Fathers provided an almost exclusive access to the Christian and classical past and were cherished in part for these reasons. As "live" representations of the past, their texts were comparable to the relics of the martyrs.[10] Yet in furnishing the Carolingians with a particular lens through which to view the past, the Church Fathers also came to play a role in the Carolingian present. Used as they were in contemporary Carolingian debates, the opinions of the Church Fathers were not simply transmitted but in the process altered and developed further. Besides setting the standards of orthodoxy, patristic authors

---

[9] The traditional dominance of Alcuin in this area is now replaced by that of Theodulf. On Theodulf's role, see Dahlhaus-Berg 1975: 39–91. See also Contreni 1983: 73–79.

[10] It is interesting that the *LC* reject the comparison between images and relics precisely because relics reflect the saints' corporeal reality, thereby foreshadowing their resurrection, whereas images are static and quite literally "dead". Cf. *LC* III ch. 24 and Chazelle 1986: 168. Patristic texts appear to contain a similar dynamic quality.

could also be judged against them. Precisely what motivated the various Carolingian debates, what kinds of arguments were used and which Fathers called upon will be the subject of the following pages.

The order of procedure in this article will oscillate between a historical and a thematic approach. Since it is impossible to cover the full spectrum of Carolingian theology, the discussion will have to be selective. We will begin by focusing on the *Libri Carolini*, a text which reflects a collaborative Carolingian enterprise. In the debate about their authorship, two figures have been most frequently mentioned. Theodulf of Orléans was probably the author of the original draft, whereas Alcuin's name is mentioned as a possible influence in their final redaction. Hence our discussion will focus first on Theodulf's and second on Alcuin's reception of the Fathers. For Theodulf we will obviously focus on the *LC*, while for Alcuin we will discuss the properly Alcuinian text *De vitiis et virtutibus (DVV)*.

From the reign of Charlemagne we will then turn to the reign of Charles the Bald, who governed during the last stage of the Carolingian renaissance. Although after the treaty of Verdun (843) the original Carolingian unity would never be restored, it is in this period of relative stability that we find a resurgence of theological activity. Although the dominant mode of this theological activity appears to have been one of controversy, whether about predestination or about the eucharist, we encounter nevertheless in the figure of Johannes Scottus Eriugena an author whose theology far transcends the limitations of this genre. Eriugena's legacy is the most imposing of the entire period. Not only does he display a remarkable originality in expressing his thought, but he is also the author who most consciously articulates the need to grapple with the divergences within the patristic tradition. It is with Eriugena that our attention will once again be turned to the Greek Fathers, who before being obliterated during the Ottonian and Capetian reign of the tenth and the eleventh centuries will make one last impressive appearance in the Irishman's writings.

In conformity with our combined historical and thematic approach, we will draw the various authors and issues together by working with two interrelated sets of questions. On the one hand we will concentrate on the presence of the Fathers in the Carolingian texts. We will look first to the use of the Fathers as a whole before studying references to individual Fathers. We will also try to contextualize the position of the Fathers by analyzing the concept of authority that each author employs in invoking the patristic tradition. The second set of questions focuses on the framework of Carolingian theology into which the Fathers are received. This framework is not a monolithic one. Theodulf uses his authors differently than Eriugena for the very reason that his text has a different intent from Eriugena's. Yet the thought-patterns of the receiving authors betray some similarity in that they all touch on anthropology as a dominant subtheme of Carolingian theology. In Theodulf we will pay special attention to memory as the human faculty by which the Fathers are remembered; in Alcuin we will pay attention to the moral recipient for whose salvation the patristic texts are cited; in Eriugena, finally, we will study the role of human reason as the faculty overseeing and coordinating the testimony of the Fathers.

Although these latter aspects are all worthy of further study, this article aptly emphasizes the Fathers themselves, regarding the anthropological themes as ancillary to highlight their role. These other themes are necessary to shift our perspective away from the Fathers as part of a fossilized past in order to reach a more precise understanding of how the past is embodied and brought to life in the Carolingian present. The Carolingian authors do not just transmit the legacy of the Fathers but in doing so, put themselves squarely in their company. It may well be among the greatest theological achievements of the Carolingian era that it was able to reconfigure the vestiges of a ravished Christian and classical culture and inaugurate a viable medieval tradition built on a relatively coherent patristic foundation.

II. *Theodulf of Orléans and the* Libri Carolini

A. *Theodulf of Orléans and the Compositional Structure of the* Libri Carolini

The *Libri Carolini*,[11] which may be more appropriately titled *Opus Caroli Regis contra Synodum*, were probably composed between 790 and 793.[12]

---

[11] *Libri Carolini sive Caroli Magni Capitulare de imaginibus*, ed. Hubert Bastgen. Ann Freeman has recently finished a new edition for MGH under the title *Opus Caroli Regis contra Synodum*, in which many of Bastgen's mistakes, among which patristic references, are corrected. I am grateful to professor Freeman for sharing her index of patristic authors with me in preparation for this article. The *LC* will be quoted according to book and chapter and the page number in Freeman.

[12] Freeman gives 790 as the likely date for the preface and 793 as the date of Charlemagne's final approval of the treatise at Regensburg. For a precise chronol-

This Carolingian text is preserved only in the incomplete autograph deposited by Charlemagne in the royal archives (Vat. lat. 7207) and in the complete copy ordered by Hincmar of Reims in the mid-ninth century (Paris, Arsenal 663). Virtually neglected throughout the Middle Ages, the *LC* are currently recognized as the most original contribution to theology during the reign of Charlemagne. Although the question of their authorship has not been solved conclusively, based on a preponderance of evidence Theodulf of Orléans is most probably the author. The presence of certain Visigothic elements in spelling and the liturgical citation of biblical texts in the Old Latin version, preserved also in Mozarabic antiphons, both point to Theodulf's Spanish roots.[13] Alcuin's stay in England during the years of the *LC*'s composition (790–793) all but excludes him as their author, although his influence may be felt in the editorial emendation of the work.[14]

The question of the use of the Fathers in the *LC* is inextricably bound up with the work's compositional history, details of which have been revealingly elucidated by Ann Freeman.[15] In 787 the second Nicene Council, presided over by Empress Irene on behalf of her young son Constantine VI, had restored the Byzantine East to an iconophile position. This decision met with the approval of pope Hadrian, who had been represented at the council by two papal legates. Some time thereafter a Latin version of the proceedings of Nicea II arrived at the Frankish court of Charlemagne where it was read out loud. Infuriated by its contents and unaware of Hadrian's approval, Charlemagne and his court theologians drew up a reply to alert the pope to the error-filled findings of the Byzantine council. A hasty list of *capitula* was made, the *Capitulare adversus synodum*, and

---

ogy of the various stages of the Carolingian debate on the images and the composition of the LC, see Freeman 1985: 105–106.

[13] Although W. von den Steinen had ventured this hypothesis as early as 1929, it was especially the groundbreaking work of Ann Freeman that all but settled the issue, see Freeman 1957. In this article Freeman also pointed out parallels with Theodulf's other works, see *art. cit.*: 688–690. Her views were most heavily contested by Luitpold Wallach, who suggested in his *Alcuin and Charlemagne* that Alcuin was the editor. See Wallach 1959: 169–177, esp. 174. In a later polemical stance he suggested Alcuin as the actual composer, see Wallach 1966: 498 and Wallach 1977: 287–294. Wallach also contested Freeman's findings of so-called Spanish symptoms, see Wallach 1977: 222–247. Theodulf's authorship is now widely accepted.

[14] See e.g. Bullough 1983: 31–39 and Dahlhaus-Berg 1975: 206–212. Freeman sees his influence but not his terminology behind *LC* IV ch. 28. See *Opus Caroli*, ed. Freeman, Introduction, p. 8.

[15] See Freeman 1985.

probably delivered to Rome in 792 by Angilbert on a mission related to the Adoptionist controversy. The contents of this capitulary
are preserved indirectly in the letter which Hadrian's *curia* wrote to
uphold Nicea II.[16] Meanwhile, Theodulf, still ignorant of the pope's
position, had set out to write a more fundamental critique of Nicea
II,—of which the hasty *Capitulare* represents a preliminary stage—
which was to contain more patristic *testimonia* and flesh out the orthodox position of the Franks. This document became the *LC*. When
Hadrian's reply was received during its composition, it must have
caused the Franks great disappointment. Rather than affecting their
theological position, however, in which agreement with the papacy
was of the greatest importance as a mark of orthodoxy, Hadrian's
reply led to a revision of and, in one interesting example, even to
the omission of references to the Fathers. Yet since the *LC* aimed
primarily at protecting the orthodoxy of believers rather than at gaining papal support, references to an earlier papal letter, which Hadrian
had sent to Constantine and Irene prior to Nicea II in 785 and
which contained a helpful collection of patristic *testimonia*, needed no
longer to be avoided.[17]

In light of this complex compositional history it is clear that the
LC represent a divided West, as the radical rejection of the adoration of images is at odds with their professed obedience to Rome.
The Carolingians not only steer a different course from that of the
East but also from that of Rome, which had allied itself with Byzantium upon the approval of Nicea II. Rather than articulate the right
to form their own judgment, however, the *LC* enunciate their position indirectly, i.e., by adducing numerous patristic authors. Since
manuscript study has revealed that the patristic testimony of the *LC*
was altered under the influence of Rome and of Charlemagne's own
court theologians,[18] the study of those instances should be especially
revealing.

---

[16] Cf. *Regesta Pontificum Romanorum*, no. 2483. The text of the so-called *Hadrianum*
is edited in MGH Epp. 5:6–57.

[17] Cf. *Regesta Pontificum Romanorum*, no. 2448. Hadrian's letter, which became incorporated in the Nicene Acts, is edited in Mansi 12: 1055–1076. Ann Freeman has
identified the following chapters, all of which were added after the *Capitulare* was
sent, as written in direct response to Hadrian's letter to Constantine and Irene:
(from Mansi 12: 1057–1059) *LC* II ch. 13; (from Mansi 12: 1065) *LC* II ch. 11; I
ch. 29, 23, 24; II ch. 16 and 17; (from Mansi 12: 1068) *LC* II ch. 15; (from Mansi
12: 1072) *LC* I ch. 19. See Freeman 1985: 85 n. 80.

[18] See Freeman 1965, Part One, *passim*.

B. *The Theology of the* Libri Carolini *and the Authority of the Fathers*

The *LC* are formally divided into four books. The central thought at
the beginning and the end of the work emphasizes the need for unity
in the Church.[19] The Carolingians regard the iconophile position of
Byzantium as a threat to that unity and consider themselves responsible for its protection. It is significant that the *LC* confront not only
the second Nicene synod of 787, which promulgated the adoration
of images, but also the synod of Constantinople in 754, which rejected
the veneration of images on idolatrous grounds. In dismissing the
iconophile alongside the iconoclast position, the *LC* opt for a defense
strategy in which the unity of the Christian Church becomes predi-
cated upon the steering of a middle course. It is this middle course
of accepting the presence of images in the churches but rejecting
their adoration which Theodulf sets out to defend.[20]

Consistent with their goal of steering a middle course, the *LC* want
to avoid such capricious decisions as made by the Greeks. At Nicea
II the Greeks had unequivocally condemned their own predecessors
who convened the iconoclast synod of 754, thereby showing disre-
spect for their own past. They are thus not to be trusted with the
leadership of the universal Church. Although for the Carolingians
the unity of the Church depends more on the avoidance of theological extremes than on the accordance of East and West, it is nevertheless crucial to present the West itself as a unified whole with a
consistent theological tradition. The *LC* do so by portraying the West
as a *pars pro toto* representative of the universal Church, whose integrity is symbolized by the obedience to Rome and by the support of
the patristic tradition. By adducing the testimony of the Fathers, the
Carolingians do not mean to emulate the ideals of the apostolic
Church,[21] as may have been the ideal of later reform movements,
nor do they want to arbitrate the debate between East and West,

---

[19] See esp. the Preface and *LC* IV ch. 28.

[20] See the end of the Preface, Freeman 102: Nos denique Esaiae vaticinio docti,
qui dicit: "Haec via, ambulate in ea, non declinabitis ab ea neque ad dexteram
neque ad sinistram," (Is. 30:12) et doctoris gentium praedicatione admoniti, qui nos
viam regiam tenere instituit (cf. 1 Tim. 2:7), imagines in ornamentis ecclesiarum et
memoria rerum gestarum habentes et solum Dominum adorantes et eius sanctis
oportunam venerationem exhibentes nec cum illis frangimus nec cum istis adoramus ... See below n. 61 for the Gregorian quality of this middle course.

[21] In Book IV ch. 20 the *LC* make the point that although every Catholic has
received the Holy Spirit, nobody possesses it "secundum apostolicae mensurae
gratiam."

although the latter reason may be cited as an apparent motive. Rather, support from the Fathers is needed to solidify the nascent unity of the West which, in the absence of a continuous history, cannot be claimed but only be evoked. Once evoked, however, this symbolic unity acquires a significance of its own and can be bolstered by various arguments. In Book I ch. 7 until II ch. 12 these are drawn mainly from Scripture and in the rest of Book II mainly from the Fathers.

The *LC*'s rhetorical approach to the task at hand, i.e., the defense of a unified Church,[22] bespeaks an ecclesiology which reaches beyond that of the Church as the harmony of its Eastern and Western phalanxes. The Church's unity is symbolically concentrated in the authority of the Roman see, but is elevated to the superior mystical status of representing the Bride of Christ. The *LC* do not always carefully distinguish between the various ecclesiological models, as the issue of the Church's horizontal accordance is flexibly connected with that of its mystical integrity. Thus they call the image-worship of the Greeks a novel constitution, the acceptance of which not only causes schism but defiles the Bride herself.[23] It is further suggested that, when the Church as the Bride of Christ is under attack, Christ himself is put at risk. Underneath the caustic criticism of Greek iconophile theology one thus finds a deeply rooted Christological sensitivity, a sensitivity by which the issue of images is transformed into the call to defend not just the honor of the Bride but of Christ himself.[24]

---

[22] The *LC* see the break-up of the Church as caused by the arrogance and ambitions of the kings and priests of the East: Inflammavit igitur ventosae arrogantiae inflata ambitio et vanae laudis insolentissimus appetitus quosdam orientalium partium non solum reges, sed etiam sacerdotes, adeo ut . . . dumque suorum gestorum ordinem volunt mandare memoriae posteritatis, discindant vinculum ecclesiasticae unitatis (Preface, Freeman 98–99).

[23] See Preface, Freeman 101, for one of Theodulf's typical syllogistic arguments: Nam si novas constitutiones ecclesiae ingerere iactantia est, scisma est, quod tamen in ecclesia fieri non debet. Quod si scisma est, macula est, quae in sponsa esse negatur. Si igitur novas constitutiones ecclesiae ingerere iactantia est, macula procul dubio est, quae in sponsa esse negatur. NB. It is significant that in Book I ch. 6 the *LC*, following the *Decretum Gelasianum* here, apply the Pauline notion of the Church as without blemish (Eph. 5:27) especially to the Church of Rome.

[24] This Christological emphasis explains why the *LC* contrast the veneration of the images with the unique Christian image of the cross, see e.g. *LC* I ch. 9, Freeman 154: Atque illi glorientur in imaginibus, nos autem "gloriemur in cruce Domini nostri Iesu Christi, per quem" nobis "mundus crucifixus est" nosque "mundo" (cf. Gal. 6:14). The cluster of images here echoes the poetry of Venantius Fortunatus, see Book II ch. 28.

As the perfect image of God, Christ has a natural link with humanity which is created in the image and likeness of God (Gen. 1:26).[25]
Theodulf's stress on humanity's specific task of living in the likeness
of God means that any serious theological role for the images is pre-
empted as he disqualifies their mediating function. If God's image is
not reflected in humans, it can surely not be found in the images
that are the mere products of human craftsmen. In highlighting the
role of humanity and especially of Christ as the image of God,
Theodulf's attack on Greek iconophile theology transforms into a
thinly veiled urge for moral reform as one of the larger Carolingian
themes.[26] Furthermore, by grafting the notion of Christ and humanity as the image of God onto the mystical vision of the Church as
Bride of Christ, the *LC* rise beyond the dilemma of an iconoclast
versus an iconophile position. Fulfilling their intended purpose of
steering a middle course, their path resembles more and more that
of the Carolingian *via regia*.[27]

The above themes demarcate the broader theological context
within which to situate Theodulf's recourse to the Fathers, by which
he communicates to his readers a certain "fullness" or "wholeness"
of the tradition. Although the reason for his belief in the authority of
the Fathers remains ultimately hidden behind the Church's mystical
veil as *sponsa Christi*, their support adds instant weight to his arguments. In the broadest terms Theodulf invokes the tradition by simply eliminating what it does not represent and stating only obliquely
what it does. While regarding the collective support of the Fathers as
an antidote against the novel doctrine of the Greeks, he underscores
each time a particular theological point. When he accuses the Greeks
of defiling the Bride in the preface, he alleges that they abandoned
"the teachings of the Fathers," who did not sanction the worship-
ping of images but accepted them for decorative purposes only.[28] In

---

[25] See *LC* I ch. 7.

[26] Cf. *LC* I ch. 17, Freeman 185: Quod vero dicunt: "per adsimilatam picturam
videre exitum conversationis sanctorum virorum," quantae sit absurditatis quantaeque
dementiae, pene infinitum est persequi, cum videlicet in imaginibus non possit sanctae
conversationis virtus videri, sed solummodo illae materiae, quibus ipsae imagines
formatae sunt. The *LC* repeatedly contrast images with Scripture on the point of
moral edification.

[27] Cf. Wallach's comments on the *via regia* in the *LC* as a typical Alcuinian notion,
in Wallach 1959: 171 and Wallach 1977: 68.

[28] See the Preface, Freeman 101: . . . relictis priscorum patrum traditionibus, qui
imagines non colere sanxerunt, sed in ornamento ecclesiarum habere siverunt, novas

Book I ch. 11 the *LC* state that the Holy Church accepts what is not reprehensible and rejects everything that is reprehensible, including this particular Greek synod, "according to the institution of the Holy Fathers." In the same chapter they say that the earlier synods of the Holy Church, called by "learned and catholic men," did not deviate from "sane and sober doctrine," but specify neither the doctrine nor the names of those catholic men.[29] Though presenting the Fathers as an anonymous force, the *LC* are convinced that, once mobilized, they only reinforce the authority of Scripture and the apostolic synods. The *LC* thus can even name them all in one breath.[30]

This compression of the Fathers into an indiscriminate force is facilitated by the fact that the *LC* regard patristic judgment as marked by incontrovertible truth. This becomes clear when the *LC* on one occasion oppose "the tradition of the venerable fathers" to the arbitrariness of the Greeks. Rather than accepting the saints upon the authority of the Church's tradition, the Greeks get entangled in their own idolatrous premises as they are forced to rank the saints according to the materials of which they are made.[31] Here the guidance of the tradition functions as a beacon of light not only in the abstract

---

et insolitas ecclesiae nituntur inferre constitutiones, quibus ei maculam potius quam decorem adscribant. Follows the syllogism quoted in n. 23 above.

[29] Cf. Freeman 159–160: Cum ergo sancta ecclesia secundum sanctorum patrum institutionem omne, quod inreprehensibile est, recipiat, omne quod repraehensibile, abiciat, hanc quoque eorum synodum, quae utique repraehensibilis est, abicit.... Illas enim synodos sancta et universalis recipit ecclesia, quae pro diversis fidei sive religionis causis diversis locis seu temporibus a doctis et catholicis viris celebratae a sana sobriaque doctrina nullatenus deviare perhibentur.

[30] See e.g. *LC* IV ch. 13, Freeman 516, against the novelties of this second Nicene synod: Habet etiam post confessionem sanctae Trinitatis confessionem quoque adorandarum imaginum inditam, quam neque in prophetarum oraculis neque in evangeliorum tonitruis neque in apostolorum dogmatibus neque in anteriorum sanctarum synodorum relatibus vel quorumlibet orthodoxorum patrum doctrinis uspiam repperimus insertam.

[31] This is the implication of *LC* I ch. 2 in which the images as *figmenta artificum* are contrasted with the truth of the saints themselves. See esp. Freeman 118: Sciscitandum ab eis est, qui tanto errore laborant, ut eas pro arbitrio suo et veritatem et sanctas et veras, et non potius secundum venerabilium patrum traditionem sanctorum imagines dicunt, quae cunctis conparata sanctior vel verior, quae omnium sanctissima aut verissima esse credenda est, quas, dum eas aequales dicere pro materiarum et magnitudinum vel operum discretione ratio non permiserit et quasdam quibusdam sanctiores et quarundam sanctissimas fateri conpescuerit, profiteri conpelluntur secundum veritatis indagatricem rationem nec veritatis capaces nec sanctas dici debere, quoniam quidem et pretio sunt inaequales, quo sibimet per conparationis gradus praeferuntur, et sanctitatis et veritatis merito aequales, qua omnes omnino carent.

world of controversial doctrine but also in the real world of Carolingian culture ravaged by war and corruption.[32]

The element of truth is what binds the authority of the Fathers closely to that of Holy Scripture. The authority of Scripture, which is ultimately embodied in the figure of Christ, who is *veritas* as well as *via* and *vita* (Ioh. 14:7), is tantamount to the voice of truth itself.[33] When attacking the Greek excuse that Scripture might have employed improper speech (*acirologia*) in Jacob's blessing of the Pharao (Gen. 47:7–10) by using the verb "benedicere" to signify "adorare", the *LC* adamantly state "that Scripture always uses pure, proper, fixed or prudent words or sayings."[34] Within the parameters of the general correspondence between Scripture and truth, Theodulf explicitly focuses on the Hebrew Old Testament. He contests the accuracy of certain Greek readings, as in Jacob's blessing of the Pharao, by testing them against the *Hebraica veritas* and the *bibliotheca Latinorum*.[35] This expression is remarkable for two reasons. First, by mentioning the Hebrew original of the Bible, it points to the old textual traditions of Visigothic Spain and reinforces the likelihood of Theodulf's authorship. Second, it reflects the Carolingian mindset in which learning and erudition are associated with the "written" quality of literacy.[36] In Theodulf's hands the Bible is turned into one of the most powerful weapons against Greek idolatry, as *scriptura* is set off against

---

[32] Freeman connects this point with Theodulf's theory of art, see Freeman 1957: 695–703, esp. 697.

[33] See the end of *LC* I ch. 2, Freeman 120: Multa enim contra huius capituli non mediocre deliramentum secundum sanctarum Scripturarum auctoritatem et secundum veritatis indagationem dici poterant, . . .

[34] See *LC* I ch. 9, Freeman 152: Sancta vero Scriptura sicut ceteros errores, ita etiam hunc loquendi modum abnuit, sed puris, propriis, fixis sive prudentibus semper verbis sive sententiis utitur . . . See also *LC* III ch. 23, Freeman 446, for the contrast between the truth of Scripture and the falsehoods of paintings: In sacris etenim litteris nihil vitiosum, nihil inconveniens, nihil inpurum, nihil falsum nisi forte id, quod perversos quosque dixisse vel fecisse sancta Scriptura commemorat, penitus invenitur; in picturis autem plura falsa, plura vitiosa, plura inconsequentia, plura inconvenientia . . .

[35] See Freeman 1957: 692–693. Although Freeman is correct in stating that Theodulf sometimes privileges the Old over the New Testament, this does not go beyond occasional formulations, as Theodulf leaves the Christological priority of the New Testament over the Old intact. See below n. 41.

[36] This does not necessarily mean that Theodulf derived all his material from written sources. As pointed out by Ann Freeman, Theodulf's citation of biblical passages is based on liturgical reminiscence, see Freeman 1957: 674–683. Nevertheless, Theodulf seems to value the literary preservation of texts. For the broader cultural significance of Carolingian literacy, see McKitterick 1989.

pictura in a contrast of truth versus falsehood. Thus Theodulf claims that Moses taught about the origin of the world through writing rather than painting.[37] He further stresses that Jesus wrote rather than drew with his finger in the sand.[38] The role of Scripture is heightened even more when it is seen not only as the reservoir of revealed, divine truth but also as the inexhaustible storehouse of the human arts.[39]

Although resembling that of Scripture, the authority of the Fathers does not have the same stature. Whereas Scripture ultimately embodies truth itself, the authority of the Fathers is based on additional criteria. Still, the evidence from Scripture and the Fathers is combined in that both are an indispensable part of the so-called *ordo testimoniorum*. In Book I ch. 5 the *LC* explain their intention to "... follow the order of testimonies, which was laid down by the Sacred Writings or the treatises of the Holy Fathers and was inordinately or improperly usurped by those who are known to have attended the aforesaid synod, with the Lord's favor in a competent order..."[40] This *ordo testimoniorum* is not an arbitrary one, as it is derived from the so-called *res christianorum*, by which the *LC* refer to the middle position of the Carolingians on the images, which is further linked to

---

[37] See *LC* II ch. 30, Freeman 305: Idem quoque Moyses originem mundi non pingendo, sed scribendo edocuit.... For Moses as the author of the Pentateuch, see Isidore, *Etymol.* VI, 2: Primus Moyses divinae historiae cosmographiam in quinque voluminibus edidit, quod Pentatiuchum nominatur.

[38] *Ibidem*, Freeman 309: qui (scil. Christus)... *digito in terra* non pinxisse, sed *scripsisse* perhibetur (cf. Ioh. 8:6).

[39] See esp. *LC* II ch. 30, Freeman 315–316, where Theodulf follows Cassiodorus, *Expositio Psalmorum*, praef. ch. 15 (De eloquentia totius legis divinae): Sed dicit forte aliquis: "Nec nomina principaliter disciplinarum nec uniuscuiusque disciplinae singillatim partes nec uniuscuiusque partis membra singillatim in sacris litteris inveniuntur." Quibus breviter respondendum est omnia in Scripturarum sanctarum amplissimis pratis per partes inveniri posse, quae artigraphi in suorum hortorum areolis posuere... Sic enim in profunditate divinarum Scripturarum liberales artes ab studiosis quibusque cernuntur, sicut vina in vitibus, segetes in seminibus, frondes in radicibus, fructus in ramis arborumque magnitudines sensu contemplantur in nucleis. On Theodulf's creative adaptation of Cassiodorus' *Expositio Psalmorum* in this chapter, see *Opus Caroli*, ed. Freeman, Introduction, pp. 52–53. See also below n. 53.

[40] See *LC* I ch. 5, Freeman 131–132:... nunc testimoniorum ordinem, qui a sanctis Scripturis sive a sanctorum patrum tractatibus digestus est et inordinate sive non proprie ab his, qui in praefata synodo sedisse noscuntur, usurpatus, ordine conpetenti Domino favente exsequamur ponentes dumtaxat summatim, quid sanctorum patrum de his definierit sententia vel quomodo a venerabilibus viris prolata sint, quae ad suum errorem astruendam illorum adglomeravit amentia. Cf. also the Preface to Book II.

the priority of the New Testament over the Old.[41] Grounded in the
res christianorum, the evidence from the Fathers proves in the final
analysis to be a subsidiary construct.

This may explain Theodulf's own freedom in proceeding with the
ordo testimoniorum. In the case of the Fathers, this is true not only in
the matter of interpreting them but also of selecting them. For unlike the text of Scripture, which in order to be accepted needs only
to be properly, i.e., spiritually received—which holds generally true
for patristic evidence as well—,[42] it seems that in the Carolingian era
the "text" of the patristic tradition is still in the process of being
woven. Theodulf actively participates in this weaving-process not just
by selecting his *testimonia* from the Nicene proceedings or Hadrian's
letter to Constantine and Irene, but especially by bringing the question
of authenticity to bear on the Fathers.[43] The fact that the question of
authenticity is raised implies that there was need for an explicit criterion on which the Carolingians could base their judgment. This
criterion is found in the *Decretum Gelasianum de libris recipiendis et non
recipiendis*,[44] which they wrongly considered a papal document.

The *LC* first bring up Gelasius in Book I ch. 6. Having concluded
that the adoration of images goes against Scripture and the Fathers,
Theodulf is ready to proceed with the *ordo testimoniorum*. Before doing
so, however, he stresses that Rome should be consulted in all matters of faith. The authority of Gelasius is connected with a quotation

---

[41] In Book I ch. 19 (Freeman 192) the *LC* coordinate the concepts of *ordo* and *res*:
Saepe in hoc opere dicere conpellimur, quod neque tabulae neque duo cherubim
nec cetera huiuscemodi ad adorandum in veteri Testamento facta fuisse credantur.
Quae quidem isti omnia relicto mediocritatis et rectitudinis calle in eo ultra, quam
ordo exposcit, extollunt, quod ea ad adorandum fuisse conlata proclamant, in eo
vero ultra, quam *res* exigit, submittunt, quod illis imagines aequiperare affectant.
About the Greeks they exclaim: Quid aliud faciunt nisi, ut imagines exaltent,
christianorum res extenuant? and accuse them of proceeding *converso ordine* by using the
Old Testament to test the New. NB. There seem to be echoes here of Augustine's
De doctrina christiana. The *LC* mention the *De doctrina* explicitly in II ch. 28 (cf. *De
doctrina* II 41, 62) and quote from it with reference to the author but not the work
in I ch. 6 (cf. *De doctrina* II, 8, 12) and II ch. 24 (cf. *De doctrina* III 7). Ann Freeman
has located an additional reference in Vat. lat. 7207, fol. 87v (II, ch. 22). On the
importance of Augustine's theory of signs in the *De doctrina* for Theodulf's theory of
art, see Chazelle 1986: 173–74.
[42] See e.g. *LC* I ch. 16 on Scripture as the *lex spiritualis*. On the Fathers, see
Freeman 1971: 605.
[43] On how the issue of authenticity affects patristic authority, see e.g. *LC* III chs.
21, 25, 26, 30. On the dubiousness of apocryphal writings, see e.g. *LC* III chs. 26,
30; IV, chs. 10, 11.
[44] See Von Dobschütz 1912: 3–61.

from *De doctrina christiana* II, 8, 12 in which Augustine extols the canonical scriptures as based on the authority of the catholic churches, especially those with apostolic sees. Theodulf further sharpens Augustine's arguments by putting the authority of Rome over that of the other apostolic sees. Despite a temporary disagreement on the issue of *celebratio officiorum*, the Western Church had never moved far away from Rome. With the unity of the holy religion thus remaining unaffected, the Western Church had recently united itself with Rome in the *ordo psallendi*.

Despite the reliance on Gelasius and the claimed adherence to Rome,[45] the role of papal authority in the *LC* appears symbolic for the unity of faith rather than determinative of the *res christianorum*. This becomes clear in Book II ch. 13 where the *LC* discuss the conduct of pope Silvester, who supposedly countenanced Constantine's adoration of images. While sympathetic to Silvester's strategy, if at all true, of elevating Constantine through visible to invisible things, the *LC* use Gelasius to argue against the Greeks that the *Acta Silvestri*, although widely read, cannot be used to prove questionable matters such as the adoration of images.[46] Thus the criterion of papal authority is curiously invoked against the Acts of a past pope, which through their alleged iconophile message appear to compromise the *res christianorum*.

On the whole, the *Decretum Gelasianum* is Theodulf's undisputed criterion in discriminating between acceptable and unacceptable authorities.[47] By using a codified list to test the authenticity of certain patristic writings, which he puts in sharp contrast with the *incontinentia oris* of the Greeks, Theodulf surely wants to proclaim their orthodoxy. Given the already established primacy of the *res christianorum*, however, this appears not to be an exclusive concern.[48] It rather seems

---

[45] Von Dobschütz argues that the use of Eph. 5:27 for the Roman Church in this chapter is influenced by Gelasius. Compare *LC* I ch. 6, Freeman 135, with *Decretum Gelasianum* III 3. See also Von Dobschütz 1912: 198, 237.

[46] In Gelasius the reluctant endorsement of the *Acta Silvestri* seems due primarily to their unidentified author: Item actus beati Silvestri apostolicae sedis praesulis, licet eius qui conscripserit nomen ignoretur, a multis tamen in urbe Romana catholicis legi cognovimus, et pro antiquo usu multae hoc imitantur Ecclesiae. The *LC* seem to turn Gelasius' reluctant support for the *Acta* into a more pointed criticism.

[47] See e.g. *LC* IV chs. 10, 11.

[48] Compare also the numerous references to the *Filioque* in the *LC*, which despite being a novel doctrine was not seen as unorthodox or at odds with the tradition. See esp. *LC* III ch. 3.

as if Theodulf wants formally to authenticate his written sources as
a precondition for their legitimate use in theological debate. The
emphasis on authentication as a way of underscoring the authority
of his sources can help us to understand certain unusual features in
the Carolingian recourse to the Fathers, found mainly in Book II.
Chronological order, for example, appears not to be a major factor.
This becomes clear when Theodulf sets out to refute the Greeks'
claim that Augustine supports their position in Book II ch. 16. Reit-
erating that man-made images should not be adored, he dwells on
the role of Christ as the true *imago dei*. He first quotes Paul (Col.
1: 12–15) and, in what appears to be a favored combination, turns
next to Augustine. Reversing chronological order, he then calls on
Ambrose to defend the "middle" position of Augustine.[49] This lack
of chronological concern became a point of contention between
Charlemagne's court and pope Hadrian, whose response to the early
Capitulare was critical of the anachronism implied by the Frankish
claim that the whole tradition agreed with Gregory the Great. Upon
review of this chapter (Book II ch. 23) the Carolingians withdrew
their appeal to Scripture and the Fathers completely.[50] If necessary,
the *res christianorum* could dispense with the *ordo testimoniorum* altogether.

The primacy of the *res christianorum* over the *ordo testimoniorum* may
go far to explain why the *LC* accused the Greeks of having "usurped"
both Scripture and the Fathers. By prescinding from any form of
authentication, they had gravely diminished the validity of their
patristic testimony. It is the *LC*'s intent to restore the texts of the
Fathers "to their original meanings."[51] In doing so they display a

---

[49] See *LC* II ch. 16, Freeman 265: Dic itaque etiam tu, sanctissime Ambrosi,
quid de hac imagine sentire te constet. Defende beatum Augustinum per te favente
Deo ad fidei rudimenta conversum, quem vides nunc ab imaginum adoratoribus
infauste criminatum. The Augustine reference is to *De diversis quaestionibus* 74. The
Ambrose-reference is to *De fide ad Gratianum* I, 7, 49–50. In the rhetorical nature of
this quotation Theodulf follows the precedent of the fifth-century sermon *Contra Iudaeos*
by the African bishop Quodvultdeus, which was used in a Homiliary composed for
Charlemagne by Paul the Deacon. See Freeman 1965: 235–237 and *Opus Caroli*, ed.
Freeman, Introduction, p. 51 n. 360. Freeman's comments on Theodulf's rhetorical
framing of his quotations to heighten the dramatic impact of the text are especially
important.

[50] See Freeman 1965: 212–213 and 1985: 91. On the complicated composition
and curtailment of the text of Book II in Vat. lat. 7207, see *Opus Caroli*, ed. Freeman, Introduction, pp. 38–43.

[51] See the Preface to *LC* II, Bastgen 60: . . . necesse est, ut in praesenti, secundo
videlicet, libro et divinae legis sane sobrieque residua commata tractaturi et quorundam
sanctorum patrum male nihilominus sententias ab illis usurpatas propriis sensibus

clear preference for Western authorities, among whom we can find Ambrose, Jerome, Augustine,[52] Hilary and Gregory the Great. Other testimonies, derived from Cassiodorus and Isidore, are sometimes cited without reference, their texts adapted freely;[53] since these authors are not in Gelasius there existed no need to mention them explicitly. Although the *LC* embrace Athanasius and Chrysostom, whose works are supported by Gelasius,[54] it is evident that on the whole they are less interested in the Greek Fathers.[55] Thus Book II ch. 17 simply states that, since the life and the preaching of bishop Gregory of Nyssa are unknown, he ought not to be considered in this debate. Although this remark may reflect Latin provincialism,[56] it is better understood as underscoring the *LC*'s call for shared sources as a condition for fruitful debate. Since Gregory of Nyssa is not listed by Gelasius, he can safely be ruled out. In Book II ch. 19, however, the *LC* go to great lengths to show that the testimony of bishop John of Constantinople, i.e., Chrysostom, cannot be construed to support image-worship by rejecting the connection between images of God and images of the Emperor.[57] When Chrysostom further states that

---

reddituri Domino favente adgrediamur. There may also be an implicit reference here to the fact that the Greeks had misinterpreted the *testimonia* in Hadrian's original letter, which after being sent to Constantine and Hadrian in 785 had become incorporated in the Nicene Acta. See Freeman 1985: 82.

[52] According to Freeman, the marginal notes in the *LC*'s original, Vat. lat. 7207, contain Charlemagne's comments on the text. She notes that Augustine is the only author whose testimony is saluted as *optimum* (twice) and *totum optime* (once) in addition to a simple *bene* once. See Freeman 1971: 607.

[53] Cassiodorus' *Expositio Psalmorum* functioned as an important source for Theodulf. On his free adaptation of this text, see *Opus Caroli*, ed. Freeman, Introduction, pp. 52-53. See also n. 39 above. To Isidore, whose *Etymologiae* and other works exercised a great influence, Theodulf owed much of his formation as a scholar, esp. his introduction to dialectic. On this, see *Opus Caroli*, ed. Freeman, Introduction, pp. 53-56.

[54] See Book II ch. 14. The passage from Athanasius' *De incarnatione verbi* here is derived from Hadrian's letter to Constantine and Irene and not from the Nicene acts. Cf. Freeman 1985: 83.

[55] Wallach makes the point that the *LC* cite on their own only one Greek patristic text that deals with an iconoclastic episode. It concerns an excerpt from a letter by Epiphanius of Salamis which was sent to John of Jerusalem in 392 and is preserved in Latin in Jerome's *Epistula* 51. *Epist.* LI, 9 is cited in *LC* IV ch. 25. See Wallach 1966: 467.

[56] Freeman 1957: 664 mentions the *LC*'s "parochial point of view." Freeman observingly remarks that Gregory of Nyssa did not feature in Hadrian's *Responsio*, which may have contributed to the *LC*'s dismissive comments here, see Freeman 1971: 600.

[57] Chrysostom is a favorite author of Theodulf's, whom he is eager to exonerate from accusations of image-worship. The quotation here does not stem from a Nicene

heaven, earth and the sea serve the image of God, the *LC* explain that by the image of God he refers to Christ or humans here rather than to man-made images. Book II ch. 20 comments on an unidentified passage from Cyril of Alexandria's commentary on Matthew which seems to imply a relation between the signifying power of parables in revealing the mysteries and the role of images, but Theodulf points out that this is not an endorsement of image-worship.[58]

The major authority for the Carolingians as well as for pope Hadrian in his alliance with Byzantium is no doubt Gregory the Great.[59] In upholding the position that images are meaningful for the instruction of the illiterate,[60] Gregory is more central than any other Father because he is not just part of the *ordo testimoniorum* but is himself an inseparable part of the *res christianorum*. It is Gregory the

---

actio, however, but from Hadrian's letter to Constantine and Irene. We are dealing in fact with two passages from Severianus of Gabala, which were conflated first in Hadrian's letter. See Freeman 1985: 84–85.

[58] On the confusion surrounding this *testimonium*, which the *LC* derived again from Hadrian's letter rather than from the proceedings of Nicea II, see Freeman 1985: 83. Theodulf comments on his difficulties in deciphering the garbled translation from the Greek here, see Freeman 1985: 79.

[59] As revealed by Ann Freeman, however, Gregory's name is linked to the question of images only in this chapter. His name is further mentioned in *LC* II ch. 9 with a reference to *Regula pastoralis* II, 6, in *LC* III ch. 2 against Tarasius' elevation to bishop with a reference to *Registrum Epistularum* IX, 219, in *LC* III ch. 25 in connection with Satanic miracles with a reference to *Homiliae in Evangelia* II, 29, 4, and in *LC* IV ch. 12 regarding another miracle with reference to *Dialogues* III, 19. See on this *Opus Caroli*, ed. Freeman, Introduction, p. 32 and n. 243. Still, quantity may not equal quality here. The importance of Gregory in the image-debate can also be seen from Hadrian's diplomatic gesture to Charlemagne in suggesting that he himself was not associated with the contents of the *Capitulare adversus synodum* but only with the *testimonium* of Gregory. See Freeman 1985: 90. Freeman notes that in the marginal notes to Vat. lat. 7207 Gregory is saluted once as *perfecte siquidem* and perhaps twice as *ecclesiastice*, see Freeman 1971: 607.

[60] On Gregory's position on images, see Feld 1990: 11–14. Citing Gregory's second letter to the iconoclast bishop Serenus of Marseille (*Registrum Epistularum* XI, 10), the *LC* mention Gregory's famous notion of *pro lectione pictura* only implicitly in the context of his opposition to the adoration of images: (Gregory advises Serenus here to gather his congregation to instruct them from Scripture that only God must be adored) ... ac deinde subiungendum, quia picturae imaginum, quae ad aedificationem imperiti populi factae fuerant, ut nescientes litteras ipsam historiam intendentes, quod dictum sit, discerent, transisse in adorationem videras, idcirco commotus es, ut eas frangi praeciperes, atque eis dicendum: Si ad hanc instructionem, ad quam imagines antiquitus factae sunt, habere vultis in ecclesiis, eas modis omnibus et offerri et haberi permittas, atque indica, quod non tibi ipsa visio historiae, quae pictura teste pandebatur, displicuerit, sed illa adoratio ... On the other hand, the *LC* show explicit support for Gregory's middle position of neither adoring nor destroying the images. On this, see Chazelle 1986: 179 and *Opus Caroli*, ed. Freeman, Introduction, pp. 31–32.

Great, after all, who first recommended the very middle course that the *LC* advocate.[61] He rejected the adoration of images, which would amount to an exhortation to idolatry, but also opposed their destruction for fear of frightening people. In a triumphant conclusion the *LC* sing the praise of Gregory as the only patristic author whose authenticity defies proof, since it coincides with his papal authority:

"See then how we, imbued with what authority and what ordinance of this venerable pontiff, do not refuse to have images in the churches, yet unconditionally reject their adoration!"[62]

C. *Remembering the Fathers*

In recent years much scholarship has focused on the role of mnemonic devices in the Middle Ages.[63] This issue has a particular significance for the *LC*, since the faculty of memory is often explicitly brought in connection with their objection to the adoration of images. I want to underline the significance of memory on two interrelated points, namely as an epistemological tool in furthering the *LC*'s arguments, and as an aid in remembering the Fathers.

On the first point, it is significant that the *LC* use memory specifically to offset the role that images play in Greek theology. The *LC* claim that images are necessary only for people with "bad memories," who are otherwise unable to remember the living tradition of the Church.[64] There seems to be a connection between the literal or carnal exegesis of Scripture, forgetfulness of the saints and the Lord himself, and spiritual weakness, all of which are negative characteristics explicitly associated with the Greeks. Against this, the *LC* celebrate the Catholic people of the West who do not need images but are so enshrouded in Christ's mystery that their memory functions independently of visual or material aids. The West with its mark of freedom (*libertatis indicium*) is contrasted with the Greeks who are

---

[61] For this it is enough to point out the identity of Theodulf's claims in the general Preface (Freeman 102, see above n. 20) with Gregory's position as the *LC* describe and endorse it in Book II ch. 23.

[62] See *LC* II ch. 23, Freeman 280: Ecce quo magisterio quove documento venerandi pontificis inbuti imagines in ecclesiis habere non rennuimus, sed earum adorationem prorsus abdicamus; cuius institutis contraire se, quisquis eas vel frangit vel adorat, modis omnibus recognoscat.

[63] See Carruthers 1990; Coleman 1992.

[64] See *LC* II ch. 22: Quod non bonam habeant memoriam, qui, ut non obliviscantur sanctorum vel certe ipsius Domini, idcirco imagines erigent.

enslaved by material images.[65] This Greek dependence on visual aids also brings on their doubtful morality (*vitium infirmitatis*). By implying that a more precious image has more representational value, they privilege the rich over the poor.[66]

Reasoning back from this role of memory regarding the *res christianorum*, i.e., the orthodox Carolingian position on images, we should take care to explain the loose handling of patristic testimony in the *LC* not just as a defect, as if the Carolingians did not know how to study their sources, but as a sign that for them a "mark of freedom" naturally leads to the confidence to interpret pre-approved authorities, such as the Fathers sanctioned by Gelasius, independently with the understanding that the full tradition supports them. It is this confidence which the *LC* so markedly betray.

III. *Alcuin of York and the* De virtutibus et vitiis

A. *The Compositional Structure of Alcuin's* De virtutibus et vitiis

The DVV was written around 800 by Alcuin for Wido, Margrave of the Marca Brittanniae, who in 799 had subjected his territory to Charlemagne. Unlike the *LC*, the *De virtutibus et vitiis* (*DVV*), whose Alcuinian authorship is undisputed, was an enormously popular treatise throughout much of the Middle Ages, as is testified by the large number of extant manuscripts.[67] In genre, the work has been compared to the so-called "mirrors for princes." Apart from its conventional dedicatory letter and a concluding epistolary peroration, the body of the work consists of two parts, the first part dealing mostly but not exclusively with virtues (chs. 1–26) and the second part summing up the eight vices (27–34). The final chapter (35) extols the importance of the four cardinal virtues: wisdom, justice, courage and temperance, describing them collectively with the term *virtus*, and leads seamlessly into the peroration.

---

[65] *Ibidem* (Freeman 277): Cum ergo mens hominis ita ei inhaerere debeat, ad cuius imaginem condita est, ut nulla creatura interposita ab ipsa veritate, quae Christus est, formetur, dementissimum est eam interpositis materialibus imaginibus, ne eius oblivionem patiatur, admoneri debere, cum videlicet hoc infirmitatis sit vitium, non libertatis indicium. NB. The phrase *nulla creatura interposita* echoes Augustine, *De vera religione* LV, 113.

[66] See *LC* IV ch. 27.

[67] See Wallach 1959: 247–251.

In his introductory letter Alcuin states to Wido that, at his repeated request, he has written him some exhortations *brevi sermone* so
that he will possess "handy sentences of fatherly admonition," which—
as he must contemplate himself in them—should excite him to the
study of eternal beatitude.[68] Thus the genre of princely mirrors folds
into the broader Augustinian and monastic theme of *scito teipsum*, which
represents a mainstay of medieval anthropology.[69] By "the handy
sentences of fatherly admonition" Alcuin seems to refer to his own
work, which is likewise the case when he recommends that Wido
store these words of his in his memory.[70] However, the casual use of
the expression *haec mea dicta* here may also intimate to us how little
difference Alcuin actually sees between his own words and those of
the Fathers, since it is clear that the *DVV* consists largely of passages
that were excerpted from patristic writers.

Whether Alcuin's moral exhortations originate with the author himself or with the Fathers, in both cases their authority is clearly differ-
entiated from that of Scripture. This becomes clear in ch. 14, where
Alcuin admonishes Wido not to postpone his conversion. In this chapter he loosely follows a sermon of Caesarius of Arles,[71] including the
passage where Caesarius ends a quotation from Eccli. 5:8 with the
words: "These are God's words, not mine." By inserting passages
from Caesarius's sermon seamlessly in his own text, Alcuin implies
that the disparity between the words of Scripture and those of either
himself or Caesarius—for he literally makes no distinction between
the two—is somehow a clearer one than the disparity between his
own words and those of the tradition.

This impression is confirmed by the fact that Alcuin habitually
introduces scriptural passages as such[72] but never once in his short
treatise mentions a patristic author by name, although the presence

---

[68] See *DVV* 613C: Memor sum petitionis tuae et promissionis meae, qua me obnixe
flagitasti, aliqua tuae occupationi, quam te in bellicis rebus habere novimus, exhorta-
menta brevi sermone conscribere, ut habeas jugiter inter manus manuales paternae
admonitionis sententias, in quibus teipsum considerare debuisses, atque ad aeternae
beatitudinis excitare studium.

[69] See McGinn 1988.

[70] See *DVV* 613D: Singulis siquidem hujus sermonis seriem distinxi capitulis,
quatenus facilius vestrae devotionis memoriae haec mea dicta inhaerere potuissent;
sciens te in multis saecularium rerum cogitationibus occupatum.

[71] See Caesarius of Arles *sermo* 18, 2–6 and Wallach 1959: 243–244, 252–254.

[72] Alcuin often introduces scriptural passages by the name of their proclaimed
author, e.g. *Psalmista* (615A; 616D) or *doctor gentium* for Paul (616B; 618C). E.g. *Dominus*
(618C), *Salvator* (617A, 617D, 622B) and *Veritas* (615D) are used for gospel passages.

of the Fathers is unmistakable. In Alcuin we thus have a form of weaving the tradition that differs markedly from the one encountered in the *LC*. Whereas Theodulf was concerned with authenticating the past by ratifying the texts of the Fathers with the authority of Gelasius, in Alcuin we witness how various strands of the tradition are literally woven together to become a new text. As an apparent side-effect of this process the difference between author and editor fades into the background. Although Alcuin has a claim on being the latter rather than the former, in the letter concluding his treatise just as in the opening epistle, he again omits any distinction between his own words and those of his sources, affirming simply that he dictated these things *brevi sermone*.[73]

B. *Alcuin's Theology and the Authority of the Fathers*

One of the issues in the debate concerning the authorship of the *Libri Carolini* focused on the question of whether the author had selected his biblical citations directly or derived them indirectly from his patristic sources.[74] Thus it was suggested that Theodulf had not been original in composing his text but slavishly copied from his patristic predecessors. Although this question is no longer immediately relevant for the *LC*,[75] the problem of composition as mindless copying from patristic sources is very much at issue in the *DVV*. Here indeed we have a work that seems more a composite than an original text, since large portions of it were obviously excerpted from patristic sources. Still, the composite nature of this treatise cannot undo the fact that a composer must have been at work in the actual arranging and weaving together of its composite parts. Underscoring a similar point, John Cavadini has aptly compared the structure of

---

[73] See *DVV* 638B: Haec tibi, dulcissime fili Wido, brevi sermone, sicut petisti, dictavi. NB. Through the repetition of similar terminology, Alcuin even seems to excerpt his own writings.

[74] See Freeman 1965: 223–269. In this section of her article Freeman also touches on the *LC*'s important borrowings from florilegia such as the pseudo-Augustinian *Speculum* or *Liber de divinis scripturis* and the mystical dictionary *Clavis Melitonis*. On the *Speculum*, see also *Opus Caroli*, ed. Freeman, Introduction, pp. 63–65.

[75] See *art. cit.* This question seems less relevant after Freeman demonstrated that the Old Latin biblical citations found in the *LC* do not derive from a corresponding (pseudo-)patristic context but stem from Spanish liturgical practice. Freeman points out that Theodulf used the *Liber de divinis scripturis* mostly in Books III and IV, esp. in *LC* III ch. 12 and IV ch. 5.

Alcuin's *De fide sanctae et individuae trinitatis* to that of a patchwork-quilt; although the pieces of it may have been pre-existent, a designer was nevertheless required to put them together. Consequently, Cavadini typifies the end-result as having "a charism all its own."[76]

The initial debate about the patristic sources used by Alcuin in the *DVV* focused in large part on the origin of his borrowings, whether he excerpted patristic texts directly or received them through an intermediate florilegium. If the use of a written florilegium can be established, it may well have been the *Liber scintillarum* of Defensor of Ligugé, a seventh century monastic *collectaneum* of patristic sources.[77] It is on this point perhaps that a more respectful look to the author as composer may help us answer some questions. As convincingly argued by Luitpold Wallach, some traits of the *DVV* are typical of Alcuin himself and cannot be relegated so easily to a prior source, i.e. Defensor. This is true, for example, of the dedicatory epistle, whose phraseology reflects that of other Alcuinian letters.[78] Wallach observed that Alcuin considered his *DVV* as something akin to Gregory's *Cura Pastoralis*, which he elsewhere referred to as a *speculum* of pontifical life. More precisely, this "mirror" was to guide Wido in the moral conflicts that he might encounter as a judge and military leader.

Aside from its opening and closing letters, which seem to be his own,[79] Alcuin's treatise poses considerable difficulties when one tries to disentangle its sources. According to H.-M. Rochais, Alcuin heavily relied on Defensor of Ligugé for the entire first part on the virtues.[80] Having proven the phraseology of Alcuin's nuncupatorial letter to be genuine, Wallach also contested Rochais on the other chapters. Although Defensor's *Liber* names its patristic sources, Wallach claimed that Defensor's quotations could have been derived from other florilegia such as Isidore of Seville's *Sententiae*. Since the *DVV* contains quotations from Isidore that were not adopted by Defensor, there is sufficient reason to think that Isidore, whom Alcuin held in high esteem, was excerpted by him directly.[81] Wallach furthermore

---

[76] See Cavadini 1991: 123.

[77] See Laistner 1931: 176.

[78] See Wallach 1959: 234.

[79] These are critically edited as letter 305 in MGH Epp. 4:464–465. Dümmler dates them around 801–804. One should keep in mind that the closing letter ends with Amen (*DVV* 638C).

[80] See Rochais 1951.

[81] See Wallach 1959: 236–238.

showed that certain parallels to longer passages in Alcuin were lifted
from pseudo-Augustinian sermons also used by Defensor. It thus
becomes plausible that Alcuin used the older source rather than the
intermediate one. As long as the authorship of the pseudo-Augustinian sermons remains unknown, however, Wallach's findings are not
conclusive. It has been claimed, for example, that some sermons are
by a later author, perhaps Hrabanus Maurus, and have become
inserted into Alcuin's text. In an attempt to defuse such claims Wallach
argued that Hrabanus' sermons contain portions of Alcuin's homilies
rather than vice versa.[82] The fact that some pseudo-Augustinian sermons can be traced back to Caesarius of Arles also diminishes the
likelihood of later inserts in Alcuin's treatise.

While the quest for Alcuin's sources can admittedly lead to infinite
regress, depending on how many layers of florilegia one is willing to
assume, the notion of Alcuin as "composer" may help us overcome
the stalemate between author and editor. Thus we can make two
further points, both of which relate to Alcuin's reputation for his
practical erudition and didactic efficiency.[83] The first touches on the
topic of the treatise itself. The *DVV* deals with the battle between the
virtues and the vices, which was itself a popular theme in the after-
math of Prudentius' *Psychomachia*. Whereas Prudentius seems not to
have been a source for Alcuin, this theme can also be found in
monastic literature, such as Cassian's *Collationes* and Gregory's *Moralia
in Job*.[84] Although Alcuin's work does not betray much originality in
borrowing from pre-existing sources, it is nevertheless important to
see how these sources are framed and elaborated. It is significant,
for example, that Alcuin chooses to apply this theme and its accompanying sources to the life of his addressee Wido, a military leader
and judge, whom he could clearly expect to be familiar with the
idea of conflicting forces.

An interesting example of how Alcuin, in consequence of the early
medieval tradition before him, adapted rather than adopted his sources
is his discussion of *pax* in *DVV* ch. 6. This chapter has now been
traced back to a pseudo-Augustinian homily and is close in content
to a quotation from Peter Chrysologus. But whereas Chrysologus, in

---

[82] See Wallach 1959: 247–251.
[83] See Einhard, *Vita Karoli Magni* XXV; see also Godman 1982: xxxvi.
[84] See Wallach 1959: 244–247. See below n. 92. In *Moralia in Iob* XXXI, 45, 91
Gregory analyzes the battle of the vices with a special eye for the role of the *miles
Dei*.

conformity with Prudentius' notion of *pax* as a virtue, exalted *pax* over the other virtues (*prae omnibus virtutibus custodienda est*), the pseudo-Augustinian homily simply stated that peace: *omnibus viribus custodienda est*, which is also the reading found in Alcuin.[85] While this reading does therefore not originate in Alcuin but in his source, it subtly hints at the moral changes that took place in a society that had been exposed to warfare. That Alcuin, likewise, kept his own addressee Wido concretely in mind can be seen from his omission of any references to the *unanimitas pacis*. When borrowing from the same pseudo-Augustinian sermon in Letter 219 to the monks of Lérins, he had emphasized unanimity as a useful point to stress to a community of saintly brethren.[86] In a statement more edifying for a judge and military commander and more attuned to his broadly Augustinian perspective, he here highlights the fact that only the evil deeds of people ought to be hated, but not the people themselves. Although they may be evil, they are still part of God's creation.[87]

While generally emphasizing the value of peace, Alcuin does not hesitate to claim that the virtues should wage a radical war on the vices. This is obvious from his terminology.[88] In ch. 34, the four cardinal virtues are suitably seen as the *duces gloriosissimi* of the virtues, set off against the *bellatores diabolicae impietatis*. The sections on the vices fittingly end with guidelines on how they each are to be overcome: *vincitur . . .*, for which pattern he could have drawn on Isidore's *Sententiae*.[89] Especially suited for a judge are the borrowings from Isidore's *Sententiae* III on judges and false witnesses in chapters 20 and 21,[90] which are preceded by a useful chapter on how to avoid deceit and fraud. Other, smaller features of the treatise are

---

[85] On the comparison between Chrysologus, Pseudo-Augustine and Alcuin, see Wallach 1959: 241–243. The borrowing is from the pseudo-Augustinian homily no. 98, 2–3 (*PL* 39: 1933). There are fewer verbal parallels with the pseudo-Augustinian *sermo* 61,3 (*PL* 39: 1859).

[86] See MGH Epp. 4:363. In this letter, which is dated around 801, the *unanimitas pacis* brings out the presence of Christ in the midst of the brothers. The notion of *unanimitas pacis* is featured in *sermo* 98, 4–5 (*PL* 39: 1933–1934), but is omitted from *DVV* ch. 6.

[87] Compare *sermo* 98, 2 with *DVV* 617B–C.

[88] See *DVV* ch. 6, 617B: Pax cum bonis, et bellum cum vitiis, semper habenda est. Cf. *Sermo* 98, 2.

[89] Wallach 1959: 245 refers to *Sententiae* II.37 (De pugna virtutum adversus vitia). Isidore lists *superbia* as the leader of the seven other vices, which he contrasts with Christ and his sevenfold grace. See on this also Gregory, *Moralia in Iob* XXXI, 45.

[90] Wallach 1959: 238 refers to *Sententiae* III, 52, 2 to III, 53, 3 (*passim*) as Alcuin's literal source for ch. 20 and to III, 54, 7 to III, 57, 6 (*passim*) for parallels with

equally effective in proving that Alcuin took some care in editing his work. It is thus interesting that ch. 1 and ch. 35 use the same quotation from Ps. 33:15 (Vg.) *Diverte a malo et fac bonum.*[91]

Despite his effective editing, Alcuin's editorial craftsmanship cannot completely conceal the fact that the catalogue of the eight vices towards the end of the treatise betrays a rather different character from the homiletic first part. Here the sources are not the homilies of pseudo-Augustine, but rather the monastic texts of Gregory the Great and Cassian. The insertion of this monastic material leads us to a second observation about Alcuin's strategy in his *DVV*, namely the unproblematic integration of a monastic with a secular morality. Although the catalogue of vices draws on monastic expertise, Alcuin takes measures which make his source-material more suited for Wido's wordly concerns. On the whole, Alcuin appears to have followed Cassian for the order of vices while he has adopted their description from Gregory. In what is a subtle difference, he has moved up *superbia* from the last position in Cassian to the rank of prime spiritual vice which it holds in Gregory. By having *superbia* as spiritual vice precede the corporeal *gula*, he gives his list a wider applicability and reveals again his Augustinian touch.[92]

At times the monastic atmosphere remains oddly visible in the *DVV*, e.g., in ch. 32 on *acedia* or sloth, where we find a warning to Wido not to be idle. Other negative qualities to be eradicated also presuppose a monastic life-style, such as the references to *taedium, murmuratio* and *instabilitas loci*. Whereas modern critics may see the presence of such vestiges as an editorial flaw, it seems Alcuin was not overly concerned with filing away at the edges of what was after all a composite tract. Instead he chose to confront this problem head on by giving a clear statement at the end of the *DVV*. Adopting

---

ch. 21. Only one slight parallel links ch. 20 (629B) with Defensor (ch. LVIIII, 14: Hysidorus dixit: non est persona iudicio consideranda sed causa).

[91] Wallach 1959: 247 points out that Alcuin copies from ch. 35 on the four cardinal virtues in his *Dialogus de rhetorica et virtutibus*. It is worth noting, however, that in the section "De virtutibus" there (*PL* 101:943C–946D) the same psalm-quote is not to be found.

[92] See *Collationes* V, 2 and V, 16, 5 and *Moralia in Job* XXXI, 45, 87–91. Alcuin's order is *superbia, gula, fornicatio, avaritia, ira, acedia, tristitia, cenodoxia*. Compared to Cassian, Alcuin has moved the spiritual vice *superbia* from the last to the first position ahead of the corporeal vice *gula*, and has further reversed the order of *acedia* and *tristitia*. The precise order of Cassian's vices was earlier adopted by Aldhelm for the allegorical confrontation between the virtues and the vices in his *Carmen de virginitate*. See on this Lapidge and Rosier 1985: 99–100. See also n. 84 above.

again the homiletic style, but this time in a voice unmistakably his own, he states that living the secular life of a layman should not deter Wido from "entering the doors of heavenly life," for the entrance to the kingdom of God is "equally open to every sex, age and person" without distinction.[93]

The desire to guide and instruct Wido on his journey to the kingdom of heaven overrides for Alcuin the need to be critical in the modern sense of explicitly citing and excerpting his sources. More important than editorial policy for Alcuin is the need to be heard: hence the haunting homiletic format of his treatise, which Wido is ordered to read frequently,[94] in which the call for immediate penance may help him save his soul.

IV. *Johannes Scottus Eriugena and the* Periphyseon

In John Scottus Eriugena we encounter the most original mind of the Carolingian era. Although such a statement is a commonplace in modern Eriugenian scholarship,[95] this article strives to bring out a different aspect of Eriugena's originality by focusing on his remarkable qualities as a synthesizer of the patristic tradition. In virtually all his works but especially in the *Periphyseon*, Eriugena engages in serious reflection upon his sources. It is the peculiar nature of the *Periphyseon*'s synthesis as an end-result, however, that makes Eriugena's reception of the Fathers so difficult to unravel. More than any other Carolingian thinker, Eriugena took great care to integrate his various patristic sources with his own frame of thought. This process is fairly easy to follow for his early work, the *On divine predestination*,

---

[93] See *DVV* 638B–C: Nec te laici habitus vel conversationis saecularis terreat qualitas, quasi in eo habitu vitae coelestis januas intrare non valeas. Igitur sicut omnibus aequaliter regni Dei praedicata est beatitudo, ita omni sexui, aetati, et personae aequaliter secundum meritorum dignitatem regni Dei patet introitus. Ubi non est distinctio, quis esset in saeculo laicus vel clericus, dives vel pauper, junior vel senior, servus vel dominus: sed unusquisque secundum meritum boni operis perpetua coronabitur gloria. Amen.

[94] Wallach reveals how Alcuin's biographer refers to the *Omelias ad Widonem*, see Wallach 1959: 244.

[95] Thus W. Beierwaltes states in the preface to the papers of the Freiburg colloquium: Johannes Scotus Eriugena ist die erstaunlichste und überzeugendste Gestalt spekulativen Denkens im frühen Mittelalter zwischen Augustinus und Anselm. See Beierwaltes 1980: 3.

where Augustine is the major theologian whose ideas are employed,[96] but becomes increasingly complex in the *Periphyseon*. Not only does Eriugena employ a wider array of western thinkers here but, in addition to western, he now also marshals eastern sources. Moreover, he is intent on establishing a perfect balance between the divergent authorities of East and West, as he wants to craft a consensus between them.[97] By integrating his sources deftly with his own theological reflections, Eriugena has in the *Periphyseon* composed what is no doubt the most difficult treatise of early medieval thought. In trying to analyze its patristic sources, not only do we lack an outward criterion, like the *Decretum Gelasianum* used by Theodulf, but we can also not isolate so easily the pieces of the patchwork, as in the quilt-design of Alcuin's text.

In discussing the reception of the Fathers in Eriugena we will thus proceed differently. We will begin by analyzing the compositional structure of the *Periphyseon*, whose dialectical method shapes the progressive unfolding of its argument. Since the *Periphyseon* represents the end of an intellectual journey for Eriugena, we will next highlight what appears to have been the most crucial stage in the development leading up to this work, namely his translation of certain Greek patristic texts. We will then come to the specific issue at hand: the authority of the Fathers and its relation to Scripture. Since Eriugena employed Western alongside Eastern theological sources in the *Periphyseon*, we will look closely to how he integrated them so as to become part of his argument. The faculty of human reason through which the voice of divine authority is communicated will receive special attention in this last segment, as Eriugena used it to craft a lasting consensus among his patristic sources.

---

[96] On the predestination-controversy in general, see Ganz 1990. On Eriugena's sometimes ambiguous and tendentious use of Augustine against Gottschalk's arguments in the *De praedestinatione*, see Mathon 1954.

[97] See *PP* IV 804D, Jeauneau 148: . . . in hac veluti controversia magnorum virorum quendam consensum velimus machinari. The immediate controversy for Eriugena here in ch. 14 is between the greatest Eastern exegete Gregory of Nyssa and the greatest Western exegete Augustine on the nature of the human body, whether it is animal/corporeal or spiritual. For Augustine's view of the body, the Disciple quotes from *De peccatorum meritis* I, 2, 2–3, 3 (quoted in *PP* IV 803B–804B) but mentions in *PP* IV 804B that this position is consistent with Augustine's teaching in the *De Genesi ad litteram* and *De civitate dei*, both of which works he quotes repeatedly; Eriugena's source for Gregory's teaching on the spiritual and superadded body is *De hominis opificio* chs. 16, 17 and 27 (from which he quotes at length in *PP* IV chs. 12–13, 793C–803B *passim*). On the further implications of the expression "consensum machinari" in Eriugena, see O'Meara 1980: 113–114 and d'Onofrio 1994: 123.

A. *The Compositional Structure of Eriugena's* Periphyseon

The *Periphyseon* was written in the final phase of Eriugena's career, between 860–866.[98] In it Eriugena sets out to investigate the all-embracing concept of *natura*, in which he includes both the things that are and those that are not. Based on the criterion of human rationality, i.e., whether or not things can be understood by the mind, the categories of being and non-being are turned into predicables of nature.[99] After this first division of nature, through which Eriugena constitutes the very object of his rational investigation, he immediately lists a second, fourfold division consisting of nature that is uncreated and creates, nature that creates and is created, nature that is created and does not create, and finally, nature that is uncreated and does not create.[100] Although intellectually less central, this last division determines the formal unfolding of the *Periphyseon*, with Eriugena devoting about a book to each of nature's forms. Book I thus deals with nature that is not created and creates, i.e., God as Cause; Book II with nature that creates and is created, i.e. the so-called primordial causes; Book III with nature that is not created and does not create, i.e., creation; and Books IV and V with nature that does not create and is not created, i.e., God as final Cause and the End to which all things aspire.[101]

Within the broad contours of this work, Eriugena's discourse fluctuates considerably by modulating from a dialectical approach in the first three books, until Book III ch. 24, to an exegetical one in the last two. The exegetical part is further subdivided into a study in

---

[98] For a summary of problems surrounding the dating of this work, see Moran 1989: 58–59.

[99] See *PP* I 441, Sh.-W. 36: Saepe mihi cogitanti diligentiusque quantum uires suppetunt inquirenti rerum omnium quae vel animo percipi possunt uel intentionem eius superant primam summamque diuisionem esse in ea quae sunt et in ea quae non sunt horum omnium generale uocabulum occurrit quod graece φύσις, latine uero natura uocitatur.

[100] See *PP* I 441B, Sh.-W. 36: Videtur mihi diuisio naturae per quattuor differentias quattuor species recipere, quarum prima est in eam quae creat et non creatur, secunda in eam quae et creatur et creat, tertia in eam quae creatur et non creat, quarta quae nec creat nec creatur.

[101] At the beginning of Book IV Eriugena sums up the contents of the earlier three books as dealing with the three forms of nature, see *PP* IV 741C–743C. In 743C (Jeauneau 4) he says that Book IV will form the conclusion: Quartus hic ab operibus sextae propheticae contemplationis de conditione universitatis inchoans, reditum omnium in eam naturam quae nec creat nec creatur consideraturus finem constituat. Due to the length of its argument it will be protracted to a fifth: suique prolixitate cogente in quintum librum porrectus (744A, Jeauneau 6).

literal exegesis in the remainder of Book III and in allegorical exegesis in Books IV and V. Beneath this formal sketch of the work's
contents, however, one finds a steadily progressing argument, as
Eriugena navigates *natura* from its original inception in God to its
final re-absorption into the divine, guided by the Neoplatonic categories of procession and return. Along the way he needs to deal
with such divergent issues as the relation of oneness to multiplicity in
creation, the ontological dependence of creation on God, the creation of humanity, the nature of paradise, the fall and the human
quest for redemption, the cosmic role of Christ, universal restoration. These issues are skillfully but imperfectly inserted into the
overarching structure of procession and return, with human reason
as the captain of the ship, charged with steering it from one item on
the agenda to the next.[102] Conforming to the priority of the first
division into being and non-being, Eriugena's epistemological enterprise clearly affects the outlook of the underlying metaphysical construct. While ontologically all created things derive from God and
will have to return to God, they rely on human reason to bring
them back to their divine origin.

This explicit role of human rationality complicates Eriugena's
reception of patristic authorities, since by inserting the Fathers in the
larger structure of the *Periphyseon*'s argument he appears to color their
testimony. Before analyzing this it may be useful briefly to mention
the authorities Eriugena adduces.[103] The Western sources Eriugena
employs are the five traditionally known ones previously encountered
in the LC, namely Augustine, Ambrose, Jerome, Hilary and Gregory
the Great,[104] from which Eriugena appears to cite directly.[105] In

---

[102] See *PP* IV 744B, Jeauneau 6: Tendenda vela navigandumque. Accelerat namque
ratio perita hujus ponti, nullas veretur minas undarum, nullos anfractus syrtesve
cautesve formidat, cui delectabilius est in abditis divini oceani fretibus virtutem suam
exercere, quam in planis apertisque otiosa quiescere, ubi vim suam non valet aperire.
Cf. the use of similar sailing imagery at the end of *LC* I ch. 30: In hoc sane articulo
hunc primum librum eludendum esse putavimus, ut, quoniam de portu mentionem
fecimus, illum quoque in hoc loco ad portum deducamus, ut retroacta navigatione
fatigati aliquantisper in portu spatiantes resumptisque viribus ad secundi libri navi-
gationem Domino auxiliante vela tendamus.
[103] For a complete list of all Eriugena's authorities, see Madec 1988c.
[104] On Eriugena's use of Hilary, Ambrose, Jerome and Gregory, see Madec 1988b.
On his use of Augustine in the *Periphyseon*, see Madec 1988a. Augustine is by far the
most important western source but ambiguously used. See also d'Onofrio 1994: 117,
who adds Marius Victorinus and Claudianus Mamertus as western sources not explicitly named.
[105] As alluded to by Madec, the manuscripts Eriugena used for his western sources
are not known. See Madec 1988b: 61. On the subject of florilegia, it is not known

addition to its Western sources, among which Augustine is the most important, the *Periphyseon* cites a remarkable spectrum of Eastern sources. Of these Pseudo-Dionysius has pride of place, followed by Maximus Confessor and Gregory of Nyssa.[106] Gregory of Nazianzen, Epiphanius, and Origen make briefer appearances.[107]

Given his articulated goal of crafting a consensus between the Fathers, two additional observations may clarify Eriugena's specific fascination with some of his sources. It has been noted that Eriugena has a very high regard for the Greek Fathers, whom he tends to regard as more astute and more articulate than the average Latin theologian.[108] Such comments could reflect his amazement at being introduced to a full-blown tradition of which he was previously unaware, and need not indicate a denegration of the Latin tradition as a whole. That this may indeed be the case becomes clear when one considers that, despite his general preference for Greek over Latin authorities, Eriugena never allows a conflict of opinion to break up the alliance between his two major authorities: Augustine in the West and Dionysius in the East.[109] The setting up of a simple hierarchy of sources is thus scarcely sufficient if one wants to gauge the meaning of patristic authority for Eriugena.[110] To put his use of his sources in context, we should next turn to his efforts as a translator.

B. *Eriugena as Translator*[111]

Eriugena's earliest foray into speculative theology came when he was asked to refute Gottschalk's theory of double predestination by archbishop Hincmar of Rheims. In his *On divine predestination (DP)*, dated

---

whether Eriugena used them, but it may be interesting to note that several florilegia of the *Periphyseon* have been discovered, see Moran 1989: 65.

[106] See Jeauneau 1983.

[107] On Eriugena's Greek sources, see Sheldon-Williams 1973. Sheldon-Williams also names John Chrysostom as a source. It is important to note that Eriugena, who calls Gregory Nazianzen the Theologian, at times confuses Gregory of Nyssa and Gregory of Nazianzen.

[108] Cf. *PP* V 955A, where in a discussion about the nature of hell, Eriugena credits the Greeks as: more solito res acutius considerantes expressiusque significantes.

[109] On the alliance of Dionysius and Augustine, see Jeauneau 1983: 145–146, Madec 1988c: 18, Otten 1993: 220 and d'Onofrio 1994: 128–129. See further *PP* V 976A and below n. 136.

[110] A better way to proceed is d'Onofrio's attempt to arrive at a "hermeneutic of the disagreement of patristic sources" in the *Periphyseon* comparable to Abelard's rules in the *Sic et Non*. See d'Onofrio 1994, esp. 124–126.

[111] For a general assessment of Eriugena's efforts as translator, see O'Meara 1988: 51–79.

around 850, he honored Hincmar's request by using Augustine, who had been Gottschalk's highest authority in this matter, to disprove the opinion of his opponent. Yet the use of Augustine seems to have been guided more by his wish to contradict Gottschalk's opinions than by his intent to provide a genuine interpretation of Augustine's view of predestination. This becomes clear from the introduction to the treatise, where Eriugena states that he will decide the problems surrounding predestination before the forum of reason,[112] which is given priority even over the authority of his main source Augustine. In the treatise itself we find Eriugena employing various rhetorical strategies, such as the argument "a contrario," to prove that Augustine actually means the opposite of what he seems to say, rather than the dialectical reasoning which is so typical of the *Periphyseon*.[113]

Suspending a more detailed judgment, one can infer from a brief reading of the *On divine predestination* that Eriugena's guidelines in arguing his position generally derive from the liberal arts, applied here effectively to win the support of Augustine.[114] In the years following the predestination-controversy,[115] Eriugena continued to be protected by Charles the Bald who next commissioned him to translate the works of Pseudo-Dionysius, which had been donated to the court of Louis the Pious by Emperor Michael Palaeologus in 827. There they had been received as authentic apostolic documents in

---

[112] See Eriugena's preface to Hincmar and Pardulus of Lyons, Madec 3–4: . . . sic uos, religiossimi patres, cum uestrae nobilitas eloquentiae ad omnes nouellarum haeresium uersutias cauendas, conuincendas, destruendas sufficiat, nostrae tamen ratiocinationis astipulationibus uestram perfectissimam de fide praedestinationis diffinitionem roborare non spreuistis, ita ut et uestrae pietatis pulcherrima uirtus omnibus pateat et nostrae oboedientiae non spernenda humilitas clarescat. See also *DP* ch. 1 where in a famous statement Eriugena posits the identity of true religion and true philosophy, yet, following Augustine's objections to the gap between private teaching and public worship in the philosophers (*De vera religione* I, 1; V, 8), embeds the use of reason firmly in an ecclesial context.

[113] In conformity with the rhetorical, rather than dialectical emphasis of the *DP*, it is fitting that Eriugena calls Augustine here: propriae translataeque locutionis doctor (*DP* ch. 11.4, Madec 69). See further O'Meara 1988: 46 and Otten 1994: 79–83. For Eriugena's deft but tendentious use of Augustine, see n. 136 below.

[114] See *DP* ch. 18.1: Madec 110–111: Errorem itaque saeuissimum eorum qui uenerabilium patrum maximeque sancti Augustini sententias confuse ac per hoc mortifere ad suum prauissimum sensum redigunt, ex utilium disciplinarum ignorantia, quas ipsa sapientia suas comites inuestigatricesque fieri uoluit, crediderim sumpsisse primordia . . .

[115] The end of the predestination-controversy was clearly not in Eriugena's favor, as he was virulently criticized by Prudence of Troyes and Florence of Lyons. See Marenbon 1990: 311–314.

the lasting confusion by which their anonymous Christian Neoplatonic author was first identified as the follower of St. Paul in Acts 17:34 only to be further equated with St. Denis, the martyred bishop of Paris. Eriugena's translation supplanted the earlier one by Hilduin, abbot of St. Denis, in that it revealed a more substantial grasp of Dionysius' ideas. Thus Eriugena had a good understanding of the structural distinction between apophatic and kataphatic theology, which had befuddled Hilduin.[116] It is no wonder that Anastasius Bibliothecarius could marvel at the achievement of this *vir barbarus* upon sending his own emendations from Rome to Charles the Bald.[117]

Eriugena, who was a novice in matters Greek when he started working on his translation,[118] proved himself a quick student in mastering this new craft. After the translation of Dionysius he also translated two works of Maximus the Confessor, namely the *Ambigua ad Iohannem*, in which Maximus explains difficult passages in Dionysius and Gregory of Nazianzus, and the *Quaestiones ad Thalassium*, to which the *Periphyseon* mistakenly refers as Maximus' "scholia."[119] He did so again at the request of Charles the Bald, it seems, "to clear up the Catholic faith for all,"[120] testifying to a changing openness toward the Greek component of the tradition which reads quite differently from the atmosphere in the *LC*. Eriugena translated at least one other Greek work, namely Gregory of Nyssa's early treatise *De hominis opificio*,

---

[116] See Roques 1975b: 120–122. For a short exposition of apophatic and kataphatic theology in Eriugena, see *PP* I 458A–B, Sh.-W. 72–74 and *PP* I 461A–462D, Sh.-W. 80–84. Cf. Dionysius, *De mystica theologia* ch. 3.

[117] See *PL* 122:1027: Mirandum est quoque, quomodo vir ille barbarus, qui in finibus mundi positus, quanto ab hominibus conversatione, tanto credi potuit alterius linguae dictione longinquus, talia intellectu capere in aliamque linguam transferre valuerit: Iohannem innuo Scotigenam ...

[118] See his own admission in the dedicatory letter to Charles the Bald accompanying his translation of Dionysius in *PL* 122, 1031C–D: Jussionibus itaque vestris neque volentes neque valentes obsistere, rudes admodum tirones adhuc helladicorum studiorum, fatemur ... ultra vires nostras, ipso tamen duce, qui est lux mentium et illuminat abscondita tenebrarum, libros quattuor sancti patris Dionysii Areopagitae, episcopi Athenarum, quos scripsit ad Timotheum, episcopum Ephesiorum, et decem epistolas ejusdem de Graeco in Latinum transtulimus ...

[119] Eriugena regarded the prologue to the scholies which preceded the text of the *Quaestiones* as a general prologue to the full text. Thus he refers to the scholies instead of the *Quaestiones*, e.g. in *PP* IV 857A, Jeauneau 266. On this confusion, see CCSG 7:xcix.

[120] In his letter to Charles the Bald (*PL* 122, 1196B), Eriugena suggests that Charles ordered his translation of the *Ambigua* for this reason: opus, quod ad communem catholicae fidei illuminationem jussistis fieri. ... Earlier in the same letter Eriugena stated how Maximus had elucidated for him the meaning of negative and affirmative theology, see 1196A.

but may also have worked on Epiphanius of Salamis' *Ancoratus* (called *De fide*) and Basil of Caesarea's *Hexaemeron*. Although Eriugena's activities as a translator seem to have inaugurated a change in his thinking that led him far from the Augustinian source-material in the *On divine predestination*, there are certain elements of continuity that bind this later "Greek" period to his earlier phase as a controversialist,[121] a period when he first showed himself as a thinker very much inclined to go his own way.

The case for such a continuity becomes more likely when we consider certain incongruities between Eriugena's translations of the Greek Fathers and his subsequent interpretations of them in the *Periphyseon*. Although Eriugena's knowledge of Greek makes him superior to his contemporaries, his translations were not without flaws. An example is the Greek adverb: οὐκοῦν, which he contradictorily translated as *non ergo* or *nonne ergo*.[122] Elementary mistakes such as these did not hamper Eriugena in drawing the right inferences from his Greek sources, as is proven by his correct understanding of Dionysius' methods of affirmative and negative theology or of Gregory of Nyssa's anthropology. In light of the discrepancies between Eriugena's translations and his interpretations, R. Roques emphasized that Eriugena was aware of his flaws as a translator but regarded his own role more importantly as that of interpreter.[123] Concerned to underscore Eriugena's correct understanding of the Fathers rather than fault his competence as a translator, Roques also showed how apparent flaws of translation were sometimes ingenuous interpretations in disguise. As an example he pointed to Eriugena's decision to translate the Greek ἀτεχνῶς in Dionysius as *valde artificialiter* in conformity with the technique of negative theology.[124]

---

[121] It is significant that in the passage from *DP* ch. 18.1, Madec 111, Eriugena attributes the wrongful interpretation of Augustine not only to ignorance of the liberal arts, but also to: . . . insuper etiam graecarum litterarum inscitia . . . In the same chapter (18.2) he provides us with the elementary Greek etymology of foreknowledge or προόρασις.

[122] In this respect it is significant that Hilduin did not make the same mistake in translating Dionysius. For this and other Eriugenian translation flaws, see Roques 1975b: 105–122, esp. 105; Jeauneau 1979: 48; O'Meara 1988: 53.

[123] See Roques 1975b: 100–104 on the distinction between *interpres* (translator) and *expositor* (commentator).

[124] See Roques 1975c: 46. The expression occurs in Dionysius, *De caelesti hierarchia* II, 1, translated in *PL* 122:1040A. Cf. also Eriugena's interpretation of this passage in *Expositiones* II, 1, Barbet 23, where he circumscribes the same Greek term as "multum artificiose."

Since the information derived from Eriugena's activities as a translator proves inconclusive if we want to determine his reception of the Fathers, which is an altogether broader concept, his earlier statements about the role of reason and the need for expertise in the liberal arts gain new interest. Aside from being an impressive original work, the *Periphyseon* can serve as a testcase to see how Eriugena, through the lens of reason and the liberal arts, responded to the challenging influence of the Greek Fathers.

C. *Reason as Arbitrator of the Fathers in Eriugena's* Periphyseon

Having concluded that Eriugena's recently acquired familiarity with Greek theology need not have replaced his initial interest in reason and the liberal arts but may have reinforced it, we must now turn to the *Periphyseon* to see how this interest helped him to confront the discrepancies between Eastern and Western Fathers. It seems that it is especially through the use of a "rational" concept of authority that Eriugena is able not just to harmonize the traditions, but to coordinate them with the higher authority of Scripture.[125]

The most extensive discussion of authority can be found in Book I. Devoted to the investigation of God as the uncreated Cause of creation, Book I discusses the applicability of Aristotle's categories to God as Cause. This discussion is found embedded in the larger context of Eriugena's fascination with Dionysius's interpretation of the Divine Names and his use of affirmative and negative theology. Having approached the matter from various angles, Eriugena reaches a final conclusion in stating that in accordance with the precepts of affirmative theology the categories only apply to God metaphorically, but that following the method of negative theology their proper sense has to be denied as an accurate description of the divine. In a subsequent interchange between the Master and his Student, the Student envisages that a conflict between Scripture and reason may arise, which would put him in an impossible position. In answering his Student's doubt, the Master states:

> Do not be afraid. For now we must follow reason, which investigates the truth of things and is not overborne by any authority, and is by no

---

[125] That the problem of Western versus Eastern Church Fathers in Eriugena is related to his view of reason versus authority is made clear by Otten 1993, Marler 1994 and d'Onofrio 1994.

means prevented from revealing publicly and proclaiming to all men the things which it both zealously searches out by circuitous reasoning and discovers with much toil.[126]

The Master next comments that the authority of Scripture is to be followed because the truth resides in it. But this is not equivalent to regarding Scripture as a book with mere literal meaning, because it uses allegory and may change the meanings of words out of condescension for the weakness of human minds.[127]

From this it is clear that Scripture has priority for Eriugena to the extent that it reveals the true nature of God which is ultimately ineffable. In this respect it provides a shortcut compared to the circuitous and laborious path of human reason. Yet this biblical shortcut, while nourishing the Christian faith, still awaits rational exposition, as the biblical allegories need to be explained.[128] It is at this point that patristic authority comes in for Eriugena, as he states:

> For concerning God nothing must be said or thought by those who live pure and pious lives and are serious seekers after the truth except what is found in Holy Scripture, and no meanings or allegorical interpretations but its own are to be used by those who either believe in or discourse about God. For who would presume to pronounce about the Ineffable Nature anything invented by himself, except such measures as it has played itself concerning itself upon its sacred instruments, I mean, the theologians?[129]

Here the same priority seems to be maintained, since by "theologians" Eriugena hints at the authors of Holy Scripture. Yet at the

---

[126] See *PP* I 508D–509A, Sh.-W. 188: Noli expauescere; Nunc enim nobis ratio sequenda est quae rerum ueritatem inuestigat nullaque auctoritate opprimitur, nullo modo impeditur ne ea quae et studiose ratiocinationum ambitibus inquirit et laboriose inuenit publice aperiat atque pronuntiat.

[127] See *PP* I 509A, Sh.-W. 188.

[128] Cf. Eriugena's famous dictum about the inexhaustibility of Scriptural texts which are like the colorful feathers of a peacock: Est enim multiplex et infinitus divinorum eloquiorum intellectus: siquidem in penna pavonis una eademque mirabilis ac pulchra innumerabilium colorum varietas conspicitur in uno eodemque loco ejusdem pennae portiunculae (*PP* IV 749C, Jeauneau 18). Books IV and V contain Eriugena's allegorical interpretation of the sixth day of creation, including the resulting fall of humanity and its expulsion from paradise.

[129] See *PP* I 509B, Sh.-W. 188: Siquidem de deo nil aliud caste pieque uiuentibus studioseque ueritatem quaerentibus dicendum uel cogitandum nisi quae in sancta scriptura reperiuntur, neque aliis nisi ipsius significationibus translationibusque utendum his qui de deo siue quid credant siue disputent. Quis enim de natura ineffabili quippiam a se ipso repertum dicere praesumat praeter quod illa ipsa de se ipsa in suis sanctis organis, theologis dico, modulata est?

same time it seems the divine voice of Scripture is modulating to blend unnoticeably with that of patristic authority. Thus Eriugena can insert a long passage from Dionysius "the theologian" here, whose authority for Eriugena resembles closely that of Scripture.[130]

Patristic authority, therefore, is secondary to but closely associated with scriptural authority for Eriugena. It rather seems as if in the tradition of the Fathers Scripture has inspired its own rational inter-pretation, leading Eriugena to postulate a remarkable continuity between the two. While Scripture is the residence of truth itself, true authority for Eriugena is the truth as it is discovered by the power of reason "and set down in writing by the Holy Fathers for the use of posterity."[131] Eriugena's abstract statement here is not unlike Theo-dulf's practise, as he used the Fathers similarly to sanction what ap-pears to have been a previously developed theological position on images. Rather than using an outward criterion, such as that of Gela-sius, however, Eriugena focuses on the substantive content embodied by both Scripture and the Fathers: truth itself. The authority of Scrip-ture differs from that of the Fathers only in that the Fathers show us their reasoning, whereas Scripture contains the truth implicitly. While Eriugena thus appears to proclaim a hierarchy of Scripture over the Fathers, at the same time he makes clear that all authority, including that of Scripture, can be traced back to reason as the uncoverer of truth. Although authority precedes reason in time, reason is ultimately prior to all authority, because it originated in the ineffable nature of God together with nature and time. Whatever priority there may be for (scriptural or patristic) authority, it is in the end only a temporal one and thus ultimately bound to disintegrate before the forum of reason, which is not determined by but prior to time.[132]

Having established the power of reason, Eriugena continues to de-rive support from the Fathers in developing his own position through-out the *Periphyseon*. The views of the Fathers which he endorses are of course rational ones. Eriugena's rationality remains nevertheless

---

[130] See *PP* I 509B–510B, Sh.-W. 188–190. Eriugena then gives a long quotation from *De divinis nominibus* I, 1–2.

[131] See *PP* I 513B, Sh.-W. 198: Nil enim aliud uidetur mihi esse uera auctoritas nisi rationis uirtute reperta ueritas et a sanctis patribus ob posteritatis utilitatem litteris commendata.

[132] See *PP* I 513B, Sh.-W. 196–198: Rationem priorem esse natura, auctoritatem uero tempore didicimus. Quamuis enim natura simul cum tempore creata sit non tamen ab initio temporis atque naturae coepit esse auctoritas, ratio uero cum natura ac tempore ex principio rerum orta est. See also Otten 1993: 220–224.

inherently unpredictable, since reason itself prevents him from following a blind scheme. The following remarks may illustrate this.
Since Eriugena regards the opinions of the Greeks as more rational
than those of the Latins, one might expect him ordinarily to follow
their views. Yet he repeatedly contradicts the Greek Father Epiphanius, because he practises literal rather than allegorical exegesis,[133]
while the Latin author Ambrose—who Eriugena associates with Origen and Gregory of Nyssa—is much preferred because of his pen-
chant for allegorical exegesis.[134] Although this exception could still be
rationally explained, there is even an inexplicable exception to this
exception. Thus Eriugena can quote extensively from Basil the Great
in Book III, whose homilies on the *Hexaemeron* as a model of literal
exegesis he surprisingly recommends.[135]

While the formidable power of Eriugena's reason at times poses
near-insoluble mysteries, giving the *Periphyseon* its idiosyncratic flavor,
Eriugena remains very focused on presenting the Christian tradition
as unified. Unlike Theodulf and Alcuin, he does so not by vertically
ordering the voices of the past, nor by horizontally sewing together
those pieces of the tradition that were available to him. Rather, he
wants to create the best possible, i.e., most rational, Christian tradition by presenting an inclusive past which embraces not only West-

---

[133] E.g. in *PP* IV 818C, Jeauneau 180 and 832D–833A, Jeauneau 212–214. In
both cases Eriugena is eager to defend the views of Origen against the literal views
of Epiphanius. In an interesting match-up, however, he pairs Epiphanius with
Gregory of Nyssa in *PP* V 899C on the issue of the resurrection as proceeding from
the collaboration between nature and grace. Here the fact that both authors are
Greek seems to unite them despite the potential discrepancy between their exegetical approaches as literal versus allegorical.

[134] There are ten references to Origen, but many more to Ambrose. Origen and
Ambrose are linked on three occasions: twice Ambrose is said to follow Origen (*PP*
IV 815C, Jeauneau 174, 832D, Jeauneau 212) and once Origen is called upon to
explain a difficult passage in Ambrose (*PP* V 930D). Yet Ambrose's closest affinity
is no doubt with Gregory of Nyssa, who is Eriugena's champion of the allegorical
reading of Genesis. After giving a series of quotations from Ambrose's *De paradiso*
(I, 5; 2, 11; 3, 12–14; 4, 24) in Bk. IV ch. 16, Jeauneau 170ff., to counterbalance
Augustine's historical reading, Eriugena concludes in *PP* IV 816D–817A, Jeauneau
176 that Ambrose's commendable interpretation of Scripture can only be understood
if we see him as having followed the highest Greek theologians, esp. Gregory of Nyssa.

[135] Of the 22 references to Basil, 17 are found in Book III. Basil's *Hexaemeron* is
an important exegetical source for Eriugena in *PP* III concerning the first five days
of creation. See Madec 1988c: 31–32. As stated in *PP* III 707B, Sh.-W. 226, Eriugena
is concerned with literal exegesis here: In his ergo omnibus nulla allegoria sed nuda
solummodo physica consideratio tractatur . . . After this Eriugena follows with a
quotation from *Hexaemeron* IV, 3. The position of Basil as a Greek author who
practises literal exegesis can thus be seen as the mirror-image of Ambrose as a Latin
author who practises allegorical exegesis. See on this d'Onofrio 1994: 117–118.

ern but also Eastern Fathers. To unify this tradition internally, he is intent on crafting a consensus between the divided heritage of East and West.[136] He does so not only by assembling what are merely separate parts but by ambitiously suggesting if not proving that a continuous tradition must rationally have preceded its unfortunate fragmentation into scattered parts.

That these parts belong naturally together becomes clear when we bear in mind that in the *Periphyseon* Dionysius as the Eastern authority "par excellence" and Augustine as his equally eminent counterpart in the West never directly contradict one another. Their harmony for Eriugena far transcends forced agreement, as it is flexibly rooted in the dialectical truth of reason itself. This can be inferred from the debate in Book II on the meaning of Divine Ignorance, where we find the Student saying:

> For what the Holy Fathers, I mean Augustine and Dionysius, most truly say about God—Augustine says that He is better known by not knowing, Dionysius that His ignorance is true wisdom—should, in my opinion, be understood not only of the intellects which reverently and seriously seek Him, but also of Himself.[137]

By pronouncing the underlying dialectical identity of divine ignorance and divine wisdom, Eriugena locates the unknowable nature of God ultimately within the purview of those who follow the right path of reason on their way to true wisdom. For those travelling this path, as for Eriugena himself, Dionysius and Augustine will guide the way.

Finally, despite its inaccuracy by modern historical standards, it is in his establishment of a connection between Dionysius and Augustine that Eriugena showed tremendous foresight. For it is precisely through

---

[136] A case in point is *PP* IV ch. 16 mentioned above on the nature of paradise. Here Eriugena starts out with a series of quotations from Augustine (*De Genesi ad litteram* VIII, 1, 1, followed by *De civitate dei* XIV, 11.48–65 and *De vera religione* XX, 38) only to arrive at the unlikely conclusion that Augustine's interpretation of paradise is not historical and perfectly reconcilable with Ambrose's allegorical reading that: . . . nihil aliud esse paradisum nisi ipsum hominem (*PP* IV 815C, Jeauneau 174). For his consequent handling of Ambrose as espousing a Greek position, see n. 134 above.

[137] See *PP* II 597D, Sh.-W. 162: Nam quod sancti patres, Augustinum dico et Dionysium, de deo verissime pronuntiant—Augustinus "qui melius" inquit "nesciendo scitur," Dionysius autem "cuius ignorantia uera est sapientia"—non solum de intellectibus qui eum pie studioseque quaerunt uerum etiam de ipso intelligendum opinor. The patristic references here are to Augustine's *De ordine* II, 16, 44 and Dionysius, *De Divinis Nominibus* VII, 3. See also Madec 1988c: 18 and Jeauneau 1983: 145.

its fascination with these different but not divergent Christian-Platonic strands of the patristic tradition in Eriugena that Carolingian theology becomes firmly linked to the intellectual revival of twelfth century Europe.[138]

Bibliography

I. *Medieval. General. Methodology*

Camille, M. 1989. *The Gothic Idol. Ideology and Image-Making in Medieval Art.* Cambridge.

Carruthers, M.J. 1990. *The Book of Memory.* A Study of Memory in Medieval Culture. Cambridge.

Chenu, M.D. 1968. *Nature, Man and Society in the Twelfth Century. Essays on New Theological Perspectives in the Latin West.* Translated by J. Taylor and L.K. Little. Chicago

Coleman, J. 1992. *Ancient and Medieval Memories. Studies in the reconstruction of the past.* Cambridge.

Cramer, P. 1993. *Baptism and Change in the Early Middle Ages, c. 200–c. 1150.* Cambridge. Cambridge Studies in Medieval Life and Thought, vol. 20.

Dodwell, C.R. 1992. *Pictorial Art of the West 800–1200.* New Haven.

Feld, H. 1990. *Der Ikonoklasmus des Westen.* Leiden. Studies in the History of Christian Thought, vol. 41.

Lubac, H. de. 1959. *Exégèse médiéval: les quatre sens de l'Écriture.* Paris. 4 volumes.

Markus, R. 1991. *The End of Ancient Christianity.* Cambridge.

McGinn, B. 1988. "The Human Person as Image of God. II. Western Christianity," in McGinn, B. and J. Meyendorff (eds.). 1988. *Christian Spirituality. Origins to the Twelfth Century.* New York. World Spirituality: An Encyclopedic History of the Religious Quest. Vol. 16: 312–330.

Riché, P. and G. Lobrichon (eds.). 1984. *Le Moyen Age et la Bible.* Paris.

Stock, B. 1983. *The Implications of Literacy. Written Language and Models of Interpretation in the Eleventh and Twelfth Centuries.* Princeton.

II. *Carolingian Culture*

Blumenthal, U.-R. (ed.) 1983. *Carolingian Essays.* Andrew W. Mellon Lectures in Early Christian Studies. Washington, D.C.

Contreni, J.J. 1978. *The Cathedral School at Laon from 850 to 930.* Munich.

—. 1983. "Carolingian Biblical Studies." In: Blumenthal 1983: 71–98.

Fichtenau, H. 1957. *The Carolingian Empire.* Translated by P. Munz. Oxford.

Gibson, M.T. and J.L. Nelson (eds.) 1990. *Charles the Bald. Court and Kingdom.* London. 2nd rev. ed.

Herrin, J. 1987. *The Formation of Christendom.* Princeton.

Laistner, M.L.W. 1931. *Thought and Letters in Western Europe.* A.D. 500 to 900. Ithaca. Reissued 1966.

Liebeschütz, H. 1967. "Development of Thought in the Carolingian

---

[138] See Chenu 1968: 49–98.

Empire," in: Armstrong, A.H. 1967. *The Cambridge History of Later Greek and Early Medieval Philosophy.* Cambridge. Pp. 565–586.

Marenbon, J. 1981. *From the Circle of Alcuin to the School of Auxerre.* Cambridge.

—. 1994. "Carolingian Thought." In: McKitterick 1994: 171–192.

McKitterick, R. 1989. *The Carolingians and the Written Word.* Cambridge.

—. (ed.) 1990. *Uses of Literacy in Early Medieval Europe.* Cambridge.

—. (ed.) 1994. *Carolingian Culture: Emulation and Innovation.* Cambridge.

Riché, P. 1976. *Education and Culture in the Barbarian West, Sixth Through Eighth Centuries.* Transl. from the 3rd French ed. by John J. Contreni. Columbia.

—. 1979. *Les écoles et l'enseignement dans l'Occident chrétien de la fin du Ve siècle au milieu du XIe siècle.* Paris.

—. 1981. *Instruction et vie religieuse dans le Haut Moyen Age.* London. Variorum Reprints.

—. 1993. *The Carolingians. A Family Who Forged Europe.* Transl. by M.I. Allen. Philadelphia.

Sullivan, R.E. 1989. "The Carolingian Age: Reflections on Its Place in the History of the Middle Ages." *Speculum* 64 (1989) 267–306.

—. (ed.) 1995. *"The Gentle Voices of Teachers." Aspects of Learning in the Carolingian Age.* Columbus, Ohio.

III. *Theodulf of Orléans and the* Libri Carolini

Primary sources:

Ambrosius. *De fide ad Gratianum Augustum.* Faller, O. (ed.) 1962. Vienna. Corpus Scriptorum Ecclesiasticorum Latinorum 78.

Aurelius Augustinus. *De doctrina christiana. De vera religione.* Martin, I. (ed.) 1962. Turnhout. Corpus Christianorum Series Latina 32.

—. De diversis questionibus octoginta tribus. Mutzenbecher, A. (ed.) 1975. *Aurelii Augustini Opera.* Turnhout. Corpus Christianorum Series Latina 44A.

Magnus Aurelius Cassiodorus. *Expositio Psalmorum I–LXX.* Adriaen, M. (ed.) 1968. Turnhout. Corpus Christianorum Series Latina 97.

von Dobschütz, E. (ed.) 1912. *Das Decretum Gelasianum de libris recipiendis et non recipiendis. In kritischem Text herausgegeben und untersucht.* Leipzig. Texte und Untersuchungen zur Geschichte der altchristlichen Literatur. 38. Band Heft 4.

Epistola Hadriani Papae Imperatoribus Missa. In: Mansi, J.D. (ed.). 1767. *Sacrorum conciliorum nova, et amplissima collectio* 12:1055–1076. Florence.

Epistolae selectae Pontificum Romanorum Carolo Magno et Ludovico Pio regnantibus scriptae. In: Hampe, K. (ed.). 1899. *Epistolae Karolini Aevi. Tomus III.* Berlin. Monumenta Germaniae Historica. Epistolarum Tomus V. Pp. 6–57.

Grégoire le Grand. *Dialogues. Tome II (Livres I–III).* Vogüé, A. de (ed.) and P. Antin. 1979. Paris. Sources Chrétiennes 260.

Gregorius Magnus. XL Homiliarum in Evangelia libri duo. In: Migne, J.P. (ed.). 1849. *Patrologia Latina* 76:1075–1312. Paris.

—. *Registrum Epistularum Libri VIII–XIV. Appendix.* Norberg, D. (ed). 1982. Turnhout. Corpus Christianorum Series Latina 140 A.

Grégoire le Grand. *Règle Pastorale. Tome I.* Rommel, F (ed.) with B. Judic and Ch. Morel. 1992. Paris. Sources Chrétiennes 381.

Eusebius Hieronymus. *Epistulae. Pars I: Epistulae I–LXX.* Hilberg, I (ed.) 1910. Vienna. Corpus Scriptorum Ecclesiasticorum Latinorum 54.

Isidorus Hispalensis Episcopus. *Etymologiarum sive Originum libri XX.* Lindsay, W.M. (ed.). 1911. Oxford. 2 vols.

Libri Carolini sive Caroli Magni Capitulare de Imaginibus. Bastgen, H. (ed.) 1924. Hanover and Leipzig. Monumenta Germaniae Historica. Legum Sectio III. Concilia. Tomi II Supplementum.

Opus Caroli Regis contra Synodum (Libri Carolini). Freeman, A. (ed.) and P. Meyvaert. 1997. Hanover. Monumenta Germaniae Historica. Concilia. Tomus II Supplementum II.

Theodulfus Aurelianensis Episcopus. De ordine baptismi ad Magnum Senonensem liber. In: Migne, J.P. (ed.) 1851. *Patrologia Latina* 150:223–240. Paris.

—. De Spiritu Sancto. Veterum Patrum sententiae, quod a Patre Filioque procedat. In: Migne, J.P. (ed.) 1851. *Patrologia Latina* 150:239–276. Paris.

Theodulfi Carmina. Dümmler, E. (ed.) 1881. Berlin. Monumenta Germaniae Historica. Poetae Latini medii aevi I:437–581.

Secondary Sources:

Chazelle, C. 1986. "Matter, Spirit, and Image in the *Libri Carolini.*" *Recherches Augustiniennes* XXI (1986) 163–184.

—. 1992–93. "Images, Scripture, the Church and the *Libri Carolini.*" *Proceedings of the PMR Conference* 16/17:53–76.

Dahlhaus-Berg, E. 1975. *Nova Antiquitas et Antiqua Novitas. Typologische Exegese und isidorianisches Geschichtsbild bei Theodulf von Orléans.* Köln-Wien.

Freeman, A. 1957. "Theodulf of Orléans and the *Libri Carolini.*" *Speculum* 32 (1957) 663–705.

—. 1965. "Further Studies in the *Libri Carolini.* I. Palaeographical Problems in Vaticanus Latinus 7207 II. 'Patristic Exegesis, Mozarabic Antiphons, and the Vetus Latina.'" *Speculum* 40 (1965) 203–289.

—. 1971. "Further Studies in the *Libri Carolini* III. The Marginal Notes in Vaticanus Latinus 7207." *Speculum* 46 (1971) 597–612.

—. 1985. "Carolingian Orthodoxy and the Fate of the Libri Carolini." *Viator* 16 (1985) 65–108.

Gero, S. 1973. "The *Libri Carolini* and the Image Controversy." *The Greek Orthodox Theological Review* 18 (1973) 7–34.

Jaffé, Ph. and G. Wattenbach (eds.) 1885. *Regesta Pontificum Romanorum ab condita ecclesia ad annum post Christum natum MCXVIII. Tomus Primus (a S. Petro ad A. MCXLIII).* Leipzig. 2nd revised edition.

Meyvaert P.J. 1979. "The Authorship of the *Libri Carolini*: Observations Prompted by a Recent Book." *Revue bénédictine* 89:29–57.

Noble, Th. F.X. 1995. "Tradition and Learning in Search of Ideology: the *Libri Carolini*". In: Sullivan 1995: 227–260.

Sahas, D.J. 1986. *Icon and Logos. Sources in Eighth-Century Iconoclasm.* An annotated translation of the Sixth Session of the Seventh Ecumenical Council (Nicea, 787), containing the Definition of the Council of Constantinople (754) and its Refutation, and the Definition of the Seventh Ecumenical Council. Toronto.

Wallach, L. 1966. "The *Libri Carolini* and Patristics, Latin and Greek: Prolegomena to a Critical Edition." In: Wallach, L. (ed.) 1966. *The Classical*

Tradition. Literary and Historical Studies in Honor of Harry Caplan. Ithaca, New York, 451–498.

—. 1977. *Diplomatic Studies in Latin and Greek Documents from the Carolingian Age.* Ithaca.

IV. *Alcuin*

Primary Sources:

Alcuinus abba et Caroli Magni Imperatoris magister. De virtutibus et vitiis liber ad Widonem comitem. In: Migne, J.P. (ed.) 1851. *Patrologia Latina* 101:613–638. Paris.

—. Dialogus de rhetorica et virtutibus. In: Migne, J.P. (ed.) 1851. *Patrologia Latina* 101:919–950. Paris.

Alcuini sive Albini Epistolae. In: Dümmler, E. (ed.) 1895. Berlin. *Epistolae Karolini Aevi. Tomus II.* Monumenta Germaniae Historica. Epistolarum Tomus IV.

Augustinus Hipponensis Episcopus. Sermones supposititii. De scripturis. In: Migne, J.P. (ed.) 1865. *Patrologia Latina* 39:1735–1972.

Iohannes Cassianus. *Conlationes XXIIII.* Petschenig, M. (ed.) 1886. Vienna. Corpus Scriptorum Ecclesiasticorum Latinorum 13.

Caesarius Arelatensis. *Sermones. Pars Prima.* Morin, G. (ed.). 1953. Turnhout. Corpus Christianorum Series Latina 103 Pars I.

Defensor Locogiacensis Monachus. *Liber Scintillarum.* Rochais, H.M. (ed.) 1957. Turnhout. Corpus Christianorum Series Latina 117,1.

Eginhard. *Vie de Charlemagne.* Halphen, L. (ed. and transl.) 1923. Paris.

Gregorius Magnus. *Moralia in Iob Libri XXIII–XXXV.* Adriaen, M. (ed.) 1985. Turnhout. Corpus Christianorum Series Latina 143B.

Isidorus Hispalensis Episcopus. Sententiarum libri tres. In: Migne, J.P. (ed.) 1862. *Patrologia Latina* 83:537–738. Paris.

Secondary Sources:

Bouhot, J.-P. 1980. "Alcuin et le *De catechizandis rudibus* de saint Augustin." *Recherches Augustiniennes* 15 (1980) 174–240.

Bullough, D. 1983. "Alcuin and the Kingdom of Heaven: Liturgy, Theology and the Carolingian Age." In: Blumenthal 1983: 1–69.

Cavadini, J.C. 1991. "The Sources and Theology of Alcuin's 'De fide sanctae et individuae trinitatis.'" *Traditio* 46:123–146.

—. 1993. *The Last Christology of the West.* Adoptionism in Spain and Gaul, 785–820. Philadelphia.

Chazelle, C. 1989. "To Whom Did Christ Pay the Price? The Soteriology of Alcuin's *Epistola 307.*" *Proceedings of the PMR Conference* 14: 43–62.

Deug-Su, I. 1984. *Cultura e Ideologia nella prima età carolingia.* Rome.

Duckett, Shipley E. 1951. *Alcuin, Friend of Charlemagne. His World and His Work.* New York.

Godman, P. 1982. *Alcuin. The Bishops, Kings and Saints of York.* Oxford.

Lapidge, M. and J.L. Rosier (transl.) 1985. *Aldhelm. The Poetic Works.* Cambridge.

Meyer, H.B. SJ. "Alkuin zwischen Antike und Mittelalter. Ein Kapitel frühmittelalterlicher Frömmigkeitsgeschichte." In: *Zeitschrift für katholische Theologie* 81 (1959) 306–350, 405–454.

Rochais, H.M. 1951. "Le 'Liber de Virtutibus et Vitiis' d'Alcuin. Note pour l'étude des sources." *Revue Mabillon* 41 (1951) 77–86.

Wallach, L. 1959. *Alcuin and Charlemagne: Studies in Carolingian History and Literature*. Ithaca, New York.

V. *Johannes Scottus Eriugena*

Primary Sources:

Ambrosius. Exameron. De paradiso. Schenkl, C. (ed.) 1897. *Sancti Ambrosii Opera*. Wien. Corpus Scriptorum Ecclesiasticorum Latinorum 32, 1.

Aurelius Augustinus. *De civitate dei libri 22*. Domhart, B. and A. Kalb (eds.) 1955. Turnhout. Corpus Christianorum series latina vols. 47–48.

—. De Genesi ad litteram libri duodecim. Zycha, I. (ed.) 1894. *Sancti Aurelii Augustini Opera*. Vienna. Corpus Scriptorum Ecclesiasticorum Latinorum 28, 1.

—. De ordine. Green, W.M. (ed.) 1970. *Sancti Aurelii Augustini Opera*. Turnhout. Corpus Christianorum Series Latina 29.

—. De peccatorum meritis et remissione et de baptismo parvulorum ad Marcellinum libri tres. Urba, C.P. and I. Zycha (eds.) 1913. *Sancti Aurelii Augustini Opera*. Vienna. Corpus Scriptorum Ecclesiasticorum Latinorum 60.

Basile de Césarée. *Homélies sur l'Hexaemeron*. Giet, S. (ed.) 1949. Paris. Sources chrétiennes 26.

Dionysius Areopagita. Opera. In: Migne, J.P. (ed.) 1857. *Patrologia Graeca* 3. Paris.

Gregorius Nyssenus. De hominis opificio. In: Migne, J.P. (ed.) 1863. *Patrologia Graeca* 44:123–256. Paris.

Iohannes Scottus. *De divina praedestinatione liber*. Madec, G. (ed.) 1978. Turnhout. Corpus Christianorum Continuatio Medievalis 50.

Iohannes Scottus Eriugena. *Carmina*. Herren, M.W. (ed.) 1993. Dublin. Scriptores Latini Hiberniae vol. 12.

—. *Expositiones in Ierarchiam coelestem*. Barbet, J. (ed.) 1975. Turnhout. Corpus Christianorum Continuatio Medievalis 31.

—. *Periphyseon (De Divisione Naturae) libri I–III*. Sheldon-Williams, I.P. and L. Bieler (eds.) 1968–1981. Dublin. Scriptores Latini Hiberniae vols. 7, 9, 11.

—. *Periphyseon. (De Divisione Natural) liber quartus*. Jeauneau, E.A. (ed.) with the assistance of M.A. Zier. 1995. Dublin, Scriptores Latini Hiberniae vol. 13.

—. *Periphyseon. The Division of Nature*. Sheldon-Williams, I.-P. and J.J. O'Meara (transl.) 1987. Montréal-Paris.

—. *Maximi Confessoris Ambigua ad Iohannem iuxta Iohannis Scotti Eriugenae latinam interpretationem*. Jeauneau, E. (ed.) 1988. Turnhout. Corpus Christianorum Series Graeca 18.

Jean Scot Érigène. Le *De imagine* de Grégoire de Nysse traduit par Jean Scot Érigène. Cappuyns (ed.) 1965. *Recherches de théologie ancienne et médiévale* 32:205–262.

Joannes Scottus. De divisione naturae libri IV–V. In: Migne, J.P. (ed.) 1865. *Patrologia Latina* 122:741–1022. Paris.
—. Versio Ambiguorum S. Maximi. In: Migne, J.P. (ed.) 1865. *Patrologia Latina* 122:1193–1222. Paris.
—. Versio operum S. Dionysii Areopagitae. In: Migne, J.P. (ed.) 1865. *Patrologia Latina* 122:1023–1194. Paris.
Maximus Confessor. *Quaestiones ad Thalassium I–LV una cum latina interpretatione Ioannis Scotti Eriugenae iuxta posita.* Laga, C. and C. Steel (eds.) 1980. Turnhout. Corpus Christianorum Series Graeca 7.

Secondary Sources:

Beierwaltes, W. 1980. *Eriugena. Studien zu seinen Quellen.* Heidelberg. Vorträge des III. Internationalen Eriugena-Colloquiums. Freiburg im Breisgau, 27–30. August 1979.
d'Onofrio, G. 1994. "The *Concordia* of Augustine and Dionysius: Toward a Hermeneutic of Disagreement of Patristic Sources in John the Scot's *Periphyseon*." In: McGinn and Otten: 115–140.
Dräseke, J. 1902. *Johannes Scotus Erigena und dessen Gewährsmänner in seinem Werke De divisione naturae libri V.* Leipzig.
Ganz, D. 1990. "The debate on predestination." In: Gibson and Nelson 1990: 283–302.
Jeauneau, E. 1979. "Jean Scot Érigène et le grec." *Archivum Latinitatis Medii Aevi (Bulletin du Cange)* XLI (1979): 5–50. Reprinted in: Jeauneau 1987: 85–132.
—. 1980. "La division des sexes chez Grégoire de Nysse et chez Jean Scot Érigène." In: Beierwaltes 1980: 33–54. Reprinted in: Jeauneau 1987: 341–364.
—. 1982. "Jean l'Érigéne et les *Ambigua ad Iohannem* de Maxime le Confesseur. In: Heinzer, F. and Chr. von Schönborn. *Maximus Confessor.* Fribourg. Reprinted in: Jeauneau 1987: 189–210.
—. 1983. "Pseudo-Dionysius, Gregory of Nyssa, and Maximus the Confessor in the Works of John Scottus Eriugena." In: Blumenthal 1983: 137–149. Reprinted in: Jeauneau 1987: 175–187.
—. 1987. *Études érigéniennes.* Paris. Études augustiniennes.
Madec, G. 1977. "L'Augustinisme de Jean Scot dans le *De praedestinatione*. In: Roques 1975. 183–190.
—. 1988a. "Le dossier augustinien du *Periphyseon* de Jean Scot". In: Madec 1988d: 73–137.
—. 1988b. "Jean Scot et les Pères latins. Hilaire, Ambroise, Jérôme et Grégoire le Grand." In: Madec 1988d: 54–62.
—. 1988c. "Jean Scot et ses auteurs." In: Madec 1988d: 9–52.
—. 1988d. *Jean Scot et ses auteurs. Annotations érigéniennes.* Paris. Études augustiniennes.
Marenbon, J. 1981. *From the Circle of Alcuin to the School of Auxerre. Logic, Theology and Philosophy in the Early Middle Ages.* Cambridge.
—. 1990. "John Scottus and Carolingian Theology: From the *De praedestinatione*, Its Background and Its Critics, to the *Periphyseon*." In: Gibson and Nelson 1990: 303–325.
Marler, J.C. 1994. "Dialectical Use of Authority in the *Periphyseon*." In: McGinn and Otten: 95–113.

Mathon, G. 1954. "L'utilisation des textes de St. Augustin par Jean Scot Érigène dans son *De praedestinatione*." In: *Augustinus Magister*. Congrès International Augustinien. Paris, 21–24 septembre 1954. Paris. Pp. 419–428.

McGinn, B. and W. Otten (eds.). 1994. *Eriugena: East and West*. Papers of the Eighth International Colloquium of the Society for the Promotion of Eriugenian Studies. Chicago and Notre Dame. 18–20 October 1991. Notre Dame. Notre Dame Conferences in Medieval Studies. Volume 5.

Moran, D. 1989. *The Philosophy of John Scottus Eriugena. A Study of Idealism in the Middle Ages*. Cambridge.

O'Meara, J.J. 1980. "*Magnorum virorum quendam consensum velimus machinari* (804b): Eriugena's Use of Augustine's *De Genesi ad litteram* in the *Periphyseon*." In: Beierwaltes 1980: 105–117.

—. 1988. *Eriugena*. Oxford.

Otten, W. 1993. "Eriugena and the Concept of Eastern versus Western Patristic Influence." In: Livingstone, E.L. (ed.). 1993. *Studia Patristica*. Louvain. Vol. 38: 217–224.

—. 1994. "Eriugena's *Periphyseon*: a Carolingian Contribution to the Theological Tradition." In: McGinn and Otten: 69–93.

Roques, R. 1975a. *Libres sentiers vers l'érigénisme*. Roma.

—. 1975b. "Traduction ou interprétation? Brèves remarques sur Jean Scot traducteur de Denys." In: Roques 1975a: 99–130.

—. 1975c. "'Valde artificialiter': le sens d'un contresens." In: Roques 1975: 45–98.

—. (ed.) 1977. *Jean Scot Érigène et l'histoire de la philosophie*. Paris. Colloques internationaux du C.N.R.S. no. 561, Laon 7–12 juillet 1975.

Sheldon-Williams, I.-P. 1973. "Eriugena's Greek Sources." In: O'Meara, J.J. and L. Bieler (eds.). 1973. *The Mind of Eriugena*. Dublin. Papers of a Colloquium. Dublin, 14–18 July 1970: 1–15.

VI. *Other Carolingian Authors on the Reception of the Fathers*

Heyse, E. 1969. *Hrabanus Maurus' Enzyklopädie "De rerum naturis."* Untersuchungen zu den Quellen und zur Methode der Kompilation. Munich. Münchener Beiträge zur Mediävistik und Renaissance-Forschung vol. 4.

Rissel, M. 1976. *Rezeption antiker und patristischer Wissenschaft bei Hrabanus Maurus*. Studien zur karolingischer Geistesgeschichte. Bern-Frankfurt/M. Lateinische Sprache und Literatur des Mittelalters vol. 7.

Tanghe, W.V. 1982. "Ratramnus of Corbie's Use of the Fathers in his Treatise *De Corpore et Sanguine Domini*." In: Livingstone, E.L. (ed.). *Studia Patristica*. Oxford. Vol. 17. 1: 176–180.

THE RECEPTION OF THE CHURCH FATHERS
IN CANON LAW

Jean Werckmeister

The Church Fathers had a major and well-known influence on Western as well as Eastern theology. Their influence on canon law is probably less well-known, despite the works of historians such as Joseph De Ghellinck or, more recently, Charles Munier.[1] The object of our work is to present a summary of what is known today of the "reception" of the Fathers in canon law.

The first difficulty we encounter on tackling this subject is to define who the Church Fathers are. As we know, the notion of "Father" evolved through the ages, and, today, the delimitation of the "patristic" period is still debated. Until the IVth century, the word *pater* only designated bishops. Augustine was the first to apply the term "Father" to a writer (Jerome) who was not a bishop. Today, for some, patristics is the study of all Christian writers of the Antiquity (until the Vth century), whatever their doctrines; for others, only Christian authors recognized as having expressed the true doctrine of the Church ought to be called "Fathers", and this independently of the time in which they lived: Isidore of Seville (VIIth century) or Anselm of Canterbury (XIth century) can thus be counted among the Fathers. We will see that, in the Middle Ages, the latter concept of "Fathers" prevailed; the Fathers were the *auctoritates* on which the Church founded its doctrine, sometimes its law, regardless of the time in which they wrote: Yvo of Chartres, in the preface to his *Decree* (end of the XIth century), would retain the name of "orthodoxi Patres"[2] for popes, as well as conciliar fathers, or Christian writers.

Another difficulty: there is not *a single* canon law, but canon laws: each Church has its own. We will see some differences between the East and the West here. We should also mention the points of view of the different Western Churches: Catholic, Lutheran, Reformed, Anglican, etc. Each of them has a different conception of theology

---

[1] See the bibliography at the end of this article.
[2] *PL* 161, col. 47.

and law, each has a different way of "receiving" the Fathers. We will only be able to make a few allusions to these differences. On the whole, we will speak of the Western Church canon law, and more precisely, for the period later than the 16th century, that of the Roman Catholic Church.

Third difficulty: canon law, be it very developed as the Catholic law, or, less so, as in the Churches issued from the Reformation, has a very broad application: organisation of the sacraments, of teaching, of the ministry; administration of property, management of conflicts, of Church government; protection of people's and communities' rights, etc. All those questions were handled by the Church Fathers, and their writings influenced the Churches. It is of course impossible to deal with all of this here. We will mainly interest ourselves in the question of marriage, on which the canon-law texts contain the most patristic texts.

Our plan will simply be chronological: starting with the Ancient Church and finishing today, touching upon the Eastern Church and the Middle Ages, we will study how the Fathers were "received" as canon law *auctoritates*.

1. *The Ancient Church*

During the first centuries, the organisational rules of the Church—not to speak of Biblical and Apostolic texts (Clement of Rome, Polycarp of Smyrna, etc.), were gathered into collections called "canonical-liturgical" or "pseudo-apostolic", because they combine, under the name of an Apostle, liturgical, moral and canonical prescriptions[3].

The most ancient texts, the *Didaché*, *The Apostolic Tradition*,[4] *The Shepherd* of Hermas,[5] the *Didascaliae Apostolorum*, the *Apostolic Ecclesiastical Constitutions*,[6] etc. are gathered as from the IVth century into collections, the most important of which is *the Apostolic Constitutions*,

---

[3] See L. Buisson, "Die Entstehung des Kirchenrechts", in *Zeitschrift der Savigny-Stiftung, Kan. Abteilung*, 52, 1966, pp. 1–175; P.F. Bradshaw, art. "Kirchenordnungen", in *Theol. Realenzyclopädie (TRE)*, 18, 1989, pp. 662–670.

[4] Latest edition: *Didaché und Traditio apostolica*, ed. W. Guerlings, Freiburg i. Br., 1991, coll. "Fontes christiani", 1.

[5] Hermas, *Le Pasteur*, ed. Robert Joly, Paris, 1958, 407 p. (coll. "Sources chrétiennes", 53).

[6] E. Tidner, *Didascaliae apostolorum, Canonum ecclesiasticorum, Traditionis apostolicae versiones latinae*, Berlin, 1975, coll. *Texte und Untersuchungen*, 75.

which is believed to have been composed in Antioch around 380.[7]

Patristics and canon law are therefore closely related in the first centuries: the Fathers, bishops and Christian writers (often anonymous) write treatises, letters, liturgical, moral and canonical rules, which are transmitted among and between the Churches. Collections transmitting those texts are often anonymous, falsely attributed to the Apostles, and filiations and influences are often difficult to establish as indeed are the texts themselves, being sometimes available in fragments, in several different versions (Syriac, Greek, Latin, Coptic, etc . . .).

It is not our aim here to develop any more on the history of this period, when canon-law is not yet autonomous.[8]

2. The Eastern Law

After the division of the Roman Empire into the Western Empire and the Eastern Empire during the IVth century—division which became final after the death of Theodosius (395), the canonical evolution of the Western Church should be distinguished from that of the Eastern Church.

The sources of Eastern canon law (we speak here mainly of the Byzantine Churches) are enumerated in the canon 2 of the *Trullian Synod* in 691.[9] The sources, which we cite in the same order as that given by the Council, are the following:

– the 85 "Apostles' canons",[10] the only part of the *Apostolic Constitutions* which the Council judged orthodox (the rest is "contaminated by heretics");

---

[7] *Les Constitutions apostoliques*, ed. Marcel Metzger, Paris, 3 vol., 1985–1986–1987, coll. "Sources chrétiennes" no. 320, 329 and 336.

[8] Besides the bibliography already mentioned, we will find a *status quaestionis* and a detailed bibliography in Alexandre Faivre, *Ordonner la fraternité*, Paris, Cerf, 1992, 555 p. (esp. pp. 361–394: "La documentation canonico-liturgique").

[9] Périclès-Pierre Joannou, *Discipline générale antique (IIe–IXe siècles)*, Rome, 1962–1963, t. I-1: *Les Canons des conciles oecuméniques*, pp. 120–125. See Charles De Clercq, *Fontes iuridici Ecclesiarum orientalium*, Rome, 1967.

[10] The *85 Apostles' Canons* is a compilation of conciliar canons dating from the end of the IVth century. They have been transmitted through the *Apostolic Constitutions*, VIII, 47. They are found in other canonical collections, such as the Syriac or Coptic *Clementine Octateuch* (ed. F. Nau, *La Version syriaque de l'Octateuque de Clément*, Paris, 1913) and of the Coptics (ed. G. Horner, *The Statutes of the Apostles or Canones ecclesiastici*, London, 1904).

- the canons of the Councils of Nicaea (325), of Ancyra (314), Neocaesarea (320), Gangra (340), Antioch (341), Laodicaea (end of the
  IVth century), Ephesus (431), Chalcedon (451), Sardica (343), Carthage (419), Constantinople I (381) and Constantinople II (553);
- 16 *canonical letters* of the following Fathers: Dionysius of Alexandria
  († 264), Peter of Alexandria († 311), Gregory of Neocaesarea, also
  called Gregory Thaumaturgus († around 270), Athanasius of Alexandria († 373), Basil of Caesarea († 379), Gregory of Nyssa († around
  395), Gregory of Nazianzus († 390), Amphilochius of Iconium
  († 394), Timothy of Alexandria († around 385), Theophilus of Alexandria († 412), Cyril of Alexandria († 444), Gennadius of Constantinople († around 495), and a canon of a synod headed by Cyprian
  of Carthage († 258);[11]
- the 102 canons of the Trullian Synod itself (691);
- were added later the 22 canons of the Council of Nicaea II (787),
  which ends the series of Eastern canonical sources.[12]

As we can see, Eastern law is essentially founded on conciliar canons. A series of letters from the "Fathers", however, constitutes a
considerable part of it. The precise list of these *canonical letters* (the
Trullian Synod only gives the names of their authors, without speci-
fying which letters are meant) will not be definitely fixed and received in the whole of the Eastern Church until the IVth century,
under the influence of canonists such as Balsamon. Moreover, Eastern Churches never established a consensus on which lists should be
recognised. But it would be too long to enter into the details of those
variations here.[13]

We should say that apart from the canonical sources indicated by
the canon 2 of the Trullian Synod, a great part of the legislation
concerning Eastern Churches comes from the imperial authorities:

---

[11] The Canonical Letters are published, in Greek with a French translation, by
Joannou, *op. cit.*, t. 2, *Les Canons des Pères grecs*, XXXVI–332 p.

[12] The Council of Constantinople III (680–681) did not produce disciplinary canons. The 27 canons of the Council of Constantinople IV were not received among
the canonical sources of the Byzantine Eastern Churches (Joannou, *op. cit.*, p. 1),
but they were admitted by the Western Catholic Churches (Saïd Elias Saïd, *Les
Eglises orientales et leurs droits*, Paris, 1989, p. 88).

[13] See the article "Droit canonique oriental", in *Petit Dictionnaire de l'Orient chrétien*,
published by Julius Assfalg and Paul Krüger, Tournhout, 1991, pp. 130–145
(= *Kleines Wörterbuch des Christlichen Orients*, hrsg. von J. Assfalg in Verbindung mit
P. Krüger, Wiesbaden, 1975). We will find here notices and a bibliography on Ar-
menian, Coptic, Nestorian, Maronite, Jacobite, Melkite, Georgian and Uniate laws.

the Theodosian *Code* (438),[14] whose book XVI is essentially dedicated to canonical questions, the *Digest* (533), the *Code* of Justinian (534),[15] etc. It is the so-called nomocanonical part of this law.

Eastern canon law therefore admitted patristic texts in its sources, and this probably as early as the Vth century: the Trullian Synod only confirmed an old practice.[16] But we should stress that this list of texts is limitative (sixteen bishops only). Some of the extracts are rather long (the 92 canons of Basil of Caeserea take up more than a third of the whole), while others are very brief (Gregory of Nazianzus only left a few lines of a poem indicating the canon of the biblical books). We can also note that these patristic texts really have a disciplinary or jurisprudential character: they are by no means *literary* patristic writings, but decisions or *canonical* consultations taken or given by the Fathers.

Thus, as well as canons of Church Councils and Synods, the Eastern law retained some patristic texts, prescriptions by some individual bishops, in view of the special authority exercised by their authors. We stress this point: it is not literary texts or Christian *writers* that were received in Eastern law, but canonical texts emanating from "Fathers" who detained institutional power within the Church. We will have to come back to this point when we speak about the Western Church.

3. *The Western Law From the IVth to the VIIth Century*

Ever since the IVth century, which marked the separation of the Western from the Eastern Church, and religious freedom for Christians, the Western canon law has been founded on two main sources: the canons of Councils, and papal Decretals.

The Councils

The Councils, easier to organize after the Constantinian peace[17], were multiplying in the East (Ancyra 314, Neocaesarea around 320, Nicaea

---

[14] Ed. Th. Mommsen and P. Meyer, Berlin, 1905.

[15] *Corpus iuris civilis*, ed. Th. Mommsen and P. Krüger, Berlin, 1954–1959.

[16] John the Scholastic (Jean of Scythopolis, Patriarch of Constantinople, † 577) had already included patristic texts in his nomocanonical collection.

[17] See H.J. Sieben, *Die Konzilidee der alten Kirche*, Paderborn, 1979 (*Konziliengeschichte,*

325, Gangra 340, Laodicaea around 400, Ephesus 431, etc.) as well as in the West (Elvira around 306, Rome 313, Arles 314, Cologne 346, Carthage 345, Toledo 400, etc.).

The Eastern councils will quickly be translated into Latin, and used in the West, especially the Council of Nicaea (to which will generally be added the canons of the Council of Sardica held in 343), and in the Vth century the other three councils, so-called Oecumenical councils: Ephesus, Chalcedon and Constantinople. These four councils will be compared, throughout the Middle Ages, to the four Gospels:

> *Inter generalia vero concilia IIII. sunt principalia, quae fere evangeliis comparantur: Nicaenum, Ephesinum, Chalcedonense et Constantinopolitanum.*[18]

> (Among the general councils, four are principal, which we can almost compare to the Gospels: Nicaea, Ephesus, Chalcedon and Constantinople.)

The Papal letters or Decretals

On the model of imperial responses, the bishops of Rome started, towards the end of the IVth century, to send *epistolae decretales* to the bishops of different countries.[19] The first known decretal is probably that sent by Siricius to Himerius, bishop of Tarragona, around 390.[20] The legislative activity of Popes tended to develop during the Vth century, with Innocent the First, Leo the Great, Gelasius . . .[21]

B). Regional councils were held since the IInd century, in the East, in Rome and in Africa (cf. Tertullian, *De Pudicitia*, X, 12). But the first Council texts we have date back to the IVth century. A detailed bibliography can be found in J. Gaudemet, *Les sources du droit de l'Eglise en Occident du IIᵉ au VIIᵉ siècle*, Paris, 1985, pp. 37–40.

[18] Etienne de Tournai, *Summa* on the Decree of Gratian (around 1170) (*Die Summa des Stephanus Tornacensis über das Decretum Gratiani*, hrsg. von Joh. Friedrich von Schulte, Giessen, 1891, pp. 2–3).

[19] Gérard Fransen, *Les Décrétales et les Collections de Décrétales*, Turnhout, 1972 (coll. "Typologie des sources du Moyen Age occidental", 2).

[20] *PL* 13, col. 1215–1236. A decretal from Damasius to the bishops of Gaul could be earlier (*ibid.*, col. 1181).

[21] Philippe Jaffe, *Regesta Pontificum romanorum*, 2 vol., Leipzig, 2nd edition revised by G. Wattenbach, 1885–1888.

The canonical collections

The first Western collections appear from the IVth century onwards (*Vetus Romana*).[22] They multiply after the Vth century, principally the African[23] and Gallic[24] collections. They contain the canons of Western and Eastern councils, and, in some cases, Papal decretals.

The great Roman collections appear by the end of the Vth century: "collection of Freising", *Quesnelliana*, and finally, in the early VIth century, the *Dyonisiana*.[25] This last collection gathers all of the "universal" law known at the time: a new Latin translation of the Eastern councils (Nicaea, Ancyra, Neocaesarea, Chalcedon, Laodicaea, etc.); African councils; Decretals of Siricius, Innocent the First, Leo the Great, Gelasius, etc. It will become the main Western collection for some centuries, sometimes competing against the *Hispana*,[26] at other times co-existing with it.

The *Hispana*, composed, as its name implies, in Spain during the VIIth century (maybe on the initiative of Isidore of Seville), cites twelve Eastern councils, eight African councils, seventeen Gallic councils, thirty Spanish councils and more than five hundred Papal decretals.[27]

* * *

Such are, during the first seven centuries of our era, the sources of canon law. As we see, there exists a parallel between the East and the West: the two *partes imperii* use the *two canonical sources* which are the councils, and Papal letters in the West, patriarchal or episcopal letters in the East.

Regarding the councils, the West added to the list used by the East, the Gallic and Visigothic Councils. It should be remembered

---

[22] Gaudemet, *Les sources . . .*, p. 76 and foll.

[23] Ed. C. Munier, *Corpus christianorum, series latina (CCSL)*, 149, Turnhout, 1974.

[24] Ed. C. Munier and C. De Clercq, *CCSL*, 148 and 148a, Turnhout, 1963. French translation by J. Gaudemet and B. Basdevant, Paris, 1977 and 1989 (coll. "Sources chrétiennes" n. 245, 353 and 354).

[25] The *Dyonisiana* is written by Dionysius Exiguus. *PL* 67; A. Strewe, Berlin, 1931, for the *versio prima*.

[26] The *Hadriana-hispanica* (VIIIth century), the *Dacheriana* (early IXth century) and the *False Decretals* (mid-IXth century) are collections derived from both the *Dyonisiana* and the *Hispana*.

[27] J. Gaudemet, *Les sources . . .*, p. 155. The *Hispana* can be found in the *PL* 84; a modern critical edition is being prepared, by G. Martinez and F. Rodriguez, *La Colección canónica Hispana*, Madrid, 5 vols. published.

too that the West rejected some canons which were accepted by the East,[28] and vice-versa.[29] Furthermore, the different Latin translations of Greek texts permitted many different interpretations, or even interpolations, to which the Greeks would certainly not have subscribed.

As for the Eastern *canonical letters*, their list differs totally from that of the West, which contains only *epistolae decretales* of Papal origin. However, as we said, the Eastern letters were those written by patriarchs or bishops. It can therefore be concluded that the main difference is that in the East there was a multitude of authors for the *canonical letters* (sixteen fathers), while in the West, only the Papal decretals were considered to have a universal import, even if initially they were addressed to one specific Church. The West, where only one patriarch, that of Rome, is to be found, was subjected from the beginning of the Vth century to a jurisdictional centralization,[30] which the East escaped.

4. *The appearance of patristic texts in the Western Canonical Collections: the Collectio Hibernensis (around 700)*

If we choose to call "Fathers", as was customary in the Middle Ages, the bishops, patriarchs and Roman pontiffs of the first centuries, and if we consider as "patristic" the canons of the ancient councils, the *canonical letters* and the *epistolae decretales*, then all of canon law is patristic.

But if we understand "Fathers" as those ancient Christian writers who produced "Christian literature", and not disciplinary texts, then there is no patristics in canon law texts until the end of the VIIth century.

The first collection in which texts from patristic literature are to be found is the *Hibernensis*. Composed in Ireland, this collection by an unknown author (some attribute it to Boniface) dates from the early VIIIth century.[31] Besides the Eastern, Gallic and Irish councils, it contains—and this is new—around 500 Biblical citations and 479

---

[28] For example, the canon 28 of the Council of Chalcedon, which raised Constantinople to the rank of "new Rome", is not repeated in the Roman collection *Dyonisiana*.

[29] The canons of the Council of Sardica are often absent from the Eastern lists.

[30] See Peter Landau, "Kanonisches Recht und römische Form. Rechtsprinzipien im ältesten römischen Kirchenrecht", in *Der Staat*, Berlin, vol. 32, 1993, pp. 553–568.

[31] *Die Irische Kanonensammlung*, ed. Hermann Wasserschleben, 2nd ed., Leipzig, 1885, LXXVI–243p.

extracts from the Church Fathers. It thus becomes a mixed, theologico-canonical[32] collection, which marks "a new step in the history of [canon] law".[33] As a matter of fact, new chapters appear, thanks to this collection, in canon law: fasting and alms-giving (books 12–14), burial (book 18), the oath (book 35), relics (books 49–50), hospitality (book 56), etc.

Here is the table, from the works of Charles Munier, of patristic quotations in the *Hibernensis*:[34]

Jerome	168 texts
Augustine	94
Isidore	65
Gregory the First	54
Origen	43
Vitae patrum	19
Gregory of Nazianzus	11
Rufinus	9
Cassian	4
Ambrose	3
Gennadius	2
Basil	3
Eucherius of Lyon	1
Sulpicius Severus	1
Orosius	1
Pelagius	1

The *Hibernensis* did not use patristic texts directly: it probably took them from a sententiary, that is, an educational collection written with a moral purpose. These biblical and patristic *excerpta* were widespread in the West from the end of the Vth century.[35]

Two-thirds of the Biblical quotations are from the Old Testament. Most of the patristic quotations, especially those from Jerome, which are most numerous, were taken from his Biblical Commentaries. We can therefore say that the authors' main concern was to confront canonical texts with Biblical texts: the Fathers were cited in their capacity as commentators of the Bible.

---

[32] Van Hove, *Prolegomena*, pp. 290–291; Fournier - Le Bras, vol. 1, pp. 62–65.
[33] C. Munier, *Les Sources patristiques du droit de l'Eglise*, p. 25.
[34] Munier, *op. cit.*, p. 30.
[35] J. de Ghellinck, *Patristique et Moyen Age*, vol. 2, Bruxelles-Paris, 1947, p. 289 and foll.

We should note another peculiarity of the Irish collection: it often refers to the Greeks Fathers (Origen, Gregory of Nazianzus, Basil . . .). As we will see, references to the Eastern Church will disappear almost completely in the following centuries.

Let us take the example of marriage: the *Hibernensis* devotes book 46 (*De ratione matrimonii*), which contains 38 *capitula*, to this question. We have noted the following sources (thus accepting what is indicated by the collection itself, or by its editor Wasserschleben, allowing for imprecisions):

13 Biblical quotations (7 from the Old Testament, 6 from the New)
11 quotations from Jerome
 9 quotations from Augustine
 2 quotations from Isidore of Seville (including one attributed to Augustine)
 2 quotations from the *Shepherd* by Hermas (attributed to Jerome)
 1 quotation from Origen
 4 canons from the Penitentials
 3 canons from the Councils (Arles, Neocaesarea, Ancyra)
 2 canons from Irish Councils
 1 canon from an undetermined Council
 5 quotations from the Decretals

As we see, Biblical and patristic quotations are much more numerous than conciliar canons. Quotations from the Pentateuch are generally indicated by "*Lex:* . . .". Many patristic quotations are Commentaries on Biblical books: for example, the Origen quotation is taken from his homily 4 on *Genesis*. We can therefore estimate that the Bible is directly used by the Irish collection as a source of law[36]. Nevertheless, many Old Testament rules are contrary to Christian usage (for example the levirate, or the polygamy of patriarchs): these contradictions, as we shall see, will be at the origin of the method of the law itself (and of theology) in the following centuries.

As for the Papal Decretals, five are cited (four by Innocent the First and one by Leo the Great), but all with a false attribution ("Synod of Rome", "Synod of Narbonne"): their Papal origin does not seem to have given them a special authority in Ireland—on the. contrary, one might say.

---

[36] See Paul Fournier, "Le *Liber ex lege Moysi* et les tendances bibliques du droit canonique irlandais", in *Revue celtique*, 30, 1909, pp. 221–234.

It has been said that the patristic content of the *Hibernensis* did not much influence the later collections.[37] This opinion should be qualified, at least concerning the subject of marriage: no less than twelve *capitula* (out of the 38 in the book 46 of the *Hibernensis*) were taken over by the *Decree* of Gratian. Out of these twelve quotations, seven are patristic. This makes for a considerable proportion.[38]

5. *From the VIIIth to the XIIth century*

As we saw, the Irish collection presents several new traits: it uses, for the first time, Biblical and patristic (including Eastern) *excerpta*; it gives only a limited importance to Papal Decretals.

These characteristics will not have an immediate influence on Western collections: Irish Christianity is isolated, and organized in such an original way that its example will not be much followed elsewhere (with the important exception of its penitential doctrine)[39].

It is only one century later that Carolingian canonists also start to make use of patristic quotations. The first example is available in the preparatory files to the Councils of Aix-La Chapelle (816) and Paris (825 and 829), which make use of the Fathers, not only for dogmatic debates, but also for disciplinary questions (such as usury, tithes, etc.).

Another example is Hincmar of Reims' recorded opinion on the divorce of Lothar II and Theutberga (in the years 860), which has recently been the object of an excellent critical edition.[40] It contains, besides Councils, Decretals and texts from the Roman law, a very large collection of Biblical quotations (six hundred, two thirds of which are from the New Testament) and patristic quotations (Ambrosiaster, Ambrose, Augustine—the most cited—, Bede, Cassiodore, Pseudo-Clement, Cyprian, Gregory the Great, Jerome, John Chrysostom, Origen, Pseudo-Prosper, Vincent of Lérins . . .), as well as quotations

---

[37] Munier, *op. cit.*, p. 31: "L'influence [des fragments patristiques de *l'Hibernensis*] sur le développement de la législation occidentale fut des plus modestes".

[38] These seven patristic extracts should be studied in more depth, so as to understand in what exact form they were transmitted in canonical collections. We could thus determine whether the *Hibernensis* or another patristic collection is at the origin of their introduction into the canonical *corpus*.

[39] *The Irish Penitentials*, ed. Ludwig Biehler, Dublin, 1975 (*Scriptores latini Hiberniae*, 5).

[40] Hinkmar of Reims, *De Divortio Lotharii regis et Theutbergae reginae*, ed. L. Böhringer, Hanover, 1992, 315 p. (*MGH, Concilia* 4, Suppl. 1). On the Biblical and patristic *auctoritates* of *De Divortio*, see the Introduction pp. 75–80, and the Indexes pp. 265–279.

from St. Benedict's *Rule*, from the *Etymologies* of Isidore of Seville, from Rabanus Maurus, Martin of Braga, etc. Hincmar's argument thus becomes both theological (that is, mainly Biblical), and canonical. But his opinion will have only a limited success. Once the problem of the divorce is solved by the death of Lothar in 869, Hincmar's work is quickly forgotten.[41] Its Biblical, patristic and canonical index, despite its richness, will therefore not be used much, at least not in canonical collections.[42]

Thus, patristic texts figure sporadically in a few canonical dossiers from the IXth century onwards. But it is only from the Xth century onwards that continental canonical *collections* begin to integrate them. Reginon of Prüm, a German Benedictine monk († 915), writes *ca.* 906 a book on the correct organization of diocesan synods, *De Synodalibus causis et disciplinis ecclesiasticis*.[43] Even though the very technical object of this work is far removed from theology, Reginon cites 43 patristic fragments, essentially from Augustine (7 texts), from Jerome (5 texts), and from the monastic *Rules* of Basil (7 texts) and Benedict (5 texts).[44]

The *Decree* by bishop Burchard of Worms (early 11th century)[45] presents around 14% of patristic texts (247 out of 1785 *capitula*). Are represented mainly Augustine (79 texts), Gregory the Great (77 texts), Isidore (31 texts), and Jerome (19 texts).[46] Like Reginon, Burchard does not hesitate to attribute many texts to those Fathers, while knowing full well that they are not their real authors and that many of the extracts come e.g. from the *Penitentials*.

In the Preface to his *Decree*, Burchard himself indicates the sources used:[47]

Ex quibus locis auctorum scriptis ecclesiastica haec decreta collegerit:
Ex canonibus, qui Corpus canonum vocantur[48]

---

[41] There is only one known manuscript (Paris, B.N. lat. 2866), published by Letha Böhringer.
[42] See the review of the publication of L. Böhringer, by J. Gaudemet, in *Revue historique de droit français et étranger*, vol. 71, 1993, pp. 609–611.
[43] Ed. Wasserschleben, 1840.
[44] Munier, *op. cit.*, p. 34.
[45] *PL* 140, col. 537–1058.
[46] Munier, *op. cit.*, p. 35.
[47] *PL* 140, col. 539.
[48] The *Corpus canonum* designates the so-called *Hadriana* collection, which is an augmented *Dyonisiana*, given by the Pope Adrian to Charlemagne in 774. Published in *PL* 67.

Ex apostolorum canone
Ex transmarinis conciliis
Ex conciliis in Germanica, Gallia, Hispania celebratis
Ex Romanorum pontificum decretis
Ex evangelicis apostolicisque Scripturis
Ex Veteri Testamento
Ex libris sancti Gregorii
Ex Hieronymo, Augustino, Ambrosio, Benedicto, Basilio magno, Isidoro
Ex Poenitentiali Romano
Ex Poenitentiali Theodori
Ex Poenitentiali Bedae.

(This Decree is composed of the following excerpts:

– the canons called "Corpus canonum"
– the canons of the Apostles
– the Overseas Councils
– the councils celebrated in Germany, Gaule and Spain
– the decrees of the Roman Pontiffs
– the evangelical and apostolical Writings
– the Old Testament
– the books of Gregory
– Jerome, Augustine, Benedict, Basil the Great, Isidore
– the Roman Penitential
– Theodorus' Penitential
– Bede's Penitential)

This list is remarkable for many reasons. Let us note especially that Burchard wants to give the sources of the *decreta* (his work is clearly canonical), that among these sources the Old and New Testaments occupy an important but by no means the first and foremost position, that Gregory the Great benefits from a special mention (he is confused neither with the other Roman Popes, nor with the Church Fathers such as Jerome or Augustine), that the list of the Fathers is very selective (only six names), that among those Fathers only one, Basil, is from the East.

We should observe, though, that most of the new patristic texts introduced by Burchard, were introduced in two of the most theological, or least canonical of his books: book 19, which is a Penitential called *Corrector* or *Medicus*, and book 20, a theological treatise called *Speculator* or *De Contemplatione*. The patristic texts, even though present also in the most canonical parts of the *Decree*, still retain an essentially theological character in Burchard's work.

After the Gregorian Reformation, patristic borrowings become more numerous and more precise: instead of copying out patristic quotations from earlier collections, or misattributing quotations from the Carolingian *Penitentials* to the Fathers, the reforming canonists seek to explore the great authors again and search for excerpts directly in their works, or at the very least, in reliable *florilegia*. The influence of Augustine becomes overwhelming: from the time of Anselm of Lucca (around 1083) the Augustinian quotations represent about two-thirds of the patristic quotations.[49]

The *Panormia*, the *Decree* and the *Collectio tripartita* of Yvo of Chartres, all composed at the end of the 11th century,[50] contain many citations from the Fathers. In the *Decree*, we find exactly 20% of patristic texts (755 out of 3760). Out of these 755 texts, 456 are by Augustine; many are wrongly attributed to Augustine by Yvo. In all, a total of more than 500 quotations is, rightly or wrongly, attributed to the Bishop of Hippo. The sources from which Yvo takes these texts are the *Decree* of Burchard and some other canonical collections, but also *florilegia* or sententiaries used in theological instruction of the time (Berenger of Tours, Lanfranc, etc.). Thus, Yvo assembles about 143 patristic texts on marriage, among which 123 are new to the canonical collections.[51] His contribution to the doctrine of the sacrament of marriage is the single most important contribution prior to Gratian. The *Panormia*, which is a condensed version of the *Decree* in 1138 *capitula*, contains around 300 patristic texts (174 from Augustine). In selecting texts for this condensed version, Yvo eliminated more conciliar canons or Decretals than patristic texts, so that the *Panormia* (25% of patristic texts) contains proportionately more than the *Decree* (20%). We can conclude that, for Yvo, patristic texts had at least as much authority as the canons themselves.

---

[49] *Anselm II. Bishof von Lucca (Anselmus Episcopus Lucensis), Collectio Canonum*, ed. Friedrich Thaner, Innsbrück, 1906–1915, 519 p. (repr. Aalen, 1965); Giuseppe Motta, "La redazione A 'Aucta' della Collectio Anselmi episcopi Lucensis", in *Studia in honorem eminentissimi cardinalis Alphonsi M. Stickler*, Rome, 1992, pp. 375–449.

[50] The *Decree* and the *Panormia* can be found in *Patrologia latina*, 161. The *Collectio tripartita* is not published.

[51] Munier, *op. cit.*, p. 71.

6. *Decree of Gratian* (1140)

We shall now concentrate our attention on the *Decree of Gratian*[52] due to its exceptional importance in the history of Western canon law. In fact, it is the most important canonical collection the Church ever had (around 4000 *capitula*). The *Decree of Gratian* was used in the Catholic Church for nearly eight centuries, that is, until the promulgation of the 1917 Code, as the first part of the *Corpus Iuris canonici*; many Churches issued from the Reformation still consider it (following Melanchthon and Calvin) as a reference if not as source of their own law.[53]

Completed *ca.* 1140 in Bologna, the *Decree of Gratian* contains, besides the usual *auctoritates* (conciliar canons, Papal Decretals, texts from the Roman law, patristic texts), the opinions of Gratian himself, in the form of *dicta Gratiani*, that is, paragraphs written by the author himself (they were printed in italics by Friedberg in his edition).[54] The *Decree* is presented in the form of a treatise of canon law, or an instruction manual, with its *dictinctiones*, its *quaestiones*, its *solutiones*: it is therefore much more than a simple collection or compilation of texts.

It borrows from its predecessors: the *Etymologies* of Isidore of Seville, the collection of Anselm of Lucca, the *Panormia* and the *Collectio Tripartita* of Yvo of Chartres, the *Polycarpus* by Gregory, the *Collectio Tripartita*, the *Liber de misericordia et iustitia* by Alger, and many others which have not been identified.[55]

We will have to examine first the patristic quotations which we find in the *Decree* (taking the example of marriage), and then study Gratian's view of *auctoritas patrum*.

---

[52] *Corpus iuris canonici*, editio lipsiensis secunda [. . .], instruxit Æmilius Friedberg. Pars prior: *Decretum Magistri Gratiani*, Lipsiae, 1879, CIV–1468 col. (anastatic reprints, Leipzig, 1922 and 1928; Graz, 1955 and 1959).

[53] Peter Landau, art. "Gratian (von Bologna)", in *Theologische Realenzyclopädie* (*TRE*), vol. 14, Berlin-New York, 1985, pp. 124–130 (with an extensive bibliography).

[54] The question concerning the authorship of the *Decree* is not resolved: is Gratian the only author, or is the *Decree* the result of a collective workshop? If Gratian is the author of the *Decree*, we ignore all of his biography. What is established anyhow, is that he was not, contrary to common belief, a Camaldule monk.

[55] The lists given by Friedberg, col. XLII–LXXV should be read as lists of concordances rather than as lists of sources. Thus, contrary to what Friedberg indicates, Gratian did not use the *Decree* of Burchard of Worms directly, nor that of Yvo of Chartres, even less the *Sentences* by Peter Lombard, which are later. See Peter Landau, "Neue Forschungen zu vorgratianischen Kanonensammlungen und den Quellen des gratianischen Dekrets", in *Ius commune*, 11, 1984, pp. 1–29; P. Landau, "Quellen und Bedeutung des Gratianischen Dekrets", in *Studia et documenta historiae et iuris*, 52, 1986, pp. 218–235.

Patristic quotations in the Decree *of Gratian*

The exact number of Gratian's *capitula* is impossible to determine: depending on the way the text is divided, and on whether or not we count the *paleae*,[56] the total varies. Besides, many texts are misattributed: for example, 582 texts are attributed to Augustine, whereas only 469 are authentic.[57] That being said, we can estimate that patristic texts account for about one third of the *Decree*: about 1200 out of the 4000 *capitula*. No canonical or theological collection previously contained such a wealth of patristic sources.

The following graph shows the share of the different Fathers in Gratian's work:

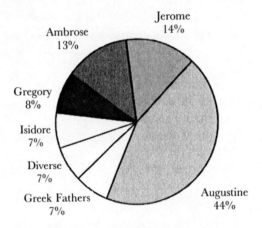

Figure 1

We can see that it is Augustine who, as usual, occupies most of the graph: about half of the patristic texts are attributed to him (582 out of 1200). Four authors (in shadow on the graph), Augustine, Jerome, Ambrose and Gregory the Great, represent together more than three quarters of the patristic texts (201 for Jerome, 148 for Ambrose, 89 for Gregory).

We therefore find the list, typical after the time of Bede, of the

---

[56] The *paleae* are *capitula* added to the *Decree* during the second part of the 12th century, by disciples of Gratian. See Jacqueline Rambaud, "Le legs de l'ancient droit: Gratien", in *L'Age classique (1140–1378). Sources et théorie du droit*, Paris, Sirey, 1965, pp. 47–129 (*Histoire du droit et des institutions de l'Eglise en Occident*, published under the direction of Gabriel Le Bras, vol. 7).

[57] Munier, *op. cit.*, p. 126.

four great Western doctors: Ambrose, Augustine, Jerome, Gregory, just as there are four main Synods, and four Gospels. Sometimes standard lists also include the names of Cyprian, Hilary, Anselm of Canterbury, or Isidore of Seville and Bede.[58] In Gratian's work Isidore (77 texts) and Cyprian (34 texts) could be added to the "great" four.

Then, in decreasing order of importance, come the Greek Fathers: John Chrysostom (33 texts are attributed to him, among which only 14 are authentic), Origen (18 authentic texts, among which 16 are falsely attributed to others, especially Jerome);[59] and Basil (14 texts, 12 falsely attributed).[60] Citations from Origen (and the Greek Fathers generally) were rare in Western canon law (with the exception of the *Hibernensis*). It is a specificity of Gratian to have introduced those few Origen texts in his *Decree*, contrary for example to Yvo of Chartres. They are in fact homilies translated by Rufinus, and falsely attributed to Jerome. These borrowings can certainly be explained by the period of good relations between the East and the West which reigned in the first half of the 12th century.

The section On Matrimony (De matrimonio) in the Decree of Gratian

The *De matrimonio* occupies the Causes 27 to 36 of the *Decree* of Gratian. It is especially interesting for us in that it is presented in the form of a treatise having its own unity, a relatively well constructed plan, and a clearly defined method.[61] The *De matrimonio* is composed of 419 *capitula*, 178 patristic quotations are to be found in 172 of them (41%).[62] As we can see, the proportion of patristic texts is even greater in the *De Matrimonio* than in the rest of the *Decree* (with an average of 30%). If we take out the false attributions and correct Friedberg's errors, we count:

---

[58] J. de Ghellinck, *Le mouvement théologique au XIIe siècle*, 1948, pp. 514–517.

[59] Charles Munier, "La contribution d'Origène au Décret de Gratien", in *Studia Gratiana*, vol. 20, 1976, pp. 241–251 (*Mélanges Fransen*, II); G. Motta, "A proposito dei testi di Origene nel Decreto di Graziano", in *Revue bénédictine*, 88, 1978, pp. 315–320.

[60] Roger E. Reynolds, "Basil and the Early Medieval Latin Canonical Collections", in *Basil of Caesera, Christian, Humanist, Ascetic*, ed. Paul J. Fedwick, Toronto, Pontifical Institute of Mediaeval Studies, 1981, pp. 513–532.

[61] We could study in the same way the *De Penitentia* (C. 33 q. 3), or the *De Consecratione*, which form well defined wholes within the *Decree* of Gratian. But they are not as well authenticated, and they present a theological rather than a canonical character. They would therefore be less representative of the place of Fathers in Church law.

[62] Let us not forget that these figures are approximate. C. Munier does not get

- 78 texts from Augustine: 11 times the *De adulterinis coniugiis*, 9 times the *De bono coniugali*, 5 times the *De nuptiis et concupiscentia*, twice the *Confessions*, once the *De libero arbitrio*, twice *De sancta virginitate*, once the *De baptismo*, 4 times the *City of God*, twice the *De fide et operibus*, four times the *De bono viduitatis*, twice the *Contra Faustum*, twice the *Contra Iulianum*, once the *De duabus animis*, twice the *Contra adversarium legum et prophetarum*, 8 letters, 3 sermons (including one apocryphal), and 19 Biblical Commentaries (*Questions on Genesis*, on *Numbers*, *Discourses on the Psalms*, *Sermon on the Mount*, etc.). We can add one quotation from an apocryphal work (*The Conflict of vice and virtue*), and 5 false attributions.
- 25 texts by Jerome: 11 times his Biblical Commentaries (*Genesis, Hosea, Joel, Matthew, Pauline Epistles*), 7 times the *Adversus Jovinianum*, 7 times the letters. We can add one apocryphal homily, and 4 false attributions of canons of unknown origin.
- 21 texts from Gregory the Great: 16 letters, 3 sermons, 2 quotations from the *Moralia*. We can add to this three false attributions and 8 apocryphal letters.
- 20 texts by Ambrose:[63] once the *Apologia David*, twice the *Expositio evangelii secundum Lucam*, once the *De Paradiso*, once the *De Cain et Abel*, 6 times the *De Patriarchis*, twice the *Hexaemeron*, twice the *De institutione virginis*, once the *De virginibus*, once the *Exhortatio virginitatis*, twice the letter no. 60 to Paternus. We can add to this list two apocryphal texts: a quotation from the *De lapsu virginis consecratae* (to be attributed to Nicetas of Remesiana?), one quotation from sermon 52.—Let us note that the false attributions to Ambrose are numerous: ten in all, mainly texts by the Ambrosiaster.
- 10 texts by Isidore of Seville:[64] 4 times the *Etymologies*, once the *Synonyms*, once the *De Ecclesiasticis officiis*, once the *Quaestiones de veteri et novo Testamento*, once the *Sentences*, one letter.
- 9 texts from the Ambrosiaster: 4 from the *Questions on the Old and the New Testament* (three of which are attributed to Augustine, and one to Ambrose), and 5 from the *Commentary on Paul's Epistle* (among which 3 are attributed to Ambrose, one to Augustine, and one to Gregory).
- 5 texts from the *Opus imperfectum in Mattheum* (attributed by Gratian to John Chrysostom).
- 2 texts from *The Shepherd* of Hermas: one is falsely attributed to Origen, the other one is a *palea*.
- 2 texts from John Chrysostom, from *Homily 4 on Matthew*. We can add

---

exactly the same totals: he finds 167 patristic quotations in 396 canons (*loc. cit.*, p. 149). See also the study and tables by Jean Gaudemet, "L'apport de la patristique latine au Décret de Gratien en matière de mariage", in *Studia Gratiana*, vol. 2, 1954, pp. 49–81 (reproduced in *Sociétés et mariage*, Strsbourg, 1980, pp. 290–319).

[63] See O. Giacchi, "La dottrina matrimonale di Sant'Ambrogio nel Decreto di Graziano", in *Sant'Ambrogio nel XVI centenario della nascita*, Milan, 1940, pp. 513–551.

[64] See Dom Séjourné, *Saint Isidore de Séville, son rôle dans l'histoire du droit canonique*, Paris, 1929.

one apocryphal text (Homily on Psalm 50), and 7 false attributions (essentially the *Opus imperfectum in Mattheum*).
- 2 texts from Cyprian, from the *De virginitate ad Pomponium*.
- 2 texts from Origen: Homily on *Numbers* (attributed to Jerome), Homily on *Genesis*. One doubtful text: *Commentary on the Epistle to the Romans*, attributed to Jerome), and an apocryphal Homily (Pseudo-Origen) on *Matthew*.
- one text from Basil, from the *Regulae fusius disputatae*.
- one Pseudo-Clementine homily.

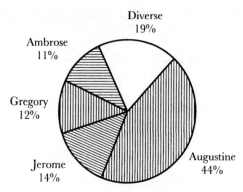

Figure 2
Distribution of the Fathers in Gratian's De matrimonio

As we see in Figure 2, the share of the "great four" (Augustine, Jerome, Gregory and Ambrose) is preponderant (more than 80% of the cited patristic texts come from their works), even more so than in the rest of the *Decree*. We can group these texts in three categories: the great treatises on marriage or virginity (Cyprian, Ambrose, Augustine . . .), Biblical Commentaries, and other works. This gives us the following, approximate repartition: 37 treatises, 62 Biblical Commentaries, and 79 diverse texts (Figure 3). As we see, despite what might be expected, the proportion of patristic treatises explicitly on marriage or virginity is not the largest. The best represented genre is by far the Biblical Commentary. We shall take up this point later.

Among the patristic treatises on marriage, we note mainly those of Augustine (*De adulterinis coniugiis, De bono coniugali, De nuptiis et concupiscentia, De sancta virginitate, De bono viduitatis* . . .), and, to a lesser degree, those of Ambrose (*De institutione virginis, De virginibus, Exhortatio virginitatis* . . .) and the *Adversus Jovinianum* of Jerome[65]. The Augustinian

---

[65] The *Adversus Jovinianum* of Jerome has been very much cited and used in the

doctrine, with its tolerance of the matrimonial institution (opposed in this to Jerome) thus left as big an imprint on Western law as it did on Western theology.[66] We could for example remind the reader of his well-known theory of the *bona* (or benefits) of marriage (the *bona matrimonii: bonum fidei, bonum prolis, bonum sacramenti*),[67] cited many times in the *Decree* of Gratian,[68] and preserved, until today, in Catholic canon law.[69] We also note that some of the great patristic treatises on marriage are ignored: the *Stromata* of Clement of Alexandria, the *De virginitate* of Gregory of Nyssa, the *Ad uxorem* of Tertullian, etc., were not recorded by medieval law. For the first two of these authors, this can be explained by the fact that they are Eastern; as for Tertullian, all his works were considered as heretical during the Middle Ages.

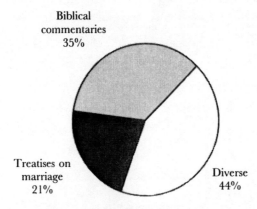

Biblical
commentaries
35%

Treatises on
marriage
21%

Diverse
44%

Figure 3
Distribution of the patristic works by genres in Gratian's De matrimonio

In the *Decree* of Gratian, we find, more or less developed, most of the subjects treated by the Fathers when discussing marriage: virginity (the vow of virginity is the object of Cause 27, which is the first Cause of the *De Matrimonio*); conjugal chastity (a specifically Christian virtue: C. 28.1); the union of Mary and Joseph (in agreement with Jerome and Ambrose, and against Augustine, Gratian considers that

---

canonical doctrine: we regret therefore that there is no critical edition (the only available edition being that of *PL*, vol. 23).

[66] See Émile Schmitt, *Le mariage chrétien dans l'œuvre de Saint-Augustin. Une théologie baptismale de la vie conjugale*, Paris, Études Augustiniennes, 1983, 318 p.

[67] Augustine expands this doctrine many times. See for example *De nuptiis et concupiscentia*, I, 17, 19 (*CSEL* 42, p. 231).

[68] For example in the *dictum post* C. 27.2.39, § 1.

[69] *Code de droit canonique* of 1983, can. 1055–1056.

this union was not really a marriage, due to lack of a sensual dimension: *dictum post* C. 27.2.2 and *dictum post* C. 27.2.29); the aim of marriage (procreation or *libido*: Gratian is rather benevolent towards the *causa explendae libidinis*, the gratification of sexual desire, C. 32.2);[70] etc.

But those themes are, of course, treated from a canonical point of view. Thus, virginity is considered under the angle of the vow attached to it and the importance this vow can have in the validity of a subsequent marriage: Gratian concludes his Cause 27.1 by estimating, against the opinion of the Lateran Synod of 1139, that the marriage of *voventes* (those who have pronounced a vow of virginity or of widowhood) is a real marriage, even if it is illicit.

On other questions, the contribution of the Fathers is less important, and sometimes negligible. For example, long excursus are dedicated to the formation of the matrimonial bond (C. 27.2), a problem which the Fathers had tackled very little, leaving this to custom or to civil law—with the exception of Ambrose, whose texts on the *pactio coniugalis*[71] are extensively cited by Gratian (C. 27.2.5 and 35). The question of marrying slaves calls for no contribution from the Fathers, with the exception of a letter from Gregory the Great, in which the Pope implies that marriages contracted with those of lower social rank can be broken:[72] the canon law teaching, especially after the IXth century, tends towards the recognition of servile or unequal marriages, which explains why recourse to the Fathers is of little use (C. 29.2).[73] Long canonical developments on impediments rely hardly at all on patristic texts, but essentially on Roman law, conciliar decrees or Papal letters; thus, Gratian devotes 23 canons to the impediment of spiritual parenthood (C. 30), among which figure 13 decretals and 5 conciliar canons, but no patristic texts. For the impediment of consanguinity and affinity (C. 35), discussed in 59 canons, we find only 3 texts from Augustine and one by Isidore of Seville. In other words, as soon as we enter the technical aspects of the law, the influence of Fathers abates, or disappears.

---

[70] Rudolph Weigand, "Die Lehre der Kanonisten des 12. und 13. Jahrhunderts von den Ehezwecken", in *Studia Gratiana*, vol. 12, 1967, pp. 443–478.

[71] Ambrose, *De Institutione virginis*, c. 6, n. 41 (*PL* 16, col. 330–331): "*Non defloratio virginitatis facit coniugium, sed pactio coniugalis.*" This position is in conformity with Roman law.

[72] Gregory the Great, Letter VII, 1 (596) addressed to Fortunatus, bishop of Naples (*CCSL* 140a, p. 443; Jaffé 1447).

[73] See R. Naz, art. "Esclave", in the *Dictionnaire de droit canonique*, vol. 5, Paris, 1950, col. 448–454.

Gratian's theory of patristic auctoritates

As we said, the *Decree* of Gratian is not only a compilation of *auctoritates*, it is also presented as a treatise of canon law. Gratian did not merely cite, as his predecessors did, the patristic *auctoritates* in his list of *capitula*. He also examined the place that should be given to the councils, the decretals and the Fathers. In fact, he elaborated a theory of the sources of the law. This is the subject of the first twenty distinctions of his *Decree*.[74]

He confronts several problems. First, who are the real Fathers of the Church? In the early VIth century, a document attributed to Gelasius (or to a synod called by Damasius, or even to Hormisdas), called *De libris legendis et reiiciendis* ("The books to be read and those to be rejected"), which had commonly been referred to as "the *Decree* of Gelasius", had given some Fathers the title of *Patres orthodoxi*, "who have not strayed from the communion of the Holy Roman Church".[75] This list will be used throughout the Middle Ages to admit or reject patristic works: it permits, for example, to recognise the orthodoxy of Cyprian of Carthage, Gregory of Nazianzus, Athanasius of Alexandria, John of Constantinople, Hilary of Poitiers, and of course Ambrose, Augustine, Jerome and their like. On the other hand, "Gelasius'" rejected the works of Tertullian, Faustus the Manichean, Cassian, etc. The list of *orthodoxi Patres* was thus well known, and Gratian simply repeated it by reproducing the *Decree* of Gelasius (D. 15.3).

Second problem: should the Fathers be admitted among the canon law authorities? Here too, Gratian's answer is a classic one. In the preface to his *Decree*, Yvo of Chartres already cited the *orthodoxi Patres* (Yvo knew and cited the *Decree* of Gelasius) among the sources of the law.[76] Gratian in his turn simply reiterated the same teaching.

Third question, more precise: should the Fathers be granted the same canon law authority as the councils or the Papal letters? The canon law *auctoritates* often contradict one another: between a council of the IVth century and a decretal of the 12th century, between a

---

[74] J. Gaudemet, "La doctrine des sources du droit dans le Décret de Gratien", in *Revue de droit canonique*, 1, 1951, pp. 5–31.

[75] Text in *PL* 59, col. 157–180, and in *Texte und Untersuchungen*, Leipzig, 1912, vol. 38–4 (*Decretum Gelasianum*, ed. E. von Dobschütz). See Charles Pietri, *Roma christiana*, vol. 1, Rome, 1976, pp. 881–884.

[76] *PL* 161, col. 47.

text by Augustine and one by Cyprian or Jerome, opinions can diverge. The *Hibernensis* already regretted this in its preface: "*Synodicorum exemplarium . . . diversitatem inconsonam, destruentem magis quam aedificantem prospiciens*" ("the dissonant variety of synodal texts tends more to destroy than to construct").[77] In case of "dissonance", of "discordance", of "*contrarietas*", which one of the authorities should be preferred? This is a new question: no theory had hitherto established a hierarchy of the different sources of the law.

Isidore of Seville, in a famous passage, had proposed the rule of the *antiquior et potior auctoritas*:[78]

> *quotiescumque in gestis conciliorum discors sentencia inuenitur, illius concilii magis teneatur sentencia, cuius antiquior et potior extat auctoritas.*

> Every time we find discordant decisions in the acts of the councils, we should retain the decision of the council whose authority is the eldest and the highest.

But this rule was difficult to apply (the jurisdictional superiority of one council over another, or its œcumenical, general or local character were not always obvious in the Antiquity), and it could concern only divergences between councils. Thus, the rule was cited in all the collections without ever really being applied.[79]

Gratian was therefore the first to examine, in his Distinction 20, the respective status of the councils, the decretals, and the Fathers. In the first *dictum* he affirms that the authority of the Papal decretals must be of equal weight to that of the conciliar canons: "pari iure exequantur". As for the Fathers, whom he calls the "expositores sacrae scripturae", the commentators of the Holy Scripture, he first recognises them as superior: their treatises benefit from "more science" (*ampliori scientia precellentes*) in that they are "more full of the grace of the Holy Spirit" (*pleniori gratia Spiritus sancti*). It was common teaching that the Fathers were considered as directly inspired by the Spirit when they wrote their translations (Jerome) or their commentaries of the Bible.[80]

---

[77] Ed. Wasserschleben, p. 1.

[78] Isidore of Seville, Letter 4 to Masson, n. 13 (*PL* 83, col. 901). This letter is of doubtful authenticity (see Dom Séjourné, *Saint Isidore de Séville, op. cit.*, pp. 74–78; G. Le Bras, in *Revue des Sciences religieuses*, t. 10, 1930, p. 255).

[79] We find the Isidorian formulation in the *Hibernensis*, and in Alcuin, Rabanus Maurus, Burchard, Anselm of Lucca, Yvo of Chartres, Alger of Liege, Abelard, in the *Polycarpus*, etc. Gratian cites it twice: D. 50.28 and C. 33.2.11.

[80] C. Spicq, *Esquisse d'une histoire de l'exégèse latine au Moyen Age*, Paris, 1944, p. 107; de Ghellinck, *Le mouvement théologique au XIIe siècle*, 1948, p. 321.

From this point of view, the Fathers therefore have a preeminence over the other sources of the law. But other criteria are to be taken into account. Especially, according to Gratian, that of science or *ratio*: "there where reason prevails, the statement seems to benefit from a superior authority" (*Quo enim quisque magis ratione nititur, eo maioris auctoritatis eius uerba esse uidentur*). This *ratio*, for Gratian, blends with the natural law, which must be placed on top of the hierarchy of laws.[81]

But Gratian adds another criterion, that of power, or *potestas*:

> *Sed aliud est causis terminum imponere aliud scripturas sacras diligenter exponere. Negotiis diffiniendis non solum est necessaria scientia, sed etiam potestas.*

> (It is one thing to decide on causes and another to comment brilliantly on the holy Scriptures. To settle a matter, science is not enough, power is also necessary.)

The Fathers are excellent at "making fine distinctions", but it is to Peter that Christ gave the power of the keys: to absolve an innocent, or to condemn the culprit, science is not enough. The power to command is also necessary (*absolutio uero uel condempnatio non scientiam tantum, sed etiam potestatem presidentium desiderant*).

The conclusion is obvious: because they are more knowledgeable, the Fathers have more authority than pontiffs to comment on the Scriptures, but they come second in the exercise of judiciary power, that is, in canon law:

> *aparet, quod diuinarum scripturarum tractatores, etsi scientia Pontificibus premineant, tamen, quia dignitatis eorum apicem non sunt adepti, in sacrarum scripturarum expositionibus eis preponuntur, in causis uero diffiniendis secundum post eos locum merentur.*

> (We see that the commentators of the divine Scriptures, although their knowledge or science is greater than that of the pontiffs, have greater authority than the pontiffs when it comes to exposition of the Scriptures but are inferior to the pontiffs when it comes to legal decisions, as they never occupied the most responsible positions.)

And Gratian concludes very clearly at the beginning of Distinction 21:

> *Decretis ergo Romanorum Pontificum et sacris canonibus conciliorum ecclesiastica negotia, et supra monstratum est, terminantur.*

---

[81] It is the object of Distinction 8.

(The ecclesiastical causes are therefore settled, as has been shown before, by the decrees of the Roman pontiffs and by the holy canons of the councils.)

Thus canon law hierarchy is established: first come the general councils, especially the four "great" ones (Nicea, Constantinople, Ephesus, Chalcedon); then, the Papal decretals (with the same legislative authority as the councils); then, in the second line, the Fathers, who do not have the power to "judge disputes". This hierarchy, of which Gratian was the initiator, was to have deep consequences later on.

7. The disappearance of patristic texts after Gratian

The *Decree* of Gratian is the medieval canonical collection containing the most patristic texts, and in the greatest proportion (if we except the *Hibernensis*). The year 1140, in which the *Decree* was probably completed, appears as the height of the Fathers' influence on the law.

A few years later, this influence was already starting to decline. A shorter version of the *Decree*, the *Abbreviato* by Omnebenus (around 1148–1155), expunges 48% of the *auctoritates* from Gratian, and almost 100% of the patristic texts.[82] One of the first decretists (commentators on the Decree of Gratian), Stephen of Tournai, gives the following list of the sources of the law in the introduction to his *Summa*,[83] written around 1169:

> *Concilia . . ., decretalis . . . Ultimo loco succedunt verba sanctorum patrum: Ambrosii, Augustini, Hieronymi et aliorum.*

> (. . . the councils, the decretals. In the last instance, come the texts of the holy Fathers: Ambrose, Augustine, Jerome, etc.)

As we see, the Fathers are not any more, as they were for Gratian, second to the councils and the pontiffs (*secundum post eos locum*), but last (*ultimo loco*): the place is the same, but the perception of it has changed. A little further, Stephen comes back to this subject; after

---

[82] Adam Vetulani and Waclaw Uruszczak, "L'œuvre d'Omnebene dans le MS 602 de la bibliothèque municipale de Cambrai", in *Proceedings of the Fourth International Congress of Medieval Canon Law, Toronto*, Vatican, 1976, p. 16.

[83] *Die Summa des Stephanus Tornacensis über das Decretum Gratiani*, hrsg. von Joh. Friedrich von Schulte, Giessen, 189 1, XXX–280 p.

reminding the reader of what conciliar canons and Papal decretals were, he adds:

> *Auctoritas etiam sanctorum patrum, qui, quamvis ius et potestatem condendi canones non habuerint, non minimum tamen locum in ecclesia habent.*

> (There is also the authority of the holy Fathers, who, even though they do not have the power and the right to edict canons, still have their place in the Church and quite an important one.)

The Fathers are almost chased from the canonical domain by this subtle understatement: *non minimum tamen* ("they still have . . .").

In fact, later canonical texts do not contain any patristic texts. Of course, the canons collected by Gratian will officially continue to belong to Church law (the *Decree* of Gratian constitutes the first volume of the *Corpus iuris canonici*, used in the Catholic Church until 1917), but the *ius novum* will be constituted only of decretals (the volume II of the *Corpus* collects the *Decretals* of Gregory IX, Boniface VIII, Clement V, etc.), and conciliar decisions (Lateran III, Lateran IV . . ., later the Council of Trent and Vatican I and II).

Many authors, ancient or modern, have heavily stressed and regretted this change of trend in medieval canon law. Roger Bacon, in the 13th century, wished that only the texts from the Scriptures and from the Fathers be present in canon law.[84] Rudolph Sohm, the great historian and Lutheran canonist († 1917), dedicated an important and interesting work[85] to this question: for him, the old canon law (*das altkatholische Kirchenrecht*) was a sacramental law: "*Das kanonische Recht ist für Gratian Sakramentsrecht [. . .]. Anderes kanonische Recht als das Recht der Sakramente gibt es nicht. Alles kanonische Recht handelt von Gott, von dem Geheimnis seines Lebens in der Christenheit*".[86] And further: "*Was die griechische Kirche Mysterium nannte, das hieß in der lateinischen Kirche Sakrament. Im Sacrament vollzieht sich etwas Geheimnisvolles*".[87] For Gratian, according to Sohm, the law essentially belonged to the theological "mystery", while the new law (*das neukatholische Kirchenrecht*), issued from the *Decretals*, tended to make Catholicism into legislation, the focal

---

[84] *Opus maius, pars secunda*, vol. 3, London, 1900, p. 38, cited by De Ghellinck, *Le mouvement théologique au XIIe siècle*, p. 17.

[85] Rudolph Sohm, "Das altkatholisches Kirchenrecht und das Dekret Gratians", in *Festschrift der Leipziger Juristenfakultät für Dr. Adolf Wach*, Munich-Leipzig, 1918, pp. 1–674.

[86] Sohm, *loc. cit.*, pp. 51–56.

[87] *Ibid.*, p. 62.

point of which were the Roman pontiffs. "Spiritual canon law" (*kanonisches geistliches Recht*) thus became mere "ecclesiastical law" (*Kirchenrecht*).[88]

Recent Catholic law has tended more and more towards legislation, with the promulgation of the 1917 Code, and then those of 1983 (for the Latin Church), and 1990 (for the Catholic Eastern Churches), which bear no direct reference to the Fathers or to Tradition.[89]

Conclusion

Research on the reception of the Fathers in canon law has, for the most part, been carried out by the many authors cited here. Especially, the work of Charles Munier on *Les sources patristiques du droit de l'Eglise du VIIIe au XIIIe siècle* ("the patristic sources of the Church law: VIIIth–XIIIth century") sets the scene for the richest period, that between the *Hibernensis* and the *Decree* of Gratian. The situation of the Eastern Churches should be researched further, as well as the post-Gratian period in the West: the influence of the Fathers on the Decretals, the modern councils, the Codes,[90] the legislation of the Churches issued from the Reformation would deserve particular attention.

The following graph sums up the major evolutions we noted: after a long period during which canon law is only composed of conciliar canons and Papal letters (in the West), with a few so-called patristic letters (in the East), but which are mainly patriarchal letters, the *Hibernensis* collection is the first to incorporate many Biblical and patristic texts. This usage will develop slowly in the West, up until the great medieval collection called the *Decree* of Gratian (around 1140), which contains around 30% of patristic texts. After the early 13th century the Fathers disappear from the new law (*Decretals* of Gregory IX), which is founded exclusively on the Popes and the councils.

---

[88] *Ibid.*, p. 95, note 6.

[89] See J. Werckmeister, "La codification du droit canonique, négation de l'histoire", in *L'Institution de l'histoire*, t. 1, directed by René Heyer, Paris, Cerf-Cérit, 1989, pp. 81–92.

[90] See for example René Metz, "Saint Augustin et le Code de droit canonique de 1917", in *Revue de droit canonique*, 4, 1954, pp. 405–419.

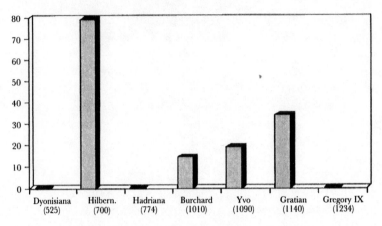

Percentage of patristic texts in a few collections

This graph only gives approximate indications: it is difficult to estimate exactly the proportion of texts from different origins in a composite collection. Even so, it allows us to visualise the major tendencies.

The *Hibernensis* (around 700), as we see on the graph, constitutes a special case: it contains more patristic or Biblical texts than conciliar or Papal texts. It is difficult to distinguish between Biblical and patristic quotations: as we said, the Fathers are often used as commentators on the Bible, and we often find in the same canon a combination of Biblical and patristic quotations.

The *Hadriana* (end of the VIIIth century), an official canonical collection of the Carolingian era, does not contain any patristic texts any more than the earlier collections (*Dyonisiana, Hispana*...).

The last three examples cited here are especially revealing: from the Decree of Burchard of Worms (1010) to the Decree of Yvo of Chartres (1090) and the Decree of Gratian (1140), the proportion of patristic texts grows regularly, until it reaches 30%.

After Gratian, legislators and canonists soon lose the habit of citing the Fathers. The Decretals of Gregory IX (1234) will only contain, as their name suggests, Papal letters. We can therefore conclude that half a millennium (VIIIth to the XIIth century) appears as an exception, during which canon law was very much influenced by the Fathers, and thus became theological law—what Sohm called "*altkatholisches Kirchenrecht*".

* * *

What can we conclude from this historical outline?

1) The Fathers had a direct influence on ecclesiastical legislation, in that most of them were bishops, and therefore legislators (either in their own Church, or during the councils). Let us remember for example the role played by Augustine in the Councils of Carthage, or by Isidore during the Councils of Toledo. Others were monks, founders of religious orders (Benedict in the West, Basil in the East): their Rules strongly influenced, if not created, legislation pertaining to monastic life.

2) The Patristic *literature* entered the law only much later, during the VIIIth century, and left it as early as the XIIIth century. The Fathers thus "received" were so essentially as commentators on the Scriptures. Through them, it was the Bible the canonists wanted to scrutinize. For Gratian especially, the purpose was to submit the institutions of his time to the critical fire of God's word. The substantial development of patristic presence in canonical collections (1200 quotations in the *Decree* of Gratian) made of these collections the main source of patristic texts for the canonists and also for the theologians of the time.[91] Peter Lombard, for example, will take a lot from Gratian for his *Sentences*.

3) After the XIth and XIIth century, for example in Alger of Liège (*Liber de misericordia*), the status of the *auctoritas* itself changed.[92] The Fathers were now cited, not to provide a definitive and authoritative answer, but rather to support an interpretation: the *auctoritas* lost its status of proof to become a mere argument. The *ratio*, reasoning, became essential for resolving differences between *auctoritates*. Abelard, at the beginning of his *Sic et non*, observes that the texts of the Fathers are not only divergent, but also often contradictory:

> *Cum nonnulla sanctorum dicta, non solum ab invicem diversa, verum etiam invicem adversa videantur* (some texts are not only divergent, but even contradictory).

It is therefore necessary to find a method of interpretation, a hermeneutic of patristic texts, to reach, if possible, a *concordia*. We will not expose here how theologians and canonists of the XIth and XIIth centuries (Bernold of Constance, Yvo of Chartres, Gratian . . .)

---

[91] de Ghellinck, *Le mouvement théologique au XIIᵉ siècle*, 1948, p. 466.

[92] Spicq, *op. cit.*, pp. 72–73; Maurice Sachot, "L'argument d'autorité dans l'enseignement théologique au Moyen-Age: les grandes étapes d'une évolution", in *Rhétorique et pédagogie*, published under the direction of O. Reboul and J.-F. Garcia, Strasbourg, 1991, pp. 111–153.

elaborated the criteria for analysis that would enable them to put those texts in a perspective and reach harmony. It was in fact the project of Gratian to reach a *Concordia discordantium canonum*, harmony of the discordant canons;[93] when the *Concordia* was published, says P. De Ghellinck, this word "[a] fait l'effet d'un cri de victoire ou de délivrance au sortir d'une difficulté vaincue".[94]

However, this relativisation of the authorities was most probably at the origin of the quick disappearance of patristic texts from the canonical *corpus*. From then on, the Papal *potestas* was to take over the patristic *auctoritas*. A modern, positivist conception finally pervaded canon law, at least in the Catholic Church: the law is the law, not because it is in conformity with the Scriptures or the Fathers, but because it has been desired and promulgated by the competent legislator, the Pope or the council. The Church Fathers, in the eyes of the Catholic Church, only belong to the historical sources of the law: their texts, today, do not have the value of laws.

The fate of patristic texts is somewhat better in the other Christian laws: the Orthodox Church, for example, has kept until today the juridical *corpus* established by the Trullian Council, and the sixteen *patristic letters* are still part of it. A future panorthodox council, in preparation now for some decades, should reform the "holy canons". What will, then, be the fate of these *letters*? Nobody knows, but it is far from probable that the Orthodox Church, after Catholicism, should codify its law by abrogating old texts. As for the Churches issued from the XVIth century Reformation, they have long been suspicious of Church law precisely because of the often centralising and autocratic character of the canon law after Gratian.[95] The renewal of interest in law in those Churches nowadays, as is shown for example by the works of Hans Dombois[96] or the *Zeitschrift für Evangelisches Kirchenrecht*, can only help revive, at least partly, the evangelical and theological law of patristic texts.

Transl. Pascale Renaud

---

[93] It is the real title of the *Decree* of Gratian.

[94] de Ghellinck, *Le mouvement théologique au XIIe siècle*, 1948, p. 478.

[95] Upon receiving the Papal bull *Exsurge Domine* which excommunicated him in 1520, Luther solemnly burnt the *Corpus Iuris canonici* before his students. Ever since then, the Lutherans have often considered the law as incompatible with the Scriptures (see R. Sohm), and relied on state laws to regulate their communities. The Reformed have generally had a less negative vision of the "canonical" discipline.

[96] Hans Dombois, *Das Recht der Gnade. Ökumenishces Kirchenrecht*, Witten-Bielefeld, 1969–1974.

Bibliography

Besides the indications given in the notes, the reader should consult the following works:

Fournier, Paul and Le Bras, Gabriel. *Histoire des collections canoniques en Occident depuis les Fausses Décrétales jusqu'au Décret de Gratien*, 2 vol., Paris, 1931–1932, XVI–463 and 386 p.

Gaudemet, Jean. *Les sources du droit de l'Eglise en Occident du IIe au VIIe siècle*, Paris, Edit. du Cerf-CNRS, 1985, 188 p. (coll. *"Initiations au christianisme ancien"*).

—. *Les sources du droit canonique, VIIIe–XXe siècles. Repères canoniques. Sources occidentales*, Paris, Edit. du Cerf, 1993, 262 p.

Ghellinck, Joseph de. *Le mouvement théologique du XIIe siècle*, 1st edition, Paris, 1914, X–409 p., 2nd edition, augmented, Bruges-Brussels-Paris, 1948, XVI–594 p.

—. *Patristique et moyen âge*, t. 2, Brussels-Paris, 1947.

—. *L'essor de la littérature latine au XIIe siècle*, Brussels-Bruges-Paris, 2nd edition, 1955, X–584 p.

Kuttner, Stephan. *Repertorium der Kanonistik (1140–1234), I. Prodromus corporis glossarum*, City of Vatican, 1937, XX–536 p. (coll. *Studi e testi*, 71).

Maassen, Friedrich. *Geschichte der Quellen und der Literatur des Kanonischen Rechts im Abendlande bis zum Ausgang des Mittelalters*, Graz, 1870, LXX–981 p.

Munier, Charles. *Les sources patristiques du droit de l'Eglise du VIIIe au XIIIe siècle*, Mulhouse, 1957, 216 p.

—. *Magistri Gratiani Decreti auctoritates Patrum*, Strasbourg, 1957 (typewritten).

Schulte, Joh. Friedrich von. *Die Geschichte der Quellen und Literatur des canonischen Rechts*, vol. 1, *Von Gratian bis auf Papst Gregor IX*, Stuttgart, 1875, VIII–264 p.

Stickler, Alphonsus M. *Historia iuris canonici latini, I. Historia fontium*, Turin, 1950, XVI–468 p.

Van De Wiel, Constant. *History of Canon Law*, Louvain, Peeters Press, 1991, 192 p. (*Louvain Theological and Pastoral Monographs*, 5).

Van Hove, Alfons. *Prolegomena*, editio altera, 1945, XXX–671 p. (*Commentarium Lovaniense in Codicem iuris canonici*, vol. 1, pt. 1).

THE CHURCH FATHERS AND THE *GLOSSA ORDINARIA*

E. Ann Matter

Introduction

Three generations of scholars have now acknowledged the fact that the *Glossa ordinaria*, printed in Migne's *Patrologia Latina* under the name of the Carolingian scholar Walafrid Strabo, is a compilation of the twelfth century.[1] As study of the *Glossa* manuscript tradition has allowed us to refine our knowledge of this important collection of medieval biblical learning, we have begun to understand its shape and its sources. One of the most important insights of this process is the awareness that the *Glossa ordinaria* to each book (or collection of books) to the Bible had an independent development, and therefore drew on different sources from earlier centuries of Christian biblical learning.

Although medieval libraries sometimes collected a complete set (or several sets) of glossed books of the Bible, there does not seem to have been a tradition of copying out an entire *Glossa ordinaria* in one manuscript or even in matching manuscripts, at least not until the age of printing.[2] There were, however, deliberate collections of the *Glossa ordinaria* in a number of medieval libraries. By the mid-twelfth

---

[1] This was first recognized by Smalley B. (1941) *The Study of the Bible in the Middle Ages* (Oxford: 1941). The argument of this book was based on a series of Smalley's earlier articles: Smalley, B. (1935) "Gilbertus Universalis Bishop of London (1128–1134) and the Problem of the 'Glossa Ordinaria' I", *Recherches de théologie ancienne et médiévale* 7 (1935) 235–262; Smalley B. (1936) "Gilbertus Universalis Bishop of London (1128–1134) and the Problem of the 'Glossa Ordinaria' II", *Recherches de théologie ancienne et médiévale* 8 (1936) 24–64; and Smalley B. (1937) "La *Glossa Ordinaria*", *Recherches de théologie ancienne et médiévale* 9 (1937) 365–400. For the most recent discussion of the development of the *Glossa ordinaria* see Gibson M. (1992). "The Glossed Bible" in *Biblia Latina Cum Glossa Ordinaria: Facsimile Reprint of the Editio Princeps Adolph Rusch of Strassburg 1480/81* (Turnhout: 1992) VII–XI. For a discussion of the false attribution to Walafrid Strabo, see Froehlich K. (1992). "The Printed Gloss", in *Biblia Latina Cum Glossa Ordinaria* (1992) XII–XXVI. For the inadequacies of the *Patrologia Latina* edition of the Gloss, published by Migne J.P. in *Patrologia Latina* 113–114 (Paris: 1879) as a work of Walafrid Strabo, see Froehlich K. (1992) XXV–XXVI.

[2] Gibson M. (1989) "The Twelfth-Century Glossed Bible", *Studia Patristica* ed. E. Livingstone 23 (1989) 232–244.

century, the library of the canons of the Duomo of Monza had a complete set with some duplications. Some of these manuscripts are French, but many were copied in Italy, and at least ten in the scriptorium of Monza itself.[3] Another twelfth-century pandect, from Messina, is now in the Biblioteca Nacional of Madrid.[4] There were at least two complete sets (with some duplications) in the mid-thirteenth-century: in the cathedral library of Toledo and the Cistercian monastery of Clairvaux.[5] A set of eight *Glossa ordinaria* manuscripts at the Roman Franciscan house of Ara Celi does not seem to have been complete, but included glossed copies of Leviticus, Numbers, Deuteronomy, Joshua, Judges, Ruth, Chronicles, Isaiah, Jeremiah, Ezekiel, Daniel, the Minor Prophets, and the Gospels. This collection was given to the house in 1277 by Pope Nicholas III (Giovanni Orsini).[6]

These sets of *Glossa ordinaria* manuscripts were collections of codices, each of which contained the gloss to one part of the Bible. The twelfth-century *Glossa ordinaria* might be found, for example, in one codex for the five books of Moses, another for the books of Tobit,

---

[3] Monza, Biblioteca Capitolare, MSS. a–4 to a–27, b–1 to b–9, e–4 to e–11, e–13, i–11, see Belloni A. and Ferrari M. (1974) *La Biblioteca Capitolare di Monza* (Padova: 1974).

[4] Madrid, Biblioteca Nacional 32–45, see *Inventario General de Manuscritos de la Biblioteca Nacional* [de Madrid], I. (1 a 500) (Madrid: 1953).

[5] The Toledo manuscripts are: Toledo, Catedral 1–31, 3–4 to 3–21, 6–1 to 6–3, 6–5 to 6–7, 6–9 to 6–24, 7–1 to 7–14, see Reinhardt K. and Gonzálvez R. (1990) *Catálogo de Códices Bíblicos de la Catedral de Toledo* (Madrid: 1990). The manuscripts of Clairvaux are now in the Bibliothèque Municipale de Troyes: MSS. 50, 54, 65, 78, 81 to 83, 87, 100, 104 to 106, 108, 110 and 111, 113, 120, 124, 139, 143, 147, 157, 183 and 184, 195, 218, 220, 228, 231, 243, 248, 251, 255, 263, 274, 388, 418, 435 and 436, 449, 453, 457, 465, 467, 474 to 478, 481, 484, 488, 490.1, 490.3, 491, 511 and 512, 517, 532, 548, 568 and 569, 573, 626, 649, 659, 670 and 671, 674, 756, 758, 815, 857, 871, 880 to 882, 904, 922, 924 to 926, 932, 934, 1023, 1026 to 1030, 1035, 1039 and 1040, 1054, 1067, 1083, 1092, 1132, 1169, 1170, 1177, 1181, 1216, 1221, 1223, 1228, 1378, 1380, 1471, 1479, 1481, 1491, 1552, 1597, 1620, 2096, 2246, and 2260, see *Catalogue général des manuscrits des bibliothèques publiques des départements* 2, *Bibliothèque Municipale de Troyes* (Paris: 1855).

[6] Vatican, Biblioteca Apostolica, MSS. 7793 to 7797, 7799 to 8001, see Casimiro Romano (1736) *Memorice Istoriche della Chiesa e Convento di S. Maria in Araceli di Roma* (Rome: 1736) 449, and Vian P. (1988) Altri codici araceolitani nella Biblioteca Vaticana," in *Miscellanea Bibliothecae Apostolicae Vaticanae, Studi e Testi* 331 (Città del Vaticano: 1988) 287–311. These manuscripts are all from France except 7800, which is Italian, see Contardi B. (1980) "Un codice di area romana della metà del Duecento," *Federico II e l'arte del duecento italiano* II (Galantina: 1980) 83, and Pace V. (1985) "Per la storia della minatura duecentesca a Roma," *Studien zur mittelalterichen Kunst 800–1250. Festchrift für F. Mütherich zum 70. Geburtstag* (Munich, 1985) 259.

Esther, Judith, and Ruth, another for the books of Solomon. It is not unusual to find a codex containing just the glossed Psalms. In the Christian canon, a single manuscript might contain the *Glossa ordinaria* to one of the Gospels, whereas the letters of Paul or the Catholic Epistles were usually copied together. Further study of the manuscript tradition of the *Glossa ordinaria* will determine which books were glossed at the same time or by the same groups of scholars. In the meantime, an investigation of the reception of the Fathers in the *Glossa ordinaria* is a multifaceted and difficult task, greatly complicated by the fact that we know much more about the gloss to some books of the Bible than others.

The *Glossa ordinaria* involved three texts, intimately related to one another on the page: the words of the Bible, written in the center in large letters; the smaller (usually in a relationship of 2:1 or 3:1) *Glossa marginalis*, framing the Bible verses; and the *Glossa interlinearis*, written between the lines of the Bible text, above key passages.[7] The relationship of the marginal and interlinear glosses to one another seems to differ from book to book, and needs to be considered separately in the case of each book of the Bible. In the final result, nevertheless, the three parts of a glossed Bible were certainly in some literary relation to one another, since they were meant to be read together. The concept of such an integrated text was not an invention of the twelfth century, but derives from a long tradition of glossed books in Latin, found in Carolingian manuscripts copied at German scriptoria, including Fulda, Saint Gall, Reichenau, and Tegernsee.[8]

What changes and is specific to the *Glossa ordinaria* is the fact that this type of integrated text actually represents a continuation of the patristic tradition of biblical commentary. The content of the commentary arranged around the biblical text in gloss manuscripts is ultimately patristic, often mediated through Carolingian compendia or reworkings of patristic exegesis, and then further selected and adapted for twelfth-century students of the Bible. Margaret Gibson has demonstrated this process of increasing "refinement" of biblical commentary from the fifth to the twelfth century in her discussions of the *Glossa ordinaria* to Isaiah and Jeremiah.[9] In the *Glossa ordinaria*,

---

[7] de Hamel C. (1984) *Glossed Books of the Bible and the Origins of the Paris Booktrade* (Woodbridge: 1984).

[8] Gibson M. (1989) 233–236.

[9] For Isaiah, see Gibson M. (1989) 239; for Jeremiah see Gibson M. (1992) VII–IX.

then, we find three historical moments of Latin biblical interpretation, the late antique world of the Latin fathers, the monastic world
of the Carolingian period, and the twelfth-century schools. It can be
said, in fact, that the *Glossa ordinaria* shows us the last moment of the
development of a tradition of compilation, done always in more
concentrated form, of patristic biblical learning. With these general
remarks in mind, let us turn to the historical development and theological content of the *Glossa ordinaria* to each of the books of the
Vulgate Bible. These discussions will necessarily vary in detail and
depth of analysis depending on the state of research on the gloss to
each book or collection of books.

1. *The Old Testament*

1.a. *The Pentateuch (Genesis, Exodus, Leviticus, Numbers, Deuteronomy)*

"The Universal Gilbert," a master at Auxerre, is the probable redactor of the *Glossa ordinaria* to the Pentateuch.[10] Gilbert's glossing of
various books of the Bible (including Lamentations, probably the Major Prophets, and possibly the Minor Prophets) was done, probably
in Auxerre, before he became the bishop of London in 1128. Gilbert
died in London in 1134.

Since the *Glossa ordinaria* represents the twelfth-century endpoint of
a centuries-old process of refinement and synthesis of the biblical
learning of early Christian authors, the sources gathered by glossators
like Gilbert are often the most obvious, celebrated, patristic commentaries on particular biblical books. It is no surprise, therefore,
that Augustine of Hippo, author of a number of commentaries on
Genesis, can be easily seen in the *Glossa* to this book. From the very
beginning of the prologue to the glossed Genesis, Augustine's reading of the days of creation in *De Genesi ad litteram* predominates and
sets an exegetical tone.[11] Although Augustine's commentary promises
a reading "according to the letter," his sense of literal, as opposed to
allegorical, readings is not that of modern exegetes. Often the interpretation verges to the christological or moral, as in the famous dis-

---

[10] Gibson M. (1992) XI, Smalley B. (1935) for Gilbert.
[11] *Biblia Latina Cum Glossa Ordinaria* (1992) vol. 1, 6–8, where Augustine's *De Genesi
ad litteram* in Migne J.P. ed. *Patrologia Latina* 34 (Paris: 1845) 245–486 is paraphrased
liberally.

cussion of the materiality of light in the interpretation of Genesis 1:3. As John Van Engen has pointed out, this advertising of a particular reading of Genesis proved enormously influential in later medieval theology.[12] In the *Glossa ordinaria* "mystical" sense, the sources are usually other than Augustine, and include selections from Isidore of Seville, the Venerable Bede and, occasionally, Jerome.[13] There are also a number of quotations from Gregory the Great in the gloss to Genesis. Most of these have been shown to come through the compendium of the biblical interpretation in Gregory's *Moralia in Job* made by his secretary, Paterius; but in some cases, it would seem that Gilbert used the compilation of Paterius to follow the quotation to the source, and provided in the *Glossa ordinaria* a more full reference to Gregory than could be found in Paterius.[14]

Exodus, Leviticus and Numbers have been glossed with an equally great range of sources. Bede and Augustine, as might be expected, are cited frequently.[15] But there are also surprises here, especially in the frequent citations of Origen of Alexandria (known through the Latin translations of Rufinus). In spite of the condemnation of Origen by the Emperor Justinian in the sixth century, the Latin versions of his works were well-diffused and much-read in the Middle Ages. For Leviticus, another unusual source is the commentary of Hesychius of Jerusalem, translated into Latin by an otherwise unknown sixth-century Jerome.[16] The glosses to Exodus, Leviticus and Numbers offer

---

[12] John Van Engen (1994) "Studying Scripture in the Early University," forthcoming in Robert Lerner ed. *Neue Richtungen in der hoch- und spätmittelalterlichen Bibelexegese* (Munich: 1994).

[13] Isidore, *Mysticorum expositiones sacramentorum, seu quaestiones in Vetus Testamentum* Migne J.P. ed. in *Patrologia Latina* 83 (Paris: 1862) 207–423. Bede, *Libri quatuor in principium Genesis* Jones C.W. ed. in *Corpus Christianorm Series Latina* 118A (Turnhout: 1967), *In Pentateuchum Commentarii. Expositio in Primum Librum Mosis* in Migne J.P. ed. *Patrologia Latina* 91 (Paris: 1850) 189–286. Jerome, *Hebraice quaestiones in libro Geneseos* Antin P. ed. in *Corpus Christianorum Series Latina* 72 (Turnhout: 1959) 1–56.

[14] Paterius, *Liber de expositione veteris et novi testamenti de diversis libris S. Gregorii M. concinatus* in Migne J.P. ed. *Patrologia Latina* 79 (Paris: 1849) 682–916. See the discussion of uses of Paterius in the *Glossa ordinaria* to Genesis in Wasselynck R. (1965) "L'influence de l'exégèse de S. Grégoire le Grand sur les commentaires bibliques médiévaux (VIIᵉ–XIIᵉ s.)" *Recherches de théologie ancienne et médiévale* 32 (1965) 186–188.

[15] Bede, *In Pentateuchum Commentarii* in Migne J.P. ed. *Patrologia Latina* 91 (Paris: 1850) 285–387. Augustine, *Questionum in Heptateuchum libri VII, Locutionum in Heptateuchum libri VII* Fraipont J. ed. in *Corpus Christianorum Series Latina* 33 (Turnhout: 1958).

[16] Origen, *In Exodum homilia* Borret M. ed. in *Sources chrétiennes* 321 (Paris: 1985), *In Leviticum homilia* Borret M. ed. in *Sources chrétiennes* 286–287 (Paris: 1981), *In Numeros homilia* Baehrens W.A. ed. in *Origenes Werke* 7 (Leipzig: 1920). Hesychius of Jerusalem, *Commentarius in Leviticum* in Migne J.P. ed. *Patrologia Graeca* 93 (Paris: 1865) 787–

excellent examples of the compressed and oft-redacted nature of the reception of the Fathers in the *Glossa ordinaria*. The use of florilegia and compendia of patristic authors in these books includes the Gregory collected by Paterius,[17] the commentary woven together from earlier sources (including Jerome, Augustine, Gregory the Great, Isidore of Seville, and Hesychius of Jerusalem) by the Carolingian abbot and bishop Hrabanus Maurus,[18] and even Walafrid Strabo's "abbreviations" of Hrabanus's compilations.[19] Deuteronomy, in contrast, is a far less full gloss, and is also less complicated, drawing its sources largely from Augustine and Gregory/Paterius.

In general the *Glossa ordinaria* to the Pentateuch is impressive in both the range of sources used and the conscious participation by Gilbert of Auxerre in the process of adaptation of patristic biblical learning for easy reference.

1.b. *Historical Books (Joshua, Judges, Ruth, 1–4 Kings, 1–2 Chronicles, Ezra, Nehemiah, Tobit, Judith, Esther)*

We do not know who was the glossator of the books of Joshua and Judges. The *Glossa ordinaria* here follows Origen's homilies (in the translation of Rufinus, usually citing the author as "Adamantius") and Augustine's *Quaestiones* and *Locutiones* on these books.[20] The influ-

---

1179. For Hesychius, see Altaner B. (1968) *Patrology* trans. H.C. Graef (New York: 1960) 389–390, no. 71.

[17] Paterius, *Liber de expositione veteris et novi testamenti de diversis libris S. Gregorii M. concinatus* in Migne J.P. ed. *Patrologia Latina* 79 (Paris: 1849) 682–916. See also Wasselynck R. (1962) "Les compliations des 'Moralia in Job' du VIIᵉ au XIIᵉ siècle," *Recherches de théologie ancienne et médiévale* 29 (1962) 5–32.

[18] Hrabanus Maurus, *Commentarium in Exodum libri quatuor, Expositionum in Leviticum libri septum, Enarrationum in librum Numerorum libri quatuor*, in Migne J.P. ed. *Patrologia Latina* 108 (Paris: 1851) 9–246, 245–586, 587–838. For a discussion of these sources see Hablitzel J.B. (1906) *Hrabanus Maurus. Ein Beitrag zur Geschichte der mittelalterlichen Exegese* (Freiburg im Breisau: 1906) 18, 70–78. See also Blumenkranz B. (1951) "Raban Maur et Saint-Augustin—compilation ou adaptation? A propos du latin biblique," in *Revue du moyen âge latin* 7 (1951) 97, and Rissel M. (1976) *Rezeption antiker und patristischer Wissenschaft bei Hrabanus Maurus*, Lateinische Sprache und Literatur des Mittelalters, 7 (Berne: 1976).

[19] Walafrid Strabo, *Abbreviatio Rabani Mauri in Exodum* Stegmüller F. *Repertorium biblicum medii aevi* vol. 5 (Madrid: 1955) no. 8318; *Epitome commentariorum Raban in Leviticum* Stegmüller no. 8319; *Abbreviatio Rabani Mauri in Numerum* Stegmüller no. 8320.

[20] Origen, *In liber Iesu Nave homilia* Baehrens W.A. ed. in *Origenes Werke* VII (Leipzig: 1921) 286–463; *In liber Iudicum homilia* Baehrens W.A. ed. in *Origenes Werke* VII (Leipzig: 1921) 464–522; Augustine, *Questionum in Heptateuchum libri VII, Locutionum in Heptateuchum libri VII* Fraipont J. ed. in *Corpus Christianorum Series Latina* 33 (Turnhout: 1958).

ence of Gregory/Paterius is also evident: Paterius only compiled two references from Gregory on Joshua and eight from Judges; these are the only citations from Gregory in the *Glossa ordinaria* to these books.[21]

The *Glossa ordinaria* to the book of Ruth is often found in codices which also contain glossed copies of Tobit, Judith, and Esther. The sources used for the gloss on Ruth will be discussed at the end of this section along with the books with which it usually traveled.

The most frequently cited source to the *Glossa ordinaria* to the books of Kings is the *Commentaria in libros IV Regum* of Hrabanus Maurus, a widely-read text still extant in more than forty copies.[22] Some of these references to Hrabanus Maurus, however, have been shown to actually correspond to the compendium of Paterius, adding to the overwhelming presence of Gregory in this part of the gloss.[23] Furthermore, as is the case with the glosses on the Pentateuch, many of the quotations from Gregory the Great begin with a selection from Paterius, but then continue with lengthy quotations from the original commentaries of Gregory. An excellent example of this is given by Wasselynck in his analysis of the *Glossa ordinaria* to 1 Kings (1 Samuel) 15:17, where the beginning of the gloss corresponds to Paterius, but the development uses no fewer than four works of Gregory the Great in the original. Since this is the method used by Gilbert of Auxerre in the *Glossa ordinaria* to the Pentateuch, Wasselynck tentatively suggests that Gilbert may have also been the author of the gloss on the books of Kings.[24]

In spite of the importance of Gregory the Great to the gloss on Kings, it is striking that Gregory's exposition of 1 Kings[25] is visible only through the mediation of Hrabanus Maurus. The *Glossa* to 3–4 Kings, in contrast, shows frequent quotations from questions on

---

[21] Wasselynck (1965) 189. Compare Paterius on Joshua in Migne J.P. ed. *Patrologia Latina* 79 (Paris: 1849) 783–786 to *Biblia Latina Cum Glossa Ordinaria* (1992) vol. 1 457–458, 785–786.

[22] Hrabanus Maurus, *Commentaria in libros Iv Regum ad Hilduinum* Migne J.P. ed. in *Patrologia Latina* 109 (1852) 9–280. For manuscripts, see Stegmüller F. *Repertorium Biblicum Medii Aevi* (Madrid: 1955) vol. 5, no. 7033.

[23] Wasselynck (1965) 189 has shown the false attributions.

[24] Wasselynck (1965) 190–191.

[25] Gregory the Great, *Expositiones in librum Primum Regum* Verbraken P. ed. *Corpus Christianorum Series Latina* 144 (Turnhout: 1963). The authenticity of this treatise has been discussed by Verbraken P. (1956) "Le commentaire de saint Grégoire sur le premier Livre des Rois," *Revue bénédictine* 66 (1956) 159–217, and Meyvaert P. (1978–79) "The Date of Gregory the Great's Commentaries on the Canticle of Canticles and on 1 Kings," *Sacris Erudiri* 23 (1978–1979) 191–216.

Kings by Bede and another set of questions on Kings attributed falsely to Bede.[26]

Hrabanus Maurus is also the primary source for the *Glossa ordinaria* on 1 and 2 Chronicles.[27] The *Glossa* sometimes cites the sources used by Hrabanus, as in 1 Chronicles 4:17, where the name Ezra is glossed with the interpretation from Jerome's *Interpretatio nominum hebraicorum,* with a citation to both Hrabanus and Jerome.[28]

The *Glossa ordinaria* on Ezra and Nehemiah (1 and 2 Ezra) is a running adaptation of Bede's commentary on these books.[29] It is possible that the pseudepigraphical books known as 3-4 Ezra were never part of the *Glossa ordinaria* tradition—at least, the *editio princeps* of Adolph Rusch does not show any glosses for these books.[30] As is the case with many mysteries of the *Glossa ordinaria,* further manuscript study will enable us to speak with more certainty on this point.

Glossed books of Tobit, Esther, Judith, and Ruth are often found copied together into one codex, making up what seems to have been a collection of favorite Bible stories.[31] The *Glossa ordinaria* to Tobit comes from Bede's allegorical interpretation, with possible influence of Hrabanus Maurus.[32] The glosses to Judith, Esther, and Ruth are made up of running selections from Hrabanus Maurus's commentaries on these books.[33]

---

[26] Bede, *In libros Regum questiones 30* Migne J.P. ed. *Patrologia Latina* 91 (Paris: 1850) 715-36, Pseudo-Bede, *Quaestiones super Regum libros* Migne J.P. ed. *Patrologia Latina* 93 (Paris: 1862) 429-456.

[27] Hrabanus Maurus, *Commentaria in libros II Paralipomenon* Migne J.P. ed. in *Patrologia Latina* 109 (Paris: 1852) 279-540.

[28] *Biblia Latina Cum Glossa Ordinaria* (1992) vol. 2, 187. This gloss must come from Hrabanus or some other intermediary source, since Jerome's work does not include a list of names for Chronicles, cf. Jerome, *Interpretatio nominum Hebraicorum* Adriaen M. ed. in *Corpus Christianorum Series Latina* 72 (Turnhout: 1959).

[29] Bede, *In Ezram et Neemiam libri III* Hurst D. ed. in *Corpus Christianorum Series Latina* 119A (Turnhout: 1969) 237-392.

[30] *Biblia Latina Cum Glossa Ordinaria* (1992) vol. 2, 305-330.

[31] Such collections are found in the following manuscripts: Bamberg, Statsbibliothek 24; Barcelona BN 496; Lilienfeld 177; Monza, BC e-6, Munich, BS clm 3803, 7933; Nürnberg C.IV.59; Paris, B.N. lat. 77, 90, 92, 118, 395, 396; Salzburg St. Peter a.viii.31; Toledo, Catedral 3-16, 3-18, 3-21, Troyes BM 113, 143, 674; Vatican BA Vat. Lat. 67, 73.

[32] Bede, *In librum Beati Patris Tobiae* Hurst D. ed. in *Corpus Christianorum Series Latina* 119B (Turnhout: 1983). Gibson (1992) raises the possibility of an unprinted commentary by Hrabanus Maurus on Tobit.

[33] Hrabanus Maurus, *Expositio in librum Iudith, Expositio in librum Esther, Commentarium in librum Ruth* Migne J.P. ed. in *Patrologia Latina* 109 (Paris: 1851) 539-592, 635-670, 1199-1224.

It is striking how much of the reception of the Fathers in the *Glossa ordinaria* to the historical books of the Bible has been mediated through Hrabanus Maurus. The glosses to the books of Kings and Chronicles, Esther Judith and Ruth all bear evidence of having been put together with the help of the Carolingian synopses of patristic learning compiled by the first *Praeceptor Germaniae*. But having recognized that only points the way for the type of source analysis that will really show us what sources were used for the standard reference gloss to these books. There is almost no secondary, critical research on Hrabanus Maurus. There are no modern critical editions of his enormously influential biblical commentaries. Perhaps the current surge of interest in the *Glossa ordinaria* will provide a long-awaited impetus for analysis of Hrabanus's sources.

1.c. *Job*

The story of the *Glossa ordinaria* to the Book of Job is a story of Gregory the Great. Obviously, here the compiler of the *Glossa ordinaria* had plenty of Gregory to choose from, almost too much Gregory. And in this case, the early medieval compilations proved of limited use. Paterius did not include Job in the *Liber testimoniorum*, so the most popular compendium does not provide any assistance. There is, however, a well-known collection of Gregory's *Moralia in Iob*, put together in the seventh-century by the Irish monk, Lathcen.[34]

Did the *Egloga* of Lathcen play a part in the *Glossa ordinaria* to Job? Investigation of this question leads to some interesting insights about the changing tastes of biblical compilers leading up to the *Glossa ordinaria*. On the one hand, Lathcen's *Egloga* could easily have been a part of the Gloss to Job; the gloss marked "allegorice" at Job 1:1, for example, is very close to Lathcen's quotation "iuxta allegoriam" from Gregory on this verse.[35] Furthermore, there are extant manuscripts of Lathcen from Laon, one dating from the eighth-ninth century, the other from the thirteenth, suggesting that this treatise was known and used in the area of the development of the *Glossa ordinaria* throughout the Middle Ages.[36] On the other hand, the Gloss to Job

---

[34] Lathcen, *Egloga* Adriaen M. ed. in *Corpus Christianorum Series Latina* 145 (Turnhout: 1969).

[35] *Biblia Latina Cum Glossa Ordinaria* (1992) vol. 2, 375 = Lathcen, *Egloga* xi.15 Adriaen M. ed. in *Corpus Christianorum Series Latina* 145 (Turnhout: 1969) 3.

[36] See the introduction of Adriaen, p. vi.

can easily be shown to have a close correspondence to the *Moralia* directly; indeed, the "allegorice" gloss to Job 1:1 could have come directly from the *Moralia* as easily as from Lathcen.[37]

In fact, the overwhelming tenor of the *Glossa ordinaria* to Job suggests that it was not taken from Lathcen. The *Glossa* is primarily concerned with the moral interpretation of the story of Job, consistently placing Gregory's last way of reading the story first, while Lathcen completely ignored the moral sense, giving only the literal and the allegorical in his compendium. Certainly the compiler of the *Glossa ordinaria* to Job had a complete text of Gregory's *Moralia* before him. He may also have had a copy of Lathcen to consult, but he did not need to do so. Everything he needed was in the original, and the interpretations that most drew him were not to be found in the compendium.

1.d. *The Psalms*

The *Glossa ordinaria* on the Psalter is attributed to Anselm, master of the cathedral school at Laon from 1080 until his death *ca.* 1117. Anselm may well have gathered together the comments which became the marginal and interlinear gloss, but he was probably not responsible for the prefatory "Prothemata in librum psalmorum" that is printed between Jerome's preface and the glossed Psalm 1, since, as A.J. Minnis has pointed out, Anselm of Laon has not been credited with prologues in the *accessus ad auctores* tradition followed by this prologue.[38] This prefatory material to the *Glossa* shows unmistakable signs of redaction in a later twelfth-century schoolroom: it conforms to the "Type C" prologue, the form of the *accessus ad auctores* which became the standard introduction to school commentaries on the Bible.[39]

In order to guide the reader in approaching the commentary, the prologue to the glossed Psalter explains in turn the *titulus, auctor, materia, intentio,* and *modus tractandi.*[40] The lengthy discussions of the title and author are woven together from selections attributed to Augustine,

---

[37] Compare to Gregory the Great, *Moralia in Iob* Adriaen M. ed. in *Corpus Christianorum Series Latina* 143 (Turnhout: 1979) 31ff.

[38] *Biblia Latina Cum Glossa Ordinaria* (1992) vol. 2, 457–458. Minnis A.J. (1988) *Medieval Theory of Authorship*, second edition (Philadelphia: 1988) 41.

[39] Minnis A.J. (1988) 40–48.

[40] *Biblia Latina Cum Glossa Ordinaria* (1992) vol. 2, 457–458.

Jerome, Cassiodorus and Remigius of Auxerre. The discussion of the *materia, intentio,* and *modus tractandi,* on the other hand, are succinctly described in material taken from Augustine's *Enarrationes in Psalmos*:

> The material is the whole Christ, groom and bride. The intention is to reform in Christ as new men those men deformed in Adam. This is the method of treatment. Sometimes he treats of Christ with regard to His head, sometimes with regard to His body, and sometimes with regard to both. With regard to the head, he speaks in three ways, either with reference to His divinity ... or with reference to his humanity ... or sometimes by transumption, as when he employs the voice of His members ... Also, he speaks of the Church in three manners: sometimes with regard to perfect men, sometimes with regard to imperfect men, and sometimes with regard to evil men who are in the Church in body but not in mind, in number but not in merit, and in name but not in spirit.[41]

The theological summary provided by the prologue is woven from and points easily to the major sources for the *Glossa* on the Psalms: the two preeminent Psalter commentaries of Latin antiquity written by Augustine and Cassiodorus.[42] Indeed, the *Glossa marginalis* to the Psalms seems at first glance to be a mere interweaving of these authors, the marginal glosses marked by alternating rubrics: "Aug." and "Cass." Sometimes these appear more like digests than quotations. Sometimes they are so intimately bound together that the sources blend into one another sometimes without clear demarcation.[43]

In general, this first impression is accurate, but a closer scrutiny of the *Glossa marginalis* soon reveals a more complex collection of sources. For one thing, the names of Jerome and Remigius appear occasionally

---

[41] "Materia est integer Christus sponsus et sponsa. Intentio homines in Adam deformatos Christo novo homini conformare. Modus tractandi. Quandoque agit de Christo secundum quod caput est. Aliquando secundum corpus. Aliquando secundum utrumque. Secundum caput tripliciter. quia vel secundum divinitatem ... Aliquando secundum humanitatem ... Aliquando per transsumptionem ut quando utitur voce membrorum ... Item de ecclesia tribus modis. Aliquando secundum perfectos. Aliquando secundum imperfectos. Aliquando secundum malos qui sunt in ecclesia corpore non de mente numero non merito nomine non numine," *Biblia Latina Cum Glossa Ordinaria* (1992) vol. 2, 458. Translation of Minnis A.J. (1988) 45.

[42] Augustine, *Enarrationes in Psalmos* Dekkers E. and Fraipont J. ed. in *Corpus Christianorum Series Latina* 38–40 (Turnhout: 1956). Cassiodorus, *Expositio Psalmorum* Adriaen M. ed. in *Corpus Christianorum Series Latina* 97–98 (Turnhout: 1958).

[43] For example, the *Glossa marginalis* on (Vulgate) Psalm 44:9, *Biblia Latina Cum Glossa Ordinaria* (1992) vol. 2, 509. Here the rubric is to Augustine, but most of the commentary can be found instead in Cassiodorus, *Expositio Psalmorum* Adriaen M. ed. in *Corpus Christianorum Series Latina* 97 (Turnhout: 1958) 408. Many of the marginal glosses echo and paraphrase, rather than quote directly.

among the sources, citing use of Jerome's homilies on the Psalms, and the unpublished commentary on the Psalms by Remigius of Auxerre.[44]

Teresa Gross-Diaz has recently shown close links between the Psalms commentaries of Gilbert of Poitiers, Anselm of Laon and the *Glossa ordinaria*. Gilbert may actually have had a hand in the compilation of the *Glossa* to the Psalms, providing another source for this complex text.[45]

The *Glossa ordinaria* on the Psalms also gives us one of the best examples of a text where the *Glossa interlinearis* is organically connected to the *Glossa marginalis*. Often, the interlinear gloss provides a clue to a longer discussion in the margin, for example, at the beginning of Psalm 41, where among the expected comments on baptism elicited by the longing of the hart for the fountains of water there appears a reference to a serpent, which is elaborated in the second marginal gloss with a citation of Cassiodorus's version of the story (ultimately from Pliny) of the stag burdened by its antlers and hair that "drinks" (*haurit*) a serpent through its nostrils, and then, burning because of the poison released by the snake, longs *ardentissime* to drink from the fountain.[46] The interlinear gloss gives us the necessary clue about the story of the snake-inhaling stag: it is an allegory of the purification of our sins through baptism.

The same process must also be required in the reading of Psalm 44. Here, the characters of the sacred nuptials, Christ and the Church, are only identified by name in the *Glossa interlinearis*, although the wedding is discussed at length in the *Glossa marginalis*.[47] In this case, it is not an exaggeration to say that the interlinear gloss is necessary

---

[44] Jerome, *In Psalmos homiliae*, Morin G. ed. in *Corpus Christianorum Series Latina* 78 (Turnhout: 1958). For Remigius, see Wilmart A. (1931) "Fragments carolingiens du Fonds Baluze," *Revue bénédictine* 43 (1931) 109; Vaccari P.A. (1945) "Il genuino commento ai Salmi di Remigio di Auxerre," *Biblica* 26 (1945) 52–99; Smalley B. (1941) 40–41.

[45] Gross-Diaz T. (1996) *The Psalms Commentary of Gilbert of Poitiers* (Leiden: 1996) 122–148.

[46] *Biblia Latina Cum Glossa Ordinaria* (1992) vol. 2, 505; Cassiodorus, *Expositio Psalmorum* Adriaen M. ed. in *Corpus Christianorum Series Latina* 97 (Turnhout: 1958) 380; Pliny, *Historia naturalis* 8.22.

[47] "Psalmus hic scriptus est tanti mysterii, tanti decoris iunctionis christi et ecclesie," *Biblia Latina Cum Glossa Ordinaria* (1992) vol. 2, 508, on interlinear gloss over 44:1 "In finem, pro iis qui commutabuntur Filiis Core, ad intellectum. Canticum pro dilecto." "Dilecto" carries a further gloss: "Christo."

to the proper understanding of the marginal gloss, and was probably intended to have been read first. This intricate connection between the two glosses may be further evidence of the hands of Anselm of Laon and Gilbert of Poitiers in the redaction of the *Glossa ordinaria* to the Psalter.

1.e. *Wisdom Books (Proverbs, Ecclesiastes, Song of Songs, Wisdom, Ecclesiasticus)*

The three prefaces to the *Glossa ordinaria* to Proverbs, Ecclesiastes, and the Song of Songs are culled from the works of Jerome: his Epistle to Chromatius and Heliodorus about the books of Solomon, a brief discussion of the three names of Solomon ("Pacificus," "Ydida," and "Christus"), and a longish excerpt from Jerome's Commentary on Ecclesiastes (to Paula and Eustochium) about the three books of Solomon.[48] The prologue to Ecclesiastes is taken from Jerome's Commentary on Ecclesiastes; and the preface to the *Glossa* on the Song of Songs weaves a selection from this same commentary into a beginning quotation from Isidore of Seville's proemium to the Solomonic books.[49]

The *Glossa ordinaria* to Proverbs, Ecclesiastes, and the Song of Songs were very often copied together into one codex.[50] Nevertheless, this probably does not mean that the *Glossa ordinaria* to the three Books of Solomon was redacted by the same author, since each manifests a very different use of the Fathers. The *Glossa* to Proverbs is taken with few changes from the commentary (itself a compilation) of Hrabanus Maurus.[51] This is also the case of the *Glossa ordinaria* to the books of Wisdom and Ecclesiasticus.[52] The *Glossa* to Ecclesiastes may be seen as a consistent sprinkling of quotations from Gregory the Great (taken from the twelfth-century continuation of the compendium

---

[48] Jerome, *Commentarius in Ecclesiasten* Adriaen M. ed. in *Corpus Christianorum Series Latina* 72 (Turnhout: 1959).

[49] Isidore, "De libris Salomonis" in *In libros Veteris ac Novi Testamenti Proemia* Migne J.P. ed. in *Patrologia Latina* 83 (Paris: 1862) 164–65.

[50] For example, Paris, B.N. lat. 124, 127–129, 470; Toledo, Catedral 6–3, 6–5, 6–7; Troyes, BM 243, 474, 491, 670, 1378, 1380, 1481; Vatican, BA Vat. Lat. 99–102.

[51] Hrabanus Maurus, *Expositio in Proverbia Salomonis* Migne J.P. ed. in *Patrologia Latina* 111 (Paris: 1852) 679–791.

[52] Hrabanus Maurus, *Commentarius in librum Sapientiae* Migne J.P. ed. in *Patrologia Latina* 109 (Paris: 1851) 671–762; *Commentarius in Ecclesiasticum* Migne J.P. ed. in *Patrologia Latina* 109 (Paris: 1851) 763–1126.

of Gregory's writings first begun by Gregory's secretary Paterius)[53] into what is essentially a running selection from Jerome's great treatise on Ecclesiastes.[54] The *Glossa ordinaria* to the Song of Songs, however, appears to be a far more complicated interweaving of earlier sources.

The interlinear gloss to the Song of Songs presents a strikingly elusive problem. Helmut Riedlinger suggests that it was essentially compiled by Anselm of Laon, and offers this as proof that the redaction of this part of the *Glossa ordinaria* comes from the so-called School of Laon.[55] The interlinear gloss does not, however, closely resemble the known and published commentary on the Song of Songs by Anselm of Laon.[56] As far as the marginal gloss is concerned, it is clear that the most important source is Gregory the Great. This should hardly be surprising, since Gregory's concern for the purity of the Church on Earth, beset by temptations and affliction, is the obvious interpretation the *Glossa* offers for the Song of Songs.

A close look at the quotations from the works of Gregory the Great reveals further information about the date and context of the *Glossa ordinaria* to the Song of Songs. As is the case for many other parts of the *Glossa*, Gregory appears largely, not totally, in selections from *collections* of his works. There is a striking congruence between the quotations from Gregory in the *Glossa*, many of which are marked with his name, and the selection of quotations on the Song of Songs in the twelfth-century Pseudo-Paterius compendium from Gregory's *Moralia*.[57] For example, Gregory's interpretation of Song of Songs 1:5, "decoloravit me sol," (from homily 17 on the Gospels), and that of 3:1, "in lectulo" (from the commentary on Ezekiel) are both taken from the Pseudo-Paterius text. Not every passage from the Pseudo-

---

[53] Pseudo-Paterius, *Liber de expositione veteris et novi testamenti de diversis libris S. Gregorii M. concinatus* Migne J.P. ed. in *Patrologia Latina* 79 (Paris: 1849) 917–1136, see also Wasselynck R. (1962) 6–7 for a discussion of this continuation.

[54] Jerome, *Commentarius in Ecclesiasten* Adriaen M. ed. in *Corpus Christianorum Series Latina* 71 (Turnhout: 1959) 249–361.

[55] Riedlinger H. (1958) *Die Makellosigkeit der Kirche in den Lateinischen Hoheliedkommentaren des Mittelalters*. Beiträge zur Geschichte der Philosophie und Theologie des mittelalters 38, 3 (Münster, West.: 1958) 125. Guy Lobrichon seems to follow this suggestion: Lobrichon G. (1984) "Une nouveauté: les gloses de la Bible," in *Le Moyen Age et la Bible*, Riché P. and Lobrichon G. ed. *Bible de tous les temps* IV (Paris: 1984) 95–114.

[56] Anselm of Laon, *Enarratio in Canticum Canticorum* Migne J.P. ed. in *Patrologia Latina* 162 (Paris: 1889) 1187–1228.

[57] Pseudo-Paterius, *Liber de expositione veteris et novi testamenti de diversis libris S. Gregorii M. concinatus* Migne J.P. ed. in *Patrologia Latina* 79 (Paris: 1849) 905–916.

Paterius collection makes its way into the Gloss, but up to Song of Songs 3:1 this is a major source, providing four lengthy passages from Gregory.

From the beginning of the third chapter of the Song of Songs until the end of the Gloss, another intermediate source for Gregory's writings is used liberally: the commentary on the Song of Songs by Robert of Tombelaine. Robert's work, a product of the monastic-based reform movement of the eleventh century, is printed in J.P. Migne's *Patrologia Latina* in two places, up to Song of Songs 1:11 under Robert's own name, and from 1:12 to the end as a continuation of the commentary of Gregory the Great, which has been extant (at least since the ninth century) only up to 1:11 (*PL* 79:493–548).[58] It should be noted that the quotations from Gregory in the *Glossa* to the Song of Songs do not come from Gregory's incomplete commentary on the Song of Songs.[59] Rather, from the third chapter on a major source is Robert's commentary, based on and accepted as Gregory. Most of these are not exact quotations, but paraphrases.

The "Gregorian" character of the *Glossa ordinaria* on the Song of Songs shows an overriding concern for which Gregory was a natural model: the purity of the Church, beset by the corruption of the world. The importance of Robert of Tombelaine's commentary to the Gloss shows how this concern was formulated in the period of the reforms of Gregory VII. And it also suggests that the *Glossa ordinaria* on this part of the Bible dates from the early twelfth century.

There are other patristic sources in this rich compilation: the prologue of the *Glossa* to the Song of Songs is made up of general discussions of the text by Isidore and Jerome. In the first book especially, there is also a good deal of material taken from Origen of Alexandria's interpretation of the Song of Songs. Origen is the author of a commentary and a set of homilies on the Song of Songs, both surviving only in part and in Latin translation, works which had a very high profile in the Middle Ages.[60] Origen's homilies on the Song of

---

[58] As Robert, *Commentariorum in Cantica Canticorum* Migne J.P. ed. in *Patrologia Latina* 150 (Paris: 1862) 1361–1370; as Gregory, continuing Gregory's commentary on the Song of Songs, Migne J.P. ed. in *Patrologia Latina* 79 (Paris: 1849) 493–548. For a discussion of Robert's text, see Matter E.A. (1990) *The Voice of My Beloved: The Song of Songs in Western Medieval Christianity* (Philadelphia: 1990) 107.

[59] Matter (1990) 94, Gregory the Great, *Expositio in Canticum Canticorum* Verbraken P. ed. in *Corpus Christianorum Series Latina* 144 (Turnhout: 1963) 1–46; Bélanger R. ed. in *Sources chrétiennes* 314 (Paris: 1984).

[60] Origen, *Commentarium in Cantica Canticorum*, translated by Rufinus of Aquileia,

Songs (extant to Song of Songs 2:14 in a translation by Jerome) is especially prolific, extant in over forty manuscripts from every century, region and type of religious life of medieval Europe.[61] Helmut Riedlinger, working from a 1588 Venetian edition of the *Glossa ordinaria* with the *Postilla* of Nicholas of Lyra, has identified over 20 citations from Origen in the Gloss, all from Origen's homilies.[62] Unlike the citations from Origen in the *Glossa* to the Pentateuch, Joshua, and Judges, these quotations are not acknowledged.

The other influence visible at almost all times beneath the surface of the Gloss to the Song of Songs is the Venerable Bede.[63] Bede's presence in the Gloss is very much like that of Robert of Tombelaine—he is seldom quoted exactly or at great length, but the interpretation of the Gloss tends to echo him. None of this should be surprising, for the concatenation of the sources: Origen, Gregory, Bede is the most common make up of ecclesiological commentary on the Song of Songs in the Middle Ages. In this way, the *Glossa ordinaria* is absolutely typical of the prevailing mode of medieval Song of Songs exegesis, the understanding of the book as the love between Christ and the Church.

In fact, although the *Glossa ordinaria* has its own strict format definition to follow, being set up as a gloss wrapping itself around the Bible text on the page, it also manages to suggest the form of a dialogue between Christ and the Church. This is an ancient tradition in Christian understanding of the Song of Songs, dating back at least to the second-century *Codex Sinaiticus*, which has a set of rubrics in the margins, dividing up the text of the Song of Songs into a dialogue, or rather, into a polylogue.[64] Bede is the most authoritative medieval source for the dialogical reading of the Song of Songs: his commentary is prefaced by two short synopses, one dividing the Song of Songs into 39 short "Capitulae," events in the action, the other rendering the text in dramatic form by means of 41 rubrics identi-

---

Baehrens W.A. in *Origenes Werke* 8 (Leipzig: 1923) 61–241; Origen, *Homiliae in Cantica Canticorum*, translated by Jerome, Baehrens W.A. ed. in *Origenes Werke* 8 (Leipzig: 1923) 26–60, *Sources chrétiennes* 37 bis (1966).

[61] Matter E.A. (1990) 25–31.

[62] Riedlinger H. (1958) 128.

[63] Bede, *In Cantica Canticorum*, Hurst D. ed. in *Corpus Christianorum Series Latina* 119B (Turnhout: 1985) 166–375.

[64] Tischendorf C. (1862) *Codex sinaiticus petropolitanus* (St. Petersburg: 1862), de Bruyne D. (1926) "Les anciennes versions latines du Cantique des Cantiques," *Revue bénédictine* 38 (1926) 118–122.

fying the speakers. The dialogue indicators in the *Glossa ordinaria* are not rubrics but internal references: "after this, the Church says," or "this is Christ".[65] The voices of the Gloss essentially follow Bede's scheme of a conversation between Christ, the Church, and the Synagogue, but with some twists. The *Glossa*, for example, is far more interested in the "Ecclesia Primitiva," a stage in the development of the ideal Church it advocates, and therefore gives more depth to the Ecclesia character. And in several places (Song of Songs 1:14, 5:3) where the text of the Song of Songs reads "ecce tu pulchra, amica mea," which Bede takes as the voice of Christ speaking to the Church, the *Glossa ordinaria* turns around the speakers and, in spite of the difficulties of gender, makes those words the Ecclesia says to Christ!

Friedrich Ohly, working from a 1634 Antwerp edition of the *Glossa ordinaria* printed with the *Postilla* of Nicholas of Lyra, finds several passages which he thinks are taken from the influential mariological/christological commentary on the Song of Songs by Rupert of Deutz.[66] There is no echo of Rupert's commentary in the *editio princeps* of Adolph Rusch, although there is a way in which the Gloss commentary, with its stress on the "Ecclesia primitiva," reminds one of the complicated allegorical interpretation of the second commentary on the Song of Songs of Honorius Augustodunensis, in which the whole allegorical mode is the stage of the primitive Church longing for the Incarnation.[67] It seems most likely that Honorius was influenced by the *Glossa ordinaria* rather than the other way around, and that his elaborate scheme was inspired by this vision of the role of the *Ecclesia primitiva* in the development of the true Church. This would suggest that the *Glossa ordinaria* to the Song of Songs was written between the death of Robert of Tombelaine *ca.* 1090, and the beginning of Honorius's work on his commentary, *ca.* 1130.

[65] Bede, *In Cantica Canticorum*, Hurst D. ed. in *Corpus Christianorum Series Latina* 119B (Turnhout: 1985) 180–181.

[66] Ohly F. (1958) *Hohelied-studien: Grundzüge einer Geschichte der Hoheliedauslegung des Abendlandes bis um 1200* (Wiesbaden: 1958); Rupert of Deutz, *Commentaria in Canticum Canticorum de incarnatione domini* Haacke H. ed. in *Corpus Christianorum Continuatio Medievalis* 26 (Turnhout: 1974).

[67] Honorius Augustodunensis, *Expositio in Cantica Canticorum* Migne J.P. ed. in *Patrologia Latina* 172 (Paris: 1854) 347–496.

1.f. *The Major Prophets (Isaiah, Jeremiah (with Lamentations and Baruch), Ezekiel, Daniel)*

The "Universal Gilbert," Gilbert of Auxerre, has also been suggested as the compiler of the *Glossa ordinaria* to the Isaiah, Jeremiah, and Ezekiel, but this attribution is not certain.[68] There are no references to Gregory the Great in the *Glossa* to Isaiah, an especially significant fact since Gilbert made such extensive use of Paterius in the *Glossa* to the Pentateuch. This suggests that the twelfth-century continuations of the compendium of Paterius were unknown to the glossator of the Major Prophets.[69]

Margaret Gibson has studied the *Glossa ordinaria* to the prophets Isaiah and Jeremiah as an example of the evolution of the sources of the *Glossa*. Beginning from the commentaries of Jerome on these books,[70] we can see the line of development of the Carolingian revisions, including the abbreviated version of Jerome on Isaiah made by Josephus Scottus, a pupil of Alcuin,[71] the still unpublished revision of Jerome done by Hrabanus Maurus,[72] and the glosses of Otfrid of Weissenberg, which were taken from Hrabanus.[73] Gibson summarizes this process as follows:

> Jerome's commentary has been adjusted to the taste of three successive annotators, in the mid-ninth century, the late tenth, and the early twelfth. Each commentator was familiar with some predecessors, though we cannot always identify them, and with Jerome. Their texts differ, but the format is unvarying and (equally to the point) the principle of adapting Jerome is also unvarying. It cannot be said that the twelfth-century *Gloss* is more learned, more profound or linguistically more sophisticated than Otfrid's marginalia in the ninth century or the anonymous annotation that was prepared for Otto III at Reichenau *c.* 1000.[74]

---

[68] Gibson M. (1992) XI.

[69] Wasselynck R. (1965) 191.

[70] Jerome, *Commentariorum in Esaiam* ed. Adriaen M. in *Corpus Christianorum Series Latina* 73–73A (Turnhout: 1963); *In Hieremiam prophetam libri vi* Reiter S. ed. in *Corpus Scriptorum Ecclesiasticorum Latinorum* 59 (Vienna: 1913) and in *Corpus Christianorum Series Latina* 74 (Turnhout: 1960).

[71] Josephus Scottus, *Epitome commentarii S. Hieronymi in Isaiam* Migne J.P. ed. *Patrologia Latina* 99 (Paris: 1851).

[72] Rabanus Maurus *Enarratio in Isaiam*, unpublished. Preface edited by Dümmler E. in *Monumenta Germaniae Historica Epistulae* 5 (Berlin: 1898).

[73] Wolfenbüttel, Herzog August Bibliothek Weissenburg 33, see Gibson (1992) VIII note 13.

[74] Gibson M. (1989) 239.

One result of this complicated source pedigree is that the sources to the *Glossa ordinaria* on Isaiah and Jeremiah is more than usually elusive. Certainly, Jerome is present, and tagged by the compilator. But is this Jerome direct, or through the filter of Josephus Scotus or (more probably) Hrabanus Maurus? In the case of Jeremiah, it seems that the *Glossa ordinaria* is quoting Hrabanus quoting Jerome;[75] the same could be true for Isaiah, but since Hrabanus's commentary remains unedited, we cannot be sure. Only more research on the manuscripts of the Carolingian compendia that are the intermediate step between the patristic age and the twelfth century will make it possible to answer this question.

Gilbert of Auxerre was very likely the redactor of the *Glossa* to the Lamentations: he is listed as the author in manuscripts, and acknowledged in the gloss with passages marked as "Gilbertus." This section of the *Glossa ordinaria* is drawn largely from the commentary of Paschasius Radbertus, abbot of the powerful Carolingian monastery of Corbie.[76] Radbertus's commentary reflects personal lamentations, since it was written either during or after a time of voluntary exile to the neighboring monastery of Saint-Riquier.

It is curious that Gilbert, who used Hrabanus so liberally in the other parts of the *Glossa ordinaria* for which he was responsible, did not make use here of a commentary by Hrabanus Maurus, the last three books of Hrabanus's commentary on Jeremiah, and the first Latin exposition of the whole of Lamentations.[77] Perhaps Radbertus's treatise, since it is the first to deal with Lamentations alone, stood out as the obvious source. Perhaps Radbertus's interpretation, which bases itself on Hrabanus, seemed to provide the most appropriate commentary on Lamentations. In any case, this gives us yet another example of the extremely complicated mediation of patristic sources in the *Glossa ordinaria*.

The book of Baruch seems to be unglossed.[78] Again, we are in need of further research on the manuscripts of the *Glossa ordinaria* to tell if this is categorically the case.

---

[75] Gibson (1992) IX.

[76] Paschasius Radbertus, *Expositio in Lamentationes Jeremiae* Migne J.P. ed. in *Patrologia Latina* 120 (Paris: 1852) 1059–1267. For a discussion of this treatise and its exegetical context, see Matter E.A. (1982) "The Lamentations Commentaries of Hrabanus Maurus and Paschasius Radbertus," *Traditio* 38 (1982) 137–163.

[77] Hrabaus Maurus, *Expositiones super Jeremiam libri viginti* Migne J.P. ed. in *Patrologia Latina* 111 (Paris: 1852) 1181–1273. See also Matter (1982) 144–149.

[78] *Biblia Latina Cum Glossa Ordinaria* (1992) vol. 3, 215–219.

Ezekiel is the one of the prophetic books most closely associated with Gregory the Great, whose series of twenty-two homilies give a running explanation of Ezekiel 1–3 and 40.[79] Gregory's homilies are incorporated into the *Glossa* where appropriate, for example, in Ezekiel 40:4–5, the vision of a man who measures a wall and a house with a line of flax and a measuring reed.[80] But the places where Gregory influenced this gloss are limited to the passages interpreted in the homilies, and there is no evidence of use the Pseudo-Paterius compendium in the formation of the *Glossa ordinaria* to Ezekiel.

Instead, the sources for the *Glossa ordinaria* to Ezekiel are overwhelmingly drawn from the exegetical tradition of Jerome. The *Glossa* to Ezekiel presents the now familiar picture of a series of commentaries tucked inside of commentaries. At the innermost place of sources are the homilies on Ezekiel of Origen of Alexandria, fourteen of which Jerome had translated into Latin.[81] The interpretations of Origen do appear in the *Glossa* to Ezekiel, in fact, his is the first source name given in the prefatory materials.[82]

Between Origen and the twelfth century, however, lies Jerome. Not only did Jerome translate Origen's homilies on Ezekiel into Latin, he was also, inevitably, influenced by Origen's interpretation as he forged his own, original, view of the most complex and passionate of the prophetic books.[83] The marks of Jerome's original interpretations of Ezekiel are clearly seen in the *Glossa*. For example, Jerome's reading of Ezekiel 44:2, which says that the eastern gate "shall remain shut; it shall not be opened, and no one shall enter by it, for the Lord, the God of Israel, has entered by it," is an allegory of both the fulfillment of the new law, and the virgin birth of Christ.[84]

Nor is Jerome's own exposition the end of the circle, since the *Glossa* attributes this gloss on Ezekiel 44:2 to Hrabanus Maurus. Once again, there is an intermediate step between the interpretations of the Latin fathers and the *Glossa ordinaria*. Once again, the intermedi-

---

[79] Gregory the Great, *Homiliae in Hiezechielem Prophetam* Adriaen M. ed. in *Corpus Christianorum Series Latina* 143 (Turnhout: 1971).

[80] Compare *Biblia Latina Cum Glossa Ordinaria* (1992) vol. 3, 295 to Gregory homily 2.2 Adriaen M. ed. in *Corpus Christianorum Series Latina* 143 (Turnhout: 1971) 226.

[81] Origen, *In Ezechielem homiliae* ed. Borret M. in *Sources chrétiennes* 352 (Paris: 1989).

[82] *Biblia Latina Cum Glossa Ordinaria* (1992) vol. 3, 221.

[83] Kelly, J.N.D., *Jerome: His Life, Writings, and Controversies* (New York: 1975) 305–308.

[84] Compare *Biblia Latina Cum Glossa Ordinaria* (1992) vol. 3, 309 to Jerome, *Commentariorum in Hiezechielem libri 14* Glorié F. ed. in *Corpus Christianorum Series Latina* 75 (Turnhout: 1964) 538. For a discussion of this passage, see Kelly (1975) 307.

ate step is the Carolingian abbot Hrabanus Maurus.[85] This commentary on Ezekiel needs further source study to determine its relationship to the *Glossa*, that is, whether this text was being used primarily and is alone responsible for the passing on of the interpretations of Origen and Jerome, or whether (as seems more likely) Hrabanus Maurus was used in tandem with his own sources. In any case, the method of glossating of Ezekiel seems quite congruent with method identified as that of Gilbert of Auxerre.

The *Glossa ordinaria* to the book of Daniel, on the other hand, seems to be an example of a direct use of Jerome. In fact, Jerome's commentary on Daniel, rather terse, historically based, and eschewing of allegorical interpretations, is one of the very few resources available in the early twelfth century.[86] Origen did not write on Daniel, and here the contribution of Hrabanus Maurus is in doubt. Hrabanus is credited with a commentary drawn from Jerome, but this survives in very few manuscripts, and has not been published.[87]

Hrabanus is, in fact, not cited openly as a source in the *Glossa*, but Walafrid Strabo is cited once, as the author behind a gloss on Daniel 11:1, but the existence of a commentary on Daniel by Walafrid is also a matter of some serious debate.[88] What did the glossator mean?

If Jerome is the major source here, references to pre-fourth century authors such as Porphyry (on the ten horns of the beast in Daniel 7:7)[89] and Tertullian (on the "seventy weeks of years" of Daniel 9:24) can be explained easily.[90]

Of course, Jerome could not have quoted Bede's *De natura rerum* on the question of the "seventy weeks of years,"[91] although Hrabanus

---

[85] Hrabanus Maurus, *Enarratio in Ezechielem* Migne J.P. ed. in *Patrologia Latina* 110 (Paris: 1852).

[86] Jerome, *Commentariorum in Danielem libri 3* Glorié f. ed. in *Corpus Christianorum Series Latina* 75A (Turnhout: 1964). See the discussion in Kelly (1975) 298–302.

[87] Hrabanus Maurus, *Enarratio in Daniel*, unpublished. The prologue has been edited by Dümmler E. in *Monumenta Germaniae Historica Epistolae* 5 (Berlin: 1898) 467–469. The one manuscript I have been able to find reference to is Karlsruhe Aug perg 208ff. 2–73, a tenth-century copy from Reichenau, see Stegmüller F. *Repertorium Biblicum Medii Aevi* vol. 5 (Madrid: 1955) no. 7057.

[88] Stegmüller gives no entry for Walafrid Strabo on Daniel, but there is one manuscript at Saint Gall, Stiftsbibliothek 41 (ninth century, second half) which has commentaries on Isaiah, Hosea, Zachariah, and Daniel attributed to Walafrid.

[89] *Biblia Latina Cum Glossa Ordinaria* (1992) vol. 3, 336.

[90] *Biblia Latina Cum Glossa Ordinaria* (1992) vol. 3, 40.

[91] Bede, *De natura rerum liber* Jones C.W. ed. in *Corpus Christianorum Series Latina* 123–123A (Turnhout: 1975) 189–234.

Maurus or Walafrid Strabo may have done. This leaves open the possibility that the compiler of the *Glossa* to Daniel was consulting Bede directly, along with Jerome and, possibly, one or more Carolingian compilations.

Again, as in the case of the *Glossa ordinaria* to the historical books of the Bible, an investigation into the sources behind the gloss is hampered by our very imperfect knowledge of the intermediate compilations through which the Fathers were received in the twelfth century.

1.g. *The Minor Prophets (Hosea, Joel, Amos, Obadiah, Jonah, Micah, Nahum, Habakkuk, Zephaniah, Haggai, Zechariah, Malachi)*

Twelfth-century witnesses attribute the *Glossa ordinaria* to the Minor Prophets to both Gilbert of Auxerre and Ralph of Laon, brother of Master Anselm.[92] The question, like many questions in the study of the *Glossa*, can only be answered by further work on the manuscripts and the sources.

The major source for these glossed texts are the series of commentaries written by Jerome over a period of almost fifteen years, but copied together in medieval manuscripts, and printed together in a modern critical edition.[93] There was very probably also an intermediate source from the Carolingian period, although probably not one put together by Hrabanus Maurus. Instead, the *Glossa* on the Minor Prophets seems to be indebted to the ninth-century school of canons at Auxerre. There is at least one commentary, variously attributed to Haimo and Remigius of Auxerre, which may be behind the particular compilation found in the *Glossa ordinaria* to the Minor Prophets.[94] The *Glossa ordinaria* to Hosea alone cites Haimo frequently

[92] Smalley (1951) 60–61. Gilbert is named as the author by Robert of Bridlington, Ralph by a manuscript from the abbey of Dore in Herefordshire.

[93] These were written, in the order Nahum, Micah, Zephaniah, Haggai, Habakkuk, Jonah, Obadiah, Zechariah, Malachai, Hosea, Joel, Amos, between 391 and 406, see Kelly (1975) 163, 220, 290. They are published together, edited by M. Adriaen in *Corpus Christianorum Series Latina* 76–76A (Turnhout: 1969–1970).

[94] *Enarratio in duodecim prophetas minores*, printed in Migne J.P. ed. *Patrologia Latina* 117 (Paris: 1852) 11–294. Three of Stegmüller's thirteen manuscripts (all twelfth century, one from Auxerre) attribute the text to Remigius, Stegmüller F. *Repertorium Biblicum Medii Aevi* vol. 3 (Madrid: 1951) no. 3088–3099. The text has been assigned to Remigius, McNally R.E. (1986) *The Bible in the Early Middle Ages* (Atlanta: 1968) 104, but Burton Van Name Edwards has pointed out that the version attributed to

by name. This also is a problem to be sorted out only by more study of the original manuscripts.

1.h. *Maccabees*

The main (and likely the only) source for the *Glossa ordinaria* to the two books of Maccabees is the commentary of Hrabanus Maurus, a treatise well-known in the Middle Ages which has not been published in full.[95]

In summary, the *Glossa ordinaria* to the books of the Hebrew Bible, although certainly put together by different scholars over the course of the first decades of the twelfth century, presents a similar set of problems, especially the difficulty of distinguishing between the patristic sources on which the *Glossa* is ultimately based and the medieval intermediaries, mostly Carolingian, through which they were known to the twelfth-century redactors. There is a pressing need for more study of these intermediary texts, in particular the vast corpus of biblical exegesis of Hrabanus Maurus.

2. *The New Testament*

2.a. *The Gospels and Acts (Matthew, Mark, Luke, John, Acts)*

The *Glossa ordinaria* to Matthew is attributed to Anselm of Laon's brother Ralph, who continued his biblical studies at Laon for another ten years after the death of Anselm.[96] The sources of this gloss follow the familiar pattern: Origen, read, revised and incorporated by Jerome, who is in turn read, revised, and incorporated by a Carolingian author.[97] The Carolingian this time is Paschasius Radbertus, whose commentary on Matthew is one of the most theologically

---

Remigius has "completely different commentaries on Hosea, Joel, Amos and Obadiah, Edwards B. (n.d.) "Carolingian Bibliography," unpublished manuscript.

[95] Hrabanus Maurus, *Commentaria in libros Machabaeorum* partially edited in Migne J.P. in *Patrologia Latina* 109 (Paris: 1851) 1125–1256. See Stegmüller F. *Repertorium Biblicum Medii Aevi* vol. 5 (Madrid: 1955) no. 7058–7059.

[96] The attribution is by Peter Comestor, see Smalley (1936) 39.

[97] Origen's commentary on Matthew is edited by E. Klostermann in *Origenes Werke* 10 (Berlin: 1935), but probably not translated into Latin until the fifth century, see Fischer B. (1963) *Verzeichnis der Sigel für Kirchenschriftsteller* (Freiburg: 1963) 387. Jerome, *Commentariorum in Matheum libri 4* Hurst D. and Adriaen M. ed. in *Corpus Christianorum Series Latina* 77 (Turnhout: 1969). See Kelly (1975) 222–225.

significant of the Middle Ages.[98] Ralph of Laon probably used the commentaries of Jerome and Radbertus side by side, since the theological thrust of Radbertus's commentary complements the historically-oriented, and sometimes hasty commentary of Jerome.

In contrast to almost every glossed book of the Old Testament and many of the New, the *Glossa* to the Gospels of Mark and Luke, and the Acts of the Apostles do not use a Carolingian commentary to convey selections from the Fathers. Perhaps this is because these commentaries are so heavily dependent on Bede. Bede is the major, and clearly demarcated, source of the *Glossa ordinaria* to the Gospel of Mark.[99] There are also a number of glosses tagged as Jerome, but these are actually taken from a Pseudo-Jerominian work from seventh-century Ireland.[100] The famous commentaries of Ambrose and Bede are the obvious sources for the *Glossa ordinaria* to the Gospel of Luke.[101] The *Glossa* acknowledges both sources throughout. The *Glossa ordinaria* to Acts is loosely related to Bede, but probably also uses the unpublished commentary of Hrabanus Maurus.[102]

Up until the thirteenth century, Anselm of Laon was thought to have edited the *Glossa ordinaria* to the Gospel of John.[103] The combination of theology and grammar in this set of glosses certainly calls to mind a twelfth-century school setting.[104] Many of the glosses, though, take as their main source the commentary of Augustine on John.[105]

In summary, among the Gospels, only that of Matthew follows the pattern of sources characteristic of the *Glossa ordinaria* to the books

---

[98] Paschasius Radbertus, *Expositio in Matthaeum* Paulus B. ed. in *Corpus Christianorum Series Latina* 56, 56B (Turnhout: 1984).

[99] Bede, *In Marcum* Hurst D. ed. in *Corpus Christianorum Series Latina* 120 (Turnhout: 1960) 427–648.

[100] Pseudo-Jerome (Cummeanus?) *Expositio in Marcum* Migne J.P. ed. in *Patrologia Latina* 30 (Paris: 1846) 589–644. See the discussion of Bischoff B. (1954) "Wendepunkte der lateinischen Exegese im Frühmittelalter," *Sacris Erudiri* 6 (1954) 189–281, reprinted in *Mittelalterlichen Studien* vol. 1, 257–259.

[101] Ambrose, *Expositio Evangelii secundum Lucam* Adriaen M. ed. in *Corpus Christianorum Series Latina* 14 (Turnhout: 1957); Bede, *In Lucam* Hurst D. ed. in *Corpus Christianorum Series Latina* 120 (Turnhout: 1960) 1–425.

[102] Bede, *Expositio Actuum apostolorum, Retractatio in Actus Apostolorum* Laistner M.L.W. ed. in *Corpus Christianorum Series Latina* 121 (Turnhout: 1983) 3–99, 104–163; For Hrabanus Maurus, *Tractatus Super Actus* see Stegmüller F. *Repertorium Biblicum Medii Aevi* 5 (Madrid: 1955) no. 7063.

[103] Smalley (1936) 39–42.

[104] Gibson (1992) X.

[105] Augustine, *in Iohannis Evangelium tractatus* Willems R. ed. in *Corpus Christianorum Series Latina* 36 (Turnhout: 1954).

of the Hebrew Bible. The Gospels of Mark, Luke, and John, and the Acts of the Apostles, are instead directly dependent on the great biblical expositors who flourished before the Carolingian age: Augustine, Ambrose, and Bede.

2.b. *The Pauline Epistles (Romans, 1–2 Corinthians, Galatians, Ephesians, Philippians, Colossians, 1–2 Thessalonians, 1–2 Timothy, Titus, Philemon, Hebrews)*

In the Middle Ages, Anselm of Laon was universally thought to be the editor of the *Glossa ordinaria* to the Pauline Epistles. If the hand was unified, however, the sources of the glosses to these books were very diverse, making use of the major commentaries of Late Antiquity where appropriate. Augustine, for example, is the author of commentaries on Romans and Galatians.[106] Jerome had written on Galatians, Ephesians, Titus and Philemon, using the Greek Origen as a source.[107] But the most common reference in the *Glossa ordinaria* to what the Middle Ages understood as the Pauline corpus is to "Amb." or "Ambr." Anselm may have thought that this referred to Ambrose of Milan, but the reference is, instead, to a still largely-unstudied anonymous fourth-century Roman author we (following Erasmus) know as Ambrosiaster.[108] The works of this figure, including the first complete commentary on the Pauline epistles in Latin,[109] circulated throughout the Middle Ages as the commentary of Ambrose. There are as well a number of Carolingian compendia to the Pauline Epistles at least one of which, that of Haimo of Auxerre, is also used by Anselm of Laon for the *Glossa ordinaria*.[110]

---

[106] Augustine, *Expositio quarundam propositionum ex epistola ad Romanos; Epistola ad Romanos inchoata expositio; Epistolae ad Galatas expositio* Migne J.P. ed. in *Patrologia Latina* 35 (Paris: 1845) 2063–2088; 2087–2106; 2105–2148.

[107] Jerome, *Commentarii in epistulam ad Galatas libri 3; Commentarii in epistulam ad Ephesios libri 3; Commentarius in epistulam ad Titum; Commentarius in epistulam ad Philemon* Migne, J.P. ed. in *Patrologia Latina* 26 (Paris: 1845) 307–438; 439–554; 555–600; 599–618.

[108] Kelly (1975) 149 for a discussion of this author.

[109] Ambrosiaster, *In epistulas s. Pauli* Migne J.P. ed. in *Patrologia Latina* 17 (Paris: 1879) 47–536.

[110] Haimo of Auxerre, *Commentarium in Epistolas Paulini* Migne J.P. ed, in *Patrologia Latina* 117: (Paris: 1852) no. 364–938; see the reference in the gloss to 1 Thessalonians 2:16, *Biblia Latina Cum Glossa Ordinaria* (1992) vol. 4, 396. Other Carolingian commentaries on the Pauline Epistles are by Claudius of Turin, Florus Diaconus, Hrabanus Maurus, and Sedulius Scottus, ed. Migne J.P. in *Patrologia Latina* 104, 119, 112, 103.

2.c. *The Canonical Epistles (James, 1–2 Peter, 1–3 John, Jude)*

The *Glossa ordinaria* to the Canonical Epistles gives us very little identification of its sources: no author tags, for example. Yet, research has shown that the major source for the *Glossa* to these books is the commentary of Bede.[111] Our sense of whether the reception of the Fathers in these epistles is more complicated than Bede alone will depend on the type of careful source study that has not yet been lavished on this part of the glossed Bible.

2.d. *The Apocalypse*

With the possible exception of the Song of Songs, the Apocalypse presents the most complicated puzzle in the study of the *Glossa ordinaria.* This is, first of all, the most unstable text of all—we still do not know for certain which of at least two versions of this *Glossa* gained currency in the twelfth century as "the" *Glossa ordinaria.*[112] Perhaps there was not just one "standard" version of this glossed Bible. Lobrichon says that this text grew slowly over the course of the twelfth century, while still maintaining an "Anselmian" (that is, of the School of Laon) appearance.[113] The *Glossa ordinaria* to the Apocalypse is a challenge awaiting an enterprising scholar of medieval exegesis.

In general, then, it is fair to say that we know far less about the sources to the *Glossa ordinaria* of New Testament books than we do about the sources of the *Glossa ordinaria* to the Old Testament. Nevertheless, it is obvious that the same sources and methods of adapting sources into glosses are at work in the New Testament as in the Old.

Conclusions

Given the predominance of Late Antique and Carolingian sources, in what sense, then, can we say that the *Glossa ordinaria* is a text of

---

[111] Bede, *In epistolas VII catholicas* Laistner M.L.W. ed. in *Corpus Christianorum Series Latina* 121 (Turnhout: 1983); Gibson (1992) VIII.

[112] Compare the Apopcalypse glosses of Munich, Bayerische Staatsbibliothek clm 3733 (Augsburg, c. 12) to Oxford, Bodleian Library MS. Auct. D. 4.12 (S.C. 2096(2)) (France, c. 13), Oxford Bodleian Library MS. Auct. D. 4.13 (S.C. 2571) (England, c. 13), *Biblia Latina Cum glossa Ordinaria* (1992) vol. 4, 541–578, and Stegmüller #11853, pp. 554–555.

[113] Lobrichon (1984) 95–114.

the twelfth century? In spite of the patristic beginnings and the influence of the Carolingian exegetes, it is possible to see the hand of twelfth-century redactors. It is best to speak of these scholars as redactors rather than authors, because, as Gibson has pointed out, there is no clear "author" of the *Glossa ordinaria*. That is, one could say that Jerome, Bede or Hrabanus are the "authors," even though the text came together centuries after their deaths.[114] We are still rather unclear about the identity of these twelfth-century redactors, although, since the time of Beryl Smalley, four masters of the early twelfth century, Anselm and Ralph of Laon, Gilbert of Auxerre, "The Universal Gilbert," and Gilbert of Poitiers have been thought to have some role in the process.

We know very little about the development of the *Glossa ordinaria* from the generation of Anselm, Ralph, and Gilbert until the middle of the twelfth century, the point at which it was possible to go to a book copier in Paris and ask for a copy of the *Glossa* to any book of the Bible. Beginning about 1160, the great masters of Paris (Peter Comestor, Peter Cantor, Stephen Langton) cited the *Glossa ordinaria* with great frequency. The *Glossa ordinaria* was frequently mentioned by the students and masters of mid-twelfth-century Paris as a reference tool, a sort of encyclopedia of biblical exegesis, even though it was never used as a school text like the *Sentences* of Peter Lombard. In this context, the *Glossa* changed through the accretion of other texts, such as the *Postilla* of Nicholas of Lyra.[115] Margaret Gibson has suggested that this transformation of the *Glossa*, in which the Parisian School of St. Victor probably played a part, is a subject worthy of an extended study in its own right.

The *Glossa ordinaria* is a particularly good example of medieval intertexuality, the conscious borrowing and re-articulating of old material in a new form. There could have been no *Glossa ordinaria* without the influence of the Fathers, but the Fathers appear in the *Glossa* in new guises. The form these ancient and early medieval Christian writings took in the *Glossa* is the heart and soul of the twelfth-century schools. When we understand this process more thoroughly, we will have learned the secrets of the medieval Latin tradition of biblical exegesis.

---

[114] Gibson M. (1992) X.

[115] As is evident in the *Biblia sacra cum glossa interlineari, ordinaria et Nycolai Lyrani Postilla* (Venice: 1588).

Bibliography

Altaner B. (1968) *Patrology* trans. H.C. Graef (New York: 1960).

Belloni A. and Ferrari M. (1974) *La Biblioteca Capitolare di Monza* (Padova: 1974).

Bischoff B. (1954) "Wendepunkte der lateinischen Exegese im Frühmittelalter," *Sacris Erudiri* 6 (1954) 189–281, reprinted in *Mittelalterlichen Studien* vol. 1, 205–273.

Blumenkranz B. (1951) "Raban Maur et Saint-Augustin—compliation ou adaptation? A propos du latin biblique," in *Revue du moyen age latin* 7 (1951) 97.

de Bruyne D. (1926) "Les anciennes versions latines du Cantique des Cantiques," *Revue bénédictine* 38 (1926) 118–122.

Contardi B. (1980) "Un codice di area romana della metà del Duecento," *Federico II e l'arte del duecento italiano* II (Galantina: 1980).

Fischer B. (1963) *Verzeichnis der Sigel für Kirchenschriftsteller* (Freiburg: 1963).

Froehlich K. (1992) "The Printed Gloss", in *Biblia Latina Cum Glossa Ordinaria: Facsimile Reprint of the Editio Princeps Adolph Rusch of Strassburg 1480/81* (Turnhout: 1992) XII–XXVI.

Gibson M. (1989) "The Twelfth-Century Glossed Bible", *Studia Patristica* ed. E. Livingstone 23 (1989) 232–244.

—. (1992) "The Glossed Bible" in *Biblia Latina Cum Glossa Ordinaria: Facsimile Reprint of the Editio Princeps Adolph Rusch of Strassburg 1480/81* (Turnhout: 1992) VI–XI.

Gross-Diaz T. (1996) *The Psalms commentary of Gilbert of Poitiers: From Lectio Divina to the Lecture Room* (Leiden: 1996).

Hablitzel J.B. (1906) *Hrabanus Maurus. Ein Beitrag zur geschichte der mittelalterlichen Exegese* (Freiburg im Breisau: 1906).

de Hamel C. (1984) *Glossed Books of the Bible and the Origins of the Paris Booktrade* (Woodbridge: 1984).

Kelly, J.N.D., *Jerome: His Life, Writings, and Controversies* (New York: 1975) 305–308.

Lobrichon G. (1984) "Une nouveauté: les gloses de la Bible," in *Le Moyen Age et la Bible*, Riché P. and Lobrichon G. ed. *Bible de tous les temps* IV (Paris: 1984) 95–114

McNally R.E. (1986) *The Bible in the Early Middle Ages* (Atlanta: 1968).

Matter E.A. (1982) "The Lamentations Commentaries of Hrabanus Maurus and Paschasius Radbertus," *Traditio* 38 (1982) 137–163.

—. (1990) *The Voice of My Beloved: The Song of Songs in Western Medieval Christianity* (Philadelphia: 1990).

Meyvaert P. (1978–79) "The Date of Gregory the Great's Commentaries on the Canticle of Canticles and on 1 Kings," *Sacris Erudiri* 23 (1978–1979) 191–216.

Minnis A.J. (1988) *Medieval Theory of Authorship*, second edition (Philadelphia: 1988).

Ohly F. (1958) *Hohelied-studien: Grundzüge einer Geschichte der Hoheliedauslegung des Abendlandes bis um 1200* (Wiesbaden: 1958).

Pace V. (1985) "Per la storia della minatura duecentesca a Roma," *Studien zur mittelalterichen Kunst 800–1250. Festschrift für F. Mütherich zum 70. Geburtstag* (Munich, 1985).

Reinhardt K. and Gonzálvez R. (1990) *Catálogo de Códices Bíblicos de la Catedral de Toledo* (Madrid: 1990).

Riedlinger H. (1958) *Die Makellosigkeit der Kirche in den Lateinischen Hoheliedkommentaren des Mittelalters*. Beiträge zur Geschichte der Philosophie und Theologie des mittelalters 38,3 (Münster, West.: 1958).

Rissel M. (1976) *Rezeption antiker und patristischer Wissenschaft bei Hrabanus Maurus*, Lateinische Sprache und Literatur des Mittelalters, 7 (Berne: 1976).

Smalley B. (1935) "Gilbertus Universalis Bishop of London (1128–1134) and the Problem of the 'Glossa Ordinaria' I", *Recherches de théologie ancienne et médiévale* 7 (1935) 235–262.

—. (1936) "Gilbertus Universalis Bishop of London (1128–1134) and the Problem of the 'Glossa Ordinaria' II", *Recherches de théologie ancienne et médiévale* 8 (1936) 24–64.

—. (1937) "La *Glossa Ordinaria*", *Recherches de théologie ancienne et médiévale* 9 (1937) 365–400.

—. (1941) *The Study of the Bible in the Middle Ages* (Oxford: 1941).

Tischendorf C. (1862) *Codex sinaiticus petropolitanus* (St. Petersburg: 1862).

Vaccari P.A. (1945) "Il genuino commento ai Salmi di Remigio di Auxerre," *Biblica* 26 (1945) 52–99.

Verbraken P. (1956) "Le commentaire de saint Grégoire sur le premier Livre des Rois," *Revue bénédictine* 66 (1956) 159–217.

Vian P. (1988) Altri codici araceolitani nella Biblioteca Vaticana, in *Miscellanea Bibliothecae Apostolicae Vaticanae, Studi e Testi* 331 (Città del Vaticano: 1988) 287–311.

Wasselynck R. (1962) "Les compliations des 'Moralia in Job' du VII[e] au XII[c] siècle," *Recherches de théologie ancienne et médiévale* 29 (1962) 5–32.

—. (1965) "L'influence de l'exégèse de S. Grégoire le Grand sur les commentaires bibliques médiévaux (VII[c]–XII[c] s.)" *Recherches de théologie ancienne et médiévale* 32 (1965) 186–188.

Wilmart A. (1931) "Fragments carolingiens du Fonds Baluze," *Revue bénédictine* 43 (1931) 109.

THE CHURCH FATHERS AND THE *SENTENCES* OF PETER LOMBARD

Jacques-Guy Bougerol

A native of the North of Italy (born in Novara around the year 1100), Peter Lombard stayed for a while at the Cathedral School of Rheims where he compiled his *Glossa in Psalmos* (published by the Franciscan Richard du Mans in Paris in 1541, reprinted in *PL* 191, 55–1296). He then went to Paris where he attended the school of Hugues de Saint-Victor. Having been appointed to a teaching post at the school of Notre Dame from 1143–1144, he compiled for his pupils the *Glossa* or *Collectanea in Epistolas Beati Pauli* (*PL* 191, 1297–192, 520). This primitive form of his teaching owes a lot to the commentary of Gilbert de la Porrée and especially to the *Expositio epistolarum Beati Pauli collecta ex libris sancti Augustini* by Florus of Lyons (approximately 835–840).[1]

Prior to 1155, Peter Lombard wanted to give his students a coherent collection such as would put their intelligence at the service of the truth. This was the first version of the *Sententiae*. Between 1155 and 1158,[2] he revised and corrected his text. The Prologue *Cupientes aliquid* (written after achieving the work), clarifies Peter Lombard's plan. In its very form, it constitutes an example of what the *Sententiae* will be like.[3] After a short quotation from Augustine, he brings in a lengthy testimony from Hilary of Poitiers,[4] then goes back to Augustine:[5] "This work must not appear to the eyes of the first lazy person who comes along, nor to those of a great scholar, as useless, because there are lots of people, of whom I am one, who have a great need of it". He intends to integrate in a short volume the opinions of the Fathers, with supporting texts, so as to prevent his students from

---

[1] On Florus of Lyons, cf. C. Charlier, "La compilation augustinienne de Florus sur l'Apôtre", in *Revue Bénédictine* 57 (1947) 132–167.

[2] This detail is supplied by I. Brady, "Pierre Lombard", *Dictionnaire de Spiritualité*, XII (1986) 1608–1609.

[3] The exact title of the work is: *Sententiae in IV Libris distinctae*. We shall subsequently refer to it as: *Sententiae*.

[4] *Prologus*, no. 3, I, 3–4. Hilarius, *De Trinitate*, X, nn. 1–2 (*PL* 10, 344 et seq.).

[5] August., *De Trinit.*, prooem., no. 1 (*PL* 42, 869; *CCL* 50, 127).

having to rustle through innumerable books by offering them a succinct text which they can read easily.[6]

The *Sententiae* are divided into four Books following both a historical and a logical order:[7] I. (48 distinctions): the Divinity, the Trinity of God, the divine essence and the three Persons, the presence of God in the world and in our lives—II. (44 distinctions): God the Creator and creatures, the notion of creation, the creation of the Angels, the fall of the bad Angels and the confirmation in grace of the good ones, the six days of creation, man and woman, the fall and its effects, grace, free will, virtue, original sin and actual sin.—III. (40 distinctions): the Incarnation and the Redemption of Christ the Mediator and liberator,[8] the virtues of Christ, faith, hope and charity, the cardinal virtues, the seven gifts of the Holy Spirit and the Ten Commandments implicitly contained in the love of God and neighbour.—IV. (50 distinctions): the seven Sacraments, the difference between the sacraments of the Old Testament and those of the New; a large place is allotted to the conditions of Christian marriage, our last end, the Last Judgment, the happiness of the just and the punishment of the wicked.

Both in its conception and its editing, Peter Lombard's work looks for a reaction against the tendency of theology to go into dialectics. Each distinction is, in fact, a conglomerate of quotations, or as he says himself, of the opinions of the Fathers.

Patristic Sources

The master theologians of the XIIth century quote a great number of texts of the Greek and Latin Fathers. The sources from which they obtain them are the canonical collections of Ivo of Chartres, Gratian and others, Abelard's *Sic et non*, the *Glossa ordinaria*. But to study closely the literal meaning of the references, one notes that the

---

[6] We translate the Latin "sententiae" by the word "opinions".

[7] The order of the material adopted by Lombard in the *Sententiae* compelled recognition by following masters and became established. Pierre de Poitiers and Raoul Ardent showed that they were dependent on it. Cf. A. Landgraf, *Introduction à l'Histoire de la Littérature théologique de la scolastique naissante*, Paris 1973, 53. We shall refer subsequently to the third critical edition of P.I. Brady, Quaracchi-Grottaferrata I, 1971 (I–II); II, 1981 (III–IV).

[8] It is to be noted that Peter Lombard gave no distinctive place in Book III to the Resurrection of Christ.

"authorities" were not all known in the XIIth century in the way that we know them today. We must first pinpoint the relative importance of these diverse "authorities" before seeking to know how Peter Lombard became acquainted with them.

The first in importance, both for the number of extracts quoted and for the preponderant influence he exercised on the theology of the *Sententiae*, is Augustine with 680 quotations—without counting the 34 quotations from the *De fide ad Petrum* of Fulgentius de Ruspe and the five texts of the *Liber sive diffinitio ecclesiasticorum dogmatum* of Gennadius. After Augustine, we find Ambrose with 66 extracts, then Hilary of Poitiers with 63. This is to say that Augustine by far outclasses the other "authorities". John Damascene, of whom we shall speak later, is quoted 26 times. To resume, in a decreasing order of quotations, we have: Augustine (680), Ambrose (66), Hilary (63), Jerome (48), Gregory the Great (41), Ambrosiaster (34), Fulgentius (34), John Damascene (26), Bede (21), John Chrysostom (14), Origen (10), Isidore (6), Leo the Great (6), Gennadius (5).

Augustine

I. Brady, in his most recent studies, has shown that Peter Lombard had no direct knowledge of more than a limited number of books by Augustine, four to be precise: the *De doctrina christiana*, the *Enchiridion*, the *De diversis quaestionibus 83*, the *Retractationes*.[9] He had no knowledge of other works by Augustine except through the *Glossa ordinaria* or the *Expositio* of Florus of Lyons.

1. – The *De diversis quaestionibus 83* is quoted 30 times in the *Sententiae*, sometimes in marginal notes as in I, d. 9, ch. 4, no. 5 (I, 107), where the extract from question 37 (*PL* 40, 27) makes precise the point that one should not say that the Son is always born, but that he was always born: "The expression 'semper natus' is better than 'qui semper nascitur', because he who is always being born has not yet been born, has never been born or will be born if he is always being born. Now the Son exists, because he was born and is always the Son; he was therefore always born".[10]

---

[9] Cf. the *Prolegomena* in volume I of the *Sententiae*, I, 118*–122*.

[10] Melior est "semper natus" quam "qui semper nascitur", quia qui semper nascitur, nondum est natus et numquam natus est aut natus erit si semper nascitur. Aliud est

– Or as in I, d. 32, ch. 2, no. 3 (I, 234), where question 23 discusses created wisdom: "When God is called 'wise', he is called 'wise' because of the wisdom without which it is false to believe that he was so or could be so; he is called 'wise' not by a participation of wisdom like the soul which may or may not be 'wise', but because he gave birth to wisdom whereby the wise man is so called;[11] but Peter Lombard is aware of the correction made by Augustine himself in his *Retractationes*, I, ch. 26 (*PL* 32, 625; *CSEL* 36, 118): "I have said of the Father in *Liber 83 Quaestionum* that he engendered wisdom whereby the wise man is so called; but I have subsequently treated this question better in the *De Trinitate*"[12] (*PL* 40, 16).

– In III, d. 11, ch. 1, no. 3 (II, 78), the extract from question 67 (*PL* 40, 66–67) comes from the *Glossa* of Peter Lombard on Rom. 8,19 (*PL* 191, 1442B): "Everything that God the Father has made through the Son is called a creature. But the Son cannot be called a creature, for through him all things were made".

– In III, d. 16, ch. 2 (II, 105), the exposé of the four states of man, prior to sin, after sin and prior to grace, in grace and in glory, the object of question 66—a theme already expounded in Book II, d. 25, ch. 6 (I, 464), following the *Summa Sententiarum* and the *De sacramentis* of Hugues de Saint-Victor—, is also to be found in the *Glossa* of Peter Lombard on Rom. 8,11 (*PL* 191, 1437C).

– In IV, d. 4, ch. 4, no. 10 (II, 258), question 62 applies the principle whereby God can supply when necessary and cause to benefit from the grace of the Sacraments a person who cannot receive them: "The goodness of the Almighty supplies for whatever was lacking in the Sacrament"[14] (*PL* 40, 53). And Peter Lombard concludes: "God has not bound His power to the Sacraments".[15]

2. – The *De doctrina christiana* is an attempt at a synthesis between Christianity and ancient culture. In the first two chapters, Augustine

---

enim nasci, aliud natum esse, ac per hoc numquam Filius est, si numquam natus est. Filius autem est quia natus, et semper Filius: semper igitur natus est.

[11] Cum sapiens Deus dicitur, et sapientia sapiens dicitur sine qua eum vel fuisse aliquando vel esse posse nefas est credere, non participatione sapientiae sapiens dicitur, sicut anima quae et esse et non esse sapiens potest, sed quod eam ipse genuerit qua sapiens dicitur sapientia.

[12] Dixi in libro *83 Quaestionum* de Patre, quod eam ipse genuit qua sapiens dicitur sapientiam; sed melius istam quaestionem in libro postea *De Trinitate* tractavi.

[13] Dicitur creatura quidquid fecit Deus Pater per Filium; qui non potest appellari creatura, quoniam per ipsum facta sunt omnia.

[14] Supplet Omnipotens benignitas quod sacramento defuerat.

[15] Deus qui suam potentiam sacramentis non alligavit.

expounds the profane and theological scientific preparation necessary to study Scripture fruitfully; book 3 deals with hermeneutics and
book 4 with homiletics. Quoted 63 times in the *Sententiae*, he opens
Book I of the *Sententiae* by laying out the programme which Peter
Lombard intended to follow—and which, in fact, he did not follow.
This is the extract where Augustine shows how all doctrine speaks
either of "things" or of "signs"; now "things" are also called "signs".
What is not destined to signify anything is properly to come under
the title of "things", whereas "signs" serve to signify: "Every doctrine
treats of things or signs. Now, one learns about things through signs.
Things are properly so called because they have no sign-value; signs,
on the other hand, are so called because it is their function to signify".[16]—In III, d. 27, ch. 5, no. 1 (II, 164), wherein Peter Lombard
studies the virtue of charity, the entire text of this no. 1 comes from
his *Glossa* on Rom. 13,9–10 (*PL* 191, 1507C and 1508B–C): "This
rule of love is instituted by God",[17] "in order that, continues the
Master of the Sentences, you may love God for Himself with all
your heart, and your neighbour as yourself, that is to say for whom
and for what reason you must love yourself".[18]
– On the other hand, in III, d. 36, ch. 3, no. 2 (II, 205), the reference
to the *De doctrina christiana* is false. The reason is that the text of the
Expositio studied by Peter Lombard contains a false directive; Florus's
original refers us more correctly to the sermon *De laude caritatis*, in
the *Glossa* on 1 Tim. 1,5 (*PL* 192, 328D–329D).

3. – The *De Genesi ad litteram*, a voluminous exposé of the first three
chapters of Genesis, and quoted 129 times, is in fact known by Peter
Lombard in the text of the *Glossa ordinaria*, whether or not Augustine's
name is mentioned. The quotations always have the note: *Super Genesim.*
Thus in the following examples, one notices that under this rubric,
the references are the most diverse:
– I, d. 35, ch. 9, no. 1 (I, 258), it is a question of the *Glossa* on
Hebr. 11,3 (*PL* 192, 489D–490A): "These visible realities, before they

---

[16] This is a reference to the *De doctrina christiana*, I, ch. 2, no. 2 (*PL* 34, 19 et seq.),
quoted in I, d. 1, ch. 1, no. 1 (I, 55): Omnis doctrina vel rerum est vel signorum.
Sed res etiam per signa discuntur. Proprie autem hic res appellantur, quae non ad
significandum aliquid adhibentur; signa vero, quorum usus est in significando.
[17] Haec regula dilectionis divinitus constituta est.
[18] Ut Deum propter se toto corde, et proximum diligas sicut te ipsum, id est ad
quod et propter quod te ipsum diligere debes. In bono enim et propter Deum te
ipsum diligere debes.

were, did not exist. So how were they known by God when they did not exist? And again: How did He make them when they were unknown to Him? He has never made anything without being aware of it. So, therefore, before they were, they both existed and did not exist: they existed in the knowledge of God, they did not exist in their own nature. I do not venture to say that they were known in a different way by God Himself as He made them; He knew them in the act of making them, *for with Him there is neither vacillation nor shadow of change*".[19]

– Another example, I, d. 37, ch. 6, no. 3 (I, 271), where the quotation is taken from the *Glossa ordinaria* on Hebr. 1,3 (*PL* 192, 406A): "Almighty God, whose immutable eternity, will and truth are always the same, moves the spiritual creature in time; he also moves the corporal creature in time; and so in this movement He governs the natures which He has created".[20]

– In book II of the *Sententiae*, the quotations are obviously very numerous, being taken from different passages of the *Glossa ordinaria*, starting from the *Prothemata* of the *Glossa*.[21]

– The most significant example is II, d. 8, ch. 1, no. 2, where Peter Lombard seeks to determine whether the angels have a body or not. The source of chapter 1 is the *Glossa ordinaria* on Genesis 1,20. In number 1, Peter Lombard expounds the thinking of certain Fathers, including Fulgentius of Ruspe,[22] Rupert of Deutz,[23] and Saint Bernard:[24] "Certain people, relying on Saint Augustine, think that all the angels before their confirmation or their fall possessed ethereal bodies composed of a purer and more superior air, and this so that

---

[19] Haec visibilia, antequam fierent non erant. Quomodo ergo Deo nota erant quae non erant? Et rursus: Quomodo ea faceret, quae sibi nota non erant? Non enim quidquam fecit ignorans. Nota ergo fecit, non facta cognovit. Proinde antequam fierent, et erant, et non erant: erant in Dei scientia, non erant in sua natura. Ipsi autem Deo non audeo dicere alio modo innotuisse cum ea fecisset, quam illo quo ea noverat ut faceret, *apud quem non est transmutatio nec vicissitudinis obumbratio.*

[20] Deus omnipotens, incommutabili aeternitate, voluntate, veritate semper idem, movet per tempus creaturam spiritualem; movet etiam per tempus et locum creaturam corporalem, ut in eo motu naturas quas condidit administret.

[21] Thus II, d. 2, ch. 5 (I, 3412); II, d. 2, ch. 1, no. 4 (I, 337); II, d. 3, ch. 4, no. 3 (I, 344); II, d. 11, ch. 2 (I, 385); II, d. 12, ch. 1, no. 2 (I, 384); II, d. 15, ch. 5, no. 2 (I, 402); II, d. 15, ch. 6, no. 2 (I, 403).

[22] Cf. *De Trinitate*, ch. 9 (*PL* 65, 505A; *CCL* 91A, 642).

[23] Cf. *De Trinitate et operibus eius: In Genesim*, I, ch. 11 (*PL* 167, 208C, 209A); where there is no mention of the name of Augustine.

[24] Cf. *De consideratione*, V, ch. 4, no. 7 (*PL* 182, 791B–C; ed. Cisterc., Roma 1963, III, 471 et seq.).

they might carry out valuable tasks, not that they might suffer".[25]
Lombard says that these authorities relied on texts of Saint Augustine. According to them, good and bad angels, before their fall or
their confirmation, had ethereal bodies, composed of a very subtle gas
which allowed them to act without ever suffering. The good angels,
confirmed in their attachment to God, have kept this body which is
so subtle that it is invisible to the eyes of men, except when they
sometimes, as it were, put on a thicker outer garment. As for the
bad angels, their bodies have lost their subtlety, becoming of such a
density and thickness that it is inflammable without ever being con-
sumed. And Lombard quotes in no. 2 of this first chapter, a long
text which he claims is taken from the *De Genesi ad litteram*, III ch.
10, nos. 14–15.[26] Now, in the *De Genesi ad litteram*, Augustine says:
"This is why even the demons are etherial beings".[27] The text quoted
by Lombard is that from the *Glossa ordinaria* on Genesis I,20: "The
demons, it is said are etherial creatures" etc.[28] Lombard read certain
authors, including Apuleus of Madaurus[29] who affirm that Augustine, in his commentary on Genesis, quotes the opinion of others:
"dicuntur", and not his own thoughts, for otherwise he would have
written: "sunt". In order to resolve this complex problem, Peter Lombard expounds the data of no. 3, before concluding with the "catholici
tractatores", that the angels have no body, although they sometimes
take on one in order to fulfil the ministries which God confides to
them; once their mission is ended, they shed this body. So we have
here the proof that Peter Lombard was not looking at the text of the
De Genesi ad litteram, but at that of the *Glossa ordinaria* which reflected
the opinion of Augustine, giving or taking a change of word.

Sometimes the name of Augustine is applied to a *Glossa* which is
foreign to him, that of Bede for example in II, d. 13, ch. 2, no. 2
(I, 390), where the text quoted is in reality taken from the *Glossa ordinaria* on Gen. 1,3.

– In II, d. 22, ch. 3, nos. 3–4 (I, 442), we are dealing with an extract from the *Expositio* of Florus of Lyons, quoted in the *Glossa* of

---

[25] Quod aliqui putant, innitentes verbis Augustini, qui dicere videtur quod angeli
omnes ante confirmationem vel lapsum corpora aëria habuerint, de puriore ac supe-
riore aëris parte formata, ad faciendum habilia, non ad patiendum.

[26] *PL* 34, 284 et seq.; *CSEL* 28–I, 72 et seq.

[27] Quapropter, etsi daemones aëria *sunt* animalia.

[28] *Biblia latina cum Glossa ordinaria*, ed. princeps A. Rusch, Strasbourg 1490–91, reprint 1992, in Gen 1,20 (I, 14): Daemones aëria *dicuntur* animalia.

[29] *De deo Socrates*, ed. P. Thomas, Leipzig 1908, III, 21.

P. Lombard on 1 Tim. 2,14 (*PL* 192, 341A–B): "The Apostle shows how Adam was a sinner in saying: *In a transgression identical to that of Adam*; he denies, moreover, that he was seduced, saying: *It was not Adam who was seduced, but the woman.* This is why, when questioned, he does not say: *The woman seduced me*, but: *she gave me to eat and I ate*; the woman, on the other hand, says: *The serpent seduced me*".[31]

Sometimes, too, the *Glossa* of Peter Lombard on the Epistles of Paul makes its appearance:

– II, d. 2, ch. 3, no. 1 (I, 338) quotes the *Glossa* on Ep. 3,10 (*PL* 192, 190C): "no created being is before time, but within time".[32]

– II, d. 11, ch. 2, no. 4 (I, 382) quotes the *Glossa* on Gal. 3,19 (*PL* 192, 127D), observing that Augustine seems to contradict Jerome: "He has not hidden from the angels the kingdom of heaven which has been revealed at the opportune time for our salvation. So to them He has made known this mystery within the space of time, for no creature exists before time, but within time".[33]

– II, d. 11, ch. 2, no. 4 (I, 382) quotes the *Glossa* on 1 Tim. 6,10 (*PL* 192, 359A–B): "For man would not be in love with money, unless he thought that this would make him more superior".[34]

– Finally, in II, d. 22, ch. 4, no. 8 (I, 444), he gives at the same time Peter Lombard's *Glossa* on Ps. 68,5 and Ps. 70,19 (*PL* 191, 629B; 649C) and the *Glossa* on Phil. 2,6 (*PL* 192, 233C) taken from the *Enarratio in Ps. 68,5*, sermo 1, no. 9 (*PL* 39, 848): "Because he did not usurp that which was not properly his own, as the devil and the first man did".[35]

Book III of the *Sententiae* offers three examples:

– III, d. 3, ch. 3 (II, 35) wherein is quoted the *Glossa ordinaria* on Hebr. 7,10 (VI, 154C): "Just as Adam was a sinner, those who were born from him had sinned, just as Abraham gave the tithe, those

---

[30] Cf. *Biblia latina cum Glossa ordinaria*, I, 14.

[31] Cum Apostolus Adam praevaricatorem fuisse ostendat dicens: *In similitudinem praevaricationis Adae*, seductum tamen negat, ubi ait: *Adam non est seductus, sed mulier.* Unde et interrogatus non ait: *Mulier seduxit me*, sed *dedit mihi et comedi*; mulier vero inquit: *Serpens seduxit me.*

[32] Nulla creatura est ante saecula, sed a saeculis.

[33] Non latuit angelos mysterium regni caelorum, quod opportuno tempore revelatum est pro salute nostra. Illis ergo *a saeculis* innotuit supra memoratum mysterium, quia omnis creatura non ante saecula, sed a saeculis est.

[34] Est enim homo, qui non esset amator pecuniae, nisi per hoc putaret se excellentiorem esse.

[35] Quia non usurpavit quod suum non esset, ut diabolus et primus homo.

who were born from him were subjected to the tithe. But that has nothing to do with Christ, although he was descended from the race of Adam and Abraham, for he was not descended from them according to the concupiscence of the flesh".[36]

– III, d. 15, ch. 1, no. 2 (II, 93) the *Glossa ordinaria* has: "It is not the body which experiences sensations, it is the soul which experiences sensations through the medium of the body, by which, as through a messenger, it receives confirmation of what is announced to it from the outside".[37]

– III, d. 17, ch. 2, no. 2 (II, 106) quotes the *Glossa ordinaria* on Gal. 5,17 (*PL* 192, 158B–C) in four extracts which clarify the problem of the will of Christ, in accordance with His two natures: "The flesh only desires something with the collusion of the soul; but it is said that it is the flesh which desires because the soul resists the spirit on account of carnal concupiscence, induced by the delectation which comes from the flesh when it encounters that delectation which is proper to the spirit".[38]

Book IV of the *Sententiae* offers eight examples from which we pick out the following:

– IV, d. 26, ch. 2, no. 2 (II, 417) refers to Hugues de Saint-Victor, *De sacramentis*, II, 11, 3 (*PL* 176, 481B and D);

– IV, d. 31, ch. 1 (II, 442) quotes the *Glossa* of Peter Lombard on 1 Cor. 7,1 (*PL* 191, 1586D): "The nuptial blessing is threefold, faith, the child and the Sacrament. In faith one takes pains not to unite oneself carnally with another after the sacramental bond. With regard to the child, one seeks to accept it with love and to educate it religiously. In the case of the Sacrament; one tries hard not to break up the marriage; and, in the case of divorce, not to enter into a union with another, not even for the sake of thc child".[39]

---

[36] Sicut Adam peccante, qui in lumbis eius peccaverunt; sic Abraham dante decimas, qui in lumbis eius erant decimati sunt. Sed hoc non sequitur in Christo, licet in lumbis Adae et Abrahae fuerit, quia non secundum concupiscentiam carnis inde descendit.

[37] Non corpus sentit, sed anima per corpus, quo velut nuntio utitur ad confirmandum in se ipsa quod extrinsecus nuntiatur.

[38] Carnalem delectationem de carne et a carne adversus delectationem quam spiritus habet.

[39] Nuptiale bonum tripartitum est, scilicet fides, proles, sacramentum. In fide attenditur ne post vinculum coniugale cum alio vel alia coeatur; in prole, ut amanter suscipiatur, religiose educetur; in sacramento, ut coniugium non separetur, et dimissus vel dimissa nec causa prolis alteri coniungatur.

– On the other hand, IV, d. 31, ch. 7, no. 1 (II, 448) refers to the *Glossa ordinaria* on 1 Cor. 7,6 which comes from the *Expositio* of Florus: "It is not because incontinence is an evil that marriage is also so".[40]
– Finally, IV, d. 49, ch. 4, no. 3 (II, 553) gives us under Augustine's name an extract from Julian of Toledo, *Prognosticon futuri saeculi*, II, 11 (*PL* 96, 479C–480A).

4. – The *Enchiridion* is an example of symbolism manifested in the three virtues of faith, hope and charity. It is quoted 117 times, and also in the four books of the *Sententiae*. Only once does Peter Lombard, relying on the *Summa sententiarum* I, 14 (*PL* 171, 1095A–B), refer erroneously to the *Enchiridion* whereas the text quoted derives its meaning partly from the *Enchiridion*, ch. 95 (*PL* 40, 276), and partly from the *De spiritu et littera*, ch. 35, no. 62 (*PL* 44, 241).

5. – The *De Trinitate*, quoted 310 times by Peter Lombard, is the crowning piece of the Fathers on the Trinity of God. The Master of the Sentences did not have at hand the complete text of Augustine's treatise; for practical purposes he uses the *Expositio* of Florus of Lyons[41] which he quoted in his *Glossa* on the Epistles of Paul.
– For example, in I, d. 46, ch. 6, no. 1 (I, 318), the reference to the *De Trinitate* XIII, ch. 16, no. 20 (*PL* 42, 1030), is to be found in fact in the *Glossa* on Rom. 8,28 (191, 1448D–1149A): "The evils caused by the wicked when piously endured help the faithful to turn from their sins, to exercise and experience the justice attached to them, and to show them the misery of this life".[42]
– In II, d. 27, ch. 8, no. 5 (I, 487), the extract from the *De Trinitate* XIII, ch. 16, no. 21 (*PL* 42, 1030), is to be found in the *Glossa* on Rom. 5,10 (*PL* 191, 1386): "So we were enemies of God inasmuch as sins are the enemies of justice; and so, once sins are forgiven, such enmity ceases and those who are justified by the Just One are reconciled".[44]

---

[40] Non enim quia incontinentia malum est, ideo coniugium.

[41] Cf. in the *Prolegomena* volume II, 53*–87*, the text of three short treatises *De Incarnatione, De corpore Christo* and *De coniugio*. The *Expositio* is published in its short form in *PL* 119, 279–420. The original text is to be found in *Ven. Bedae Opera* VI, Coloniae Agrippinae 1688, 31–823.

[42] Illa etiam mala quae ab iniquis fideles pie perferunt, ipsis utique prosunt, vel ad demenda peccata, vel ad exercendam probandamque iustitiam, vel ad demonstrandam huius vitae miseriam.

[43] Alia sunt ea quae creduntur, aliud est fides qua creduntur.

[44] Ita ergo inimici eramus Deo sicut iustitiae sunt inimica peccata; et ideo, remissis peccatis, tales inimicitiae finiuntur, et reconciliantur iusto quos ipse iustificat.

– In III, d. 11, ch. 1, no. 2 (II, 78), it is a question of the *Glossa* on 1 Cor. 8,6 (*PL* 119, 332): "As we are speaking of Christ, the prudent, attentive and pious reader must understand what is said, in what sense and why it is said".[45]

– In I, d. 31, ch. 15, no. 1 (I, 230), we read in the *Glossa* on Phil. 2,11 the *De Trinitate*, VI, ch. 3, nos. 4–5 (*PL* 42, 926): "I do not know if one finds in Scripture the expression 'only form one' with regard to beings of differing natures. When it is a question of several beings of an identical nature but with different feelings, they do not form only one inasmuch as they differ in their feelings. So the expression 'one', when it is not made precise as to which 'one' it is a question of and when one qualifies as 'one' several things identical in nature and essence, implies neither dissimilarity nor difference".[46]

– In II, d. 24, ch. 5, no. 5 (I, 454), the *Glossa* on Col. 3,12 appeals to the *De Trinitate*, XII, ch. 7, no. 12 (*PL* 42, 1004): "The superior part of reason is attached to eternal reasons, contemplates them and is inspired by them; the inferior part, on the other hand, stoops to directing temporal realities".[47]

– Finally, in I, d. 45, ch. 4, no. 3 (I, 308–309), the *Glossa* on Hebr. 1,7 brings in the *De Trinitate*, III, ch. 4, no. 9 *PL* 42, 873): "Therefore the will of God is the primary and supreme cause of every form and action susceptible to sensitivity. Nothing happens without the Master of all things, having given from the depths of His invisible and immaterial palace, the order or permission for it in conformity with His ineffable justice".[48] So the *Expositio* of Florus of Lyons gave Peter Lombard a considerable number of texts taken from the *De Trinitate* which he integrated into his *Glossa* on Paul's Epistles and which he used again in the *Sententiae*. The short treatises published by I. Brady in the *Prolegomena* of the third edition of Peter Lombard's

---

[45] Cum de Christo loquimur, quid, secundum quid et propter quid dicatur, prudens et diligens ac pius lector intelligere debet.

[46] Nescio utrum inveniatur in Scripturis dictum, unum sunt, quorum est diversa natura. Si autem et aliqua plura eiusdem naturae sint et diversa sentiant, non sunt unum in quantum diversa sentiunt. Cum ergo sic dicitur unum ut non addatur quid unum, et plura unum dicuntur, eadem natura atque essentia, non dissidens neque dissentiens, significatur.

[47] Rationis autem pars superior aeternis rationibus conspiciendis vel consulendis adhaerescit; portio inferior ad temporalia gubernanda deflectitur.

[48] Voluntas igitur Dei prima et summa causa est omnium specierum atque motionum. Nihil enim fit, quod non de interiore atque intelligibili aula summi Imperatoris egrediatur secundum ineffabilem iustitiam.

Sententiae show how Peter Lombard made use of the *Expositio*; there are so many texts which come from the *Expositio* of Florus of Lyons.[49]

6. – The *Retractationes*, quoted 32 times, are a source of information on the whole of Augustine's literary activity up to 427. Several quotations from the *Retractationes* were written in the margin of the text of the *Sententiae*, which does not mean that Peter Lombard was not the author of these marginal notes; Peter Lombard doubtlessly added them during the incessant work of correcting and perfecting which he carried on until the end of his life. These notes have been published in smaller print by I. Brady.

– For example, I, d. 2, ch. 1, no. 2 (I, 61) where Peter Lombard corrects Augustine in the latter's own words; making the same distinction, ch. 2, no. 2 (I, 62) Augustine corrected his text: "Where I said of the Father and the Son 'The one who begets and the one who is begotten is one'; one should say 'are one'".[50]—In I, d. 32, ch. 2, no. 3 (I, 235), we have already mentioned the marginal note wherein is published the correction made by Augustine to the text of qu. 23 of the *De diversis quaestionibus 83* on the wisdom begotten by the Father.

– In II, d. 27, ch. 2, no. 1 (I, 481), Peter Lombard confirms by means of a text in the *Retractiones*, that if man could fall spontaneously and by his own free will, he could not rise again by himself.

– In III, d. 15, ch. 1, no. 5 (I, 481), the *Retractationes* throw light on a passage in the *De libero arbitrio* in order to show that Christ did not share in our miseries which are the result of sin and which are the affliction of mankind.

– In IV, d. 4, ch. 4, no. 4 (II, 256), Peter Lombard makes clear that in his *Retractationes*, Augustine did not retract his opinion at all. He simply wanted to correct the unfortunate interpretation of the episode about the good thief on the subject of forgiveness received outside baptism.

FLORUS OF LYONS

The deacon Florus of Lyons composed between 816 and 855,[51] an *Expositio epistolarum beati Pauli* where he assembled together the major

---

Cf. note 41.
[50] Ubi dixi de Patre et Filio: *Qui gignit et quem gignit unum est*, dicendum fuit *unum sunt*.
[51] On Florus of Lyons, cf. C. Charlier, "La Compilation augustinienne de Florus sur l'Apôtre", in *Revue Bénédictine* 567 (1947) 132–167, in this context 159.

part of the texts in which Augustine comments on the Pauline Epistles. Whilst the principal texts of this *Expositio* are to be found in the patrology *PL* 119, 279–420, one can read the entire text within the works of the Venerable Bede.[52] Moreover, the new edition of the *De Trinitate* in the collection *Corpus Christianorum. Series latina*, 50 and 50A, gives in the *Prolegomena* (50, XLVIII–LXX) a concordance with the sources, including that of Florus. Further, one finds in the Tables (50A, 594–595), a list of all the references to the *Expositio* of Florus. The rigour with which Florus selected the Augustinian commentaries and the precision of his references, brought out by C. Charlier, makes his monumental work a source from which a number of masters drew, including Peter Lombard. Fr. I. Brady has edited three extracts from Lombard's primitive *Glossa* on the Pauline Epistles in his Introductions to the third critical edition of the Book of Sentences: the *De processione Filii et Spiritus sancti*, a commentary on Rom. 11,36,[53] the *Tractatus de Incarnatione* which is a long commentary on Rom. 1,3[54] and the *De corpore Christi*, a commentary on 1 Cor. 11,25.[55] These three extracts are a clear proof of the rôle played by Florus. To give even clearer evidence of this, it is sufficient to quote alongside the text, the four books of the *Sententiae*.

The Expositio *of the Epistle to the Romans*

– I, d. 46, ch. 6, no. 1 (I, 318): "These evils piously borne, as Augustine says in the book *De Trinitate*, help the faithful to rid themselves of their sins, to exercise and experience their justice, and to show them the wretchedness of this life".[56]

This text comes from the *De Trinitate*, XIII, ch. 16, no. 20 (*PL* 42, 1030; *CCL* 50A, 409): "These evils, piously borne, help the faithful to rid themselves of their sins, to exercise and experience their justice, and to show them the wretchedness of this life".[57]

---

[52] Ven. Bedae *Opera*, VI, Coloniae Agrippinae 1688, 31–828.

[53] I, 86*–88*.

[54] II, 54*–77*.

[55] II, 77*–84*.

[56] Illa etiam mala quae ab iniquis fideles pie perferunt, ut ait Augustinus in libro *De Trinitate*, ipsis utique prosunt, vel ad demenda peccata, vel ad exercendam probandamque iustitiam, vel ad demonstrandam huius vitae miseriam.

[57] We give the text of the critical edition published in *CCL 50 and 50A.*: Prosunt autem ista mala quae fideles pie perferunt, vel ad emendenda peccata, vel ad exercendam probandamque justitiam, vel ad demonstrandam hujus vitae miseriam.

It is quoted by Lombard in his *Glossa* on Rom. 8,18 (*PL* 191, 1449A): "These evils, piously borne, therefore help the faithful to rid themselves of their sins, to exercise and experience their justice, and to show them the wretchedness of this life".[58]

This text comes from Florus in h.l. (*PL* 119, 290): "So ... although bodily death originated in the sin of one man ... this was so that they might apprehend the true life".[59]

– II, d. 27, ch. 8, no. 5 (I, 487): "The things which are believed are not the same as the faith by which they are believed".[60]

The same text is to be found in III, d. 23, ch. 3, no. 1 (II, 143), but it relies on the Glossa on Eph. 4,5 (*PL* 192, 197C–D). We shall come to it later.

This text is to be found in the *De Trinitate*, XIII, ch. 2, no. 5 (*PL* 42, 1016; *CCL* 50A, 386): "What they believe is one thing, the faith by which they believe is another".[61]

This is quoted in Lombard's *Glossa* on Rom. 1,17 (*PL* 191, 1323D): "For the faith by which one believes what one does not see is properly called 'faith'".[62]

The source is Florus in h.l. (*PL* 119, 308): "One truly understands faith by which one believes what one does not see ... of eminent truth".[63]

– III, d. 15, ch. 1, no. 2 (II, 93): "For he took from what is ours in order that he might grant us that which is from him, so as to take away that which is ours. For he took on that which is old in us so that he might pour his newness into us. He accepted the old, that is punishment, so as to destroy both our faults and our punishment".[64]

This text is a summary of a long text in the *De Trinitate*, IV, ch. 3, nos. 5–6 (*PL* 42, 889; *CCL* 50, 163–166): "For the moment, as far as God will grant it, this is what has to be explained: how 'one' in our

---

[58] Prosunt igitur ista mala, quae fideles pie perferunt, vel ad demenda peccata, vel ad exercendam probandamque justitiam, vel ad demonstrandam huius vitae miseriam.

[59] Quamvis enim et ipsa mors carnis de peccato primi hominis originaliter venerit etc. ... ut apprehendant veram vitam.

[60] Alia sunt ea quae creduntur, aliud est fides qua creduntur.

[61] Sed aliud sunt ea quae creduntur, aliud fides qua creduntur.

[62] Est enim fides qua creduntur quae non videntur, quae proprie dicitur fides.

[63] Intelligitur quidem fides qua creduntur ea quae ... praestantissime veritatis.

[64] Suscepit enim de nostro ut de suo nobis tribueret, ut nostrum tolleret. Suscepit enim nostram vetustatem, id est poenae, ut nostram duplam consumeret, id est poenae et culpae.

Lord and Saviour Jesus Christ, corresponds in a certain way with 'two' in us, by virtue of our salvation. . . . This is how the unique death of our Saviour saves us from our two deaths and how His unique resurrection assures our two resurrections. His body has been administered to us as a sort of homeopathic remedy, in two forms: in death and resurrection, as a sacrament for the inner man and an example for the outer man".[65]

This is quoted in the *Glossa* on Rom. 6,6 (*PL* 191, 1405A–B): "Let us see how that which is old in us was destroyed on the Cross. The old in us constitutes our curse, in our faults and punishment. Thus it is said that he was made our curse by destroying in us our faults and our punishment, for that which is doubly old in us has been destroyed by his one death".[66]

One can read this text in Florus in h.l. (*PL* 119, 290): "It is to the sacrament of our inner man that this cry belonged: 'My God! My God! why have you forsaken me?' . . . so that he who speaks the truth in his heart may dwell on God's holy mountain".[67]

– III, d. 19, ch. 6, no. 2 (II, 123): "We were enemies of God inasmuch as our sins are the enemies of justice: once these sins have been forgiven, such enmity ceases; and those whom the just one himself justifies are reconciled with him."[68]

This text comes from the *De Trinitate*, XIII, ch. 16, no. 21 (*PL* 42, 1030; *CCL* 50A, 411): "We were enemies of God inasmuch as our sins are the enemies of justice: once these sins have been forgiven, such enmity ceases; and those whom the Just One himself justifies are reconciled with him."[69]

---

[65] Verum quod instat in praesentia quantum donat Deus edisserendum est, quemadmodum simplum Domini et Salvatoris nostri Iesu Christi duplo nostro congruat et quodam modo concinat ad salutem . . . Una ergo mors nostri Salvatoris duabus mortibus nostris saluti fuit, et una eius resurrectio duas nobis resurrectiones praestitit cum corpus eius in utraque re, id est in morte et in resurrectione, et in sacramento interioris hominis nostri et exemplo exterioris medicinali quadam convenientia ministratum est.

[66] Qualiter autem vetustas nostra in cruce consumpta sit videamus. Vetustas nostra sicut et maledictio in duobus consistit, scilicet in culpa et in poena. Unde dicitur factus maledictum, et utrumque in nobis consumpsit, quia nostram duplam vetustatem sua simpla consumpsit.

[67] Interioris enim hominis nostri sacramento data est illa vox etc. . . . ut inhabitet in monte sancto Dei qui loquitur veritatem in corde suo.

[68] Ita ergo inimici eramus Deo sicut iustitiae sunt inimica peccata; et ideo, remissis peccatis, tales inimicitiae finiuntur, et reconciliantur iusto quod ipse iustificat.

[69] Nec inimici eramus Deo, nisi quemadmodum iustitiae sunt inimica peccata, quibus remissis tales inimicitiae finiuntur, et reconciliantur iusto quos ipse iustificat.

This is quoted in the *Glossa* on Rom. 5,10 (*PL* 191, 1386C): "For we were not enemies of God except in the way that sins are the enemies of justice; and therefore once sins have been forgiven, such enmity ceases, and those whom the just one justifies are reconciled with him".[70]

Florus in h.l. (*PL* 119, 308): "So why should the death of Christ not have occured? Indeed, why, out of the innumerable ways the Almighty had of freeing us ... is it just that through the holiness of one, he should leave all of us uncondemned who are regenerated by the pure and spiritual grace of the second Adam".[71] It is the whole of no. 21 which Florus quotes in his *Expositio*.

– III, d. 23, ch. 3, no. 1 (II, 142): "What they believe is one thing, the faith by which they believe is another. What they believe is to be found in present, past or future events: faith is to be found in the soul of the believer and is only visible to the person who possesses it".[72]

This text comes from the *De Trinitate*, XIII, ch. 2, no. 5 (*PL* 42, 1016 et seq.; *CCL* 50A, 386): "What they believe is one thing, the faith by which they believe is another. What they believe is to be found in present, past or future events: faith is to be found in the soul of the believer and is only visible to the person who possesses it. It is also found in others, but it is not the same faith, it is a similar faith".[73]

Florus on Eph. 4,5 (*PL* 119, 377): "What one believes is one thing, the faith by which one believes them is another etc.... Each one, by the consciousness he has of himself, recognizes this will as his own, not by any means because he believes it, but because he sees it very clearly".[74] The reference here is to the end of no. 5 of Augustine's text.

---

[70] Non enim inimici eramus Deo, nisi quemadmodum justitiae sunt inimica peccata, et ideo remissis peccatis tales inimicitiae finiuntur, et reconciliantur justo, quos ipse justificat.

[71] Cur ergo nor fieret mors Christi? Immo cur non praetermissis aliis innumerabilibus modis etc.... ut propter hunc unum dimittat omnes per ipsius immaculatam gratiam spiritualem regeneratos.

[72] Aliud sunt ea quae creduntur, aliud fides qua creduntur. Illa enim in rebus sunt, quae vel esse vel fuisse vel futurae esse dicuntur: haec autem in animo credentis est, ei tantum conspicua cuius est.

[73] Sed aliud sunt ea quae creduntur, aliud fides qua creduntur. Illa quippe in rebus sunt quae vel esse vel fuisse vel futura esse dicuntur: haec autem in animo credentis est, ei tantum conspicua cuius est, quamvis sit et in aliis, non ipsa sed similis.

[74] Aliud sunt ea quae creduntur; aliud fides qua creditur etc.... sed plane pervidet voluntatem.

– III, d. 27, ch. 7 (II, 167): "Although there are two commandments of love, often one is put forward for both of them. This is not unreasonable, for one cannot love God without one's neighbour, nor one's neighbour without God".[75]

This text comes from the *De Trinitate*, VIII, ch. 7, no. 10 (*PL* 42, 956; *CCL* 50A, 284–285): "Although there are two commandments on which hang the whole of the Law and the Prophets—the love of God and the love of one's neighbour—it is not without reason that Scripture normally mentions only one for both of them. Sometimes it speaks only of the love of God, witness this passage . . . Sometimes Scripture reminds us only of the love of neighbour, witness this passage. . . . It necessarily follows therefore that first of all he must love God".[76]

This is quoted by Lombard in his *Glossa* on Rom. 13,8 (*PL* 191, 1507C): "And note that although there are two commandments of love on which hang the whole of the Law and the Prophets, just one is mentioned for both, and not without reason, for one cannot love God without one's neighbour nor one's neighbour without God".[77]

The *Expositio* of Florus gives this text in h.l. (*PL* 119, 313): "This is true love, to be attached to the truth etc. . . . for first of all he loves God".[78]

The Expositio *on 1 Cor.*

– I, d. 32, ch. 2, no. 4 (I, 235–236): "If the Son is the only one to possess intelligence, both for himself and for the Father and the Holy Spirit, we fall into holding the absurd opinion that the wisdom of the Father does not come from himself, but from the Son, that wisdom did not engender wisdom but that the Father has his wisdom from the wisdom which he engendered. For where there is no intelligence

---

[75] Cum autem duo sint praecepta caritatis, pro utroque saepe unum ponitur. Nec immerito, quia nec Deus sine proximo, nec proximus sine Deo diligi potest.

[76] Cum enim duo praecepta sint in quibus tota Lex pendet et Prophetae, dilectio Dei et dilectio proximi; non immerito plerumque Scriptura pro utroque unum ponit: sive tantum Dei, sicuti est illud etc. . . . Sive tantum proximi dilectionem Scriptura commemorat, sicut est illud . . . Consequens ergo est ut praecipue Deum diligat.

[77] Et nota quia cum duo sint praecepta charitatis, in quibus tota lex pendet et prophetae, pro utroque saepe unum ponitur, non immerito, quia Deus, nec sine proximo, ne proximus sine Deo diligi potest.

[78] Haec est autem vera dilectio, ut inhaerentes veritati etc., . . . ut praecipue Deum diligat.

there cannot be wisdom: consequently, if the Father does not possess intelligence, himself and for himself, but if the Son has intelligence for the Father, then it is the Son who gives wisdom to the
Father. And if in God, to be is to have wisdom, if in him the essence is identical to wisdom, it is no longer the Son who receives the
divine essence from his Father—which, however, is true,—it would
be rather the Father who receives it from the Son, which is the
height of absurdity and error".[79]

This text appears *ad verbum* in the *De Trinitate*, XV, ch. 7, no. 12
(*PL* 42, 1065-1066; *CCL* 50A, 476).

In his *Glossa* on 1 Cor. 1, 24, Peter Lombard quoted it: "Be careful to understand that the Son is called the wisdom of God not as if
he alone were intelligent or wise both for himself, and for the Father
and for the Holy Spirit. For if the Son alone is wise both for himself, and for the Father and for the Holy Spirit, one arrives at the
absurdity that the Father is not wise of himself, but by the Son; and
wisdom would not engender wisdom, but the Father would be called
wisdom by the wisdom which he engendered. For where there is no
intelligence, there cannot be wisdom. And therefore if the Father
does not have intelligence of himself, but if he has it from the Son,
it is certainly the Son who makes the Father wise; and if in God, to
be is to have wisdom, if in him the essence is identical to wisdom,
it is no longer the Son who receives from his Father, it would be
rather the Father who receives it from his Son, which is the height
of error".[80]

Now the *Expositio* of Florus in h.l. has (*PL* 119, 319): "For if only

---

[79] Si solus ibi Filius intelligit, et sibi et Patri et Spiritui Sancto, ad illam reditur
absurditatem, ut Pater non sit sapiens de se ipso, sed de Filio; nec sapientia sapientiam genuerit, sed ea sapientia Pater dicatur sapiens esse quam genuit. Ubi enim
non est intelligentia, nec sapientia potest esse. Ideoque, si Pater non intelligit ipse
sibi, sed Filius intelligit Patri, profecto Filius Patrem sapientem facit. Et si hoc est
Deo esse quod sapere et ea illi essentia quae sapientia, non Filius a Patre, quod
verum est, sed a Filio potius Pater habet essentiam: quod absurdissimum est atque
falsissimum.

[80] Cave ne intelligas Filium dici sapientiam Dei tanquam ipse solus sit intelligens,
vel sapiens sibi, et Patri, et Spiritui sancto. Si enim ibi solus Filius intelligitur sapiens, et sibi, et Patri, et Spiritui sancto, ad illam reditur absurditatem, ut Pater nec
sit sapiens de seipso, sed de Filio; nec sapientia sapientiam genuerit, sed ea sapientia
dicatur Pater sapiens esse, quam genuit. Ubi enim non est intelligentia, nec sapientia
esse potest. Et ideo si Pater non intelligit ipse sibi, sed Filius intelligit Patri, profecto
Filius Patrem sapientem facit; et si hoc Deo esse quod sapere, et ea illi essentia quae
sapientia, non Filius a Patre quod verum est, sed a Filio potius Pater habet essentiam
quod falsissimum est.

the Son possesses intelligence, etc. . . . which the Father is".[81] It is a question here of an extract from no. 12, a longer extract than those quoted previously.

– I, d. 5, ch. 1, no. 8 (I, 83): "This is why Christ is the power and the wisdom of God because he is the power and wisdom of the power and the wisdom which is the Father, as he is light from the light which is the Father, and the source of life in God the Father who, certainly, is the source of life. The Son is therefore wisdom from the Father who is wisdom, as he is 'light from light', 'God from God', as the Father is light on his own account; the Son is also light on his own account. God the Father individually, the Son also individually is wisdom. Finally, just as both together are only one light, one God, so both together are only one wisdom".[82]

The source is the *De Trinitate*, VII, ch. 3, no. 4 (*PL* 42, 937; *CCL* 50, 251), quoted word for word.

One finds this text in Lombard's *Glossa* on 1 Cor. 1,24 (*PL* 191, 1545B): "We preach that Christ is the wisdom of God and the power of God. Be careful to understand that the Son is the wisdom of God not as if he alone were intelligent and wise, for himself, for the Father, and for the Holy Spirit. . . . God the Father is therefore wise, from his own wisdom; and the Son is wise from the wisdom of the Father from the wisdom which is the Father by whom the Son is begotten. So the Father possesses intelligence through his own intelligence, the Son through the intelligence of the Father, is intelligent from the intelligence which is the Father from which he is begotten".[83]

Florus is the source of the foregoing (*PL* 119, 320), but he inserted into this *Expositio*, not book VII, ch. 3, no. 4 of the *De Trinitate*, VII, ch. 3, no. 4, but book XV, ch. 7, no. 12 (*PL* 42, 1066).

– I, d. 27, ch. 3, no. 4 (I, 206): "The Word, inasmuch as he is

---

[81] Si enim solus ibi Filius intelligit etc. . . . quod est Pater.

[82] Ideo Christus dicitur virtus et sapientia Dei: quia de Patre virtute et sapientia, etiam ipse virtus et sapientia est, sicut ipse lumen de Patre lumine est, et ipse fons vitae est apud Deum Patrem fontem vitae. Filius ergo sapientia de Patre sapientia est, sicut Filius lumen de lumine Patre et Deus Filius de Deo Patre, ut et singulus sit lumen, et singulus sit Deus, et singulus sapientia, et simul unum lumen, unus Deus, una sapientia.

[83] Praedicamus Christum esse Dei sapientiam, et Dei virtutem. Cave ne intelligas Filium dici sapientiam Dei tanquam ipse solus sit intelligens, vel sapiens sibi, et Patri, et Spiritui sancto. . . . Est ergo Deus Pater sapiens, ea quae ipse est sua sapientia; et Filius sapientia Patris est sapiens, de sapientia quae est Pater de quo genitus est Filius. Sic et Pater est intelligens ea quae ipse sua intelligentia, Filius autem intelligentia Patris, est intelligens de intelligentia quae est Patri, de qua genitus est.

wisdom and essence, is what the Father is; as Word, he is not what the Father is, for the Word is not the Father, and the Word is used relatively, like the Son".[84]

This text is taken from the *De Trinitate*, VII, ch. 3, no. 4 (*PL* 42, 937; *CCL* 50, 251):

"Certainly, if this temporal and ephemeral word which we give utterance to manifests itself and manifests what we are speaking of, how much more so does the Word of God through whom all things were made? He manifests the Father exactly as the Father is, for he himself is as he is and as is the Father, inasmuch as he is wisdom and also essence, for as Word he is not what the Father is: the Word is relative, like the Son, which obviously is not what the Father is".[85]

This text is also to be found in Lombard's *Glossa* on 1 Cor. 1,24 (*PL* 191, 1545B) quoted earlier.

Peter Lombard's source is the *Expositio* of Florus (*PL* 119, 320).
– III, d. 20, chs. 3–4 (II, 126–127): "So, power followed the resurrection, for, having died, he lives again so as never to die again".[86]

We can find this text in the *De Trinitate*, XIII, ch. 14, no. 18 (*PL* 42, 1028; *CCL* 50A, 407): "So, by power, having died, he came back to life so as to never die again".[87]

The text appears also in the *Glossa* on 1 Cor. 2,7–8, from which Peter Lombard took it: "If he had not also been the Son of Man, etc."[88] (*PL* 119, 320).

Florus quotes this text in his *Expositio*.
– IV, d. 45, ch. 6, no. 4 (II, 528): "His own perfection is sufficient in itself in order to know all that he knows. It is true that God has his messengers, the angels: not, however, to announce to him what he does not know, for there is nothing that he does not know; but it is for their own good that the angels take note of the truth when

---

[84] Verbum, secundum quod sapientia est et essentia, hoc est quod Pater; secundum quod Verbum, non hoc est quod Pater, quia Verbum non est Pater, et Verbum relative dicitur sicut Filius.

[85] Si enim hoc verbum quod nos proferimus temporale et transitorium, et se ipsum ostendit, et illud de quo loquimur, quanto magis Verbum Dei, per quod facta sunt omnia? Quod ita ostendit Patrem sicuti est Pater: quia et ipsum ita est, et hoc est quod Pater, secundum quod sapientia est et essentia. Nam secundum quod Verbum, non hoc est quod Pater: quia Verbum non est Pater, et Verbum relative dicitur, sicut Filius, quod utique non est Pater.

[86] Post vero in resurrectione secuta est potentia, quia revixit mortuus, nunquam postea moriturus.

[87] Potentia vero, quia revixit mortuus, nunquam postea moriturus.

[88] Nisi ipse esset et filius hominis, etc. . . . cum loqueretur in terra.

they act; when it is said that they announce certain things to God, it is not that they inform him about them, it is that they learn them from him through the intermediary of the Word, without anything being spoken. They announce what God wills, having been sent by him to whom he wills, receiving from him through his Word, that is, finding in the divine truth what they must do, what they must announce, to whom and when they must do so".[89]

This text is taken from the *De Trinitate*, XV, ch. 13, no. 22 (*PL* 42, 1075; *CCL* 50A, 494), and is quoted ad verbum.

It is also to be found in Lombard's *Glossa* on Phil. 4,6, in the same terms.

Florus quotes it in his *Expositio* on Phil. 4,6, and it is from there that Peter Lombard took it. Florus transcribed a large part of no. 22 of the *De Trinitate* (*PL* 119, 388).

One can see from these few examples that the Master of the Sentences took a lot from the *Expositio* of Florus of Lyons when he made his commentary on the Epistles of Saint Paul. He practically derived what he knew of Augustine's *De Trinitate* by reading the extracts given in the *Expositio*. When he started to edit the *Sententiae*, in one fell swoop he took the texts he had assembled in his *Glossa*, completing them when necessary with new borrowings from the *Expositio* of Florus.

John Damascene

Peter Lombard is aware that in introducing John Damascene, he is introducing a completely new "auctoritas" in the West. He feels the need to support it with pontifical patronage, as he says in I, d. 19, no. 9 (I, 167): "This is why John Damascene, a great Doctor among the Greeks, wrote in a book on the Trinity which pope Eugenius had translated: Common and universal things are attributed to particular subjects. Common reality is therefore attributed to substance, particular reality to hypostases, that is to say, to the person. The

---

[89] Ad omnia quidem scienda sufficit Deo sua perfectio. Habet tamen nuntios, id est angelos, non qui ei quae nescit annuntient: non enim sunt ulla quae nesciat, sed bonum eorum est de operibus suis eius consulere veritatem. Et hoc est quod ei dicuntur nonnulla "nuntiare": non ut ipse ab eis discat, sed ut ab eo ipsi, per Verbum eius sine corporali sono. Nuntiant etiam quod voluerit, ab eo missi ad quos voluerit: totum ab illo per illud Verbum eius audientes, id est in eius veritate invenientes quid sibi faciendum, quid, quibus et quando nuntiandum sit.

particular is so called, not because it possesses a part of nature, but because it is, in number, an atom, that is to say, an individual. (Pay attention to this!) It is in fact by number, and not by nature, that hypostases differ."[90] We are treating here with an extract from the *De fide orthodoxa*, III, ch. 6 (PG 94, 1002C; versio Burgundionis, ch. 50, no. 1 (ed E. Buytaert, 186). The Greek text consists of four parts; but the version of Burgundio of Pisa is divided into 100 chapters. The title of this version illustrates what Peter Lombard said of it: "From John, a priest of Damascus, begins the Mansur Book in which is to be found the certain tradition of the orthodox faith. This book is divided into a hundred chapters from Greek into Latin by Burgundio, Judge of the city of Pisa, at the request of Pope Eugenius III of blessed memory".[91]

The 25 quotations which we can find in the *Sententiae* are taken from chapters 46–52 of the version by Burgundio of Pisa. It seems therefore that Peter Lombard did not know the entire work by John Damascene. According to I. Brady,[92] he became acquainted with the *De fide orthodoxa* during his journey to Rome in 1154–1155. Now, Books I and II date from the years 1155–1156, Books III and IV from the years 1157–1158. His hasty reading of a few chapters did not give him the grounds for including John Damascene among the usual authorities, as we shall see.

– I, d. 19, chs. 9–12 (I, 167–171). In making an extremely important distinction, Peter Lombard tries to expound as clearly as possible the equality of the three Persons of the Trinity. In chapters 1–9, he expounds the Catholic position, starting with a text from the *De fide ad Petrum*, the work of Fulgentius of Ruspe, falsely attributed to Augustine; then Augustine makes his appearance in several texts taken from the *De Trinitate*, the *Confessiones* and the *Enarrationes in Ps. 101*, Hilary's *De Trinitate* is also quoted. In chapter 3, he calls on John Damascene to witness to the Catholic faith according to the *De fide orthodoxa*,

---

[90] Unde Ioannes Damascenus, inter Graecorum doctores magnus, in libro quem de Trinitate scripsit, quem et Papa Eugenius transferri fecit: Communia et universalia praedicantur de subiectis sibi ipsis particularibus. Commune igitur substantia est, particulare vero hypostasis, id est persona. Particulare autem dicitur non quoniam partem naturae habet, sed particulare numero, ut atomum, id est individuum (Diligenter attende!) Numero enim, et non natura, differre dicuntur hypostases.

[91] Iohannis presbyteri Damasceni qui Mansur Liber incipit in quo est traditio certa orthodoxae fidei capitulis divisa centum a Burgundione Iudice cive Pisano de graeco in latinum Domino tertio Eugenio beatae memoriae papae translatus.

[92] Cf. *Sententiae*, I, Prolegomena, 121*; II, Prolegomena, 13*–18*.

ch. 50, no. 2 (ed. E. Buytaert, 187): "We confess that the whole
nature of the deity is found perfectly in each of the hypostases, that
is to say, of the Persons: thus the Father is perfectly God, the Son is
perfectly God, the Holy Spirit is perfectly God".[93] In chapter four,
Hilary expounds how each of the Persons is totally in the other two.
Peter Lombard expresses his conclusion in no. 2 of chapter 9 I, 167
12): "From all the foregoing, it is clear that the three Persons are the
divine essence".[94]

It is now that Peter Lombard introduces John Damascene, as we
cited earlier, stressing that the *De fide orthodoxa* seems to contradict
Augustine: "Quae praemissae sententiae Augustini penitus contradicere
videntur. Quid ergo dicemus ad haec?" (ch. 9, no. 3—I, 168 12–13).
Chapters 9–12 will attempt to understand John Damascene's exposition by penetrating the difference in terminology which can render
the mystery of the Trinity complex and even obscure. Peter Lombard
cleverly takes up Augustine's attitude again, repeating perfectly the
possible explanations so as thus to make them more familiar to us,
"if one repeats them often while reflecting on them, they become
more familiar to us".[95] (*De Trinitate*, VIII, no. 1—*PL* 42, 947; *CCL*
50, 268.) The laborious exposé of distinction 19 ends thus: "We have
therefore shown sufficiently that no Person in the Trinity surpasses
another in grandeur".[96]

– In the preceding distinction, Peter Lombard referred the reader to
a later distinction, d. 19, ch. 10, no. 2 (I, 169 29–30): "we shall deal
in the following distinction with the difference between the Persons
according to their properties".[97] It is a question of the distinction of
Book I, d. 27, ch. 3 (I, 205–206). John Damascene is brought in
with extracts from chapters 49, 50 and 51 of Burgundio's version
to expound how their personal properties are appropriate to each
of the Persons and determine them by differentiating them, without
however separating them: "We recognize the difference of the hypostases, that is to say, of the Persons in three properties, that is to say,

---

[93] Confitemur deitatis naturam omnem perfecte esse in singulis suarum hypostaseon,
id est personarum: omnem in Patre, omnem in Filio, omnem in Spiritu sancto;
ideoque perfectus Deus Pater, perfectus Deus Filius, perfectus Deus Spiritus sanctus.

[94] Ex praemissis patet quod tres personae dicuntur divina essentia.

[95] Saepius versando repetantur, familiarius quidem innotescunt.

[96] Ecce iam ostendimus sufficienter qualiter in Trinitate aliqua persona aliam non
superet magnitudine.

[97] De quarum distinctione secundum proprietates in sequenti tractabitur.

paternal, filial and processional".[98] (ch. 3, no. 2; I, 205 29–31). It is chapter 49 of Burgundio's version that is referred to here.

– In Book II, d. 32, ch. 2, no. 2 (I, 513–514), Peter Lombard lets us hear the opinion of those who hold that in baptism in water and the Spirit, the soul is purified and the flesh delivered from the contagion of concupiscence. This opinion is quoted in the *Glossa ordinaria* on Acts 1,5 (*Biblia*, 451b–452a): "By the invocation of the name of Christ, the interior virtue of the Holy Spirit purifies the souls and bodies of the baptized".[99] Now, we find the same opinion expressed in the *De fide orthodoxa*, ch. 82, no. 1 (ed., 294 38–40): "Because in fact man is composed of soul and body, so he gives us a double purification by water and the Spirit".[100] Peter Lombard does not quote John Damascene here, out of ignorance of the text.

– In Book III, the count of quotations from John Damascene comes to 16. We shall examine two of them.

– III, d. 22, ch. 3, no. 2 (II, 139): "Thus John said: "The whole Christ is perfect God, but not exclusively God: for he is not only God, he is man; in the same way, the whole Christ is perfect man, but he is not exclusively man, he is also God. 'Totum' represents the nature, 'totus' the hypostasis; as 'aliud' belongs to the nature, 'alius' to the hypostasis".[101] The reference is to chapter 51, no. 5 (ed., 194 59–63) which enables Peter Lombard to confirm that in the tomb, Christ was "totus" in hell, "totus" everywhere, as he is now "totus" everywhere, but not "totum".

– III, d. 9, ch. 1, no. 4 (II, 70), where chapter 52, nos. 3–4 (ed., 196–197, 18–38) of the *De fide orthodoxa* is quoted to confirm that the humanity of Christ is adored in a single adoration, that of the Person of the Word: "The natures of Christ are two, different in reason and mode, but united according to the hypostases. Therefore Christ is one, perfect God and perfect man, whom we adore with the Father and the Spirit with his unsullied flesh; we say that this flesh is

---

[98] Differentiam hypostaseon, id est personarum, in tribus proprietatibus, id est paternali et filiali et processibili, recognoscimus.

[99] sed invocato nomine Christi interior virtus Spiritus sancti baptizatorum animas et corpora purificat.

[100] Quoniam enim duplex homo ex anima et corpore, duplicem nobis dedit et purgationem, per aquam et Spiritum.

[101] Unde Ioannes: Totus est Christus Deus perfectus, non autem totus Deus est: non enim solum Deus est, sed et homo; et totus homo perfectus, non autem totum homo: non solum enim homo, sed et Deus. "Totum" enim naturae est repraesentatitivum, "totus" autem hypostaseos; sicut "aliud" quidem est naturae, "alius" autem hypostaseos.

not adorable: for it is adored in the hypostasis of the Word which is an engendered hypostasis; we do not witness to any veneration of the creature. For we do not adore naked flesh, but flesh united to the deity in the single hypostasis of the Word of God in which the two natures are united. I fear to touch a piece of coal when the wood has caught fire. I adore both natures with a single adoration of the flesh united to the deity. For I am not creating a fourth Person in the Trinity, but I confess a single Person, that of the Word and his flesh".[102]

HILARY OF POITIERS

Hilary of Poitiers died in 367 whereas Augustine was born in 354. This means that Augustine knew and read Hilary's *De Trinitate* as he gives us to understand in his own *De Trinitate*, VI, ch. 10, no. 11 (*PL* 42, 931; *CCL* 50, 24): "An author who wanted to explain the characteristics of each of the Persons of the Trinity in a few words said: Eternity is in the Father, form in the Image, enjoyment in the Gift. We are dealing with a man whose authority carries weight in the interpretation of the Scriptures and the demonstration of the faith. As far as I could, I have dug out the hidden meaning of these terms: Father, Image, Gift, form, enjoyment. I do not believe that I have strayed away from his thinking about the word 'eternity' by understanding it in this way: the Father has no father from whom he proceeds; the son, on the contrary, receives from the Father both his existence and his coeternity with him".[103] Hilary's text to which Augustine refers is to be found in his *De Trinitate*, II, ch. 1 (*PL* 10, 10, 51).

---

[102] Duae sunt naturae Christi ratione et modo differentiae, unitae vero secundum hypostasim. Unus igitur Christus est, Deus perfectus et homo perfectus, quem adoramus cum Patre et Spiritu una adoratione cum incontaminata carne eius; non inadornabilem carnem dicentes: adoratur enim in una Verbi hypostasi, quae hypostasis generata est; non creaturae venerationem praebentes. Non enim ut nudam carnem adoramus, sed et unitam deitati in unam hypostasim Dei Verbi duabus reductis naturis. Timeo carbonem tangere propter ligno copulatum ignem. Adoro Christi mei simul utraque propter carni unitam deitatem. Non enim quartam appono personam in Trinitate, sed unam personam confiteor Verbi et carnis eius.

[103] Quidam cum vellet brevissime singularum in trinitate personarum insinuare propria: Aeternitas, inquit in Patre, species in imagine, usus in munere. Et quia non mediocris auctoritatis in tractatione scripturarum et assertione fidei vir exstitit Hilarius enim hoc in libris suis posuit, horum verborum, id est Patris et Imaginis et Muneris, aeternitatis et speciei et usus, abditam scrutatus intelligentiam quantum valeo, non

Thus Peter Lombard wished to recall Augustine's reflection so as to permit himself to render precise the exact meaning of the terms used by Hilary, terms which Augustine did not sufficiently exploit. He also wanted to insert in its entirety Hilary's text in I, d. 31, ch. 2, no. 2, presenting, among others, this admirable expression of Hilary's: "There is an ineffable embrace between the Father and the Image, an embrace which is not without delight, without love, without joy".[104] And Peter Lombard adds in no. 3: "You know now how Hilary's words are to be understood, although they are so profound that the human spirit can hardly understand them even when expounding them; the explanation which Augustine gave presents in fact a great deal of difficulty and ambiguity".[105]

The *Sententiae* include 63 quotations from the *De Trinitate* in Book I, 16 in Book III. Besides, the *De Synodis* appears 8 times in Book I and once in Book III. We shall come back to this later.

The De Trinitate

– I, d. 5, ch. 1. Peter Lombard asks himself if the Father engenders the divine essence, if the divine essence engenders the Son. This question was contested by Joachim of Fiore, but the IVth Lateran Council (1215) again affirmed it. The problem is complex and in order to answer it, Augustine is called upon to witness. But it seems that Hilary's position contradicts that of Augustine: the Son possesses the divine essence, it is completely in him so that it seems that the divine essence is born. Hilary's texts are taken from several books of the *De Trinitate*; they are quoted in nos. 9–11 in the following order: IV, no. 10 (*PL* 10, 103A) and V, no. 37 (*PL* 10, 155A), IX, no. 51 (*PL* 10, 322B–323A), IX, no. 53 (*PL* 10, 324A), IV, no. 14 (*PL* 10, 107C), V, no. 37 (*PL* 10, 155A–B). Hilary's position is clearly expounded: the truth of the nature of the Father is found in the Son since in him God is God, "For there is one in one and one from one".[106] In

---

eum secutum arbitror in aeternitatis vocabulo nisi quod Pater non habet Patrem de quo sit, Filius autem de Patre est ut sit atque ut illi coaeternus sit.

[104] Est autem ineffabilis quidam complexus Patris et Imaginis, qui non est sine perfruitione, sine caritate, sine gaudio.

[105] Ecce habes qualiter verba Hilarii praemissa accipienda sint, licet tantae sint profunditatis, ut etiam adhibita expositione vix aliquatenus ea intelligere valeat humanus sensus, cum et ipsa eorum explanatio, quam hic Augustinus edidit, plurimum in se habeat difficultatis et ambiguitatis.

[106] Est enim unus in uno et unus ab uno.

chapter 2 of the same 5th distinction, Hilary is quoted to show that the Son was not born "ex nihilo"; in chapter 3, Peter Lombard quotes Hilary in conclusion: "He is son by nature, for he possesses the same nature as the one who begat him".[107]

– I, d. 12, ch. 2, no. 5. Hilary is quoted here (*De Trinitate*, XII, nos. 55–57 (*PL* 10, 469A–471 et seq.)) to explain how the Holy Spirit is from the Father through the Son and is sent from the Father through the Son: "In the Holy Spirit, issuing from you and sent through him".[108] "Before the beginning of time your Only One dwelt, having been born from you, so that your Holy Spirit is from you through him; what I do not perceive through my senses, I maintain nevertheless through my conscience: for before your spiritual realities I am numb".[109] Peter Lombard specifies in conclusion how the words of Hilary are to be understood: "One should not understand these words as if the Holy Spirit is from the Father and the Son and that he is sent from both; but in this sense that the Son receives from the Father, that through him the Holy Spirit is and is sent. This is what Hilary intended to convey, making a verbal distinction to show that authority is vested in the Father".[110]

– I, d. 34, ch. 1. Here Peter Lombard expounds the conclusion of the controversy between Gilbert de la Porré and his accusers at the Consistory of Rheims (1148). In support of his thesis, Gilbert quoted texts from Hilary to distinguish between the nature of God and the person; the divine essence cannot at the same time be the Father and the Son without causing confusion. The Master of the Sentences, following the Consistory of Rheims in this, re-established Hilary's orthodox opinion by quoting from the *De Trinitate*, VIII, nos. 21–22 (*PL* 10, 252A–253A): "We are all spiritual beings if the spirit of God is in us. But this spirit of God is the spirit of Christ, so that if the spirit of Christ is in us, it is the spirit which brought Christ back to life. Thus if the spirit of him who brought Christ back to life is in us, it is the spirit of Christ which is in us; however, the spirit which

---

[107] Natura filius est, quia eandem naturam quam ille qui genuit habet.

[108] In Sancto Spiritu tuo, ex te profecto et per eum misso.

[109] Ante tempora Unigenitus tuus ex te natus manet, ita quod ex te per eum Sanctus Spiritus tuus est; quod etsi sensu non percipiam, tamen teneo conscientia: in spiritualibus enim rebus tuis hebes sum.

[110] Quod non est intelligendum, quasi a Patre et Filio est et mittitur ab utroque; sed hoc ipsum habet Filius a Patre, ut ab ipso et sit et mittatur Spiritus Sanctus. Hoc ergo voluit significare Hilarius, distinctionem faciens in locutione, ut ostenderet in Patre esse auctoritatem.

is in us is also the spirit of God ... and thus God and the spirit of God are not the same thing".[111] A discussion is then engaged in which leads to the conclusion: "Thus in the Trinity we must not distinguish between nature and the matter of nature as in the case of created realities, for, as Hilary says 'to compare terrestrial realities with God serves no purpose; and if one provides some examples in this comparison, no-one considers that these examples contain in themselves the perfection of absolute reason'; 'God is not to be spoken of in human words'".[112]

The De Synodis

As we have already said, the De Synodis is quoted 8 times in Book I and once in Book III. I. Brady has remarked that Peter Lombard only read Hilary's treatise after he had edited the Sententiae. This is why, as he became acquainted with it, he inserted the texts in marginal glosses. Once, in I, d. 31, ch. 1, no. 3 (I, 224), the expression "resemblance is a non-different essence"[113] appears in the first edition of the Sententiae, whilst in the second edition one reads "resemblance is a non-difference",[114] as though Peter Lombard meant that the Father and the Son are called similar because they are not different.

Moreover, I. Brady has picked out in the third edition of the Sententiae the marginal glosses added by Peter Lombard after the definitive compilation of the Sententiae.

The Use of Patristic Sources

A quick analysis of the principal patristic sources of the Sententiae testifies to a fairly broad knowledge of the texts. It is certain that

---

[111] Spirituales omnes sumus, si in nobis est spiritus Dei. Sed et hic spiritus Dei est et spiritus Christi. Et cum Christi spiritus in nobis est, eius spiritus in nobis est qui suscitavit Christum. Et cum eius qui suscitavit Christum in nobis est spiritus, et spiritus in nobis est Christi; nec tamen non Dei est spiritus qui in nobis est ... et secundum hoc non idem est Deus et quod Dei.

[112] Itaque in Trinitate non ita distinguendum est inter naturam et rem naturae sicut in rebus creatis, quia ut ait Hilarius, "comparatio terrenorum ad Deum nulla est; et si qua comparationum exempla interdum afferuntur, nemo ea existimet absolutae in se rationis perfectionem continere"; "non enim humano sensu de Deo loquendum est".

[113] Similitudo est indifferens essentia.

[114] Similitudo est indifferentia.

Peter Lombard read a number of documents in order to compile the commentaries on the Psalms and on the Epistles of St. Paul. Apart from the *Glossa interlinearis* and the *Glossa ordinaria*, he availed himself of the works of his predecessors, some of whom had been his teachers, from the *De sacramentis christianae fidei* of Hugues de Saint-Victor to the *Summa sententiarum*, taking in the most diverse *Sententiae*, the *Summa divinae paginae* of Peter of Poitiers and the writings of Abelard.

As we have often had occasion to stress, the knowledge of the Fathers which he had acquired, was a partial one. The exact position of Augustine, Hilary and John Damascene on certain very complex questions was difficult to unravel, with the result that Peter Lombard handed down to the Middle Ages "opinions" that were often far from certain. Certainly, throughout the *Sententiae*, he was able to show proof of an uncommon balance, removed from all polemics or risky opinions.

In each of the books of the *Sententiae* we have chosen a distinction, the analysis of which will enable us at one and the same time to realize the genius of Peter Lombard and a sense of tradition which is, moreover, in conformity with medieval methodology. The influence of Abelard often makes itself felt in the conciliatory way in which Peter Lombard resolves divergent texts: "texts which seem to contradict each other, we so resolve them".[115]

I, d. 16

Let us take as an example distinction 16 of Book I on the visible mission of the Holy Spirit. The distinction is divided into two chapters; from the beginning of the first chapter, the difference between the two ways in which the mission is unfolded is expounded: the visible mission and the invisible mission.[116] No. 2 quotes an extract from Augustine's *De Trinitate*, ch. 5, no. 10 (*PL* 42, 851; *CCL* 50, 93) to show how the temporal movement of the Holy Spirit signifies his spiritual mission: "One then immediately sees why one speaks also of mission with regard to the Holy Spirit. A visible form has been extracted from time to permit the Holy Spirit to manifest himself visibly, as on the occasion of his descent on Christ under the appearance of a dove or, when, ten days after Christ's Ascension, the day of

---

[115] Quae sibi contradicere videntur sic determinamus.
[116] Cf. Peter Lombard's primitive *Glossa* on Rom. II (I, 90* 10–11).

Pentecost, there suddenly broke out a sort of violent storm in the heavens and one saw tongues of fire divide and settle on each of the Apostles. It is that intervention, manifested visibly to the eyes of mortal men, which has been called the mission of the Holy Spirit. It was not a question of the Holy Spirit showing himself in his own substance—as such he is invisible and immutable like the Father and the Son—but to strike the hearts of men by an external demonstration in order to bring them from the temporal demonstration of him who was coming to the mysterious eternity of him who is always present".[117] In no. 3, Peter Lombard then poses the inevitable question: in this temporal manifestation the Holy Spirit does not appear in his substance, but within the forms of a concrete image, a dove or tongues of fire. Does this manifestation mean that the Holy Spirit is lesser than the Father, exactly as the Son is, inasmuch as he has been sent on a mission? No. 4 expounds moreover how the Son is lesser than the Father—inasmuch as he is one who is sent—with the help of an extract from book IV of Augustine's *De Trinitate*, ch. 19, no. 26 (*PL* 42, 905; *CCL* 50, 194), which Peter Lombard read in the *Expositio* of Florus: "*God sent his Son fashioned from a woman, fashioned under the Law*, so small that he was 'fashioned' and sent on account of having been 'fashioned'. But if it is the superior who sends the inferior, let us too recognize that he who is fashioned or made is inferior, inferior inasmuch as he is made, made inasmuch as he is sent".[118] As the Son is less than the Father, inasmuch as he is sent, can the Master then answer the question asked: why not say the same thing of the Holy Spirit? The answer has to be "no", because the Holy Spirit did not become a dove whereas the Son did become

---

[117] In promptu est intelligere de Spiritu sancto cur missus est et ipse dicatur. Facta est enim quaedam creaturae species ex tempore, in qua visibiliter ostenderetur Spiritus sanctus, sive cum in ipsum Dominum corporali specie columbae descendit, sive die Pentecostes factus est subito de caelo sonus, quasi ferretur flatus vehemens, et visae sunt illis linguae divisae sicut ignis, qui et insedit super unumquemque eorum. Haec operatio visibiliter expressa et oculis oblata mortalibus, missio Spiritus sancti dicta est: non ut appareret eius ipsa substantia, qua et ipse invisibilis et incommutabilis est sicut Pater et Filius, sed ex exterioribus visis corda hominum commota, a temporali manifestatione venientis ad occultam aeternitatem semper praesentis converteruntur. Cf. The *Florilegia* of Florus Lugdunensis and the primitive *Glossa* on Rom. II,36.

[118] *Misit Deus Filium suum factum ex muliere, factum sub Lege*: usque adeo parvum, ut factum; eo itaque missum quo factum. Fateamur ergo factum minorem, et in tantum minorem, in quantum factum, et in tantum factum, in quantum missum. Cf. the primitive *Glossa* on Rom. II,36 (I, 91*32–35).

man. And to quote in support of this a text from book II of the *De Trinitate*, ch. 6, no. 11 (*PL* 42, 851–852; *CCL* 50, 93–94): "Nowhere does Scripture say of God the Father that he is superior to the Holy Spirit, or of the Holy Spirit that he is inferior to God the Father. The reason is that the creature assumed to manifest the Holy Spirit is not analogous to the case of the Son of Man in whom the person of the divine Word himself became present to us. We must not believe that the Son of Man in fact possessed the Word of God in the way of the other wise men and saints, although "unparalleled among his rivals", nor that he possessed it to a greater extent to the point of surpassing the other saints in wisdom; but that he was the Word of God himself. Indeed, the Word in flesh and the Word made flesh are not the same thing; in other words, there is a difference between the Word in man and Man-the-Word. Here the word flesh is synonymous to "man": *The Word was made flesh*, as in this text: *All flesh shall see the salvation of God.* It is not a question here of flesh without soul or spirit, but "all flesh" means "every man". Certainly, the creature in which the Holy Spirit manifested himself was not assumed as was flesh and humanity in the womb of the Virgin Mary. The Holy Spirit did not fill the dove with joy, nor the wind, nor the fire; nor did he definitively join these beings to his personal individuality".[119]

In chapter 2, no. 1 continues the discussion: the Son made man is less than the Father and the Holy Spirit. This is confirmed in no. 2 by a text from book I of the *De Trinitate*, ch. 7, no. 14 (*PL* 42, 828; *CCL* 50, 45), a text which Peter Lombard read in the *Expositio* of Florus: "This was a source of error for people insufficiently attentive to examine Scripture and take account of the totality of the sacred text. They tried to transpose what Scripture says of Christ Jesus as man to his nature which was eternal before the Incarnation and which

---

[119] Ideo nusquam scriptum est quod Deus Pater maior sit Spiritu sancto, vel Spiritus sanctus minor Deo Patre, quia non sic est assumpta creatura in qua appareret Spiritus sanctus, sicut assumptus est filius hominis, in qua forma ipsius Dei Verbi persona praesentaretur: non ut haberet Verbum Dei, sicut alii sancti sapientes, sed prae participibus suis; non utique quod amplius habebat Verbum ut esset quam ceteri excellentiore sapientia, sed quod ipsum Verbum erat. Aliud est enim Verbum in carne, aliud Verbum caro, id est aliud Verbum in homine, aliud Verbum homo. Caro enim pro homine posita est in eo quod ait: *Verbum caro factum est.*, sicut et illud: *Et videbit omnis caro salutare Dei.* Non enim sine anima vel sine mente, sed ita omnis caro ac si diceretur "omnis homo". Non ergo sic est assumpta creatura in qua appareret Spiritus sanctus, sicut assumpta est caro illa et humana forma ex Virgine Maria. Neque enim columbam beatificavit Spiritus, vel illum flatum vel illum ignem sibique et personae suae in unitatem habitumque coniunxit in aeternum.

is still eternal. They claim that the Son is inferior to the Father because the Lord himself said in the Scriptures: *The Father is greater than me.* But truth shows that in the same sense the Son is inferior to himself. How, in fact, would he not have become inferior to himself, he who *emptied himself, taking on the condition of a slave?* He by no means took on the condition of a slave by losing his condition as God, in which he was equal to the Father. So if he took on the condition of a slave without losing the condition of God, since as slave and as God he is the same and unique Son of God the Father—as God, equal to the Father, as slave, the mediator between God and men, the man Christ Jesus—who does not see that, as God, he is superior to himself, and as a slave inferior to himself? Scripture is therefore justified in making these two affirmations: The Son is equal to the Father, the Father is greater than the Son. In the one, one sees a consequence of his divine condition, in the other a consequence of his condition as a slave, without any confusion";[120] and in no. 3, another text from book II, ch. 1, no. 2 (*PL* 42, 845; *CCL* 50, 81): "The Son of God and the equal of the Father as far as his divinity is concerned, which is his essential condition, and as inferior to the Father in accordance with his state as a slave which he assumed and which made him become inferior, not only to the Father, but also to the Holy Spirit, indeed 'inferior to himself'".[121] Peter Lombard adds to this text an extract from the *Contra Maximinum*. In fact it is an extract from the *Epistola 170 ad Maximum medicum*, no. 9 (*PL* 33, 750; *CSEL* 44, 629): "This is why he became inferior, not only to the Father, but also to

---

[120] Erraverunt homines minus diligenter scrutantes vel intuentes universam seriem scripturarum, et ea quae de Christo Iesu secundum hominem dicta sunt, ad eius substantiam quae ante incarnationem sempiterna erat et sempiterna est transferre conati sunt. Et illi quidem dicunt minorem Filium esse quam Pater est quia scriptum est ipso Domino dicente: *Pater maior me est.* Veritas autem ostendit secundum istum modum etiam se ipso minorem Filium. Quomodo enim non etiam se ipso minor factus est, qui *se ipsum exinanavit formam servi accipiens?* Neque enim sic accepit formam servi ut amitteret formam Dei, in qua erat aequalis Patri. Si ergo accepta est forma servi ut non amitteretur forma Dei, cum et in forma servi Dei idem ipse sit Filius unigenitus Dei Patris, in forma Dei aequalis Patri, in forma servi mediator Dei et hominum homo Christus Iesus, quis non intelligat quod in forma Dei etiam ipse se ipso maior est, in forma autem servi etiam se ipso minor est? Non itaque immerito Scriptura utrumque dicit, et aequalem Patri Filium, et Patrem maiorem Filio. Illud enim propter formam Dei, hoc autem propter formam servi sine ulla confusione intelligitur.

[121] Dei Filius et aequalis Patri secundum Dei formam in qua est, et minor Patre secundum formam servi quam accepit, in qua forma non solum Patre, sed etiam Spiritu sancto, neque hoc tantum, sed etiam se ipso minor inventus est.

himself and the Holy Spirit, and *became slightly lower than the angels*".[122]
A new text of the *De Trinitate*, taken from book I, ch. 7, no. 14 (*PL*
42, 829; *CCL* 50, 46), to be found in Florus, ends this long list of
authorities: "The Son of God is thus by nature the equal of the
Father, in his state inferior to God the Father, in the condition of a
slave which he assumed".[123] Peter Lombard can therefore conclude
that the Son, in the form of a servant is less than the Father, less
than himself and less than the Holy Spirit.

In no. 4, the Master of the Sentences seems to come back to his
conclusion when he expresses a doubt experienced in reading Hilary
of Poitiers. According to the latter, the Father is called greater than
the Son by virtue of his "authority", because he possesses in himself,
as Father, the power to beget; moreover, the Son confesses this, saying:
The Father is greater than me; and St. Paul confirms this: *Donavit ei nomen
quod est super omne nomen* (Phil. 2,9). Paul's reflection is another way of
saying what Jesus said. There then follows, as though in conclusion,
a long extract from Hilary's *De Trinitate*, no. 54 (*PL* 10, 325A–B):
"So if the Father is greater than the Son on account of the power
which he has to enable him to be what he is, would the latter be
inferior from the fact that he recognizes that he has received this?
The one who gives is greater, but the one who receives is not inferior, for it is given to him to be one with the Father. In fact he says:
The Father and I are one. If it had not been given to Jesus to be proclaimed as being *in the glory of God the Father*, he would be inferior to
the Father; but if it has been given to him to dwell in the glory
which is that of the Father, at one· and the same time you take note
that the Father is greater, from the fact that he has the power to
make a gift to the Son, and that both are one, from the fact that we
proclaim that it is given to Jesus to be in the glory of the Father. So
that is why the Father is greater than the Son. Oh yes he is greater
than the one to whom he bestows to be all that he is himself; he is
greater than the one to whom he grants, through the mystery of his
birth, to be the image of the Unborn One; greater than him whom
he begets of himself, in his divine state".[124] And Peter Lombard adds

---

[122] Propter quam, non tantum Patre, sed etiam se ipso et Spiritu sancto minor
factus est, et etiam *minoratus paulo minus ab Angelis*.

[123] Est ergo Dei Filius, Deo Patri natura aequalis, habitu minor, id est in forma
servi quam accepit. Cf. the *Glossa* of Peter Lombard on Phil. 2,6–7 (*PL* 192, 234A–B).

[124] Si igitur, donantis auctoritate Pater maior est, numquid per doni confessionem
Filius minor est? Maior itaque donans est, sed minor iam non est cui unum esse

in conclusion: "You have heard, reader, what Hilary says on this subject. Note his words attentively wherever they are to be found and piously understand them".[125] The way in which the material amassed in this distinction is presented is to be found in most of the distinctions of the *Sententiae*.

We see six texts of Augustine quoted, taken from books II, IV, II, I, II, I of the *De Trinitate*. These texts, in reality, are not without a strong connecting thread. The last quotation comes from Book I and reproduces the essentials of the "regula ex Scriptura" enounced by Augustine. And, moreover, Hilary's text is very well chosen by Peter Lombard, as witness to the tradition which he inherited.

II, d. 17

Book II of the *Sententiae* is devoted to the work of creation. Distinction 17 researches how souls are created. The essential texts will be borrowed from Augustine's *Super Genesim*. We have already seen that Peter Lombard unvaryingly attributes to Augustine all the texts of the *Glossa*, giving them this general title. These texts are sometimes borrowed from the *De Genesi ad litteram*. We shall realize this when we read distinction 17 of Book II.

In chapter 1, no. 1 raises the question of the origin of the soul: is it created from something or not, when is it created, what grace does it receive at its creation? The initial biblical text is Gen. 2,7: *Formavit Deus hominem de limo terrae et inspiravit in faciem eius spiraculum vitae.* Thus God formed the body of man from the slime of the earth and "breathed" into him a soul, or, as the Septuagint version has it, "flavit" vel "sufflavit".

In no. 2, Peter Lombard quotes Bede's commentary on Gen. 2,7 (*PL* 91, 42C–D and 43B–C; *CCL* 118A, 44 et seq.): "We do not hold that God physically fashioned his body with corporeal hands or

---

donatur. Ait enim: *Ego et Pater unum sumus.* Si non hoc donatur Iesu, ut confitendus sit *in gloria Dei Patris*, minor Patre est; si autem in ea gloria ei donatur esse qua Pater est, habes et in donantis auctoritate quia maior est, et in donati confessione quia unum sunt. Maior itaque Pater Filio est, et plane maior, cui tantum donat esse quantus est ipse; cui innascibilitatis esse imaginem sacramento nativitatis impertit, quem ex se in forma sua generat.

[125] Audisti, lector, quid super hoc dicat Hilarius, cuius verba, ubicumque occurrunt, diligenter nota pieque intellige (I, 141 21–22). We shall study later how Peter Lombard quotes Augustine's *De Trinitate* in his *Glossa super epistolas beati Pauli*. Here Peter Lombard repeats what he said in his *Glossa* on Ps. 138,16 (*PL* 191, 1217B).

that from his throat he breathed in the soul";[126] the *Glossa interlinearis* (*Biblia*, 19b) translates the "formavit" of the Bible by the words "iubendo, volendo" used by Bede who continues: "that he was made corporeally, that is to say soul and body from slime, but rather that the soul was created from nothing by the breath of God . . . Thus God fashioned man from slime, that is to say that by his word he commanded that he should be made from slime. He breathed on to his face a breath of life, that is the substance of the soul and spirit by which he would live, thus he created it".[127] (*Biblia*, 20b). In no. 4, following Augustine, Peter Lombard expounds the position of heretics; without quoting it, he summarizes what is expounded in the *Glossa ordinaria* (*Biblia*, 20b–21a).

In no. 5, Augustine's reply is given to the position of heretics. Now, we are dealing with Bede's commentary reproduced in the *Glossa ordinaria* (*Biblia*, 21a): "One must not listen to those who think that the soul is part of God. For if this were so, (man) could not be deceived either by himself or another, nor be led to do wrong or to suffer, nor to change for the better or the worse. The breath which animated man comes from God, but it is not God. And the breath of man is not part of the one who made him".[128]

In chapter 2, the question is raised as to the moment of the creation of the soul, whether before the body or at the same time? Augustine's opinion is quoted first, according to the "*Super Genesim*", which the *Glossa ordinaria* reproduces word for word, which makes one think that the text of no. 2 is not by Augustine, but is attributed to him in the *Glossa*: "We are trying to find out if the soul was forcibly incorporated. But it is better to think that this was done naturally when God created it; as it is natural for us to want to live. To live a bad life is not natural, but comes from a perverse will"[129]

---

[126] Non ergo carnaliter putemus Deum corporeis manibus formasse corpus vel faucibus inspirasse animam.

[127] Factus sit corpore, scilicet et anima et corpus de limo, anima vero de nihilo Deo inspirante creata est . . . Formavit ergo de limo hominem, id est verbo suo de limo fieri iussit. Inspiravit in faciem eius spiraculum vitae, substantiam, scilicet animae et spiritus in qua viveret, creavit.

[128] Non sunt audiendi qui putant esse partem Dei. Si enim hoc esset, nec a se, nec ab alio decipi posset, nec ad malum faciendum vel patiendum compelli, nec in melius vel deterius immutari. Filius autem quo hominem animavit factus est a Deo, non de Deo. Nec flatus hominis pars ipsius est quem facit non de se ipso.

[129] Quaeri solet utrum si velit incorporari compellatur? Sed melius traditur hoc naturaliter velle, id est sic creari ut velit: sicut naturale nobis est velle vivere. Male autem vivere non naturae, sed voluntatis perversae.

(*Biblia*, 21a). The text of this *Glossa* is slightly different from that given by Peter Lombard which is the following: "God wished it naturally, that is to say that he created the soul as he wished, as it is natural for us to want to live. To want to live a bad life is not a natural thing, but comes from a perverse will".[130]

No. 3 expounds the opinion of other authorities, including Bede and Hugues de Saint-Victor, on the text: "He breathed on his face a breath of life, that is the substance of the soul and spirit by which he will live; thus he created it"[131] (*Biblia*, 20b). Peter Lombard rejects this opinion in no. 4 and in no. 5 comes back to Augustine's opinion: "It has to be said that the soul too was not created, because of advance knowledge as to what its future would be, just or unjust"[132] (*Biblia*, 21a).

Chapter 3, except for Peter Lombard's conclusion, is to be found in the *Glossa ordinaria* under the name of Augustine: "One wonders if God suddenly created man in his virile state, making him perfect and making him grow in age, as now he fashions him in the womb of his mother. In whatever way God acts, he does so in a way which is in corformity with his omnipotence and wisdom. Thus he issued temporal laws with their types and their qualities, in such a way that his will is established over all things. In fact, by his power, he fixed the number of creatures, he did not bind his power to things, but he fixed the days when the rod of Moses would be changed into a serpent. Such things are not against nature, unless the natural course of things appears to us in a different way from that in which it appears to God who created it. Thus Adam was created as an adult; he made him in accordance with the causal reason following which he created up to then; otherwise he would not have created him in his work of six days. He did not make him against his predisposition, although for he was in the first condition of causes. Thus man could have been created, but it was not necessary. For creation was not up to the creature, it was the work of the good pleasure of the Creator whose will has necessarily to be followed. We know the nature of creatures from experience, but we do not know how they will evolve

---

[130] Naturaliter illud voluit, id est creata fuit ut vellet, sicut naturale nobis est velle vivere. Male autem velle vivere non naturae, sed voluntatis est perversae.

[131] *Inspiravit in faciem eius spiraculum vitae*, substantiam scilicet animae et spiritus in qua viveret, creavit.

[132] Dicendum est etiam animam non sic esse creatam ut praescia esset operis futuri, iusti vel iniusti.

in the future. In nature, the young man normally grows old, but we do not know if that is the will of God. What happens, happens according to what he wishes and knows in advance. A lot of things will take place in accordance with inferior causes: but in the foreknowledge of God, they are not in the future. In other words, future things are as he who cannot err has foreseen them"[133] (*Biblia*, 20b).

In chapter 4, Peter Lombard, relying on the Bible, affirms that man created outside paradise was then placed in it.

Chapter 5 seeks to define the nature of this paradise with the help of the *Glossa ordinaria* which he transcribes word for word: "Three opinions about paradise have been expressed: the first is that of those who only understand it in a physical way; the second is that of those who understand it spiritually; the third comprises both ways. I confess that the third opinion pleases me most: man formed from slime was placed in a bodily paradise, which enables us to understand that Adam is the man of the future, for he is man in his own nature"[134] (*Biblia*, 21a). As to the time of the creation of paradise, Bede replies in the *Glossa ordinaria* reproduced by Peter Lombard: "At that time God planted paradise. He ordered that the earth, emerging from the waters, should produce herbs and trees"[135] (*Biblia*, 21a). The conclusion

---

[133] Quaeritur utrum Deus repente hominem in aetate virili fecerit: an perficiendo et aetate augendo, sicut nunc format in matris utero? Sed quidquid horum fecerit, hoc fecit quod Deum omnipotentem et sapientem decuit. Ita enim temporum leges generibus qualitatibusque rerum distribuit: ut voluntas sua super omnia sit. Potentia enim sua numeros creaturarum dedit: non ipsam eis alligavit, nec exspectati sunt dies, ut virga Moysi verteret in draconem. Nec talia contra naturam sunt, nisi nobis quibus aliter naturae cursus innotuit, Deo autem est natura quod fecit. Sic Adam in aetate virili continuo factus est; quem tamen fecit secundum causalem rationem in qua prius factus est, alioquin enim eum in sex dierum operibus non fecerat. Neque enim contra dispositionem suam faceret: erat enim in prima causarum conditione. Sic hominem fieri posse: sed non ibi erat necesse. Hoc enim non erat in conditione creaturae, sed in beneplacito creatoris: cuius voluntas necessitas est. Nos autem in rebus temporaliter exortis scimus quid cuiusque natura sit: quod experimento accipimus, sed utrum futurum sit, ignoramus. In natura iuvenis est ut senescat: sed utrum in Dei voluntate sit, nescimus. Hoc enim necessario futurum est, quod vult et praescit. Multa vero secundum inferiores causas futura sunt: sed in praescientia Dei futura non sunt. Si autem ibi aliter sunt, potius futura sunt sicut ibi sunt ubi praescit qui non potest falli.

[134] Tres generales sententiae de paradiso sunt: una eorum qui corporaliter tantum intelligi volunt. Alia eorum qui spiritualiter tantum. Tertia vero eorum qui utroque modo paradisum accipiunt. Tertiam mihi placere fateor, ut homo factus ex limo quod corpus humanum est: in paradiso corporali locatus intelligatur quomodo Adam, et si aliud significat, quia est forma futuri: in natura propria homo accipitur.

[135] Ab illo principio plantavit paradisum: quo terram omnem remotis aquis, herbas et ligna producere iussit.

of this chapter summarizes the *Glossa* of Bede and of Strabo.

Chapter 6 expounds what the tree of life planted in paradise was, following the *Glossa* of Bede: "The tree of life is so called because it was given such a strength that he who ate of it would receive stable bodily health, and that he would not be affected by any sickness and could not be struck by the passing of years or old age"[136] (*Biblia*, 21b).

Chapter 7 describes the tree of the knowledge of good and evil, with the help of Augustine from whom Peter Lombard quotes two long passages taken from book VIII of the *De Genesi ad litteram*, passages summarized in the *Glossa ordinaria* (*Biblia*, 21b): "So the tree was not bad, but it is called the tree of the knowledge of good and evil, because after being forbidden, it was in this future transgression that man would learn by experience what constituted obedience with regard to good and disobedience with regard to evil; its name does not come from the fruit which it would bear, but from what would follow transgression".[137]

So in this distinction 17, Peter Lombard has scarcely done other than to use the *Glossa ordinaria* on Genesis. It would be necessary to study in detail the relationship which exists between the *Glossa ordinaria* and the *De Genesi ad litteram* in order to determine precisely what is derived from Augustine and what is Lombard's compilation.

III, d. 19

In the Christology which takes up Book III of the *Sententiae*, distinction 19 deals with the question of Christ the Redeemer and Mediator in seven chapters. We have here a very significant example of the use Peter Lombard made of patristic sources through his *Glossae* on the Psalms and the Epistles of St. Paul. Very often, he departs from the *Glossa interlinearis* or the *Glossa ordinaria* of unknown authorship, to finish with the text of the *Sententiae*. This will become clear as we analyse distinction 19.

---

[136] Lignum vitae dictum est quia divinitus accepit hanc vim, ut qui ex eo manducaret, corpus eius stabili sanitate firmaretur, nec ulla infirmitate, vel aetate in deterius vel in occasum laberetur.

[137] Arbor ergo non erat mala, sed scientiae dicta noscendi bonum et malum, quia post prohibitionem erat in illa transgressio futura: qua homo experiendo disceret, quid esset inter obedientiae bonum et inobedientiae malum, nec de fructu qui nasceretur inde positum est nomen: sed de ipsa re quae transgressionem secuta est.

Chapter 1 of this distinction expounds how Christ by his death delivers us from Satan and from sin. The question is formulated in no. 2 to which the *Glossa* on Rom. 5,8 (*PL* 191, 1383–1387) proffers the reply: "Because by his death, as the Apostle says, he is commended to us, that is to say that the marvellous and loving kindness of God towards us is made apparent inasmuch as he sent his son to die for us sinners . . . Therefore the death of Christ justifies us now that through it love is enkindled in our hearts".[138]

In question here is a summary of Peter Lombard's *Glossa* (= *Glossa PL*) on Rom. 5,8–10 (*PL* 191, 1386C) which comes from Augustine's *De Trinitate* via Florus of Lyons: "But if God loved us beforehand, how are we reconciled to him through the death of Christ and freed from his wrath? We say to this that the wrath of God which judges gently is nothing other than his just vengeance . . . From which follows rightly: for if by the death of his Son, as if he said: truly living he could save those who were his friends".[139] We have to add to this the *Glossa PL* on Rom. 6,3–5 (*PL* 191, 1403B–D): "For the death of Christ and his resurrection are not only realities, they are sacraments. For every act of Christ on the Cross, in his tomb, in the Resurrection, in the Ascension, in his sitting on his throne at the right hand of the Father, is such an act that it configures the Christian life in its mystical reality".[140] This last Gloss is taken from Augustine's *Enchiridion*.

In no. 3, the same conclusion is taken up again in different terms via the *Glossa PL* on Rom. 3,25 (*PL* 191, 1362B), starting with the *Glossa interlinearis* (*Biblia*, IV, 281a): "By faith in his blood, that is to say by faith in his Passion, or rather by faith and by his Passion; the one does not go without the other".[141] The *Glossa PL* takes up these terms again: "By faith in his blood, that is to say by faith in his

---

[138] Quia per eius mortem, ut ait Apostolus, commendatur nobis caritas Dei, id est apparet eximia et commendabilis caritas Dei erga nos, in hoc quod Filium suum tradidit in mortem pro nobis peccatoribus . . . Mors igitur Christi nos iustificat, dum per eam caritas excitatur in cordibus nostris.

[139] Sed si ante nos diligebat Deus, quomodo per mortem Christi ei sumus reconciliati, et ab ira liberati? Ad quod dicimus, quod ira Dei, qui cum tranquillitate judicat, nihil est aliud quam justa vindicta . . . Unde recte sequitur: Si enim per mortem Filii, quasi dicat: Vere jam vivens poterit amicos factos salvare.

[140] Mors enim Christi et resurrectio, non tantum res, sed etiam sacramenta sunt. Quidquid enim gestum est in cruce Christi, in sepultura, in resurrectione, in ascensione, et in sedere ad dexteram Patris, ita gestum est, ut his rebus mystice non tantum dictis, sed gestis, configuretur vita christiana.

[141] Per fidem in sanguine eius, id est per fidem passionis vel per fidem et per passionem; neutrum enim sine altero valet.

Passion without which nothing is pleasing to God. Or rather, by faith in his blood, that is to say by faith and by his Passion. He joins the two together, for neither one goes without the other".[142]

In no. 4, we leave the *Glossa interlinearis* (*Biblia*, II, 538a), and go on to Ps. 68,5: "This is gratuitous: I have not sinned and I have suffered; I have not stolen, and this because it so pleases you",[143] which Peter Lombard paraphrases somewhat.

In no. 5, the exposition is headed: *Augustinus in libro de baptismo parvulorum*. In actual fact, it has to do with an explanation of the *Glossa PL* on Hebr. 2,14 (*PL* 192, 421B–D): "We had fallen under the dominion of the prince of this age who seduced Adam and made him his slave, and began to possess us as his slaves. But the Redeemer came who vanquished the seducer. And so, what did the Redeemer do? He laid a trap, he presented his Cross as a prey, his blood . . . He shed his blood so as to wash us from our sins".[144] Peter Lombard has quoted word for word his *Glossa* on Hebr. 2,14, and continues: "So the devil had us, but he was conquered by the blood of the Redeemer: for he held us by the bonds of our sins, like the chains of captives. The Redeemer came, *he held him* by the bonds of his Passion; he entered *into his house*, that is to say into the hearts where he dwelt, and destroyed *his power*, that is to say us, whom he had filled with his bitterness. Our God, destroying his power and making it his own, dissipated the bitterness and filled us with gentleness by his death, redeeming us from our sins and making us sharers in his glory".[145] The text of Matthew 12,29 is thus proposed in the *Glossa interlinearis* (*Biblia*, IV, 44b) by Florus of Lyons: "He bound the

---

[142] Per fidem in sanguine eius, id est per fidem passionis, sine qua nihil places Deo. Vel, per fidem in sanguine ipsius, id est per fidem et passionem. Haec simul jungit, quia neutrum sine altero valet.

[143] Hoc est gratis: non peccavi, et penas dedi; non rapui, vel hoc ideo quia tibi placet.

[144] Incideramus enim in principem huius saeculi qui seduxit Adam et servum fecit, et coepit nos tanquam vernaculos possidere. Sed venit Redemptor et victus est deceptor. Et quid fecit Redemptor? Tetendit muscipulam, crucem suam posuit ibi quasi escam, sanguinem suum . . . Ille quippe sanguinem suum fundit, ut peccata nostra deleret.

[145] Unde ergo diabolus nos tenebat, deletum est sanguine Redemptoris: non enim tenebat nos nisi vinculis peccatorum nostrorum. Istae erant catenae captivorum. Venit ille, *alligavit fortem* vinculis passionis suae; intravit in *domum eius*, id est in corda eorum ubi ipse habitabat, et *vasa eius*, scilicet nos, eripuit; quae ille impleverat amaritudine sua. Deus autem noster, vasa eius eripiens et sua faciens, fudit amaritudinem et implevit dulcedinem per mortem suam a peccatis redimens et adoptionem gloriae filiorum largiens.

strong one, restrained his seduction of the elect and weakened his power".[146]

Chapter 2 is headed: *Cur Deus homo et mortuus.* The point of departure is the *Glossa ordinaria* on Hebr. 2,11 (*Biblia*, IV, 426a): "And he, in the same vein, shared in what was theirs, being a man who would conquer the devil: not in justice, but in violence, man would wrest his power from him; but if man were to conquer, losing his rights as a man, so that man should be the victor, it was necessary that God in him should make him sinless. For if it were a case of man on his own or an angel in man, he would easily sin. Thus it is evident that he knew himself to possess both natures".[147] Whence we have the *Glossa PL* (*PL* 192, 421D) in almost identical terms.

Chapter 3 raises very briefly the question: how and with what suffering did Christ deliver us by his death? Two glosses answer this, the first is the *Glossa PL* on Rom. 8,23 (*PL* 191, 1445A): "Thus, as to what adoption would mean, he expounds in speaking of the *redemption of our body*, that is to say that he redeems his body from death".[148] The second gloss is the *Glossa PL* on Rom. 6,6 (*PL* 191, 1405D): "I do not say that he should be no more, but that we should not be constrained to slavery, and indeed we are not any more . . . and so rising again in righteousness, we walk in a new way of life, we rise from virtue to virtue until we reach the right hand of God and see the God of gods as he is".[149]

Chapter 4 attempts to explain how Christ bore our punishment. The text of the *Sententiae* is composed of two extracts, the first from the *Glossa PL* on Rom. 3,26 (*PL* 191, 1362B–1363A). This is the text of the *Glossa interlinearis*: "Who bears our sins, that is to say the punishment due to our sins".[150] And this is the second text which shows how Christ bore the sins of those who preceded him: "Fulfilling his Passion he showed that he was the Just One in a manifestation

---

[146] Alligaverit fortem, a seductione electorum compescuerit potestatem ademerit.

[147] Et ipse similiter participavit eisdem nisi homo esset qui diabolum vinceret: non iuste, sed violenter homo ei tolleretur, sed si homo cum vincit, iure hominem perdit, et ut homo vincat necesse est ut Deus in eo sit qui faciat eum sine peccato esse. Si enim homo per se vel angelus in homine, facile peccaret cum et utramque naturam per se constat se scivisse.

[148] Deinde quid dixerit adoptionem exponit scilicet, *redemptionem corporis nostri*, scilicet ut ipsum corpus redimatur a mortalitate.

[149] Non dico ut non sit, sed ut non cogamur servire, et vere non cogimur . . . et sic ad bona resurgentes in novitate vitae ambulemus, de virtute in virtutem ascendentes, quousque in dextera Dei locati Deum deorum sicut est videamus.

[150] Qui peccata nostra, id est penam pro peccatis debitam.

necessary not only for the forgiveness of the sins of those present, but also for the forgiveness of the sins of those who had preceded his coming, the forgiveness of the sins of those who lived when God, without punishing them, was waiting to redeem them. This deferment on the part of God occurs when the sinner is not immediately punished, but when God in his patience calls him to repentance".[151]

Chapter 5 seems to be Peter Lombard's own compilation in order to show that Christ is at one and the same time the only Redeemer and the only Mediator. This text is worth quoting: "Thus he is properly called the Redeemer of the world and the Mediator between God and men. Now, the Son alone is termed Mediator in the Scriptures. Sometimes the Father and the Holy Spirit are called redeemers, simply because they manifest their power, not because they show humility and obedience. For it is in using his power and demonstrating his obedience, that the Son is rightly called the Redeemer, because he accomplished in himself that by which we are justified, and he carried out this justification by the power of his divinity with the Father and the Holy Spirit. He is therefore the Redeemer inasmuch as he is God through his power and inasmuch as he is man through his humility. He is more often called the Redeemer in accordance with his humanity, for in accordance with his humanity and in it, he received and celebrated the Sacraments which are the source of our Redemption. Thus the Son is correctly called the Redeemer".[152]

The study of Christ the Mediator starts with chapter 6. The introductory material reproduces the *Glossa PL* on 1 Tim. 2,5 (*PL* 192, 339A): "Stop at these words and read this: for there is *only one God*, as if he said: Truly he wishes all men to be saved, for there is only

---

[151] Quod cum implevit justum se esse ostendit, quae ostensio necessaria fuit, non solum pro remissione praesentium, sed etiam propter remissionem praecedentium delictorum, scilicet eorum quae praecesserunt Christi adventum, delictorum dico existentium in sustentatione Dei, Deo, scilicet patiente et non puniente tunc. Sustentatio enim Dei est, ubi peccator non statim punitur ut peccat, sed per patientiam Dei adducitur ad poenitentiam.

[152] Unde ipse vere dicitur mundi redemptor et Dei hominumque mediator. Sed mediator in Scriptura dicitur solus Filius; redemptor vero aliquando etiam Pater vel Spiritus sanctus, sed hoc propter usum potestatis, non propter exhibitionem humilitatis et obedientiae. Nam secundum potestatis simul et obedientiae usum, Filius proprie dicitur redemptor, quia in se explevit per quae iustificati sumus, et ipsam iustificationem est operatus potentia deitatis cum Patre et Spiritu sancto. Est igitur redemptor in quantum est Deus potestatis usu, et in quantum humilitatis effectu. Et saepius dicitur redemptor secundum humanitatem, quia secundum eam et in ea suscepit et implevit illa sacramenta quae sunt causa nostrae redemptionis. Proprie igitur Filius dicitur redemptor.

one God, the creator of everything, namely the Blessed Trinity; and *also a single mediator between God and men,* that is to say in order to establish peace as an intermediary arbitrator, namely *Christ Jesus,* made man for all men in order to be a mediator. He can only be an intermediary through man. This is the arbiter Job wished for when he said: *that he might be an arbiter for us".*[153]

In no. 2, we find a text from Augustine's *In Iohannem* taken up again in the *Glossa PL* on Rom. 5,10 (*PL* 191, 1384A–B) which comes from Florus, and likewise a second text from the *De Trinitate* reproduced from Florus in the same *Glossa PL* (*PL* 191, 1386C). These are the two texts: "That we should be reconciled with God through the death of Christ does not mean that Christ reconciles us with himself so as to start loving those whom he hated previously, as an enemy is reconciled with his foe in order that they should become friends and that those who previously hated each other should henceforth love each other . . . we were at enmity because of sin. Christ loved us so much even when we were at enmity with him by practising iniquity".[154] The very text of the *Sententiae* reproduces word for word that of the *Glossa PL.* This is the second text: "We were only enemies of God to the extent that our sins are enemies of justice: once these sins are forgiven, such enmity ceases; and those whom the Just One himself justifies are reconciled with him".[155]

No. 3 contains Peter Lombard's theological conclusion.

No. 4 asks the question why, if our sins are forgiven by the sole mediation of the Son, the Father and the Holy Spirit cannot also be

---

[153] Insiste litterae, et junge sic: *unus Deus* enim. Quasi dicat: Vere omnes homines vult salvos fieri, quia unus est Deus, creator omnium scilicet sancta Trinitas; et *unus est mediator Dei et hominum,* id est ad componendum pacem quasi medius arbiter, scilicet *Christus Jesus,* pro omnibus factus homo, ut sic esset mediator. Non enim aliter quam per hominem mediat. Hic est arbiter ille quem Job desiderat dicens, uter *"esset nobis arbiter".* It is interesting to compare the text of this *Glossa* with the text of no. 1 of the *Sententiae:* "Qui solus dicitur mediator, non Pater vel Spiritus sanctus. De quo Apostolus: *Unus mediator Dei et hominum, homo Christus Jesus,* id est per hominem quasi in medio arbiter est ad componendam pacem: id est ad reconciliandum homines Deo. Hic est arbiter quem Iob desiderat: *Utinam esset nobis arbiter".*

[154] Quod ergo nos reconciliati sumus Deo per mortem Christi, non sic est intelligendum, quasi ideo nos reconciliaverit ei Christus, ut jam inciperet amare quos oderat, sicut reconciliatur inimicus inimico, ut deinde sint amici, et se invicem diligant qui ante se invicem oderant . . . propter peccatum inimicitias habebamus. Habebat enim ille caritatem erga nos, etiam cum inimicitias exercebamus adversus eum, operando iniquitatem.

[155] Non enim inimici eramus Deo, nisi quemadmodum justitiae sunt inimica peccata, et ideo remissis peccatis tales inimicitiae finiuntur, et reconciliantur justo, quos ipse justificat.

called mediators. The answer takes up again what was said previously, namely that the entire Trinity is reconciled with us by its power, the Son in his humanity by his obedience.

Thus we come to the last chapter, chapter 7, in order to study in which nature Christ is mediator.

In no. 1, a preliminary answer is given by the *Glossa PL* on Gal. 3,20 (*PL* 192, 130A): "There cannot be a Mediator between God and God, for there is only one God, but between God and man, as though between two extremes".[156] The text which follows is taken from the *Confessiones*, transcribed in the *Glossa PL* on 1 Tim. 2,5 (*PL* 192, 339A–B): "The Mediator between God and men must have something resembling God and something resembling men; if he were completely like men, he would be too far away from God; if he were completely like God, he would be too far away from men—thus he would not be a Mediator. The true Mediator, Christ, between mortal sinners and the immortal Just One, made his appearance, immortal among men, just with regard to God".[157] An interpolation is taken from the *Glossa PL* on Ps. 29,2 (*PL* 191, 292C): "For in him that which is infirm brings him near to us".[158]

In no. 2, there is an intervention by the *Contra Eutychen* of Vigilius, transcribed in the *Glossa PL* on Gal. 3,20 (*PL* 192, 130C): "If then according to you, you heretics, Christ has only one nature, show how it comes about that he is the mediator between us and this nature: how does it come about that he is the mediator if he does not possess both natures? For you can only admit such a mediator between God and men if he is God through his divine nature and man through his human nature; you cannot show otherwise how men are reconciled with God. For, in coming, Christ united in himself the human and the divine by the communion of the two natures in one person. He thus reconciled all the faithful with God the Father by curing from the impiety of pride those who loved the humility of Christ by believing in him and imitated him in loving him".[159]

---

[156] Mediator autem esse non potest inter Deum et Deum, quia unus est Deus: sed inter Deum et hominem, quasi inter duo extrema.

[157] Mediator autem inter Deum et homines oportebat aliquid simile Deo, et aliquid simile hominibus, ne per omnia hominibus similis, longe esset a Deo, aut per omnia Deo similis longe esset ab hominibus, atque ita mediator non esset. Verax itaque mediator Christus inter mortales peccatores et immortalem justum apparuit immortalis cum hominibus, justus cum Deo.

[158] In eo enim quod infirmus, propinquat nobis.

[159] Si ergo Christus secundum vos, o haeretici, unam tantum naturam habet, osten-

The third and last paragraph, no. 3 consists of Peter Lombard's conclusion on the Mediation of Christ: "This is what has been somewhat explained why Christ alone is called the Mediator between God and man; and according to which nature he so is, namely his human nature; and with whom, namely the Triune God. For he reconciled us with the Trinity through his death, by which he redeemed us from slavery to the devil. For, as Peter says, *we are redeemed, not by corruptible gold and silver, but by the precious blood of the immaculate Lamb*".[160]

Thus distinction 19 of Book III is comprised of an assembly of texts which are derived directly from the *Glossa PL*. These texts come from Augustine or other authors, generally through Florus of Lyons.

IV, d. 2

Distinction 2 of Book IV offers us an example of the putting together of disparate texts, and, above all, the opportunity to underline the fact that one of Peter Lombard's opinions was not maintained in the Schools, as evidenced by a mention in a manuscript from the beginning of the XIIIth century. In this case it has to do with determining the number of the sacraments and establishing the difference between John's baptism and that of Jesus.

In chapter 1, no. 1 establishes the number of the sacraments: baptism, confirmation, the Blessing of the Bread or eucharist, penance, Extreme Unction, orders and marriage, seven sacraments in all. Some sacraments, such as baptism, says Peter Lombard, remit sins and confer the aid of grace; others are only a remedy, such as marriage; still others endow us with grace and strength, such as the eucharist and orders. The list of seven is given an official status by Peter Lombard in this distinction, whereas in the history of sacramental theology, opinions were still vague.

---

dite unde sit medius inter nos et illam: unde enim medius erit, si utramque non habuit? quia nisi talem dederis inter Deum et homines, qui ita sit medius ut Deus sit propter divinitatis, et homo propter humanitatis naturam, quomodo humana reconcilientur divinis, non ostendis. Nam ipse veniens, prius in seipso humana divinis sociavit, per utriusque naturae communionem in una eademque persona. Deinde omnes fideles Patri reconciliavit Deo, dum sanati sunt ab impietate superbiae, quicumque humilitatem Christi credendo dilexerunt, et diligendo imitati sunt.

[160] Ecce hic aliquatenus insinuatur quare Christus solus dicitur mediator Dei et hominum; et secundum quam naturam mediet, scilicet humanam; et cui mediet, scilicet Deo Trinitati. Trinitati enim nos reconciliavit per mortem; per quam etiam nos redemit a servitute diaboli. Nam ut Petrus ait, *non corruptibilibus auro et argento redempti* sumus, *sed pretioso sanguine Agni immaculati.*

No. 2 replies to the question as to why the Sacraments were not given to mankind immediately after the original fall. It was necessary to await Christ through whom grace and truth came to us (Jn. 1,17). In addition, it was essential for man to be convinced that natural law and the written law could not suffice for his salvation.

No. 3 specifies that only marriage was instituted before sin, both as a sacrament and a service. After sin, it also became a remedy for concupiscence. But this will be considered in its appropriate place.

Chapter 2 will study baptism, as stated in no. 1.

No. 2 speaks immediately of the baptism of John who baptized only with water, as is made clear by the *Glossa interlinearis* on Mt. 3,11 (*Biblia*, IV, 12a): "with water only, not with the Spirit",[161] as though John said what the *Glossa ordinaria* says about the same Gospel (*Biblia*, IV, 12a): "I only wash the body for I cannot remit sins",[162] or as the *Glossa ordinaria* on Lk. 3,16 puts it (*Biblia*, IV, 151a): "He baptizes with water and not with the Spirit because only Christ can do this".[163]

The difference between the baptism of Christ and that of John is established in chapter 3. John's baptism was a baptism of repentance and not of forgiveness, Christ's baptism was a baptism of forgiveness. This is affirmed by the *Glossa ordinaria* on Mt. 3,11 (*Biblia*, IV, 12a): "He is greater than me. For I baptize for repentance, but he baptizes for forgiveness. I have the Spirit, but he gives it. I preach the Kingdom of Heaven, but he confers it".[164]

No. 4 poses the question as to whether in these conditions the baptism of John was really of use. Yes, as states the *Glossa ordinaria* on Mt. 3,11 (*Biblia*, IV, 12a): "As in my birth I precede him in my preaching, so in baptizing those whom by this sign I distinguish as the penitent as opposed to the impenitent, I direct them to the baptism of Christ".[165]

Then chapter 5 enquires whether John's baptism was a sacrament or not. It precursed the baptism of Christ.

Then an interesting question is raised in chapter 6, namely as to

---

[161] In aqua tantum, non in Spiritu.

[162] Tantum corpora lavo, quia peccata solvere nequeo.

[163] Aqua non Spiritu baptizat, quod solius est Christi.

[164] *Fortior me.* Quia ego baptizo in poenitentiam, ille in remissionem. Ego Spiritum habeo, ille dat. Ego regnum caelorum praedico, ille dat.

[165] Sicut nascendo praedicando praecurro, sic baptizando ut poenitentes quos ego hoc signaculo ab impoenitentibus discerno, ad baptismum Christi dirigam.

the status of the baptized spoken of in Acts 19,2–6. What was the formula used by John, asks no. 1.

In no. 2, Peter Lombard appeals to Jerome who declares in his commentary on the prophet Joel, reproduced in the *Glossa ordinaria*, (*Biblia*, III, 379a): "The man who affirms that he believes in Christ and does not believe in the Holy Spirit has not got his eyes open to the vision of God's salvation. Thus those who were baptized by John in the name of Him who was to come, that is the Lord Jesus, said: We have never heard that there is a Holy Spirit. They were re-baptized, moreover they received the true baptism".[166]

In no. 3, Peter Lombard comes to an original conclusion: "Those who had not placed their hopes in the baptism of John and who believed in the Father, the Son and the Holy Spirit, were not baptized again; they received the laying on of hands from the Apostles which conferred the Holy Spirit upon them. The remainder who did not thus believe were baptized with the baptism of Christ, as is stated".[167] Thus Peter Lombard establishes here an exegesis of Acts 8,16–17 which remains proper to him: the imposition of hands was sufficient for the baptized who did not yet know of the existence of the Holy Spirit. This opinion was not recognized by the Masters, as is evidenced a hundred years later by St. Bonaventure (II, praelocutio, 2a): "There are eight propositions, two per Book, in which the position of the Master is no longer accepted ... In Book IV, one position concerns that of John's baptism".[168] Already in the Gloss of the Vat. lat. manuscript 691, f. 223va, we read the same declaration: "Here we do not follow the Master".[169]

This means that Peter Lombard's exegesis was not accepted by those who nevertheless followed his *Sententiae* to the letter and made

---

[166] Qui se dicit in Christum credere et non credit in Spiritum sanctum, nondum habet claros oculos ut videat salutare Dei. Unde baptizati a Ioanne in nomine venturi, id est Domini Iesu, quia dixerunt: Sed neque si Spiritus est audivimus, iterum baptizantur, immo verum baptisma accipiunt.

[167] Illi vero qui spem non posuerunt in baptismo Ioannis, et Patrem et Filium et Spiritum sanctum credebant, non post baptizati fuerunt; sed impositione manuum ab Apostolis super eos facta, Spiritum sanctum receperunt. Alii vero, qui non ita credebant, baptizati sunt baptismo Christi, ut praedictum est.

[168] ... his dumtaxat exceptis, in quibus Magister communiter non sustinetur, immo communis opinio tenet contrarium. Haec autem sunt octo, ita quod in quolibet sunt duae de illis positionibus. ... In quarto similiter duae reperiuntur: una de baptismo Ioannis ...

[169] Hic Magister non tenetur. On the Vat. lat. 691 manuscript, cf. J.G. Bougerol, "La Glose sur les Sentences du Manuscrit Vat. lat. 691", in *Antonianum* 55 (1980) 108–173.

them the framework of their teaching until the time of Cardinal Cisneros at the beginning of the XVIth century.

Conclusion

The Place of Peter Lombard in the History of Theology

Peter Lombard has a unique place in the history of nascent scholasticism for several reasons. First of all because he is a very objective witness of the theological knowledge of his age. One can affirm that Peter Lombard truly belonged to the XIIth century, that he never claimed to propound a personal theology, but that he wished to assemble in a kind of *Summa* the theology which was common in his time. As J. de Ghellinck writes: "A bright spirit who sees things justly, both prudent and judicious, Peter Lombard is capable of disenmeshing tendencies and their conclusions, as of the ways to utilize or moderate them. It is one of the original features of his work that he was able to present us with such a complete tableau of existing opinions. It was another to have continually given a judicious assessment and found his way through this maze".[170] On the one hand, in his commentary on the Psalms as in his Gloss on the Epistles of St. Paul, he clarified the Scriptural text by placing around it the commentaries of the Fathers. The various analyses that we have been able to carry out, as well as many soundings with regard to the Book of the Sentences, have shown that the first source of the *Sententiae* is to be found in Scripture commentaries.[171] On the other hand, Peter Lombard has very often inserted in the *Sententiae* long extracts from the *Glossae*, not only in order to quote from the Fathers, but also to expound theological problems and their solution.[172]

The other primary sources of the *Sententiae* come from contemporaries or certain predecessors of the Master of the Sentences. His tremendous merit lies in having found a legitimate formulation, equally distanced from the errors of Gilbert de la Porrée and the outrageous views of Abelard, and to have embedded it in a collection of patristic texts suitable to clarify the doctrine of faith already grasped in a

---

[170] J. de Ghellinck, "Pierre Lombard", in *DTC*, 1985–1986.
[171] On the history of the Glosses of Peter Lombard, cf. the *Prolegomena* of I. Brady, *Sententiae*, I, 46*–90*.
[172] Cf. pp. 116–125 *supra*.

semi-instinctive and mannered way in the literal-mindedness of the "authorities". Obviously, the absence of metaphysics makes itself felt in the expounding of certain trinitarian doctrines where the texts of Augustine, transmitted by Florus of Lyons, make up for the lack of rational reflection. It appears that Peter Lombard wished to present a theology where dialectics would not play the excessive rôle to which it laid claim. His moderate attitude relies upon a very extensive choice of patristic texts in order to make a judicious use of Augustine's formulae rather than enunciate his thought in personal terms. A.M. Landgraf points out a gloss on the 1206 Troyes Latin manuscript which severely criticizes the interpretation of Augustine given by Peter Lombard.[173] This is a very rare case.

Whatever deficiencies we can find today in Peter Lombard's work, the fact remains that it suggests a vast amount of reading and extra-ordinary reflection. As J. de Ghellinck stresses: "The use of another's expressions is not made without a certain autonomy of thought, a very subtle sense of the nuance to be conveyed, sometimes an inde-pendence when it comes to appreciation, which make the psycho-logical analysis of the author very complex and which usually make this analysis redound to his honour".[174] Moreover, the fact that theo-logical reflection developed for four centuries after the commentary of the *Sententiae* witnesses to the intrinsic value of the work of Peter Lombard. The Glosses and Commentaries of Peter Comestor, Peter of Poitiers and Stephen Langton up to William of Auxerre and Philip the Chancellor are evidence of its success. The *Summa fratris Alexandri*, the collective work of the Franciscan study centre in Paris under the direction of John of La Rochelle, also relies on the *Sententiae*.[175]

The Fathers Seen through the Eyes of Peter Lombard

The relative poverty of libraries and the often faulty copying of patristic texts lead to an essential question: are the "opinions" presented by Peter Lombard in the *Sententiae* an exact reflection of the thinking of the Fathers? This is a big question and is worth being asked. In fact,

---

[173] Cf. A.M. Landgraf, "Die Stellungnahme der Frühscholastik zur wissenschaftlichen Methode des Petrus Lombardus", in *Collectanea Franciscana* 4 (1934) 513–521.

[174] Cf. J. de Ghellinck, "Pierre Lombard", in *DTC*, 1986.

[175] Cf. *Summa fratris Alexandri*, IV, Prolegomena (V. Doucet), Quaracchi 1948, 92, 132. V. Doucet has listed 321 explicit quotations and 548 implicit quotations in the first four volumes.

we are dealing here with a pseudo-problem. Indeed, if we take the case of Augustine's *De Trinitate*, we have to admit that Peter Lombard knew the text through the *Expositio* of Florus of Lyons. The authenticity of the Augustine presented by the *Sententiae* depends on the authenticity of the Augustine presented by Florus. Now, we know from historians that Florus was perfectly acquainted with Augustine's text and that he was able to choose extracts suitable to present a faithful picture of his work.[176] This faithfulness rebounds therefore on the authenticity of Peter Lombard's presentation.

Another example is to be found in the way in which Peter Lombard quotes the *De Trinitate* of Hilary of Poitiers. Unlike that of Augustine, he has Hilary's text before him, he knows it well and has weighed its profundity, witness the reflection which he adds to his words: "You, the reader, have heard what Hilary says about this. Wherever you find his words, note them with care and understand them with piety".[177] This permits us to think that at the time when Peter Lombard compiled the *Sententiae*, Scripture was not read, nor were the Fathers, in the way that we read them today. We have Hilary addressing his prayer to the Father to respond to his poverty by opening up to him an understanding of the mystery: "We poor people, we beg for what we lack and with a stubborn zeal we scrutinize the words of your prophets and Apostles, and we knock at the door of minds which are closed to us: but it is for you to reply to our prayer, to be present when we beg you to be, to put up with our insistence. We are discouraged by the paralysing stupour of our nature, and we are prevented from entering into the understanding of your mystery by the demands of our ignorance and the poverty of our spirit: but the study of your teaching builds up in us the sense of your divine knowledge, and the obedience of faith carries us beyond our natural opinions".[178] Such a prayer can only take root in the heart of a man for whom the reading of Scripture and the Fathers has above all to

---

[176] Cf. C. Charlier, "La compilation augustinienne de Florus sur l'Apôtre", in *Revue Bénédictine* 57 (1947) 132–167.

[177] Audisti, lector, quid super hoc dicat Hilarius, cuius verba, ubicumque occurrunt, diligenter nota pieque intellige. Cf. pp. 137–140 *supra*, and esp. p. 146, n. 125.

[178] Nos quidem inopes ea quibus egemus precabimur, et in scrutandis prophetarum tuorum apostolorumque dictis studium pervicax afferemus, et omnes obseratae intelligentiae aditus pulsabimus: sed tuum est, et oratum tribuere, et quaesitum adesse, et patere pulsatum. Torpemus enim quodam naturae nostrae pigro stupore, et ad res tuas intelligendas ignorantiae necessitatem ingenii nostri imbecillitate cohibemus: sed doctrinae tuae studia ad sensum nos divinae cognitionis instituunt, et ultra natu-

nourish his faith and pass it on to others. Peter Lombard was very much on the same lines as Hilary or Augustine.

Of course, the search for the "Sitz im Leben" of the Fathers is completely foreign to the mediaeval mind as is the criticism of texts or their exegesis. Oral civilization conditioned the minds of masters and students, as of all men of the time, in such a way that it was unthinkable to dwell at length on the literal meaning of quotations rather than to extract their meaning. The way in which the *Glossa interlinearis* was inserted between the lines of Scripture in manuscripts and in the first incunabula of the *Biblia latina* represents an attempt at an exegesis of the sacred text, not in order to institute a critique of it, but to explain its continuation.

In the prologue *Cupientes* which Peter Lombard wrote after compiling the first edition of the *Sententiae*, he makes his own the words of the *De Trinitate* of Augustine, III, prooemium, no. 2 (*PL* 42, 869; *CCL* 50, 128): "I expect more than a benevolent reader: an independent critic, especially in these writings where, please God, may the importance of the subject produce as many solutions as it raises objections!".[179] Peter Lombard chose to express his profound thinking in the terms which Augustine used. He could not have expressed himself better.

Transl. D. Gathercole

Bibliography

Biblia latina cum Glossa ordinaria, ed. princeps A. Rusch, Strassburg 1490–1491, reprint 1992 (Brepols, Turnhout).
J.G. Bougerol, "La Glose sur les Sentences du Manuscrit Vat. lat. 691". In: *Antonianum* 55 (1980) 108–173.

---

ralem opinionem fidei obedientia provehit. Hilary of Poitiers, *De Trinitate*, I, no. 37, (*PL* 10, 49). It has to be noted that Hilary's texts which appear in the third edition of the *Sententiae* do not always correspond to the critical edition of Smulders in the *Corpus Christianorum*.

[179] Non solum pium lectorem sed etiam liberum correctorem desiderim, multo maxime in his ubi ipsa magnitudo quaestionis utinam tam multos inventores habere posset quam multos contradictores habet. The Latin text transcribed here is that of the critical edition of *CCL* 50, 128. The text given in the third Quaracchi-Grottaferrata edition is slightly different: Non solum pium lectorem, sed etiam liberum correctorem desiderio, maxime ubi profunda versatur veritatis quaestio: quae utinam tot haberet inventores, quot habet contradictores! (I expect more than a benevolent reader, an independent critic, much more in these writings where the profound question of the truth is posed, which should produce as many solutions as objections!)

I. Brady, "Pierre Lombard", in the *Dictionnaire de Spiritualité*, 12 (1986) 1604–1612.

C. Charlier, "La compilation augustinienne de Florus sur l'Apôtre". In: *Revue Bénédictine* 57 (1947) 132–167.

M. Colish, *Peter Lombard*, Leiden, 1994.

The article by J. de Ghellinck, *Pierre Lombard*, in the *Dictionnaire de Théologie Catholique*, 12 (1935) 1941–2019 still has its value today. The author has taken up again some of his points in *Le Mouvement théologique du XIIe siècle*, Bruges, 1948, 113–296.

PH. Delhaye, *Pierre Lombard, sa vie, ses œuvres, sa morale*, Montreal-Paris, 1961.

A.M. Landgraf, *Introduction à l'histoire de la littérature théologique de la scolastique naissante*, Paris, 1973.

—, "Die Stellungnahme der Frühscholastik zur wissenschaftlichen Methode des Petrus Lombardus". In: *Collectanea Franciscana* 4 (1934) 513–521.

Petri Lombardi Sententiae in IV Libros dispositae, 3a editio (I. Brady), Quaracchi-Grottaferrata 1971–1981, 2 vols.

G. Mathon, "Pierre Lombard". In: *Catholicisme*, 11 (1988) 386–390.

C. Munier, *Les sources patristiques dans le droit de l'Église du VIIIe au XIIe siècle*, Mulhouse, 1957.

Summa fratris Alexandri, IV, Prolegomena (V. Doucet), Quaracchi, 1948.

SIC ET NON: PATRISTIC AUTHORITY BETWEEN REFUSAL AND ACCEPTANCE: ANSELM OF CANTERBURY, PETER ABELARD AND BERNARD OF CLAIRVAUX

Burcht Pranger

Introduction

In view of the overwhelming presence of the Church Fathers in early medieval theology a discussion of their influence would seem to amount to a discussion of that theology itself. Clearly it cannot be the purpose of this article to undertake such a task. After the previous chapters dealing with the developments of the technical implements (the gloss, the Sentences, the *Decretum* etc.) which increasingly enabled scholars—theologians and others—to see the Fathers in their pastness, I propose to focus on three thinkers who can be said to have been hovering between the new and the old: Anselm of Canterbury, Bernard of Clairvaux and Abelard.[1] Anselm and Abelard are widely seen as having contributed to the emergence of the scholastic method whereas Bernard's name is associated with a firm rejection of that same development. And indeed, there is no point in denying the general correctness of that assumption. Contrary to this, however, my article intends to demonstrate that an assessment of the attitude of those three thinkers towards the Fathers may somehow reveal a common stance. All three are "modern" in that they belong to a cultural climate in which technical sophistication in the field of textual studies was on the increase. The very boldness with which they applied those freshly developed technical implements to biblical and patristic authority also displays a kind of self-consciousness, a sense of belonging to the illustrious company of the Fathers themselves, that was characteristic of a past which was soon to vanish.

To capture this moment in which the acceptance of traditional authority and the rise of modernity in the eleventh and twelfth centuries coalesce—that being the limited scope of this study—, I first

---

[1] In this article I focus on Anselm and Bernard, only referring to Abelard to illustrate the formers' position.

give a rough outline of the emerging scholastic theology. Thence I turn to Abelard. Next I move back in time to Anselm, to end up once more in the twelfth century with an analysis of Bernard's view of both Anselm and Abelard, and of the Fathers.

1. *Scholastic Theology*

The twelfth century witnessed the birth of so-called scholastic theology. Two distinctive features of this theology are its location and its method. As for the location, it was exclusively practised in the urban schools, and later on, at the universities. Scholastic theology distinguished itself from the world of monastic learning together with which it had hitherto constituted one and the same pattern of culture. As for its techniques, it developed an interest in "authentication of sources, in authorial intention, and in historical criticism"[2] all of which had so far been unheard of. This new critical attitude is symbolised by the title of Peter Abelard's work in which he tried to assess apparent contradictions in the Bible and the Church Fathers: *Sic et non*. However true it may be that canonists developed similar methods of critical scrutiny in the same period, it is the theologians who were the more radical of the two. Where the canonists were bent on seeking "harmony from dissonance"[3] when confronted with opposing authorities, the theologians were much more prepared to leave contradictions unsolved or even "to reject authorities point blank if it could be shown that they were irrelevant, outmoded or plainly incorrect."[4] As a result, scholastic theology manifested itself above all as a method.[5] As such it ought not to be confused with later, humanist and early-modern, interest in past authors, which was believed to be not just critical in terms of method but also intrinsically rational without the need for a supreme authority of faith. In the course of the thirteenth

[2] Colish, M.L. (1991) ". . . *Quia hodie locum non habent*: Scholastic Theologians Reflect on their Authorities", in *Proceedings of the PMR Conference* vol. 15 (Villanova: 1991) 2.

[3] Colish, M.L. (1991) ". . . *Quia hodie locum non habent*: Scholastic Theologians Reflect on their Authorities". In: *Proceedings of the PMR Conference* vol. 15 (Villanova: 1991) 2. Colish here refers to the title of Stephan Kuttner's book.

[4] Colish, quoting Beumer, disagrees with Landgraf who sees the theologians as more conservative. *Proceedings of the PMR Conference* vol. 15 (Villanova: 1991) 2.

[5] Cf. Grabman's classic: Grabmann, M. (1909–11) *Geschichte der scholastischen Methode*, I–II, (Freiburg: 1909–11; reprint Graz: 1957).

century this "scholastic method" developed into a lengthy process of learning in which the student was trained in a "critical" use of the sources of Christian faith: the Bible and the Church Fathers. In the end, he had to be able independently to apply the *sic et non* to those sources—and for that matter, to the sources of philosophical knowledge—and, in addition, to instruct the next generation in the same combined principles of authority and methodological doubt.

Striking examples can be given of a critical and sometimes bold handling of the Bible. Yet it should be realised that the newness of the scholastic approach mainly lies in the application of new methods, such as the treatment of New Testament authors as "theologians in their own right".[6] As for boldness in the interpretation of the Bible, I intend to demonstrate that earlier theologians had been no less daring than their predecessors and can even be said to have felt freer precisely because of the absence of any fixed "scholastic" method.

The attitude of the scholastic theologians toward the Church Fathers has been summed up by Marcia Colish as follows:

> Next, we have the patristic authors. This group of authorities includes the Latin church fathers, as well as those Greek fathers available in translation. It also includes the popes who had made rulings for the early church and the decrees of the early church councils. On the one hand, the fathers, as a group stand under the Bible. On the other hand—and this is a point stated the most clearly by Hugh of St. Victor—they are attached to the Bible. The meaning of the Bible is not self-evident; and these authorities often have to be brought to bear on it in grasping the sense of the text. It should be appreciated here that the twelfth-century scholastics are not interested in discussing the relations between scriptural and patristic authority, or in placing them in a clear hierarchy vis-à-vis each other. Rather, they see the Christian message as a message that was begun to be interpreted within the New Testament itself, a process which was then continued by the church fathers and by the theologians of successive ages. All the witnesses are seen as part of a single organic conception of authority. For the scholastic of this period, antiquity is not, of itself, a test of authority. Antiquity is no guarantee that an authority was correct, in his own day, or plausible, nowadays. Thus the church fathers, and the early popes, like anyone else, have to stand up to scrutiny on the grounds of their content and their cogency.[7]

---

[6] Colish, *Proceedings of the PMR Conference* vol. 15 (Villanova: 1991) 3.

[7] Cf. Colish, *Proceedings of the PMR Conference* vol. 15 (Villanova: 1991) 3–4.

Now in the late twelfth century this scholastic method developed into a *scientia*, a real science organised according to the principles of Aristotle's philosophy. Ideally, this did not imply any decrease in the authority of the Bible and the Church Fathers. Rather, the great scholastic theologians such as Thomas Aquinas and Bonaventure succeeded in merging the traditional with the modern, the wisdom (*sapientia*) of the Fathers with the new science of scholasticism. Their very success, however, as well as the fact that their theology not only became the dominant force in the thirteenth century but has been influential ever since—at least up to the beginning of this century—, has tended to be in the way of an unbiased assessment of their immediate predecessors. Too often the latter were seen either as precursors of scholastic theology or as the last representatives of a waning period. Anselm of Canterbury, for instance, has often been called the "Father of Scholasticism" whereas Bernard of Clairvaux was given the epithet "the last of the Fathers". In a sense both honorific titles tell us more about the history of Roman Catholic theology than about those authors themselves. Anselm's fatherhood is supposed to announce the birth of a scholastic system which, in the view of its defenders, provided Christian faith with a solid, sound and definite structural framework. Calling Bernard a "father", on the other hand, is meant to express a feeling of nostalgia for a period which, in the view of the critics of scholasticism, had not yet been corrupted by the aridity of scholastic, philosophical language. In that view the Fathers, of whom Bernard was considered to be the last but not the least, have come to symbolize a kind of authority by which later history was to be judged. The criteria for such a judgment were made up of a cluster of authoritative notions which enabled post- and antischolastic theologians to draw a line vis-à-vis their scholastic opponents. This cluster basically consisted of the view that the Bible was the source of faith, that the life of the early Church was exemplary of the way this Bible-based faith ought to be put into practice[8] and that the Church Fathers in their writings had produced a most successful and effective reflection on both Christian faith and life. In the Preface to his edition of the works of Bernard, Jean Mabillon gave the classic definition of this concept of "patristic" authority:

---

[8] See Certeau, M. de. (1963) "De Saint-Cyran au Jansénisme, conversion et réforme", *Christus, Cahiers Spirituels* 10 (1963) 399–417, and Olsen, G. (1969) "The Idea of the Ecclesia Primitiva in the Writings of the Twelfth-Century Canonists", *Traditio* 25 (1969) 61–86.

> Those are called Fathers by the Church whose sanctity, teaching and antiquity it holds in reverence. By "teaching" I mean teaching of Scripture and tradition rather than philosophy ... Those may be called Fathers who are made venerable thanks to the authority they already commanded and to their non-philosophical approach.[9]

It is clear, then, that, from a retrospective point of view, the use of the word "father" with regard to both Anselm and Bernard reflects the emergence of a crisis in the history of Christian theology in which differences of opinion between the various schools of thought concerning issues of authority and philosophical autonomy became increasingly irreconcilable. In view of this later development a fair assessment of the position of the Church Fathers in the eleventh and twelfth century proper should start with an attempt to disentangle the knot in which the different semantic levels of notions such as "fathers", "antiquity", "authority", "cogency" and "rationality" are mixed up and tied together. What is required here is a thorough and finely-tuned *archéologie du savoir*. A first and necessary step in that direction is a firm refusal to consider the pre-scholastic period as just preparing the ground for later developments. In other words, there are insufficient grounds to consider the history of theology in this period exclusively as part of an emancipatory process leading up to a more independent use of reason vis-à-vis biblical and patristic authorities. Nor should critics of the emerging scholastic theology like Bernard be credited with, or for that matter, be accused of an anti-rational stand based on an allegedly blind acceptance of a fixed concept of biblical and patristic authority.

2. *Abelard's roots*

The fact that the problem of biblical and patristic authority appears inextricably intertwined with a theological view of history requires an analysis of the influence of the Church Fathers in Anselm and Bernard to go beyond a mere tracing and appreciation of sources. As for those sources, a fairly accurate survey can be given. Augustine is the main force of inspiration in Anselm whilst there is a strong presence of Boethius in the more philosophical parts. In Bernard's

---

[9] Mabillon, Preface to the edition of the works of Bernard of Clairvaux; *PL* 182:25–6.

case things look a bit more diffuse. The influence of Origen is all-pervasive as is Gregory the Great's and Augustine's. Other Church Fathers do make their appearance, albeit on a much more incidental basis than those mentioned.

Yet identifying those sources tells us little or nothing about the relation between those sources and the authors who used them. For one thing, even when quoted, the Church Fathers are rarely mentioned by name. The same, although to a lesser degree, obtains for biblical quotations. Of course, no one would deny the usefulness of modern editions in which references to the sources are given. Yet it should be realised that the desire for further information is a concern of the modern reader and not Anselm's or Bernard's. Rather than to a primitive attitude towards their source-material their silence with regard to the sources points to a capacity and a freedom to absorb the past in one's own writings which was to be increasingly lacking in later, more "historically" orientated products of scholastic theology.

To illustrate this point, let us turn to someone who is generally considered the first important representative of scholastic theology: Abelard. In his *Historia calamitatum* he tells the following story.[10] After his preparatory studies in the arts he decided to do his final training—that is, the interpretation of the Bible, with the famous master Anselm of Laon. Soon, however, he was bored both with his teacher's method and the teacher himself. Boasting in a tavern that he could do better, he was challenged by his fellow-students to take a commentary by the Fathers on an obscure text from Ezekiel and lecture on it. To their astonishment he invited them on the spot to come to his lecture the next morning and hear the results. Rather than wasting time in consulting other authorities, he decided to use the short cut of the intellect, to work *non per usum sed per ingenium*. Thus he was able to accomplish in one day what for his fellow-students could only be the result of hard labour marked by the detour of submitting themselves to the authority of an ineffective master.

Now this passage can be interpreted on different levels. First, we may assume Abelard to have applied to the text a "modern-scholastic" reading according to the principles laid down in the preface to his *Sic et non*. This would have consisted of a critical approach to the

---

[10] Abelard, *Historia calamitatum*, Monfrin, J. (ed.) (Paris: 1959) 68–9.

biblical and patristic authorities involved. Surely, Abelard would not have spent his brief night of preparation collecting other patristic authorities and glosses on the Ezekiel-text. What he would have done, was to "scrutinize the source-material on its content and cogency", distinguishing the author's intention, for instance, through an assessment of the circumstances in which the text was produced. From this scrutiny a sense of historical distance may have emerged which made it possible for Abelard to take the text for what it was and which set him apart as an interpreter from the patristic authorities he was commenting on. However, a second, equally important, dimension of this story suggests precisely the opposite. The very fact that Abelard claimed to proceed *non per usum sed per ingenium* would seem to imply a unity of logical and linguistic space in which problems and inconsistencies caused by differences of space and time could be solved.[11] In that case, there would be as little reason for Abelard to be concerned about the historical nature of his sources, about their "otherness", as there is for a logician to worry about the applicability of his formal system of inference to the external world. But Abelard was concerned about the past, both his own and that of others, pagans and christians alike.[12] His handling of patristic texts with the flair of *ingenium* cannot therefore be judged in terms of later scholastic theology, where there is a more balanced view of the relationship between authorities and rational scrutiny. For Abelard, as for his monastic predecessors, the corpus of biblical and patristic texts first and foremost represented the enduring presence of the past with such overwhelming intensity and diversity that no part of human language and thought could be imagined as being unrelated to it. And as for Abelard's modernist and "historical" approach to those texts, his search for logical cogency and for the intention of past authors is to be considered an intrinsic part of the dynamic interplay between textual authorities and the scrutinizing mind. Whatever sense of historical distance is created in the process, remains within those bounds.

---

[11] Coleman, J. (1992) *Ancient and Medieval Memories. Studies on the Reconstruction of the Past* (Cambridge: 1992) 272.
[12] See Cramer, P.J. (1993) *Baptism and Change in the Early Middle Ages c. 200–c. 1150* (Cambridge: 1993) 263-6.

3. *Anselm as reader of Augustine*

Let us take a step back in time and turn to Anselm of Canterbury. Before his use of the Church Fathers can be discussed, a different question must be answered. In view of the fact that he has been called "the Father of Scholasticism", what did he contribute to Abelard's and others' "modern" approach to historical sources? The answer seems simple: nothing whatsoever. Anselm and Abelard lived in different worlds, the one in the monastery, the other in the city. Accordingly, their minds moved in different directions, the one reflecting monastic calm,[13] focusing on the rational coherence and cogency of the main themes of Christian faith, the other reflecting urban diversity.[14] The latter deals with a great number of subjects ranging from logic to ethics and theology. Consequently, Anselm's influence on the scholastic method appears to be constricted to the use of reason in matters of faith, symbolised by the famous motto of Augustine, *fides quaerens intellectum*, faith searching for understanding. Where Anselm refused to go beyond faith, Abelard—so it is often said, in particular by his opponents—gives the impression of being intellectually curious for curiosity's sake.

However, without denying the differences between the two thinkers, they must be said to belong to one and the same cultural world to a much greater degree than has hitherto been supposed. Admittedly, Anselm does not allow for modern concerns such as the intention of the author and the interest in the circumstances in which texts came into existence. But both he and Abelard do face similar problems in their use of past authors. Both refuse to consider the works of the Church Fathers as external authorities containing clear-cut opinions which might be used as such in scholastic disputations. In fact, Anselm's rational flair in applying his method of *sola ratione* to the issues of Christian faith compels him, like Abelard, to make past authorities part of a game—a search for cogency and clarity—which prevents him from reading them in their pastness and historical otherness. But then it should be realised that "pastness" and

---

[13] For a brilliant description of Anselm's life and thought, see Southern, R.W. 1990 *Anselm of Canterbury. Portrait in a Landscape* (Cambridge: 1990).

[14] See Luscombe, D.E. (1969) *The School of Peter Abelard. The Influence of Abelard's Thought in the Early Scholastic Period* (Cambridge: 1969) and Luscombe, D.E. 1988. "From Paris to the Paraclete: the Correspondence of Abelard and Heloise". *Proceedings of the British Academy* LXXIV (1967) 247–283.

"otherness" are not the exclusive property of the modern, twentieth-century mind. In other words, if we do not find our concept of "pastness" and "otherness" in Anselm and, even if Abelard's tentative curiosity with regard to the intention of past authors is to be appreciated in a different context from modern concepts of the past, they cannot be said to have had no sense of the past. On the contrary. The reciprocity between the scrutinizing mind and the biblical and patristic sources which I attributed earlier on to Abelard and which is even more strongly present in Anselm, is based on a greater confidence in bringing past sources to life than many a modern historian would dare dream of.

In his first big treatise, the *Monologion*, Anselm offers a theology of the Trinity which is entirely based on Augustine's *De trinitate*. After taking his point of departure in the neo-platonic reduction of the diversity of good things we find in reality to the one and supreme good which is God, he discusses the divine properties such as infinity, speech, intellect and creative power, all of which culminate in the trinitarian shape of the divine. Here the Augustinian notions are in place: the Trinity is nothing but God remembering, understanding and loving as the Father, the Son and the Holy Spirit respectively. Thus the three persons are related to each other in a permanent process of reciprocal activities.

Anselm himself is quite outspoken about his indebtedness to Augustine. In the preface to the *Monologion* he tells the reader in so many words that nothing new is to be expected:

> Frequently checking my text I was unable to find myself saying anything that would not be in accordance with the works of the catholic fathers, most of all, with those of Augustine. Therefore, if anyone thinks that in this work I have put forward something which is either too new or contrary to truth, I beg him not to call me instantly a presumptuous innovator or a defender of falsehood but, rather, to look diligently at the work of the aforementioned doctor Augustine, *De trinitate*. May he then judge my little work accordingly.[15]

Of course, in view of its place in the preface, this passage is first of all to be considered as an expression of literary modesty. Were it taken quite literally, the question might arise whether it makes sense

---

[15] Anselm of Canterbury, Preface to the *Monologion*; *S. Anselmi Cantuariensis Archiepiscopi opera omnia*, ed. Schmitt F.S. (Stuttgart-Bad Canstatt: 1968) I, 8.

at all to write after what has been said by the Fathers themselves. But even apart from the rhetorical setting that question cannot be avoided. In the dedicatory letter to his *Cur deus homo* which he sent to pope Urban II, Anselm does indeed feel the need to state why research into matters of faith is legitimate after what has been said by the apostles and the Church Fathers:

> Although after the holy apostles and doctors many of us have had to say this and that about the meaning of our faith in order to confute foolishness and to break the hardness of the infidels, and to pasture those whose heart had already been purged by that same faith with the help of the rationality of the same faith. . . . so that we neither in our times nor in the future may hope to achieve similar results in the contemplation of truth, I do not think it reprehensible if anyone, standing firm in faith, wants to embark on the exercise of the rational scrutiny of faith. For, since "the days of man are brief," even the apostles and doctors have not been able to say all they could have said if they had lived longer. Moreover, the rational meaning of truth is so wide and so deep that it can never be exhausted by us mortals . . .[16]

Here Anselm gives the traditional patristic reasons in favour of further reflection on matters of faith in addition to the knowledge revealed to us by the Bible. And the specifically Augustinian setting becomes even more unmistakable when he goes on to interpret the inexhaustibility of the *veritatis ratio* in terms of the *credo ut intelligam*, that is, the drive inherent in faith to strive for greater clarity and understanding. Finding himself, in his intellectual capacity, located between faith and vision (*fides* and *species*) the best man can do is to use his intellect as a vehicle to articulate rationally what he has faithfully accepted as true (ranging from the existence of God to the necessity of Christ's incarnation). It is not only the Augustinian unrest of the soul which makes itself felt in this intellectual pursuit but also his "eudaemonianism", that is, the idea that intellectual exercise is a matter of pleasure (*delectatio*) consisting of the joy derived from discerning the rational structure of the inexhaustible truth.

Now if we compare those two passages by Anselm, we face the following question. What are we to make of Anselm's claim in the preface to the *Monologion* that he is saying nothing which is out of tune with Augustine's *De trinitate*? How is this claim to be related to the concept of intellectual progress as formulated in the dedicatory

---

[16] Schmitt II, 41–2.

letter to *Cur deus homo*? What does Anselm mean when he asks the reader to judge his work "according to Augustine's books on the Trinity"?

First, there are the facts. Augustine's *De trinitate* does indeed figure prominently in the *Monologion* as is made abundantly clear by the many references in Schmitt's edition. But then it should be stated once more that such references are made for the benefit of the modern reader who knows how to distinguish between sources as historical data and their use. Such was clearly not Anselm's idea of fidelity to Augustine's text. For him, fidelity is to be linked to cogency, that is, to a certain degree of coherence between Augustine's text and his own. This coherence, in turn, is not supported by a *tertium* which might be used as a criterion of fidelity. Reading Augustine in Anselm's manner means to scrutinize the text (*diligenter perspiciat*) in the hope that, by focusing intensely on it, dimensions may be brought out that lay in hiding waiting to be revealed by the sympathetic reader.

Let us now test Anselm's claim to be faithful to Augustine and examine whether the *Monologion* can be seen as a seamless imitation of *De trinitate*. Of all the subjects discussed in both works there is one which may be particularly helpful with regard to this comparison, and that is memory. For human memory is the faculty which bridges the gap between the past and the present. Accordingly, it is supposed to help us account for the difference between the past and the present. At the same time it underlies, for Augustine as well as for Anselm, the very structure of the Trinity in its eternity. What, then, are we to think of the divine memory? Considering its timelessness, how is distance being created and maintained?

In his *De trinitate* Augustine coined the definition of the Trinity as consisting of God the Father as memory, God the Son as intellect or wisdom and God the Holy Spirit as love or will. This trinitarian structure is reflected in the human soul, which is thus somehow capable of knowing God through itself and knowing itself through God. Of course there are fundamental differences between the timeless memory of God and the time-bound memory of man. In book XV Augustine points out one of these differences when stressing the fact that, in contrast to human knowledge, the persons of the Trinity do not need one another to exercise their faculties of memorizing, understanding and willing.[17] In other words, the Father does not need the Son if he

---

[17] Augustine, *De trinitate* XV, VII, 12; CCL 50A, 477.

wants to understand either the Son or the Holy Spirit if he wants to love; nor do they need the Father in order to remember.

Anselm's chapter on memory in the *Monologion* is much along the lines of Augustine's argumentation.

> What are we to think of memory? Should we say that the Son is the understanding of memory, or the memory of the Father, of the memory of memory? Further, since it cannot be denied that the supreme wisdom remembers itself, it is most becoming to assume that the Father is understood in terms of memory as is the Son in terms of "word" since the word seems to spring from memory. And that can clearly be observed in our mind. For since the human mind does not always think itself in the same way it always remembers itself, it is obvious that the word it produces is born from its memory when it thinks itself . . .[18]

In this process of continuous remembering the Word which proceeds from the memory of the Father as a child from its parents takes on the latter's function, that is, his being memory. So, like Augustine, Anselm holds the view that it is not only the Father who remembers, the Son who understands and the Spirit who wills. The Son also remembers, just as the Father also understands.

> In the same way as the Son is understanding and wisdom, he also belongs to the memory of the Father. But what the Son knows in his wisdom and understands, he also remembers. The Son is, therefore, [the product of] the memory of the Father and the memory of memory, that is, the memory remembering the Father who is memory, just as he is wisdom of the Father and wisdom of wisdom . . .[19]

Like Augustine Anselm realises that this is not the way the human faculties of memory, intellect and will operate:

> For in that which is memory of itself [i.e. Christ being *memoria memoriae*] memory does not exist in its own memory in the same way as one thing exists in another, as, for instance, the things which are in the memory of the human mind. Those things exist in such a manner as to be not identical with our memory.[20]

The point Anselm here makes is that the objects of remembering and of the other faculties of the human mind are in a sense inanimate in that they do not actively participate in the process of remembering. The implication would seem to be that, if we were able

---

[18] *Monologion* c. 48; Schmitt I, 63.
[19] *Monologion* c. 48; Schmitt I, 64.
[20] *Monologion* c. 48; Schmitt I, 64.

to understand correctly, we would understand and remember things, as the Trinity understands and remembers itself, or, even, that we would understand things such as the Trinity. This last conclusion is not as far-fetched as it seems. In his treatise *De veritate* Anselm argues that whatever statement of truth we make in language, thought and sense-perception, it only becomes effective if seen as a statement of, and in, the supreme truth. It is only then that statements of truth on whatever level of knowledge (sense-perception, proposition etc.) are able to "do what they ought to do", that is, to be true within their limited scope of being a true perception or a true proposition.

"If we were to understand correctly . . ." This is precisely the point where Augustine and Anselm seem to part ways. As for Augustine, his reflections on memory are part of the grand design of his "theology of creation". By "creation" I mean his view of the relationship between God and man, which encompasses the relationship between the persons of the Trinity themselves as well as the relationship between the faculties of the human mind. Both in Augustine's *Confessiones* and in his *De trinitate* we are presented with the dynamics of those relations as they develop from the depth of memory, human and divine. In the process, Augustine is, of course, aware of the differences between the human and divine minds. But that is not the kind of problem he really cares about, nor does he attempt to articulate those differences. For Anselm, on the other hand, the concept of linguistic cogency is fundamental. This does not mean that he distinguishes clearly between the divine and the human as far as language is concerned. Rather, for him our language and thought is, as I have pointed out earlier, governed by the supreme, divine truth which is supposed to be all—pervasive in whatever utterances the human mind makes. In the daily practice of linguistic life, however, we turn out to be inadequate in rendering this presence of the divine in words. In his works, Anselm gives many examples of the inaccuracies of human speech which, unless corrected through rational scrutiny, tend to obscure our view of truth. One example may suffice. If we deal with the problem of free will and necessity, we should be careful not to interpret our way of speaking (the *usus loquendi*) in terms of a literal truth. To say, for instance, that "Hector is conquered by Achilles" means, from a grammatical point of view, that Hector is the acting subject. From the viewpoint of truth, however, it is Achilles who acts whereas Hector is the passive party. Since this example is found in the context of a discussion about necessity with regard to

God, there is reason to assume that the problems Anselm cites concerning this issue derive largely from grammatical errors. These differ
from the confusion about Hector and Achilles in scale rather than in
principle.[21]

There is no major issue of the Christian faith which Anselm
does not subject to this principle of correctness. The status of truth,
the freedom of the will, the fall of the devil, the existence of God,
the necessity of the Incarnation, all are scrutinized on their degree
of rational and linguistic cogency. By discussing the inconsistencies
of our speech habits (*usus loquendi*), Anselm brings the true outlook of
all those issues to the fore. Rather than representing a choice between two alternatives, as human language would seem to suggest,
freedom of will consists in "doing the right thing". Rather than being at liberty to deny the existence of God as language suggests,
man is forced by reason to admit the necessity of His existence. Rather
than being subjected to the power of the devil as our religious *usus
loquendi* suggests, man is solely responsible for his own misbehaviour.
Realising all this, requires accurate linguistic analysis and exercise.
Only upon such thorough examination do things, both human and
divine, reveal themselves as they really are.

But does this Anselmian concept of cogency imply that in the last
resort the human mind works according to the same principles as
those through which the persons of the Trinity communicate? Are,
for instance, the products of our memory such as our thoughts about
God and His creation eventually to be seen as "memory of memory",
as part of a reciprocal process of knowledge? In terms of a general
theory of knowledge, the answer has to be negative. After all, Anselm
clearly states that "man requires materials or images drawn from
external sources to formulate his thoughts whereas God is completely
original and there is no distinction between his thought and his expression."[22] Yet from the viewpoint of the enclosed space of his
monastic ruminations, there is a sense in which Anselm can be said
to go beyond Augustine by applying his principle of rational cogency
to human language and thought. In doing so, he does not deprive
the human mind of external sources to articulate its thoughts. In-

---

[21] See, for instance, *Cur deus homo* II, c. 17; Schmitt II, 123 and *De veritate* c. 8;
Schmitt I, 188.

[22] Coleman, J. (1992) *Ancient and Medieval Memories. Studies on the Reconstruction of the
Past* (Cambridge: 1992) 167.

stead, he firmly reduces those thoughts, once formulated, to their agents, to the mind producing them, to the memory of the monastic mind in search of God, which is intellect as well as will. This then appears to be the ultimate meaning of Anselm's famous adage *sola ratione* which he announces in the majestic opening lines of the *Monologion* only to bring it to perfection in the *Proslogion*.

> If anyone, either by not having heard of it or by not believing, does not know of one nature and further happens to be ignorant of most of the other things we necessarily believe about God and His creation,— that supreme nature which is the highest of all that is, autarchic in its eternal beatitude, giving and making through His omnipotent goodness the very being or the well-being of all other things, then I believe such a person, even if of a modest intellectual capacity, to be able to convince himself of the truth of most of all this by reason alone.[23]

Here Anselm presents us with a precise itinerary of the monastic mind. Whatever part of reality is touched by the mind, the *sola ratione* reveals this reality, in spite of the latter's provenance from the realm of images, to be part of "the supreme nature and the other things we necessarily believe about God and His creation." To think of that nature and of those "other things" *sola ratione* means to draw them from memory right through the oblivion caused by the inaccuracies of our normal speech habits. If then in the *Monologion* and the *Proslogion* he proves in different ways the existence of God, he does so by reducing the vague and obscure knowledge we have about God from our (sense and image) experience to a "memory of memory", that is, "to an activity of the mind remembering being remembered by God". Ultimately, it is in the complete reciprocity between the mind and its object and the object and its mind, that the *sola ratione* brings out the presence of God. This presence embraces both the forgetfulness of the mind caught up in the sinful obscurities of language and thought, and the happiness it enjoys after it has completed its mission of remembering God and His creation.

Surely, this kind of reasoning by way of reason alone is far beyond Augustine's view of the human mind as somehow reflecting the dynamics of the trinitarian process. Yet Anselm's view cannot be said to be un-Augustinian. On the contrary. It is Augustinian in a suspiciously seamless manner. Narrowing down Augustine's rhetorical

---

[23] *Monologion*, c. 1; Schmitt I, 13.

improvisations to the sharply confined space of monastic thought, Anselm produces a kind of cogency which justifies his claim of fidelity to Augustine. At the same time he appears to be involved in an experiment no less daring and new than Abelard's *non per usum sed per ingenium*.

By applying his own principle of cogency to Augustine's text Anselm's reading of Augustine in no way implies the inability on his part to see the past in its otherness or, for that matter, to disagree with the Fathers. In his *Cur deus homo*—the treatise dealing with the necessity of Christ's Incarnation—he demonstrates in no uncertain terms his willingness to go against the grain. After discussing, in the first chapters of the treatise, the objections raised by the infidels against the needlessly complicated structure of the Christian faith—why, so they argue, did the omnipotent God not just order reconciliation rather than going about the complicated business of sending Christ to take upon him the sin of mankind?—he goes on to settle the score with his fellow-Christians, both past and present.

> But as for what we are used to saying about God (*Sed et illud quod dicere solemus*), that He had to act against the devil through justice rather than by force in order to set man free, so as to have the devil, by killing Him in whom death did not lawfully reside and who was God, rightly lose the power he exercised over the sinners—in all other cases God would have brought unjustified violence upon the devil since the latter rightly held the ownership of man whom he had not drawn into his possession by force; man had rather offered himself to the devil of his own accord—, I do not see how such a view can hold (*non video quam vim habeat*).[24]

This is a blunt statement. True to his *sola ratione*-method Anselm does not quote authorities either pro or con. If he had done so, there would have been a long list of Church Fathers and contemporaries upholding the view of the devil as the rightful owner of man, and none in favour of rejection of that view. Irenaeus, Augustine, Leo the Great and Gregory the Great,[25] all somehow thought of man as being the prisoner of the devil waiting to be delivered from that power by divine intervention. What is more, the phrase *illud quod dicere solemus*/"what *we* are used to saying", makes it crystal clear that Anselm realises what he is doing here. Not only does he dis-

---

[24] *Cur deus homo* II, c. 7; Schmitt II, 55–6.
[25] For the references see Schmitt II, 54.

agree with past and present masters, he is conscious of the fact that he proposes something entirely new. After briefly stating his new position he argues at some length—in view of the brevity of Anselm's style that amounts to a few lines—against those who base their opinion on biblical authority, in this case, St. Paul's letter to the Colossians. But there again a proud "I do not see it that way" rings out:

> If one objects that "the bond with its legal demand (*chirographus decreti*)" of which the apostle says that "it stood between us" (Coll. 2,14) is cancelled and if one takes this text to mean that the devil, before Christ's passion, as if under the terms of a bond, rightfully demanded from man sin as a mortgage payable because of the first sin into which he had lured man, and as a punishment for sin, in order to demonstrate by that his rights over man, my considered opinion is that it should not be so understood (*nequaquam ita intelligendum est*).[26]

Unlike Hilary of Poitiers, Ambrose, Augustine, Leo the Great and Gregory the Great all of whom had interpreted "legal demand" (*decretum*) as referring to the devil's rights,[27] Anselm argues that it is God's *decretum* which is meant here rather than the devil's. So, even though we have here one of the rare occasions on which Anselm comments *expressis verbis* on a biblical text, he does not use it as a preset authority. Biblical authority too is scrutinized *sola ratione* on whether it makes sense or not before being allowed to carry weight against other, patristic, authorities who fail to pass the test of rational cogency.

Now that Anselm has excluded the devil from the process of redemption on rational grounds, one might like to know exactly what those grounds are. What does an argument look like that justifies the majestic "I do not see it that way"? With regard to this question Anselm, in his usual succinct fashion, states his case as follows:

> For since both man and the devil belong exclusively to God and neither of them can exist outside God's power, what reason should there be for God to act with, about and in what is His own other than punishing this servant of His, who has persuaded his fellow-servant to desert their common Master and go over to him, and who had welcomed him as a traitor welcomes a fugitive, as a thief welcomes a thief with the booty of his lord?[28]

---

[26] *Cur deus homo* II, c. 7; Schmitt II, 58.
[27] For the references, see Schmitt II, 58.
[28] *Cur deus homo* II, c. 7; Schmitt II, 56-7.

Cum suo, de suo, in suo . . . Here a parallel can be drawn with Anselm's reading of Augustine's *De trinitate*. The principle of rational cogency is based on reciprocity between the mind and its object. Whether this principle is applied to biblical and patristic authorities or to the subject-matter of faith itself does not make any difference. Within Anselm's monastic mentality it is all in the game. Consequently, statements with regard to sources from the past are actualised into statements about the present. Thus Anselm's imitation of Augustine's *De trinitate* on the one hand and his stance against the tradition of the Fathers, indeed against a *communis opinio* of past and present masters, on the other, represent the same position. What we would call "a sense of the pastness of the past" is, for Anselm, a communication of minds remembering, understanding and willing. Just as in the *Monologion* the monastic memory somehow echoes the memory of the Trinity in a more cogent way than for Augustine, so Anselm in his *Cur deus homo* moves the argument about redemption away from the influence of vague, demonic and "impersonal" powers, limiting it instead to the active participants involved: God and man, or, to put it even more strictly, *cum suo, de suo, in suo*. This is the very basis on which the principle of *sola ratione* operates. Thanks to this close coherence between God and His creation, the Incarnation of Christ is seen, from the human viewpoint, as a memory of memory, as "an activity of the mind remembering being remembered by God." For Anselm, it is only within that structure of close harmony that the omission of a missing link caused by sin becomes the catastrophic threat it is. Arguing from that same rational harmony, Anselm is able to make the case that such a threat must be necessarily averted. In doing so he proves the consistency of the Christian doctrine of redemption.

4. *Bernard's* NON

Discussions of biblical and patristic authority in the twelfth century tend, so I argued above, to isolate Bernard from the general development of religious thought in that era. He is often assumed not to have participated in the search for rational cogency which, the differences between thinkers such as Anselm and Abelard notwithstanding, shaped the common cause of early scholasticism. And even though, admittedly, the epithet "the last of the Fathers but not the least" reflects the romanticized patristic, and anti-scholastic, mood of later generations, Bernard himself seems to have made it abundantly clear where he stood: on the side of the defenders of tradition versus the experimental innovators.

Yet things are much more complex than that. For only if what is meant by tradition and bibilical and patristic authority on the one hand and the quest for rational cogency on the other were unambiguously clear, we could leave the matter at that. However, just as we have seen that for Anselm the principle of *sola ratione* does not contradict the authority of Augustine, so Bernard's claim not to go beyond the Fathers does not preclude a non-authoritarian use of his own principle of cogency.

If we look at the eleventh and twelfth century theologians from a broad perspective, we can see them at work in different constellations with the same ingredients. All are somehow educated in the liberal arts. All are imbued with biblical language. All have read and absorbed a certain amount of patristic literature. But expressing themselves in religious terms they did not have at their disposal another a separate body of religion on which they might comment. In other words, authority, tradition and the search for cogency, belonged to the same cultural pattern within which many different configurations could be produced in the absence of one single external criterion for fidelity to truth and religion. The place and function of authorities from the past is part and parcel of this complex and can thus not be expressed independently from it. Whether we see Abelard excel in logic, search for clarity in theology and ethics and write hymns and laments as re-creations of biblical drama, or whether we see Hugh of St. Victor reconstruct the arc of Noah with the help of patristic tools, or Bernard reenact in his sermons the major events from the life of Christ, it is all done with different mixtures of the same materials: the Bible, the Fathers and the arts.

It is with this flexible framework in mind, then, that differences of opinion with regard to the authority of the Bible and the Fathers and the use of reason should be addressed. And differences of opinion there certainly were, fierce clashes even, the most famous of which being of course the confrontation between Bernard and Abelard at the council of Sens in 1140.

The story as such is quickly told. Alarmed, as on other important occasions, by his friend William of St. Thierry about certain bold statements by Abelard with regard to the Trinity, the power of the devil and other doctrinal issues, Bernard enters the ring. He does so timidly, he says in Letter 189 to pope Innocent II, like David confronting the heavily armed Goliath. After thus assuming biblical authority in a very special disguise, he feels free to accuse Abelard of a-typical behaviour. In fact, Bernard's intervention at the council of Sens was so effective as to bring about Abelard's condemnation.

In his accusation Bernard tries to depict his opponent as someone who fails to strike the right balance between the study of the arts on the one hand and biblical and patristic authority on the other:

> We have in France a new theologian, a student of the old master, who since his childhood has dabbled in logic and has now gone mad studying the holy Writ. Doctrines which had been condemned in the past and silenced, both his and others', are brought back to life by him. Moreover, he adds new ones to them. He claims not to be ignorant of whatever is to be found in heaven above or on earth below, excepting the phrase "I do not know". He puts his mouth into the heavens and examines the divine heights, and, returning to us, he utters words inexpressible. Being prepared to use reason in order to account for everything, even for that which surpasses reason, he proudly sins against reason, and against faith. For what is more against reason than trying to go beyond reason by reason? And what is more against faith than refusing to believe what cannot be grasped by reason? ... For that faith in God has any merit if human reason provides it with experience is denied by the blessed pope Gregory. He praises the apostles who decided to follow the Redeemer on the basis of one single order.[29]

After this vivid introduction Bernard goes on to point out that Abelard mistakenly holds the "Arian" view that there are degrees within the Trinity. The details of that discussion need not concern us here. Suffice it to know that allusions to the Fathers are scarce. Leclercq, in his edition, identified only a few: one to Jerome, one to Ps.-Athanasius, one to the *symbolum* of Athanasius, one to Augustine. There is even a comparatively modest use of biblical quotations and allusions. Bernard's argumentation presupposes the existence of a general knowledge of, and a "catholic" consensus with regard to doctrinal issues.

The next issue on which Bernard takes Abelard to task is by now a familiar one. Following Anselm, Abelard, in his Commentary on the letter to the Romans, had rejected the view according to which man is rightly subjected to the power of the devil from which he was to be delivered by the Son of God.

---

[29] *Epistola* 190, I, 1. *Sancti Bernardi Opera.* Leclercq, J., C.H. Talbot and H.M. Rochais (eds.) (Rome: 1957–1977) 8 vols. Volume VIII, 17–8.

Before dealing with the subject-matter proper I want to look at to the rhetorical frame in which Bernard's attack is wrapped. In this particular case it is above all the radical application of the *sic et non-* method which incurred Bernard's wrath. For the issue at stake is not just that the Fathers have different opinions which should be reconciled by the present commentator. Rather, Abelard has gone all out against the entire patristic tradition by opposing his personal *non* to the unanimous *sic* of the Fathers. As we know from *Cur deus homo*, and as Abelard, quoted here by Bernard, had not hesitated to admit in his Commentary, all the Fathers agreed on this issue. But, so he adds wryly, "as it seems to me (*ut nobis videtur*) the devil never held any right over man, except perhaps by God's permission, in which case the guard rather than the son of God should have taken on flesh in order to set man free."

For Bernard this is several bridges too far. Behaving as he does, Abelard should be condemned for having gone "beyond the ancient boundaries set by our Fathers (*transgredi terminos antiquos, quos posuerunt patres nostri*)". This hybrid use of the *sic et non* is met with the full force of Bernard's sarcasm:

> All, so he [Abelard] admits, say: so it is (*sic*). But I say: it is not so (*non sic*). What do you mean? Can you do better? What greater subtleties can you come up with? Do you boast that something has been secretly revealed to you that has been overlooked by the saints and has escaped the attention of the wise?[30]

Next Bernard contrasts Abelard's refusal to accept the authority of tradition with his own humble attitude of obedience to the Gospel, the real one that is, not "the gospel according to Peter [Abelard]." Finally, he proposes to argue on the basis of biblical authority (*ad Prophetas te ducam*). For of what use is it to refer to the "faith and doctrine of the doctors [of the Church]" to someone who is willing "shamelessly to disagree with them on an issue with regard to which they are unanimous?"

This entire episode is telling with regard to Bernard's attitude toward tradition and authority, although his rhetorical fireworks tend to block direct access to his final intentions. I should like to draw attention to several important features in this debate.

First, Bernard's remark about his adherence to biblical authority rather than that of the Fathers, as a debater's concession to Abelard

---

[30] *Epistola* 190, V, 11; Leclercq VIII, 26.

refusing to accept patristic authority, should be taken with a grain of salt. Nowhere in his extensive oeuvre does Bernard explicitly argue on the basis of patristic authority. That is not to say that the Fathers are not present in his texts. As we shall see in the next paragraph, Bernard's writings not only *reflect* influences from the Fathers. There is also a sense in which they can be called creative reproductions of patristic literature. Just as Anselm had rightly characterised his *Monologion* as an imitation of Augustine's *De trinitate*, so there are passages in Bernard's oeuvre which can be read as a rewriting of Origen and the other Fathers. However, this patristic presence is an indirect and organic one. As a consequence, Bernard's boasting to Abelard that he respects patristic authority—"the ancient boundaries set by our Fathers"—does not imply that he has an arsenal of preset arguments at his disposal which he can use against his opponent. As for the actual debate, Bernard—like Anselm and not unlike Abelard in the Ezekiel-episode—is quite confident that he can handle the case on his own.

This brings us to a second observation. Since Bernard clearly uses neither the *sola ratione*—nor the *sic et non*—methods, in what does his confidence dwell? There is only one answer to this question: biblical authority. And where we have seen that biblical references were rather scarce in the passage about the Trinity, with regard to the argument about the devil's power Bernard more than fulfils his promise *ad Prophetas te ducam* by showering the reader with biblical quotations. But how is this appeal to biblical authority related to Bernard's so-called confidence? Do we not have here a blatant contradiction? Exactly what, then, does biblical authority mean for him?

Basically, Bernard's use of the Bible does not differ from Anselm's respectful re-writing of Augustine. Where Anselm draws Augustine's text within the rules and games of grammatical and rational scrutiny, Bernard makes the biblical discourse part of the rhetorical drama he is in the process of creating. Both authors are "modern" in that they "frame" biblical and patristic texts with the help of the liberal arts (grammar, logic and rhetoric).[31] Accordingly, Bernard's biblical references are no longer, or, more precisely, not yet *"Probestellen"*. Their being quoted is supposed to have the reader participate in an ongoing discourse which, even if it is presented in the guise of an

---

[31] Of course, that is what the Fathers did too. The important difference lies in the explicit role of the arts.

argument or a debate, owes its continuity and consistency to the art-
ful intentions and the manipulative skills of the writer.

An example. To prove his point of the devil's power Bernard quotes,
and comments on the biblical texts as follows:

> The Lord said to his captors: "This is your hour and the power of
> darkness" (Luke 22,53). That power [of the devil] was not hidden to
> him [St. Paul] who said: "Who delivers us from the powers of dark-
> ness and brings us to the kingdom of the Son of his clarity" (Coll.
> 1,13). The Lord did not even deny the presence of the devil's power
> in Himself nor, for that matter, of Pilate's power, who was a crony of
> the devil (*qui membrum erat diaboli*) when He said [to Pilate]: "You would
> not have power over me unless it were given to you from above" (Joh.
> 19,11).[32]

What comes to the fore here is not the fact that the devil is identified as the personification of the power of darkness. Rather Bernard
wants to impress on his reader, through a litany of quotations, the
dramatic presence of evil in human existence by which man is dominated. Accordingly, far from simply looking for texts in which the
devil figures, he tries to charge texts as the ones quoted by highlighting their dramatic potential. The effectiveness of this method is mainly
achieved by bombarding the reader with text-examples but it also
shows through in the little asides. The name of Pilate, who is mentioned in passing as a crony of the devil (*membrum diaboli*), electrifies
the enumeration of biblical authorities. All of a sudden we see the
devil personified manifesting his power. This line of thought is continued in the next paragraph where yet another *membrum diaboli* is
introduced in a spectacularly dramatic setting: Laban who rightly
kept his nephew Jacob in captivity.[33] Ultimately, the entire sequence
of biblical references serves only one purpose: to bring about the
majestic appearance of Christ as the liberator of man. Through a
repetitive use of the rhetorical figure of antithesis,[34] man's domination by the devil thus evokes the overwhelming presence of its counterpart: divine mercy and liberation. Christ's coming to mankind would
have made little or no sense if it had not been not to deliver man
from the domination of the devil. In Bernard's discourse this devil is
far from being a mythological figure. Nowhere does he present us

---

[32] *Epistola* 190, V, 14; Leclercq VIII, 29.
[33] Cf. Genesis 36.
[34] *Epistola* 190, VI, 15–16; Leclercq VIII, 29–30: *Iuste igitur homo addictus, sed misericorditer liberatus* etc.

with a dramatised picture of man kept in captivity by the devil proper
with the same degree of intensity with which he evokes the scenes of
Pilate and Jesus, Laban and Jacob.

By using biblical authorities in this way, ranging from incanta-
tional quotation of texts to supreme dramatisation, Bernard probably
felt he was true to the Fathers. And indeed he was, since he be-
haved as if he were one of them. Adhering to the "boundaries" drawn
by them, that is, to the mixture of respect for biblical authority
and the freedom to play with biblical notions within the framework
of the liberal arts, he applied his own concept of rhetorical cogency
to the past. It may be true, then, that the conflict between Bernard
and Abelard can still be appreciated within the context of a balance,
however delicate, between the arts and biblical and patristic authority.
The emergence of theology as a science (*scientia*), however, asked for
a far more formalized concept of authority. In that respect not only
Bernard but Abelard too may be called "the last of the Fathers".

There is a third feature in Bernard's dealings with Abelard which
deserves attention. Witty though the parody of Abelard's *non sic* against
the unanimous *sic* of the Fathers may be, the latter's "it seems to me
that the devil did not hold power over man" is nothing but a literal
repetition of Anselm's "I do not see it that way" concerning the
same issue. This then raises the following question. If all Abelard's
boldness boils down to is to have echoed the views of Anselm, why
did Bernard not include the latter in his attack? Here we touch upon
a complicated matter.[35] The question we do have to face regards the
nature of Anselm's authority. Exactly what does Bernard mean by
"the ancient boundaries set by our Fathers"? Of course, there is no
problem with regard to the *terminus a quo*, but what about the *terminus
ad quem*? How far does the "ancient", the *antiquitas*, reach for Bernard? It is clear that in Bernard's days Anselm was held in high
esteem. Bernard's contemporary John of Salisbury, for instance, wrote
a *Vita* as a contribution to the process of canonisation. And although
sainthood and esteem as such did not qualify a person as "Father"
(or a "doctor"), Bernard's silence with regard to Anselm hints at
some embarrassment on his part. Apparently, apart from many other
things, Anselm had somehow managed to become "a doctor" if not

---

[35] For an interesting discussion of Abelard's attitude toward Anselm, see Clanchy
M.T. (1990) "Abelard's Mockery of St. Anselm", *Journal of Ecclesiastical History* 41
(1990) 1–23.

"another Augustine"—just as Hugh of St. Victor was to be called *alter Augustinus* by his contemporaries—, and thus to carry a kind of authority which could not be ignored. To ignore Anselm, however, is exactly what Bernard did, and thus he reveals a crack in the *sic* of the patristic consensus with which he attacked Abelard's *non*. And if that is not true, the least that can be said is that, as long as patristic authority was approached from the viewpoint of self-conscious continuity, the problem of the *terminus ad quem*—of the "antiquity of the Fathers"—stood no chance of being solved.

5. *Bernard's* SIC

After analysing Bernard's view of patristic authority in his polemics against Abelard, I want to conclude by giving an example of his "reproducing" the Fathers in his own discourse. This is the most difficult part since, as I have pointed out above, rather than quoting from the Fathers in support of his views, Bernard's discourse presents itself as an amalgam of biblical language in a patristic setting. It is not the identification of patristic allusions as such which is problematic. That is, after all, a problem which can be solved by tenacious research. We here face the same problem as when examining Anselm's claim of fidelity to Augustine's *De trinitate*. Like Anselm, Bernard's creativity is such as to leave the reader puzzled on account of its seamless imitation of the original. In other words, it is the self-conscious feeling of continuity on Bernard's part which now requires further assessment.

If it is true that, generally speaking, Bernard owes much to Augustine, his language of mystical union and desire appears to be heavily influenced by Gregory the Great and Origen.[36] When during the bride and bridegroom's rest in a mutual embrace there is a "silence in heaven lasting half an hour", this allusion to the Apocalypse can be traced back to Gregory and Origen.[37] When Bernard, in Sermon 74 on the Song of Songs, tells about his personal experience of the visits by the Word, similar phrases can be found in Origen.[38]

---

[36] Obviously, the entire infrastructure of Bernard's language is modelled according to the exegetical principles developed by those Fathers and others (such as Ambrose).

[37] Gilson, E. *La théologie mystique de Saint Bernard* (Paris: 1947) 128.

[38] Brésard, L. 1983 *Bernard et Origène commentent le Cantique* (Forges: 1983) 64; Deroy, J.P.Th. (1963) *Bernardus en Origenes* (Haarlem: 1963).

Since we have concentrated so far on the theme of tradition and authority, it seems proper to concentrate on an example which deals with the very problem of the past. In Sermon 2 on the Song of Songs Bernard reflects on the unfulfilled desire of the Old Testament Fathers for the coming of Christ. His fellow-monks ought to be ashamed if they would take the trouble to look back from their comfortable position of fulfilment at the vain attempts of the Fathers to hasten the arrival of the Redeemer. Bernard next goes on to identify himself with the impatience of the Fathers:

> For a perfect person might have said: "What do I care for those streams of words uttered by the Prophets? I would much rather be kissed by the handsomest of men. Let him himself kiss me with the kiss of his mouth. I refuse to listen to Moses any longer for he suffers too much of a speech impediment. Isaiah's lips are unclean, Jeremiah does not know how to speak up because he is a young boy. In fact, all prophets are poor speakers. He himself, he whom they speak about, let himself speak. May he himself kiss me with the kiss of his mouth . . . I therefore rightly refuse to accept any more visions and dreams, I do not want any more symbols and riddles. I even get tired of the pretty shapes of angels. My Jesus surpasses them in stature and beauty. I do not ask for anyone else, no angel, no man, but only for himself to kiss me with the kiss of his mouth.[39]

This passage clearly derives from Origen both in wording and in content:

> For how long will my bridegroom go on to send his kisses through Moses? For how long will he go on to send his kisses through the Prophets? It is the lips of the bridegroom himself I long for. May he himself come, may he himself descend (Hom. PG 13:39).

> He should stop talking to me through his servants, the angels and the Prophets. He should rather come himself and kiss me with the kiss of his mouth . . . It is him to whom I shall listen when he talks to me, it is him whom I shall see when he teaches me.[40]

Continuity between the two passages there certainly is. Origen's text and Bernard's imitation of it relate to each other as a score being performed by a musician who adds his own phraseology and writes his own cadenza. And for the moment it might even seem that in Bernard, whom we just saw actualising the Bible in his dispute with

---

[39] *Sermones super Cantica Canticorum*, 1, I, 2, Leclercq I, 9.
[40] Origen, *In Canticum Canticorum*, I; PG 13, 85A. Cf. Brésard, L. (1983) *Bernard et Origène commentent le Cantique* (Forges: 1983) 51.

Abelard and whom we now see imitating Origen's biblical drama-
tisations, there is no trace of any sense of the past whatsoever. All
that counts is the immediate performance of biblical drama in patristic
disguise. Yet Bernard's drawing a line vis-à-vis Abelard, and, by implication, vis-à-vis Anselm, suggests otherwise. Somehow and somewhere
an idea of historical distance makes itself felt. In the event, in Bernard's
use of Origen all the problems concerning biblical and patristic authority we have discussed above coalesce. Both Origen and Bernard
are in a position to take the Old Testament Prophets for what they
are worth. Theirs is the vantage-point of the *perfectus*, that is, the
hypothetically perfect person in the past who, in the present, happens to be none other than the author scrutinising Scripture. Imitating Origen, Bernard behaves as his equal. Together they share the
same sense of the one and only historical distance that counts, that
is the fulfilment of the Scriptures in Christ, which, in turn, provides
later generations with the room and opportunity for endless ruminations. Being part of an unbroken chain, the literary-religious products of those later generations have to be judged accordingly. There
is, in other words, a principle of cogency which can be applied to
the past and the present. That same principle of cogency contains
both the spiritual freedom of the reader of the Bible and his humble
obedience to authority.

But what about Anselm and Abelard? What are we to think of
Anselm's and Abelard's self-conscious "I do not see it that way" against
the unanimous patristic tradition? The irony of the matter is that,
for all their modernity,—"modernity" being a kind of *vaticinium ex
eventu* anyway—their proud *non* somehow echoes the impatience of
the Old Testament Prophets in Origen's and Bernard's versions as
well as their refusal to "accept any more symbols and riddles." Admittedly, the principles of rational and rhetorico-biblical cogency were
destined to move into entirely different directions. That, however,
should not prevent us from remembering their common provenance
from biblical Utopia where symbols and riddles can, in a sense, be
said to have gone ever since the coming of Christ. It is this concept
of fulfilment as laid down in Scripture and taken up by the Fathers
that constitutes authority while at the same time creating a "textual"
continuity in which it can be scrutinised, commented upon and, if
need be, contradicted. To argue *sola ratione* as Anselm did, or *non per
usum sed per ingenium* in Abelard's way, still reflects this moment of
fulfilment underlying the writings of the Fathers. In a similar vein,

Bernard's flair for imitating the Bible and Origen is equally rooted in the knowledge of being "one of them".

This common denominator, however frail, which links the eleventh and twelfth-century protagonists discussed above, allows us to characterise their attitude toward the Church Fathers. A delicate balance between self-confidence and a sense of authority: that is the key in which the reading of the Fathers is set before the storm of scholasticism caused those elements to drift apart.

Bibliography

Peter Abelard. *Historia calamitatum.* ed. Monfrin, J. (Paris: 1959).

—. Sic et non. In: *PL* 178: 1359–1610.

—. *Sic et non*, ed. Boyer B.B. and R. McKeon. (Chicago: 1976).

Anselm of Canterbury, *S. Anselmi Cantuariensis Archiepiscopi opera omnia*, ed. Schmitt F.S. (Stuttgart-Bad Canstatt: 1968).

—. *Monologion, Proslogion, Debate with Gaunilo, Meditation on Human Redemption*, vol. I, ed. and transl. Hopkins J. and H. Richardson (New York: 1974).

Bernard of Clairvaux. *Sancti Bernardi Opera*. [SBOP] eds. Leclercq, J., C.H. Talbot and H.M. Rochais (Rome: 1957–1977) 8 vols.

Origen. *Homiliae in Canticum Canticorum.* ed. Rousseau, O. (Paris:1953) Sources Chrétiennes 37.

—. *In Canticum Canticorum.* PG 12, 83–216.

Beumer, J. (1952) "Der theoretische Beitrag der Frühscholastik zu dem Problem des Dogmenfortschritts", *Zeitschrift für katholische Theologie* 74 (1952) 205–26.

Benson, R.L. and G. Constable (eds.) (1982) *Renaissance and Renewal in the Twelfth Century* (Oxford: 1982).

Brésard, L. (1983) *Bernard et Origène commentent le Cantique* (Forges: 1983).

Buytaert, E.M. (1974) "Abelard's Trinitarian Doctrine". In: *Peter Abelard*, ed. E.M. Buytaert (Leuven: 1974) 127–52.

Certeau, M. de. (1963) "De Saint-Cyran au Jansénisme, conversion et réforme", *Christus, Cahiers Spirituels* 10 (1963) 399–417.

Chenu, M-D. (1957) *La théologie au douzième siècle* (Paris: 1975).

Clanchy, M.T. (1990) "Abelard's Mockery of St. Anselm", *Journal of Ecclesiastical History* 41 (1990) 1–23.

Coleman, J. (1992) *Ancient and Medieval Memories. Studies on the Reconstruction of the Past* (Cambridge: 1992).

Colish, M.L. (1968) *The Mirror of Language, A Study in the Medieval Theory of Knowledge* (New Haven: 1968).

—. (1991) ". . . *Quia hodie locum non habent*: Scholastic Theologians Reflect on their Authorities". In: *Proceedings of the PMR Conference* vol. 15 (Villanova: 1991) 1–17.

Constable, G. (1982) "Renewal and Reform in Religious Life: Concept and Realities" in Benson and Constable (Cambridge: 1982) 37–68.

Cramer, P.J (1993) *Baptism and Change in the Early Middle Ages c. 200–c. 1150* (Cambridge: 1993).

Deroy, J.P.Th. (1963) *Bernardus en Origenes* (Haarlem: 1963).

Grabmann, M. (1909–11) *Geschichte der scholastischen Methode*, I–II, (Freiburg: 1909–11; reprint Graz: 1957).

Evans, G.R. (1978) *Anselm and Talking about God* (Oxford: 1978).

—. (1980) *Anselm and a New Generation* (Oxford: 1980).

—. (1981) "St. Anselm and sacred history", in *The Writing of History in the Middle Ages*, eds. R.H.C. Davis and J.M. Wallace-Hadrill (Oxford: 1981) 187–210.

—. (1983) *The Mind of Bernard of Clairvaux* (Oxford: 1983).

Gilson, E. (1947) *La théologie mystique de Saint Bernard* (Paris: 1947).

Kuttner, S.G. (1960) *Harmony from Dissonance: An Interpretation of Medieval Canon Law* (Latrobe: 1960).

Landgraf, A.M. (1953) "Diritto canonico e telogia nel secolo XII", *Studia Gratiana* 1 (1953) 371–413.

Lubac, H. de. (1959) *Exégèse médiévale. Les quatre sens de l'Écriture* (Paris: 1959).

Luscombe, D.E. (1969) *The School of Peter Abelard. The Influence of Abelard's Thought in the Early Scholastic Period* (Cambridge: 1969).

—. (1988) "From Paris to the Paraclete: the Correspondence of Abelard and Heloise", *Proceedings of the British Academy* LXXIV (1967) 247–283.

Morrison, K.F. (1969) *Tradition and Authority in the Western Church* (Princeton: 1969).

Olsen, G. (1969) "The Idea of the Ecclesia Primitiva in the Writings of the Twelfth-Century Canonists", *Traditio* 25 (1969) 61–86.

Paré, G. and A. Brunet and P. Tremblay (1933) *La Renaissance du XIIe siècle: Les écoles et l'enseignement* (Paris: 1933).

Pieper, J. (1960) *Scholasticism. Personalities and Problems of Medieval Philosophy* (London: 1960).

Rousseau, O. (1953) "Le dernier des Pères". *Bernard Théologien. Analecta Sacri Ordinis Cisterciensis* 9 (1953) 306–8.

Southern, R.W. (1990) *Anselm of Canterbury. Portait in a Landscape* (Cambridge: 1990).

Stock, B. (1983) *The Implications of Literacy: Written Language and Models of Interpretation in the Eleventh and Twelfth Centuries* (Princeton: 1983).

Thomas, R. (ed.). (1980) *Petrus Abaelardus (1079–1142).* Trierer theologische Studien 38 (Trier: 1980).

Zerbi, P. (1975) "San Bernardo di Chiaravalle e il concilio di Sens. In: *Studi su S. Bernardo di Chiaravalle nell' ottavo centenario della canonizzazione. Convegno internazionale-Certoza di Firenze, novembre 1974* (Rome: 1975) 49–73.

PART TWO

PATRISTIC SOURCES AND THEIR USES IN
THE LATER MIDDLE AGES

ROBERT GROSSETESTE AND THE CHURCH FATHERS

Neil Lewis

Introduction[1]

It is perhaps difficult for the modern reader to appreciate fully the regard in which Grosseteste was held in his day. Like many other important thinkers of the middle ages, he has been eclipsed in our memory by geniuses such as St. Thomas Aquinas or Duns Scotus. Yet he was the dominant figure in English intellectual life in the first half of the thirteenth century. The chronicler Salimbene referred to him as one of the "greatest clerks of the world." He was revered by the English Franciscans, of whom he was the first teacher. His death was followed by repeated, though unsuccessful attempts at his canonization. Roger Bacon (*c.* 1214–*c.* 1292) and John Wycliffe (*c.* 1330–84) ranked him with the greatest thinkers of the past.[2] At the basis of this esteem lay Grosseteste's truly remarkable contributions to thirteenth-century intellectual life, both as a student of natural science and Aristotle, and as a theologian, translator, and commentator. It is in these latter roles that he played a key part in the reception of the fathers. His theological writings made a use of the Greek fathers unparalleled in his contemporaries or predecessors. To the Latin West he introduced for the first time a number of Greek patristic texts in Latin translation or critical revisions of already extant translations. His commentaries on the works of Pseudo-Dionysius displayed a level of textual criticism unheard of in previous or subsequent medieval commentary.[3]

---

[1] I would like to thank my colleague Fr. Denis Bradley and Prof. James McEvoy for their helpful comments on an earlier version of this paper. All translations in this paper, unless otherwise noted, are my own. The dating of Grosseteste's works is a difficult matter. When possible, I have provided the dates suggested by his recent editors.

[2] Salimbene, *Chronica*, ed. O. Holder-Egger (Leipzig: 1905) 233; John Wycliffe, *Trialogus*, ed. G.V. Lechler (Oxford: 1869) 83; Roger Bacon, *Opus tertium*, 22, in *Fr. Rogeri Bacon Opera Quaedam Hactenus Inedita*, ed. J.S. Brewer, vol. 1 (London: 1859) 70.

[3] See Thomson (1940) for the range of Grosseteste's writings.

Grosseteste was born in England between about 1168 and 1175. His life before 1225 is largely unknown. It is not known whether he taught at Oxford before this date or where he obtained his training in the arts or theology; he perhaps studied theology in Paris during the dispersal of scholars from Oxford between 1209 and 1214, but this is at best conjecture. It is known that he taught theology in the secular schools at Oxford between about 1225 and 1230, and left this position in 1230 or 1231 to teach the Franciscans recently established at Oxford. He may not, as is sometimes said, have been the first chancellor of Oxford, but he certainly took on the duties of chancellor at some point, if not the official title.[4] In 1231 he resigned all his preferments, except his prebend in Lincoln cathedral, and devoted himself to his studies and the instruction of the Franciscans. In 1235 he was made Bishop of Lincoln, a position he occupied until his death in 1253. He was known to later medievals as *Lincolniensis*.[5]

Grosseteste on Patristic Authority

James McEvoy has observed that Grosseteste was a man swimming against the theological currents of his day.[6] In response to the encroachment of Peter Lombard's *Sentences* at Oxford, Grosseteste urged the Oxford regent-masters to base their ordinary lectures on Scripture alone, the source of the doctrinal foundation stones upon which the masters were to erect the house of God.[7] Although theology became increasingly speculative and dialectical in the thirteenth century, Grosseteste, after working in speculative theology *c.* 1225–30, countered this trend in his own writings. He turned to pastoral concerns and a form of scriptural exegesis that made heavy use of the "holy expositors," but eschewed the increasingly popular dialectical methods such

---

[4] See Southern (1992) xxix–xxxii.

[5] For Grosseteste's career, see the contrasting accounts given in McEvoy (1982) and Southern (1992). Details in much of the literature pertaining to Grosseteste's biography and the dating of his works must be used with caution.

[6] McEvoy (1975) 62.

[7] See letter 123, in *Roberti Grosseteste episcopi quondam Lincolniensis epistolae*, ed. H.R. Luard (London: 1861) 346–47. On Lombard's *Sentences* see Fr. Bougerol's contribution to this volume. Raedts (1987) 124 suggests that Grosseteste was reacting against the Dominican, Richard Fishacre, the first to use Lombard's *Sentences* in theological instruction at Oxford.

as the *quaestio* or syllogistic structuring of the text of Scripture.

Grosseteste never expressly lists those he takes as fathers and only occasionally uses the term. More often he uses the expression "holy expositor," by which he refers to the saints who have interpreted Scripture. Under this head he employs material from all of the Greek and Latin fathers listed in *Decretum Gelasianum* (with the exception of Cyprian, Theophilus of Alexandria, and Prosper of Aquitaine),[8] as well as material from Gregory the Great, John of Damascus, Isidore of Seville, Bede, and other figures who play a lesser role in his writings. In addition, in his Dionysian commentaries he frequently refers to Pseudo-Dionysius the Areopagite as the "most holy" or "most wise father."

Grosseteste had an unusually deep veneration of these men and, despite the power and originality of his thought, a great humility regarding his own contributions. He described himself as walking in the footsteps of the fathers.[9] Throughout his theological writings he emphasizes his mental limitations in comparison with them. He alludes to their role in his theological inquiries in the treatise *De cessatione legalium* (*On the Cessation of the Ceremonial Laws*), written *c.* 1231-35. Here he develops a series of arguments for the view that even had man not fallen there would still have been a God-man.[10] He begins by noting that the fathers had not settled this matter:

> Yet, if my memory does not fail me, in those books of theirs that I have so far looked at none of the holy expositors determine whether there would have been a God-man even if man had not sinned.[11]

After presenting arguments that there indeed would have been a God-man even had man not fallen, he concludes:

> By these and similar arguments it seems that it can be proved that there would have been a God-man even if man had never sinned. Yet I am quite sure [*scio*] that I do not know whether this is true, and my ignorance on this matter pains me in no small degree. For as we said above, I recall having seen nothing determined on this by our authorities. Nor do I wish or dare to assert anything on so difficult a question

---

[8] Namely the Greeks Gregory of Nazianzus, Basil, Athanasius, Chrysostom, and Cyril; and the Latins, Hilary of Poitiers, Ambrose, Augustine, and Jerome.

[9] *De cessatione legalium*, III.i.30, ed. R.C. Dales and E.B. King (Oxford: 1986) 132.

[10] Grosseteste was an early proponent of this view, but it may be found before him. See Moiser (1973). I am indebted to Denis Bradley for this reference.

[11] *De cess. leg.*, III.i.1 (*ed. cit.*, 119).

without express authority, since a plausible argument can easily deceive my paltry mental ability and knowledge.[12]

In Grosseteste's day there was a growing desire to return to the complete texts of the fathers—the so-called *originalia patrum*—and to place less reliance on the extracts from them to be found in the biblical glosses or collections of excerpts known as *florilegia* or *sententiae*; the Greek fathers, in any case, were poorly represented in such materials.[13] As the above passage indicates, Grosseteste shared this desire and made a practice of inspecting the original books of the holy expositors on issues with which he was concerned. On matters of theological importance he sought the backing of their authority. If they were silent or arrived at no definite conclusions, he would only present his views, no matter how well argued, as possibilities. His concern to arrive at truth and avoid falsity in such matters and his humble conception of his own mental abilities led to a characteristic tentativeness in his writings.

Although Grosseteste took himself to be "following in the footsteps of the fathers," he saw that often they appeared to be walking in different directions. Given their importance in his theological works, he could hardly avoid trying to conciliate such apparent doctrinal differences. He did so, however, not by the use of dialectical techniques, but by the careful inspection of the fathers' writings in their linguistic and historical contexts.

In the second recension of *De libero arbitrio* (*On Free Choice*), written *c.* 1225–30, for example, following what he thought to be the doctrine of St. John Chrysostom,[14] Grosseteste held that the Father causally precedes the Son, thereby suggesting the heterodox view that the Son was lesser than the Father. He emphasizes, however, that although Chrysostom's words may appear heterodox, they are not and to interpret them thus "is our presumption and vice, and it is not because he himself understood anything impious in them."[15] He

---

[12] *Ibid.*, III.ii.1 (*ed. cit.*, 133).

[13] On *originalia* see Rouse (1991) 249–51 and references cited therein. Callus (1954) describes the turn in England to complete texts, and notes the development in the second half of the thirteenth century of compendia containing extracts from the Greek Fathers.

[14] It was in fact the teaching of John Scottus Eriugena in his homily on the prologue of John, *Vox spiritualis aquilae*, which Grosseteste wrongly ascribes to Chrysostom in a number of works. See McEvoy (1987).

[15] Latin text in *Die Philosophischen Werke des Robert Grosseteste, Bischofs von Lincoln*, ed.

goes on to point out that Augustine's reference to the Father as principle in relation to the Son may also suggest such a doctrine; it too must be correctly understood.

In a later note he appended to his translation of the Greek father St. John of Damascus' *Trisagion* (his discussion of the hymn "Holy, Holy, Holy") Grosseteste discusses the conflict between the Greek and Latin Churches over the Latins' doctrine that the Holy Spirit proceeds from the Father and the Son (*Filioque*). He holds that the price for finding genuine disagreement here is to reckon one side or the other to be heretics. But

> ... who is so foolhardy as to accuse the author of this work, John Damascene, together with the Blessed Basil, Gregory the Theologian, Gregory of Nyssa, Cyril, and other such Greek Fathers, of heresy? And who on the other hand dares to make a heretic of Blessed Jerome, Augustine, Hilary, and other such Latin doctors?

The solution of the apparent conflict again lies in a careful investigation of the language of the fathers:

> It is probable consequently that the opposing statements quoted do not correspond to any real conflict between the Saints; for this reason, that what is said is said in a variety of ways; for example, in this context "of this person," and similarly "from this or that person," or again "by him"; and it may be that if this wide range of expressions were more subtly understood and analysed, it would emerge clearly that the doctrine which finds opposing expressions is in fact the same.[16]

In these works Grosseteste's attitude to the Latin and Greek fathers is ecumenical, "consisting in a respect for all the Fathers, not just for those of his own immediate tradition."[17] His great respect for and use of the Greek as well as Latin fathers marks his mature theological works.

In the above passages Grosseteste seeks concord through the idea that verbal differences may correspond to a sameness of meaning. In *De cessatione legalium* he employs the same strategy in his extended discussion of the conflict between Jerome and Augustine on the

---

L. Baur (Münster: 1912) 186. The first recension is reedited in Lewis, N., "The First Recension of Robert Grosseteste's *De libero arbitrio*," *Mediaeval Studies* 53 (1991) 1–88.

[16] For Grosseteste's work toward the reconciliation of the Greek and Latin Churches, see McEvoy (1975), whose translation (45) I have used above.

[17] McEvoy (1975) 52.

ceremonial laws.[18] But in this discussion he also mentions another irenic strategy to which he more frequently appeals. Not only must the meaning of the fathers' words be carefully scrutinized, but also the use to which they put them. They do not always speak assertorically; often they simply mean to pose possibilities:

> It should be noted that the holy writers in most cases were not so much concerned to assert what was the case as to point out what was possible, and their statements are generally not so much statements of fact as statements of possibility, even though they may appear to us to have been made assertorically and to state facts.[19]

This strategy allows for genuine differences of meaning in the fathers' statements without logical incompatibility, since statements of alternative possibilites may be true together.

Grosseteste has little to say about the basis of the epistemological authority of patristic texts. He appears to have taken them at least in some cases as divinely inspired. He describes Jerome and Augustine, for example, as reeds through whom the Holy Spirit breathes.[20] But he also admits that in those cases in which we simply cannot reconcile their views they may be in genuine conflict. In these cases, however, their words may not be divinely inspired. Because there is some value in this for later readers, the Holy Spirit may leave them to their own devices.[21] Unfortunately Grosseteste provides no principled way of determining when the fathers are writing under divine inspiration and when not.

John Wycliffe admired Grosseteste's irenic approach and set him up as an example sorely neglected by many writers of his day who were more prepared to criticize the fathers than sympathetically interpret their words.[22]

---

[18] His reconciliation of the conflict between Jerome and Augustine on the ceremonial laws is usefully summarized and contrasted with more dialectical approaches in Smalley (1955) 90–94.

[19] *De cess. leg.*, IV.iii.4 (*ed. cit.*, 165).

[20] *Ibid.*, IV.iii. (*ed. cit.*, 164–65).

[21] *Ibid.*, IV.iii.3 (*ed. cit.*, 165).

[22] See John Wycliffe, *De Trinitate*, ed. A. du Pont Beck (Colorado: 1962) 145: "Would that modern writers would pay more attention to the writings and opinions of this good man, whose intention was to reconcile the ancient doctors of the Church, gathering together their Catholic opinions and expounding them in a favourable and pious sense, rather than attacking dead men by forcing them into equivocal positions, so that their writings may be trampled on and those of their critics glorified, as is the odious fashion of too many nowadays" (Southern's (1992) 300 translation, slightly modified).

The Use of the Fathers in Grosseteste's Writings

Grosseteste's writings cover a wide range, and we can give only a brief survey of the role the fathers play in them.

We may pass quickly over works from before about 1230. They were either scientific in nature or concerned with speculative theology.[23] The former works display no overt patristic influence, although many of their characteristic positions undoubtedly owe much to patristic thought.[24] The writings in speculative theology are generally quite short, with the exception of *De libero arbitrio*.[25] Despite a concern with issues much debated by Grosseteste's contemporaries, they rarely refer to their views. Instead, as in all Grosseteste's works, "the great authority of the great Augustine" looms large;[26] in addition, Anselm of Canterbury and Bernard of Clairvaux exert a strong influence.

In the early 1230s or perhaps the late 1220s Grosseteste shifts his attention to pastoral concerns or biblical exegesis. *De decem mandatis* (*On the Ten Commandments*), a work of the former genre, is intended for the instruction of those who have the cure of souls.[27] It draws on Scripture and the Latin patristic writers, especially Augustine. From the Greek fathers, however, we find only a single quotation from Chrysostom.

De cessatione legalium, another work of this period, argues that the ceremonial laws ceased to be binding upon the death of Christ. Grosseteste's juxtaposition of *rationes* and *auctoritates* recalls *De libero arbitrio*, but he makes a far greater use of patristic texts, primarily the Latin fathers Augustine, Gregory the Great, and Jerome, but also the Greeks, most of whom, however, he had found in Burgundio's twelfth-century translation of John of Damascus' *De fide orthodoxa*.

Despite their increasing use of patristic material these works contain little that is novel in the use of the fathers. Matters change,

---

[23] The chronology of Grosseteste's scientific writings is still in a state of flux; the recent tendency has been to shift dates back from those proposed by earlier scholars; this is especially true of the Aristotelian commentaries. See McEvoy (1982) 505–19 and Southern (1992) 120–40.

[24] See McEvoy (1982) 158–62, 326–45.

[25] These works are edited in Baur, *ed. cit.* The *Quaestiones theologicae* ascribed to Grosseteste in Callus (1948) are, in my view, by some other author.

[26] See letter 1 to Adam Rufus in Luard, *ed. cit.*, 1–2. For Augustine's influence see McEvoy (1982) 51–68.

[27] McEvoy (1991) analyses this work in detail. A *Moralitates in Evangelia* has also been ascribed to Grosseteste, but see Dobson (1975) for an attack on the ascription.

however, with Grosseteste's biblical exegesis, which displays a deepening engagement with both the Latin and Greek fathers. His exegetical works include glosses on the Pauline letters and commentaries on Galatians, the first one hundred Psalms, the first two chapters of Genesis (*Hexaemeron*), and Ecclesiasticus 43: 1–5. The Pauline glosses are no longer extant, although portions can be reconstructed from quotations made by Thomas Gascoigne in the fifteenth century. Only the *Hexaemeron* and commentary on Ecclesiasticus have been published; in addition to them, only the *Commentary on the Psalms* has been studied to any large degree.[28] The works on the Pauline letters and Psalms 1–79 probably date from before *c.* 1231, as they show little sign of the Greek learning found in Grosseteste's other exegetical works.[29] The commentary on Ecclesiasticus was probably written *c.* 1230–35. The commentaries on *Galatians* and the *Hexaemeron* display an increasing command of the Greek patristic literature and the Greek language, and probably date from the period *c.* 1232–35.

The exegetical works are concerned to expound the senses of Scripture, and in particular the literal sense. As noted, Grosseteste avoids using a dialectical method of biblical exegesis. He rejects attempts to formulate the text of Scripture in accordance with a rational epistemological structure of premises and conclusions, holding that since the things said in the text are

> . . . equally credible, we should not care which is said first or second, nor ought we to syllogize one from another, for given that they are credible in this way, none is better known than another.[30]

---

[28] For the Pauline glosses see Smalley (1955). Some of Gascoigne's quotations from these glosses were published by J.E.T. Rogers in *Loci e Libro Veritatum* (1881). Thomson (1940) 74–75 incorrectly identified the MS Cambridge, Gonville and Caius 439 as containing Grosseteste's *Commentary on Romans*; the attribution is rejected in Smalley (1955) 76, n. 2. The *Hexaëmeron* has been edited by R.C. Dales and S. Gieben (Oxford: 1982); J. McEvoy has edited the commentary on Ecclesiasticus in "The Sun as *res* and *signum*: Grosseteste's Commentary on *Ecclesiasticus* ch. 43, vv. 1–5," *Recherches de théologie ancienne et médiévale* 41 (1974) 38–91. Editions by J. McEvoy of the *Commentary on Galatians* and by R.C. Dales of Gascoigne's extracts from Grosseteste's Pauline glosses are forthcoming in the series *Corpus Christianorum Continuatio Mediaevalis*.

[29] See Smalley (1955). It is possible, however, that Grosseteste's Greek studies go back some years before 1231 (Dionisotti [1988]), and the dating of works on the basis of the Greek learning they display must be done with considerable caution. The commentary on Psalms 1–79 in all likelihood dates from before 1231, as it is contained in the MS Durham A.iii.12, parts of which must have been composed before that date; see Hunt (1955).

[30] *Hex.*, I.ii.2, *ed. cit.*, 51.

Yet if dialectic plays little role in Grosseteste's interpretation of Scripture, the fathers play a key role. Grosseteste notes in his short commentary on Jerome's introduction to the Bible that the sense of sacred Scripture is hidden and indicated by signs, and admits no easy entry without a guide.[31] The fathers are Grosseteste's guides to the sense of scripture. His commentaries on Galatians and Genesis, in particular, are largely based on the Greek and Latin fathers' writings on these books.

The growing presence of the Greek patristic tradition and of Grosseteste's Greek learning is evident in the *Commentary on the Psalms*.[32] The commentary on Psalms 1 to 79 is uneven in focus and displays a great interest in the natural world, as do so many of Grosseteste's works. Its patristic sources are primarily Augustine and Gregory the Great, and to a lesser extent Jerome, Cassiodorus, and Chrysostom. In the commentary on Psalms 80 to 100, however, Grosseteste is no longer as concerned with the natural world and starts to make extensive use of Greek patristic sources. This part of the commentary, unlike the earlier part, seems to have been written not as notes in the margins of his copy of the Psalms, but as a full-scale commentary. Augustine and Gregory retain the most prominent role, but Grosseteste starts to refer to "Gregory of Nazianzus, Basil, Athanasius, and, above all Cyril and Theodoret."[33] His quotations, however, are not from translations then extant in the Latin West. M.R. James first noted this fact and suggested that Grosseteste possessed a Greek *catena* or collection of extracts of the Greek fathers on the Psalms, as well as a Greek Psalter, from each of which he made short translations, though probably, at this early stage of his Greek studies, with the aid of assistants.[34]

If the *Commentary on the Psalms* marks a turning point in Grosseteste's intellectual life, the *Hexaemeron* shows him to have well rounded the corner. In this commentary Grosseteste works through the first two chapters of Genesis, discussing at length the various interpretations that have been placed on their contents by both the Greek and Latin fathers. He continually has his eye on apparent conflicts in their views or difficulties that might confront their interpretations.

---

[31] *Ibid., Prooemium* 3 (*ed. cit.*, 18).
[32] I am indebted in the following remarks to Southern (1992) 113–19.
[33] Southern (1992) 117.
[34] James (1922).

Although he does not neglect the spiritual sense of Scripture, his primary concern is for the literal sense. It provides occasion for discussion of physical issues, in many cases ones that he had previously raised in his physical works, though he now introduces where relevant the fathers' views on these matters. In addition we find numerous discussions of questions concerning the translation and interpretation of Greek terms, which display Grosseteste's by now quite considerable knowledge of Greek.[35]

The Greek father St. Basil plays a key role. Grosseteste quotes Basil's *Hexaemeron* second only to the combined quotations of Augustine. Whether Basil's *Hexaemeron* helped stimulate the writing of the *Hexaemeron* or instead was consulted as a step in its preparation, Grosseteste clearly saw its value for hexaemeral studies. He had at some point obtained a copy of this work in Eustathius' Latin translation from the monks of Bury St. Edmunds in exchange for a manuscript containing Parisian glosses on Scripture.[36] Earlier medieval writers had employed Basil's *Hexaemeron*, but not to the degree found in Grosseteste's *Hexaemeron*. The usual practice was to quote a few proof texts, but Grosseteste quotes long passages. He discusses Basil's views at length and perhaps translates some material himself from the Greek text of Basil.[37] In addition to the hexaemeral writings of Basil and Augustine (*De Genesi ad litteram*), he employs Ambrose's *Hexaemeron* and *De paradiso*, and Bede's *Hexaemeron* (which he often ascribes to Jerome), and makes wide use of Jerome, Gregory the Great, Isidore of Seville's *Etymologies*, and John of Damascus' *De fide orthodoxa*.[38]

Much of the commentary is driven by the differences of view presented by the patristic tradition, but the discussion of them avoids dialectical methods and is often inconclusive. The discussion of whether the heaven mentioned in Genesis 1:1 is above or identical to the firmament is characteristic. After quoting extensively from their writings, Grosseteste notes that Jerome, Strabus, Bede, and John of

---

[35] The nature of this commentary is discussed in Raedts (1987) 122–37. For the unusual depth of the philological notes in Grosseteste's writings, see Dionisotti (1988).

[36] See Hunt (1955).

[37] See Southern (1992) 207. Rizzerio (1992) reveals that in the *Commentary on Galatians* Grosseteste makes translations from Chrysostom and his commentator Theophylact, as well as from the Greek NT. She also discusses Chrysostom's influence on this commentary.

[38] On Grosseteste's sources in the *Hexaemeron* see Muckle (1951) and (1945), and the editors' introduction.

Damascus believe that it is different, whereas Josephus, Gregory of Nyssa, and "other expositors" take them to be the same. In this case he notes with his usual modesty that "it is not [his] place to deter-mine this controversy," although he holds that if we adopt the former view the heaven must be immobile, and proceeds to explain why. In another passage, considering the question of nature of the waters above the firmament, he explains the differing views on this matter and, having arrrived at no definite conclusion, asks what the point of setting out these opinions is "given that they are incompatible." Appealing to an irenic strategy noted above, he replies that they let us know "the possible ways in which the waters may happen to truly exist above the firmament," so that we may

> . . . reply to those who try to prove that there cannot be waters above the heavens, and show them the several ways in which what Scripture says can be the case. The holy expositors wrote these things not so much to assert them to be the case, as to show the possible ways in which what Scripture says may be so.[39]

The *Hexaemeron* is the last of Grosseteste's major theological works. After *c.* 1235 he turned to translation and commentary. A word, however, must be said about a number of sermons written in this later period. Some of these sermons are of great value for an under-standing of Grosseteste's mature theological and psychological views. Most important for us is the fact that they display the influence, little present in the earlier works, of Pseudo-Dionysius, whom Grosse-teste was studying and translating in the late 1230s and early 1240s. We may briefly consider the sermon *Ecclesia sancta celebrat* (*The Holy Church Celebrates*), which Grosseteste probably wrote *c.* 1242–44.[40] It concerns the resurrection, especially the spiritual resurrection, and outlines at some length Grosseteste's account of the two lives of nature and grace. Pseudo-Dionysius' influence is evident both in Grosseteste's choice of language and his thought, although, as McEvoy notes, the latter is subordinated to the thought of Augustine. An example must suffice. In his account of the soul's ascent to God, Grosseteste is greatly influenced by Pseudo-Dionysius' neoplatonic conception of the hierarchy of being and his mystical sensibility, but he does not adopt his view that the vision of God is mediated by created theophanies; instead he adopts the Latin conception of a direct vision of God, as

---

[39] *Hex.*, III.iii.6 (*ed. cit.*, 105).
[40] Edited and discussed in McEvoy (1980). My remarks are indebted to this article.

he does in his commentary on Pseudo-Dionysius' *Mystical Theology*.[41]

Grosseteste's extensive use of the Greek and Latin fathers was made possible by the large library he had built up. Parts are still extant, others can be reconstructed. He definitely possessed copies of Augustine's *City of God*, Gregory's *Moralities on Job*, the letters of Jerome, and Eustathius' translation of Basil's *Hexaemeron*, and these works are all heavily cited in his writings. His translational projects led him to acquire Greek manuscripts containing works such as the *Testaments of the Twelve Patriarchs*, the Pseudo-Dionysian corpus with the scholia of Maximus and John Scythopolitanus, and works by John of Damascus.[42]

His use of complete texts allowed Grosseteste to acquire a deeper understanding of patristic thought than could be gained through the use of compendia. But in his day turning to the originals had its drawbacks. The manuscripts containing them had no modern indexes; the handwriting was often abbreviated and hard to decipher; and they could be cluttered with marginal and interlinear comments. As a result it could be difficult to locate material quickly in them. In response to this difficulty Grosseteste devised an ingenious system of indexing signs by which he annotated his books.[43] Each sign indicated a topic and was associated with a table listing scriptural, patristic, and secular (separately in the margin) references on that topic. Written in the margins of manuscripts these signs not only allowed the reader to know what kind of material was contained in that part of the manuscript, but also, by reference to the table, to locate parallel material in other authors; this material in turn could be quickly located by looking for the sign in manuscripts of their writings.

The table probably dates from *c.* 1230, and shows that by this date, before he had embarked on his major exegetical works, Grosseteste had already engaged in a wide range of reading in the patristic and secular literature, including most of the vast Augustinian corpus, and a lesser range of Greek patristic texts then available in transla-

---

[41] For Pseudo-Dionysius' influence see McEvoy (1982).

[42] See Dionisotti (1988) and Hunt (1955) for estimates of Grosseteste's Greek and Latin library.

[43] It is extant in the MS Lyons 414, together with Adam Marsh's additions. An edition by Philipp Rosemann will be included with the editions of the *Commentary on Galatians* and Pauline glosses mentioned in n. 28. For descriptions of the system see Thomson (1955) and (1934), Southern (1992) 186–95, and Rosemann (forthcoming). Rouse (1991) shows how this system was part of a broader development of reference tools by thirteenth-century scholars.

tion, most notably John of Damascus' *De fide orthodoxa* and numerous works by Chrysostom. After his death, Grosseteste's books and writings were deposited in the Franciscan convent at Oxford, and the English Franciscans used his indexing system in the second half of the thirteenth century, and in this small way became acquainted with his patristic learning. But the system required an intimate familiarity with the approximately four hundred signs it contained and its use seems to have been limited to the Franciscans.[44]

Richard Dales has indicated another way in which Grosseteste's use of patristic sources influenced later writers. Grosseteste's contemporaries Richard Rufus of Cornwall and Richard Fishacre referred to his works in their commentaries on the *Sentences* of Peter Lombard. These works suggest how Grosseteste's use of the Greek fathers may have helped to transform the range of authorities cited in the later thirteenth century.[45] The citation of passages from a given father depended to a large degree on their availability in earlier Latin works, notably in glosses on the Bible and collections of *sententiae*. Beryl Smalley has noted how the presence of quotations or references in the biblical glosses assured authors a place as commonly used authorities, whereas those who were not quoted were not so used.[46] St. Basil is a case in point. He was rarely referred to in the glosses, but Richard Fishacre, upon reading Grosseteste's *Hexaemeron*, became acquainted with material from Basil's *Hexaemeron*, and incorporated some of it verbatim in his *Commentary on the Sentences*. Richard Rufus also drew many quotations from Grosseteste's *Hexaemeron*, and provided precise references to the authors Grosseteste had quoted, tracking down for himself the material from the Greek fathers Grosseteste had been using.[47]

Patristic Translations and Commentaries

The Nature of Grosseteste's Translations and Commentaries

After his elevation to the episcopacy, Grosseteste directed his intellectual energies to his projects of translation and commentary. They

---

[44] For uses of this system see Hunt (1952–3).
[45] Dales (1971) has made some initial observations; see also Raedts (1987).
[46] Smalley (1938) 105.
[47] See Dales (1971).

were undoubtedly his most significant contribution to the reception of patristic thought. Roger Bacon notes that the Latins had lacked countless books by the Greek and Hebrew expositors of Scripture, including books by Basil, Gregory of Nazianzus, John of Damascus, (Pseudo-) Dionysius, and Chrysostom, and that Grosseteste alone in the previous seventy years was the first to translate such authors, and the first ecclesiastic since Pope Damasus to be interested in advancing the Church through translations.[48]

Grosseteste probably began to study Greek in the early 1230s, perhaps even earlier, and, despite Roger Bacon's asseverations to the contrary, seems to have had a considerable command of the language by the middle of the decade, although his earlier efforts at translation—occasional passages found in his exegetical works, for instance— probably involved the help of Greek-speaking assistants, including Nicholas the Greek and John of Basingstoke.[49] His patristic translations and commentaries were written after he became bishop, between 1235 and 1245. His translations of Aristotle and related works may have largely paralleled these over the years c. 1237–46.[50]

Grosseteste translated works by St. John of Damascus, St. Ignatius the Martyr, Pseudo-Dionysius the Areopagite, the scholia of St. Maximus the Confessor on the works of Pseudo-Dionysius, and the *Testaments of the Twelve Patriarchs*; he also made a paraphrase of some material perhaps by St. Basil. He added important full-scale commentaries to his translations of the Pseudo-Dionysian corpus, and explanatory notes to a number of the other translations. I shall survey this material in the next section.

We know little about Grosseteste's motivations for the study of Greek or for the extensive project of translation and commentary he took up late in life during his activist episcopacy. It has been suggested that he learned Greek because of an interest in biblical exegesis; this would also explain occasional references we find to his knowing some Hebrew.[51] His interest in Greek no doubt also ties in with the

---

[48] *Compendium Studii Philosophiae*, ed. Brewer, *op. cit.*, 474. It was St. Damasus (*c.* 304–84) who commissioned Jerome to produce a revised translation of the Bible.

[49] For Grosseteste's assistants see Russell (1933). Bacon's statement in his *Opus tertium c.* 25 (*ed. cit.*, 91) that Grosseteste could only translate unaided toward the end of his life is rejected by modern scholars. Dionisotti (1988) provides the best account of Grosseteste's Greek studies.

[50] See McEvoy (1982) 474–75. This is a revisionist view; scholars have previously viewed the Aristotelian translations as written after the patristic material.

[51] See Southern (1992) 181–86 and Dionisotti (1988). On the question of his

fact that from the earliest days of his Greek studies, and probably even before them, Grosseteste had a strong realization of the difficulties involved in understanding a text in translation. He clearly thought that the meaning of Greek texts could not be fully grasped in translation by someone with no knowledge of Greek. In his important prologue to his translation and commentary on Pseudo-Dionysius' *Celestial Hierarchy* he writes:

> It must be realized that in a Latin translation, and especially one that, so far as the translator is capable, is made word for word, it is quite often necessary for many things to be expressed ambiguously and in a variety of senses, even though they cannot have a variety of senses in the Greek idiom. This is why, when ambiguities of this kind present themselves to him, an expositor of this book who does not have or know the Greek text must remain largely ignorant of the author's meaning, which cannot be hidden to someone who has a moderate or even minimal command of Greek.[52]

Grosseteste's remedy for the loss or confusion of meaning that results from translation, and especially from word for word translation, was not, as one might expect, a less literal mode of translation. As a translator Grosseteste desired to present the Latin reader with a translation as close as possible to the original Greek, which required a word-for-word translation. This was no doubt motivated in part by a reverence for the words of the original, but, it has been argued, was also due to his view that an author's meaning cannot simply be lifted out from under the words of one language and dressed in those of another, but is intimately bound up with its original mode of expression.[53] Ideally we should learn the language in question and consult the original text. Short of this, the translator should produce

---

knowledge of Hebrew see Callus (1955b) 34–36. A MS from the Franciscan convent at Lincoln, containing Grosseteste's indexing symbols, has a note that reflects the attitude of Grosseteste's circle: "Note on the basis of the points made here and in what follows the virtually unavoidable necessity of a knowledge of the Greek and Hebrew tongues for an understanding of Scripture, and especially of Greek" (text in Hunt (1952–3) 244, n. 6).

[52] I have used the Latin text in McEvoy (1975) 54–55, n. 31. Versions are also published in Grabmann (1926) 465 and Ceccherelli (1955). It may be noted that in *De cess. leg.* Grosseteste shows that he had already been comparing translations of the Ps.-Dionysius' *Celestial Hierarchy*. He refers to "another translation" of a passage, which his editors think was probably made by an assistant (*ed. cit.*, xxvi). In addition he had a bad copy of the *Celestial Hierarchy*. Perhaps we have here the seeds of his interest in retranslating the Ps.-Dionysian corpus?

[53] See McEvoy (1981) 589.

a translation as close to the original as possible, and remedy the aforementioned problems by the provision of commentaries or glosses that explain in depth the details of the translation.

It might be thought that Grosseteste would have been interested in retranslating works by authors such as Basil and Chrysostom, of which he probably had Greek copies. But he was generally content to use the existing translations of their works. Why then did he translate the works he did? The answer seems to be that with the exception of the works of John of Damascus, his patristic translations are of works that he and his contemporaries took to be authentic texts from the apostolic or pre-apostolic eras, or scholia on such. He appears to have focussed on them because of their incalculable importance in the history of Christianity.

Following common medieval practice, Grosseteste prepared his translations on the basis of previous ones; some of his translations were themselves later put to the same use.[54] But his preparation for his translations displays a critical sensibility rare in the middle ages, especially before his day.[55] In order to secure a reliable Greek text he attempted to obtain and collate as many Greek manuscripts as he could. He was aided in this by his assistants, who no doubt also helped him to construct tables of word-correspondences and the like. In addition, Grosseteste compared existing translations and carefully studied the language and thought of the author. He was the only great medieval translator, besides Eriugena, who was also a powerful original thinker, and his superior mind equipped him well in the case of the difficult writings of Pseudo-Dionysius.

Grosseteste took the common practice of word-for-word translation to an extreme. Aiming to uncover the *mens auctoris et venustas sermonis*— the author's meaning and the character of his speech—he provided a "scrupulously exact word for word translation,"[56] striving to achieve uniformity in the translation of a given term and to retain the word-order of the original Greek. He realized the difficulties this involved when Greek terms or grammatical structures had no Latin parallel, and notes that in such cases "it will not be without value to sacrifice Latinity in order to make clearer the author's meaning."[57]

---

[54] See e.g. Backus (1986).

[55] One author greatly influenced by Grosseteste's critical sensibility was Roger Bacon.

[56] McEvoy (1982) 77.

[57] He makes these remarks in his prologue to his translation of the Ps.-Dionysius' *Celestial Hierarchy*. I have used the Latin text in McEvoy (1975) 57, n. 39.

These sacrifices have made some of Grosseteste's translations valuable witnesses to the lost Greek manuscript traditions upon which they were based,[58] but as one might expect they were hard to read, and their poor Latinity could hardly have made the author's meaning clearer to readers without Greek—Grosseteste's intended audience. His translations were criticized in his day for "obscurity and deformity," which helps to explain their relatively limited use. The criticisms stung, but Grosseteste thought that these difficulties were inevitable and the criticisms unfair.[59] He did not intend his translations to be read alone, but rather to form a single unit in the manuscripts containing them with commentaries or notes in which the text of the Latin translation was discussed in great detail.[60]

This, in addition of course to the explanation of Pseudo-Dionysius' teaching, was in large part the aim of Grosseteste's Dionysian commentaries. They may well have begun as marginal notes he had made, as was his practice, in his translations concerning peculiarities of the translation, or etymological, grammatical, or theological explanations of terms in the text, which he later worked up into full-scale commentaries. These commentaries, however, retain the marks of their origin. James McEvoy notes that they focus "upon the words of the Greek text and [are] dedicated to the recovery of every nuance of meaning present in it."[61] They work through the text line by line and contain few references to other authors, save occasional references to other commentaries, and little direct expression of Grosseteste's own views.[62]

By contrast St. Albert's commentary on Pseudo-Dionysius' *Divine Names*,[63] written *c.* 1250, follows a rigid order and displays the sensibility of a man steeped in the scholastic method of the *quaestio* and distinction. The text is laid out, related to the preceding text, and divided into subsections of Albert's device. Albert then proceeds to raise questions stemming from the text in the medieval *quaestio* format.

---

[58] See e.g. Lightfoot (1885) 78–80.

[59] See McEvoy (1975) 57, n. 40.

[60] Dionisotti (1988) 28 describes the format of the Dionysian translations-cum-commentaries: "The text [of the translation is] divided into sections, each followed by the relevant bit of Greek scholia, and then by Grosseteste's running commentary, while the margins are reserved for individual points of detail in the language or content."

[61] McEvoy (1982) 84.

[62] For Grosseteste's translational practices see Callus (1955b), Dionisotti (1988), McEvoy (1981) and (1982), and Franceschini (1933–4).

[63] *Super Dionysium de Divinis Nominibus*, in *Alberti Magni Opera Omnia*, ed. P. Simon, vol. 37 (Aschendorff: 1972).

He cites numerous authorities and continually introduces his own views on the topics at issue. His concern is essentially doctrinal, not philological. He has no interest in textual criticism or in the text as an object of interest in itself, and being ignorant of Greek accepted the text as it stood.

An Overview of Grosseteste's Translations and Commentaries, and their Diffusion

ST. JOHN OF DAMASCUS (*c.* 675–*c.* 749)

The first of Grosseteste's projects of translation was works by the Greek father St. John of Damascus. John's most important work, the *Fount of Wisdom,* had three parts: the *Dialectica* (*Dialectic*), which is concerned with elements of Aristotelian philosophy; *De centum haeresibus* (*The Hundred Heresies*); and *De fide orthodoxa* (*The Orthodox Faith,* also know to medieval thinkers as the *Sententiae*), which presents the main teachings of the Greek fathers on Christian doctrine. Grosseteste translated these works, as well as an anonymous prologue to them.[64] In addition he translated John's *Disputatio Christiani et Saraceni* (*Disputation between a Christian and Saracen*), which was appended to *De centum haeresibus; Introductio dogmatum elementaris* (*An Elementary Introduction to the Dogmas); De his quae in Christo duabus voluntatibus et operationibus* (*On the Two Operations and Wills in Christ*), which is included as part of the *Introductio;* and the *Trisagion.*

These translations probably date from between about 1235 and 1239. The translation of the *De fide orthodoxa,* the most important of these translations and the only one expressly ascribed to Grosseteste in any manuscript, was largely a corrected version of Burgundio of Pisa's twelfth-century translation,[65] although it includes material lacking in Burgundio's translation. Grosseteste appears to have translated the remaining texts directly from the Greek; they do not seem to have been available in Latin translation in his day.

---

[64] Due to its incorrect title *Prologus translatoris* Thomson (1940) 81 wrongly thought it to be Grosseteste's note on his translations.

[65] The texts of the two translations are compared in Hocedez (1913a). Grosseteste refers to his having "recently translated into Latin" the *Trisagion* in his *Commentary on the Celestial Hierarchy;* see Thomson (1940) 51. The other texts are unascribed and we know of no cross-references to them in Grosseteste's works. Holland (1983), the most recent discussion of the translations of John of Damascus, has strengthened Thomson's already strong case for ascribing them to Grosseteste.

Grosseteste wrote no commentaries on these works, but he did add numerous marginal notes to his translations. The note on the *Filioque* appended to the *Trisagion* achieved some fame. It was reproduced in full by John Duns Scotus in his *Opus oxoniense*, and closely paraphrased by John Wycliffe in his *De Trinitate*.[66] To his translation of *De centum haeresibus* Grosseteste added marginal notes containing material relating to the various heresies discussed, including translations he had made from Josephus' *Hypomnesticon*, a Greek work included in his manuscript containing the Greek text of the *Testaments of the Twelve Patriarchs*.[67]

The translation of the *De fide orthodoxa* was known by the middle of the thirteenth century. Both Roger Bacon and Salimbene mention it, although neither seems to make use of it in their works. Such use as the translation had was primarily by English authors, though not to the exclusion of Burgundio's translation.[68] Duns Scotus, Wycliffe, and John Hus all employ it, but it did not greatly influence them. The translation of the *Dialectica* is used by a number of Franciscans, including William of Alnwick, Matthew of Aquasparta, and William of Ockham. There is little evidence of use of the translations of the remaining works, although the manuscript tradition suggests that uses are waiting to be found.[69] The diffusion of Grosseteste's translations of John of Damascus will be easier to determine with the publication of Meridel Holland's projected edition of these works.

St. Basil (*c.* 330-79)

In a letter written to the Abbot and Convent of Bury, probably *c.* 1238-40, Grosseteste notes that he had occupied some leisure time by reading a Greek work on the *Life of Monks*, a paraphrase of which

---

[66] Scotus *Opus oxoniense*, ed. in *Opera Omnia*, vol. 5 (Vatican City: 1959) 3; John Wycliffe *De trinitate, ed. cit.*, 174. The text is also printed in McEvoy (1975) 44, n. 15.

[67] See Holland (1983). Grosseteste translated the latter work in 1242. Marginal cross-references in the Dionysian commentaries indicate that the *De fide orthodoxa* and the *Trisagion* preceded them, but Holland has conjectured that Grosseteste set aside the project of translating John of Damascus and worked on the Dionysian translations and the *Testaments* before returning to the translation of the *Heresies* after 1242.

[68] See Hocedez (1913b) and De Ghellinck (1948) 392-93.

[69] We know of thirteen MSS of the *Dialectica*, eleven of the *De fide orthodoxa*, nine of the *Introductio*, and six each of the *Trisagion* and *De centum haeresibus*. See Thomson (1940) 45-51.

he includes in the letter. Thomson has suggested that the work in question "is a paraphrase of sections from the longer Rules of St. Basil."[70] The paraphrase is found only in this letter, although Grosseteste's letter collection enjoyed some popularity in the later middle ages.

ST. IGNATIUS THE MARTYR (*c.* 35–*c.* 107)

There is some controversy over the ascription to Grosseteste of Latin translations of the middle recension of the letters of St. Ignatius the Martyr, and of the four spurious letters that purport to relate Ignatius' correspondence with St. John and the Virgin.[71] In 1644 Archbishop Ussher argued that Grosseteste was responsible for the translation of the middle recension. Lightfoot accepted and further defended this conclusion in his edition of the letters. He argued, however, that the four spurious letters were in all likelihood a Latin forgery. In response, Thomson argued that the ascription of the translation of the middle recension to Grosseteste was "unsubstantiated," whereas the evidence was "final in favour of Grosseteste's authorship of the translation of these spurious letters."[72]

Scholars have, however, generally found persuasive the case for an ascription to Grosseteste of the middle recension. As for the spurious letters, the evidence for Grosseteste's having translated a Greek forgery is twofold: a "contemporary and explicit MS ascription" to Grosseteste,[73] and a remark Lightfoot reports made by Cotelier (1624), that he had seen an entry "in a catalogue of manuscripts belonging to the church of St. Peter at Beauvais" listing "two or three letters of the Blessed Ignatius the Martyr to the Blessed Virgin Mary and to St. John, which were found at Lyon at the time of the Council of Pope Innocent IV, and turned from Greek into Latin."[74] If indeed Grosseteste translated these, he would have done so when he was at this Council in 1245. The middle recension, if translated by Grosseteste, would probably date from before 1241, when Grosseteste completed his commentary on Pseudo-Dionysius' *Celestial Hierarchy*, in which he quotes from the translation of the middle recension.

---

[70] Thomson (1940) 71.
[71] On the recensions of letters ascribed to Ignatius see Lightfoot (1885) chs. 2, 4; Thomson (1940) 58–62.
[72] Thomson (1940) 60.
[73] *Ibid.*, 60–61.
[74] Latin text in Lightfoot (1885) 224, n. 2.

The translation of the middle recension had virtually no impact. It is extant in a single manuscript, but is known to have been present in another, now lost manuscript. The fourteenth-century English Franciscans John Tyssington and (through him) William Wodeford quote it. Wycliffe also quotes from this translation in his *De apostasia* (*On Apostasy*), but merely repeats the passage found in Grosseteste's *Commentary on the Celestial Hierarchy*.[75]

The apocryphal Ignatian correspondence, if by Grosseteste, would have been one of his most successful translations, since it enjoyed great popularity on the Continent in the fourteenth and fifteenth centuries. Over fifty manuscripts are known to exist. Most date from after the middle of the fourteenth century and are of continental provenance.

PSEUDO-DIONYSIUS (*c.* 500)

Grosseteste's translations and commentaries on the Pseudo-Dionysian corpus were his most important contribution to the reception of patristic thought. Between 1239 and 1241 he translated and commented on *The Celestial* (or *Angelic*) *Hierarchy* and *The Ecclesiastical Hierarchy*. He followed them with translations and commentaries on *The Divine Names* and *The Mystical Theology*.[76] Grosseteste possessed a Greek copy of the ten letters of Pseudo-Dionysius, but did not translate them so far as we know.[77]

Grosseteste and his contemporaries took the works of Pseudo-Dionysius to have been written by Dionysius the Areopagite, whom Acts 17:34 records St. Paul converting to Christianity in Athens. The ascription is false, as these works are influenced by Proclus (411–85) and probably date from no earlier than 500, but Grosseteste and his contemporaries, being ignorant of this, took them to have an authoritative status second only to Scripture. These works were an extremely

---

[75] See Lightfoot (1885) 77, 80–84 and Southern (1992) 311.

[76] See Callus (1947).

[77] We possess the MS Grosseteste used for his translations of Ps.-Dionysius. It displays the critical manner in which he went about translation; indeed it approaches a critical edition of the Greek text. It was copied in France and extensively collated with three other manuscripts; the margins contain numerous variant readings, some in Grosseteste's own hand. See Barbour (1958). No doubt much of this work was done by his assistants, whose help he refers to at the end of his *Commentary on the Angelic Hierarchy*. (Callus (1955b) 43).

important conduit for the infusion of neoplatonic ideas into medieval
thought and had an immense influence throughout the middle ages.

Two other Latin translations of the Dionysian corpus were being
used in Grosseteste's day, those made by the great Irish scholar John
Scottus Eriugena in the ninth century, and by John Saracen in the
twelfth. Parts of the corpus were commented upon by Hugh of
St. Victor in the twelfth century; and by both Thomas Gallus, Grosseteste's friend, and Albert the Great in the mid-thirteenth century,
and others thereafter.

Grosseteste's Dionysian translations and commentaries were more
widely diffused than his translations of John of Damascus, but faced
stiff competition from the earlier translations and other commentaries, especially on the Continent. Dondaine has noted that, since they
were completed only in 1243, they arrived a little late to be used by
the great scholastics in their dealings with Dionysius.[78] There is no
trace of them in such major thirteenth-century continental figures as
Thomas Aquinas, Albert the Great, Bonaventure, or Henry of Ghent,
but they were employed in Paris later in the century by the Franciscans
Peter John Olivi and Matthew of Aquasparta, and in the fourteenth
century John of Ripa used them extensively in his *Lectura on the Sentences* and other works.[79]

Grosseteste's version of the Dionysian corpus found more use in
England. Thomas of York cites both the translation and commentaries, and they are often quoted by Franciscan thinkers, including Roger
Marston, William de la Mare, Peter Baldewille,[80] John Duns Scotus,
William of Alnwick, and William of Nottingham (fl. *c.* 1315). Further
uses will undoubtedly turn up as more works of English, and especially Franciscan theology are edited.

Callus notes that in the mid-fourteenth to fifteenth centuries
Grosseteste's version of the Dionysian corpus had some success among
mystical writers, and cites the example of Rudolph de Biberach's use
of it in *De septem itineribus aeternitatis.*[81]

---

[78] Dondaine (1953) 34.
[79] He is the rare example of someone who expressly uses the translations and
commentaries together, as Grosseteste intended. His use of Grosseteste's Dionysian
corpus would merit study.
[80] 30th lector to the Oxford Franciscans; he refers to Grosseteste's *Commentary on
the Angelic Hierarchy* in his inception. See Little, A.G. and Pelster, F., *Oxford Theology
and Theologians c. A.D. 1282–1302* (Oxford: 1934) 249, 356.
[81] Callus (1955b) 61.

St. Maximus the Confessor (c. 580–662)

St. Maximus, the Greek theologian and ascetic writer, composed a prologue and scholia to the works of Pseudo-Dionysius. As part of his translation of the Dionysian corpus, Grosseteste produced an incomplete translation of these scholia, as well as of scholia by John Scythopolitanus, which were mixed in with them.[82]

Grosseteste did not realize the true authorship of the prologue and scholia, but on the basis of material appended to his copy of the ten Pseudo-Dionysian letters he incorrectly concluded that they were written by Archbishop Dionysius of Alexandria (d. c. 264).[83]

Testaments of the Twelve Patriarchs

The *Testaments of the Twelve Patriarchs* is an apocryphal work purporting to relate the message given by each of the twelve sons of Jacob to his descendents on his death bed. Whether it was Christian or Jewish in origin is disputed; it undoubtedly contains Christian material, though it is perhaps a later interpolation. Colophons of several early manuscripts indicate that Grosseteste took the work to be of Jewish origin and to contain prophecies of Christ.[84] Hearing that John of Basingstoke had seen this work in Athens, Grosseteste sent to Greece to obtain a copy. He translated it in 1242, with the aid of Nicholas the Greek.

Matthew Paris, the source of this information, gives an idea of the work's great appeal. He thought that it "clearly was of the substance of the Bible" and had "for a long time been unknown and hidden through the envy of the Jews, because of the clear prophecies of the Saviour it contains," but Grosseteste had "fully and evidently" translated this "glorious treatise so as to strengthen the Christian faith and make greater the embarrassment of the Jews."[85]

The translation appears to have been intended for popular consumption. Unlike Grosseteste's other translations, it is neither written in a word for word style, nor accompanied by notes or commentaries.[86]

---

[82] See Franceschini (1933).

[83] For the Latin text where he mentions this see Thomson (1940) 52.

[84] Thomson (1940) 42. See De Jonge (1991) for the most recent discussion of Grosseteste's translation of the *Testaments*.

[85] *Chronica maiora*, in *Matthaei Parisiensis, Monachi Sancti Albani, Chronica Maiora*, ed. H.R. Luard, vol. 4 (London: 1872–83) 5:285, 4:232–33.

[86] See Dionisotti (1988) 29.

The most popular of Grosseteste's translations, it is extant in almost eighty manuscripts dating from the thirteenth to the seventeenth centuries. It was frequently published from the fifteenth to eighteenth centuries, and was employed as the basis of many translations into vernacular tongues.

St. Jerome (*c.* 342–420)

The preface to Grosseteste's *Hexaemeron* is a gloss of two letters of St. Jerome, letter 53 to the priest Paul, and 28 to Desiderius. These texts, which amount to an introduction to the Bible, commonly preceded the text of Genesis in medieval manuscripts of the Bible. The gloss outlines these letters first in general, and then in great detail. It makes much use of Isidore of Seville's *Etymologies*, and displays a fair degree of Greek learning. It is not organically connected to the rest of the *Hexaemeron*, which contains a separate introduction on the subject matter of theology.[87]

Conclusion

The importance of Grosseteste's role in the reception of the Fathers is clear. Far less clear, however, are the diffusion and influence of his contributions to patristic studies. These matters have been little studied, but the evidence as it stands presents a rather disappointing picture. There is no doubt that Grosseteste's example helped to spur a growing interest in the Greek fathers in thirteenth-century England, but there is little evidence that his discussions of their works greatly influenced their interpretation by later authors. His most important translations and commentaries were not in general use on the Continent, and in England appear to have been primarily employed by the Franciscans, and the depth of their influence on them is difficult to gauge. His patristic learning and personality greatly impressed both Roger Bacon and John Wycliffe, each of whom, like Grosseteste, was a forceful personality in his own right and had a deeply conservative conception of theology. But the powerful impression he made does not seem to have been accompanied by a powerful influence on the formulation of their thought or understanding of the fathers.

[87] Dales and Gieben (1968) describe this work in detail.

Appendix

Works incorrectly ascribed to the fathers by Grosseteste

This appendix, largely compiled from published editions or studies of Grosseteste's *Tabula*, provides a provisional list of works incorrectly ascribed by Grosseteste to the fathers, as well as to some other authors. On the left is listed the author to which the work is wrongly ascribed, followed by the title used by Grosseteste (if he uses a title), the work's correct author, if this is known, followed by information concerning editions. Finally, works by Grosseteste in which the ascription occurs are listed. In their case an * indicates that the title given is employed by Grosseteste in the material in question, + that the material in question is expressly ascribed to the author in question, and # that Grosseteste, according to his editors, possibly refers to this work in his ascription of material to the father in question (I would note, however, that the absence of mention of such a work in the *Tabula* provides strong reason to think Grosseteste is not referring to it). Many of the incorrectly ascribed works listed in Grossetetse's *Tabula* are not employed in those of his works that are currently edited, but they may yet turn up in unedited material.[88] In most cases the works below were standardly misascribed by medieval writers to the author mentioned.

St. Ambrose

De dignitate conditionis humanae (Alcuin, *c.* 735–804)
Ed. *PL* 17, 1015–18, and 100, 565–68. *De intelligentiis* + (ed. Baur).
In epistula ad Romanos (Ambrosiaster)
Crit. ed., H.I. Vogels, *CSEL* 81.1, 4–497; *PL* 17, 45–184. *De cess. leg.* IV vii 5+.

---

[88] Works referred to and ascribed in Grosseteste's *Tabula* are listed in Thomson (1955) and Hunt (1955). I have benefited greatly from a draft of Philipp Rosemann's forthcoming edition of the *Tabula*, which he kindly supplied me. I have also found invaluable P. Glorieux's *Pour revaloriser Migne. Tables rectificatives*, Melanges de Science religieuse, IXe Annee 1952, Cahier Supplémentaire, in which further references regarding many of the above works may be found. It should be noted that some of the works Hunt lists as spuriously ascribed to Augustine are authentic: *De penis purgatoriis* is part of the *Ennarationes in Psalmos*, *De penitentia* is *Sermo* 351, and the *Soliloquia* is probably not the inauthentic *Soliloquia animae ad Deum*, but the authentic work by Augustine, from which Grosseteste quotes in *De veritate*.

St. Anselm of Canterbury

Similitudines (Alexander of Canterbury, *fl.* 1120?)
Ed. *PL* 159, 605–708. *Tabula**+.

St. Athanasius

De trinitate et spiritu sancto (Lib. i–vii: St. Eusebius of Vercelli, d. 371; lib. viii: luciferian addition; lib. ix: St. Gregory of Elvira, d. after 392; lib. x–xii: anon.)
Crit. ed. (lib. i–vii), V. Bulhart, *CCSL* 9, 3–99; *PL* 62, 237–334. *Tabula**+.

St. Augustine

De conflictu virtutum et viciorum (Ambrose Autpert, d. 784)
Crit. ed., R. Weber, O.S.B., CCCM 27B, 909–31; *PL* 40, 1091–1106. *Tabula**+.

De definitionibus rectae fidei (Gennadius of Marseilles, *fl.* 470)
Also known as *Liber ecclesiasticorum dogmatum; Liber de ecclesiasticis dogmatibus*. Ed. C.H. Turner, *Journal of Theological Studies*, 7 (1905–6), 78–99 and 8 (1906–7), 103–14; *PL* 42, 1215–22. *De lib. arb.* c. 15/16*+(rec. I/rec.II); *Hex.* I xxii 1*+; *Tabula**+.

De differentia animae et spiritus (Alcher of Clairvaux, *fl.* 1165)
Also known as *De spiritu et anima*. Ed. *PL* 40, 779–832. *Hex.* II x 1#, VIII vii 1+, VIII xi 1+; *De cess. leg.* III i 22*+; *Tabula**+.

De fide ad Petrum (St. Fulgentius of Ruspe, 468–533, or perhaps c. 462–527)
Crit. ed., J. Fraipont, *CCSL* 91A, 711–60; *PL* 40, 753–80. *Tabula**+.

De igne purgatorio (St. Caesarius of Arles, c. 470–542)
Sermo 179. Crit. ed., G. Morin, O.S.B., *CCSL* 104, 724–29; *PL* 39, 1946. *Tabula**+.

De mirabilibus divinae scripturae (Anon.)
Ed. *PL* 35, 2149–2200. Probably written in Ireland in 661 by an author named Augustine. Its inauthenticity is noted by Aquinas in ST IIIᵃ. q.xlv.a. 3. *Hex.* II v 2*+; *Tabula**+.

Hypomnesticon (St. Prosper of Aquitaine?, c. 390–c. 463)
Ed. *PL* 45, 1611–64. *De libero arbitrio* c. 10/11*, 15/16+, 17*+, 19*+, 20*+; *De decem mandatis* IX 2*+; *Hex.* VIII xxi 1*+; *Tabula**+.

Liber contra quinque haereses (St. Quodvultdeus, d. c. 453)

Also known as *Adversus quinque haereses*. Crit. ed., R. Braun, *CCSL* 60, 261–301; *PL* 42, 1101–16. *Comm. in Galatas* IV 37*[+]; *Tabula**[+].
Principia dialecticae   (Anon.)
Ed. *PL* 32, 1409–20. *Hex.* I xviii 3[#].
Quaestiones ex veteri testamento   (Ambrosiaster)
Ed. *PL* 35, 2207–2386. *Hex.* VIII x 2[#].

The following works are ascribed, as titled, to Augustine in the *Tabula* but remain unidentified.

In catalat' consuet'
According to Dr. Rosemann's forthcoming edition of the *Tabula*, a work of this title is frequently ascribed to Augustine. Hunt appears to have read *Catholica confutatio* here, a work he identifies with Prosper of Aquitane's *Responsiones ad capitula obiectionum vincentianarum* (ed. *PL* 51, 177–86). Thomson reads *In catalogo confutacionum*, and suggests this may be the *De incarnatione et confutatione Iudaeorum*.
Contra reprehensores nuptiarum.
De bono virginali.
De praedestinatione contra Pelagium.
Dialogus contra Manichaeos.
In scripto suo ad Marcell.
Super ad Colosios.
Super ad Corinthios.

St. Bede

Super ad Rom., Eph., Thess., Hebr., Coloss., Timoth., Petr., Iac.
(Florus, *c.* 790–*c.* 860)
Ed. *PL* 119, 279–470. *Tabula**[+].

St. Bernard of Clairvaux

De cognitione humanae conditionis   (Anon.)
Ed. *PL* 184, 485–508. *Hex.* VIII vi 3[#].
In the *Tabula* Grosseteste ascribes to Bernard an unidentified *In dictis*.

St. Chrysostom

Super "in principio erat verbum" (John Scottus Eriugena, *c.* 810–*c.* 877)
Also known as *Homilia in prologum Ioanni: "Vox spiritualis aquilae."*
Crit. ed., E. Jeauneau, *Homélie sur le prologue de Jean* (Paris, 1969);

PL 122, 283–96. This work was not well known and the misascription seems peculiar to Grosseteste; see McEvoy (1987). *De lib. arb. c.* 8/9*⁺, 15/16⁺; *Hex.* I viii 6⁺, V xxi 3⁺; *De operationibus solis* (= *Comm. in Ecclus.*, 43:1–5) 11*⁺ (ed. J. McEvoy, *Rech. Théol. anc. méd.* 41 [1974], 38–91)); *Comm. in Psal.*, MS Bologna, *Bibl. Com. dell'archiginnasio* A.983, fol. 158c⁺; *Tabula**⁺.

St. Jerome

Commentarius in Pentateuchum   (Ps.-Bede)
Ed. *PL* 91, 189–394. *Hex.* I xiii 2⁺, IV ii 3⁺, V xix 2⁺, VII xii 2, VIII vii 2⁺, VIII xxxii 1⁺, VIII xxxv 7⁺, XI ix 2⁺, XI xxviii 1⁺.

Epistula ad Demetriadem or *Epistula 47*   (Pelagius, *fl.* 400)
Also known as *Liber de institutione virginum.* Ed. *PL* 30, 15–45 and 33, 1099–1120. Ascribed by Bede in *In Cantica Canticorum* (*CCSL* 119B, 175) to the pelagian, Julian of Eclanum. *De lib. arb. c.* 12/13⁺, 15/16*⁺; *De cess. leg.* I vii 3*⁺; *Tabula**⁺.

Hexaemeron   (Bede)
Crit. ed., Ch. W. Jones, *CCSL* 118, 1–242; *PL* 91, 9–190. *Hex.* I xxii 1⁺, II i 2⁺, II iv i⁺ (also cited as Bede), IV ii 3⁺, VIII xiii 1⁺, VIII xxiv 1⁺ (also cited as Bede), VIII xxxii 1⁺ (also cited as Bede), XI xiv 2⁺.

Rabanus Maurus (776/784–856)

De corpore et sanguine   (St. Paschasius Radbertus, *c.* 790–865)
Crit. ed., B. Paulus, O.S.B., CCCM 16, 13–131; *PL* 120, 1267–1350. *De cess. leg.* III i 30*⁺; *Hex.* XI iv 1⁺, XI viii 3*⁺; *Comm. in Galatas* III 29*⁺; *Tabula**⁺.

De cruce
Probaby a scribal slip for a work of the same name that Grosseteste correctly ascribes to St. John Chrysostom. *Tabula**⁺.

De libero arbitrio
Probably works of the same name by Augustine or Bernard. *Tabula**⁺.

Strabus

Hexaemeron   (Bede)
Ed. as above. *Hex.* XI i 1# (also cited as Bede).

Bibliography

This survey is especially indebted to the work of McEvoy, Southern, Callus and Thomson. The vast expansion in Grosseteste studies in recent years has led to many revisions in our understanding of Grosseteste and his works. The excellent books by McEvoy (1982) and Southern (1992) together give the best picture of the current state of Grosseteste studies. Callus (1955b), despite the need for revision in some regards, remains the best overview of Grosseteste's scholarly activity. Thomson (1940) contains a wealth of bibliographical information, which is partially brought up to date and corrected in McEvoy (1982). Francheschini (1933a) is the classic, though somewhat outdated study of Grosseteste's translational activity. The bibliography in Gieben (1969) is updated in Gieben (forthcoming); McEvoy (1982) contains an update to the year 1980. The literature on Grosseteste is regularly reviewed in the *Bulletin de Théologie ancienne et médievalé*. Section A of the bibliography lists modern editions; they are, however, in many cases uncritical. Some material unavailable in modern editions, the translation of *De fide orthodoxa*, for example, may be found in much older editions, for details of which see Gieben (1969).

A. *Editions of Grosseteste's Translations and Commentaries on The Fathers*

JOHN OF DAMASCUS

i. *Translations*

Dialectica, ed. M. Holland, *An Edition of Three Unpublished Translations by Robert Grosseteste of Three Short Works of John of Damascus.* Ph.D. dissertation, Harvard University, 1980; ed. O.A. Colligan, *St. John Damascene, Dialectica, Version of Robert Grosseteste* (St. Bonaventure, N.Y.: 1953).
Trisagion, Introductio dogmatum elementaris, De centum haeresibus, De duabus voluntatibus, extract from *Disputatio Christiani et Saraceni,* ed. Holland, *op. cit.*
Prologue to the *De fide orthodoxa,* ed. Holland, *op. cit.*; PG 94, col. 489–98.

ii. *Note*

Note on the *Filioque,* ed. in John Duns Scotus, *Opera Omnia,* vol. 5 (Vatican City: 1959) 3.

ST. BASIL

Paraphrase of extracts from *Longer Rules* (?), in letter 57, ed. H.R. Luard, *Roberti Grosseteste episcopi quondam Lincolniensis epistolae* (London: 1861) 173–78.

ST. IGNATIUS THE MARTYR

Translations of the middle recension of the letters, and of the four spurious letters to the Virgin and St. John, ed. J.B. Lightfoot *The Apostolic Fathers. Part II. S. Ignatius. S. Polycarp,* 2d. ed., vol. 3 (London: 1889) 3–72.

PSEUDO-DIONYSIUS

i. *Translations*

Celestial Hierarchy, ed. D. Chevallier *et al. Dionysiaca*, 2 vols. (Paris-Bruges:
1937–50); chaps. 1–9, ed. J.S. McQuade, *Robert Grosseteste's Commentary on
the "Celestial Hierarchy" of Pseudo-Dionysius the Areopagite.* Ph.D. thesis, Queen's
University Belfast, 1961; chaps. 10–15, ed. J. McEvoy, *Robert Grosseteste on
the Celestial Hierarchy of Pseudo-Dionysius. An Edition and Translation of his Commentary, chapters 10 to 15.* Master's thesis, Queen's University of Belfast,
1967.
Divine Names, Mystical Theology, ed. Chevallier, *op. cit.*
Ecclesiastical Hierarchy, ed. C. Taylor Hogan, *Robert Grosseteste, Pseudo-Dionysius
and Hierarchy: A Medieval Trinity, Including an Edition of Grosseteste's Translation
of, and Commentary on, "De Ecclesiastica Hierarchia."* Ph.D. thesis, Cornell University, 1991, 3 vols.; ed. Chevallier, *op. cit.*

ii. *Commentaries*

On the Celestial Hierarchy, chaps. 1–9, ed. J.S. McQuade, *op. cit.*; chaps. 10–
15, ed. J. McEvoy, *op. cit.*; extracts ed. in Dondaine, H.-F., "L'objet et le
'medium' de la vision béatifique chez les théologiens du xiiiᵉ siècle,"
Recherches de théologie ancienne et médiévale 19 (1952) 60–130; Pouillon, D.,
"La Beauté, propriété transcendentale, chez les Scholastiques (1220–1270),"
Archives d'histoire doctrinale et littéraire du moyen âge 15 (1946) 263–329; Ruello,
F., "La *Divinorum Nominum reseratio* selon Robert Grosseteste et Albert le
Grand, *Archives d'histoire doctrinale et littèraire du moyen âge* 34 (1959) 99–197.
On the Divine Names, bk. 1, ed. Ruello, *art. cit.*; extracts in id., *Les "Noms
Divins" et leurs "Raisons" selon Saint Albert le Grand Commentateur du "De divinis
nominibus"* (Paris: 1963) 155–73.
On the Mystical Theology, ed. U. Gamba, *Il Commento di Roberto Grossatesta al
"De Mystica Theologia" del Pseudo-Dionigi Areopagita* (Milan: 1942).
On the Ecclesiastical Hierarchy, ed. Taylor Hogan, *op. cit.*

Testaments of The Twelve Patriarchs

Translation ed. in PG 2 (Paris: 1886) cols. 1025–1150

ST. JEROME

Commentary on letter 53 to the priest Paul and letter 28 to Desiderius, ed.
R.C. Dales and S. Gieben, *Hexaëmeron* (Oxford: 1982) 17–48.

B. *Modern Studies*

Backus, I. (1986) "John of Damascus, *De fide orthodoxa*: Translations by
Burgundio (1153/54), Grosseteste (1235/40) and Lefèvre d'Etaples (1507),"
Journal of the Warburg and Courtauld Institutes 49 (1986) 211–17.
Barbour, R. (1958) "A Manuscript of Ps.-Dionysius Areopagita Copied for
Robert Grosseteste," *Bodleian Library Record 6* (1958) 401–16.

Callus, D., ed. (1955a)* *Robert Grosseteste, Scholar and Bishop* (Oxford: 1982).
(1955b)* "Robert Grosseteste as Scholar," in Callus (1955a) 1–69.
(1954)* "The Contribution to the Study of the Fathers made by the Thirteenth-Century Oxford Schools," *The Journal of Ecclesiastical History* 5
(1954) 139–48.
(1948) "The *Summa Theologiae* of Robert Grosseteste," in *Studies in Medieval
History Presented to Frederick Maurice Powicke*, ed. R.W. Hunt *et al.* (Oxford: 1948) 180–208.
(1947) "The Date of Grosseteste's Translations and Commentaries on
Pseudo-Dionysius and the Nichomachean Ethics," *Recherches de théologie
ancienne et médiévale* 14 (1947) 186–210.
Carabine, D. (forthcoming) "Robert Grosseteste on the *Mystical Theology* of
the Pseudo-Dionysius," in McEvoy (forthcoming).
Ceccherelli, I. (1955) "Roberto Grossatesta studioso di greco, e una consid-
detta sua introduzione grammaticale allo studio della lingua greca," *Studi
Francescani* 52 (1955) 426–44.
Dales, R.C. (1971) "The Influence of Grosseteste's 'Hexaemeron' on the
'Sentences' Commentaries of Richard Fishacre, O.P. and Richard Rufus
of Cornwall, O.F.M.," *Viator. Medieval and Renaissance Studies* 2 (1971)
271–300.
Dales, R.C. Gieben, S. (1968) "The *Prooemium* to Robert Grosseteste's *Hexae-
meron*," *Speculum* 43 (1968) 451–61.
Dionisotti, A.C. (1988) "On the Greek Studies of Robert Grosseteste," in
The Uses of Greek and Latin: Historical Essays, ed. A.C. Dionisotti *et al.* (Lon-
don: 1988) 19–39.
Dobson, E.J. (1975) *Moralities on the Gospels. A New Source of the Ancrene Wisse*
(Oxford: 1975)
Dondaine, H.-F. (1953) *Le Corpus Dionysien de l'Université de Paris au xiiie siècle*
(Rome: 1953).
Franceschini, E. (1933–4)* "Roberto Grossatesta, vescovo di Lincoln, e le
sue traduzioni latine," *Atti del Reale Istituto Veneto di scienz, lettere ed arti, 93,*
2 (Venice: 1933–4) 1–138; repr. in idem, *Scritti di filologia latina medievale*
(Padua: 1976) II, 409–544.
(1933) "Grosseteste's Translation of the Prologus and Skholia of Maximus to the Writings of the Pseudo-Dionysius Areopagita," *The Journal
of Theological Studies 34* (1933) 355–63.
Gamba, U. (1944) "Roberto Grossatesta traduttore e commentatore del
De Mystica Theologia' dello Pseudo-Dionigi Areopagita" *Aevum* 18 (1944)
100–32.
Ghellinck, J. De (1948) *Le Mouvement théologique du xiie siècle*, 2d. ed. (Bruges:
1948).
Gieben, S. (1969) "Bibliographia universa Roberti Grosseteste ab an. 1473
ad an. 1969," *Collectanea Franciscana* 39 (1969) 362–418.
(forthcoming) "Robert Grosseteste: A Bibliography 1970–1991," in McEvoy
(forthcoming).
Grabmann, M. (1926) *Mittelalterliches Geistesleben*, vol. 1 (Münster: 1926).
Hill, K.D. (1976) "Robert Grosseteste and his Work of Greek Translation,"
The Orthodox Churches and the West, ed. D. Baker (Oxford: 1976) 213–22.
Hocedez, E. (1913a) "Les trois premières traductions du *De Orthodoxa Fide*,"
Le Musée Belge 17 (1913) 109–23.

(1913b) "La diffusion de la 'Translatio Lincolniensis' du '*De orthodoxa fide*' de saint Jean Damascene," *Bulletin d'ancienne littérature et d'archéologie chrétiennes* 3 (1913) 189–98.

Holland, M. (forthcoming) "Aspects of Grosseteste's Greek Translations, with Special Reference to *College of Arms MS Arundel 9*," in McEvoy (forthcoming).

(1983)* "Robert Grosseteste's Translations of John of Damascus," *Bodleian Library Record* 11 (1983) 138–54.

Hunt, R.W. (1955) "The Library of Robert Grosseteste," in Callus (1955a) 121–45.

(1952–3) "Manuscripts Containing the Indexing Symbols of Robert Grosseteste," *Bodleian Library Record* 4 (1952–3) 241–55.

James, M.R. (1922) "Robert Grosseteste on the Psalms," *The Journal of Theological Studies* 23 (1922) 181–85.

Jonge, M. de (1991) "Robert Grosseteste and the Testaments of the Twelve Patriarchs," *Journal of Theological Studies*, NS 42 (1991), 115–25.

Lightfoot, J.B. (1885) *The Apostolic Fathers. Part II: S. Ignatius. S. Polycarp*, 2d. ed., vol. 1 (London: 1885).

McEvoy, J., ed. (forthcoming) *Robert Grosseteste. New Perspectives on his Thought and Scholarship* (Brepols).

(1991) "Robert Grosseteste on the Ten Commandments," *Recherches de théologie ancienne et médiévale* 58 (1991) 167–205.

(1987) "John Scottus Eriugena and Robert Grosseteste: An Ambiguous Influence," in *Eriugena Redivivus*, ed. W. Beierwaltes (Heidelberg: 1987) 192–223.

(1982)* *The Philosophy of Robert Grosseteste* (Oxford: 1982).

(1980) "Robert Grosseteste's Theory of Human Nature With the Text of His Conference 'Ecclesia Sancta Celebrat'," *Recherches de théologie ancienne et médiévale* 47 (1980) 131–87.

(1981) "Language, Tongue and Thought in the Writings of Robert Grosseteste," in *Sprache und Erkenntnis im Mittelalter*, vol. 2 (Berlin-New York: 1981) 585–92.

(1975)* "Robert Grosseteste and the Reunion of the Church," *Collectanea Franciscana* 45 (1975) 39–84.

Moiser, J. (1973) "Why Did the Son of God Become Man?," *The Thomist* 37 (1973) 288–305.

Muckle, J.T. (1951) "Did Robert Grosseteste Attribute the *Hexameron* of St. Venerable Bede to St. Jerome?," *Mediaeval Studies* 13 (1951) 242–44.

(1945) "Robert Grosseteste's Use of Greek Sources in his *Hexameron*," *Medievalia et Humanistica* 3 (1945) 33–48.

Raedts, P. (1987)* *Richard Rufus of Cornwall and the Tradition of Oxford Theology* (Oxford: 1987).

Rizzerio, L. (1992) "Robert Grosseteste, Jean Chrysostome, et l'*expositor graecus* (= Theophylacte) dans le commentaire *super epistolam ad Galatas*," *Recherches de théologie ancienne et médiévale* 59 (1992) 166–209.

Rosemann, P. (forthcoming) "Robert Grosseteste's *Tabula*," in McEvoy (forthcoming).

Rouse, M.A and R.H. (1991) "Development of Research Tools in the Thirteenth Century," in *Authentic Witnesses: Approaches to Medieval Texts and Manuscripts*, ed. M.A. and R.H. Rouse (Notre Dame, Indiana: 1991) 221–55.

Russell, J. (1933) "The Preferments and 'Adiutores' of Robert Grosseteste," *Harvard Theological Review* 26 (1933) 161–72.

Smalley, B. (1955)* "The Biblical Scholar," in Callus (1955a) 70–97.

(1938) "A Collection of Paris Lectures of the Later Twelfth Century in the Ms. Pembroke College, Cambridge 7," *The Cambridge Historical Journal* 6 (1938) 103–13.

Southern, R. (1992)* *Robert Grosseteste: The Growth of an English Mind in Medieval Europe*, 2d. ed. (Oxford: 1992).

Taylor Hogan, C. (forthcoming) "Pseudo-Dionysius and the Ecclesiology of Robert Grosseteste: A Fruitful Symbiosis," in McEvoy (forthcoming).

Thomson, S.H. (1955) "Grosseteste's Concordantial Signs," *Medievalia et Humanistica* 9 (1955) 39–53.

(1940)* *The Writings of Robert Grosseteste, Bishop of Lincoln 1235–1253* (Cambridge: 1940).

(1934) "Grosseteste's Topical Concordance of the Bible and the Fathers," *Speculum* 9 (1934) 138–44.

THE PATRISTIC SOURCES OF THE *LEGENDA AUREA*: A RESEARCH REPORT

Barbara Fleith

> ". . . nam Legendas Sanctorum in uno volumine compilavit, multa adiciens in eisdem de Ystoria Ecclesiastica, de Ystoria Tripartita et de Ystoria Scolastica et de Cronicis diversorum auctorum".[1]

I. *Introduction*

For a long time, researchers had taken for granted that the author of the Legenda Aurea had made use of a considerable amount of primary sources; here they meant the writings of the fathers of the church across the centuries. The present essay aims to summarize the various contributions of researchers and to characterize the present situation; from this, it should be possible to define the main lines of research for the future. It is impossible to trace and evaluate all published research articles for the 177 legends. Consequently I have confined myself to presenting here those articles which I personally have knowledge of. None of the works can be considered as definitive or exhaustive.

1. *The Author, Jacobus de Voragine*

The name of the author[2] of the Latin Legenda Aurea is usually given as "Jacobus de" or "a Voragine",[3] which refers to his place of birth, a small town on the coast between Genoa and Savona, known nowadays under the name of "Varazze". Born around 1230,[4] Jacobus de

---

[1] Quotation from Jacobus de Voragine, Chronica Januensis, published for the first time by Muratori (1726); critical edition by Monleone (1941); quotation vol. II, p. 404.

[2] For more details, see Fleith (1991), 9–11; Maggioni's important work (1995) appeared too late to be taken into account here.

[3] See Airaldi (1988), and the Atti "JdV" (1987).

[4] Quétif (1719), 454.

Voragine entered the newly founded Dominican order in 1244. After his studies, which took place either in Bologna[5] or in Genoa,[6] and a few years of activity as a teacher and preacher, he became successively the prior of the convents of Como, Bologna and Asti.

From 1267 until 1277 and from 1281 until 1285/86 Jacobus de Voragine was the prior of the province of Lombardy. He was appointed to the rank of archbishop of Genoa in 1295. He died in the night of the 13th of July 1298 and was buried in the Dominican church of Genoa.

In the Chronica Januensis, written by Jacobus in 1295–1297, Jacobus de Voragine gives an overview of his literary works: he mentions first the Legenda Sanctorum, then two volumes of sermons for saints' days, and one volume of Sunday sermons, one of Lenten sermons, one of sermons on Mary and finally his Chronicle.[7]

2. The Legendary

The Legenda Aurea was probably completed in 1260.[8] The earliest recorded manuscript Metz, Bibl. mun. 1147* is dated 1273 but has since been burnt. The oldest extant and clearly dated manuscript dates from 1281 (Paris, B.N.F. nouv. acq. lat. 1800). For the 13th century as a whole, 70 manuscripts have been identified.

As may be inferred from the quotation at the beginning of this essay, the Legendary bore initially no specific name but only the generic term of "Legendae sanctorum".[9]

However, in the 13th century manuscripts already, the titles "legenda aurea" (cf. Paris, B.N.F., lat. 16054) and "Historia lombardica" also appear, two names which later on would become characteristic of the Legendary.

As specified by Jacobus himself, the book was compressed into one volume. It is a "short legendary" which is arranged "per circulum anni",[10] which means that the individual legends are ordered accord-

---

[5] Richardson (1935), vol. I, 5.

[6] Monleone (1941), vol. I, 35.

[7] Cf. Monleone (1941), vol. II, 404. For each work in particular, cf. Kunze (1983), 449.

[8] For details, see Fleith (1991), 12. On the question of dating cf. W. Williams-Krapp's review in: Mittellateinisches Jahrbuch 29, (1995), 164–168.

[9] On the title question, see Fleith (1991), 25.

[10] Cf. Philippart (1977).

ing to the Church year. At the time it was written, a universal calendar of holy days had not yet been created. As compared to the
Dominican calendars then in use, Jacobus de Voragine rather followed the old Roman calendar which became universally recognized
from the 16th century on.[11] Through this adjustment to saints who
might, in the future, receive worship in many regions, the author
possibly intended to secure a good starting basis for the wide spread-
ing of his legendary among clerical circles in all regions.

Jacobus de Voragine included not only holy legends but also spiritual meditations on days dedicated to the Lord, to Mary and other
religious holidays. Thus the work begins with a text for Advent followed by the legend of Andrew and so on and ends with a text for
the harvest festival of late November. This Church year is divided
into five parts: a prologue and four chapters. Particular attention is
devoted to the Passion of Christ. Characteristically, almost all the
legends contained within the Legenda Aurea are accompanied by
etymologies of names.

Analysis of most of the thousand or so Latin manuscripts of the
work demonstrates that the original consisted of 176 legends. All of
these legends are included in Theodor Graesse's 1846 edition,[12] which
is so far the only modern edition of the Latin text. Six of the legends
present in Graesse do not belong to the original body of legends:[13]
Sophia (Graesse 48), Timotheus (Graesse 52), Fabian (Graesse 64),
Apollonia (Graesse 66) and Bonifacius (Graesse 71), and the legend
of Elizabeth. The latter however was included in the Legendary already in the 13th century and has since been an integral part of the
Legenda Aurea. Hence, the "vulgate" version contains 177 legends.

The legends of Cornelius (Graesse 132) and Lambertus (Graesse
133) were placed in the wrong order by Graesse. The legend of Cornelius should stand before Eufemia's (Graesse 139) and the legend of
Lambertus should come after Eufemia's.

It has been observed that the work, due to its considerable scope,
is frequently divided into two volumes (a Winter Volume and a Summer Volume), which often circulated separately.

---

[11] Cf. Fleith (1991), 342.
[12] Graesse, 1. ed. (1846), 2. ed. (1850), 3. ed. (1890); Reproduction 1965, "bad
print of the Dresden incunabulum 180 (1°) destroyed in 1945, according to the
catalogue of manuscripts, identical with M. Wenssler's print, Basle n.d. (before 1474;
cop., No. 6399, Seybolt, No. 8)" acc. Kunze, 1983, 453.
[13] Cf. in detail Fleith (1991), 30.

The original Legendary, during its transmission through the years, was constantly modified to varying degrees by additions, rearrangements and deletions, possibly with the aim of adapting it to the specific purposes of the countries or orders through which it passed. These interventions occasionally went so far as to render the original book unrecognizable amidst the multitude of subsequently added legends.[14]

3. *Use*

The characteristics of the contents—encyclopedic conception and emphatically didactic features—together with recent studies about historical transmission suggest that the work was used for many different purposes.

The traditional situations where such a legendary would be used, such as its use in Chapter House and Refectory can be proven also for the Latin Legenda Aurea.[15]

Mainly however it was used for the preparation of sermons; the Legenda Aurea can in some cases even be proven to be the source for collections of sermons.

A context for use of the Legenda Aurea, barely recognized until now, is its use in the school environment.[16] This would explain the didactic elements of the work, but also serve as an interpretation for the historical discovery that a large part of the manuscripts originated from the school/university areas. 30 years after its appearance the Legenda Aurea belonged to the manuscripts strictly controlled by the University, which were copied in the Parisian Pecia System, and which were intended for use by the University of Paris.

Not until the work was translated into the vernacular[17] did it gain any real importance as educational literature, not only with clerics and convents but also in lay circles. This educational function also becomes visible on a superficial level in the manuscripts so that they come to contain many more illustrations. In the Latin manuscripts

---

[14] Cf. Fleith (1991). Studies about the historical transmission record data on the preserved Latin manuscripts, take into account the mutations of the original corpus and give a list of the legends which were added to the original corpus and which can be found in the manuscripts of the Legenda Aurea.

[15] Compare to Fleith, more exact account (1991), 39ff.

[16] First discussed by Boureau (1984), 24f.

[17] Compare the article to the translations and history of use in the individual regions. Transmission and inclusion in the Lexikon des Mittelalters (1991).

miniatures are only seldom to be found; the vernacular translations on the other hand, above all the Vignay translation, are to a certain extent artistically decorated.[18]

II. *General Remarks on Trends in Research*

1. *Roze and Benz—The Traditional Perspective*

In the Legenda Aurea there are often references to older texts and their authors. Boureau (1984) counted 1186 such explicit references to earlier texts, with the result that the Legenda Aurea in his opinion constitutes "a veritable encyclopedia of references and quotations" [75] "In fact the liturgical chapters, which represent slightly less than a quarter of the total volume of the Legendary, contain 640 of the 1186 quotations. Out of the 153 biographical chapters, 88 contain no reference: this is the case with the lives of most martyrs, virgins, confessors and abbots (. . .). The lives of apostles and doctors of the church abound in references". [77] For Boureau these are references, but not exploited sources. He puts them together in 3 information-yielding lists [78–83].[19] What Boureau expressly referred to as "References" was judged as a list of sources in the early stages of research into the Legenda Aurea. Roze in 1867 put together the following sources on the strength of the quotations.[20] "Here is a list of those who are quoted in the Golden Legend. We classify them chronologically:

All the books of the Bible, including the Book of Jashar, mentioned in Joshua, X, 13.

1st century – Joseph, priests and deacons of Achaia, saint Dionysius the Areopagite, saint Clement, saint Linus.
II century – Saint Ignatius of Antioch.
III century – Origen, Cyprian.
IV century – Saint Hilary, saint Basil, saint John Chrysostom, Eusebius of Caesarea, Eutropius, saint Athanasius, Palladius, saint Ambrose, Amphilochius of Iconium, Sedulius, saint Gregory of Nyssa.
V century – Saint Augustine, saint Jerome, Prosper, Orosius, Cassian,

---

[18] Compare to Verdier, 1986, 95–99, and Maddocks, 1986, 155–169.
[19] Although Boureau emphasized that it was not a question of source indications, he wrote two plates with "Christian sources" [80] and "non-Christian sources" [83].
[20] See criticism in Analecta Bollandiana 22 (1903), 81f.

Macrobius, saint Gelasius, Prudentius, saint Leo, saint Paulinus of Nola, Pelagius, Gennadius, saint Eucherius of Lyon, saint Severus, Sulpicius, Socrates, Sozomenes, Theodoret.

VI century – Saint Gregory the Great, Cassiodorus, saint Fulgentius, the Lives of the Fathers, saint Gregory of Tours, Dorotheus, Boethius, Elpis.

VII century – Saint Isidore of Seville, John the deacon, Mohammed.

VIII century – Saint John of Damascus, Venerable Bede, saint Germain of Constantinople, Paul the deacon.

IX century – Saint Walfrid-Strabo, the Gloss, Methodius, Hincmar, Haymo, Usuard, Alcuin, Eginhard, Amalarius, John the Scot, Heiric, Turpin.

X century – Remigius of Auxerre, Nolker, saint Odo of Cluny.

XI century – Saint Peter Damian, saint Gerald, Fulbert of Chartres, Hermann the Lame, Adalbodius.

XII century – Bernard of Clairvaux, Petrus Comestor, Saint Anselm, Peter of Cluny, Richard of St. Victor, Peter Lombard, Hugh of St. Victor, Sigebert of Gembloux, Pope Callistus, William of Saint-Thierry, Arnold of Bonneval, Gilbert, Eckbert, Peter the Chanter, Leo of Ostia, Honorius Augustudinensis, Gratian.

XIII century – Innocent III, saint Hugh of Cluny, Helinandus, John Beleth, William of Auxerre, Godfrey of Viterbo, Vincent of Beauvais, Henry of Ghent, Sicard of Cremona, Maître Prévost.

Other books which could not be classified:

Gospel of Nicodemus – Infancy Gospels – Apocryphal book attributed to St. John the Evangelist. – Abdias. – John and Mark. – Hegesippus. – Melito or Mellitus of Laodicea. – The doctors of Argos. – the Sibylline books – Rabbi Moses. – Bartholomew. – Timothy. – Peter of Ravenna. – Sulpicius of Jerusalem. – Theotymus – Hubert of Besançon. – Constantine. – Saint Cosmas Vestitor. – Peter of Compostella. – Richard – Albert. – The Apocryphal History of Pilate. – History of Antioch. – An Apocryphal History of the Greeks. – An Ancient History. – Several Chronicles. – Acts of the Holy Pontiffs. – Glossaries. – Book of the Saints Gervasius and Protasius. – The Miracles of the Holy Virgin. – Book of Miracles of the Saints. – The Ambrosian Missal. – Hymns."[21]

---

[21] Roze (1867) 46–47 and Roze (1902) XIVff.

Roze expressly emphasizes that Jacobus de Voragine,—as he says himself in his Chronicle[22]—worked as a compiler.[23] "Therefore it is quite simply a compilation: therefore the style is that of a copyist who, finding a narrative in the works of an author, reproduces it much as he encountered it."—". . . it is our duty to declare that Jacobus de Varazze had copied *almost everywhere, compilavit. . . .*" When a legend was found in its entirety in the works of a Father of the Church, it had been copied *in extenso*: such as in the Life of Saint Paula by Saint Jerome and in the account of the Virgin of Antioch by Ambrose.[24]

Benz also compiled a list of the sources used in the Legenda Aurea, in total 250 titles, which he appended to the Latin bibliography in the 2nd volume of the first edition of his German translation.[25] In contrast to Roze, however, Benz was convinced that Jacobus de Voragine had remodeled these sources and adapted them to his personal style. "One must know the sources of Jacobus de Voragine: not only their enormous number, but also their endlessly varied quality, in order to measure the scope of his creative endeavor: hundreds of styles have been brought into one."[26]

2. *Research Problems*

With these two contrary research positions the foundation was laid for further treatment of the question of sources for the Legenda Aurea:

Did Jacobus de Voragine quote word for word from these sources or did he remodel them in his own style?

Did Jacobus de Voragine really make direct use of this impressive quantity of sources or did he use compilations from which he also drew the quotations of the original sources?

When he used compilations, to what extent? Did he know the original sources despite this? Which compilations are involved here?

Are the answers to these questions the same for every text of the Legenda Aurea—the spiritual observations, the legends of the Fathers, the legends of the martyrs, virgins, confessors and the modern legends?

---

[22] Chronicle quotation Monleone (1941), vol. II, 404 at the beginning of the article on hand: "compilavit".

[23] Roze, 1867, 43f.

[24] Roze, 1867, 44–45.

[25] Benz, 1917–1921, vol. 2. pp. 557–630 Latin bibliography; pp. 631–642 Source Indications.

[26] Benz, (8) 1975, XXV.

As long as the intention was to determine the sources in the traditional way, i.e. by comparing them with the original texts, the same
answer came up again and again; Jacobus de Voragine used an
enormous number of source texts.

The discoveries of the last fifty years have shown however that in
determining the sources for the Legenda Aurea the following points
are important:

a) In many cases one should speak mainly of indirectly used sources,
   which means that here material is assembled which had accumu-
   lated over the centuries and had reached the authors of the 13th
   century through anonymous intermediary writers.

b) The question of direct use of sources and the answers to the
   questions above are progressively gaining in importance through
   increasing knowledge of 13th century hagiographic literature.

   The more the degree of knowledge of other Legendaries of the
   period, and in particular "short legendaries", increased, the more
   precisely the position regarding direct sources of the Legenda Aurea
   could be defined.

c) At the same time it was observed, and becomes clear also through
   Boureau's list of references, that certain legends were transmitted
   in a relatively fixed form, i.e. were hardly modified through additional information from other sources. This applies above all to
   the old legends of the Martyrs, Virgins, Confessors and the Fathers
   of the Desert, which are referred to as "Primary legends", whereas
   the legends of the Apostles and the biographies of the great church
   preachers were more subject to modification by the authors; in
   our context they should be called "Commentary Legends".

d) The genesis of the legends of the saints of the 13th century—the
   "modern" saints—took place under special conditions, and should
   be discussed under its own heading.

Investigations into the spiritual observations of the Legenda Aurea, a
quarter of the total text, are to my knowledge not yet available, but
offer a rich field of research for the history of the effects of the original texts.

3. *The Search for New Answers*

Today it can be said with certainty that the sources for any "primary" or "commentary" Legend of the Legenda Aurea which is also

to be found in other Legendaries of the 13th century, cannot be determined without comparison with these contemporary Legendaries. The main problem consists in access to them, given that their existence has only become known to a wider circle since the works of Poncelet (1910) and Philippart (1977). So far, no critical editions of them are available.

3.1. *Three "Short Legendaries" of the 13th Century*
To determine the precedents of the Legenda Aurea a comparison with the following legendaries appears indispensable:

3.1.1. Johannes de Malliaco (Jean de Mailly, OP.), *Abbreviatio in gestis et miraculis sanctorum* (Abbreviatio), first version appeared in 1225–1230; an expanded edition appeared in 1243.[27] The text has been available since 1947 in the French translation by Dondaine. In the introduction the translator answers the question of whether Jacobus de Voragine knew the Abbreviatio: "The close relationship of the two works {Abbreviatio and Legenda Aurea}, in their literary form and in their content, scarcely leaves room for doubt. ... It appears that he {Jacobus de Voragine} was inspired by the *Gestures and Miracles* throughout his work."[28] A year earlier Dondaine[29] had still cautiously declared the Abbreviatio to be the principal source of the Legenda Aurea, however with this modification: "The source, let it be well understood, is not so much the material used by Jacobus de Voragine, ... as the creative idea of the Golden Legend." Out of the 177 chapters in the Legenda Aurea 136 were also to be found in the Abbreviatio "in depth, form and language, sometimes down to the very letter."[30]

But Dondaine warns against seeing the Abbreviatio simply as a prototype of the Legenda Aurea: "In general, the foundation of common legends is obtained from the same sources, there is no doubt about that. However, it would be premature to state that Jacobus de Voragine copied his forerunner."[31] Sometimes the legends of the

---

[27] See regarding Abbreviatio: Dondaine (1946), (1947), Philippart (1974), (1979), Geith (1985), (1987), (1993) and Maggioni (1987), (1990).

[28] Dondaine (1947), 14. "The basic text of the translation is chiefly that of the Latin manuscript 10843 of the French National Library, probably one of the most ancient which has reached us". [21]

[29] Dondaine (1946), 54.

[30] *Ibid.*, 91.

[31] *Ibid.*

Abbreviatio are more detailed, at other times those of the Legenda Aurea.

For the Abbreviatio Dondaine believes to have proof from the example of the Ursula Legend that Jean de Mailly was really the author of his short legends, and not merely the imitator of existing compilations.[32] On pages 97 to 99 Dondaine compiles a list of the works used by Jean de Mailly "Comparing it {the list} to the catalogue of works used by Jacobus de Voragine in the *Golden Legend* this list would appear to us to be rather impoverished.[33]

For the following work I have used the Abbreviatio Text with the help of a microfilm of the manuscript in the University Library in Basle B.III, 14.

3.1.2. Bartholomew of Trent OP, Epilogus in Gesta Sanctorum (Epilogus) written in 1245 in Trent. The text is available in the edition of D. Gobbi (1990) which is in fact a diplomatic transcript of the Klosterneuburg Manuscript.[34]

Boureau expressly points out, that Jacobus de Voragine knew the Epilogus: "he {Jacobus de Voragine} explicitly quotes it in the chapter on the nativity of the Lord; he probably borrowed from it an anecdote on Dominic which he could find nowhere else, he copied (without naming his source) the text of his chapter on Saint Patrick.[35]

3.1.3. Vincentius Bellovacensis' (Vincent of Beauvais OP), Speculum Historiale constitutes the third part of his encyclopedia entitled Speculum maius. "In fact, out of the 3800 chapters which make up his Speculum historiale, almost 900 relate the lives and miracles of the saints . . ." "It remains nevertheless true that this is a work of general history and not properly a legendary. . . ."[36]

Poncelet believes that the Speculum Historiale was published for the first time in 1244 and that in 1250 or somewhat later Vincent of Beauvais wrote a second edition.[37] The first edition was already used

---

[32] *Ibid.*, 87.

[33] *Ibid.*, 99.

[34] For Batholomew of Trent cf. Dondaine (1971), (1975), Boureau (1990) with further references, and Maggioni (1987), (1990).

[35] Boureau (1990), 24.

[36] Poncelet (1910), 20.

[37] Petitmengin (1984), 147 refers to a difference in the counting of books for the Speculum Historiale: In contrast to the printing of Johan Mentelin, Strasbourg, 1473 the first book is missing from the 1624 Douai edition (reprinted in Graz 1965), with the result that here the counting is one book behind that of the Mentelin edition.

by Jean de Mailly before its publication.[38] The work of Dondaine (1946) showed that the first edition of the Speculum Historiale which has not reached us did not appear before 1244, i.e. at a time when the Abbreviatio had already reached its second edition[39] and could in no way have been used by Jean de Mailly.

For this reason Dondaine assumes that the dependency should be defined in the opposite manner: Vincent of Beauvais takes a large part of the chapters of the Abbreviatio word for word into his Speculum Historiale;[40] as Vincent worked with the support of secretaries, Jean de Mailly may have been one of his secretaries.[41] Results which lead us further are to be hoped for from the work of the "Atelier Vincent of Beauvais" in Nancy.[42]

3.2. *Results of Research up to the Present Day*

First of all it should be pointed out that the researchers only seldom really concerned themselves with the works of their predecessors especially those from countries other than their own, or those who worked primarily on vernacular texts, perhaps because it was not expected that research into sources in the vernacular could have repercussions on the Latin versions.

Not until the ground-breaking work of Dondaine in 1946/7 could the inclusion of the Abbreviatio for the determination of sources be expected. Previously it was only too understandable to wish to trace the Legenda Aurea texts directly back to their "original sources", so that Wilhelm in 1907 saw the Thomas legend of the Legenda Aurea as a short version of an old Passio sancti Thomae, and in so doing did not take into account the influence of the Abbreviatio, which was quite unknown to him.

Surprisingly, studies of sources which include the comparison with the Legendaries mentioned above can be established quite early.

Already in 1909 Monteverdi noticed for the Eustachius legend that Abbreviatio, Speculum Historiale and Legenda Aurea were indirectly

---

[38] Poncelet (1910), 20.
[39] Dondaine (1946), 85.
[40] *Ibid.*, 60.
[41] *Ibid.*, 89.
[42] Compare to the note in the Dominican History Newsletter, II, 1993, pp. 22–23, in which reference is made to the research of E. Meyrignac, "Le Légendier du Speculum Historiale".—On Vincent de Beauvais as compilator compare A.J. Minnis, Late-medieval discussions of *compilatio* and the role of the *compilator*.—In: Beiträge zur Geschichte der deutschen Sprache und Literatur 101 (1979), 385–421.

transcribed through a version which is now lost, which must have been the common source of these three legendaries.

In 1925 Petersen raised this problem once again and likewise emphasized the similarity between Abbreviatio, Speculum Historiale and Legenda Aurea; Speculum Historiale was, however, more detailed than Abbreviatio. On the basis of Poncelet's theory of a later 2nd edition of the Speculum Historiale text Petersen declared that the wider-reaching Eustachius legend of the Speculum Historiale was the result of the later drafting of the Vincent of Beauvais.

Hug (1929) took particularly rewarding pains with the Peter and Paul legends (according to our classification "commentary" legends) of the Legenda Aurea. Here the traditional search for sources is combined with the comparison of legendaries from the same period; the latter gave Hug doubts about the methods hitherto used to compare the Legenda Aurea texts with the old sources:

"The decomposition of the Peter and Paul legends has permitted Jacobus to be considered as a skilful and many-sided mosaic artist. From sources of writers of almost every century before him he collected his material and tried to create a literary work out of it. . . . Not very many pieces of work can demonstrate his activity as a compiler to the same extent as these two. However the possibility still exists that Jacobus had another set of texts unknown to us available to him. As a result of literary value of the following research a further dependency relationship can be established between Jacobus and Bartholomew of Trent and in addition a very probable literary dependency on the "Abbreviatio in gestis et miraculis" of Ms. 1731 of the Mazarine."[43] For these two commentary legends the connection with the short legendaries could be established as well as a dependence on other older sources.

The most all-encompassing study of sources was compiled by Zuidweg in 1941. He knew the Speculum Historiale but not the Abbreviatio, which could be explained by the fact that his investigations preceded those of Dondaine by 4 years.

Zuidweg found himself in the same undecided situation as Hug. He also attempted to verify the old sources for a certain number of legends, noticed however that texts similar to the Legenda Aurea were also to be found in other legendaries; in Ado's Martyrologium, but above all in Speculum Historiale.

---

[43] Hug (1929), 623f.

For his investigations Zuidweg uses mainly the texts of the Patrologia Latina of Migne (*PL*) and the Acta Sanctorum without making reference to the difficulties of the constitution of the text in these two editions. The texts are not critically edited in the two collections, but are very often put together from different intermediary writers: "Martyrium e Ms. Fuldensi cum aliis exemplaribus collato" (Cf. p. 270 below).

Although of indisputable value as collections, neither Migne nor the Acta Sanctorum provided a sound basis for investigation of sources. Zuidweg does not seem to have been aware of this. He examined approximately 60 legends (primary and commentary legends) of the Legenda Aurea down to their sources, i.e. compared them with the original texts, and came to the following conclusions: In no way can one talk of a unified personal style of Jacobus de Voragine; [9] nowhere does the personality of the author come to the forefront and everywhere the text has been taken from existing written sources [25] with the result that on the whole we must speak of a great dependence on sources. His quotations are second-hand quotations [26], even the etymologies are taken from other sources, partly from Isidore [40]. Jacobus de Voragine had a "circle of simple readers" [17] in mind; for this reason he leaves out geographical names, dates and unimportant personal names. For him it is more a matter of reporting the sensational, [17] and of recounting "wonders". [15] He copies the text of his sources word for word when it is short and simple, when the source is too detailed, he shortens it; when it is too complicated, he simplifies it; when it is too strange, he looks for more familiar ways of formulating it. [17] Jacobus de Voragine's particular achievement lies in his method of choosing, i.e. in finding in his sources what his readers wanted to hear. [33]

Here Zuidweg reports doubts as to his own method of proceeding, as it can certainly not be assumed that Jacobus de Voragine used his sources directly. An intermediate step must be assumed to exist. In this case it is even possible that the collation of the texts is not Jacobus de Voragine's own work, but that he made use of a compilation which was in circulation at the time but which is now lost. [36] The main reason for Zuidweg's assumption lies in the fact that he noted a great deal of common traits between the Legenda Aurea and the Speculum Historiale; both must have used the same sources. Jacobus de Voragine knew the Speculum Historiale, which he mentions explicitly in the Legenda Aurea (Legenda Aurea 494.21 and 503.17) [38].

Indeed Zuidweg shows in his investigations that Legenda Aurea is often nearer to the original texts or more detailed than Speculum Historiale, cap. 39, 41, 61, 122 etc. with the result that Legenda Aurea did not always use Speculum Historiale. Since it is in any case unimaginable that both produced the same excerpt independently of one another from an enormous wealth of sources, it must be assumed that they used a common source, an "anonieme acta". [39] Zuidweg did not know the works of Monteverdi and Hug!

At the end of the 2nd chapter Zuidweg presents a list of methods used by Jacobus de Voragine in evaluating sources. I quote from the French summary [155]:

"A. *Several sources are used in more or less equal proportions, in such a way that it is not possible to determine a principal source.*
Method 1. The sources are reproduced freely: here and there there is literal or almost literal copying." Cap. 18, 19, 124, 166.
"Method 2. Sources are copied word for word or nearly so; here and there the sources are reproduced more freely." Cap. 21, 114, 149.
"B. *Besides a principal source, other secondary sources have been used.*
Method 3. The main source and the secondary sources are reproduced freely; here and there there is literal or almost literal copying." Cap. 23.
"Method 4. There is literal or almost literal copying of the main source and secondary sources; here and there the sources are reproduced more freely." Cap. 24, 39, 63, 113, 146, 152.
"C. Only one source was used.
Method 5. The author allowed himself complete or extensive liberty." Cap. 15, 27, 56, 84. "It must be noted however that it is not impossible that the author used in this case a version unknown to us, the context of which approached more that of the Golden Legend than the source we have identified.
Method 6. The copying is literal or almost literal: here and there the source is reproduced more freely." Cap. 16, 38, 74, 79, 122, 126, 138, 150, 167, 180. "In this last chapter the source was considerably shortened.
Method 7. The author gives a series of anecdotes and aphorisms rather than a legend or biography proper; the anecdotic episodes, borrowed from only one source, follow one another in an arbitrary fashion." Cap. 175, 176, 177, 178, 179.
"Method 8. Copying is entirely verbatim or almost verbatim." Cap.

29, 41, 61, 62, 78, 80, 82, 101, 106, 111, 133, 148, 154, 171. "In chapter 29 copying is literal to excess, to the point where Jacobus de Voragine retained the word *ego*, which refers to the source author! In this chapter the omission of various fragments of the source harms the legend as a whole in a particularly regrettable manner."

At the end of the 1960s, a new generation of hagiographic investigations got under way, whose object was to show the passing on of a single legend on the basis of all extant versions. For the Legenda Aurea first of all Orywall (1968) should be mentioned, who dealt above all with French versions of the Margaret Legend, and who for this reason only mentioned the Latin account incidentally. She pointed out the identity of the Margaret text in Abbreviatio and Speculum Historiale [61]; this text was also carried over to a large extent into the Legenda Aurea version, in any case Jacobus de Voragine also knew the source text of Abbreviatio/Speculum Historiale [86]. Orywall's results led us to suppose that the same excerpt was used by all three authors.

Kunze's (1969) investigation of the legend of Mary of Egypt, groundbreaking for the hagiographic research method, deals with the version in Speculum Historiale,[44] which possibly served as a source for the Legenda Aurea for this legend.[45]

Haubrichs pointed out in 1979, that the Legenda Aurea for the St. George legend takes the text of the Abbreviatio, which is also in Speculum Historiale, but in addition to this works with several other sources.[46]

A result similar to Orywall is to be found in the work of Petitmengin (1984):

For the Pelagia legend the Legenda Aurea text reveals numerous deviations from the Abbreviatio, but also shows knowledge of the "Original text" of the legend.[47]

Zehnder (1987) assumed that Jacobus de Voragine composed for the Ursula legend a mixed text from old texts and the Speculum Historiale. Zehnder apparently did not know the Abbreviatio, as this mixed text is already in the Abbreviatio and Dondaine had paid particular attention to the Ursula legend.[48]

---

[44] A Maria Aegyptiaca legend is not contained in the Abbreviatio.
[45] Kunze (1969), 30f.
[46] Haubrichs (1979), 295.
[47] Petitmengin (1984), 153.
[48] Dondaine (1946), 86f.

Maggioni devoted two essays (1987 and 1990) and Geith three to
the interdependence between Legenda Aurea and Abbreviatio; in the
first two (1985 and 1987) Geith demonstrated after examining the
Juliana legends in Abbreviatio and Legenda Aurea that the Legenda
Aurea text was taken and shortened directly from the Abbreviatio.
However, in 1993 Geith found two hitherto untraced passages in the
Epilogus in Gesta Sanctorum,[49] thus establishing it as a likely source.

Merrilees noted in 1986 that the legend of the seven sleepers came
into both the Legenda Aurea and Speculum Historiale from the Abbreviatio. In 1992 Löffler showed that the Alexius legend, which is not
contained in the main body of the Abbreviatio, was compiled from
several sources, perhaps also from the Magnum Legendarium Austriacum. The Speculum Historiale relates a version which is similar to
one of the Legenda Aurea sources.

3.3. Different Use of Sources for Primary and Commentary Legends

Although Boureau (1984) expressly insists that it was not his intention
to examine the sources of the Legenda Aurea, he nevertheless devotes
several pages to this problem and in my opinion comes to an important conclusion, even if he does not appear to have examined the
legends individually down to their sources or have dealt extensively
with existing research. On pages 89–91 Boureau suggests an approximate categorization of possible sources of the Legenda Aurea, while
pointing out the limitations of this attempt, as long as an investigation of sources is not tackled systematically.

"The chapters on the saints are divided into three categories according to the method of use of previous texts:—71 chapters out of
153 are no doubt derived from a common source. They adapt either
the Martyrologium hieronymianum or the Liber Pontificalis for the
shortest chapters, or the columns of the Martyrologium of Ado, or
the ancient Acts, illustrated vitae, or finally the Vitae Patrum.—In
37 chapters Jacobus de Voragine completes a fundamental source by
various glosses or by accounts of posthumous miracles. [87]—33
chapters offer a synthesis of narrative elements and doctrinal traits,
in the midst of a didactic whole." [88] This categorization shows
that Jacobus de Voragine worked sometimes as an abbreviator, at
other times as a commentator, or as a compiler. "The longest and
most substantial chapters, which concern the 'original' saints and the

---

[49] For the discussion of the last essay of 1993 see below.

doctors, present in most cases an original elaboration, while the accounts devoted to the martyrs of the great persecutions and the first confessors tend to abridge earlier narratives." [92] Here we see again the difference between primary and commentary legends, which one could surely formulate in a crass and overly generalized manner: the primary legends are put together from the short legendaries mostly without great modifications; the commentary legends show a greater degree of revision with the aid of the most diverse sources, but can in their essence also have originated from the short legendaries.

3.4. *Present State of Conflicting Research Trends in the Works of* S.L. *Reames and K.E. Geith*

Again and again it has been emphasized throughout the history of research that Jacobus de Voragine abridged his sources. S.L. Reames made this observation the central theme of her work of 1985, in which she sets down what Jacobus de Voragine omitted from his sources, and to what extent these omissions characterize the intentions of the author. To present these omissions, the author compares Jacobus de Voragine's text directly with the old source texts; in so doing she uses as a point of departure the direct use of sources by Jacobus de Voragine, which is not free from controversy in the research with which she concerns herself. She recognizes less influence of the earlier short legendaries on the creative wishes of Jacobus de Voragine as an abbreviator. [69] "Jacobus' characteristic omissions might conceivably have arisen from his continual dependence on earlier abridged legendary or legendaries with just the same set of priorities. Should a source of that description come to light, an attempt to explain the selectivity of the Legenda in terms of Jacobus' career and personal temperament may look rather foolish in retrospect. But from the evidence I have seen, the risk seems well worth taking. The two earlier legendaries with which the Legenda should presumably have most in common, those of Jean de Mailly and Bartholomew of Trent, resemble it a good deal less than has been claimed. So do the [70] accounts of the saints in Vincent of Beauvais' Speculum historiale. Even in those chapters and parts of chapters where Jacobus seems actually to be following one of these works, most often Jean's Abbreviatio, his priorities are recognizably his own, not theirs. And for most major legends (...) he seems to have had access to reasonably complete texts. In fact, his accounts in the Legenda are full of passages that are not abridged at all, but taken verbatim from the original

lives of the saints (. . .)." The knowledge of these original sources is
also to be found in Jacobus de Voragine's sermons. Although the formation of the two legendaries Abbreviatio and Legenda Aurea was
not always so strongly contrasted as in the case of the Dominic legends,
Jean de Mailly treats his legends in a different way from Jacobus de
Voragine: "Almost uniformly (. . .) his {Jean de Mailly} abridgments
are better balanced than those in the Legenda—less apt to substitute
political propaganda for religious teaching, more restrained in their
use of the marvelous, and more intent on the role of the saints as
models for imitation. Thus Jean shows very little of Jacobus' inclina-
tion to prove the saints' glory by emphasizing the wondrous ease of
their victories. In the Abbreviatio even the martyrs, the great heroes
of the church, tend to appear as recognizable human beings whose
greatness consists in suffering, endurance, and dependence on God."
[205] Reames provides examples for this from the legends of Anastasia,
Sebastian, Eusebius, Augustine and Agnes. [205–207] The difference
between the two legendaries, which shows itself on the level of the
individual selection and formulation of the recounted episodes, points
really to a fundamental difference between the two legendaries: "In
a very real sense the two books are identified with two different movements in the late medieval church: the Abbreviatio, with the general
trend toward liberalization and inclusiveness that reached its height
in the early thirteenth century; the Legenda, with the reasserting of
conservative, clerical values that followed." [207]

   In her work Reames risks an attempt, which previously, because
of the uncertainty as to sources, had been made only for individual
legends for which the sources had already been identified. She tries
to interpret the particular "abridging" style of Jacobus de Voragine;
she provides this interpretation for the three commentary legends of
Benedict, Ambrose and Augustine, and for the "modern" legend of
Dominic, concentrating thereby on particular types of legends in the
Legenda Aurea. For the three commentary legends she compares
the Graesse text with editions of the original church texts, and comes
to very interesting conclusions (see the individual chapters). It is astonishing however that she never confronts her findings with the earlier
source investigations, e.g. Zuidweg, whose work she knows. Besides
she does not consider the problem that several passages and omissions of the Legenda Aurea which she presents as a basis of interpretation for Jacobus de Voragine's intentions as a narrator, are to be
found verbatim in the Abbreviatio or were also omitted by it (see
the individual chapters concerned).

In his last article "Jacobus de Voragine—independent author or compiler"[50] K.E. Geith expressly calls for a further examination of the problem of the dependence of the Legenda Aurea on the Abbreviatio through further individual investigations. While Dondaine saw dependence only on the level of inspiration, Geith sees many legends of the Legenda Aurea as directly dependent on the Abbreviatio.

Geith had pointed out this dependence in 1985/1987 through the example of the Juliana legend; more recently he compared the texts of the Legenda Aurea in the Graesse edition and the Basle manuscript of the Abbreviatio. "In fact, the comparison of the work of Jean de Mailly with the Golden Legend shows that the greater part of the *Abbreviatio* text appears more or less faithfully reproduced in the work of Jacobus de Voragine. Out of the 200 columns of the Basle Manuscript, 132 reappear in the text of the Golden Legend, that is to say 66%. In this way it turns out that the work of Jean de Mailly is the main source of the Golden Legend." [28] Geith conceded however that this dependence can only be proven by precise studies.[51]

Both investigations provide the picture which is already outlined above: a large proportion of the Legenda Aurea legends are taken directly from the short legendaries, other legends are also transcribed

---

[50] Geith (1993).

[51] 1. The following chapters are not mentioned by Geith (1993) because they are not contained in the Abbreviatio: Cap. 1 Adventus Domini, 15 Paulus erem., 18 Macarius, 26 Basilius ep., 27 Johannes elem., 29 Paula, 30 Julianus (not present in the Basle manuscript), 31 Septuagesima, 32 Sexagesima, 33 Quinquagesima, 34 Quadragesima, 35 Ieiunium IV temporum, 50 Patricius, 53 Passio Domini, 54 Resurrectio Domini, 55 Secundus, 56 Maria Aegyptiaca, 60 Marcellinus, 62 Virgo Antiochena, 63 Petrus mart., 72 Adscensio Domini, 73 Spiritus Sanctus, 84 Marina, 88 Leo pp., 92 Theodora, 98 Christina, 105 Martha, 136 Prothus et Jacinctus, 138 Johannes Chrysostomus, 144 Forseus, 147 Remigius, 149 Franciscus, 152 Thais, 157 Crisantus et Daria, 163 Commemoratio animarum, 168 Elizabeth, 174 Jacobus interc., 175 Pastor, 176 Johannes abb., 177 Moyses abb., 178 Arsenius abb., 179 Agathon abb., 180 Barlaam et Josaphat, 181 Pelagius, 182 Dedicatio ecclesiae.

2. The following chapters are so short in Abbreviatio that a comparison of the text with Legenda Aurea was not possible: Cap. 8 Stephanus, 28 Conversio Pauli ap., 69 Johannes ante portam latinam, 95 Praxedis, 164 Quatuor coronati, 165 Theodorus.

3. The following chapters show after the comparative work of Geith no relationship with Abbreviatio: Cap. 4 Lucia, 7 Anastasia, 13 Circumcisio Domini, 14 Epiphania, 37 Purificatio, 44 Cathedra Petri, 51 Annunciatio Dominica, 70 Letania mai. et min., 76 Pancratius, 83 Quiricus et Julita, 85 Gervasius et Prothasius, 86 Johannes Baptista, 87 Johannes et Paulus, 91 Septem fratres (Felicitas), 94 Alexius, 109 Machabei, 119 Assumptio Mariae, 121 Timotheus, 124 Augustinus, 142 Cyprian

from the short Legendaries in their essence, with extracts from a large number of other sources.

The problem becomes difficult where the Legenda Aurea contains the same excerpts as the other short Legendaries, but is textually closer to the original sources.

4. The Legends of "Modern" Saints

This section concerns the legends of Francis, Dominic, Elizabeth and Peter the Martyr. Here the question is above all whether Jacobus de Voragine, partly a contemporary, fellow member of the order or compatriot, produced the life story of these saints of the 13th century himself, whether he reaches back to oral tradition, or whether he remained faithful to authorized written sources. The various positions on this issue are listed in the list of sources for the individual chapters.

The stylistic characterization of these four life stories is that of Vauchez, who devoted a study to the treatment of modern saints in the Legenda Aurea.[52] Vauchez notes that Jacobus de Voragine al-

---

et Justina, 156 Lucas, 162 Omnes sancti, 170 Clemens pp., 171 Crisogonus, 172 Catharina.

4. The following chapters are according to Geith similar to the Abbreviatio: Cap. 3 Nicolaus, 6 Nativitas Domini, 9 Johannes ap. et ev., 10 Innocentes, 11 Thomas eps., 12 Silvester, 21 Antonius abb., 23 Sebastianus, 45 Matthias, 46 Gregorius pp., 47 Longinus, 57 Ambrosius, 59 Marcus ev., 65 Philippus, 67 Jacobus, 77 Urbanus, 89 Petrus ap., 90 Paulus ap., 96 Maria Magdalena, 99 Jacobus ap., 100 Christophorus, 102 Nazarius et Celsus, 107 Germanus, 112 Inventio Stephani, no comment by Geith; in my opinion this legend is similar to the Abbreviatio, 115 Donatus, 118 Hippolitus, 120 Bernhardus, 123 Bartholomeus, 125 Decollatio Johannis bap., 137 Exaltatio crucis, 140 Matthaeus ap., 141 Mauricius, 145 Michael, 146 Hieronymus, 148 Leodegarius, 150 Pelagia, 153 Dionysius, 166 Martinus, 169 Caecilia.

5. For the following chapters according to Geith the Abbreviatio was an important source: Cap. 2 Andreas, 5 Thomas, 16 Remigius, 17 Hilarius, 19 Felix, 20 Marcellus, 22 Fabianus, 24 Agnes, 25 Vincentius, 36 Ignatius, 38 Blasius, 39 Agatha, 40 Vedastus, 41 Amandus, 42 Valentinus, 43 Juliana, 49 Benedictus, 58 Georgius, 61 Vitalis, 68 Inventio crucis, 74 Gordianus, 75 Nereus et Achilleus; in the Basle Manuscript of the Abbreviatio this legend appears under the name "Domicilla virgo" (27r), 78 Petronilla, 79 Marcellinus, 80 Primus et Felicianus, 81 Barnabas, 82 Vitus et Modestus, 93 Margareta, 97 Appolinaris, 101 Septem dormientes, 103 Felix pp., 104 Simplicius et Faustinus, 106 Abdon et Sennes, 108 Eusebius, 110 Petrus ad vincula, 111 Stephanus pp., 114 Sixtus, 116 Cyriacus, 117 Laurentius, 122 Simphorianus, 126 Felix et Adauctus, 127 Savinianus, 128 Lupus, 129 Mamertinus, 130 Aegidius, 131 Nativitas Mariae, 132 Cornelius et Cyprianus, 133 Lambertus, 134 Adrianus, 135 Gorgonius, 139 Eufemia, 143 Cosmas et Damianus, 151 Margarita, 154 Calixtus, 155 Leonardus, 158 Undecim milia virgines, 159 Symon et Judas, 160 Quintinus, 161 Eustachius, 167 Briccius, 173 Saturninus.

[52] Vauchez (1986), 27–56.

ways refers to official texts, which were either approved by Rome or by the General Chapters.

In addition the author is content to recount the pattern of events as they were established through his sources. He also avoids references which are historically too precise, especially personal names. "The procedure of Jacobus de Voragine therefore has nothing to do with that of a historian or even a chronicler. His work is that of a double abbreviator or an excellent narrator." [48] All that did not suit his narrative purpose was left out, e.g. characters of lesser importance. Moreover a tendency towards simplification or emphasis is noticeable (in this way not yet dead people become dead). "He also insists on the marvelous and the edifying." [49]

III. *Sources Used*

I have compiled in the following section the chapters for which there are investigations into the sources available, summarized them and finally added Geith's conclusions. I have put some observations in curly brackets.˙

It should again be indicated at this point that verbatim comparisons of texts between the Latin Legenda Aurea and other texts always suffer from the lack of a critical edition; all researchers and I myself have relied upon the Graesse edition while being aware that this edition should be evaluated like any manuscript witness, although somewhat more reliable than most. This can be explained by the fact that the Legenda Aurea manuscripts which are not summaries or compilations, represent a fairly faithful transmission of the text, despite great differences in the corpus.

The Individual Chapters

Cap. 5 De sancto Thoma apostolo (pp. 32–39)
Wilhelm (1907), 37–41: Speculum Historiale, lib. 10, 62–66, is alleged to be a summary of the Passio sancti Thomae; this Passio was also used by Jacobus de Voragine with extensive abridgments as a source and in any event expanded with material from other sources. "He also put the etymology of the name at the beginning and added to the section on etymology a quotation from Prosper's book De vita contemplativa MSL. 59, 496 C. At the very end of the Abgar Legend

he added the text from Pseudo-Isidore concerning the mission areas of Thomas and to these a reference to Chrysostom MSG. 56, 638. In the account of the punishment of the cup-bearer, the part in question is taken from Augustine's Contra Faustum XXII, 79 and presented *in extenso*. In the story of the transmission of the bones of the Apostle several points were newly added, e.g. that the event occurred in 230 A.D. Moreover it is added that Edessa was previously called Rages, which directly or indirectly refers back to Tobias. 1,16; 3,7; 4,21; 5,9 etc." [39] {These last two additions are however already to be found in the Abbreviatio}. In comparison to Speculum Historiale the Legenda Aurea excerpt is considered to be of poorer quality. "The often mentioned brevity of Jacobus definitely does not appear in its best light here. . . . The excerpt is in places poorly thought out and often shows great lack of clarity." [41] Cf. Gounelle (1994) and Fleith (1996).
Geith (1993) Abbreviatio text transcribed in the Legenda Aurea.

Cap. 7 De s.Anastasia (pp. 47–49)
Maggioni (1987), 174: Largely dependent on the Epilogus.
Geith (1993): No relation to the Abbreviatio.

Cap. 15 De s.Paulo eremita (pp. 94–95)
Zuidweg (1941), 48–51: Source : Jerome, Vita s.Pauli primi eremitae, *PL* t. 23, col. 17–30, greatly abridged. Speculum Historiale, lib. 11, cap. 85, 86, 87, 88 also uses Hieronymus. "There is in this case absolutely no evidence that this author and Jacobus were dependent on each other." [51]
Not present in Abbreviatio.

Cap. 16 De s.Remigio (pp. 95–97)
Zuidweg (1941), 131–132: Source: Condensed excerpt from Hincmar, Vita Sancti Remigii, *PL* t. 125, which was also used in Speculum Historiale, lib. 20, cap. 100 and lib. 21, cap. 5–8. {The common source for the Legenda Aurea and the Speculum Historiale is to be found—as my investigations showed—in Abbreviatio.}
Geith (1993): Abbreviatio text transcribed in the Legenda Aurea.

Cap. 18 De s.Macario (S. 100–162)
Zuidweg (1941), 132–133: Source: Vitae of two different people, Macarius Aegyptius and Macarius Alexandrinus are conflated. Source 1: Vita to be found in *PL* t. 74, col. 243ff. under the title: "Heraclidis eremitae

Paradisus, incerto sed veteri interprete." The text in the Legenda corresponds to its cap. VI: "Vita duorum magnorum Macariorum." Source 2: Verba Seniorum in the Vitae Patrum, lib. V, {*PL* 73}. Missing in the Abbreviatio.

Cap. 19 De s.Felice (pp. 102–103)
Zuidweg (1941), 134: Vitae of various people: Cassianus, Felix the Roman martyr (unknown source), Felix confessor (presbyter Nolanus, Ass. Ianuar, T.I. 937–950). (Source: Gregory of Tours, De Glor. Mart I, 104) and Felix confessor (presbyter Romanus, Ass Ianuar, T.I. 950–952) are put together here. The report of the Legenda Aurea on the last mentioned saint is thought to have been close to the Acta ex veteribus Mss, Ianuar, T.I. 951, the Speculum Historiale, lib. XVIII, cap. 39 and 40, and Ado, Martyriologum, sub 14 Jan., {*PL* 123}. Geith (1993): Abbreviatio text transcribed in the Legenda Aurea.

Cap. 21 De s.Antonio (pp. 104–107)
Zuidweg (1941), 52–56: Source: 1. Athanasius, Vita beati Antonii, translated into Latin by Evagrius, transcribed in the Vitae Patrum, lib. I, *PL* t. 73, col. 125–170.—2. Verba Seniorum of the Vitae Patrum, lib. V and VI {*PL* 73}, for Legenda Aurea 105, 36–106, 27 and 107, 20–28. The many common points with Legenda Aurea and Speculum Historiale, lib. 13, cap. 91, 92, and 93 would suggest that a common excerpt was used for Athanasius; Jacobus took many more details from it.
Geith (1993): Similar to Abbreviatio. {Abbreviatio does not contain the extracts from the Verba Seniorum}.

Cap. 23 De s.Sebastiano (pp. 108–113)
Wilmart (1936), 177: The Ambrose quotation 113, 13–16 came from the Prefationes to the Ambrosian Missal.
Zuidweg (1941), 134–35: Source: Ambrose, Acta S.Sebastiani Martyris, transcribed in the Appendix ad Opera S. Ambrosii, *PL* t. 17, col. 1–23. Apart from the Etymology and the conclusion (112, 36 until the end) the entire legend is alleged to have been taken from this source; deviations and omissions can be explained by a desire for simplification.
Geith (1993): Similar to Abbreviatio.

Cap. 24 De s.Agnete virgine (pp. 113–117)
Wilmart (1936), 177/178: The Ambrose quotation 117, 6–9 came from the Prefationes to the feast day in the Ambrosian Missal and was transcribed in an abridged form.

Zuidweg (1941), 56–59: 1. Epistola I, to be found under Epistolae ex Ambrosianarum numero segregatae, *PL.* t. 17, col. 813–821.—2. Ambrose, De Virginibus, lib. I, cap. 2, *PL* t. 16, col. 200 and 201; this text is thought to have been transcribed verbatim.

Geith (1993): Abbreviatio text transcribed in the Legenda Aurea.

{The final part in Legenda Aurea which was taken from the liber de Virginibus is missing in the Abbreviatio. As for the first part of the text, which is transmitted in both works, it is established after an investigation that in some parts it is the Abbreviatio, in other parts it is the Legenda Aurea which is closer to the Epistola text. Abbreviatio was not unequivocally the source of the Legenda here}.

Cap. 25 De s.Vincentio (pp. 117–120)

Wilmart (1936), 178: The Ambrose quotation 120, 11–15 came from the Prefationes to the feast day in the Ambrosian Missal; "Voragine was content to quote the key sentence of the Milan preface." [178] Geith (1993): Abbreviatio text transcribed in the Legenda Aurea.

Cap. 27 De s.Johanne Eleemosinario (S. 126–133)

Zuidweg (1941), 59–64: Leontius, Vita S. Johannis Eleemosinarii, translated into Latin by Anastasius, transcribed in the Vitae Patrum, lib. I, *PL* t. 73, col. 337–384. The same source is thought to have been used in Speculum Historiale, lib. 22, cap. 108–110, verbatim. The Legenda Aurea deviates in form from both texts, one feels "his usual tendency to shorten and simplify; many details are left out, many particulars have been left out, many expressions have been replaced with others" [60], with the result that one can speak neither of completely liberal treatment nor of simple copying.

Not present in the Abbreviatio.

Cap. 29 De s.Paula (pp. 135–140)

Zuidweg (1941), 64–68: Source: Hieronymus, Epistola CVIII, ad Eustochium virginem, epitaphium Paulae matris, *PL* t. 22, col. 878–906; the Legenda Aurea text was taken word for word from this.

Boureau (1984), 29–30: Cap. 29 and 62, "are the only ones in the Golden Legend where a source is transcribed literally without either adding or deleting anything." [29] Jacobus' specific use of sources is, however, alleged to be the compilation of several sources. For this reason the authenticity of Legend is to be questioned.

My examination of the remaining manuscripts however shows quite clearly that the Paula legend belongs to the original body of the text

(Compare to Fleith (1991), 30–37).
Not present in Abbreviatio.

Cap. 30 De s.Juliano (pp. 140–145)

Not present in the Basle manuscript of the Abbreviatio; the Legend
is however to be found in Dondaine's Corpus (1947), 94–98. Geith
(1987), 296, believes that the Abbreviatio was also used here as a
source. However the various Julian legends appear in the Legenda
Aurea in a different order to that of the Abbreviatio; moreover a
passage about Julian the Apostate has been transcribed.

Cap. 38 De s.Blasio (pp. 167–169)

Zuidweg (1941), 135: Source: Prima Acta ex vetustissimis mss., Acta
Sanctorum Feb. T.I., sub 3 Feb., pp. 366ff. Both the paraphrasing
with abridgments and the literal transcription are nearly identical to
Speculum Historiale, lib. 12, cap. 45 and 46. However Legenda Aurea
is more detailed in comparison to Speculum Historiale.
Geith (1993): Abbreviatio text transcribed in the Legenda Aurea.

Cap. 39 De s.Agatha virgine (pp. 170–173)

Wilmart (1936), 178: The Ambrose quotation 173, 26–32 comes from
the Prefationes to the Feast Day in the Ambrosian Missal. "The
Golden Legend omits the entire first sentence." [178]
Zuidweg (1941), 135–136: Apart from the etymology and 173, 25–
32 mostly taken verbatim from the Acta s.Agathae, Acta Sanctorum
Febr. T.I. sub 5 Febr., 615ff. Legenda Aurea and Speculum Historiale,
lib. 11, cap. 42–44 are for the most part identical, Legenda Aurea is
sometimes more detailed. In the Acta the sentence 173, 11–13 is
missing, which could have been seen as a personal interpretation of
Jacobus de Voragine; the sentence is however to be found literally in
Speculum Historiale {and in Abbreviatio}.
Geith (1993): Abbreviatio text transcribed in the Legenda Aurea.

Cap. 41 De s.Amando (pp. 174–176)

Zuidweg (1941), 136: possible sources of materials: 1. Baudemundus,
Vita s.Amandi, Acta Sanctorum Febr. T.I., sub 6 Febr, pp. 815ff. 2.
Vita auctore Aquitano anonymo, ex ms. Andreae du Chesne, Acta
Sanctorum l.c., pp. 854–855. The excerpt which emerged from these
sources coincides in the main with Speculum Historiale lib. 21,
cap. 119 and 120. Sometimes either the Legenda Aurea or the Speculum Historiale transmits more detailed indications of the source,

i.e. both must have used a common extract from the above named sources. That the baby says "Amen" during baptism (175, 19–20) is not mentioned in Speculum Historiale {and in Abbreviatio}. In contrast to the sources, Legenda Aurea, Speculum Historiale {and Abbreviatio} all state that Amandus stayed 15 years at Martinus' grave (175, 4–5).

Geith (1993): Abbreviatio text transcribed in the Legenda Aurea.

Cap. 43 De s.Juliana (pp. 177–178)
Geith (1985), 95–104: Abbreviatio is the shortened version of a proto-type from the "Contaminated Family", distributed mainly in France, a mixture of the texts of C and G; the original legend of this family has been condensed by the Abbreviatio into "essential actions and facts." [100]

Geith (1987), 289–302: The comparison between Abbreviatio and Legenda Aurea shows that Jacobus "to a great extent copied {the Abbreviatio text} directly with slight linguistic simplification and in some places further shortened or summarized it." [293] For this reason the Abbreviatio was further shortened by roughly a third, above all in the action and dialogue sections between Juliana, her father and the Prefect Eleusius. In two passages however, Jacobus provides information which is not present in Abbreviatio: 177, 30–33, a description, which is fully recounted in the original Juliana legend, and 178, 17, in which the devil appears "in specie juvenis".

Geith (1993), 27–28: These two parts which are not contained in the Abbreviatio are nonetheless present in the Legendary of Bartholomew of Trent and could have been taken into the Legenda Aurea from there.

Cap. 45 De s.Mathia (pp. 183–188)
Gaiffier, 1973, 265–272: The source reference "Historia apocrypha" 184, 2 for the Judas story refers to a text, which is known to have circulated in manuscripts already in the 11th century. The question whether Jacobus also found there the critical comment 185, 29–32 or devised it himself, must remain open. "In any case, to solve the problem, it is necessary to be sure that the compiler of the Golden Legend was not following a manuscript where the copyist had already alerted the reader of the Historia." [271]. Cf. Gounelle (1994) and Fleith (1996).

Geith (1993): Similar to Abbreviatio.

Cap. 49 De sancto Benedicto (pp. 204–213)

Reames (1985): Jacobus de Voragine partly copies anecdotes verbatim from his source, Gregory's *Dialogues*, but omits the accompanying moral lessons. [85] The biography too appears different in several places. So, for example, the affirmations of the introduction that only the wondrous would be reported [88] so that the success of the saint might seem easier and more marvelous were omitted. Other omissions served to make clear the power of the saint and how rapid and effective the use of "force" [89] was, e.g. in the punishment story [Legenda Aurea 206, 10f.] {In my opinion this episode is also to be found, albeit not verbatim, in Jean de Mailly}. The demonstrations of the source of love and pity towards other human beings were left out; although the saint still shows certain virtues, the most prominent message of the Legenda Aurea has to do with power and privileges of being in a ruling position. [90] Benedict's experiences are separated from the life of the community (this becomes evident e.g. in the episode of food provision [Legenda Aurea 210] {in my opinion the same as Abbreviatio}); it has to do with overcoming the desires of the flesh and the devil (compare with the Story of the Memory of a Woman [Legenda Aurea 205] {in my opinion also the same as Abbreviatio}) Concentrating on passages that are not to be found in the Abbreviatio the author states: "The patterns we have been tracing—the separation of the saint from the community, the willingness to identify him with a rather harsh kind of justice, the insistence on his privileges and powers but not on his ability to teach or reform or heal other human beings, the prominence of confrontations—are found in nearly every chapter of the *Legenda* I have examined." [97] {Here a list of these legends would have been particularly helpful.} The interpretation of the abridgments in the Benedict legend therefore gives as a central motive "the vindication of the saint against his adversaries" [97], which brings the author to conclude about the Legenda Aurea in view of the time of its compilation: "that the Legenda was not compiled to provide edification and reassurance to Christians at large, but to arm preachers for battles against some current enemy or enemies of the saints and their sponsors." [99] Geith (1993): Abbreviatio text transcribed in the Legenda Aurea.

Cap. 53 De passione domini (pp. 223–235)

Gaiffier (1973), 265–272: The source reference "historia apocrypha" 231, 21 for the Pilate story refers to a text, which could already be established in manuscripts of the 11th century. The question whether

Jacobus also found there the critical comment 234, 27–28 or devised it himself, must remain open. "In any case, to solve the problem, it is necessary to be sure that the compiler of the *Golden Legend* was not following a manuscript where the copyist had already alerted the reader of the *Historia*." [271]. Cf. Gounelle (1994) and Fleith (1996). Geith (1993): Not present in Abbreviatio.

Cap. 56 De s.Maria Aegyptiaca (pp. 247–249)
Zuidweg (1941), 137: Vita S.Mariae Aegyptiacae meretricis auctore Sophronio interprete Paulo Diacono; this version was printed by Heribertus Rosweydus, Vitae Patrum, lib. I, Antwerp 1615 (many times), pp. 381–392, transcribed in *PL* 73, col. 671–690. (Bibliotheca Hagiographica Latina 5415). Because of the common points between Legenda Aurea and Speculum Historiale, lib. 15, cap. 65–73, their authors must have used a short legend from the tradition of Diaconus, "probably an excerpt from the draft of the Vitae Patrum".
Kunze (1969), 27–31: Source: Anonymous Latin translation (M1) (Bibliotheca Hagiographica Latina 5417, 5417a, 5417b), i.e.—against Zuidweg—not Paul the Deacon. It is possible that M1 "was already present in the version of the Vitae Patrum, which the Spanish abbot Valerius undertook in the second half of the 7th century" [28]. M1 was taken into the Speculum Historiale almost unchanged and "perhaps from here, but greatly shortened, found its way into the Legenda Aurea." [30/31] Cf. R. Maniglia, Studi sul testo latino della "Vita sanctae Mariae Aegyptiacae", Testi di Laurea dattiloscritta sostenuta presso l'Università degli studi di Milano nell' a.a. 1988–1989.
Not present in Abbreviatio.

Cap. 57 De s.Ambrosio (pp. 250–259)
Reames (1985): Principal source was the Vita S.Ambrosii by Paulinus [117]. Reames characterizes in the following way the process of selection by Jacobus de Voragine: "(. . .) the miracle stories with harsher implications loom very large. For in this chapter of the Legenda the saint's human adversaries are not usually just humbled; they are subjected to punishments ranging from exile to maiming and torture to violent death." [118]. This selection can be explained by the special circumstances of the 13th century and the role of the early Dominicans, defined thus: "no small resemblance to a military order—an army of preachers, missionaries, and, when need dictated, inquisitors, in the service of the pope." [118] In Jacobus de Voragine's shorter version there are only three enemies to be overcome: "de-

mons, heretics and temporal rulers who challenge the authority of the church." [120] Jacobus de Voragine expands and abridges Paulinus' list of the virtues of Ambrose, however he completes this list from extra sources (among others, Historia Ecclesiastica, Decretum Gratiani). {In the few places where Abbreviatio and Legenda Aurea transmit the same text, two observations must be made: on one hand, compared to, for example, the story of the heretical girl [Legenda Aurea 251], the Legenda Aurea makes more abridgments than the Abbreviatio, and thus reaches the effect postulated by Reames; on the other hand, the abridgments by Jacobus de Voragine reported by Reames are also already to be found in the Abbreviatio, cf. the chariot story, and for example the Day of Exile: Legenda Aurea p. 251 "sed Dei judicio ipso die"; Abbreviatio Fol. 22 rb: "sed judicio ipso die"; in the Vita of Paulinus only on the first birthday after the attack}.

Geith (1993): similar to Abbreviatio.

Cap. 58 De s.Georgio (pp. 259–264)

Wilmart (1936), 178: The Ambrose quotation 263, 21–28 comes from the Prefationes to the Feast Day in the Ambrosian Missal.

Haubrichs (1979), 294–295: Speculum Historiale and Legenda Aurea both used the Abbreviatio; moreover Jacobus knew "the 'Decretum Gelasianum', as well as Bede's Martyrologium and used for the interpretation of the name of his hero the Enkomion of Andreas of Crete, which he came to know either through the intermediary of PP or through the Sermo of Peter Damian; he reports the fight with the dragon and wonders at the contradictions between the various accounts of the Legend which he has seen. (Zc, a version of the X-Type, JM [= Abbreviatio], BT). He finally uses the "Liber epilogorum" of the Dominican Bartholomew of Trent (BT), which contained a short St. George legend, and quotes Prefationes of the Ambrosian liturgy, as well as Gregory of Tours. He relates after the "Historia Antiochena" the crusade anecdote of St. George's help in the taking of Jerusalem. [295]

Geith (1993): Abbreviatio text transcribed in the Legenda Aurea.

Cap. 59 De s.Marco ev. (pp. 265–271)

Wilmart (1936), 179: The Ambrose quotation 267, 21–28 comes from a later version of the Prefationes to the Feast Day in the Ambrosian Missal.

Geith (1993): similar to Abbreviatio.

Cap. 61 De s.Vitali (pp. 272–273)
Zuidweg (1941), 137–138: Source: Passio ex Ms. Coenobii Bodecensis
Ordinis Regularium S.Augustini in diocesi Paderbornensi, Acta Sanctorum Aprilis t. III, pp. 562–565. The Legenda Aurea is closer to
this source than Ado's Martyrologium, PL t. 123, which has many
points in common with the Legenda Aurea. The Legenda is however
more detailed than the Martyrologium. The Speculum Historiale,
lib. 9, cap. 50, uses the same excerpt as the Legenda Aurea, but makes
more abridgments. As unclear points in the Legenda Aurea (examples
272, 31 and 33), which could only be clarified by the original source,
are also to be found in the Speculum Historiale, they should not be
traced to Jacobus but to the source of the short Legendaries.
Geith (1993): Abbreviatio text transcribed in the Legenda Aurea.

Cap. 62 De virgine quadam Antiochena. (pp. 273–277)
Zuidweg (1941), 68–71: Source: Ambrose, De Virginibus, lib. II, cap.
4 and the beginning of cap. 5, PL t. 16, col. 224–228, copied almost
literally.
Boureau (1984), 29–30: Cap. 29 and 62 "are the only ones in the
Golden Legend to copy a source in its entirety, without making any
additions or omissions." [29] Jacobus de Voragine's specific use of
sources is, however, the putting together of several sources; he normally quotes only briefly from the Liber de Virginibus. For this reason the authenticity of the Legend is questionable.
According to Fleith (1991), 30–37, this Legend belongs to the original body of text.
Not present in Abbreviatio.

Cap. 63 De s.Petro martire (pp. 277–291)
Zuidweg (1941), 26, 72–82: Sources: 1. Thomas de Lentino, Vita
Sancti Petri Martyris, Acta Sanctorum, Aprilis T.III, S. 686–719. 2.
Gerardus Frachetus Lemovicensis, Vitae Fratrum Ordinis Praedicatorum. Monum. Ord. Fr. Praed. Hist., Lovanii 1896. "Also for this
chapter, the author does not provide the slightest personal contribution; it is simply an exact transcription." [26]
Dondaine (1953), 66–162: Thomas de Lentino is not the source for
the Legenda Aurea, but the Legenda Aurea is one of the main sources
for Thomas. [109] Sources for Legenda Aurea: 1. Canonization Bull
of March 24th, 1253. This Bull was transcribed almost completely
by Vincent de Beauvais into the context of the already completed
Speculum Historiale, lib. 31, cap. 103 and 104, immediately after its

promulgation. [114] 2. Gerardus Frachetus, Vitae Fratrum, a compilation of material from the General Chapters of the Dominican Order of Milan 1255 and Paris 1256.

The work was completed between 1259 and the Strasbourg chapter at Pentecost 1260. [114/115] Despite this a certain originality of Jacobus de Voragine should be mentioned: the legend in Legenda Aurea contains apart from the references to the sources named above, reports about miracles, which were only briefly mentioned in earlier sources. "The authority of this contribution is undeniable." [118] Zuidweg minimized too strongly the personal role of Jacobus de Voragine; this mistake comes about because Zuidweg did not examine the sources of the life story in the Bibliotheca Hagiographica Latina. [118, note 27].

Vauchez (1986), 27–56: The fact that the text of Thomas de Lentino is longer than that of Jacobus de Voragine and in certain passages relates not only new miracles, makes Vauchez doubt Dondaine's theory with regard to the dependence of these two texts, as it is difficult to imagine that a shorter text served as a source for a longer one.

Vauchez sees a solution to the contradiction between Zuidweg and Dondaine in accepting that Jacobus de Voragine could have used the earlier version (before 1274) of the Lentino text. [38]

Not present in Abbreviatio.

Cap. 67 De s.Jacobo ap. (pp. 295–303)
Gaiffier, 1973, 265–272: The reference to the source "historia apocrypha" 299, 14–15 and 301, 13 refers to a text, which could already be established in manuscripts of the 11th century. The question whether Jacobus also found there the critical comment 301, 36–37 or devised it himself, must remain open. "In any case, to solve the problem, it is necessary to be sure that the compiler of the Golden Legend was not following a manuscript where the copyist had already alerted the reader of the Historia." [271]. Cf. Gounelle (1994) and Fleith (1996).

Geith (1993): Similar to Abbreviatio.

Cap. 68 De inventione crucis (pp. 303–311)
Cf. Gounelle (1994) and Fleith (1996).

Geith (1993): Abbreviatio text transcribed in the Legenda Aurea.

Cap. 74 De s.Gordiano (pp. 337–338)
Zuidweg (1941), 138: Possible source of material: Acta Martyrii ex

pervetustis mss. codicibus, Acta Sanctorum Maii T.II, sub 10 Maii, pp. 552–553; no literal correlation; however much in common with Speculum Historiale, lib. 14, cap. 37.
Geith (1993): Abbreviatio text transcribed in the Legenda Aurea.

Cap. 77 De s.Urbano (pp. 341–342)
Lühmann (1968), 20–30 decides that the following is a source for the Legenda Aurea: "Passiones SS. Ceciliae et Urbani (9th century?) [22]; these two legends do not appear separately in the Legenda Aurea. [21] Lühmann did not deal with other short legendaries of the same period.
Geith (1993): Similar to Abbreviatio.

Cap. 78 De s.Petronella (p. 343)
Zuidweg (1941), p. 132, note 1: Source: Acta Nerei et Achilei; strong correlation with Speculum Historiale lib. 9, cap. 38; both legendaries probably followed the same extract here.
Geith (1993): Abbreviatio text transcribed in the Legenda Aurea.

Cap. 79 De s.Petro exorcista et Marcellino (pp. 343–344)
Zuidweg (1941), 138–139: Source unknown. Points in common with Ado, Martyrologium, sub II Junii, PL t. 123, however Legenda Aurea is more detailed. On the other hand the contents are those of the Speculum Historiale, lib. 12, cap. 74 and 75 as is the text.
Geith (1993): Abbreviatio text transcribed in the Legenda Aurea.

Cap. 80 De s.Primo et Feliciano (pp. 345–346)
Zuidweg (1941), 132, note 1: Literally the same as Speculum Historiale lib. 12, cap. 69. Both legendaries probably followed the same extract here.
Geith (1993): Abbreviatio text transcribed in the Legenda Aurea.

Cap. 82 De ss.Vito et Modesto (pp. 350–351)
Zuidweg (1941), 139–140: Source of material: Passio sancti Viti et Modesti, Acta Sanctorum 15 junii T.II pars II, pp. 1013ff., Shortening and liberal rewriting of the text. Legenda Aurea and Speculum Historiale, lib. 12, cap. 70 and 71, are thought to have used the same extract because of the similarities. {My investigations gave the result that Legenda Aurea and Speculum Historiale are very similar, but there is a more literal similarity to be found between Speculum Historiale and Abbreviatio.}
Geith (1993): Abbreviatio text transcribed in the Legenda Aurea.

Cap. 84 De s.Marina virgine (p. 353)
Zuidweg (1941), 140: Source: Vita sanctae Marinae virginis, unknown author, Vitae Patrum, lib. 1 *PL* t. 73; Legenda Aurea follows this source with abridgments.
Geith (1993): Not present in Abbreviatio.

Cap. 87 De ss.Johanne et Paulo (pp. 364–367)
Wilmart (1936), 183: The Ambrose quotation 367, 13–17 comes from the Prefationes to the Feast Day in the Ambrosian Missal.
Geith (1993): No similarity to Abbreviatio.

Cap. 89 De s.Petro ap. (pp. 368–379)
Hug (1929), 604–624: Sources for etymology: Isidore, Ethymologiae, *PL* 82, col. 287, Beda Ven. *PL* 94, col. 221 and Bartholomew of Trent. [606] Proven sources of the legend: 1. The apocryphal Martyrium beati Petri apostoli a Lino episcopo conscriptum of Linus. In: Acta apostolorum apocrypha. Post Constantinum Tischendorf denuo ediderunt Ricardus Adalbertus Lipsius and Maximilianus Bonnet. Pars prior. Lipsiae 1891 (= Lips. A. app. apc. I), pp. 1–22.—2. Marcellus, Passio sanctorum apostolorum Petri et Pauli., in: Lips. A. app. apc. I, pp. 119–177.—3. Hegesippus, i.e. the Latin translation of Josephus Flavius' Bellum Judaicum, which comes from an old account of Ambrose, De excidio urbis Hierosolymitane, lib. II, caput. II., *PL* 15, col. 2068–2070.—4. Acta Nerei et Achillei, Acta Sanctorum Maii t. III, 10a.—5. Bartholomew of Trent.—5. Pseudo-Clement, Recognitiones, VII, 6, II, 9, 20, 23, 36 and III, 46 and 63 (according to the edition of Gersdorf, Leipzig 1838).—6. Dionysius Areopagita, Epistola ad Timotheum, Analecta sacra, IV, 261–271.—7. Historia Apocrypha—8. Chronicle of Hieronymus-Eusebius, *PL* 27, 587–588 ad a. 66.—9. Gregorius Magnus, Dialog. lib. III cap. 25, *PL* 77, 280; lib. IV, cap. 13 and 11, *PL* 77, 340/41 and 336/7.— 10. Mitrale, allegedly by Sicardus of Cremona, *PL* 213, col. 417.— 11. Hieronymus, *PL* 26, col. 176.—12. Isidore, *PL* 83, col. 149.—13. Haymo, *PL* 117, 654 (in contents).—14. "Leo vel Maximus" *PL* 57, col. 405.

Jacobus de Voragine himself provides for many of the pieces of text from 1 and 2 the source "Leo" which means that he had a source available to him which was in circulation under the name of Pope Leo. [609] "The pieces originating from Marcellus were used freely by Jacobus de Voragine. To some extent he removed them from their original context and brought them into another context in the body of his legends. Many a section is related quite freely or in a strongly condensed form, many are copied literally. His intention was only to include texts which contained action.—He leaves speeches of any kind almost untouched or uses only what is necessary for the course of the narrative." [609]

A striking similarity can be established between 372, 32–373, 26 as a whole piece and the Abbreviatio. Legenda Aurea has here 373, 10–13 in addition to the Abbreviatio text and is in this way closer to Marcellus. [610] 371, 12–371, 26 likewise correspond to the Abbreviatio; this time the Legenda Aurea has less text, and for this reason inserts the sentence 371, 20–21, which is identical to Bartholomew of Trent. 379, 29–33 is repeated almost verbatim in Abbreviatio, and is similar in Bartholomew [620/621]. For 377, 29–36 Bartholomew may be considered as a possible source due to the common expressions. "Despite this, the possibility of a common third source remains open." [617] For correlation between the two legendaries Hug gives still more examples [618–619]. "As a result of literary value of the research in question a definite (. . .) relationship of dependence between Jc. and Bartholomew Trid. and a very probable literary dependence on the 'Abbreviatio in gestis et miraculis' (. . .) can be established." [624]
Gaiffier, 1973, 265–272: The source reference "historia apocrypha" 326, 6 and 26 refer to a text which could already be established in manuscripts of the 11th century. Cf. Gounelle (1994) and Fleith (1996). Geith (1993) "The principal source of this account is the work of Jean de Mailly" (= Abbreviatio). 371, 9–12 do not originate—as Jacobus claims—from Beleth, but from Bartholomew of Trent, like several other parts of this legend.

Cap. 90 De s.Paulo ap. (pp. 380–396)
Hug (1929), 604–624: Sources for etymology: 1. Isidore, Ethymologiae, *PL* 82, col. 287f.—2. For correlation with Speculum Historiale lib. 7. cap. 9 compare Petrus Comestor, Hist. Schol.—3. Hrabanus Maurus, commentary on the second Letter to the Corinthians c. 1. *PL* 112, col. 160.—Bede, Commentary on the Acts of the Apostles c. 13, *PL* 92, 973. [606/607]—Proven sources for the Vita: 1. Linus, Passio sancti Pauli apostoli, Lips. A. app. apc. I, pp. 23–44. 2. Dionysius Areopagita, Epistola ad Timotheum, Analecta sacra,. IV, 261–271.— 3. Gregorius Magnus, Epistolae lib. IV, *PL* 77, 703, 704, 705.—4.

Gregorius Turonensis, Miraculorum, lib. I, cap. 29, *PL* 71, 729/30. The same account is present in Speculum Historiale lib. VIII, cap. 21.—5. Johannes Beleth, Rationale divinorum officiorum, *PL* 202, col. 143 (cap. 138 de festo apostolorum Petri et Pauli).—6. Mitrale, allegedly from Sicardus de Cemona, *PL* 213, col. 416/7.—7. Chrysostomus, Homil. I–VII, PG 50, 473–514.—8. Bartholomew of Trent. What Hug says about the dependence between Legenda Aurea, Abbreviatio and Bartholomew of Trent about the Peter legends also applies to the Paul legends.

Geith (1993): Similar to Abbreviatio.

Cap. 93 De sancta Margaretha (pp. 400–403)
Orywall (1968): In Abbreviatio and Speculum Historiale there is an almost identical version of the legend, which goes back to the version I(c) of "Passio Theotimo" (Bibliotheca Hagiographica Latina 5305) and probably the so-called Caligula version. [64]. This Abbreviatio version was used by Jacobus de Voragine for the Legenda Aurea, as Jacobus de Voragine quoted from it the double death date [85]; however as the Legenda Aurea transmits several passages which are not in the Abbreviatio, Jacobus de Voragine must have used the version I(c) of "Passio Theotimo" directly. [86] In this way the research into the sources of the Margaretha legend confirmed the results of Dondaine and Zuidweg who say that, besides the shortened texts of the Abbreviatio and the Speculum Historiale, their immediate sources should also be put forward to explain the correlation with the Legenda Aurea. [85]

Geith (1993): Abbreviatio text transcribed in the Legenda Aurea.

Cap. 94 De s.Alexio (pp. 403–406)
Löffler (1992), 32, 96–103: Source: Version C, Acta Sanctorum, julii IV, pp. 251–253 (Bibliotheca Hagiographica Latina 286), the most often rewritten, shorter version of an older Latin account. [32] Within this version Legenda Aurea follows both Group VI [97] and Group IX [99]. On the basis of his analysis of the whole account of the Vitae of Alexius, Löffler comes to the conclusion that Jacobus de Voragine had definitely used several sources for a single legend, but that he could work with a single source in a different way, i.e. partially rewriting exactly a preceding text, partly condensing it through abridgment. "Even brief expansions of the text are not to be excluded, through the mere addition of adverbs." [103] Besides, Löffler points out the possibility that Jacobus de Voragine could have used

the Magnum Legendarium Austriacum at least for his Alexius legend [103, note 1]. The Speculum Historiale depends on the C-Edition, which Vincent followed verbatim with little deviation and only greatly shortened at the end [96]. For two points in the text we must think of a precedent from the L version [96 note 1]. An Alexius legend is not present in the main corpus of the Abbreviatio, but in two of the manuscripts; these however were not models for the Legenda Aurea. [97].

Cap. 97 De s.Apollinari (pp. 417–418)
Wilmart (1936), 184–185: The Ambrose quotation 419, 3–16 was taken verbatim from the Prefationes to the Feast Day in the Ambrosian Missal.
Geith (1993): Abbreviatio text transcribed in the Legenda Aurea.

Cap. 100 De s.Christophoro (pp. 430–434)
Wilmart (1936), 186–188: The Ambrose quotation 434, 24–37 was taken from the Prefationes to the Feast Day in the Ambrosian Missal.
Geith (1993): Similar to Abbreviatio.

Cap. 101 De septem dormientibus (pp. 435–438)
Zuidweg (1941), 140: Because of the strong correlation between Legenda Aurea and Speculum Historiale, lib. 11, cap. 45 and lib. 20, cap. 31–33, both authors must have used the same extract. {The controversy regarding the number of years slept (Legenda Aurea: 377 and 372 or 196 years; Speculum Historiale: 192 and 142 years) is also an adaptation of the statement in Abbreviatio: 372 and 193 or 194 years.}
Merrilees (1986), 122: L1, one of the four in: Hüber, Die Wanderlegende von den Siebenschläfern, Leipzig 1910, 59–84, different Vulgate versions were the source of the Abbreviatio and were taken from there into the Speculum Historiale and Legenda Aurea. The sleeping time in L1 is 372 years [128].
Geith (1993): Abbreviatio text transcribed in the Legenda Aurea.

Cap. 102 De ss.Nazario et Celso (pp. 439–442)
Wilmart (1936), 188–189: The Ambrose quotation 442, 1–24 was taken from the Praefationes to the Feast and Vigil Day in the Ambrosian Missal. Jacobus de Voragine also rewrites here an extract from the Praefationes to the Translation report of Nazarius.
Geith (1993): Similar to Abbreviatio.

Cap. 105 De s.Martha (pp. 444–447)
Dumont (1951): Speculum historiale is one of several sources.
Not present in Abbreviatio.

Cap. 106 De ss.Abdon et Sennen (p. 447)
Zuidweg (1941), 82–83: Speculum Historiale lib. 11, Cap. 49 corresponds almost word for word to Legenda Aurea 447, 15–27. We must therefore assume that they had a common source.
Geith (1993): Abbreviatio text transcribed in the Legenda Aurea.

Cap. 111 De s.Stephano papa (p. 461)
Zuidweg (1941), 140: Speculum Historiale lib. 11, Cap. 60 are almost literally identical to Legenda Aurea; therefore one can assume that both used the same excerpt from the old Vita Acta Sanctorum, Augustus T.I., pp. 139–146 {?} as a source.
Geith (1993): Abbreviatio text transcribed in the Legenda Aurea.

Cap. 113 De s. Dominico (pp. 466–483)
Bangemann (1919), 7–30: Sources: 1. Constantinus Urbevetanus. 2. Humbertus de Romanis. 3. Gerardus de Fracheto. 4. Bartholomaeus Tridentinus. Jacobus de Voragine follows a main source, but uses in addition several other secondary sources. [25] Only literal correlation could be used as proof of sources for the Legenda Aurea, as Jacobus de Voragine copies word for word, except when he condenses the exhaustively treated material of his source. [26] "He almost always reproduces faithfully the names of places, people and other proper names. He mostly leaves out the expressions of feeling, be they of the protagonists, of the writers of earlier texts, and the moral observations. He recounts one anecdote after another without connections. What he offers is virtually bare facts. One looks in vain for any personal comment from him—a personal style is also lacking—as he copies word for word." [26/27]

Because of the lacking literal correlation there are a few places in the Vita which could not have come from the above named sources (e.g. 470, 1–38 and 477, 20ff.). [21] The Legenda Aurea has these extracts, among others, in common with the Legendary of Rodericus Cerratensis (appeared around 1270).
Zuidweg (1941), 83–94: {Zuidweg did not know the work of Bangemann!} Sources: 1. Constantinus Urbevetanus, Legenda Dominici (ca. 1242–1247); 2. Humbertus de Romanis, Vita S. Dominici (before 1254), all printed in MOPH, t. 16, Monum, Hist. S.P.N.

Dominici, Fasc. II, Romae 1935. 3. Gerardus de Fracheto, Vitae Fratrum Ordinis Praedicatorum (before 1260), MOPH, Fratris Gerardi de Fracheto O.P. "Vitae Fratrum Ordinis Praedicatorum", Lovanii 1896. 4. Bartholomaeus Tridentinus, Liber epilogorum in gesta Sanctorum (ca. 1244–1251). From this Jacobus de Voragine compiled his Vita, without making use of the oral tradition. Speculum Historiale lib. 29, cap. 94–96, 104–105, lib. 30, cap. 65–77, 110–116, 118–120 and the Legenda Aurea correspond where both used Urbevetanus. Nor can Zuidweg provide a precise source for all the passages: the places which were already considered questionable by Bangemann are indicated by Zuidweg to have been taken from Gerardus, but "the form stands out to a considerable degree" [87]. The naming of the frater Raynerius Lausanensis is not to be found in Gerardus. For the whole episode, 477, 20–478, 18 an unknown source must have been used or else Jacobus de Voragine worked independently here. [92] It cannot, however, be a question of an oral source, as parts of the narrative are also present in Bartholomew and Gerardus. Zuidweg believes that Jacobus de Voragine simply retells in more detail what he found in his sources. [94]

Reames (1985): As the legend was often revised and enriched in the 13th century, no certain statement can be made on whether the Legenda Aurea depends on an earlier text or is based on oral sources. It is not however the author's intention to locate the exact points in the text for single passages, but to examine "the larger relationship between the way this legend developed, during the first half of Jacobus de Voragine's lifetime, and the priorities that govern the Legenda." [164] Reames noted that Jordan's image of Dominic changes during the years 1235–1260, due to ever more reports of miracles, but progressively fewer realistic details from the Libellus and the canonization documents with the goal of cultivating the saint and legitimizing his own order. Jacobus de Voragine's version "seems to represent an extreme development of a few strands within the tradition, at the expense of the rest." [166]

Therefore the author compares the Legenda Aurea text with its main source, the Vita of Constantinus Urbevetanus, the Abbreviatio (which Petrus Ferrandus used as a source) and Epilogus, noting that they were written for a public outside the order. [167] The difference is, that Jean de Mailly and Bartholomew of Trent promote the interests of the order and deliver further lessons, which Jacobus de Voragine does not do. [167] The function of the Abbreviatio and

Epilogus is "to defend the new order against the common charge that it represented an unjustifiable departure from the laws and traditions of the church" [169]. In Jacobus de Voragine such miracle reports are also to be found but in a much more striking form, where the main theme comes to be showing the foundation of the order as God's will and not as human intention [169], which, for example, happens through visions. Here the mission of the Dominicans with the support of the Franciscans is interpreted as the final salvation before the end of the world, an argument which is, compared with other texts, more dramatic, extreme and controversial. Jean de Mailly describes Dominic relatively realistically; his legend invites the reader "to embrace Dominic's ideals and follow him." [177] In Epilogus, in addition to this, the example of active "charity" is indicated through Dominic [177]; there the aim is not so much to encourage the imitation of the saint as to encourage a vision of him as father and leader of his brothers in the order, who is accompanied by God and loves his brothers. This can be explained by the fact that due to increasing criticism of the Dominican order the holiness and importance of the order's founder had be ever more strongly underlined and belief in one's own order reactivated. [177–180] Bartholomew of Trent's miracle reports after Dominic's death told mostly of healing, with the result that through the death of the saint and his canonization a new possibility would be created for the transmission of divine love in the world. In Constantinus' version this tendency to retell a large number of short miracle reports was noticeable [183], which above all served to encourage the brothers in their daily work; moreover Dominic's role as Inquisitor was dealt with clearly for the first time, which was taken up and emphasized by Humbert [184] and which was understandable due to the historical circumstances of the 1250s. Jacobus de Voragine's version shows stronger interference: "Dominic's image as a father is impaired somewhat by Jacobus de Voragine's customary focus on supernatural power for its own sake; but enough stories are retold about the founder's care for his followers and for other pious Christians who honor his memory so that this chapter of the Legenda conveys an unusually clear invitation to join one of those groups and reap the benefits. The crucial change from earlier accounts is the extent to which Jacobus de Voragine redefines the purpose of the order, abandoning the once-central ideal of apostolic preaching." [185/186] In the Legenda Aurea moreover the interminable combat against stubborn heretics becomes the dominant motif [188], where a certain God-given inquisitional authority is attributed to the saint. [191] At the same time Jacobus de Voragine produces the image of the saint who thoroughly renounces the world and is loyal to the ideal of poverty, which he leaves to his brothers as a heritage [192]. Reames views these affirmations together with interpretation results of other legends and deduces from this the mental state of the author "as a discouraged son of Dominic, an idealist who lost all his faith in human nature and some of his faith in God when apostolic preaching failed to win over the enemies that confronted the order." [193] Cf. Interpretation in: Boureau (1984), pp. 225–237.

Vauchez (1986), 27–56, concurs with Zuidweg's results; he also does not know the work of Bangemann. As Jacobus used the Vitae Fratrum and this was not approved until 1260, the composition of the text by Jacobus de Voragine cannot have occurred before 1261. [33] {The Vitae text however was in existence since 1255 and in my opinion Jacobus could have used it before the approval. Cf. Tugwell in: The Journal of Theological Studies 44/1 (1993), 395–397.}

The non-use of the canonization and order foundation documents shows that Jacobus de Voragine "did not want to do the work of a historian, but provide his colleagues with material easy to use for preaching and to his listeners—or readers—a collection of accounts illustrating the action of God in this world through his servants." [36]
{No similarity to Abbreviatio.}

Cap. 114 De s.Sixto (pp. 483–484)
Zuidweg (1941), 95: Source for the Sixtus legend 483, 11–32: Martyrium e ms. Fuldensi {cum aliis exemplaribus collato}, Acta Sanctorum Aug. T.II, sub 6 Aug. p. 140f. Speculum Historiale lib. 11, Cap. 92 is mostly identical to the Legenda Aurea, but the latter is more detailed. Source for the observation about the Transfiguratio Christi 483, 32–484, 14: Sicardus, Mitrale, sive Summa de officiis ecclesiasticis, lib. IX, cap. 38, *PL* t. 213 {col. 419}.
Geith (1993): Abbreviatio Text transcribed in Legenda Aurea {Investigations showed that the Legenda Aurea is sometimes closer to the original text than Speculum Historiale and Abbreviatio}.

Cap. 119 De assumptione beatae Mariae virginis (S. 504–527)
Cf. Verdier (1986): sources without any references. Cf. Gounelle (1994) and Fleith (1996).

Geith (1993): No similarity to Abbreviatio.

Cap. 122 De s.Simphoriano (pp. 539–540)
Zuidweg (1941), 141: Original source: Vita sancti Simphoriani (used by Gregory of Tours), Acta Sanctorum Aug. T.IV, pp. 496–497. Legenda Aurea and Speculum Historiale, lib. 11, cap. 115 tally for the most part, however the Legenda Aurea is somewhat more detailed, i.e. both used the same excerpt from the original source. Legenda Aurea, Speculum Historiale {and Abbreviatio} all refer in the beginning to "Gregorius Turonensis", proof that the quotation reference was taken from the common source.
Geith (1993): Abbreviatio text transcribed in Legenda Aurea.

Cap. 123 De s.Bartholomeo (pp. 540–548)
Wilmart (1936), 190–192: The Ambrose quotation 545, 34–546, 25 comes from the Prefationes to the Feast Day in the Ambrosian Missal. Maggioni (1987), 177–182: Largely taken over from the Abbreviatio; the Epilogus was also used. On the sources cf. details in: Maggioni (1990).
Geith (1993): Similar to Abbreviatio.

Cap. 124 De s.Augustino (pp. 548–566)
Zuidweg (1941), 96–118: Several sources: used partly freely, partly verbatim: Possidius, Vita S. Aurelii Augustini, *PL* t. 32, col. 33–36; Augustinus, Confessiones; Philippus de Harveng, Vita beati Augustini, *PL* t. 203, col. 1205–1234.

After the description of Augustine's death follow quotations from fathers of the church about Augustine (560, 4–561, 16), out of which Zuidweg has only examined the following: 560, 13–15 Volusianus Ep. 2 = 135, Acta Sanctorum p. 360 C, 560, 15–20 Hieronymus, Epist. 134 ad Augustinum, *PL* t. 22; 560, 20–24, Epistola de duodecim doctoribus, *PL* t. 23; 560, 24–34, Hieronymus, Epist. 141 and 102 ad Augustinum, *PL* t. 22; 560, 34–39 Gregorius, Ep. 37, Acta Sanctorum 362 B.C.; 561, 15–16 Bernardus, sermo 80 in Cantica, Acta Sanctorum, p. 362 C. [114/115]. All quotations given here were transcribed literally apart from small deviations, which could however also be variations or mistakes in the rewriting. For the Translation report 561, 16–562, 4 Petrus Oldradus, Epistola, Acta Sanctorum pp. 366ff. was the source, greatly abridged by Jacobus de Voragine, and also Philippus. For the passage 561, 16–31 (Impossibility of moving the coffin and the construction of a church in the name of the saint at every nightly resting place) no source can be determined. In Philippus this incident is to be found only once, exactly as in Speculum Historiale {and in Abbreviatio!}. The sources for the miracle reports Cap. 2–13 (which are absent from the Abbreviatio) are the "Variae Sancti Apparitiones", Acta Sanctorum 380ff. or unknown sources. In a closing observation 565, 36–566, 25 Jacobus de Voragine quotes from Augustine, Soliloquy I, 10, *PL* t. 32.

To sum up it can be said that the reports on Augustine and citations from fathers of the church are mostly quoted literally; places which however were taken from Possidus and the other sources were rewritten more freely. The miracle reports are not to be traced to earlier sources, with the result that for this one should rather assume independence on the part of Jacobus de Voragine. "The point in favor of Jacobus' taste and sensitivity is that he has given in his compilation a place to some of the finest parts of the Confessions." [97]

Only for a few parts of the text can correlation with Speculum Historiale lib. 17, cap. 46–52, lib. 20, cap. 28, lib. 23, cap. 148 be established.

Colledge, 1985: The author puts forward the interesting theory that Jacobus de Voragine did not write his Legenda Aurea alone, but assigned the task to a team of collaborators, who worked with varying degrees of care. [300], which shows for example in the compiling of extracts from Augustine's work; "yet not all the information with which James was supplied was equally reliable" [301]. "Misstatements of the types we have commented on—of fact (Augustine was born at Tagaste, not Hippo), of emphasis (the bishop did not say 'Vade secura . . .' to Monica), of attribution (Prosper did not write De Vita Contemplativa, Augustine never complained that God 'posuit me ad amplustram')—have been found in the earlier portion of the work." [313] Regarding the use of sources an alternation between exact knowledge and complete carelessness can be established [312].

In the second half of the work, so long as it is a question of cult and miracle reports from Northern Italy—and here Colledge is opposed to Zuidweg's argument that Jacobus de Voragine used only written sources—Jacobus de Voragine worked above all from oral tradition [306ff.]. In the last part of the legend Jacobus produces "a story more stereotyped, where, perhaps, he relies less upon his editorial staff for materials than at the beginning." [313] Finally Colledge explores the question of in what way Jacobus de Voragine presents Augustine as one of the principal teachers of the universal Church.

"A balanced answer seems to be that, given the space at its disposal and the preferences and prejudices of the readers, the Legenda has done its best to draw a faithful picture." [313] Jacobus gives his reader a representative overview of Augustine's literary activity; he does not merely limit himself to the *Confessions*, but adds well chosen extracts from the Soliloquies. On the other hand Jacobus says relatively little about Augustine's role as a fighter against heresy and lawgiver and wisely avoids repeating any further known statement. ". . . it may be the verdict of others who know Augustine at first hand that James has achieved, both by selection and omission, freedom from every charge that he has misrepresented the great advocate of love of God and neighbor." [314].

Reames (1985): The Augustine chapter shows like no other Jacobus de Voragine's religious values [135]. "The Legenda account itself contains a long series of testimonials to Augustine's profundity and importance as a theologian (pp. 560–61); and for his life Jacobus supplements the standard Vita with dozens of quotations from Augustine's own writings. (. . .) The emphasis falls (. . .) on Augustine's personal experience and on his virtues. The implication may be that this particular narrative (. . .) was meant for the edification of the clerics who used the Legenda directly" [135] The more important function however is to present Augustine as "a sort of advertisement for the religious life, and especially for the Order of Preachers—a natural enough connection, since it was the Rule of St. Augustine which Dominic and his first followers had adopted as the foundation of their own constitutions." [138] In the conversion story divine influence plays a lesser role [138], on the other hand the autonomy [139] and initiative [141] of the saint are brought into prominence. After the conversion Jacobus de Voragine shows Augustine's holiness "by associating him with a 'divine love', which is as otherworldly as possible and by insisting on his indifference to all earthly pleasures and rewards." [142] The use of the Soliloquia is characterized in the following manner by Reames: "For he {Jacobus de Voragine} does not just cite the most negative statements from the Soliloquies, ignoring the original qualifications. He actually presents these statements as his climatic examples of Augustine's sanctity, as if there were nothing more splendid in the saint's whole career than his pre-baptismal renunciation of wealth, honors and the rest" [145] as concentration on the supernatural, where Jacobus de Voragine however plays on the ideal of poverty of the begging orders, which—when it is lived out—was a sign of completeness in the succession of the saints [149]. Further, preferences—against the sources—for the vita contemplativa, the isolation from society, a form of self-determined love of one's neighbor [156] and denial of the beauty of the world [158] can be deduced, which Reames believes could be defined them as "puritanical." [158]. The psychological effect of such reading—and the reading of many other legends in this style—is a desire to imitate on the part of the reader.

Geith (1993): No similarity to Abbreviatio.

Cap. 126 De ss.Felice et Adaucto (p. 575)
Zuidweg (1941), 141: For this legend it can be determined that Ado's Martyrologium, Speculum Historiale lib. 12, cap. 80, Legenda Aurea {and Abbreviatio} must have all been derived from the same source. {The similarities presented by Zuidweg between Ado and the Legenda Aurea 575, 12 and 21 against the Speculum Historiale, and between Speculum Historiale and Legenda Aurea 575, 16–18 against Ado are also partly recounted in Abbreviatio}.

Geith (1993): Abbreviatio text transcribed in Legenda Aurea.

Cap. 133 De s.Lamberto (pp. 596–597)
Zuidweg (1941), 132, note 1: Legenda Aurea and Speculum Historiale are identical; both legendaries probably followed the same excerpt here.

Geith (1993): Abbreviatio text transcribed in Legenda Aurea.

Cap. 138 De s.Johanne Chrysostomo (pp. 611–620)
Zuidweg (1941), 118–119: Source: Cassiodorus, Historia Tripartita, lib. IX, cap. 48, lib. X, lib. XI, cap. 17 and lib. XII, cap. 13 and 14, PL t. 69; faithful rewriting of contents with abridgments, simplification and various deviations in form.

Not present in Abbreviatio.

Cap. 139 De s.Eufemia (pp. 620–622)
Wilmart (1936), 192–194: The Ambrose quotation 622, 9–19 was taken from the Praefationes to the Feast Day in the Ambrosian Missal.

Geith (1993): Abbreviatio text transcribed in Legenda Aurea.

Cap. 140 De s.Matthaeo (pp. 622–628)
Maggioni (1987), 174–176, 182–184: Largely an adaptation of the Abbreviatio.

Geith (1993): Similar to Abbreviatio.

Cap. 141 De s.Mauritio et sociis suis (pp. 628–632)
Wilmart (1936), 194–195: The Ambrose quotation 631, 16–27 was
taken from the Praefationes to the Feast Day in the Ambrosian Missal.
Geith (1993): Similar to Abbreviatio.

Cap. 146 De s.Hieronymo (pp. 653–658)
Zuidweg (1941), 141–142: Various sources: 1. Divi Hieronymi Vita,
under the name of "Eusebius Cremonensis", *PL*, t. 22, col. 235–238;
this Vita is in Migne and the Acta Sanctorum, Sept. T.VIII, sub 30
Sept., not fully reproduced [Note 1]. 2. Vita Divi Hieronymi incerto
auctore, *PL* t. 22, col. 201. 3. Hieronymus, Epistola 22 ad Eustochium,
Paulae filiam, *PL* t. 22, col. 398 and 399, § 7.4.4. Hieronymus, Epistola
76 ad Abigaum, *PL* t. 22, col. 689. 5. Isidorus, Selecta veterum
testimonia, *PL* t. 22, col. 218. Also Speculum Historiale lib. 16, cap.
18–88; lib. 17, cap. 62, lib. 18, cap. 12 and 35, rewrites the legends,
however only the lion chapter from lib. 16 bears any great resemblance to the Legenda Aurea. For 658, 2–5 no source has been found.
Geith (1993): Similar to Abbreviatio. {The meditations on Jerome's
death are absent from Abbreviatio.}

Cap. 148 De s.Leodegario (pp. 660–662)
Zuidweg (1941), 132 note 1: Verbatim correlation with Speculum
Historiale, lib. 23, cap. 124–125; sometimes Legenda Aurea is more
detailed, sometimes Speculum Historiale; both legendaries probably
followed the same excerpt here.
Geith (1993): Similar to Abbreviatio.

Cap. 149 De s.Francisco (pp. 662–674)
Baumgartner (1909), 17–31: Thomas de Celano, Vita minor (= Chorus
legend) (appeared after 1230, designed for liturgical use [20]), literal
copying from this source. 2. The same, Legenda Secunda (appeared
1245–1247). 3. The same, Tractatus de Miraculis (appeared around
1250). 4. Bonaventura, Legenda Major (appeared 1260–1263) "here
however investigation proves to be somewhat more difficult, as Bonaventure had likewise used the works of Fr. Thomas of Celano." [27]
Baumgartner deduces this dependence from the partly verbatim correlation, which could however come from the original sources, but
above all from the common rewriting of three parts which are not to
be found in the original sources. Baumgartner uses this dependence
on Bonaventura to establish the terminus post quem of the composition of the Legenda Aurea as 1263, in which Bonaventure's legend
was approved. {In my opinion however it is quite possible that

Jacobus could have used the Legend before its approval, if he used it at all, and that the three particular sections presented by Baumgartner do not come from a source used jointly by Legenda Aurea and Bonaventure.}

"These sources are, with the exception of five sentences, used so literally, that Jacobus, following the purpose of his work, condenses that which is treated in detail, but otherwise copies almost word for word." [30] The five sentences refer to a part of the etymology, which Baumgartner sees as a personal contribution of Jacobus.

"We possess (...) in the Francis legend of Voragine a very old description of the saint's life, compiled from the best sources." [31] Cf. the important study of the Patres Collegii S. Bonaventurae, art. "Jacobus de Voragine, Vita Sancti Francisci, Legendae S. Francisci Assisiensis", in: Analecta Franciscana sive Chronica aliaque varia documenta ad Historiam Fratrum Minorum. Vol. IX, Ad Claras Aquas, Florence, 1926–41, 680–693. The study, based on the analysis of several manuscripts concludes that the legend was transmitted in two different versions within the framework of the Legenda Aurea. Zuidweg (1941), 142–143, emphasizes that Baumgartner's results confirmed his own conclusions regarding Jacobus' use of sources.
Vauchez (1986), 27–56 comes to the same conclusion as Baumgartner without quoting the evidence. The Chorus legend of Thomas de Celano, a summary for liturgical use, seems to have been particularly practical and easy to use to Jacobus, as he copied some passages out of it word for word, referring to incidents unrelated by any other source. [40]
Not present in Abbreviatio.

Cap. 150 De s.Pelagia (pp. 674–676)
Zuidweg (1941), 143–144: Original source of material: Jacobus Diaconus Edessenus, Vita c.Pelagiae meretricis, allegedly translated by Eustochius and taken into the Vitae Patrum, lib. I, *PL* t. 73, col. 663–670, extremely shortened and simplified retelling of the contents. Speculum Historiale lib. 11, cap. 96 and 97 show strong, partly literal similarity to Legenda Aurea, which means that both used a common extract; the Legenda Aurea is more detailed in parts. Petit-mengin (1984), 146–157: Abbreviatio follows version B, often verbatim. [149] Some of his expressions are to be found in the Group Nz, which above all consists of the Northern Italian manuscripts and witnesses of the Cistercian Liber de Nataliciis [149]. Speculum Histo-

riale copied the text of the Abbreviatio, setting it in a historical context. [146/147]

The Pelagia legend of the Legenda Aurea, shorter compared to the Abbreviatio, reveals numerous borrowings from the Abbreviatio. But Legenda Aurea concentrates more on the character of Pelagia, "Jean de Mailly on the contrary, closer to the original, attached more importance to Nonnus and his deacon." [154] Jacobus, however, also used the original text of the legend, his source must have been a report B, source of many formulations from A' or a combination of A' and B [154]. "To us modern readers, the text of Jacobus de Voragine appears clumsy: he lingers with bad taste on the melodramatic passages, he reiterates the shedding of tears, while he skips factual details, such as the Nonnus' gaze on Pelagia, for reasons to do with morality." [154]

Geith (1993): Similar to Abbreviatio.

Cap. 152 De s.Thaisi meretrice (pp. 677–679)
Zuidweg (1941), 121–122: Vita s.Thaisis meretricis, auctore incerto, Vitae Patrum lib. 1, *PL* t. 73, col. 661–662, until 679,24 the Legenda was copies this source literally.—The last 8 sentences go back to the Verba Seniorum of the Vitae Patrum lib. V, libellus 10, § 21, {*PL* 73}; the texts correspond completely in content and form.
Not present in Abbreviatio.

Cap. 154 De s.Calixto (pp. 686–687)
Zuidweg (1941), 132, note 1: Quite identical to Speculum Historiale, lib. 11, cap. 124; both legendaries probably followed the same excerpt here.
Geith (1993): Abbreviatio text transcribed in Legenda Aurea.

Cap. 158 De undecim millibus virginum (pp. 701–705)
Zehnder (1987), 41: The Ursula legend is based on the Speculum Historiale, supplemented by a second Passio Ursulae ("Regnante domino") from the early 12th century, and the Revelationes of Elizabeth of Schönau (mid-11th century). "The character of a mixed form (. . .) already becomes clear in the second sentence of his (Jacobus de Voragine's) text, when he reports both the name Nothus from the Passio Ursulae and the name Maurus from the Revelationes of Elizabeth." Then the legend of the second Passio follows, until the text borrows the names of "men in her following" as well as the names of the superior accompaniment from the Revelations of Elizabeth.

The Cyriacus passage, as well as the chronology, are also borrowed
from Elizabeth, as is the story of Etherius, who travels to meet his
bride. On the other hand, the story of Cordula is borrowed from
the revelations of the pious nun Helmdrude von Neuenhersee. Jacobus
de Voragine reports the year of martyrdom as 238, but immediately
follows this report with a critical comment". {Zehnder does not seem
to know the Ursula legend of the Abbreviatio, as all his conclusions—
apart from the critical comment on the year of death—apply also to
the Abbreviatio, with the result that Jacobus did not produce this
mixed text, but appropriated it either from the Abbreviatio or a
common source}. Cf. Dondaine (1946), 86f.
Geith (1993): Abbreviatio text transcribed in Legenda Aurea.

Cap. 161 De s.Eustachio (pp. 712–718)
Petersen, 1925, 62–65: The Abbreviatio contains a short Latin version, which is likewise present in the first four of the five chapters of
the Speculum Historiale. Following Poncelet, Petersen assumes that
the Abbreviatio version came from a first version of the Speculum
Historiale, and that the current Eustachius legend of the Speculum
Historiale is that of a corrected second version. "So far as our legend is concerned, the disagreement observed between the two texts
towards the end could well be explained by a revision made by Vincent in his 'second edition'". The Legenda Aurea text is similar to
Abbreviatio and Speculum Historiale in many respects. For this Petersen quotes Monteverdi, 1909, 402–4, according to whom all three
texts were derived from a "literal Latin version", "through the intermediary of a version, lost today, which would have been their common
source." Petersen, on the other hand, suggests that, instead of pre-
suming the existence of an unknown Latin source text, which no-one
has seen, it would be more accurate to assume that Jacobus used the
Abbreviatio or the first version of the Speculum Historiale and in
addition the old "literal Latin version". Cf. also A. Boureau, Narration cléricale et narration populaire. La légende de Placide-Eustache.
In: Les saints et les stars. Le texte hagiographique dans la culture
populaire. Paris 1983, 41–64.
Geith (1993): Abbreviatio text transcribed in Legenda Aurea.

Cap. 166 De s.Martino episcopo (pp. 741–750)
Wilmart (1936), 195–196: The Ambrose quotation 750, 20–23 was
taken from the Praefationes to the Feast and Vigil Day in the Ambrosian Missal. "The primitive version flows easily and without obstacles

across the three themes of the shared coat, the thirst of the martyr and the marvels produced by apostolic zeal. The copy shows almost gross gaps which are not excused by the demands of a rapid adaptation. Moreover, the absence of a link between the first sentence of the quotation and the following sentences is now plain. Voragine put together extracts which came from two distinct contexts; hence the double use of the theme of miracles. This material disparity is all the better explained as the two prefaces "Qui ut infidelitatis" and "Nos te omnipotens", do not belong to the same liturgical context (. . .)" [174]

Zuidweg (1941), 144–145: Four fifths of the text were appropriated from the following works of Sulpicius Severus: 1. De vita B. Martini. 2. Dialogi II. 3. Dialogi III. 4. Epistolae, *PL* t. 20–5. In addition Beleth, Odo and Ambrose were quoted. Legenda Aurea 745, 26–28 does not come from these sources {this sentence is, however, present almost verbatim in Abbreviatio}.

Reames (1981): Jacobus de Voragine gives a "condensed version of the narrative" of the life of Sulpicius Severus up to Martin's ordination as a bishop; for the following events he combines material from the Vita, the Dialogues and the letters of Sulpicius Severus "selecting and arranging the events to form a single narrative. He omits a number of events from Martin's episcopacy, but he adds virtually nothing except a brief series of posthumous miracles, drawn mostly from Gregory." {Gregory of Tours} [147] On closer examination it emerges however that Jacobus de Voragine chose and shortened his sources according to a definite principle, with the result that his own priorities become apparent: an increase in frequency of miracle reports, in which the power of the saint in connection with supernatural power becomes visible [147], the saint becomes more lonely and heroic, and separated from his historical context [148]; several of the conflict situations are left out [149], above all those with other representatives of the church [152]. "The Martin portrayed by Jacobus is no longer 'one of us' at all, but a remote and wondrous figure who stands above and apart from the human condition, performing his acts of power." [156] Reames confronts these observations with an analysis of Jacobus sermons and takes the way he interprets Martin as an expression of his personal creativity. (Cf. also Boureau (1984), pp. 215–216.)

Geith (1993): Similar to Abbreviatio.

Cap. 167 De s.Briccio (pp. 751–752)
Zuidweg (1941), 145–146: Gregory of Tours, Hist. Franc., lib. II, cap. 1, *PL* t. 71.
Geith (1993): Abbreviatio text transcribed in Legenda Aurea.

Cap. 168 De s.Elizabeth (pp. 752–771)
Research is in agreement that this legend was added to the main body approximately 20 years after the writing of the Legendary, and that the version printed in Graesse already belonged to the Vulgate version of the Legenda Aurea at the end of the 13th century [cf. Fleith, 1991, 340–341].
Vauchez (1986), 41, 45–49, believes in the authorship of Jacobus, divides the legend into 59 episodes, out of which 36 or 37 are based on the Libellus de dictis quattuor ancillarum, 9 episodes on the Miracula felicis Elizabeth, written in 1235 by Bishop Konrad II of Hildesheim and the Cistercian abbot Hermann von Georgenthal, and 8 or 10 episodes can be traced to the Summa vite of Conrad von Marburg from the years 1232–1233. For the episodes 752, 15–13, 754, 32–25, 758, 25–28, 761, 18–762, 17 and 765, 9–766, 6 no sources have been identified.
Vidmanova (1993): Although there exists in Speculum Historiale lib. 30, cap. 136 a summary of the legend with miracles like those in the Legenda Aurea, it could not have been the source of the Legenda due to differences in form and style. The original source for the etymology was Jerome, Liber interpretationis Hebraicorum nominum. The unknown author of the legend tried through the addition of an etymology to remain in the style of Jacobus, although the author of the Elizabeth legend was more artistic and worked more consciously in a rhetorical manner.
Not present in Abbreviatio.

Cap. 169 De s.Caecilia (pp. 771–777)
Wilmart (1936), 197: The Ambrose quotation 773, 25–31 was taken from the first part of the Praefationes to the Feast Day in the Ambrosian Missal.
Geith (1993): Similar to Abbreviatio.

Cap. 170 De s. Clemente (pp. 777–788)
Cf. Gounelle (1994) and Fleith (1996).
Geith (1993): No similarity to Abbreviatio.

Cap. 171 De s.Crisogono (pp. 788–789)
Zuidweg (1941), 122–123: 1. A somewhat shortened but generally accurate rendering of Ado, Martyrologium, 24 November, *PL* t. 123,—2. For 788, 18–23 Chrysogonus, Epistola, without indication of sources.
Geith (1993): No similarity to Abbreviatio.

Cap. 175 De s.Pastore (pp. 803–805)
Zuidweg (1941), 123–124: Taken entirely from the Vitae Patrum, lib. V (Verba Seniorum), Libellus 1, 4, 8, 9, 10 {*PL* t. 73}.—Speculum Historiale lib. 15, similar to cap. 79ff., but Legenda Aurea is closer to the source.
Not present in Abbreviatio.

Cap. 176 De s.Johanne Abbate (pp. 805–806)
Zuidweg (1941), 124–125: Taken entirely from the Vitae Patrum, lib. V (Verba Seniorum), Libellus 1, 4, 10 {*PL* t. 73}.—Speculum Historiale lib. 15, similar to cap. 79ff., but Legenda Aurea is closer to the source.
Not present in Abbreviatio.

Cap. 177 De s.Moyse Abbate (pp. 806–807)
Zuidweg (1941), 125–126: Taken entirely from the Vitae Patrum, lib. V (Verba Seniorum), Libellus 2, 5, 9, 11, 15 {*PL* t. 73}.—Speculum Historiale lib. 15, similar to cap. 79ff., but Legenda Aurea is closer to the source.
Not present in Abbreviatio.

Cap. 178 De s.Arsenio Abbate (pp. 807–809)
Zuidweg (1941), 127: Taken entirely from the Vitae Patrum, lib. V (Verba Seniorum), Libellus 2, 3, 4, 6, 12, 18 {*PL* t. 73}; lib VI, 3.—Speculum Historiale lib. 15, similar to cap. 79ff., but Legenda Aurea is closer to the source.
Not present in Abbreviatio.

Cap. 179 De s.Agathon abbate (pp. 809–811)
Zuidweg (1941), 127: Taken entirely from the Vitae Patrum, lib. V (Verba Seniorum), Libellus 4, 7, 10, 11, 12, 15, 17 {*PL* t. 73}.—Speculum Historiale lib. 15, similar to cap. 79ff., but Legenda Aurea is closer to the source.
Not present in Abbreviatio.

Cap. 180 De ss.Barlaam et Josaphat (pp. 811-823)
Zuidweg (1941), 128-130: Jacobus gives as the source the Greek author
Johannes Damascenus, of whom he must have used the same Latin
translation—probably from the Vitae Patrum—as Speculum Historiale,
lib. 15, cap. 1-64; in some places there is more transcription of text
in Legenda Aurea, in others in Speculum Historiale; but Legenda
Aurea abridges and condenses more than the Speculum; that Jacobus
appropriates that which is told in the form of comparisons and in
this way can be understood by everyone, is typical of the author of
the Legenda Aurea.
Not present in Abbreviatio.

IV. *Suggestions for Further Research*

The overview presented here shows that Jacobus de Voragine proceeded in varied ways in the writing of his text:

1. Few texts are copied absolutely word for word from a single source.
2. For the commentary legends it was observed that they partly come
   in their essence from other collections of legends, but were greatly
   enriched with comments from often different patristic sources, or
   that they were considerable abridgments of the old Vitae. The
   exact definition must be worked out for each legend individually
   on the basis of a separate narrative history.
3. Primary legends are—sometimes with single comments added—
   appropriated verbatim or with abridgments from other collections
   of legends, above all the short legendaries.
4. "Modern" legends have their own specific histories of development.

Personal formulations of the author are at the most to be seen in the
form of abridgement or simplification of the source text. In this process
one can discover and interpret a creative wish particular to the author, provided that the sources of the text in question are adequately
established. Otherwise Jacobus de Voragine quotes mostly verbatim,
with the result that criticism, misunderstandings and references are
transferred wholesale from his models and predecessors.

The most interesting question seems to me personally to be the
question of use of the short legendaries, because on the one hand
there appears to be no question that Jacobus de Voragine used the

legendaries of the same period, while on the other hand it has been repeatedly observed that the Legenda Aurea is in parts more detailed and nearer to the patristic sources than its sister legendaries.

Zuidweg emphasized again and again that Speculum Historiale and Legenda Aurea come from the same, as yet unknown, excerpt. For this it must at first be proven that in these places Speculum Historiale was not the source for Legenda Aurea (in some places Speculum Historiale was the source in any event, as Jacobus de Voragine expressly quotes Vincent of Beauvais, cf. cap. 56 Maria Aegyptiaca). Further it must be investigated whether the excerpt suggested by Zuidweg could be the Abbreviatio. In this case Legenda Aurea and Speculum Historiale used the Abbreviatio independently of one another, or—more probably—the Legenda Aurea used Abbreviatio, Speculum Historiale and Epilogus (cf. for example cap. 43 Juliana). Other researchers have emphasized that Jacobus de Voragine also knew the sources of the Abbreviatio (cap. 93 Margaret, cap. 150 Pelagia, cap. 161 Eustachius); if this is true, there must have been an early short legendary, an "original short legendary", which was used by all four Dominican authors. It is however highly improbable that no traces of such a legendary known to the four authors have survived. Here, in the final analysis, only a synoptic view of the four known short legendaries in a critical edition in comparison to the "original sources" will be able to give reliable information.

Sources for the meditations on the church feasts, a feature totally absent from the short legendaries, promise a rich field of research.

Without critical editions however, all statements about the sources used must remain hypothetical.

Transl. Liam McCarney
Ed. Silke Cornu

Bibliography

AB: Analecta Bollandiana, Paris—Brussels 1882.—
ACLA 1: Legenda Aurea: Sept Siècles de diffusion. Actes du colloque international sur la Legenda Aurea: texte latin et branches vernaculaires à l'Université de Québec à Montréal 11–12 May 1983. Work published under the direction of Brenda Dunn-Lardeau (Cahiers d'Etudes Médiévales. Cahier spécial—2). Montreal—Paris 1986.

ACLA 2: Legenda aurea—la Légende dorée (XIII^c–XV^c s.). Actes du Congrès international de Perpignan (séances "Nouvelles recherches sur la *Legenda aurea*") publiés par Brenda Dunn-Lardeau (Le moyen français 32), Montréal 1993.

Acta Sanctorum (ASS): Acta Sanctorum quotquot orbe coluntur..., published by J. Bollandus, G. Henschenius, among others Antwerp, Basle, Tongerloo, Paris, 1643ff.

Airaldi (1988): G. Airaldi (Published): Jacopo da Varagine tra santi e mercanti. Milan 1988.

Alatri (1962): M. D'Alatri, Dalla Legenda Aurea. La Legenda dei Santi Cristoforo, Benedetto, Gregorio. Pescara, 1962.

Altaner (1922): B. Altaner, Der heilige Dominikus. Untersuchungen und Texte (= Breslauer Studien zur historischen Theologie, 2. Breslau und Habelschwerdt, 1922.

Atti <JdV> (1987): Jacopo da Varagine. Atti del I Convegno di Studi (Varazze, 13–14 April 1985). Published by G. Farris and B.T. Delfino, Comune di Varazze, Centro studi Jacopo da Varagine, 1987.

Bangemann, (1919): F. Bangemann, Mittelhochdeutsche Dominikuslegenden und ihre Quellen. Dissertation, Halle 1919.

Battle (1972): C. Battle, Die Adhortationes sanctorum Patrum ("Verba Seniorum") im Lateinischen Mittelalter. Überlieferung, Fortleben und Wirkung (= Beiträge zur Geschichte des alten Mönchtums und des Benediktinerordens, 31). Münster, 1972.

Baumgartner (1909): E. Baumgartner, Eine Quellenstudie zur Franziskuslegende des Jacobus de Voragine Ord. Praed., in: Archivum Franciscanum Historicum, 2 (1909), 17–31.

— (1912): E. Baumgartner, Die Franziskuslegende des Jacobus de Voragine O.P., in: Archivum Franciscanum Historicum, 5 (1912), 210–236.

Benz (1917, 1925, 1975): R. Benz, Die Legenda Aurea des Jacobus de Voragine aus dem Lateinischen übersetzt. First edition, Jena, 1917–1921; Second printing 1925, Eighth printing Heidelberg, 1975.

Bollandus (1643): J. Bollandus, Acta vetera Sanctorum a Latinis collecta. Legenda Aurea defensa, Paragraph IV in the Praefation generalis to the Acta Sanctorum, in : ASS, ian. vol. 1, XIX–XXI.

Boureau (1984): A. Boureau, La Légende dorée. Le système narratif de Jacques de Voragine (+ 1298). Paris, 1984.

— (1990): A. Boureau, Barthélemy de Trente et l'invention de la "Legenda nova".—In: Raccolte di vite di santi dal XIII al XVIII secolo. Structure, messagi, fruizioni. A cura di Sofia Boesch Gajano (Università degli Studi di Roma "La Sapienza" Collana del Dipartimento di Studi storici dal Medioevo all'età contemporanea 5), Brindisi 1990, 23–39.

Butler (1899): P. Butler, Legenda Aurea—Légende dorée—Golden Legend. Baltimore, 1899.

Colledge (1985): E. Colledge (ed.), "James of Voragine's Legenda Sancti Augustini and its Sources".—In: Augustiniana 35 (1985), 281–314.

Dondaine (1946): A. Dondaine, Le Dominicain français Jean de Mailly et la "Légende dorée", in: Archives d'histoire dominicaine, 1 (1946), 53–102.

— (1947): A. Dondaine (Ed.), Jean de Mailly, O.P., Abrégé des Gestes et Miracles des Saints, traduit du latin, Paris 1947.

— (1953): A. Dondaine, Saint Pierre Martyr, in: Archivum Fratrum Praedicatorum, 23 (1953), 66–162.

— (1971): A. Dondaine, L' "Epilogus in Gesta Sanctorum" de Barthélemy de Trente, in: Studia mediaevalia et mariologia P. Carolo Balic, OFM ... dicata. Rome, 1971, 333–360.

— (1975): A. Dondaine, Barthélemy de Trente, O.P.—In: Archivum Fratrum Praedicatorum 45 (1975), 79–105.

Dumont (1951): L. Dumont: La Tarasque: essai de description d'un fait local d'un point de vue ethnographique. Paris 1951.

Fleith (1991): B. Fleith, Studien zur Überlieferungsgeschichte der lateinischen Legenda Aurea (= Subsidia Hagiographica, 72). Bruxelles, 1991.

— (1996): B. Fleith, Die Legenda Aurea und ihre dominikanischen Bruderlegendare—Aspekte der Quellenverhältnisse apokryphen Gedankenguts. In: Apocrypha 7 (in the press).

Gaiffier (1973): B. de Gaiffier, L' "Historia apocrypha" dans la Légende dorée, in: AB, 91 (1973), 265–272.

Geith (1985): K.E. Geith, Die Juliana-Legende in der Abbreviatio in gestis et miraculis sanctorum von Jean de Mailly, in AB, 103, (1985), 95–104.

— (1987): K.E. Geith, Die "Abbreviatio in gestis et miraculis sanctorum" von Jean de Mailly als Quelle der "Legenda Aurea", in AB, 105, (1987), 289–302.

— (1993): K.E. Geith, Jacques de Voragine—auteur indépendant ou compilateur? in: ACLA 2, 17–31.

Gobbi (1990): D. Gobbi (Ed.), Bartolomeo da Trento domenicano e agiografo medievale. Passionale de sanctis. Textus—Index. Trento (Bibliotheca civis III), 1990.

Gounelle (1994): R. Gounelle, Sens et usage d'apocryphus dans la Légende dorée.—In: Apocrypha 5 (1994), 189–210.

Graesse (1846, 1965): T. Graesse, Jacobi a Voragine Legenda Aurea vulgo Historica Lombardica dicta ad optimorum librorum fidem recensuit. First edition, Dresden, 1846; Reprinting of the third edition, Osnabrück, 1965.

Haubrichs (1979): W. Haubrichs, Georgslied und Georgslegende im frühen Mittelalter. Text and reconstruction (Theorie-Kritik-Geschichte vol. 3). Königstein 1979.

Hug (1929): W. Hug, Quellengeschichtliche Studie zur Petrus- und Pauluslegende der Legenda Aurea, in: Historisches Jahrbuch der Görres-Gesellschaft, 49 (1929), 604–624.

Klinck (1970): R. Klinck, Die lateinische Etymologie im Mittelalter (= Medium Aevum, 17). Munich, 1970.

Kunze (1969): K. Kunze, Studien zur Legende der heiligen Maria Aegyptica im deutschen Sprachgebiet (Philologische Studien und Quellen, 49). Berlin, 1969.

— (1983): K. Kunze, Article Jacobus a (de) Voragine (Varagine), in: Verfasserlexicon, Die deutsche Literatur des Mittelalters. 2., thoroughly revised Edition, published by K. Ruh, together with G. Keil (among others), Berlin—New York, vol. 4, 1983, 448–466.

Lexikon des Mittelalters, Articles Legenda Aurea B. Überlieferung und Rezeption. A. Vitale-Brovarone: Italy; B. Fleith: France; D. Briesemeister: Iberian Peninsula; K. Kunze: Germany; M. Görlach: England; J. Deschamps:

Mid-Netherlands area; P. Meulengracht Sørensen: Scandinavia; G. Barone: Bohemia and Mähren; K. Liman: Poland. Vol. V. Munich-Zürich, 1991, 1797–1801.

Löffler (1992): R. Löffler, Alexius. Studien zur lateinischen Alexiuslegenda und zu den mittelhochdeutschen Alexiusdichtungen. Diss. Freiburg 1992.

Lühmann (1968): W. Lühmann, St. Urban. Beiträge zur Vita und Legende, zum Brauchtum und zur Ikonographie (Quellen und Forschungen zur Geschichte des Bistums und Hochstifts Würzburg, vol. XIX). Würzburg 1968.

Maddocks (1986): H. Maddocks, Illumination in Jean de Vignay's Légende dorée, in ACLA 1. 155–169.

Maggioni (1987): G.P. Maggioni, Il codici novarese di Jean de Mailly e la Legenda aurea.—In: Novarien 17 (1987), 173–184.

— (1990): G.P. Maggioni, Aspetti originali della "Legenda Aurea" di Iacopo da Varazze.—In: Medioevo e Rinascimento. Annuario del Dipartimento di Studi sul Medioevo e il Rinascimento dell'Università di Firenze, IV/ n.s. I, 1990, 143–201.

— (1995): G.P. Maggioni, Ricerche sulla Composizione e sulla Trasmissione della "Legenda Aurea" (Biblioteca di "Medioevo Latino" Collana della "Società internazionale per lo studio del Medioevo Latino" 8), Spoleto 1995.

Merrilees (1986): B. Merrilees, Reductio ad capitulum: le cas des sept dormants d'Ephèse. In: ACLA 1, pp. 119–130.

Monleone (1941): G. Monleone, Iacopo de Varagine e la sua Cronaca di Genova dalle origine al MCCXCVII (= Fonti per la storia d'Italia, publication of the Istituto Storico Italiano per il Medioevo. Scrittori. Secolo XIII, nos. 84–86). 3 volumes, Rome, 1941.

Monteverdi (1909): A. Monteverdi, La Legenda di S. Eustachio, in: Studi Medievali III (1909), 392–498.

Muratori (1726): L.A. Muratori, Chronicon Genuense, in: Rerum Italicarum Scriptores, vol. IX, Milan, 1726, 5–56.

Orywall (1968): I. Orywall, Die alt- und mittelfranzösischen Prosafassungen der Margarethalegende. Diss. Cologne, 1968.

Pagano (1936): A. Pagano, Etimologie medievali del b. Jacopo da Varazze, in: Memorie dominicane, 53 (1936), 81–91.

Petersen (1925): A. Petersen, Deux versions de la vie de saint Eustache en vers français du moyen âge. Critical edition, phil. Diss. Helsinki 1925.

Petitmengin (1984): P. Petitmengin and P.-Y. Lambert, Les Vies Latines Abrégées, in: P. Petitmengin (Published), Pélagie la pénitente. Métamorphoses d'une légende, t. II: La survie dans les littératures européennes. Paris 1984, 145–163.

Philippart (1974): G. Philippart, Le manuscrit 377 de Berne et le supplément au Légendier de Jean de Mailly, in: AB, 92 (1974), 63–78.

— (1977): G. Philippart, Les Légendiers Latins et autres manuscrits hagiographiques (= Typologie des sources du Moyen-Age occidental, Fasc. 24–25). Turnhout, 1977.

— (1979): G. Philippart, Le Légendier de Jean de Mailly à Meillerie sur le Léman en 1447, in: AB, 97 (1979), 128.

Poncelet (1910): A. Poncelet, Le Légendier de Pierre Calo, in: AB 29, (1910), 5–116.

Quétif (1719): J. Quétif et J. Echard, Article Jacobus de Voragine, in: Scriptores ordinis Fratrum Praedicatorum recensiti notisque historicis et criticis illustrati, vol. 1. Paris 1719.

Reames (1981): S.L. Reames, Saint Martin of Tours in the "Legenda Aurea" and Before, in: Viator 12 (1981), 131–164.

— (1985): S.L. Reames, The Legenda Aurea: A reexamination of its paradoxical history. Madison, 1985.

Richardson (1935): E.C. Richardson, Materials for a life of Jacopo da Varagine. New York, 1935.

Roze (1867): J.-B. Roze, La Légende d'or.—In: Revue de l'art chrétien, 11 (1867), 38–52.

— (1902): J.-B. Roze, (ed.), Jacques de Voragine, La Légende Dorée, nouvellement traduite en français avec introduction, notices et notes et recherches sur les sources par J.-B. Roze, Paris 1902, 3 volumes. (see the Recension in AB 22 (1903), 81f.)

Steinmeyer (1926): E. v.Steinmeyer, Die Historia apocrypha der Legenda Aurea, in: Münchner Museum für Philologie des Mittelalters und der Renaissance, 3 (1926), 155–166.

Sudhoff (1951): Die Legende der heiligen Katharina von Alexandrien: Untersuchungen und Texte unter Zugrundelegung der Bielefelder Handschrift. Diss. Tübingen, 1951.

Vauchez (1986): A. Vauchez, Jacques de Voragine et les saints du XIII^c s. dans la Légende dorée. In: ACLA 1, pp. 27–56.

Verdier (1986): P. Verdier, Les textes de Jacques de Voragine et l'iconographie du couronnement de la Vierge, in: ACLA 1, 95–99.

Vidmanová (1993): A. Vidmanová, Autour de l'auteur de la "Vie de Ste Elisabeth" dans la Legenda Aurea, in: ACLA 2, 33–47.

Wilhelm (1907): Fr. Wilhelm, Deutsche Legenden und Legendare. Texte und Untersuchungen zu ihrer Geschichte im Mittelalter. Leipzig 1907.

Wilmart (1936): A. Wilmart, S. Ambroise et la Légende Dorée, in Ephemerides liturgicae, 50 (1936), 169–206.

Zehnder (1987): F.G. Zehnder, Sankt Ursula: Legende—Verehrung—Bilderwelt. Cologne 1987.

Zuidweg (1941): J.J.A. Zuidweg, De werkwijze van Jacobus de Voragine in de Legenda aurea. Dissertation, Amsterdam, 1941.
(Summary by B. de Gaiffier, in AB, 61 (1943), 313–315.)

THE CHURCH FATHERS AND *AUCTORITATES* IN SCHOLASTIC THEOLOGY TO BONAVENTURE

Jacques-Guy Bougerol

"The Authorities" in The Middle Ages

The contemporary reader is often surprised by the treatment medieval writers gave to cited texts. The way they use the Fathers or authors recognised as "authentic" does not seem to chime in with the role they impose on them. Be that as it may, these authors constituted "authorities" and the Middle Ages remained faithful to the principle of tradition.[1] After the scriptural proof, the argument from authorities was the later Medieval masters' ultimate weapon, so that it sometimes assumed an even greater importance than the Scriptures.[2] What do we mean by the tradition argument? Was it really argument in the usual sense of the term? Historical investigation as we understand it should bring several testimonies to converge, their coincidence offering ground to argumentation. But nowhere do we find such a scientific attitude in the master's works. Not even when they confront two different versions of the same text do they worry about which one of them is authentic. We have found only one exception, *In III Sent.*, d. 35, a. un., q. 1 (III, 773), where two translations of Pseudo-Dionysius' *De divinis nominibus*, c. 4, § 1 (PG 3, 867), that of John Scot Erigena and that of John Sarrazin, are collated so as to give rise to a third interpretation. To answer the "scientificity" objection, we must say that the religious situation in the Middle Ages did not make this sort of enquiry necessary. Everyone could use the tradition as he chose. If sometimes one had to consult past authors about a controversy, no overt mention of this was made in the final version of the list of authorities compiled. It is also rather surprising to notice with what credulity the masters admitted, beside the most authentic monuments of tradition, works such as the *De spiritu et anima*,

---

[1] See J. de Ghellinck, "Patristique et argument de tradition au bas moyen âge", in *Aus der Geisteswelt des Mittelalters*, 403–426.

[2] One example is *In I Sent.*, d. 8, p. 1, a. 2, q. 1 (I, 156–157), where all the "pro" arguments are taken from Aristotle or Richard of Saint-Victor.

the exact origin of which nobody can determine to this day.

Theologians did not actually try to reduce the contradictions they found in the texts of the "authorities". All followed the example of Peter Lombard, who merely juxtaposed the texts, or tried to reconcile dissonant assertions by what has been called a benign interpretation, the origin of what was to become later the usual treatment of the "authentici" doctors, generally referred to as "reverenter" or "pie exponendum" (reverent or pious interpretation). This is why the great theologians of the Middle Ages touched only lightly upon the problem of the development of Christian dogma.[3] There was indeed a confusion between the argument from tradition and the argument from authority. As Bonaventure stressed, authority has no value in a proof unless faith, too, be present, so that the solidity of an argument is founded on faith. Thus, when we look for the certainty of our future resurrection, we establish its proof by the holy Scriptures and the word of the prophets who announced it. If we want to go further and prove that what they said is true, we must answer that we know their word to be true, because the Holy Spirit inspired them. Thus the faith they received from God gave them authenticity. And we are sure of this authenticity, continues Bonaventure, because we received the same faith from the same God.[4] Since this is settled, why accumulate citations of the Fathers? One authority is enough, provided we interpret it correctly. But let us not be deceived. If the mediaeval theologians did not pay attention to the genesis of theological questions, their conception was not without wisdom and subtlety: they claimed that instead of appealing to the "authorities" of the saints in our reasoning, we should submit our reason to the authority of the saints, where it shows no manifest absurdity.[5]

---

[3] Cf. Marcolino, "Elemento di desenvolvimento dogmatico secondo san Bonaventura", in *S. Bonaventura 1274–1974*, 177–219.

[4] Bonaventure, *In III Sent.*, d. 23, dub. 5 (III, 505): Auctoritas autem nullius est efficaciae in probando nisi per fidem; et ita tota firmitas argumenti ad fidem redit. Unde, si aliquis quaerat, utrum resurrectio sit futura, probatur et per auctoritatem sacrae Scripturae et per verba prophetarum qui ita dixerunt. Sed si quaerat ulterius, ut probem ei quod ipsi verum dixerunt, respondebitur ei quod scimus ipsos verum dixisse, quia a Spiritu sancto illuminati fuerunt, et ita certificati fuerunt per fidem quam a Deo receperunt; et nos certificamur de eorum certificatione per fidem quam ab ipso Deo accipimus.

[5] Bonaventure, *In I Sent.*, d. 15, p. 1, a. un., q. 4: Non debemus auctoritates sanctorum trahere ad nostram rationem, sed magis e converso rationem nostram auctoritatibus sanctorum subiicere, ubi non continent expressam absurditatem (I, 265).

After Peter Lombard

In the conclusion to our study on the reception of the Fathers in the *Sentences* of Peter Lombard, we stressed that theological reflexion developed over four centuries, through commentaries of the *Sententiae*, and that this testified to the intrinsic value of Peter Lombard's work: "The Glosses and the Commentaries of Peter Comestor, Peter of Poitiers and Stephen Langton, up to William of Auxerre and Philip the Chancellor are there to testify of its success".[6] We are now going to verify this assertion by a succint analysis of the reception of the Fathers by the Scholastic masters up until Bonaventure.

The minute study done by Dom O. Lottin on free will and freedom from Anselm until the end of the XIIIth century,[7] makes clear the different guises under which the Fathers were received by the successive masters. Without a doubt, Anselm was inspired by a text of Augustine to define free will in his Dialogues *De libero arbitrio*.[8] Peter Lombard[9] borrowed his definition of free will from the *Summa Sententiarum*,[10] which had extracted it from the *Miscellanea* of Hugh of St. Victor.[11] It would seem that the terms of the definition come from Anselm of Laon: "The freedom of the will is the voluntary free judgement. This judgement is made by distinction, and by the deliberation of reason to determine whether this or that is to be done or not to be done".[12] We can also affirm that all the passages in the *Sentences* which treat of the free will of God and the angels are most probably inspired by Abelard, whereas the passages concerning the diverse modalities of free will are taken from Hugh of St. Victor.

Robert of Melun starts with the text by Peter Lombard, *II Sent.*, d. 25, c. 1, n. 2 (I, 461): "Liberum de voluntate iudicium", and makes a critical exposition of it.[13] Gandolph of Bologna, between 1160 and 1170, also cites the definitions in the order in which Lombard gives

---

[6] Cf. J.G. Bougerol, "The Sentences of P. Lombard", *supra*, pp. 113–163.

[7] Cf. O. Lottin, *Psychologie et Morale aux XIIᵉ et XIIIᵉ siècles*, I, 1957, 9–389.

[8] *PL* 158, 489. Augustine's text is in the *De correptione et gratia*, c. 1 (*PL* 44, 917).

[9] *In II Sent.*, d. 24, c. 3 (I, 452–453).

[10] Cf. *Summa Sententiarum*, III, 8 (*PL* 171, 1129B; 176, 101C).

[11] Cf. Hugh of St. Victor, *Miscellanea*, I, n. 175 (*PL* 177, 574A). Cf. O. Lottin, *op. cit.*, I, 28s.

[12] Cf. O. Lottin, *Psychologie et Morale*, V, 345: Libertas arbitrii est liberum ex voluntate iudicium. Iudicium vero est discretio et deliberatio rationis, utrum hoc scilicet vel illud sit faciendum vel non faciendum.

[13] Cf. MS *Bruges, Ville 191*, f. 175v b–180r a.

them. Peter of Poitiers (211, 1031B), establishes a connexion between those definitions which he designates as being the definitions of philosophers and those of theologians. Alan of Lille uses these definitions too, as well as Prevostinus of Cremona and Stephen Langton.

William of Auxerre and the Summa aurea

Analysing the text of the four books of the *Summa Aurea* we cannot help but note that the Fathers are cited with varying frequency. Augustine is in first position with 1242 quotes, the ordinary and interlinear Gloss is far behind with 552 quotes. Then come Gregory the Great with 218 entries, Pseudo-Dionysius with 100 entries, Jerome with 97 entries, Boethius with 83 entries, John of Damascus with 77 quotations in Burgundio of Pisa's version, Ambrose with 53 entries, Anselm with 37 entries, Ambrosiaster with 33 entries. Hilary closes the list of the Fathers with 13 citations. We will now briefly examine a sample of passages from the *Summa aurea* containing patristic quotations.

I, Tractatus VIII, c. 6 (I, 140)
Augustine is cited: "The Father and the Son are the one and only principle (or origin) of the Holy Spirit".[14] This text comes from the *De Trinitate*, V, c. 14, n. 15 (*PL* 42, 921). It was probably copied by William of Auxerre from Peter Lombard *I Sent.*, d. 19, c. 2, n. 4 (I, 216), even though the Master of the *Sentences* does not cite it in the same terms as in the *Summa aurea*, as his source is the preceding chapter of the *De Trinitate*, V, c. 13, n. 124 (*PL* 42, 920): "Eternally the Father is the principle of the Son by generation, the Father and the Son are the one and only principle of the Holy Spirit". This incidentally is why Augustine says in the book V of *De Trinitate*: "The Father is called Father relatively and in the same way he is said to be the principle relatively; . . . when we say that the Father is the principle and that the Son is the principle, we do not say that they are two principles of the creature, because the Father and the Son are in relation to the creature the same and only principle, the unique creator".[15]

---

[14] Et dicit Augustinus quod "Pater et Filius sunt unum principium Spiritus sancti".
[15] Dicitur relative Pater, idemque relative dicitur principium; sed Pater ad Filium dicitur, principium vero ad omnia quae ab ipso sunt. Et principium dicitur Filius.

I, Tr. VIII, c. 7 (I, 150)

Glossa Lombardi, in Col. 1, 13. This gloss comes from Augustine, *De Trin.*, XV, c. 17, n. 27 (*PL* 42, 1080): "In the same way, in God are all goods; therefore in God are maternal love and free love; of natural love the Apostle says: *He transferred us to the kingdom of the Son of His love.* Here love is understood in its essence, because if it were taken in a personal sense for the Holy Spirit, the Son would then be son of the Holy Spirit".[16] This text, indeed, seems to be an extract from Lombard, *I Sent.*, d. 10, c. 3 (I, 113–114): "This is why Augustine says in the book XV of the *De Trinitate*. . . . Because the Apostle says of God the Father: *He transferred us to the kingdom of the Son of his love.* If then in the Trinity, God's charity is only in the Holy Spirit, the Son is also Son of the Holy Spirit. But because this is absolutely absurd, there remains that, not only is there charity of the Holy Spirit down below, but after all that I said, the Spirit is properly called charity".[17] However, Peter Lombard also cites extracts from *De Trinitate*, XV, c. 19, n. 37 (*PL* 42, 1086s.), with many omissions and transpositions, in his *Gloss* on Col. 1, 13 (*PL* 192, 262C).

II, Tr. IV, c. 1 (I, 85)

The following definition of hierarchy is attributed by William to Pseudo-Dionysius: "Because the (angelic) orders are distinguished by hierarchies, one should start with the hierarchy thus described by the blessed Dionysius: the hierarchy is for the sacred things and for those endowed with reason the ordained power which maintains its sovereignty over them (in relation to the first Sovereign)". This definition was also used by Alexander of Hales without reference to Pseudo-Dionysius and as if it were his own remark.[18] Bonaventure,

---

Cum enim diceretur ei: *Tu quis es*? respondit: *Principium, qui et loquor vobis.* Sed numquid Patris principium? Immo creatorem se voluit ostendere, cum se dixit esse principium, sicut et Pater principium est creaturae, quia ab ipso sunt omnia. Pater et Filius simul ad creaturam unum principium est, sicut unus creator.

[16] Item, in Deo sunt omnia bona; ergo in Deo est amor naturalis et amor gratuitus; de naturali dicit Apostolus: *Transtulit nos in regnum dilectionis suae.* Ibi dilectio sumitur essentialiter, quia si sumeretur personaliter pro Spiritu sancto, ergo Filius esset filius Spiritus sancti; ita dicit Augustinus.

[17] This is part of the text given by Lombard (I, 113–114): "Si caritas, inquit, qua Pater diligit Filium et Patrem diligit Filius, . . . Ait enim Apostolus de Deo Patre: *Transtulit nos in regnum caritatis suae.* Si ergo non est in illa Trinitate caritas Dei nisi Spiritus sanctus, Filius est etiam Spiritus sancti. Sed quia hoc absurdissimum est, restat ut non solum ibi sit caritas Spiritus sanctus, sed propter illa de quibus satis disserui, proprie sic vocatur.

[18] Alexander of Hales, *Glossa in II Sent.*, d. 9, n. 1 (II, 83): Sed quoniam novem

who qualified it as a "definition by a master", had in all likelihood no idea of its origin.[19]

II, Tr. IV, c. 1 (II, 85–103)

William of Auxerre discusses the explanations given by Gregory the Great of the nine angelic hierarchies. In the solution (87), he states: "The authority of Gregory is to be understood as follows: each order is called by a name which stands fully for the function it encompasses". This text, situated in the *In Evangelium*, II, hom. 34, n. 14 (*PL* 76, 1255C),[20] is cited by Peter of Poitiers, *Sententiae*, II, C. 5 (*PL* 211, 952D). We also find it in Lombard, *II Sent.*, d. 9, c. 3, n. 2 (I, 372) and in the *Summa Sententiarum*, II, 5 (*PL* 171, 1113C; 176, 86B) which gives an explanation different from Gregory's.[21]

II, Tr. IX, c. 1, q. 4

Searching for the exegesis of *Genesis* 1, 26: *Let us make a man in our image and likeness*, William cites Augustine and Hilary: "According to the blessed Augustine and the blessed Hilary, these two terms *faciamus* and *nostram* not only mean the plurality of persons, but also the unity of essence by virtue of designating only one operation of the three persons. In the same way, the terms *image* and *likeness*, not only designate the unity of essence according to Hilary, but also the plurality of persons. The meaning of the text is therefore: Let us make a man in our image and likeness, that is, the likeness whereby we are similar among us. Also, the term *image* means: Let us make a man in our image, that is, in the image by which we imitate each other".[22] It

---

ordines angelorum pertinent ad hierarchiam, oportet cognoscere quid sit hierarchia et quid est quod dicitur hierarchia. Secundum rationem nominis, idem quod sacer principatus. Ratio autem dicens quid est esse, est haec: Hierarchia est rerum sacrarum et rationabilium ordinata potestas, in sibi subditis debitum retinens dominatum.— On this subject, see J.G. Bougerol, "Saint Bonaventure et la hiérarchie dionysienne", in *AHDLMA* 36 (1969), 131–167.

[19] Cf. Bonaventure, *In II Sent.*, d. 9, praenotata (II, 238): Hierarchia est rerum sacrarum et rationabilium ordinata potestas, in subditis debitum retinens principatum.

[20] Gregory, *In Evangelium*, II, hom. 34, n. 14: Auctoritas Gregorii est sic intelligenda: "Unusquisque ordo illius rei censetur nomine quam plenius accepit in munere", plenius respectu inferiorum, ordinum; vel sic, quam plenius accepit in munere, id est in officio sive ministerio.

[21] Cf. Peter Lombard, *In II Sent.*, d. 9, c. 3, n. 3 (I, 373 and note 1).

[22] Secundum autem beatum Augustinum et secondum beatum Hylarium iste due dictiones "faciamus" et "nostram" non tantum significant pluralitatem personarum sed etiam unitatem essentie, per hoc scilicet quod designant unam operationem trium personarum; similiter per ista: "imaginem" et "similitudinem", non tantum unitas essentie designatur secondum beatum Hylarium, sed pluralitas personarum. Similitudo

seems that William of Auxerre reproduces here the explanation given by Lombard, *I Sent.*, d. 2, c. 4, n. 2–3 (I, 64–65).

II, Tr. XIV, c. 2 (515–518)

To define original sin, William of Auxerre relies on Lombard through Stephen Langton, *Quaestiones*, from the manuscript Paris B.N. lat. 14556, f. 164vb, of which we find a transcription in O. Lottin, *Psychologie et Morale*, IV, 100. But in discussing the definition of original sin, he cites a text from Augustine, *Sermo 151*, c. 5 (*PL* 38, 817), which we find in Lombard. Here is what William says: "Also, Augustine says that the original sin is concupiscence which makes the child prone to concupiscence, the adult concupiscent"; thus the original sin is an urge, seeing as concupiscence is an urge.[23] Peter Lombard is in fact more explicit: "By the name of concupiscence, Augustine did not mean the act of concupiscence, but the original vice, as he calls it 'the law of the flesh'. This is why he says in *De verbis Apostoli*: There is always struggle in this mortal body, because concupiscence with which we are born, cannot end till we die; it can diminish daily, but can never end. What is this concupiscence with which we are born? It is a vice that makes the child capable of concupiscence, and the adult concupiscent". In being transmitted by Lombard, Langton and William of Auxerre, Augustine has become considerably simplified.

III, Tr. IX, c. 1 (104–112)

John of Damascus in the version of Burgundio, c. 71 (272–274)[24] is brought in in the discussion of the exact condition in which Christ was alive during the *triduum* of his death: "Anathema to him who affirms that the Son of God, because he took on human nature, shed it again during the three days after his crucifixion". The conclusion is then: in the *triduum* he was united with his human nature and was therefore a man. Lombard, *III Sent.*, d. 21, c. 1, n. 8 (II, 133) cites Augustine, or rather Vigilius of Thapsus, *Contra Felicianum Arianum de unitate Trinitatis*, c. 14 (*PL* 62, 280A) who expresses the same opinion.

---

enim in divina essentia non tantummodo se habet in habitudine ad hominis gratuita, sed designat mutuam distinctionem personarum. Unde is est sensus: *Faciamus hominem ad ymaginem et similitudinem* nostram, id est ad ymaginen qua ymitatur nos ad invicem.

[23] *Summa aurea*, II, tr. 14, c. 2: Item dicit Augustinus quod "peccatum originale est concupiscentia que parvulum facit concupiscibilem, adultum conccupiscentem"; et ita peccatum originale est fomes, quia fomes nichil aliud est quam concupiscentia.

[21] Anathema sit qui dixerit Filium Dei, ex quo semel assumpsit hominem, deposuisse hominem.

III, Tr. XLII, c. 1, q. 1 (791)

William cites the definition of virtue by Augustine: "Virtue is a good quality of the mind by which we live rightfully, that no-one can put to bad use, and that is infused in us, without our aid, by God".[25] He read this definition in Lombard, *II Sent.*, d. 27, c. 1 (I, 480), in a slightly different form. For Dom O. Lottin, the definition in the *Sentences* is probably that of Lombard himself, who combined a text by Augustine and an Augustinian idea, that of the gratuity of grace: "Virtue is a good quality of the mind, by which we live rightfully, which can never be put to bad use, and by which God only acts in man", says Lombard.[26]

IV, Tr. V, c. 2, q. 1

Setting out to prove that the baptismal character forms faith and charity, William relies on Pseudo-Dionysius, *In Eccles. Hierarch.*, c. 2, in the version of Scot Erigena (*PL* 122, 1074C).[27] According to Pseudo-Dionysius, the ineffable creation is the baptism which makes us similar to God, because we had no access to God prior to it. This regeneration is the main impulse of our faith, by which we believe in the divine realities. This same regeneration makes us carry out God's commandments, seeing as through baptism we acquire charity. This is why the Apostle says that faith operates in love. William cites also another translation of Pseudo-Dionysius, that by John Sarrazin: "The primary movement of the soul is the love of God".[28] He adds a passage from the *Extractio in Hier. cael.*, c. 2 by Thomas of Vercelli (ed. Alonso, Lisboa, 1957, 561): "The inner man is shaped and formed to a habitus greater and more useful".[29] He thus accumulates a variety of interpretations, more or less removed from Pseudo-Dionysius, so as to reaffirm the standard doctrine.

---

[25] Virtus est bona qualitas mentis, qua recte vivitur, qua nemo male utitur, quam Deus infundit in nobis sine nobis.

[26] Virtus est, ut ait Augustinus, bona qualitas mentis, qua recte vivitur et qua nullus male utitur, quam Deus solus in homine operatur.—Cf. O. Lottin, *Psychologie et Morale*, III, 100–102.

[27] Ait communis magister—et communem magistrum vocat vel ierarcheum, qui fuit magister dictorum apostoli, vel ipsum Paulum—secundum intellectum in divina primordialis est motus divinaque dilectione in divinas operationes divinorum mandatorum principalissima processio essendi nos divinitus ineffabilissima creatio.

[28] Cf. *Dionysiaca*, II, 1107–1108: primordialis motus anime est dilectio Dei.

[29] Dicit Glossa: Figuratur et formatur homo interior ad maiorem et utiliorem habitudinem.

IV, Tr. XI, c. 1 (269)

William cites the definition of satisfaction avowedly according to Augustine: "To satisfy is to destroy the causes of sins and no longer be subject to their workings".[30] The text is in fact by Gennadius of Marseille (*De ecclesiasticis dogmatibus*, c. 24 (*PL* 58, 994C)), which Lombard also cites, *IV Sent.*, d. 15, c. 3 (329).

These few examples enable us to see how William of Auxerre made use of the sources available to him to have access to the Fathers. The distinction between the used source and the Fathers in question is in most cases blurred and indeed of no interest to William himself.

Philip the Chancellor and the Summa de bono

Taking as his opening the story of Ruth who went to glean in Boaz' field, Philip the Chancellor affirms that it is not enough to repeat what others have said, but that their opinions should be discussed and should then be the basis for one's own enquiry. This is the prologue to the *Summa de bono*, first published in a critical edition by Nicolas Wicki.[31] The work of Philip is remarkable for its clarity and depth. It also constitutes a collection of important patristic texts. There are 590 quotes from Augustine, but the number of quotes from the different Biblical *Glosses* amounts to a total of 597. In fact, the *ordinary Gloss* appears 307 times, the *interlinear Gloss* 108 times, which amounts to a total of 415. Furthermore, Philip calls upon Peter Lombard's *Gloss on the Psalms* 105 times and his *Gloss on Paul's Epistles* 77 times. Naturally, the citations from the various *Glosses* include a great many extracts from Augustine and other Fathers. Similarly, in our study on Peter Lombard we showed the way in which many texts by Augustine had reached the Master of the Sentences through Florus. After the *Glosses* and Augustine, Pseudo-Dionysius is cited 111 times, Bede 110 times, Gregory 103 times, John of Damascus 79 times. Examples chosen from the 179 questions of the *Summa de bono* show how Philip uses his patristic sources.

---

[30] Satisfacere est causas peccatorum excidere et suggestionibus earum additum amplius non indulgere.

[31] Philippi Cancellarii Parisiensis *Summa de bono, ad fidem codicum primum edita* studio et cura Nicolai Wicki, Bern 1985, I, 3: Absque rubore quidem dicta sequitur aliorum quod non est tantum recitator, sed si que dismissa sunt discutit et inquirit.

De bono gratiae. I. De gratia in generali. Q. 1 De diversis acceptionibus gratie et eius rationibus (355–357)

In his definition of *gratia*, Philip stresses that the word has many senses. Grace is defined as "grace imparted freely" and "grace imparting God freely". Philip refers to Lombard in *II Sent.*, d. 27, c. 3 (482): "Since from grace come merits, we understand grace imparting freely, that is, imparting God, or rather grace imparted freely. Also in *Romans* 3,24: *Justified by God's free grace*, the *Gloss*: that is, by his free gifts.[32] Grace is actually a gift of God, of the Holy Spirit. Or, grace is the will, the free will of God. *Ephesians* 2,8–9: *For it is by his grace you are saved, through trusting him; it is not your own doing. It is God's gift, not a reward for work done*; the *Gloss*: That is, the gracious will of God;[33] and again the *Gloss*: That is, faith doesn't come from you, that is, by the force of your nature, because it is the gift of God and not something due to your own efforts. The Master of the Sentences identifies "grace" and "faith" in *II Sent.*, d. 26, c. 2 (472). Also in his *Gloss* on *Heb.* 13,9: *It is good that the heart be fortified by grace and not by food*; he says: that is, that you have perfect faith by believing that everything is pure for those who are pure (*PL* 192, 513B)". The *Gloss* of Peter Lombard is cited again for other senses of "grace": firstly that of "remission of sins", "*Rom.* 1,7: *Grace and peace to you*; *Gloss*: Grace, that is remission of sins (*PL* 191, 1316B); or gift of the Holy Spirit, 1 Tim. 1,2: *Grace, mercy and peace*; *Gloss*: Mercy means here what in the other Epistles is called grace, that is, remission of sins (*PL* 192, 327B); or grace rendering acceptable, as in *Eph.* 1,6: *The glory of his gracious gift, so graciously bestowed on us in his Beloved, might redound to his praise*; the *Gloss* here is: That is, it makes us agreable. We note here the effect of the first preordination which belongs to justice (*PL* 192, 172D); or "eternal life", *Rom.* 6,23: *For sin pays a wage, and the wage is death, but God gives freely, and his gift is eternal life*; and the *Gloss*: We must recognize that the grace of God is called here eternal life, because eternal life is deserved by the grace given to man; (*PL* 191, 1412D)". For the same meaning, Philip cites the *Gloss* of Lombard on *John* 1,16: *We have received grace upon grace*; the *Gloss*: "The grace of glory for the grace of justification not due to us" (*PL* 191, 1413A). Philip goes on to study the diverse senses of

---

[32] *Biblia*, IV, 281a.
[33] *Biblia*, 371a.

grace under the aspect of the four causes. After calling upon the testimony of John Chrysostom, or rather that of the Pseudo-Chrysostom of the *Opus imperfectum*,[34] he cites again three times the *Gloss* of Lombard, on *Ep.* 1,13: "*When you had heard the message of the truth, and had believed it, you received the seal of the promised Holy Spirit; Gloss*: By the image of God formed again in you (*PL* 192, 175A); on *1 Cor.* 12,4–7: *There are varieties of gifts . . . In each of us the Spirit is manifested in one particular way, for some useful purpose; Gloss*: It is the efficient cause, that is, grace is that in which the Spirit is manifested (*PL* 191, 1652B); on *Ps.* 103,15: *Bless my soul, the Lord . . . oil to make their faces shine; Gloss*: Grace is the shining of the soul which reconciles holy love (*PL* 191, 236A)".

De bono gratiae in angelis. G. II, 1. Quid sit hierarchia (378–487)

Philip's passage on the angelic hierarchy contains many citations from Pseudo-Dionysius, cited 111 times in the *Summa de bono*. The *Celestial Hierarchy* is cited 10 times in the translation of Scot Erigena, and 7 times in the translation of John Sarrazin, who is called by Philip the "Commentator". Thus when he comes to explain what Ps.-Dionysius says in chapter 8 (*Dionysiaca II*, 871–872) on the domination of the superior hierarchies over the inferior ones and that of the inferior hierarchies over men, the passage in question being: "This is why the name holy sovereignties means, I think, a spiritual elevation . . . superior to any belittling servitude, ignoring all compromise and free from any difference, tending with a firm vigour towards the real Sovereignty and the Principle of all sovereignties"—Philip cites the "Commentator", who says: "Even before we expose this text, we must find why it stresses the freedom from any difference, given that all angels are perpetually united to God" (ms. Paris, B.N. lat. 1619, f. 97va–vb).

De caritate. Q. X. De ordine caritatis (721–732)

Philip studies the order of charity at length, by relying on the different *Glosses*, the ordinary *Gloss* on *Deut.* 6,5: *You shall love the Lord your God* etc.; *Gloss*: "All are to be loved equally, but because we cannot provide for the needs of all, we must love those who are close to us in

---

[34] Cf. Pseudo-Chrysostom, *Opus imperfectum in Matth.*, hom. 28 (PG 56, 779). Cf. also J. Chrysostom, *In Epist. ad Rom.*, hom. 10, n. 2 (PG 60, 476).

time and space (*Biblia*, I, 381b); on *Ezech.* 44,6–7: *Let there be an end to all your abominations, in admitting foreigners, uncircumcised in heart and flesh, to be in my sanctuary, profaning it; Gloss* of Jerome: The foreigners uncircumcised of heart, of ears, of lips, of eyes, of taste, of smell, shouln't enter the sanctuary (*Biblia*, 310a); on *Mark* 2,27: *The Sabbath was made for the sake of man and not man for the Sabbath; Gloss* of Bede: The sabbath must be kept according to the precept, but in case of necessity, the precept is not violated (*Biblia*, IV, 96a); on *Luke* 8,21: *My mother and my brothers—they are those who hear the word of God and act upon it; Gloss* after Ambrose, *Expositio ev. Lucae* VI, n. 38 (*PL* 15, 1678): He did not abusively neglect his mother and did not deny her, her to whom he spoke from the cross (*Biblia*, IV, 169b)".

De bono nature intellectualis creature. Q. X. De ymagine (105–108)

Philip had excellent knowledge of the *De fide orthodoxa* of John of Damascus in the translation of Burgundio of Pisa. In the passage explaining why angels were created in God's image, the definition of the angel is taken from *De fide orhodoxa*, II, c. 3 (PG 94, 868), in the version of Burgundio c. 17 (ed. E. Buytaert, 69–74): The angel is an intellectual substance, always mobile, endowed with free will, incorporeal, serving God according to grace, not nature, immortal, etc. This chapter II, 3 of John of Damascus is, so to speak, looted by Philip to explain the nature of the angel and his mobility.

De iustitia Q. VI. De partibus iustitie et primo de latria. 3. De ymaginibus (972)

The cult of images is evoked by Philip with the aid of abundant quotations from chapter IV, 16 of the *De fide orthodoxa* of John of Damascus: "As Basil, the divine and great interpreter of the divine realities, says: Honor rendered to the images attains to the prototype, because what is depicted in the image is derived from the prototype . . ." (vers. Burgundio c. 89, ed. E. Buytaert, 331, 9–11).

Thus Philip, as all the examples show, cites abundantly and accurately the Fathers from those of their works that are familiar to him and from the *Glosses*.

Alexander of Hales, the Glossa super Sententias, *the* Quaestiones disputatae antequam esset frater, *the* Summa fratris Alexandri

Alexander of Hales is the first Parisian master to have composed a Gloss on the four books of the *Sentences* by Peter Lombard,[35] in the years 1220–1225. Before he entered the Franciscan Order, thus taking on the charge of the brothers' studium in 1236, he had also disputed on the *Quaestiones*.[36] On becoming lecturer at the School of the Friars, he also disputed on many *Quaestiones* and gave John of La Rochelle the task of composing the *Summa theologica* which bore the name of its initiator, the *Summa fratris Alexandri*.[37] Father Victorin Doucet preceded the edition of the book IV of this *Summa*, with *Prolegomena* where he studied at length all the problems arising from this unfinished work,[38] and especially that of its sources. This is how he came to count 4814 explicit quotations and 1372 implicit quotations from Augustine, more than one quarter of the texts cited in the body of the *Summa*. But the primary interest of Alexander of Hales is that he was the first to quote abundantly from the work of Anselm. The *Glossa super Sententias* contains in its four volumes 241 quotations from Anselm, the *Quaestiones antequam esset frater* have 76. As for the *Quaestiones postquam fuit frater*, not edited yet, the *Prolegomena* gives their list and content, notably the five questions *De peccato originali*, studied at length by Dom O. Lottin.[39]

Glossa super I Sent.
In the distinction XII on the procession of the Holy Spirit, chapter 2, n. 5 (I, 120), where Peter Lombard cites *De Trinitate* by Hilary of Poitiers, Alexander invokes *De processione* by Anselm, c. 9 (*PL* 158, 301A): "To receive from the Father the essence from which proceeds the Holy Spirit, and to receive the Holy Spirit is not the same

---

[35] Magistri Alexandri De Hales, *Glossa in quatuor Libros Sententiarum Petri Lombardi*, nunc demum reperta atque primum edita, I–IV, Quaracchi 1951–1957.

[36] Magistri Alexandri De Hales, *Quaestiones disputatae "Antequam esset frater"*, nunc primum editae, I–III, Quaracchi 1960.

[37] Doctoris Irrefragabilis Alexandri De Hales Ordinis Minorum *Summa Theologica*, I–IV, Quaracchi 1924–1948.

[38] Doctoris ... *Summa Theologica seu sic ab origine dicta "summa fratris Alexandri"*. Tomus IV, Prolegomena, Quaracchi 1948.

[39] O. Lottin, "Le traité du péché originel chez les premiers maîtres franciscains", in *Ephemerides Theologicae Lovanienses* 18 (1941) 26–64; O. Lottin, *"Les théories sur le péché originel de saint Anselme à saint Thomas d'Aquin"*, in *Psychologie et Morale aux XIIe et XIIIe siècles*, IV-3, 11–280; cf. on Alexander of Hales, *ibid.*, 171–212.

thing. The first alternative means no indigence in the Son; the second suggests that, if the Son receives from the Father the Holy Spirit he does not have by himself, then he possesses something less than the Father and receives from him the ability to give the Holy Spirit; but it does not follow necessarily that it is the Son who lacks the Spirit, the converse could equally well be the case". Again, Alexander cites *De processione*, c. 16 (*PL* 158, 309 B): "Let us say that the Holy Spirit in proceeding from the Father, also proceeds from the Son, just as the things done by the Father through the Word, are also done by the Word". Two other citations from the *De processione*, c. 19 and 20 (*PL* 158, 312 and 314), specify the exact meaning of *John* 15,26 where Jesus says: *When the Counsellor comes, who proceeds from the Father.* "Why does he not add *and from the Son?* It should be answered that in the Scriptures, what is attributed to one person of the Trinity should not be attributed to either of the other two persons. When the Lord tells Peter: *Blessed are you, Simon Bar Jona . . . but my Father who is in heaven* (*Mat.* 16,17); or: *No one knows the Father except the Son and any one to whom the Son chooses to reveal him*; or: *When the spirit of truth comes, he will guide you into all the truth; for he will not speak of his own authority* (*John* 16,13)—the attribution in each case is made to only one person although the discourse involves all three". Chapter 20 of *De processione*, treating the question of knowing whether the Holy Spirit, according to the Scripture, proceeds from the Father, answers that it is never said in the Old or New Testament whether he proceeds from the Son. "However, in John 5,26 where it is said: *For the Father has life in himself, so he has granted the Son also to have life in himself,* as well as in *John* 17,3: *And this is eternal life, that they know thee the only true God, and Jesus Christ whom you have sent,* the Holy Spirit is not excluded by the fact that he is not named". Thus by interpreting Hilary. with the aid of Anselm's exegesis, Alexander arrives at the standard, Western doctrine of double procession.

Glossa super II Sent. De peccato originali

In the *Glossa super sententias*, distinction 30, the note 7 starts with a quotation from *De conceptu virginali* of Anselm: "We will see now what is the original sin. Anselm, *De conceptu virginali*: It is a sin that everybody bears in his nature since his origin; and it is a sin that everybody commits once he is a person distinct from others. It is natural, not because it belongs to the essence of this nature, but because it is the corruption of it. . . . The original sin is the absence or the nudity of justice due, by the disobedience of Adam, and which induces the absence of beatitude".[40] Alexander appropriates Anselm's thesis according to which Adam transgressed the interdiction to enter the terrestrial paradise, not only as a private individual, but also and especially as father of the whole of human race.[41] And to clarify his position, he cites no less than eight texts from Anselm.

In the *Quaestiones postquam fuit frater De peccato originali*, Alexander repeats the accounts of the *De conceptu virginali* of Anselm, by abundantly citing them.[42]

Glossa super III Sent.
Anselm appears again in the *Gloss* of Book III of the *Sentences*, where the Incarnation of God's Son is considered. Since the d. 1, n. 10 (III, 14), Alexander comments on Lombard's text, III Sent. d. 1, c. 3, n. 1 (II, 26): "Some say that the actions of the Trinity are inseparable; if the Son took on flesh, then the Father and the Spirit also took on flesh". Three texts by Anselm come to throw light on the matter. All three are taken from the *Cur Deus homo*, II, c. 22 (*PL* 158, 430C); c. 8 (*PL* 158, 405B and C): If it is required that for the sin of man, man must satisfy, then it is necessary that he who satisfies also be a sinner or one of his kind. Alexander concludes that deity cannot unite itself to any creature other than man.

Distinction 12 of the same Book III, in chapter 2 (II, 81), answers the question of whether the Father could have taken on a man other than the Son. Alexander cites the *De incarnatione Verbi* of Anselm, c. 4 (*PL* 158, 276A): "If a man is one person among many others, it is necessary that many persons who are distinct from one another be one and the same person, which is impossible. For the same reason, it is impossible that God incarnated in one particular person, be incarnated in another". Alexander concludes that the Father cannot take on the particular man who was taken on by the Son. To prove that it is not possible for God to take on a man not from Adam's race, Alexander cites *Cur Deus homo*, II, c. 8 (*PL* 158, 405D–406A).

---

[40] Alexander of Hales, *Glossa in II Sent.*, n. 7 (II, 286–287): Nunc superest videre quid sit ipsum originale peccatum. Anselmus, De conceptu virginali: Est peccatum quod quilibet trahit cum natura in ipsa sui origine; et est peccatum quod ipse facit postquam est persona ab aliis discreta; et dicitur naturale non quod sit ex essentia ipsius naturae, sed ex ipsius corruptione. . . . Originale est carentia vel nuditas debitae iustitiae per inobedientam Adae facta, quam concomitatur beatitudinis carentia.— This definition is from the *De conceptu virginali*, c. 27 (*PL* 158, 461A–B). It is found also in the anonymous question of the manuscript Douai 434, f. 387ra.

[41] Id., *ibid.*, d. 33 (312–325).

[42] Anselm, *De conceptu virginali*, cc. 24, 25, 27 (*PL* 158, 457C; 459C; 461A).

Also, in the gloss on chapter 3 of Lombard (II, 82), Alexander answers the doubt of whether the man as taken on can lie or not be God, by a quotation from *Cur Deus homo*, II, c. 10 (*PL* 158, 408 D–409 A): "All power follows will. When he says: I can speak, he means 'if I want to'; therefore as he could not want to lie, he could not lie".

Glossa super IV Sent., d. 4, n. 25, *d* and *l* (IL, 94–96)
Lombard, *IV Sent.*, d. 4, c. 7, n. 4 (II, 262) proposes as an objection that baptized children do not yet have charity and faith. Are they just?—he asks. Alexander finds in the *De conceptu virginali* of Anselm, c. 29 (*PL* 158, 462C; 463s.), both the question and the answer. "If justice is the rectitude of will observed in itself, as it is said in the *De veritate*, c. 12 (*PL* 158, 482B), how can the child not be unjust even after baptism? To which it should be answered that as long as children do not have justice only because of their original helplessness, they are not unjust, because there is not in them absence of *due* justice. In fact, sin has to be present for due justice to be absent. This is why, if children die, they are not damned as being unjust, but the justice of Christ who gave himself away for them, and the justice of the Mother Church which believes for them, make them just".

Quaestio antequam esset frater. Q. XV. *De incarnatione*, disp. I, membrum 1, n. 9 and 16 (195–197)
We will take only one example in the *Quaestiones antequam esset frater*, where St. Anselm appears again. The Q. XV has four disputations. In the first one, n. 9 (195), Alexander objects to the *De incarnatione Verbi* of Anselm: "The Father, the Son and the holy Spirit do not differ in the simple essence. Therefore, if this essence can be united to the human nature, the Father and the holy Spirit must also be united to the human nature. To which Anselm answers himself: God took on a man, not as one nature, divine and human, but as one person, God and man". Alexander concludes that because this person is distinct from the other persons, the two natures should be distinguished in him.[43]

The authority of Anselm was ignored before Alexander introduced him in his *Glossa super Sententias*, in his *Quaestiones antequam* and *postquam*, and in his *Summa fratris Alexandri*.[44] In this last work, of which John

---

[43] Anselm., *De incarnatione Verbi*, c. 4 (*PL* 158, 272s.; 275C): Deus assumpsit hominem, non sic ut una natura esset Dei et hominis, sed ut una persona esset Dei et hominis et eadem.

[44] Cf. De Ghellinck, *Le mouvement théologique du XIIe siècle*, Paris 1914.

of La Rochelle was an initiator, Anselm appears with 501 explicit quotations. In Book I, the treatise *De Deo* calls upon *Monologion, Proslogion*, the *De processione Spiritus sancti*, the *De veritate*, the *De concordia praescientiae et praedestinationis*. In the treatise on man of Book II, the *De libero arbitrio* is often cited. In the treatise *De malo* in Book III, appear the *De casu diaboli* and the *De conceptu virginali*. Finally in Book IV, we have seen that two treatises of Anselm are cited, the *De incarnatione Verbi* and the *Cur Deus homo*. If Augustine is considered by the Franciscan masters as the "Doctor praecipuus", as Matthew of Aquasparta states in his *Quaestiones disputatae de gratia* (Quaracchi 1935, CLIX), Anselm is called by Roger Marston, in his *Quaestiones disputatae* Augustine's "secutor", or "successor" (Quaracchi 1932, 117). Many more authorities appear in the work of Alexander of Hales. We only wanted to stress the primary importance given to St. Anselm, who was thus to make his first appearance in scholastic theology.

St. Bonaventure

To determine the number of books which Bonaventure had available to him as "sententiarius", let us not forget that he had on his table the "lectura" by Eudes Rigaud on the first three Books of the *Sentences* and, without a doubt, that of Albert the Great. It is therefore probable that many authorities are from those two earlier masters. Similarly, it is common knowledge that St. Thomas had read the "lectura" of the *Sentences* of Bonaventure when he, in turn, lectured on Lombard's *Sentences*. We shall now examine some of the most important authorities cited by Bonaventure.

St. Augustine

St. Augustine was to Bonaventure "the greatest of the Latin Fathers",[45] the greatest interpreter of the holy Scripture,[46] surpassing all the other Fathers by the purity of his doctrine.[47] No one had described better

---

[45] Bonaventure, *In III Sent.*, d. 3, p. 2, a. 2, q. 1, concl.: Augustinus, praecipuus doctor Latinus (III, 86s.).

[46] Bonaventure, *Sermo "Unus est magister"*, n. 19 (V, 572): Uterque autem sermo, scilicet sapientiae et scientiae, per Spiritum sanctum datus est Augustino, tanquam praecipuo expositori totius Scripturae, satis excellenter, sicut ex scriptis eius apparet.

[47] Bonaventure, *Epist. de tribus quaestionibus*, n. 12 (VIII, 335): Nam nullius melius

the nature of time and matter, than Augustine when he inquired into and discoursed on them in the *Confessiones*; no one had written better on forms and the propagation of things than Augustine in *De Genesi ad litteram*; no one had exposed matters to do with the soul and God better than Augustine in *De Trinitate*; no one had described the creation of the world better than Augustine in *De civitate Dei*. In a word, nearly all theological questions find their solution in the works of Augustine.

Bonaventure inherited from Augustine a cast of mind described by Augustine himself in *Sermo 43*, n. 7 (*PL* 38, 258):[48] "They are quite right, those who say to me: "I must understand first, to be able to believe". I am equally right when I reply in the words of the prophet: "Believe, so that you can understand". Both views are right. Therefore, understand to believe, believe to understand. No need to say more; strive to have faith, to understand my preached word; have faith so that you can have understanding, of the word of God". This is echoed by Bonaventure, speaking of the joy of the disciples in contemplating the risen Christ: "As Jeremiah (15, 16) says: *Thy words became to me a joy*. The word of God, once it is perfectly believed, becomes a delectable source of joy and elation for the heart of him who understands it".[49]

The Augustinianism Bonaventure inherited from his masters Alexander of Hales, John of La Rochelle, Eudes Rigaud was not the pure Augustinianism of Augustine. St. Anselm, Hugh and Richard of Saint-Victor, Gilbert of Porrée had constructed a more abstract, more technical platonism, but still open to receive everything that the 13th century was to bring to it. Peter Lombard, with his *Liber Sententiarum*, was to offer the theological schools a program of study,

---

naturam temporis et materiae describit quam Augustinus, inquirendo et disputando in libro Confessionum; nullus melius exitus formarum et propaginem rerum quam ipse super Genesim ad litteram; nullus melius quaestiones de anima et de Deo quam ipse in libro De Trinitate; nullus melius naturam creationis mundi quam idem in libro De civitate Dei. Et ut breviter dicam, pauca aut nulla posuerunt magistri in scriptis suis, quin illa reperias in libris Augustini.

[48] Augustine, *Sermo 43*, n. 7 (*PL* 38, 258), in the translation by H. Marrou, *Saint Augustin et la fin de la culture antique*, Paris 1958, 643.

[49] Bonaventure, "Sermo Dominicae in octava Paschae", n. 11, in *Sermones Dominicales*, ed. J.G. Bougerol, Grottaferrata 1977, 295: Et de hoc dicitur Ieremiae 15, 16: Factum est verbum tuum in gaudium et laetitiam cordis mei. Verbum divinum, postquam perfecta fide creditur, ita miro modo delectat, cum intelligitur, ut fiat in gaudium et laetitiam cordis intelligentis.

a genuine book of chosen texts where Augustine occupies the most prominent place. The vocabulary of Augustine became a theological commonplace. Augustinian subjects too became the common property of theologians. Moreover, we must not forget the simultaneous rise of Aristotelianism and Avicennism, the doctrines of which were to mingle so as to constitute a variety of Augustinianisms, so aptly analysed by Etienne Gilson. Gilson distinguished notably Aristotelian Augustinianism represented by Alexander of Hales, John of La Rochelle and Bonaventure; and Avicennan Augustinianism represented by William of Auvergne, Roger Bacon and Robert Grosseteste.[50] Rather than looking for the most judicious adjective to qualify the Augustinianism of Bonaventure, it would be more helpful to the reader if we mention here the Augustinian doctrines which he adopted, stamping them with his own genius: theory of the "veritas exprimens" in the *Questiones De scientia Christi*, q. 3 (V, 13–16), of seminal reasons in *In IV Sent.*, d. 43, a. 1, q. 4, concl. (IV, 888), of intellectual illumination in *De scientia Christi*, q. 4 (V, 17–27),[51] of exemplarism, etc. Moreover, Bonaventure's particular fidelity to the Augustinian doctrine of illumination allowed him to go further than Anselm and to show that the ontological argument itself stemmed necessarily from God and Being: man would not be capable of arguing thus for God's existence, had his being not been determined by Being itself or God.[52]

Saint Bonaventure cited Saint Augustine more than 3050 times. Some works are represented by fewer than 10 quotations, some by only one. But others are privileged: *De Trinitate*, 559 quotations; *Tractatus in Iohan. evang.*, 318; *De civitate Dei*, 299; *De Genesi ad litteram*, 2231; *Sermones*, 182; *Enarrationes in Psalmos*, 179; *Epistolae*, 156; *Enrichidion*, 126; *De libero arbitrio*, 107; *De diversis quaestionibus 83*, 99; *Confessiones*, 98; *De doctrina christiana*, 84. The *Retractationes* appear 48 times.

Of course, the works of Augustine were more extensively cited in those works of Bonaventure which touch on typically Augustinian themes. This is how the *Tract. in Iohan.* was quoted most frequently in the *In Iohannem* of Bonaventure; the *De Trinitate* in the *In I Sent.*,

---

[50] Cf. E. Gilson, "Pourquoi saint Thomas a critiqué saint Augustin", in *Archives de l'histoire doctrinale et littéraire du Moyen Age* 1 (1926–1927) 80–111.

[51] Cf. J.M. Bissen, *L'exemplarisme divin selon saint Bonaventure*, Paris 1929; H. Urs Von Balthasar, *La gloire et la croix*, II-1, Paris 1968, 237–323.

[52] Cf. E. Gilson, *L'esprit de la philosophie médiévale*, Paris, 1944, 59–60; Bonaventure, *De mysterio Trinitatis*, q. 1, a. 1, concl. (V, 49); and the capital text *Itin.*, c. 5 (V, 308–310).

and in the *Quaestiones disputatae de mysterio Trinitatis*; the *De Genesi ad litteram* in the *In II Sent.*

One example will suffice to show how Bonaventure appropriated Augustine's authority. Enquiring into whether angels knew their own creation in the Word, called the "cognitio matutina", in *In II Sent.*, d. 4, a. 3, q. 1 (II, 138–140), Bonaventure notes at least two solutions, depending on whether one refers to *De Genesi ad litteram* or to *De civitate Dei*. If we follow *De Genesi ad litteram*, IV, c. 22, n. 39; c. 35, n. 56 (*PL* 34, 311ss.), we read that the good angels were created and glorified at the same time, so that they knew all things in the Word and the eternal reasons. But, if we turn to *De civitate Dei*, IX, c. 21 (*PL* 41, 274), we find an exactly opposed answer, with Augustine asserting that a certain space of time elapsed between the creation of the angels and their fall or their glorification, such that the good angels could not have the "cognitio matutina" at the moment of their creation. Bonaventure then tackles the exegesis of these two texts and concludes by distinguishing two different senses of "cognitio matutina": the general sense (as used in *De civitate Dei*), which is the knowledge in the creature itself by a contemplation of things lower than itself, but which the reference to God in glory transforms from "cognitio vespertina" into "cognitio matutina". The other, correct sense (as in *De Genesi ad litteram*), is the immediate knowledge in the Word and the eternal reasons. Bonaventure adds: "This way of stating the issue is more courteous towards Augustine, rather than dwelling on the inconsistencies of his interpretation ... It is not believable that such a great man contradicted himself, especially as he never included the question in his *Retractationes*".[53] Bonaventure's knowledge of Augustine is detailed and profound from as early on as the *Quaestiones disputatae de scientia Christi*. Already, his "lectura" of the *Sentences* shows the extent and depth of his familiarity with the Bishop of Hippo. In the questions themselves, an analysis of arguments in favour of the thesis put forward, allows us to appreciate the importance of Augustine's authority as well as the sheer number of works of other Fathers and authorities referred to.

A. Stohr says that "despite the great influence of the African Father on nearly all aspects of Bonaventure's teaching, it is difficult to

---

[53] Bonaventure, *In II Sent.*, d. 4, a. 3, q. 1 (II, 140): Et hoc curialius est dicere quam dicere quod Augustinus dicat contraria et tanquam instabilis modo dicat hoc, modo contrarium. ... Non est tamen credendum quod tantus homo sibi contradicat, maxime in his quae non retractat.

find any trace of Augustinian spirit in Bonaventure's doctrine of the Trinity".[54] Greek influence was essential here. Bonaventure knew John of Damascus in the version by Burgundio of Pisa and Gregory of Nazianzus in a still unidentified version.[55] He knew above all Richard of Saint-Victor and his *De Trinitate* and Alexander of Hales whose *Quaestiones antequam esset frater* expose the trinitarian theology of the Greeks. The Greek formulation "per Filium in Spiritu sancto" appears in the *Breviloquium*.[56] We must also underline the great importance accorded by Bonaventure to the text of Hilary mentioned in the *Sentences* by Peter Lombard. As a matter of fact, in *I Sent.*, d. 31 both Hilary and Augustine are cited. In chapter 2, n. 2 (I, 225), Lombard explains his appropriation of Hilary by quoting an extract from *De Trinitate* of Augustine, VI, c. 10, n. 11 (*PL* 42, 931), which attributes eternity to the Father, form to the Son and enjoyment or joy to the Holy Spirit. In n. 8 (I, 228), we find a long excerpt from Hilary's *De synodo*, n. 59–60 (*PL* 10, 521A–C): "The head, principle of all things, is the Son; the head, principle of Christ, is God". Bonaventure read and studied these words. He made them the theme of the *dubium* 7 of *In I Sent.*, d. 31 (I, 551s.). We know that the *dubia* are in reality short questions which arise from Lombard's text. Arguments are stated briefly and are followed by a conclusion that sheds light on the reading. These *dubia* might well have been the *lectio cursoria* of the sententiarius, because in some manuscripts they are separate from the *Commentary on the Sentences* for Books I and II. Thus, in his *dubium* on the Trinity Bonaventure sought to resolve a doubt. He starts out by examining the meaning of Hilary's statement: "The head of all things is the Son". This expression seems ambiguous at first sight. Either "head" is said by reference to divinity, or to the sameness of nature. In the former case, the Holy Spirit could also be called "head"; moreover, "head" of the Son could not be God, because the "head" has a primacy which the Father does not have with regard to the Son, as there is no degree between the Father and the Son. If "head" is said because of sameness of nature, the Son sharing his nature only with men, could not be "head" of *all* things. To this

---

[54] Cf. A. Stohr, *Die Trinitätslehre des hl. Bonaventura*, Münster i. Westf., 1923, 34.

[55] Cf. H. Dausend, "Die St. Gregor von Nazianz-Stellen in der Werken des hl. Bonaventura", in *Fransk. Stud.* 3 (1916) 151–160.

[56] Bonaventure, *Brevil., prol.*, n. 5 (V, 202): Cum mera fide ad Patrem luminum accedamus, flectendo genua cordis nostri, ut ipse per Filium suum in Spiritu sancto det nobis veram notitiam Iesu Christi. . . .

problem, Bonaventure brings a carefully studied solution, which contains the germ of his teaching on the *Verbum Increatum* as an exemplar of creation. His answer is that the word "head", taken in its proper sense, bears the idea of influence and of sameness of nature. In this sense, Christ is the head of the whole Church. But Hilary broadens the sense of the word, by saying that "head" means "original principle". Because God the Father is the principle of the Son, and the Son is principle of all things so that he produces and is produced, he is a head himself, and has a head himself. But the Father who does not have a head because he is unknowable, is head of all things; he is therefore the source from which emerge all things and to which, by the Son, all things return. In this return there is a difference of degree between things and the Son; but between the Son and the Father there is no difference of degree, only that of order and origin. This is why Hilary does not say "his gradibus", but "hoc gradu",[57] concludes Bonaventure. We should note here that Hilary is heavily dependent on Greek thought.

Pseudo-Dionysius the Areopagite

Among the authors often cited and referred to by Bonaventure, Pseudo-Dionysius holds an important place. At the very beginning of the treatise on angels in the *In II Sent.*, d. 9, Bonaventure sets out to justify the preference he gives to the Dionysian classification over that of Gregory: "We should rely on what Dionysius says, because he learned directly from Paul and reports what he heard, because Gregory himself refers to him, and finally because Dionysius founded the distinction of hierarchies on what is intrinsic and essential to the angelic spirits themselves, he therefore distinguished the orders as

---

[57] Bonaventure, *In I Sent.*, d. 31, dub. 7 (I, 551s.): Item quaeritur de hoc quod dicit: "Caput enim omnium Filius est". Videtur enim male dicere, quia aut dicitur "caput" ratione deitatis, aut ratione conformitatis naturae.... Dicendum quod "caput", secundum quod proprie accipitur, importat rationem influentiae, et conformitatis naturae: et sic dicitur Christus caput esse totius Ecclesiae; sed Hilarius extensiori modo accipit, prout "caput" dicit originale principium. Et quoniam Deus Pater est principium Filii, et Filius principium omnium, ita quod Filius producitur et producit, ideo est caput, et habet caput. Sed Pater quoniam caput non habet, cum sit innascibilis, est caput omnium; et ideo dicitur fontale principium, a quo omnia et in quem omnia per Filium reducuntur. Et in hac reductione gradus est, comparando creaturas ad Filium; sed ultra comparando Filium ad Patrem non est gradus, sed ordo et origo. Et ideo Hilarius non dicit "his gradibus", sed "hoc gradu".

they are established in heaven".[58] Years later, in 1273, when pronouncing the *Collationes in Hexaemeron*, studying the "docta ignorantia", the final stage of wisdom, Bonaventure cited Paul in 2 Cor. 6–10, and added: "Paul taught this wisdom to Dionysius, Timothy and to other perfect ones; he concealed it from the others".[59] Thus, since Hilduin, priest of Saint-Denys, confused the three Dionysiuses, the one converted by Saint Paul, the founder of the Church of Paris and the mysterious author of the *Corpus areopagiticum*, medieval theologians had a great veneration for Dionysius. Who is he? Nobody knows. We suppose he is a writer who lived in the Syrian circles of the first quarter of the VIth century.[60]

The Dionisian problem is two-fold: it is first of literary order: when we encounter a quotation from Pseudo-Dionysius, we have to determine in which version it has come down to us. Five versions exist in fact, and are presented in a parallel edition[61] in the *Dionysiaca*: the version of Hilduin (circa 832: H); that of John Scotus Erigena (circa 867: E); that of John Sarrazin (circa 1167: S); that of Robert Grosseteste (circa 1235: R); finally the *Extractio* of Thomas Gallus (circa 1238: V).

The second problem is doctrinal.[62] Bonaventure cites the work of Dionysius 248 times. The version E appears 31 times, E modified 58 times, E corrected by S 29 times, version S 20 times, S corrected by V twice, E corrected by S and R 3 times and the original version once. The obvious conclusion is that there was in the School of the Friars an original version of the Dionysian Corpus, a version revised at some time between Alexander of Hales and Bonaventure, as

---

[58] Bonaventure, *In II Sent.*, d. 9, prooem. (II, 241): Et dicendum ad hoc, quod magis innitendum est dicto Dionysii, tum quia ipse didicit, sicut dicitur, a Paulo, et ita tradidit sicut audivit; tum quia Gregorius in confirmationem eorum quae de hac materia dicit ipsius auctoritatem; tum etiam quia, sicut ex praedictis patet, Dionysius distinctionem hierarchiarum sumsit penes ea quae sunt ipsis angelicis spiribitus intrinseca et essentialia; et ideo sic ordines distinxit sicut habent collocari in caelis.

[59] Bonaventure, *Hexaem.*, coll. 2, n. 28 (V, 340–341): Quarta facies sapientiae est difficillima, quia est nulliformis, quod videtur destructivum praecedentium, non tamen est. De hac enim dicit Apostolus primae ad Corinthios secundo: Sapientiam loquimur inter perfectos . . . etiam profunda Dei. Hanc sapientiam docuit Paulus Dionysium et Thimotheum et ceteros perfectos, et ab aliis abscondit.

[60] Cf. H. Dondaine, *Le corpus dionysien de l'Université de Paris au XIIIᵉ siècle*, Rome, 1953, 25; G. Thery, *Etudes dionysiennes. I. Hilduin traducteur de Denys*, Paris 1932.

[61] *Dionysiaca*, ed. dom Chevalier, Bruges I, 1937: II, 1950.

[62] Cf. J.G. Bougerol, "Saint Bonaventure et le Pseudo-Denys l'Aréopagite", in J.G. Bougerol, *Saint Bonaventure. Etude sur les sources de sa pensée*, Variorum, Northampton, 1989, 33–123.

Alexander ignores R, while Bonaventure finds it at his disposal and uses it 3 times. At the doctrinal level, it is interesting to analyse one or two texts from each of the Dionysian treatises

De divinis nominibus
DN, c. 4, § 15 (Dionysiaca, 225):

E: We call love be it divine, angelical, intellectual, animal, or natural, a virtue which unites and forms a continuous whole.

S: We call love . . . a virtue which assembles.

Bonaventure cites this text 15 times following version E, except in the sermon *De regno Dei*, n. 21 (V, 544s.), where we found the exact text of version S. The interest of this text lies in that it defines love, or rather loving desire, as a power of unification and connexion which drives superior beings to exercise their providence towards their inferiors, just as it drives those of equal rank to entertain mutual relations, and those who are at the bottom of the scale, to turn towards those who have more strength and are above them. Dionysius, here, gives a glimpse of what he will teach in the *Celestial Hierarchy*.

DN, c. 4, § 1 (Dionysiaca, 146).

As essential Good, it spreads its goodness to all beings.[63]

We know the Latin translation which became widespread in the early XIIIth century: "Bonum diffusivum sui". Who is the author of this version? In trying to go back, starting with Bonaventure, we find Alexander of Hales, William of Auvergne, William of Auxerre and finally Philip the Chancellor in the *Summa de bono*, q. 1.[64] Bonaventure cites the axiom 26 times, 10 times in support of a conclusion or a reflection, eight times in an argument against the given thesis, seven times in an argument for the thesis, once as main argument of a demonstration. We can classify these texts under three headings: some specify the notion of diffusion, others apply the axiom to the trinitarian diffusion, others still apply it to the diffusion of creation. Diffusion is the actual communication of an inherent or infused power. Diffusion in God is not necessary in that, God being the Good, the Good is diffused without God wanting it, but as God is sovereignly fruitful

---

[63] Translation of M. de Gandillac, *Oeuvres complètes du Pseudo-Denys l'Aréopagite*, Paris, 1943, 94.

[64] Philippus Cancellarius, *Summa de bono*, ed. N. Wicki, I, 6: Item de verbis Dionysii, in libro de divinis nominibus, in principio tractatus de bono potest extrahi: Bonum est multiplicativum aut diffusivum esse.

and a fecond source, his sovereign Goodness spreads just like his Wisdom and his Power.

The Trinitarian diffusion is of capital importance in the trinitarian theology of Bonaventure. In God diffusion is sovereign, it produces within God himself the persons by an ever ongoing communication. It is also natural because Goodness in him is his nature, voluntary because in him will and goodness are one and the same reality, liberal because issuing from his will, necessary because God cannot prevent himself from communicating, without end being ever ongoing, perfect because it gives everything to him who can receive it.

As for the diffusion of creation, it issues from the firm will of God to spread his goodness, when as the efficient principle he creates everything in conformity with himself as exemplary cause and for himself as the final cause, bringing back to him all that he created.

Theologia mystica

The most interesting text is from the c. 1, § 1 (*Dionysiaca*, 567–569). It is cited 5 times by Bonaventure. The most complete quotation is in the *Itinerarium*, c. 7, n. 5 (V, 313): "And we should say with Dionysius to God-Trinity: Supra-essential and supra-divine Trinity, eminent guide of Christians to divine wisdom, take us to where the new, absolute and enduring mysteries of God's science are hiding in the radiant darkness, in the midst of silence where his secrets are revealed. Because this profound obscurity is the brightest, the clearest evidence. Thus far for God. But to the friend to whom this is addressed let us say with Dionysius: For you, my friend, strengthen yourself in the ways of mystical contemplation; let your senses work, and the operations of your intelligence, the sensible and the invisible, what is and what is not; and, by this non-knowledge, reintegrate yourself, as much as you can, into the unity of him who surpasses all essence and all science. It is in this limitless detachment of yourself and of the world, in this absolute purity of your soul, that ecstasy will bring you to the supra-essential ray of the divine darkness, bare and free of all ties".[65] This text establishes the foundations of the

---

[65] Bonaventure, *Itin.*, c. 7, n. 5 (V, 313): Dicendo cum Dionysio ad Deum Trinitatem: Trinitas superessentialis et superdeus et superoptime Christianorum inspector theosophiae, dirige nos in mysticorum eloquiorum superincognitum eet superlucentem et sublissimum verticem; ubi nova et absoluta et inconvertibilia theologiae secondum superlucentem absconduntur occulte docentis silentii caliginem in obscurissimo, quod est manifestissimum, supersplendentem, et in qua omne relucet,

"docta ignorantia", which goes beyond contemplation and transcends the sensible world and the soul itself, in a "transitus", a passage in Jesus Christ the Crucified reposing in the sepulchre, leaving behind the operations of intelligence, and transforming in God the "apex affectus", the peak of our affections. This ascension, as Bonaventure notes in the *Hexaemeron*, coll. 2, n. 29–34 (V, 341–342), begins with the assertion: "I attribute to God the best and the highest that I can understand", and ends in the negation: "Love issues from the negation when I say of God: God is not this, or not that, just as he who sculpts a figure does not add anything to the stone, nay, he takes out, and leaves in the stone a noble and beautiful form".

Hierarchia caelestis

Among the Dionysian schemas used by Bonaventure, that of hierarchy is of prime importance. We find it in fact in his trinitarian theology, in angelology, in ecclesiology as well as in spiritual theology; that is, Bonaventure does not hesitate to universalize the hierarchy even more than Dionysius. Bonaventure presents three Dionysian definitions, commenting on them, before summing up his position in the magisterial definition taken from Alexander of Hales. These three definitions are in Dionysius, in the c. 3 of the *Hierarchia caelestis*: c. 3, § 1 (Dionysiaca, 785–786); c. 3, § 2 (Dionysiaca, 787–788), in the order cited by Bonaventure.

The first one defines the uncreated hierarchy: "The hierarchy is the divine beauty, which is simple, perfect, consummated or capable of consummation".[66] Bonaventure, while citing the version E literally, still transforms Dionysius' meaning, because the Areopagite never introduced a definition of uncreated hierarchy to shed light on the notion of celestial hierarchy. He never even used the term "hierarchy" to designate the divinity, but the word "thearchy". It is therefore a deliberate transformation that Bonaventure imposes on the Dionysian text. The commentary he gives, explains even better his intention of

---

et invisibilium superbonorum splendoribus superimplentem invisibiles intellectus. Hoc ad Deum. Ad amicum autem, cui haec scribuntur, dicatur, cum eodem: Tu autem, o amice, circa mysticas visiones, corroborato itinere, et sensus desere et intellectuales operationes et sensibilia et invisibilia et omne non ens et ens, et ad unitatem, ut possibile est, inscius restituere ipsius, qui est super omnem essentiam et scientiam. Etenim te ipso et omnibus immensurabili et absoluto purae mentis excessu, ad superessentialem divinarum tenebrarum radium, omnia deserens et ab omnibus absolutus, ascendes.

[66] Ps.-Dionysius, *Caelestis Hierarchia*, c. 3, § 1 cited in *In II Sent.*, d. 9, praenotata (II, 237).

going further than the trinitarian theology of Dionysius. The Trinity does not prejudge of the unity, nor the unity of the Trinity. But unity is the perfection of Trinity, and Trinity that of unity. In fact, unity in the Trinity is expressed by these words: "The hierarchy is the divine beauty. Now, beauty consists in plurality and equality, as Augustine put it.[67] But plurality does not prejudge of the unity, nor unity of plurality, because unity is such in God that it is at the same time sovereign goodness, source of a perfect communication. Finally, unity is the perfection of plurality and plurality that of unity, which means that the absolute and sovereign perfection resides in Trinity and unity". Bonaventure, therefore, means to chain up the whole universe of the created hierarchies to the divine Hierarchy, as "analogies", in the Dionysian sense.

The second definition given is, in fact, the only one also found in Dionysius: "The hierarchy is the divine order, knowledge and action, resembling God's image as much as possible, and ascending to the divinely conferred illuminations, in proportion to the image of God borne".[68] The way in which Bonaventure presents this definition after he has situated the divine Hierarchy at the top and at the origin of the hierarchical universe, allows him to underline the "egressus" aspect of angelic hierarchy. It "springs" from God as image and resemblance, just as man does. It comes from God in the mode of an image. The theology of the divine appropriations sheds light on this process: as order or ordained power, the angelic hierarchy is brought back to the Father, as knowledge to the Son, and as activity to the Holy Ghost. Bonaventure even adds: according to memory, intelligence and will, thus linking his commentary to the explanation he gave of the Augustinian assignation of the image, *In I Sent.*, d. 3, p. 2, a 1 (I, 80-87). The hierarchy also comes from God by resemblance. It is at the same time a habitus, a stable disposition—deiformity—and an act, the return to God by divine illuminations.

The third definition put forward is in fact the one used by Dionysius himself to describe the purpose of the hierarchy: The hierarchy is, as much as possible, similarity and unity with regard to God (God being the guide of holy knowledge and action); it defines everything in

---

[67] Augustine, *De vera religione*, c. 3, n. 56 (*PL* 34, 46s.)

[68] Pseudo-Dionysius, *C.H.*, c. 3, § 1 (Dionysiaca, 785-786), cited in *In II Sent.*, d. 9, praenotata (II, 237): Hierarchia est ordo divinus, scientia et actio, deiforme quantum possibile similans, et ad inditas ei divinitus illuminationes proportionaliter in Dei similitudinem ascendens.

terms of his divinity; as much as possible, it re-forms those who praise it.[69] Bonaventure, as a matter of fact, does not misinterpret Dionysius' meaning. For Dionysius, it is the purpose of the hierarchy; for Bonaventure it is the "regressus", the return to God. The hierarchy bears in itself this return as a requirement, as a habitus, and lives it in its actuality, led by God. This unchanging return has such a plenitude of grace and charity that its fecundity, its hierarchy can help others.

Gathering all those elements analysed in the three Dionysian texts: hierarchical character of the divine hierarchy, notion of hierarchy in its "egressus" in God, in his image and semblance, in his "regressus" in plenitude to unity, Bonaventure borrows from Alexander of Hales a "quaedam definitio magistralis", coming in fact from Prevostinus of Cremona (ms. Todi 71, f. 91b), cited by William of Auxerre, *Summa aurea*, II, tr. 4, c. 1 (ed. J. Ribaillier, II, 85), taken from William by Alexander of Hales, *Glossa in II Sent.*, d. 9, n. 1 (II, 83), finally repeated by Bonaventure as a magisterial definition: "The hierarchy is an ordained power of sacred and rational realities, which exercises due sovereignty over its subjects".[70]

Hierarchia ecclesiastica, c. 2, § 1 (Dionysiaca, 1106–1107)
Bonaventure cites this text of Dionysius in the version E, *In IV Sent.*, d. 3, p. 1, q. 1, ad 4 (IV, 66), to define the "res sacramenti" of baptism: "What is the principle of the sacred commandments that accompany the sacred act? To form our animal habitus to welcome the divine word and the divine actions so that we are led to celestial rest".[71] This text was copied literally by Bonaventure from Alexander of Hales, *Glossa in IV Sent.*, d. 3, n. 5 (IV, 50). Alexander, and subsequently Bonaventure, greatly modified Dionysius' text. But Alexander was not entirely responsible for the modification, as he himself had borrowed the text from William of Auxerre, *Summa aurea*, IV, tr. 5, c. 2, q. 1 (ed. J. Ribaillier, IV, 77).

---

[69] Ps.-Dionysius, *C.H.*, c. 3, § 2 (*Dionysiaca*, 787–788): Hierarchia est ad Deum, quantum possibile est, similitudo et unitas, ipsum habens scientiae sanctae et actionis ducem, et ad suum divinissimum definiens; quantum vero possibile est, reformat suos laudatores.

[70] Hierarchia est rerum sacrarum et rationabilium ordinata potestas, in subditis debitum retinens principatum.—Cf. J.G. Bougerol, "Saint Bonaventure et la hiérarchie dionysienne", in *AHDLMA* 36 (1956) 131–167.

[71] Ps.-Dionysius, *E.H.*, c. 2, § 1 (*Dionysiaca*, 1106–1107): Quoddam ergo est ad principium sanctissimorum mandatorum sacrae actionis? Ad aliorum divinorum eloquiorum et sacrorum actionum susceptivam opportunitatem formans animales nostros habitus, ad supercaelestis quietis anagogen nostrum iter faciens.

But although Alexander and Bonaventure cite the same text, they comment it very differently. For Alexander the text contains three main points: the soul lives a spiritual life; living spiritually, it can understand and act rightly; this understanding and this right action then lead the soul to celestial rest. But Bonaventure sees in this definition the "res sacramenti" of baptism. This reality is the grace invigorating the soul, and subsequently giving it the power of contemplative virtue. We see here the beginning of Bonaventure's theology of virtues and gifts which lead the soul to wisdom, through grace.

In conclusion, we might say that Bonaventure received from Pseudo-Dionysius a certain spirit which we could call the hierarchical spirit. Although the idea of "egressus" and of "regressus" was not the exclusive property of Bonaventure, as St. Thomas made it the outline of his *Summa Theologica*, it was still Bonaventure who first used this idea as the basis for his metaphysical and theological vision of the relationship between God and his creation.

Dionysius gave Bonaventure a method that was to become totally transformed, because there is far more in Bonaventure than in Dionysius. The Franciscan's theology evolves on three levels: the symbolic level, which teaches the right use of the sensible, the speculative level which teaches the right use of the intelligible, and the mystical level, which takes us towards rapture and ecstasy of the soul. Whereas in the *Breviloquium*, speculative theology is cataphatic or affirmative and founded on necessary reasons, in the *Itinerarium*, symbolic theology is at first cataphatic, grounded on exemplaristic metaphysics, and from chapter 7 onwards, apophatic, that is, negative, seeking to reach intellectual contemplation in so far as possible. From then on, the gift of wisdom introduces the believer to experimental knowledge of sapiential contemplation. Thus Bonaventure systematised Dionysius' thought and used it to show how speculative theology becomes mystical theology.

Dionysius also furnished Bonaventure with some key-concepts of trinitarian theology, that of transcendence in particular. But Scriptures and the Masters (Augustine, Anselm, Richard of Saint-Victor) make Bonaventure go beyond the static and apophatic contemplation of Dionysius, to reach an essentially dynamic synthesis of God's Trinity, with the Father a spring of life and basic plenitude, and the Word incarnate a unique Mediator because of being the median person in the Trinity. Dionysius' christology thus underwent an important transformation, as is shown by the text we are about to cite, and which could *prima facie* come from Dionysius. However, Bonaventure takes it, in fact, from Augustine, *De vera religione*, because it perfectly illustrates his thought, in *In I Sent.*, d. 27, p. 2, a. 1, ad 5 (I, 486): "The Father is the principle to which we are driven back, the Son, the form we imitate, the Spirit, the grace which reconciles us".[72]

We saw how Bonaventure constructed his treatise on angels by founding it on Dionysius, but profoundly transforming the latter's doctrine, stressing the correlation of the celestial and the terrestrial Church.[73] Similarly, Bonaventure's ecclesiology, in its hierarchical construction, depends very much on Pseudo-Dionysius. However, unlike Pseudo-Dionysius, Bonaventure introduces a theology of history into the framework of his otherwise non-historical ecclesiastical hierarchy, by saying in *In IV Sent.*, d. 24, p. 2, a. 2, q. 4, concl. (IV, 635): "The kingdom of the Church is brought to God the Father by the Son and the Holy Spirit, when it is reduced to the supreme unity of the Father, after which it can rise no higher".

Finally, Bonaventure's spiritual theology also seems to have been very much marked by the Dionysian notion of the hierarchical acts, or spiritual ways. However, here too Bonaventure shows himself to be the master of his sources, in the way he uses Dionysius in his conception of return to God. Neither Hugh of Saint-Victor, nor even Robert Grosseteste, had admitted the coexistence of the three ways of the soul. Bonaventure, on the contrary, can conceive of them only as degrees of assimilation to God. For him, the divinisation of man is a dynamic process in which are constantly combined the three hierarchical acts until peace, truth and charity reach perfect unity in the Spirit. It would certainly be possible to prove that the *De triplici via* constitutes a more authentic comprehension of Dionysius than that of Hugh of Saint-Victor or Robert Grosseteste.[74]

As Bonaventure stresses in *De reductione artium ad theologiam*, Richard of Saint-Victor too is Dionysius' heir, so that the transformation, that

---

[72] Cf. Augustine, *De vera religione*, c. 55, n. 113 (*PL* 34, 172): Pater est principium ad quod reducimur; Filius forma quam sequimur; Spiritus sanctus gratia qua reconciliamur.

[73] Cf. Y. Congar, "Aspects ecclésiologiques de la querelle entre mendiants et séculiers dans la seconde moitié du XIIIᵉ siècle et le début du XIVᵉ", in *AHDLMA* 28 (1961) 115–127.

[74] Cf. R. Roques, "Denys", in *Dict. Spir.*, 281; V. Lossky, *La notion des analogies chez Denys le pseudo-Aréopagite*, in *AHDLMA* 5 (1930) 279–309.

he, Bonaventure imposes on the Dionysian thought is facilitated by the contribution of Augustine, Anselm, Bernard of Clairvaux, as well as the Victorines, Hugh and Richard. The authority which the Middle Ages granted to Pseudo-Dionysius has, as we saw, no sound historical basis; however, it is a fact we should consider in researching Bonaventure's sources. It is also a fact the value of which should not be underestimated. Dionysius gave to the Middle Ages, poor in Latin versions of Plato, the opportunity of getting into contact with the platonism of Plotinus, Proclus and Iamblicus. He also transmitted in his theology the best of the Greek Fathers, from Basil to Gregory of Nyssa.

Saint Anselm

It has been said that Bonaventure seems to have been the best commentator of Saint Anselm.[75] If this is so, the question we should ask is: what influence did Saint Anselm have on Bonaventure?

Saint Anselm was a metaphysician of Christian dogma. The time in which he wrote, 1069–1109, the environment in which he lived, are crucial for our understanding of him. His departure from the Abbey of Bec for Canterbury in 1093 might explain why his work did not become influential for some time. The importance he assigns to reason in the understanding of faith, "fides quaerens intellectum"— the very title of the *Proslogion*—, his attachment to the Augustinian tradition, as well as his open-minded attitude towards the problems of his time, made him into a pioneer. Even though he never considered writing a theological *summa*, the monographs he wrote and re-wrote form a whole.

Anselm finally emerged in the early 13th century, thanks to Philip the Chancellor. Some, e.g. Alexander of Hales, Bonaventure and the Franciscan masters up until John Duns Scotus, welcomed him as an "authority", others, e.g. Tomas Aquinas, detested his "rationes necessariae" and contested the importance of the argument developed in the *Proslogion*. The attachment of the "pro-Anselmians" to the spirit of Platonism, and of the "anti-Anselmians" to Aristotle, partly accounted for their attitude. Until Kant and Karl Barth, Anselm was to remain subject either to admiration or to sharp criticism.

---

[75] P. Rousseau, *Oeuvres philosophiques de saint Anselme*, Paris, 1947, 36.

Bonaventure took 274 quotations from Anselm. It is little, compared to the 461 he took from Bernard. But the analysis of these borrowings shows that the influence of Anselm on Bonaventure is extremely important, far more so than that of Aristotle. The most cited work is *De conceptu virginali* from which Bonaventure drew a doctrinal complement on rectitude of the will and the notion of justice on as many as 49 occasions. The *Cur Deus homo* appears 48 times in the treatise of Incarnation-Redemption. Although the *Monologion* is cited only 28 times and the *Proslogion* 25 times, these two treatises were of very great importance to Bonaventure.

The *Monologion* appears in a variety of passages, especially in the *In I Sent.*, d. 27, where Anselm is cited 5 times in question 1, where Bonaventure justifies the place he gives to the Word in relation to creation: "Because the Word exists in God, the creation can exist as word 'ad extra', an image of the Son".[76]

The *Proslogion* is favoured by Bonaventure. Eight times, he cites the chapters 26–28 and he makes them into the conclusion to the *Breviloquium*, the *Soliloquium* and *De perfectione vitae ad sorores*. But the main idea borrowed from Anselm is the ontological argument on which Bonaventure founds his doctrine of the evidence of God's existence, in the lecture *In I Sent.*, d. 8 and in the *Quaestiones disputatae de mysterio Trinitatis*, q. 1, a. 1.

Thus three specific topics in Bonaventure's work witness the influence of Anselm: the "necessary reasons", the concept of rectitude and the Anselmian ontological argument.

The concept of "necessary reasons" means that theological knowledge differs from simple knowledge of faith in that it looks for the intelligiblity of the realities, which faith reveals. This intervention of reason wants, first, to make explicit what was implicit, by deducing theological conclusions from the articles of faith; secondly, it wants to prove, that is, make intelligible, these same articles of faith by means of reasons or analogies.

It is possible to have knowledge of and faith in one and the same proposition. Theology or theological reasoning does not supplant faith, which has still to assent, with all the difficulties and virtues that this entails. However, rational arguments, scientific demonstrations and

---

[76] Cf. A. Gerken, *La théologie du Verbe*, French tr., Paris 1970, 67; *ibid.*, 58–83, the development of these texts in *In I Sent.*, d. 27, p. 2, to which are added those of the *Quaestiones disputatae de mysterio Trinitatis* and of the *Collationes in Hexaemeron*.

the knowledge arising from them are all compatible with faith. We thus find in the *Breviloquium* a magisterial demonstration of the argument by necessary reasons, designed to bring about the understanding of faith. The terms used show it clearly: *Ratio autem ad haec intelligendum haec est*... In accord with his basic intention, Bonaventure does not leave the realm of faith. The Scriptures teach us that God is the first principle. This we believe with certitude by the faith infused in our hearts. The authority of God who reveals who he is, gives our faith an infallible certitude, on which reason builds so as to aquire a further understanding of faith. Of course, the conclusion to which we are thus led is the work of reason working within faith, but it is first of all the work of reason, so that the conclusion reached does not stem from infallibility of faith. The theologian is fallible. To remain truthful and eliminate all risk of error, he has to be absolutely rigorous. Advancing step by step, acquiring a better understanding as he progresses, he may not deduce from revealed truth more than it contains.

We could cite every chapter of the *Breviloquium*, because in each the starting point of the explanation is the article of faith: God is the first principle. Each deduction made by Bonaventure, until the very last, is attached to the preceding one as part of the process of understanding.

This dialectic constitutes a blend of intuitive knowledge and rigorous logic. On the one hand, the connexion perceived by the believing mind between the successive steps in the chain is a priori intelligible, due to the light of faith infused in us by our inner Master. On the other hand, reason exercised by a long period of training in grammar and logic aids this intuitive knowledge by its rigour.

The audacity of this endeavour makes for the originality of the *Breviloquium*. No theologian before Bonaventure had attempted to build a synthesis of theology on this dialectical model. Saint Anselm had got no further than perfecting a *method* of demonstration which we find in Bonaventure, not only in vocabulary, but also in the internal structure, even though the Anselmian axioms are in some respects different from those of the *Breviloquium*. "Convenientia", "necessitas", "rationes necessariae", are Anselm's words taken over by Bonaventure, while the terms "concatenatio", "contextio" (that is, the chains of reasons) do not appear under Bonaventure's pen.

We could also find some connexion between the deep intention of the *Breviloquium* and the terms in which Saint Anselm presented *Cur*

Deus homo to Urban II.[77] However, Bonaventure came more than one hundred years after Anselm. The *Fides quaerens intellectum* of Anselm certainly found a resonance in him, but Anselm never set out to demonstrate faith in the way Bonaventure did. Bonaventure went further than Anselm, and, reaching in the *Breviloquium* the culmination of the analogy of faith, he situated his dialectic beyond the realm of philosophy and in the realm of faith. The light of faith could not supply e.g. the rational arguments for God's existence but it could exercise a regulative function in philosophical dialectics.

The Notion of Rectitude

The notion of rectitude appears often in Bonaventure's work, but the text of the *prooemium* of *In II Sent.* seems to be the most significant here: "It is obvious that God not only made man capable of attaining rectitude by giving him His image, but He made him upright (*rectus*) by directing him towards Himself. Man finally attains to rectitude, when his will conforms to the sovereign goodness by love, and his merit becomes an extension of the sovereign power, by an act. This is accomplished when man turns to God by and in his whole self".[78] Bonaventure develops this theme, taking each of the three elements of the conversion, the three being (1) man's understanding of the absolute truth, (2) the conforming of the human will to the absolute goodness, by love, (3) merit becoming an extension of the divine (absolute) power by an act. Beatitude is the end: "This will happen in glory when our merit rejoins the divine merit. Then we will be the all-powerful masters of our will, just as God is master of his: we will be kings. This is why to all men is promised the kingdom of heaven".[79] Of course, sin deprived man of this three-fold rectitude.[80]

---

[77] Cf. R. Roques, "La méthode du Cur Deus homo de saint Anselme de Cantorbery", in *Structures théologiques de la Gnose à Richard de Saint-Victor*, Paris 1962, 243–293.

[78] Bonaventure, *In II Sent.*, prooem. (II, 4): In hoc verbo ostenditur, quod Deus non tantum fecit hominem possibilem ad rectitudinem, suam ei imaginem conferendo, sed etiam fecit hominem rectum, ipsum ad se convertendo. Tunc enim homo rectus est, quando intelligentia adaequatur summae veritati in cognoscendo, voluntas conformatur summae bonitati in diligendo, et virtus continuatur summae potestati in operando. Hoc autem, quando homo ad Deum convertitur ex se toto.

[79] Bonaventure, *In II Sent.*, prooem. (II, 4): Hoc erit in gloria, quando virtus nostra continuabitur divinae virtuti; tunc erimus omnipotentes voluntatis nostrae, sicut et Deus suae, et ideo omnes reges; et ideo omnibus promittitur regnum caelorum.

[80] Bonaventure, *Brevil.*, p. 3, c. 5, n. 2 (V, 234).

The return to God consists therefore in this "rectificatio", that is, the ordering of our powers towards their proper end.[81]

Anselm's Argument

The third Anselmian theme, probably the most important in Bonaventure's thought, is, as we said, the ontological argument of the *Proslogion*. Bonaventure was familiar with Anselm's work when he started his reading of the *Sentences* as bachelor during the school year of 1250–1251. The order in which he "read" Lombard was: I, IV, II, III.[82] The first four questions *De scientia Christi* were the "inceptio" of Bonaventure as *licentiatus* during the first part of the year 1253–1254. The questions disputed in *De mysterio Trinitatis* followed during year 1254–1255. And all these works, read or disputed, show how well Bonaventure knew Anselm.

The most important text is the *lectura* of *In I. Sent.*, d. 8, p. 1, where article 1 is devoted to the truth of God. In the q. 1, the foundations on which the demonstration is constructed are taken from Augustine and Anselm. But the conclusion will take shape in two stages, as Bonaventure makes a separate exegesis of the two authorities. Following Augustine, he concludes that truth is the property of God only in the sense that only in God there is pure indivision without the blend of any diversity, only in God there is pure imitation and resemblance without the admixture of any dissemblance, only in God there is the sovereign expression of light without darkness. We have here the idea of truth as taught by Augustine.

Following Anselm now, and in a very different mode, his exegesis of *De veritate* leads Bonaventure to say that the word "true" can be used only with respect to the exemplary cause, just as that of the word "good" can be used only in relation to the final cause. This is why all created truth is true, not in its essence, but by its participation in the uncreated truth. It is under the influence of the sovereign light that true things find their voice. If the divine light stopped its

---

[81] Bonaventure, *In III Sent.*, d. 34, p. 1, a. 2, ad 4 (III, 749): Rectitudo enim consistit in ordine potentiae ad obiectum.

[82] Cf. B. Distelbrink, "De ordine chronologico IV Librorum Commentarii S. Bonaventurae", in *Coll. Franc.* 41 (1971) 288–314; I. Brady, "The Opera omnia of Saint Bonaventure" (1882–1902), in Il *Collegio S. Bonaventura di Quaracchi*, Grottaferrata 1977, 132–134.

influence, all the other beings would also lose their truth. Truth is therefore the property of the divine essence because it is appropriate only to the divine essence, which is its sole *raison d'être*. This is why essence is not a property of truth. This is inherent to our human language and to the "modi significandi". Essence and truth do not mean the same thing. Essence tells us what a thing is, truth tells us the condition in which it is in relation to God. Of course truth and essence are one and the same in God but they are not synonyms for men, retaining their fundamental distinction in human thought and language. Just as created truth is the property of and reason for the knowledge of created essence, uncreated truth, in our thought and in our language, is the reason for the meaning of and the knowledge of uncreated essence. There is thus a close link between logical and ontological reality, for Anselm as well as for Bonaventure.

Thus Bonaventure can tackle the question 2. Foundation 1 is taken from the *Proslogion*, c. 2: "God, according to the common principle, is a being greater than which cannot be thought. Yet, what cannot be thought as not being, is greater than what can be thought as not being. Therefore as nothing can be thought greater than God, the divine being is such that He cannot be thought as not being".[83] And the foundation 4 confirms the argument of Anselm: "Our intellect can seize nothing otherwise than by the light and with the aid of the first truth: therefore all act of the intellect thinking that something is not is due to the first light. Yet under the influence of this primary light, we cannot think that this very light or primary truth does not exist. Therefore in no way can we think that the primary truth is not".[84]

It would seem that this *fundamentum* constitutes an epistemological support to the ontological argument. The conclusion makes everything appear self-evident. The fool thinks falsely that the divine being is not. But besides this extreme case, man can be blinded or ignorant, so that his knowledge God fails; and he can suddenly find

---

[83] Bonaventure, *In I Sent.*, d. 8, p. 1, a. 1, q. 2, fund. 1 (I, 153): Deus secundum communem animi conceptionem est quo nihil maius cogitari potest; sed maius est quod non potest cogitari non esse, quam quod potest; ergo cum Deo nihil maius cogitari possit, divinum esse ita est, quod non potest cogitari non esse.

[84] Bonaventure, *In I Sent.*, d. 8, p. 1, a. 1, q. 2, fund. 4 (I, 153): Intellectus noster nihil intelligit nisi per primam lucem et veritatem, ergo omnis actio intellectus, quae est in cogitando aliquid non esse, est per primam lucem; sed per primam lucem non contingit cogitare, non esse primam lucem sive veritatem: ergo nullo modo contingit cogitare, primam veritatem non esse.

himself not knowing *who* God is. However, he cannot not know that God is. Yet because he fails often in the knowledge of who God is, he thinks that God is what he is not, for example an idol, or that God is not what he is, for example a just God. Thus by denying that beatitude is in God, we deny His existence.

Man's knowledge can also be deficient because its object is not knowable, either because it is not always present, or because it is not everywhere, or because it is not present completely. What is not always is sometimes and sometimes is not and therefore it sometimes can be thought as non-existent. Also, what is present in part is in part absent. Yet God is always, he is everywhere and, as a whole, always and everywhere. He can therefore not be thought as non-existent.

The un-knowability of something can be due to lack of evidence. Yet the truth of the divine being is obvious, because when we know the terms of the first principle, we know the principle too. In this sort of proposition the predicate is included in the subject: God or the sovereign truth is Being itself such that we cannot conceive of better: therefore he cannot not be, nor be thought not to be, because the predicate (existence) is included in the subject (God).

Furthermore, the existence of the divine being is an obvious conclusion of any demonstration, given that all created truth proves the existence of divine truth, because if there exists a being by participation, then it follows that there is a being by or in essence. Moreover, all correct knowledge includes innate knowledge of God, because all knowledge is knowledge only due to there being divine truth.

We must concede that the truth of the divine being is such that the latter cannot be thought as non-existent, unless we do not know what "God" means. The question 1 of the *De mysterio Trinitatis* tackles the problem in a more systematic and mature way: The truth of the existence of God is incontrovertibly self-evident, because it is the first truth and sovereignly immediate. Existence which is attributed to the subject is absolutely identical with it. This is why, just as no intelligence can think that the same being can exist and not exist at the same time, the division of what is perfectly one and indivisible eludes our power of reason in the same way. Just as it is evidently false to say that the same being is and is not at the same time, or that the being which is Being itself does not exist, it is evidently true to say that the primary and supreme being does exist.[85]

---

[85] Bonaventure, *De myst. Trinitatis*, q. 1, a. 1, concl. (V, 49). Cf J. Chatillon, "De

The profound sympathy between Anselm and Bonaventure is to do with the identity of their reasoning: neither Anselm nor Bonaventure went directly from *the idea* to *being*, because in their eyes, the idea is no more than the mode of presence of being in thought. God's knowability helps our intellect to acquire knowledge of it, all the more so as it is not something external to our powers of knowledge that we have to perceive like any other object, but something intrinsic to our capacity to know, its very source, one might say. That such a process can take place only within the context of faith was obvious to Anselm as it was to Bonaventure: to contemplate God perfectly, the intellect and the heart had to be purified by faith which makes man just. Faith purifies the intellect just as justice purifies the heart.

Bernard of Clairvaux

One century separates Bernard of Clairvaux and Saint Bonaventure. Bernard was born in 1090 and died in 1153. Bonaventure, born in 1217, died in 1274. In the course of one century Christian thought underwent a drastic change. The powerful personality of Bernard dominated for some time the religious revival of the 12th century. One century later, he is an "authority" whose texts are transmitted through the masters.

How did Bonaventure see Bernard? Bernard preferred wisdom to science and condemned all curiosity in men of God. He was imbued by the Scriptures, which gave a great elegance to his style. Bonaventure was sensitive both to the goal pursued by Bernard and to the means he had used to attain it. For Bonaventure, to understand the mystery of Christ amounts to three points, all to be found in the Scriptures: eternal generation and the incarnation of Christ, the rule of life, and finally the union of the soul with God. The effort of the doctors must concentrate on the first point, that of preachers on the second, that of contemplation on the third. Generation and incarnation of Christ was covered mainly by Augustine, the rule of life by Gregory, and the union of the soul with God by Dionysius. Augustine's successor was Anselm, Gregory's Bernard, and Dionysius' Richard of

Guillaume d'Auxerre à saint Thomas d'Aquin. L'argument de saint Anselme chez les premiers scolastiques du XIIIe siècle", in *Spicilegium Beccense*, Paris 1959, 209–231.

St. Victor; Anselm was master of reasoning, Bernard of preaching, and Richard of contemplation. As for Hugh of St. Victor, he excelled in all three disciplines.[86] Thus for Bonaventure, Bernard was first of all a preacher teaching the rule of life. We notice that this latter term covers a multitude of meanings for Bonaventure. The preacher, in fact, must not only speak about what he sees or hears from Jesus Christ, but also listen to the Spirit talking to his heart. The doctrine he preaches must stem both from his reflection and his spiritual experience and, so that his words have the power to convince, he must testify by his life the truth of what he says. The knowledge which moves his intelligence, the elegance with which he speaks, life-experience which accords with knowledge and rhetoric, are the three qualities indispensable to him who wants to preach God's Word.[87] To preach without knowing what should be said is dangerous, to say it without elegance is inefficient, to preach without practising is contemptible.

The main works of Bernard cited or referred to by Bonaventure are the following: first the *Sermones de Tempore et de sanctis* cited 99 times, of which the sermon *In dom. oct. Assumptionis* alone is cited 15 times. Then come the sermons *In laudibus Virginis Mariae*, otherwise called the *Super Missus est*, which yield 49 quotations, including 48 textual ones. The sermons *De diversis* offer 17 quotations and the sermons *Super Cantica* appear 102 times. It should be remarked that the latter are never cited in the sermons on Mary by Bonaventure, because Bernard's sermons *Super Cantica* are not mariological. The themes in Bernard's *Super Cantica* that interest Bonaventure are those of image (10 times) and humility (12 times).[88]

As for the didactical opuscules of Bernard, they too are variously cited: the *De gradibus humilitatis* is important in the theme of evangelical perfection (16 quotations), the *De diligendo Deo*, cited 13 times in the central text of c. 7, n. 17—twice in *In II Sent.*, d. 26 and d. 27—

---

[86] Cf. Bonaventure, *De reductione artium ad theologiam*, n. 5 (V, 321): Unde tota sacra Scriptura haec tria docet, scilicet Christi aeternam generationem et incarnationem, vivendi ordinem et Dei et animae unionem. Primum respicit fidem, secundum mores, tertium finem utriusque. Circa primum insudare debet studium doctorum, circa secundum studium praedicatorum, circa tertium studium contemplativorum. Anselmus sequitur Augustinum, Bernardus sequitur Gregorium, Richardus sequitur Dionysium, auique Anselmus in ratiocinatione, Bernardus in praedicatione, Richardus in contemplatione. Hugo vero omnia haec.

[87] Cf. *Sermo 22 Pent.*, n. 1 (ed. J.G. Bougerol, *Sermones dominicales*, 467).

[88] Cf. J.G. Bougerol, "Saint Bonaventure et saint Bernard", in *Variorum*, IV 3–79.

was remarkably well commented on by E. Gilson.[89] The *De gratia et libero arbitrio* is cited 32 times, including 22 times in the *In II Sent.*, and twice in the *In IV Sent.* The *De consideratione* appears only 52 times, the *Epistolae* 47 times.

Bonaventure came to know the works of Saint Bernard already in his university period, and he knew them better than his predecessors. The presence of textual quotations from Bernard in otherwise undated sermons by Bonaventure indicates by and large that they date from before 1257.

The main themes that Bonaventure takes from Bernard are: image, love, humility and mariology. The image theme is treated by Bonaventure with great freedom, given that the positions of the two theologians on the issue are very dissimilar: Bernard founds the image in free will, while Bonaventure takes as its foundation the tripartite soul.

In expounding his doctrine of love-charity, Bonaventure takes his basic ideas from William of Saint-Thierry, whose works he knew under the name of Bernard.[90] It is significant to notice that the fundamental quotations are taken from the *De Contemplando Deo*, the *De natura et dignitate amoris* and the *Epistola ad Fratres de Monte Dei*, all works by William. But many of Bernard's own expressions are to be found in Bonaventure, such as "curvitas", "condescensio", "dignatio".

The most important theme seems to be that of humility, foundation of evangelical perfection. The first of the *Questiones disputatae de perfectione evangelica*, q. 1 *De humilitate quoad actum ipsius* (V, 117–124) is founded on Bernard, including the definition of humility: "Humility is the virtue by which man despises himself in the very true knowledge of himself".[91]

On the theme of free will Bonaventure constructs his own system taking Bernard as a starting point: free will is an habitus of the soul, conjunction of reason and will, and having power over the acts of both capacities as an arbiter between two parties. Three authorities are cited to support Bonaventure: Augustine, Anselm and Bernard.

Bonaventure's mariology owes a great deal to Bernard, even though the latter could be accused of preventing Bonaventure from accept-

---

[89] Cf. E. Gilson, *La théologie mystique de saint Bernard*, 72 and note 1.

[90] Cf. J.G. Bougerol, "Saint Bonaventure et Guillaume de Saint-Thierry", in *Antonianum* 46 (1971) 298–321.

[91] Cf. Bonaventure, *De perfectione evangelica*, q. 1 (V, 117): Humilitas est virtus qua homo verissima sui cognitione sibi vilescit.

ing Augustine and Anselm on the question of sanctification of the Virgin Mary.[92]

In conclusion, we might say that Bonaventure discovered in Bernard the theologian he wished to become himself: profoundly influenced by the Bible, looking there first for the answer to the problems he posed himself or was given to solve, deeply aware, also, that theology must help man not to know more, but to love better.

Among the themes which our analysis allowed us to group together, there is one whose absence we can deplore, that of paschal love, central to Bernard's mystical theology. This is a fact, but we should not conclude too readily that Bonaventure rejected the doctrine. The absence could simply be due to a difference of theological context.

Bonaventure finds in Bernard a congenial spirit. He is happy to discover in his works admirable phrases, delightful in their spiritual depth and elegance of their expression. Bonaventure, far from being insensitive to the charms of language, knows that the rigour which he endlessly strives for can be allied to the beauty of form. He praises Bernard for it, because he himself admires it.

More precisely still, Bonaventure finds in Bernard not a justification of the specific vocation for the Franciscan life, but a justification of the evangelical renewal of which the Franciscan vocation is an original and concrete expression. In taking from Bernard the foundations of evangelical perfection, Bonaventure marks an important stage in the development of evangelical life of the Church.

The Victorines

The School of Saint-Victor, founded in the early XIIth century by William of Champeaux near the river Seine, at the gates of medieval Paris, kept during its too short existence an open mind and a unity of aspiration, which is what made it influential. It marked and conditioned, one century later, the first Franciscan School of Paris and gave it its own tone, with the arrival of Alexander of Hales among the Friars minor.

The history of how Alexander of Hales came to Paris to obtain

---

[92] Cf. J.G. Bougerol, "Saint Bonaventure et saint Bernard", 62–64. The problem emerges mainly in *In III Sent.*, d. 3, p. 1, q. 1–3 (III, 61–72).

his degrees at the Arts Faculty, probably also the Faculty of canon law and the Faculty of theology remains to be written. However, we know that in 1147–1148, Pope Eugene III had reformed the Saint-Genevieve abbey and had left it in the care of ten Saint-Victor monks under the guidance of prior Odo. It would seem that the chair of theology was also transferred to Mount Saint-Geneviève.[93] Was Alexander of Hales the student of Thomas Gallus between 1209 and 1218 (until Thomas left for Vercelli), before he took over the chair himself, becoming the first-ever lecturer on the *Sentences* of Peter Lombard (1223–1127) as well as disputing the *Quaestiones antequam esset frater* (1220–1236)? Did he deprive the School of Saint-Victor of the chair by becoming a Franciscan? The fact is that Gregory IX, in a bull dated 26 January 1237 in Terni, gave the abbey the right to open a theology school.[94]

What appears certain is the importance of the Victorines in the published work of Alexander of Hales. The *Glossa* cites Hugh 72 times, Richard 56 times; the *Quaestiones* call upon Hugh 39 times and Richard 22 times. As for the *Summa fratris Alexandri*, the first three books cite Hugh 346 times and Richard 142 times.

The analysis of the quotations from Hugh and Richard in the work of Bonaventure shows that there is almost complete continuity between the Victorines and the School of the Friars minor during the first twenty years of the latter's existence.

Hugh of Saint-Victor

Among the works of Hugh, Bonaventure cites the main ones, namely: *Didascalion de studio legendi, In Hierarchiam caelestem, De sacramentis christianae fidei, De arrha animae, De quatuor voluntatibus in Christo, In Ecclesiasten.*

Didascalion de studio legendi (*PL* 176, 739–838; ed. F.X. Buttimer, Washington 1939)
Bonaventure recommends the reading of the *Didascalion*: If you want to know fully how to study, read the *Didascalion* of Hugh.[95] F. Delorme's edition of the *Collationes in Hexaemeron* mentions three quotations from

---

[93] Cf. Fourier Bonnard, *Histoire de l'Abbaye royale et de l'Ordre des Chanoines réguliers de Saint-Victor de Paris*, Paris 1904, I, 160–170.

[94] Cf. *Chart. Univ. Paris.*, I, n. 111, p. 159.

[95] Bonaventure, *Hexaem.*, ed. F. Delorme, visio 3, coll. 4, n. 7 (181–182): Si vis ad plenum scire studendi modum, lege librum Hugonis, Didascalicon.

the *Didascalion*. But it is mainly the *De reductione artium ad theologiam* which makes use of the *Didascalion*, even though it modifies greatly its classification, its spirit and its aim.[96] Sermons seem to depend on the *Didascalion* as much as on Richard's *Liber exceptionum*.[97]

In Hierarchiam caelestem (PL 176, 923–1154)

The most important quotation is to be found in *In III Sent.*, d. 14, a. 1, q. 3, concl. (III, 304); it deals with the question, much debated at the time, of whether Christ's soul, as that of the blessed, sees God's face in eternal light or in some inferior, intermediate light. The question is treated by Bonaventure in Book III, where he goes more deeply into explaining the content and mode of Christ's human knowledge, relying also on the *Glossa* of Alexander and on the *lectura* of Eudes Rigaud. In his "determinatio", he combats the opinion of those who refuse to admit that a creature can have vision of God, and cites Gregory's *Moralia in Iob*, XVIII, c. 54, n. 90 (*PL* 76, 93) in support of his view. Others, whom Bonaventure calls "moderniores", even though they assert the realisation of God's vision, still assert that the radiance of eternal light is attenuated by the mediation of theophanies. Against their assertions Bonaventure cites Hugh's text.[98]

De sacramentis christianae fidei (PL 176, 173–618)

The *De sacramentis* constitutes the main source upon which Bonaventure drew, thus following the example of his masters. 155 quotations are distributed as follows: 5 in *In I Sent.*, 38 in *In II Sent.*, 22 in *In III Sent.*, 86 in *In IV Sent.*, 4 in the *Quaest. disputatae de mysterio Trinitatis*, 4 in the *Breviloquium*, one each in the sermon *Unus est Magister*, in *In Ioannem*, in *In Lucam*, and in two other sermons. Often, Bonaventure makes criticisms or goes beyond Hugh's opinions.

In the treatise on faith, *In III Sent.*, d. 23, a. 1, q. 1, arg. 1 (III, 470), Bonaventure borrows from Hugh his definition of faith: "Faith is the evidence of things not seen, beyond opinion and below science",[99] and this definition is to be found three times. But the largest number of borrowings is to be found in the *In IV Sent.*

---

[96] Cf. *De red. art. ad theol.*, ed. P. Michaud-Quantin, Paris 1971, 11–23.

[97] Cf. *Sermones de Tempore*, ed. J.G. Bougerol, Paris 1990, *Sermo 155*, 219–221. In n. 8, we read: Mulier haec significat animam rationalem quae habet decem drachmas, id est novem partes scientiae philosophicae et decima drachma est sapientia divina, scilicet sacra theologia.

[98] Cf. H.F. Dondaine, "L'objet et le médium de la vision béatifique chez les théologiens du XIIIe siècle", in *RTAM* 19 (1952) 60–130.

[99] Hugo, *De sacramentis*, I, p. 10, c. 2 (*PL* 176, 330C): Fides est certitudo de rebus absentibus, supra opinionem et infra scientiam constituta.

De arrha animae (*PL* 176, 951–970)

To define and deepen his vision of love Bonaventure preferred the thought of Hugh of Saint-Victor to that of Bernard. Five times we find the definition: I know, O my soul, that love is your life. That love is a transforming force is to be found 6 times. That it unites him who loves to the loved one is found 5 times. That love is the only possible response to love, once. Finally, married love is defined five times, but not in the sense intended by Bernard: "O my soul, if you would deign to conceive how arrogant are those round you who have not deserved to put into action the grace given to them. Because he has chosen you above all the others, he who is your spouse, your loved one".

De quatuor voluntatibus in Christo (*PL* 176, 841–846)

This very short opuscule gives Bonaventure the occasion to give an interpretation of Hugh's position. How many wills does Christ have? John of Damascus counts two of them, a divine will and a human will. Peter Lombard counts three, according to the powers of willing: divine, rational, pertaining to the senses. Hugh distinguishes four wills according to the mode of willing: divine will, the will of reason, the will of piety, the will of the flesh.

In Ecclesiasten (*PL* 175, 113–126)

When writing his *Commentary* on *Ecclesiastes*, Bonaventure seems to have had Hugh's open before him. He is charmed by the beauty of the language and the depth of the thought. He cites this admirable phrase from the second homily (*PL* 175, 142D): "All beauty, all joy, all sweetness of created things can affect the human heart, but none can satisfy it, only the sweetness for which it is created". He repeats this idea in the *Soliloquium*, c. 1, n. 6 (VIII, 31).

In conclusion, we can say that for Bonaventure, the master Hugh of Saint-Victor is master of reasoning, of preaching and of contemplation. It is from him that Bonaventure learned to measure the importance of wisdom.[100] We have underlined the links between the two masters. It is certain that Bonaventure took from *De sacramentis* a great deal more than just the odd notion or general idea. He was above all sensitive to the dynamic nature of Hugh's exposition of doctrine, very far removed from the rigidity of Peter Lombard. For Hugh,

---

[100] Cf. R. Baron, *Science et sagesse chez Hugues de Saint-Victor*, Paris, 1957.

christianity is above all a living narrative. We find the same conception in the *Breviloquium* and even more explicitly, in the *Hexaemeron*.

Richard of Saint-Victor

The importance of Richard is of a different order. He is the master of contemplation. His speculative mysticism entices Bonaventure, who cites the *De Trinitate* 35 times, a figure which belies the importance of the treatise for the Franciscan.

De Trinitate (*PL* 176, 887–994; ed. J. Ribaillier, Paris 1958)
Richard's treatise, I, c. 2 (ed. J. Ribaillier 875–882) is cited in the *De mysterio Trinitatis*, q. 1, a. 2, concl. (V, 56b), including the fundamental text: "We hold on to nothing more constantly than to that which we learn through faith". Richard is also the source for Bonaventure's exposition of the distinctness of the divine person. In God, the persons are distinguished by origin, in angels by quality, in mankind by origin and quality. The notion of origin which Alexander of Hales also insisted on, provides the basis for Bonaventure's doctrine of the Trinity.

Alexander of Hales drew from the *De Trinitate* of Richard of Saint-Victor the essential part of his teaching, and the early Franciscan school continued to pay the same respect and the same attention to the Victorine master. Bonaventure, by dividing each of his questions in *De mysterio Trinitatis* into two articles so as to establish how the Trinity of persons accords with the unity of substance, and with attributes such as simplicity, infinity, eternity and primacy, obviously follows Richard of Saint-Victor.

General Conclusion

Hans Urs von Balthasar, wanting to stress the importance of Bonaventure in the long history of the search for God, says that he is the "lieu privilégié de convergence et de confluence de tous les courants et de toutes les conceptions du monde qui, de tous côtés, irriguent et fécondent le milieu du treizième siècle".[101] Bonaventure is indeed a focus of confluence and convergence. Not one of the theologians who

---

[101] Cf. H. Urs von Balthasar, *La gloire et la croix*, II, 328.

had a share in the construction of his doctrines is to be found there *qua* himself, so great is the unifying power which allowed Bonaventure to attain to the supreme simplicity of his own system of thought. This unifying power, is, we would like to claim, none other than that of Francis of Assisi.[102]

Transl. Pascale Renaud

Select Bibliography

Primary Sources

Magistri Alexandri de Hales, *Glossa in quatuor Libros Sententiarum Petri Lombardi*, I–IV, Quaracchi, 1951–1957.
—, *Quaestiones disputatae antequam esset frater*, I–III, Quaracchi, 1960.
Summa fratris Alexandri, I–VI, Quaracchi, 1924–79, 6 vols.
—, Tom. IV. *Prolegomena*, ed. V. Doucet, Quaracchi, 1948.
Biblia latina cum Glossa ordinaria. Facsimile reprint of the Editio Princeps Adolph Rusch of Strasbourg 1480/81, Turnhout, 1992.
Bonaventurae Opera omnia, Quaracchi, 1882–1902, 10 vols.
Dionysiaca. Recueil donnant l'ensemble des traductions latines des ouvrages attribués au Denys de l'Aréopage, ed. P. Chevalier, Bruges, 1937–50, 2 vols.
Magistri Guillelmi Altissiodorensis Summa aurea, cura et studio, Jean Ribaillier, Paris-Grottaferrata 1980–1987, 7 vols.
Philippi Cancellarii, *Summa de bono*, ed. N. Wicki, Bern 1985, 2 vols.

Secondary Literature

H. Urs von Balthasar, *La gloire et la croix*, Paris, 1965–83, 8 vols.
San Bonaventura (1274-1974), Grottaferrata, 1973–74, 5 vols.
R. Baron, *Science et sagesse chez Hugues de Saint-Victor*, Paris, 1957.
J.M. Bissen, *L'exemplarisme divin selon saint Bonaventure*, Paris, 1929.
J.G. Bougerol, "Bonaventure de Bagnoregio et la première école franciscaine", in *Carthaginensia* 2 (1986), 170–171.
—, *Saint Bonaventure, Etudes sur les sources de sa pensée*, Variorum, Northampton, 1989.
I. Brady, "The Opera omnia of Saint Bonaventure (1882–1902)", in *Il Collegio S. Bonaventura di Quaracchi*, Grottaferrata, 1977, 132–134.
Y. Congar, "Aspects ecclésiologiques de la querelle entre mendiants et séculiers dans la seconde moitié du XIIIe siècle et le début du XIVe siècle", in *Archives de l'histoire doctrinale et littéraire du Moyen-Age*, 28 (1961).

---

[102] Cf. J.G. Bougerol, "Bonaventure de Bagnoregio et la première école franciscaine", in *Carthaginensia* 2 (1986) 170–171.

J. Châtillon, "De Guillaume d'Auxerre à Saint Thomas d'Aquin. L'argument de saint Anselme chez les premiers scolastiques du XIIIe siècle", in *Spicilegium Beccense*, Paris, 1959, 209–231.

H. Dausend, "Die St. Gregor von Nazianz-Stellen in den Werken des hl. Bonaventura", in *Fransk. Stud.* 3 (1916) 151–160.

B. Distelbrink, "De ordine chronologico IV Librorum Commentarii S. Bonaventurae", in *Collectanea Franciscana* 41 (1971) 288–314.

H.F. Dondaine, "L'objet et le médium de la vision béatifique chez les théologiens du XIIIe siècle", in *Recherches de théologie ancienne et médiévale* 19 (1952) 60–130.

H. Dondaine, *Le Corpus dionysien de l'Université de Paris au XIIIe siècle*, Rome, 1953.

C. Fourier Bonnard, *Histoire de l'abbaye royale et de l'Ordre des Chanoines réguliers de Saint-Victor de Paris*, Paris, 1904.

M. de Gandillac, *Oeuvres complètes du Pseudo-Denys l'Aréopagite*, Paris, 1943.

A. Gerken, *La théologie du Verbe. La relation entre l'incarnation et la création selon saint Bonaventure. Trad. de l'allemand par J. Gréal*, Paris, 1970.

J. de Ghellinck, "Patristique et argument de tradition au bas moyen âge", in *Aus der Geisteswelt des Mittelalters. Studien und Texte Martin Grabmann zur Vollendung des 60. Lebensjahres von Freunden und Schülern gewidnmet*, hg. A. Lang, J. Lechner, M. Schmaus (*Beiträge zur Geschichte der Philosophie und Theologie des Mittelalters*, Supplementband 3), Münster, 1935, 403–426.

—, *Le mouvement théologique du XIIe siècle*, Paris 1914.

E. Gilson, *L'esprit de la philosophie médiévale*, Paris, 1944.

—, "Pourquoi saint Thomas a critiqué saint Augustin", in *Archives de l'histoire doctrinale et littéraire du Moyen-Âge*, 1 (1926–1927) 80–111.

—, *La théologie mystique de saint Bernard*, Paris, 1934 (2nd ed.: Paris, 1947).

V. Lossky, "La notion des analogies chez Denys le pseudo-Aréopagite", in *Archives de l'histoire doctrinale et littéraire du Moyen-Âge*, 5 (1930) 279–309.

O. Lottin, *Psychologie et Morale aux XIIe et XIIIe siècles*, Louvain, Gembloux, 1942–60, 6 vols.

—, "Le traité du péché originel chez les premiers maîtres franciscains", in *Ephemerides Theologicae Lovanienses*, 18 (1941) 26–64.

R. Roques, "La méthode du Cur Deus homo de saint Anselme de Cantorbéry", in R. Rocques, *Structures théologiques de la Gnose à Richard de Saint-Victor*, Paris, 1962, 243–293.

—, "Denys", in *Dictionnaire de spiritualité ascétique et mystique*, t. III (Paris, 1957), col. 244–286.

P. Rousseau, *Oeuvres philosophiques de saint Anselme*, Paris, 1947.

A. Stohr, *Die Trinitätslehre des hl. Bonaventura*, Münster i. West., 1923.

THOMAS AQUINAS AND THE FATHERS OF THE CHURCH

Leo J. Elders

By the term "the Fathers of the Church" we mean those spokesmen of the Christian tradition who distinguished themselves by their learning and sanctity and who were acknowledged to represent the early, fundamental tradition of the Church. Nowadays the tendency prevails, at least in the Catholic Church, to acknowledge 16 Fathers of the Church, eight of whom are from the East, eight from the Latin West, and to end the patristic period with Isidore of Seville in the West and John Damascene in the East.[1] However, Thomas Aquinas and other medieval theologians do not know of such a clearcut chronological delimitation of the historical period of the Fathers.

Several historians have pointed out that there is a close connection between the teachings of the Fathers and medieval theology.[2] This applies to such theologians as Anselm, Hugh of St. Victor, Albert the Great and Bonaventure and, as we shall see, especially to Thomas Aquinas. To obtain a more profound understanding of the thought of Aquinas as well as of the method he used in theological studies it is imperative to know his relationship to the Fathers. A point of special interest is the way in which Thomas tried to bridge the gap between the pastoral teachings of the Fathers, often expressed in a literary style, and the rigorously scientific theology of the scholastics of his time. The study of Aquinas's attitude to the Fathers was initiated at the beginning of this century with a series of articles by A. Gardeil[3] and by Martin Grabmann's *Geschichte der scholastischen Methode* but, long before, the important theologian M. Scheeben attracted attention to this question. Further early literature[4] will be mentioned in the footnotes and the bibliography.

---

[1] Theologians such as Origen and Tertullian who do not satisfy the three conditions outlined above are called ecclesiastical authors.

[2] See A. v. Harnack, *Lehrbuch der Dogmengeschichte*, III[3], Freiburg 1897. Cf. also M. Scheeben, *Handbuch der katholischen Dogmatik*, I 428–430.

[3] *Revue thomiste* 11 (1903) 197–215; 428–457; 12 (1904) 207–211; 486–493; 583–592; 13 (1905) 194–197. Studies by von Hertling and J. de Ghellinck are also helpful.

[4] Notably the work of Ignaz Backus.

The Fathers and the Middle Ages

Whereas most works of such Latin Fathers as Ambrose, Augustine, Gregory the Great, Hilary and Jerome were known to theologians in the West throughout the entire period, the same cannot be said of the writings of the Greek Fathers. In his *Sentences* Peter Lombard quotes Augustine about 1000 times, Ambrose and Hilary respectively 90 and 85, Gregory[5] and Jerome 55 and 50 times, but there are only 27 references to John Damascene and 17 to Chrysostom.[6] However, acquaintance with the Greek Fathers varied according to the different Latin authors: in his *De divisione naturae* John Scot Eriugena refers to several Greek Fathers.[7] Paschasius Radbertus and Ratramnus show a fairly good knowledge of them, as does Gilbert of La Porrée.

Even when an author such as Anselm of Canterbury hardly ever quotes a Father, he developed his thought against the background of and in continuity with St. Augustine. Lanfranc of Bec explicitly defended the Fathers against false representations of their doctrine.

Parallel to the innovation of philosophical studies brought about by the arrival of the *Corpus aristotelicum* in the Latin West, in the twelfth century Greek theological thinking began to exercise a considerable influence on Latin theologians:[8] the idea of a hierarchically ordered universe and the concept of the divinisation of nature in Christ met with widespread acclaim.

The collections of *Sentences* composed during the 12th century were intended to bring together the Fathers' best insights. During the same period Italian translators were engaged in making Greek patristic works available to the Latin West.

Terms to Signify the Fathers in Aquinas' Works

Thomas does not use the expression *patres Ecclesiae*. In *S.Th.* I 1, 8 ad 2 the term *alii doctores Ecclesiae* occurs, meaning the Fathers and perhaps other great theologians. The expression *sancti Patres*, which occurs 39 times, signifies the patriarchs of the Old Testament, but

---

[5] Throughout this paper "Gregory" stands for Gregory the Great.
[6] See J.G. Bougerol, "The Fathers in the *Sentences*", *supra*, pp. 113–164.
[7] Cf. W. Otten, "The Texture of Tradition", *supra*, pp. 3–50.
[8] See M.-D. Chenu, *La théologie au douzième siècle*[2], Paris 1966. pp. 290ff.

sometimes also refers to the early anchorites of the Egyptian and Syrian deserts and the bishops participating in the Oecumenical councils.[9] The expression *sancti doctores*, on the other hand, occurring 50 times, is quite close to our "the Fathers of the Church", except for the fact that Aquinas does not limit these doctors to the first six centuries. When in the context of a particular passus one of the Fathers has been mentioned by name, he uses *alii doctores* to denote other Fathers.[10]

The Authority of the Fathers According to Aquinas

In the first question of the *Summa theologiae*, article 8, the reply to the second objection, Thomas sets forth his view of the authority and role of the Fathers in sacred theology. He observes first that it is especially proper to sacred theology to argue from authority, inasmuch as its principles are received by revelation. Theology also makes use of human reason, not in order to prove the faith, but to make clear other things that are set forth in this doctrine. This explains why sacred doctrine resorts to the authority of philosophers in those questions in which they were able to know the truth by natural reason. Thomas wrote: "Nevertheless sacred doctrine makes use of these authorities as extrinsic and probable arguments, but properly uses the authority of canonical Scriptures as a necessary demonstration and the authority of the doctors of the Church as one that may properly be used, yet merely as probable. For our faith rests upon the revelation made to the apostles and prophets, who wrote the canonical books, and not on the revelations (if any such there are) made to other doctors".[11]

According to this text, the arguments of philosophers, even if true, are extraneous to theology, since sacred theology proceeds from revelation. However, one should not say that as a source of doctrine the writings of the Fathers are to be placed between those of the philosophers and Sacred Scripture: in the eyes of Thomas the Fathers

---

[9] III 2, 3; *De potentia* 9, 4; 10. 4 ad 13. In the opuscule *In symbolum apostolorum*, 2, Thomas writes: "apostoli et sancti Patres posuerunt inter articulos fidei. . . ."

[10] I 35, 5 ad 1; III 27, 4 ad 2: "Origenes et quidam alii doctores".

[11] Translation by A.C. Pegis, *Introduction to St. Thomas Aquinas*, New York 1945, p. 15. This volume contains texts from the *Summa theologiae* and the *Summa contra gentiles*.

are on the side of the Bible, for under the inspiring influence of the same Spirit the Scriptures were written and *explained*.[12] However, the writings of the Fathers as such do not carry absolute authority, but are sources of doctrine insofar as they convey what is contained in the Bible and their doctrine has been received by the Church.[13] The Fathers are witnesses to the faith of the Church and expound what is contained in Sacred Scripture: there is a continuity of thought between them and the Bible and they represent the authority of the Apostles.[14] The Fathers explain Sacred Scripture; to do so they may use philosophical ideas. Their arguments are developed at the level of theological science but do not possess absolute authority.

While Augustine did not always attribute a special authority to some of the Fathers as interpreters of Holy Scripture,[15] Aquinas is more positive. To benefit from the full meaning of the Scriptures we need the explanations proposed by the Saints, even if not all of their comments may be of great value and if some are mistaken, when they say things which do not belong to the faith:[16] "In things which do not belong to the faith we may have different opinions". In fact, Jerome, Hilary and Gregory of Nazianzus said that the angels were created before the material world, while Augustine holds that all things have been created simultaneously.[17] Thomas adds that one must not reject without more ado the opinion of Gregory of Nazianzus who enjoys such great authority that no one ever slandered him.[18] As he did with regard to the writings of the philosophers, Thomas attempts to glean whatever insights can be gained from the texts of the Fathers. A theologian, he writes, must apply his mind with care, assiduity and reverence to the texts of the great doctors of the past without neglecting or despising what they say.[19] The Preface to the

---

[12] *Quodlib.* XII, art. 26 (q. 17, art., un.): "Dicendum quod ab eodem Spiritu Scripturae sunt expositae et editae".

[13] The Church is the medium in and through which Christians believe. Cf. II–II 5, 3.

[14] See J.G. Geenen, "Le fonte patristiche come "autorità" nella teologia di S. Tommaso", in *Sacra doctrina* 77, 7–67, p. 18.

[15] *Epist.* 82, I 3 to Jerome: "Alios autem ita lego, ut quantalibet sanctitate et doctrina praepolleant, non ideo verum putem, quia ipsi ita senserunt; sed quia mihi vel per illos auctores canonicos vel probabili ratione quod a vero non abhorreat, persuadere potuerunt" (*PL* 33, 296); cf. *Epist.* 148.

[16] *Quodl.* XII, art. 26 ad 1.

[17] *In II Sent.*, d. 2, q. 1, a. 3.

[18] I 61, 3.

[19] II–II 49, 3 ad 2.

opuscule *Contra errores graecorum* conveys Thomas's position very neatly: "Since certain statements in the works of the Fathers seem dubious, they may become the occasion for error or for strife and slander; therefore, I intend to *explain* first what is doubtful in these texts and to *show* next how we can take them as our starting point to teach and defend the catholic faith."

In this opuscule as well as in other works, Thomas explains why certain texts in the works of the Fathers appear of dubious truth to us: their opinions are sometimes influenced by erroneous philosophical theories, such as certain tenets of Platonism.[20] But more important is the fact that it is only after heresies had made their appearance, that the Fathers were obliged to express themselves with the utmost care. For example, prior to Arianism they did not speak so explicitly about the unity of divine essence as later doctors did. This even happened to that most eminent doctor, St. Augustine, who after Pelagianism had begun to spread, expressed himself more carefully with regard to the freedom of the human will than in the books he wrote against the Manichaeans to defend free will.[21] As a matter of fact, in fighting heresies the Fathers sometimes go to the opposite extreme.[22]

A fine example of this reverent way of correcting or refining certain statements by the Fathers is a remark on Chrysostom's view that Mary was somewhat ambitious and tried to attract the attention of others. In these words, Thomas says, Chrysostom went beyond good measure ("in verbis illis excessit"), but he adds that a correct explanation of this text is possible.[23] Likewise one should *interpret* Damascenus's view that the Holy Spirit does not proceed from the Son[24] or that divine nature became flesh.[25] Origen's position on the subordination of the Son is to be discarded. It also happens that a Church Father proposes an opinion without realizing that it has been rejected already by a general Council.[26] On the other hand, when the Fathers put forward different views on issues which are not revealed doctrine, it is best to respect their liberty and to explain

---

[20] Cf. *In II Sent.*, d. 14, q. 1, a. 2.

[21] *Contra errores Graecorum*, n. 1029.

[22] *In evangelium Ioannis*, ch. 1, lesson 7, n. 174: "Nam antiqui doctores et sancti, emergentes errores circa fidem ita persequebantur, ut interdum viderentur in errores labi contrarios".

[23] III 27, 4 ad 3: Chrysostom might express what people are likely to think.

[24] I 36, 2 ad 3.

[25] *De fide orth.* III, ch. 6.

[26] III 2, 6.

what they say with due consideration.[27] Different views on certain points can be of great help. To explain *1 Tim.* 2,4 ("God wills all men to be saved") Thomas quotes the main comments by the Fathers, as he does with regard to other difficult issues. Indeed, the search for truth is a common undertaking requiring the collaboration of many.

According to Thomas not even the consensus of a number of Fathers creates absolute certitude. Only the doctrine of Church is the absolute criterion to evaluate the truth of the teachings of the Fathers: the Church gives definite value to their views, as the council of Chalcedon did with regard to the doctrine set forth in Pope Leo the Great's *Letter* 28.[28] Likewise (ps.) Athanasius' exposé of the faith (the *Quicumque*) was received by the authority of the pope and so it is considered a rule of the faith.[29]

Concern About the Authenticity of Certain Works

In assigning certain works to individual Fathers, Thomas usually follows the prevalent convictions of his time which were sometimes mistaken. Fulgentius's *De fide ad Petrum* is attributed to Augustine, the creed *Quicumque* to Athanasius, an unfinished commentary on the *Gospel according to Matthew* (*Opus imperfectum in Matthaeum*) is said to be the work of Chrysostom. Despite these and some other minor mistakes Thomas considered the question of the authenticity of the writings very important. The book *De spiritu et anima* is not by Augustine, he writes, and for that reason it has no authority.[30]

The Sources of St. Thomas's Knowledge of the Works of the Fathers

An important question is whether Thomas obtained most of his knowledge directly from the texts or, rather, from collections of the

---

[27] II–II 1, 2.

[28] See *Q. d. de potentia*, 10, 4 ad 13.

[29] II–II 1, 10, ad 3.

[30] *Q. d. de anima*,. q. un., a. 9 ad 1; III 35, 6 ad 3. Thomas uses such expressions as "auctoritatem non habet", "non est authenticus". On this question see G. Geenen, "Saint Thomas d'Aquin et ses sources pseudoépigraphiques", in *Ephemerides theol. lovan.*, 1943, 71–80.

teachings of the Fathers. Until the entire Leonine edition of all the works of Aquinas has been completed the answer to this central question must remain uncertain. It varies, moreover, from work to work. In so far as the *Quaestiones disputatae* render academic disputes, the references to the Fathers in many of the arguments may have been suggested by the participants and represent what was generally known of certain Fathers in university circles. In works later than the *Catena aurea* Thomas sometimes quotes the Fathers according to the text of the *Catena*. Many years ago J. de Ghellinck argued that in most cases the theologians of the 12th and 13th centuries borrowed their quotations from the Fathers from collections such as the *Tabulae in Augustinum* or the *Tabulae in Damascenum* which, for a certain time, were indeed widely used. De Ghellinck also asserted that the sometimes contrasting or conflicting statements provided welcome material for dialectical exercises.[31]

It is certainly true that a good number of such collections were in circulation and that works such as Alexander of Hales's *Summa fratris Alexandri* provided handy access to important texts. Certain sayings were probably standard knowledge for students in theology. In this connection one must also mention the different biblical glosses, of which the *Glossa ordinaria*,[32] the *Glossa Petri Lombardi* and the *Glossa interlinearis* were used by Thomas. Those glosses carried a good number of texts from the Fathers.

Despite the availability of such chrestomathies, certain theologians made a real effort to see the works of the Fathers with their own eyes and did not hesitate to travel to different monasteries to consult these rare manuscripts. Albert the Great read extensively in the works of the great Latin doctors. It seems certain that at some time during his life Aquinas himself read the main works of the Latin Fathers, although he may not always have had them to hand while writing or dictating his treatises or *summae*. He could rely on his fabulous memory, though, for references. Sometimes we find a quotation from a Father in a context where there is no explicit reference to any of his works. In I–II 72, 7 sins are divided into sins of the mind, of the mouth and in works, a division ascribed to Jerome; in II–II 161, 1 Origen is quoted to confirm that humility is a virtue; these references

---

[31] "Le traité de Pierre de Lombard sur les sept ordres ecclésiastiques: ses sources, ses copistes", in *Revue d'hist. ecclésiastique*, X (1909) 290ff.

[32] Cf. E.A. Matter, "The Fathers in the *Glossa ordinaria*", *supra*, pp. 83–112.

are quite isolated. In these and similar cases Thomas is likely to quote from memory or use one or the other of the above mentioned collections or the passages he brought together in his own *Catena aurea*. On the other hand, when he gives precise quotations in a doctrinal context, indicating the title and the book or chapter he may have had that work to hand.

Thomas never refers to Minucius Felix or to Lactantius; Tertullian is mentioned seven times. He criticizes the latter severely for his materialistic view of the soul and even of God, calling him a heretic. Thomas may not have read his works, and probably relied on second hand information.

Thomas and the Greek Fathers

Thomas did not know enough Greek to read Greek texts. Nevertheless he uses a great number of works of Greek ecclesiastical authors in Latin translations. These works are far more numerous than those known by any of his Latin predecessors or contemporaries. In his *Catena on the Gospel of Luke* he quotes authors thus far unknown to the West and in his christology, *S. Th.* part III, he uses texts from Athanasius and Cyril of Alexandria, part of which at least he had found in the *Acts* of the Council of Ephesus. In fact, Thomas is the first Latin theologian to quote *verbatim* from the *Acts* of the first five ecumenical councils, which he seems to have discovered (in Latin translations) in the early sixties in Italy (Monte Cassino; the archives of the Papal Court).[33] However, references to the early apologists and Clement of Alexandria are almost absent.

What translations did Thomas use? From an early date a number of scriptural commentaries and homilies as well as Origen's *De principiis* were known to the West in the translations of Rufinus and Jerome. Certain homilies of St. Basil and of Chrysostom had likewise been translated. Around the middle of the twelfth century John Burgundio of Pisa produced *de verbo ad verbum* translations of Chrysostom's homilies on the *Gospel according to St. John*, of those on *Genesis* and of his commentary on the *Gospel according to Matthew*.[34]

---

[33] For references see the *Index in Summam theologiae et Summam contra gentiles* of the Leonine Edition (under "auctoritates citatae a Sancto Thoma").

[34] See P. Classen, *Burgundio von Pisa*, Heidelberg 1974.

To this must be added a translation of part of the *De natura hominis* of Nemesius, a treatise which was attributed to Gregory of Nyssa, and of the third part of John Damascene's *Fons scientiae*. This work was given the Latin title *De fide orthodoxa* and exercised a considerable influence on Latin theological thinking, also providing many references to other Greek authors.

With regard to the works of the Ps. Dionysius,[35] Thomas used different translations. In the *Summa contra Gentiles*, Dionysius[36] is quoted in the translation of Sarrazin, elsewhere often in that of John Scot Eriugena. Basil's *Homilies on the Hexaemeron* were available in the translation of Eustathius.[37] Cyril of Alexandria's *Letter to the Monks of Egypt* as well as his *Letter on Peace to John of Antioch* could be found in the *Collectio turonensis* and in Cassino. Many quotations from Cyril in the *Catena in evang. Lucae* were borrowed from the *Catena in Lucam* by Nicetas of Heracleia. In addition to these works Thomas had some Greek works translated into Latin.[38]

Quoting the Fathers

At the beginning of the century G. von Hertling suggested that many quotations from Augustine in Aquinas's works are purely decorative.[39] The same has been said of many biblical references.[40] However, this way of stating the issue is not very felicitous and misses the point entirely. The numerous quotations from works of the Fathers served the purpose of anchoring Thomas's doctrinal elaborations in the solid foundation of the most authentic tradition of the Church and of showing the underlying unity of all authentic Christian thought. Thomas is not so much interested in a historical study of the doctrine of the Fathers as in discovering, with their help, a deeper understanding of the mysteries of the faith. As Ignaz Backus writes, "the

---

[35] Cf. also Philippe Chevalier, *Dionysiaca. Recueil donnant l'ensemble des traductions latines des ouvrages attribués à Denys l'Aréopagite*, 2 vols., Bruges 1937–1950.

[36] In the following pages "Dionysius" stands for the Pseudo-Dionysius, the Areopagite.

[37] See Irena Backus, *Lectures humanistes de Basile de Césarée. Traductions latines (1439–1618)*, Paris 1990, 83–95.

[38] See below our observations on the *Catena in evang. sec. Lucam*.

[39] *Sitzungsberichte d. Bayr. Akad. d. Wiss., philos. philol. histor. Klasse*, 1904, 535–602.

[40] W.G.M.B. Valkenberg, *Did not our Heart Burn! Place and Function of Holy Scripture in the Theology of Aquinas*, Utrecht 1990.

Fathers must secure the road on this excursion into the profound mysteries and provide some light in the darkness. Thomas wants to obtain some knowledge from them, but knowledge of what they said in order to know the Incarnate Word of God".[41]

Throughout the *Summa theologiae* one discovers a certain strategy in the redaction of the *Sed contra* arguments: in matters directly connected with the faith Thomas quotes scriptural texts or, when the appropriate passages were difficult to find, statements of the Fathers. But in these quotations there is a certain pattern: Augustine, Ambrose, Gregory and other Doctors are assigned fields in which they have a special competence.

Especially in the *Disputed Questions* and in the *Summa theologiae* a great number of quotations from the Fathers in the objections at first sight appear to contradict the thesis of the *Sed contra* argument and the *corpus articuli*. The purpose of presenting these texts is not just to practice dialectics, but rather to delve into their deeper meaning and to "recover" them so as to secure the harmony of Christian doctors. Differences and apparent errors are sometimes due to the insufficiency of linguistic expression or to faulty terminology. Real errors may also have crept in, but in most cases there is some hidden sense in which texts can be understood correctly. In order to explain discrepancies, Thomas uses subtle distinctions and resorts to the different meanings in which terms can be used.

The Fathers are also quoted as sources of information on philosophical views and historical events in antiquity. In *S.Th.* I 1, 5 obi. 2, Thomas mentions a passage from Jerome which is not free from some exaggeration: "The ancient doctors (of the Church) used so many sayings of the philosophers that it is hard to say whether their knowledge of those secular authorities deserves more praise than their knowledge of Holy Scripture", a quotation which serves as a starting point to determine how far theologians may use philosophy.

A Table of Patristic References in Aquinas's Main Works

The table below is based on the *Index thomisticus*. With regard to some of the abbreviations used, "EBT" refers to the *Expositio in Boetii De*

---

[41] *Die Christologie des hl. Thomas von Aquin und die griechischen Kirchenväter*, Paderborn 1931, p. 123.

	ORIGENES	LEO Pope	JOHN Dam.	JEROME	ISIDORE	HILARY	GREGORY of Nys.	GREGORY of Naz.	GREGORY the Gr.	EUSEBIUS	EPIPHANIUS	DIONYSIUS	DIDYMUS	CYRIL Al.	CYPRIAN	CHRYSOSTOM	BASIL	AUGUSTINE	ATHANASIUS	AMBROSE
SN1	7	0	64	20	5	82	0	0	29	0	0	148	0	0	0	3	2	325	4	37
SN2	2	0	38	33	4	8	2	1	67	0	1	192	0	0	0	3	5	339	0	20
SN3	7	7	152	27	9	18	4	0	88	0	0	101	0	0	0	2	4	263	10	30
SN4	7	6	81	118	41	6	3	0	210	3	1	222	0	1	9	34	4	591	2	83
SCG	19	10	7	0	0	8	6	0	19	0	0	44	1	5	0	0	2	37	3	2
ST1	28	0	81	34	9	43	5	1	91	0	0	238	0	0	0	20	32	722	16	20
1-2	4	0	75	17	31	5	35	0	66	0	0	96	0	0	1	11	1	536	0	26
2-2	17	7	33	161	89	7	6	0	373	0	0	106	0	2	12	83	12	908	6	125
3	20	36	139	91	13	30	2	10	96	4	0	102	2	21	11	126	3	635	14	96
Ver	13	0	118	32	7	11	12	0	87	0	0	197	0	0	0	6	7	696	0	106
Pot	16	1	39	8	1	32	5	2	23	0	0	63	0	4	0	0	17	254	13	102
Malo	0	0	36	25	18	1		0	102	0	0	100	0	0	0	15	2	409	0	17
Un.V	0	2	9	0	0		0	0	0	0	0	4	1	0	19	0	0	12	2	0
CTMT	332	26	5	848	4	343	2	0	184	2	0	6	0	5	0	1281	1	705	2	197
CTMC	12	1	0	239	0	3		0	40	1	0	1	0	4	1	204	0	100	0	6
CTLC	159	0	10	14	9	0	80	25	198	81	6	4	9	382	1	417	120	307	44	1
CTJO	166	0	0	6	0	82	0	0	117	1	0	0	2	1	1	790	6	966	0	12
EVJO	91	1	2	15	0	46	0	0	54	0	0	11	0	0	1	259	3	426	5	20
EVMT	94	2	5	174	0	41	0	0	46	0	0	7	0	0	4	184	0	260	0	5
EBT	4	0	5	9	1	5		0	6	0	1	31	0	0	0	0	2	66	0	7
CDR	3	0	0	19	0	1	4	6	23	1	0	3	0	1	0	10	3	32	1	0
CEG	6	0	1	2	0	3	2	0	3	0	8	1	0	32	2	9	24	17	60	2
CoTh	1	0	0	2	0	0	0	0	5	0	0	7	0	0	0	4	0	14	0	1
Job	1	0	2	1	2	0	0	0	2	0	0	5	0	0	0	0	0	8	0	6
Isai	1	0	3	17	0	2	0	0	4	0	0	2	0	0	0	1	0	8	0	
Rom	0	2	2	6	0	2	0	0	4	0	0	2	0	0	0	10	0	63	1	6

Trinitate, "UnV" to the *Quaestio disputata de unione Verbi*, "CoTh" to the *Compendium theologiae*, "CDR" to the *Contra doctrinam retrahentium* and "CEG" to the *Contra errores graecorum*.

A representative selection has been given of the various types of works such as systematic studies, opuscules, disputed questions and scriptural commentaries. The *Expositio in De divinis nominibus* has not been listed, since it has only very few quotations: 9 from Augustine, 1 from Damascene and 2 from Origen.[42] Evidently one must not look for references to the Fathers in Thomas's Aristotelian commentaries nor in purely philosophical treatises.

Occurrences of 20 patristic authors in 26 works have been listed. More Greek authors will be mentioned in the section on the *Catena aurea*. The figures given are approximate: a passage in Thomas's works may have been inspired by a patristic text without an explicit reference being given. Moreover, errors occur in assigning particular texts to certain Fathers, as we have pointed out above. Another example, Theophylactus is quoted sometimes as Chrysostom or as Bede. In some cases, Thomas mentions a name without referring to a text.[43]

Under "Leo Papa" and "Gregory the Great" a very small number of references to Pope Leo IV and to Gregory II, Gregory III and Gregory VII are also listed. The latter are so few that it was not worthwhile to check the very considerable number of occurrences of "Gregorius" in all those works to deduct the "spurious" references.

The considerable number of quotations from Basil, Chrysostom and Cyril of Alexandria in some works must be explained by the fact that translations of their respective commentaries were available, such as those on the gospels according to Matthew, Luke and John.

The quotations from works of the Fathers in the *Catena*, *Contra errores graecorum*, *Summa contra gentiles*, *Summa theologiae*, etc. will be discussed in greater detail below.

The Catena Aurea

The *Catena aurea* of St. Thomas occupies a special place and deserves to be studied by itself. In the 12th century several glosses on Scripture

---

[42] For the presence of the Fathers in the *Quaestio disputata de malo* see our "Les interlocuteurs de saint Thomas d'Aquin dans les *Questions disputées sur le mal*", in *Doctor communis*, 1993, 40–52.

[43] Cf. II–II 124, 2 obi. 3 on Cyprian.

were in use, that is, collections of short comments which had frequently been taken from the works of Augustine, Jerome, Gregory, Bede, etc. Also available were the works of certain Fathers on the gospels, often in the form of homilies (Hilary, Chrysostom, Origen, Augustine, Gregory the Great), but a good deal of these texts dealt only with selected passages from the gospels and frequently contained long arguments on moral issues. So the idea arose to compose a continuous, more balanced commentary on the entire text of the Gospels with excerpts from the works of the Fathers.

Pope Urban IV asked St. Thomas (1262) to write just such a new type of a practical commentary on each passus of the four gospels consisting of quotations from the Fathers. Thomas successively composed these *Catenae* in about four years. The respective length of them in the Marietti Edition is 416 pages for Matthew, 134 for Mark, 315 for Luke and 268 for John. Because of its outstanding quality the work came to be called the *Catena aurea*.

In his dedication of the *Catena* of the First Gospel, addressed to Urban IV, Thomas explains that he put together or compiled a continuous explanation of this Gospel, taken from the writings of the various doctors. He added a few lines here and there in the interest of coherence. Although he often abbreviated these texts somewhat, he succeeded in maintaining their particular style and even wording. Here and there he changed the order of sentences. He placed the name of the respective Father or theologian before the quotation, usually omitting from which work the text is borrowed. The reader understands that the main commentary or series of homilies of this author on the Gospel in question is meant. However, if a quotation is taken from a new or different work, it is indicated.

In writing these *Catenae*, Thomas's intention was to bring out the literal sense of the Scriptural text, to indicate the mystical sense as well as to refute certain errors concerning the faith and to confirm the catholic doctrine. This is important, he writes, because it is above all in the gospels that the form of the catholic faith and the rule of our entire Christian life are proposed. Explanations on the mystical sense are introduced by "mystice autem".

In the *Catena*, Thomas does not sharply distinguish between the Fathers of the Church and later authorities. While the early Christian authors before 200 are absent, later authors are quoted repeatedly. Besides the authors mentioned on the previous table, Cassian, the Council of Ephesus, Maximus, Theodotus, Theophylactus, Dionysius of Alexandria, John the Bishop, Gennadius, Titus of Bosra, Bede, Hrabanus, Remigius and Severianus are quoted.

In the preface to the *Catena* on the Second Gospel—dedicated to Cardinal Annibaldo d'Annibaldi (Pope Urban had died in the meantime)—Thomas added that he had certain passages from the Greek doctors translated into Latin ("in Latinum feci transferri"). As Geenen calculated Thomas quoted twenty-two Latin and fifty-seven Greek authors throughout the *Catena*. In particular in the comments on *Luke* the presence of Greek authors is very remarkable.[44]

The study of the texts of the Greek Fathers and authors had a great impact on Thomas's later work, in particular on the trinitarian theology and christology of the *Summa theologiae*.

In the nineteenth century a number of Oxford scholars, among whom John Henry Newman, produced an English translation of the *Catena aurea*. One of them, M. Pattison of Lincoln College, wrote: "All former glosses had been partial and capricious, dilating on one passage, and passing unnoticed another of equal or greater difficulty. But it is impossible to read the Catena of St. Thomas without being struck with the masterly and architectonic skill with which it is put together. A learning of the highest kind, not mere literary book-knowledge. . . . ., a thorough acquaintance with the whole range of ecclesiastical antiquity; . . . a familiarity with the style of each writer, so as to compress into a few words the pith of a whole page, and a power of clear and orderly arrangement in this mass of knowledge, are qualities which make this Catena perhaps nearly perfect as a conspectus of Patristic interpretation. Other compilations exhibit research, industry, learning, but this, though a mere compilation, evinces a masterly command over the whole subject of theology".[45]

It looks as if Aquinas gradually obtained more translations of Greek authors while working on his *Catena*. In the commentary on *Mark* Theophylactus[46] enters on the scene (with 362 references); he and Bede are the main sources. This is probably due to the fact that not so much other material was available. Theophylactus will also prove a useful source of documentation in the comments on the last two

---

[44] "Saint Thomas et les Pères", *Dict. de théol. cath.*, XV 1, 743.

[45] *Commentary on the Four Gospels by S. Thomas Aquinas*, vol. I, 1, 2nd ed. (Oxford & London 1864), Preface iii–iv quoted after J. Weisheipl, *Friar Thomas D'Aquino. His Life, Thought and Works*, Washington² 1983, p. 171.

[46] Constantinople, eleventh century. Theophylactus mostly follows Chrysostom.

Gospels.[47] In the *Catena on Luke* the full impact of Greek patristic sources can be felt: Cyril of Alexandria, Gregory of Nyssa, Gregory of Nazianzus, Eusebius and Titus of Bosra are frequently quoted. If we leave out the glosses, the *Catena on Luke* has more quotations from Greek authors than from Latin theologians.

For his *Catena on John*, Thomas could avail himself of much material from Fathers and authors such as Augustine, Chrysostom and Theophylactus. The passages quoted are often longer than those in the other *Catenae*. Thomas is willing to use any good text. For instance, where bishop Haymo has something worthwhile to say on a passage of the Gospel, Thomas will quote him.

Tracing all the texts and translations used by Thomas in writing his *Catena aurea* will have to wait until the Leonine Edition has been completed.

The Treatise Contra Errores Graecorum

At about the same time Thomas began work on the *Catena* Pope Urban asked him to evaluate a treatise with excerpts of Greek Fathers and theologians which had been translated into Latin and had attracted attention because of a number of unusual and unorthodox statements. This booklet had been written by Nicholas of Durazzo, bishop of Crotone in Southern Italy, who intended to show the agreement of the Greek Fathers with Western theological thought on certain disputed questions such as the *Filioque* and the primacy of the pope. Thomas limited himself to a study of the text of the *Libellus* as it was and did not check whether the author is reliable in attributing certain passages to some of the Fathers.

Thomas deals first with doubtful statements of the Fathers that cannot be accepted without correction. Difficulties are due to the fact that the Fathers sharpened the verbal expression of the mysteries of the faith only after heresies appeared and were refuted; a further difficulty is caused by the fact that certain words are translated by different Latin terms and misunderstandings occur. In the second part of this opuscule Thomas explains the catholic doctrine of the procession of the Holy Spirit. When Gregory of Nazianzus calls the

---

[47] Out of a total of 1035 references to Theophylactus in Thomas's works, 1033 are found in the *Catena*.

Holy Spirit "ingenitus" he does not deny that the Spirit proceeds from the Father. Likewise when the Holy Spirit is called by some Greek Fathers the image of the Father, this is just a less felicitous way of stating the issue.[48] But because Thomas considers it pretentious to correct such great doctors, he suggests a sense in which one may say that the Holy Spirit is the image of the Father and the Son: insofar as he proceeds from them he must have a certain resemblance with his origin. In the final chapters Thomas defends the authority of the Roman pontiff. In his epilogue he warns again against using the wrong Latin terms to translate certain Greek words and observes that one must not exaggerate by calling the Fathers "patres fidei". We must respect certain of their ways or expressions but not make these our own.

In the *Contra errores graecorum* 205 references or quotations occur from the Greek Fathers, only five of which belonged to the texts which at that time were known in the West; 200 are new and were taken over by Thomas from Nicholas of Durazzo's *Libellus*.

The Expositio in Boetii De Trinitate

Before turning to a study of the use of the Fathers in the two *Summae* we must first consider an early work, viz. the commentary on the first pages of Boethius's theological treatise on the Trinity. The use of the Fathers is limited to what was general practice in academic circles. Jerome is a source of information on Origen. Thomas quotes *Hom. 15 De fide* of Basil, refers once to an anecdote in Eusebius's *Historia ecclesiastica* and has six quotations from Gregory's *Moralia* and *Homilies on the Gospels*. Besides some remarkable sentences from Hilary[49] there are more than sixty quotations from some twenty different works of Augustine. The texts stress that God enlightens the human intellect as the sun does the air, but they give also a number of striking statements and definitions such as: "virtus est ars bene recteque vivendi"; "gaudium de veritate cognita est beatitudo"; "vera religio est qua unus Deus colitur"; "vera immutabilitas soli Deo convenit";

---

[48] "Apud Latinos non consuevit dici quod Spiritus Sanctus sit imago Patris vel Filii".

[49] *De Trinitate* 2, 10: "qui infinita prosequitur, etsi non contingat aliquando, tamen semper proficiat prodeundo"; "Pater maior Filo, maioritas non importat inaequalitatem sed auctoritatem principii".

"primus error circa divina est ea quae de corporibus noverunt, ad divina transferre". Thomas may have had some of these books of Augustine to hand, although the sentences quoted are likely to have figured also in the *Tabulae* and in such other works as the *Summa fratris Alexandri*. The references to texts of the Fathers in the *Scriptum super libros Sententiarum* follow a pattern which was quite standard at the time and need not be discussed.

Quotations from the Fathers in the Summa Contra Gentiles

Even if this important work is theological in its design, the sections dealing with purely philosophical arguments occupy such a considerable part of it, that one does not expect many references to the Fathers.

There are nevertheless quite a few quotations. Some of these occur in Book IV in purely theological arguments, such as those on the procession of the Holy Spirit. In IV 24 Thomas first quotes some texts from Scripture implying the procession of the Holy Spirit from the Son, and then refers to passages from Cyril and Didymus and concludes with this ringing statement: "The same is also found in what the Fifth Council has determined: 'On all points of doctrine we follow the Holy Fathers and Doctors of the Church, Athanasius, Hilarius, Basilius, Gregory the Theologian and Gregory of Nyssa, Ambrose, Augustine, Theophilus, John of Constantinople, Cyril, Leo, Proclus,[50] and we accept everything which they have explained about the true faith and the condemnation of the heretics'. Now from a great number of texts by Augustine, especially from his book on the Trinity and that on the Gospel according to John, it is obvious that the Holy Spirit proceeds from the Son. We must, therefore, admit that the Holy Spirit proceeds from the Son as he does from the Father".[51]

---

[50] Patriarch of Constantinople in 434.

[51] "Sequimur per omnia sanctos patres et doctores Ecclesiae, Athanasium, Hilarium, Basilium, Gregorium Theologum et Gregorium Nyssenum, Ambrosium, Augustinum, Theophilum, Ioannem Constantinopolitanum, Cyrillum, Leonem, Proclum; et suscipimus omnia quae de recta fide et condamnatione haereticorum exposuerunt. Manifestum autem ex multis auctoritatibus Augustini et praecipue in libro De Trinitate et Super Joannem quod Spiritus sanctus sit a Filio. Oportet igitur concedi quod Spiritus Sanctus sit a Filio."

Other groups of references occur at the end of a good number
of chapters of the first three Books. They are introduced by such
expressions as "hanc etiam veritatem catholici doctores professi sunt;
ait namque Hilarius . . ."; "huic etiam auctoritas consonat"; "quam
quidem veritatem expresse tradit . . ."; "in hanc sententiam etiam
catholici tractatores conveniunt". At one point Thomas writes that
the fact that only God can create is confirmed by the Scriptures and
by Damascenus. In II 23 Thomas shows that God does not act out
of natural necessity invoking both the Holy Scripture and Hilary in
support. In III 65 the chapter on the conservation of things by God
ends with a text from Scripture and Augustine's assertion that God
is the "causa subsistendi omnis creaturae". In III 96 Thomas argues
that the immutability of divine providence does not exclude the
necessity of prayer of petition. The texts from Scripture on prayer
are corroborated by Augustine's saying "bonus Dominus qui non
tribuit saepe quod volumus ut quod mallemus attribuat". At the end
of ch. 100 the argument is confirmed by a text from Augustine: "Deus
nihil contra naturam facit, quia id est naturale cuique rei quod facit".
In III 93 Thomas argues that there is no destiny ruling the world
other than the plan of divine providence. Texts from Augustine and
Gregory at the end of the chapter are quoted in confirmation: "Si
quis voluntatem vel potestatem Dei fati nomine appellat, sententiam
teneat, linguam corrigat" and "Absit a fidelium mentibus ut fatum
aliquid esse dicant".

Other quotations relate to insights which are accessible to natural
reason, such as certain texts by Dionysius on love and its effects, or
by Augustine on the soul and on God. Some examples of the second
group: in connection with the argument for God's existence from
finality, Damascenus writes that "it is impossible that discordant or
even contrary things work together most of the time or always, unless they are directed by some one" (I 13). We find many striking
quotations from Augustine's works at the level of philosophical arguments: "Quia Deus bonus est sumus"; "non erunt tunc volubiles
nostrae cogitationes"; peace is "ordinata concordia".

In III 46 Thomas argues that the soul has no knowledge of itself
through its own essence. He quotes two texts from the *De Trinitate*:
even Augustine accepts this. In this life we cannot know the essence
of God. Some texts by Augustine seem to say the opposite, but "non
est autem credendum quod Augustinus hoc in praemissis verbis sen-
serit" (III 47). In III 83 Gregory is invited to remind us that God

also governs the world: "Mundum per seipsum regit qui per seipsum condidit".

Some Old Testament texts intimate that evil as well as good things come from God. Thomas explains the expression "creare malum" (Jes. 45,6) with a beautiful text by Gregory: "Creare mala dicitur cum res in se bonas creatas nobis male agentibus in flagellum format" (II 41) (we say that God creates evil when he uses creatures good in themselves to punish us for our evil actions).

Throughout the *Summa contra gentiles* the Fathers are quoted as sources of information. In II 64 we read that Gregory of Nyssa (= Nemesius) ascribes to a certain Dinarchus the view that the soul is a harmony. Augustine is quoted in IV 82 on theories of cyclical return.

Despite appearances to the contrary Thomas had the doctrine of the Fathers constantly in mind while writing his great *Summa*. This can also be concluded from his declaration of intent in the opening chapters (I 2), where he says that he wants to set forth the truth of the catholic faith to the best of his powers, just like St. Hilary in his *De Trinitate*, who writes: "I am aware of this most important duty and mission in my life which I owe to God, sc. that all my words and all my thoughts speak of Him".

The Summa Theologiae

The *Summa theologiae* is generally considered as Thomas's main work and masterpiece, a work which at the same time is the most profound, best ordered and most thoroughly catholic theological study of the entire Christian tradition. It brought about a total renewal of theology and has not yet lost anything of its value. Thomas's solutions and answers have for the greater part been generally accepted. The recent *Catechism of the Catholic Church* shows an astonishing continuity of thought with Aquinas.[52] Considering the importance of the *Summa theologiae* we must now examine the role the theology of the Fathers plays in it.[53]

As we shall see, the individual Fathers quoted vary somewhat in

---

[52] See *Catechism of the Catholic Church*, Libreria Editrice Vaticana, 1994.

[53] Cf. C. Pero o.p., *Le Fonti del Pensiero di Tommaso d'Aquino nella Somma Theologica*, Torino 1979.

the three parts which make up the *Summa* (Part I, Part I–II & II–II and Part III). We must furthermore distinguish between references to the Fathers in the objections at the beginning of each article and quotations in the *Sed contra* arguments and in the *corpus articuli.*

We shall deal successively with these three Parts. It is obvious that both on account of the enormous mass of material and of the limits imposed on this paper, we must make a selection. The figures refer to the Part, question and article under discussion.

First, the quotations in the objections of the first 26 questions will be considered. In I 2, 1 the difficulty is raised whether God's existence is evident to man. Damascenus seems to say so ("omnibus cognitio existendi Deum naturaliter est inserta"). Thomas avails himself of the opportunity to clarify the issue and to make plain in which sense this statement must be understood. The same happens on countless other occasions. In I 1, 8 (on the question whether theology is an argumentative science) we hear Ambrose say (obi. 1) "Tolle argumentum, ubi fides quaeritur". In his answer Thomas explains the limits but also the use of arguments from reason in theology. In I 6, 4 Augustine asserts that God *is* the goodness of each good thing (obi. 1). Thomas replies that this applies to God as the exemplary and final cause of things. When Augustine writes that the Spirit of God moves itself,[54] although not in place nor in time, Thomas observes that he is speaking here according to Plato, who said that the First Mover moves itself, calling every operation a movement (I 9, 1 ad 1). In certain texts Augustine seems to assert that we shall see God with our own eyes. However, in these passages "Augustinus loquitur inquirendo in verbis illis et quasi sub conditione" (I 12, 3). Speaking of our knowledge of God Thomas quotes Augustine's saying "Deus movet spiritualem creaturam per tempus".[55] Thomas notes that it applies only to natural knowledge, not to the beatific vision. Are we able to know anything about God by natural reason (I 12, 12)? In his younger years Augustine denied such a possibility, but in his *Retractationes* he changed his mind: "multos etiam non mundos multa scire vera".

In his *Commentary on Romans*, Origen writes "that something is not going to happen because God knows it, but that God knows these things because they are going to be". This text gives a totally wrong

---

[54] "Spiritus Creator movet se".
[55] This text from *Super Genesim ad litt.* VIII 20 occurs 14 times in Thomas's works.

view of divine science, which in reality is based only on God's causal action. Thomas saves it somehow by saying that Origen is speaking of what is called the *scientia simplicis intelligentiae* in God (I 14, 8). Whether God wills evil to happen is a difficult issue. Texts from Augustine and Dionysius seem to favour an affirmative answer, although elsewhere Augustine himself writes that no sensible person wants evil. Thomas proposes the correct solution in his formula "Deus vult permittere mala fieri") (I 19, 9). As appears from these examples, Thomas wants the Fathers to be actively involved in the elaboration of his *Summa*. He also quotes them to have an opportunity to explain difficult texts and to show in which sense these texts must be understood.

The use of texts of the Fathers in the *Sed contra* arguments is different: this class of arguments in the *Summa* differs from references in the objections. Theology is a discipline based upon authority. In strictly theological questions the argument from authority is decisive. The *corpus articuli* serves the purpose of explaining or confirming this truth by means of analogous reasoning or philosophical arguments. In such articles the *Sed contra* will bring a relevant text from Scripture, or, if this is not available, from one of the Fathers. Augustine, Hilary, Dionysius, Jerome, Damascenus, Ambrose and others provide such texts. Out of a great number of these in the first twenty-six questions of Part I, the following examples illustrate what has been said: Augustine: "Deus vere et summe simplex est" (I 3, 7); Hilary: "esse non est accidens in Deo sed subsistens veritas" (I 3, 4); Gregorius: "Deus communi modo est in omnibus rebus praesentia, potentia et substantia" (I 7, 3); Jerome: "Deus solus est qui exordium non habet" (I 10, 3); Ambrose: "Sunt quaedam nomina quae evidenter proprietatem divinitatis ostendunt" (I 13, 3).

Some of these texts recur elsewhere in Thomas's works; others are exclusive to a particular article. This means that Aquinas searched for them purposely.

We must turn now to the questions concerning the Trinity (27–43). Some critics have argued that Aquinas's doctrine of the Trinity is centered entirely on Western views and starts from a consideration of God's essence by resorting to the processions. Augustinian impersonalism is said to be its foundation.[56] As is often the case, such

---

[56] Cf. V. Lossky, *Essai sur la théologie mystique de l'Orient*, Paris 1944, p. 55.

generalisations are based on a misunderstanding and are erroneous. Thomas organizes his treatises differently to Augustine. The first question he asks is whether there are processions in God and from there he passes on to that of the relations. In this connection one should notice that in the *Contra errores graecorum*, ch. 4, Thomas corrects certain statements of the Fathers that the divine essence produces: generation and spiration can only be said of a personal *principium quod*. The processions do not constitute the divine Persons: "Persona agens praeintelligitur actioni" (the acting person is conceived as prior to his action).[57] This is not to deny the importance of the Greek Fathers for the theological works of Aquinas but it shows how certain critics of Thomas were misled both with regard to what he actually said and with regard to the views of some of the Greek Fathers.

Of the 78 articles which make up this treatise, two have no *Sed contra* argument. Of the remaining arguments, 17 are biblical texts and one a dogma of the Nicene Council, two state the praxis of the Church in liturgy, 27 are borrowed from Augustine, 7 from Athanasius, 5 from Hilary, 1 from Damascenus and 1 from Gregory. Athanasius (the *Quicumque*) testifies that the Holy Spirit also proceeds from the Son (I 36, 2); Damascenus is quoted as an authority on the question of notions in God (32, 2).

A particularly difficult problem concerns the appropriation of certain operations to the individual Persons in God, operations which in reality belong to God's essence. Augustine is not always clear in his explanations. Thomas indicates the solution: when we speak about God in the way we do about created things, we first consider God himself, next we study God insofar as he is one; then we ponder his power to operate and finally consider his relation with his effects (I 39, 8).

Aquinas reproaches Origen for holding that the Father and the Son are different substances, a view which is in line with Arius who followed the Platonists (I 32, 1 ad 1). In fact, as Augustine says "non errare alicubi periculosius est quam in Trinitate" (Nowhere the danger to fall into error is greater than in the study of the Trinity, I 32, 4).

Questions 44 to 119 deal with the procession of creatures from God. I 48 and 49 study the problem of evil. Dionysius provides a number of key texts such as "malum non est existens neque bonum" and "malum est praeter rationem esse". He is moreover, together

---

[57] *Q. d. de potentia* 8, 3.

with Gregory the Great, the foremost authority on the treatise on angels. He confirms the immateriality and incorruptibility of the angels, their great number and their absence of discursive thinking. Dionysius asserts also that the demons never lost their splendid natural gifts: "Non sunt natura mali" (I 63, 4)—they are not evil by nature, he says.

In Q. 63 Thomas begins his study of material things. In the questions on the *Hexaemeron*, Augustine, Chrysostom and Basil are quoted. Texts from Origen and Jerome are also brought forward.[58] Large sections of the treatise on man are philosophical. However Augustine is present in many articles, with Gregory of Nyssa (Nemesius) providing some arguments. Augustine is the foremost authority on the state of the first men and on man as the image of God (qq. 93–102). Gregory, on the other hand, is Thomas's foremost authority regarding whether angels can influence each other and man.

As we have seen, certain Fathers are quoted with regard to particular questions on which they had a special authority or made important statements. As a conclusion to our survey of this part of the *Summa theologiae*, I would suggest that a good number of the references to the Fathers are derived from Thomas's own personal reading of the main works of the Latin Fathers and of some of works of the Greek Fathers. While preparing and dictating the text, he may not always have had these works to hand, but the references are nevertheless based upon a first hand knowledge. Some quotations, probably the smaller part, may have been borrowed from *Tabulae*, chrestomathies and compilations. In many cases we shall never be quite sure from which source a particular quotation was taken.

The Second Part of the *Summa theologiae* deals with man's actions in view of his end. The first five questions consider man's final end, happiness. Augustine is introduced as an authority on the issue of man's final end, on the question of what happiness consists in and on how to attain it. In Questions 6 to 17 on human actions in general, Damascenus is asked to define what is a voluntary act ("actus qui est operatio rationalis, I–II 6, 1) and to explain what the "circumstances" of the human act are. Q. 11 deals with the act called enjoyment (*fruitio*): obviously Augustine is the chief authority on all four articles. In some of the following articles Damascenus and Gregory

---

[58] See also G. Bardy, "Sur les sources patristiques grecques de saint Thomas dans la Iᵉʳᵉ partie de la *Somme théologique*", in *RSPT* XII (1923), 493–502.

of Nyssa (= Nemesius) contribute a text each for the *Sed contra*. Augustine does so on the issue of the act of the will whereby the will is said to *use* other faculties (*usus*). I–II 16, 1: "Uti est assumere aliquid in facultatem voluntatis"; art. 2: "Uti aliqua re non potest nisi animal quod rationis est particeps". But one cannot "use" the last end, for "Deo nullus recte utitur" (art. 3), in other words, no creature can put God to the right *use*.

In the remarkable treatise on the passions (qq. 24–48), Augustine is an important witness. He confirms that love is the first of the passions (q. 25, 2: "Amor enim inhians habere quod amatur cupiditas est; id autem habens eoque fruens laetitia est"). Likewise texts from Augustine are quoted in q. 27 on the cause of love: "Non amatur certe nisi bonum"; "Nullus potest amare incognitum"; omnes aliae affectiones animi ex amore causantur (nothing can be loved but the good; no one can love what he does not know; love is the cause of all other feelings ≈ *De civ. Dei* 14, 7). However, in q. 28 on the effects of love such as union, ecstasy, fervor and a passion which wounds the soul, Dionysius provides five of six *Sed contra* arguments: "Amor est virtus unitiva"; "Divinus amor extasim facit", etc. (love is the force that unites; divine love leads to ecstasy).

In the treatise on virtues in general, a central question is whether virtue is a good habitus and makes us good. Augustine answers: "Nemo autem dubitaverit quod virtus animam facit optimam" (q. 55, 3). Ambrose informs us about the moral virtues as cardinal virtues, Gregory declares that there are four of these cardinal virtues (q. 66, 1 & 2); these Fathers also confirm the connection of all the virtues (q. 65, 1). On the gifts of the Holy Spirit, Gregory, Ambrose and Augustine are authorities (q. 68), while the authority on the beatitudes (q. 69) is Augustine. The latter is asked also to determine what a vice is: "Vitium est qualitas secundum quam malus est animus" (q. 70, 1). Gregory instructs us about a division of sins as well as about the various capital sins (qq. 72 & 84), but Augustine is the main authority in the entire question of the *subject* of sin (q. 74).

Isidore remained in the background in the preceding questions, but in the study of positive law and law in general he enters the scene (qq. 90 ff.). Other authorities are Cicero, Aristotle, the *Digesta* and Augustine (on eternal law, in particular, q. 93).

The last section of the *Prima Secundae* of the *Summa theologiae* is concerned with the external principle of human actions which is divine grace. In qq. 109–114 Augustine is again the most important authority and several of his works are quoted: *Retractationes, De natura et gratia, De perseverantia, De correptione et gratia, De haeresibus.*

The *Secunda Secundae* (II^a–II^{ae}) deals with the virtues and vices in particular. QQ. 1–16 are concerned with faith. There are relatively few quotations from the Fathers except in qq. 8 and 9 on the gifts of understanding and science, where Gregory and Augustine intervene. The latter also declares that unbelief is the greatest of sins (q. 10, 3). In 14, 1 Thomas lists the opinions of several Fathers regarding the sins against the Holy Spirit. Augustine is very much in evidence.

In q. 20, 4, obi. 3 Thomas quotes a text from Augustine on the convenience of the Incarnation, an insight he also used in *S.C.G.* IV: "Nihil tam necessarium fuit ad erigendum spem nostram quam ut demonstraretur nobis quantum nos Deus diligeret" (there is nothing more necessary to build up our faith than to have demonstrated to us the extent of God's love).

In qq. 23–27 on charity there is a considerable number of quotations from Augustine: "Caritatem voco motum ipsum animi ad fruendum Deo propter ipsum"; "caritas est virtus quae cum nostra rectissima affectio est, coniungit nos Deo, qua eum diligimus"; "caritas meretur augeri ut aucta mereatur et perfici" (I call charity the impulse of the mind to love God as himself; love is a force which, as our supreme feeling, binds us to God; it is that which makes us love him; charity should be increased, and having been increased, it should be perfected). These and similar texts are taken from a great number of different works so that Aquinas displays his exceptional acquaintance with Augustine's thought. Some of these quotations are explained in the course of the discussion, so that a misunderstanding is prevented.

If Augustine is conspicuous in the treatise on the virtues, he is even more so in q. 40 on war and in q. 47 on prudence which is defined as "cognitio rerum appetendarum et fugiendarum". Augustine provides *Sed contra* arguments with regard to the morality of numerous acts in the field of justice, varying from whether one is allowed to own property (66, 2) to whether a lawyer can demand a fee for his services (71, 4) or whether a businessman can sell goods at a higher price than the one he paid for them (77, 4). In *Matthew* 5,34f. Jesus forbids to take an oath; Thomas consults Jerome and Augustine on the meaning of these words (89, 2). Likewise Augustine is the main authority in determining the sinfulness of lying (q. 110) and superstition (qq. 92–93). In q. 161 on humility, Augustine is a keywitness to tradition; furthermore he provides some texts on patience, (136), temperance (q. 141), chastity (q. 151). On virginity (q. 152) and modesty (168), on the other hand, Ambrose is a primary authority. On pride (162, 1) Thomas quotes Isidore ("qui vult supergredi quod est superbus est") and Augustine ("superbia est perversae celsitudinis appetitus"). In 162, 2, on the sin of the first parents, the *Sed contra* argument is from Origen, while long quotations from Augustine explain the way in which Adam and Eve were tempted (165, 2).

Curiosity may easily become a vice. Jerome writes: "Do you not agree that one yields to vanity and gets his mind involved in darkness when he vexes himself day and night in the art of dialectics or, when studying the physical world, lets his eyes move from one end of the skies to the other?" (167, 1).[59] Thomas outlines the correct attitude with regard to profane studies, referring to several texts from Augustine.

Gregory supplies a good number of texts on temperance, justice and fortitude and sheds light on the nature of several vices.[60] Isidor, on the other hand, is quoted to furnish simple definitions of certain concepts. For instance, in II–II 57, 1, his division of law is given: "Ius aut naturale est aut civile aut gentium". In qq. 171 on prophecy and in 179–182 on the contemplative and active life, Gregory is the main authority.

In the Second Part of the *Summa theologiae* Thomas seldom refers to the Greek Fathers but in the study of Christ (Part III) the latter are present throughout and contribute to the development of certain themes. I. Backus mentions the questions of the composite person of Christ (q. 2, 4), the *communicatio idiomatum* (16, 4–5), the will of Christ (18), the attribution of the conception of Christ to the Holy Spirit (32), the circumstances of the birth of Christ (35), the incorruptibility of the body of Christ in the tomb, where John Damascene is likely to have influenced Aquinas. The arguments that Christ adopted human nature to redeem it, are also found in Damascenus, as is the rejection of the monophysitism of Eutyches.[61]

---

[59] "Nonne vobis videtur in vanitate sensus et obscuritate mentis ingredi qui diebus et noctibus in dialectica arte torquetur, qui physicus perscrutator oculos trans caelum levat?"

[60] On the presence of Gregory in the *Quaestiones disputatae de veritate* and *De malo*, see Enzo Portalupi, *Studi sulla presenza di Gregorio Magno in Tommaso d'Aquino*, Fribourg 1991.

[61] See the study of I. Backus (notes 4, 41 and bibliography).

The Alexandrian doctrine of redemption through the assumption of human nature and the rejection of Apollinaris were likewise used by Thomas. On account of his knowledge of the *Acts* of the Council of Ephesus he acquired a much better understanding of Arianism. Furthermore, Thomas's finesse in his analysis of Nestorius, despite his lack of knowledge of the Greek sources[62] is yet another indication of his unique theological genius.

However, Thomas surpassed Damascenus and others in his extremely clear presentation of Christian doctrine and in his sharp-sighted analysis of such concepts as person, individual, nature and the way they are applied to Christ. Thomas appears to have some reservations with regard to the Greek doctrine of the deification of the human nature of Christ through the hypostatic union, but he did develop the doctrine of the fulness of grace in Christ.

I. Backus concludes his observations by pointing to another aspect of Thomas's genius: his understanding of the positive method in theology, his high respect for Greek theology and his capacity to penetrate the world of the Greek Fathers.[63]

The christology of the *S.Th.* III is followed by the treatise of the sacraments which allow us to enter into a communion with Christ. In qq. 60–62 on the nature, the necessity and the main effects of the sacraments Augustine is the first authority. Some well-known texts are the following: "The visible sacrifice is the sacrament, that is the sacred sign of the invisible sacrifice"; "In no known religion, regardless of whether it is true or false, can people be brought together, unless they are bound by sharing some visible signs and symbols".[64] When Augustine writes that "verbum operatur (in sacramentis) non quia dicitur sed quia creditur" (the word is efficacious in the sacraments not because it is uttered but because it is believed) Thomas explains: it is not a question of the external sound of the words but of their meaning which we know by the faith. He also quotes Augustine's observation "from where comes this stupendous power of the water that it touches the body and washes clean the heart if it does not do so through the word, (and that) not because it is said, but

---

[62] Backus, *o.c.*, 181.
[63] *O.c.*, p. 326.
[64] "Sacrificium visibile invisibilis sacrificii sacramentum, id est sacrum signum est"; "In nullum nomen religionis, seu verum seu falsum, coadunari homines possunt, nisi aliquo signaculorum vel sacramentorum visibilium consortio colligentur".

because it is believed" and "the word is joined to the element and the sacrament is there".[65]

In the following questions on the individual sacraments, their form, matter and ministration, Thomas mentions a great number of decrees and decisions by councils, synods and popes and refers also to the liturgical use of the Church. Occasional quotations from the Fathers occur such as Ambrose's words in 75, 8: "Where the consecration is added, bread becomes the body of Christ"[66] and a passage from Cyril in 75, 1: "Do not doubt their truth, but rather accept in faith the words of the Saviour; since He is the Truth, he speaks no falsehood".[67] In 90, 4 Augustine provides the last *Sed contra* argument of this (incomplete) Third Part.

Indeed, throughout the *Summa theologiae* Augustine is the Father of the Church who enjoys the greatest authority and is quoted most, over four times more than Gregory and over five times more than Dionysius. One may say that Thomas composed his works in an uninterrupted dialogue with Augustine. He had read, meditated on and memorised the writings of Augustine so well that he could present a chrestomathy of the most characteristic, profound and beautiful texts of the Bishop of Hippo Regius.[68] The reader is struck by Aquinas's broad acquaintance with these numerous works: with a perfect mastery of an immense documentation he quotes not only the better known works of Augustine but also his sermons, letters and treatises which nowadays are almost forgotten.[69] On account of their importance, several texts are mentioned more than once. On a few occasions Thomas is mistaken regarding the title of the work and this might mean that he is quoting from memory.

As to philosophical issues which are in some way connected with the doctrine of the faith (such as the spirituality of the soul) Thomas likes to corroborate his theses with the authority of Augustine but,

---

[65] "Unde ista est tanta virtus aquae ut corpus tangat et cor abluat nisi faciens verbo, non quia dicitur sed quia creditur" (60, 6) and "accedit verbum ad elementum et fit sacramentum" (60, 4).

[66] "Ubi accedit consecratio, de pane fit corpus Christi".

[67] "Non dubites an hoc verum sit, sed potius suscipe verba Salvatoris in fide; cum enim sit veritas, non mentitur".

[68] See my study "Les citations de saint Augustin dans la *Somme théologique* de saint Thomas d'Aquin", in *Doctor communis*, 1987, 115–165.

[69] A glance at the *Index of the Summa theologiae and the Summa contra gentiles* of the Leonine Edition (under "Auctoritates citatae a sancto Thoma") will show the enormous number of Augustine's works quoted by Aquinas.

on a number of points, he corrects the latter's statements noting that "in hoc sequitur opinionem Platonis" or "et hanc opinionem, scil. Platonicorum, tangere videtur Augustinus".[70] As we have shown above, Aquinas explains certain texts which might cause misunderstandings.[71] Indeed, when we compare his presentation of many points of doctrine with the works of Augustine we notice considerable progress in the analysis of problems and the elaboration of solutions. Nevertheless, Augustine had provided a great number of texts which offer profound insights into the truth and are remarkable for the beauty of their literary expression. Thomas must have appreciated them, for he multiplies the quotations as so many pearls of Christian wisdom and literary beauty of which Augustine had the secret.

Augustine has a special authority on certain questions: with Jerome, Chrysostom and Origen he is the undisputed master with regard to the interpretation of the New Testament. Augustine is also an authority on the interior life of the Christian. Above all, he is the good pastor, our reliable guide in the most difficult ethical questions. Finally, he is an important source of information about antiquity and the non-Christian philosophers.

Thomas was full of admiration and gratitude with regard to the gigantic personality of the greatest of the Fathers of the Church, even if in his references there is no servile flattery, for truth is the only thing that mattered to Thomas.

A Concise Bibliography

The Fathers of the Church are referred to and quoted in the wording found in the works of Thomas Aquinas. For Thomas's works the Leonine Edition was used insofar as it is now available. For the other works, such as the *Catena aurea*, the *Commentaries on the Gospel according to Matthew* and the *Gospel according to John* the Marietti Edition was used.

Ignaz Backus, *Die Christologie des hl. Thomas von Aquin und die griechischen Kirchenväter*, Paderborn 1931.
Irena Backus, *Lectures humanistes de Basile de Césarée. Traductions latines (1439–1618)*, Paris 1990.
G. Bardy, "Sur les sources patristiques grecques de saint Thomas dans la Ière partie de la *Somme théologique*", in *RSPT* XII (1923), 493–502.

---

[70] I 66, 2 ad 1; 84, 6. Cf. the *Qaest. disp. de spir. creat.*, q. un., 10 ad 8.
[71] These texts are mostly quoted in the objections at the beginning of the articles.

J.-G. Bougerol, "The Fathers in the *Sentences* of Peter Lombard", *supra*, pp. 113–164.

P. Classen, *Burgundio von Pisa, Richter-Gesandter-Übersetzer*, Heidelberg 1974.

M.-D. Chenu, *Le théologie au douzième siècle*[2], Paris 1966.

P. Chevalier, *Dionysiaca. Recueil donnant l'ensemble des traductions latines des ouvrages attribués à Denys l'Aréopagite*, 2 vols., Bruges 1937–1950.

G. Conticello, "San Tommaso ed i Padri: la *Catena aurea super Ioannem*", in *Archives d'histoire doctrinale et littéraire du Moyen Âge* 65 (1990), 31–92.

L. Elders, "Les citations de saint Augustin dans la *Somme théologique* de saint Thomas d'Aquin", in *Doctor communis*, 1987, 115–165.

A. Gardeil, "La réforme de la théologie catholique. La documentation de saint Thomas", *Revue thomiste* 1903, 5–19; 197–215; 1904, 207–211; 583–592; 1905, 194–196.

J.G. Geenen, "Le fonte patristiche come "autorità" nella teologia di S. Tommaso", in *Sacra doctrina* 77, 7–67.

Id., "Saint Thomas d'Aquin et ses sources pseudoépigraphiques", in *Ephemerides theol. lovan.*, 1943, 71–80.

J. de Ghellinck, "Le traité de Pierre de Lombard sur les sept ordres ecclésiastiques: ses sources, ses copistes", in *Revue d'hist. ecclésiastique*, X (1909) 290ff.

A. v. Harnack, *Lehrbuch der Dogmengeschichte*, III[3], Freiburg 1897.

G. von Hertling, *Sitzungsberichte d. Bayr. Akad. d. Wiss., philos. philol. histor. Klasse*, 1904, 535–602.

V. Lossky, *Essai sur la théologie mystique de l'Orient*, Paris 1944.

E.A. Matter, "The Fathers in the *Glossa ordinaria*", *supra*, pp. 83–112.

W. Otten, "The Texture of Tradition. The Role of the Church Fathers in Carolingian Theology", *supra*, pp. 3–50.

C. Pera, o.p., *Le Fonti del Pensiero di Tommaso d'Aquino nella Somma Theologica*, Torino 1979.

Enzo Portalupi, *Studi sulla presenza di Gregorio Magno in Tommaso d'Aquino*, Fribourg 1991.

M. Scheeben, *Handbuch der katholischen Dogmatik*, I 428–430.

W.G.M.B. Valkenberg, *Did not our Heart Burn! Place and Function of Holy Scripture in the Theology of Aquinas*, Utrecht 1990.

J. Weisheipl, *Friar Thomas D'Aquino. His Life, Thought and Works*, Washington[2] 1983.

THE RECEPTION OF AUGUSTINE IN THE LATER
MIDDLE AGES

Eric Leland Saak

The year 1506 was pivotal for Augustine scholarship in the later Middle Ages. Johannes Amerbach had been working in Basel since 1490 on the first edition of Augustine's *Opera Omnia*. Reaching its completion in 1506, the Amerbach edition "signified at the same time a break and a new beginning in the history of Augustine's reception."[1] Martin Luther and Andrew Karlstadt were soon to seize the fruits of this monumental achievement and claim Augustine as their own. Two years later, in 1508, the statutes of the University of Wittenberg instituted the *via Gregorii* as the designation of the *via moderna*, alongside the "old ways" of the *via Thomae* and the *via Scoti*.[2] Henceforth Wittenberg students could be taught in the tradition of the fourteenth-century Augustinian friar, Gregory of Rimini (d. 1359). Gregory's famous sixteenth-century Wittenberg confrère "Brother Martin" extolled his forebearer as having stood alone "in the battle for Scripture and Augustine against the scholastic doctors."[3] Ten years after the Amerbach edition, Erasmus of Rotterdam defended the superiority not of Augustine, but of Jerome as *summus theologus* and as the model for the humanist ideal.[4] When Erasmus' own edition of

---

[1] "... die Amerbachedition bedeutet zugleich Zäsur und Neuanfang in der Geschichte der Augustinrezeption." Heiko A. Oberman, *Werden und Wertung der Reformation. Vom Wegestreit zum Glaubenskampf*, (Tübingen, 1977; 2nd ed. Tübingen, 1979), 90. Cf. H.A. Oberman, *Masters of the Reformation*, trans. by Denis Martin, (Cambridge, 1981), 71.

[2] See Heiko A. Oberman, "Headwaters of the Reformation: *Initia Lutheri—Initia Reformationis*," in H.A. Oberman, *The Dawn of the Reformation. Essays in Late Medieval and Early Reformation Thought*, (Edinburgh, 1986), 39–83; 65–80. Originally published in *Luther and the Dawn of the Modern Era: Papers for the Fourth International Congress for Luther Research*, ed. H.A. Oberman, SHCT 8, (Leiden, 1974), 40–88; Manfred Schulze, "Via Gregorii in Forschung und Quellen," in *Gregor von Rimini. Werk und Wirkung bis zur Reformation*, SuR 20, (Berlin-New York, 1981), 1–126.

[3] H.A. Oberman, "Headwaters of the Reformation," 45.

[4] H.A. Oberman, *Werden und Wertung*, 93–95. On Jerome's influence in the later Middle Ages, see Berndt Hamm, "Hieronymus—Begeisterung und Augustinismus vor der Reformation. Beobachtungen zur Beziehung zwischen Humanismus und Frömmigkeitstheologie (am Beispiel Nürnbergs)," in *Augustine, the Harvest, and Theology*

Augustine appeared in 1529, it was simply one in a series of Church Fathers the humanist produced. Even though shortly thereafter John Calvin saw himself as standing with Augustine on the ruler of faith,[5] the late medieval Augustinian Renaissance was at an end.

Yet the appearance of the Amerbach edition marks a turning point in another sense. Precisely when the scholarly apparatus was available to facilitate research on the entire corpus of Augustine's works as never before, Luther and Karlstadt made the antipelagian Augustine the standard, thereby distancing themselves from the historical Church Father.[6] If the symphony of late medieval Augustinianism crescendoed to a climax in the Wittenberg theology and its *via Gregorii*, it came to a close in unison on the dominant note of Augustine's antipelagianism.

Since the turn of the 20th century, Luther has provided the catalyst for research that has broadened and deepened our knowledge of Augustine's heritage. Scholars have sought either to illumine the late medieval sources of Luther's Reformation theology, or to preserve Luther's originality from the taint of his scholastic past.[7] Yet conclusive proof of Luther's exact dependence on or independence from the tradition(s) of his Order still lies beyond our grasp. The extent to which Luther was influenced by the likes of Gregory of Rimini, Hugolino of Orvieto, or Simon Fidati of Cascia remains the subject of speculation and debate.[8]

(1300–1650). Essays Dedicated to Heiko Augustinus Oberman in Honor of his Sixtieth Birthday, ed. Kenneth Hagen, (Leiden, 1990), 127–233.

[5] See Luchesius Smits, *Saint Augustin dans l'oeuvre de Jean Calvin*. I: *Étude de critique littéraire*, (Assen, 1957).

[6] "Modern scholarship cannot but agree with Melanchthon against Luther when he argues that *sola fide* does not characterize Augustine's doctrine of justification. Indeed, to be immersed in and to emerge from late medieval Augustinianism does not *ipso facto* mean a better grasp of the historical Augustine." H.A. Oberman, "Headwaters of the Reformation," 72–73. See also, Bernhard Lohse, "Zum Wittenberger Augustinismus. Augustins Schrift De Spiritu et Littera in der Auslegung bei Staupitz, Luther und Karlstadt," in *Augustine, the Harvest, and Theology*, 89–108.

[7] For an overview of the scholarship from the later 19th century to present, see Manfred Schulze, "Via Gregorii in Forschung und Quellen,"; David C. Steinmetz, *Luther and Staupitz. An Essay in the Intellectual Origins of the Protestant Reformation*. Duke Monographs in Medieval and Renaissance Studies 4, (Durham, N.C., 1980): 16–27; and Eric Leland Saak, "Religio Augustini: Jordan of Quedlinburg and the Augustinian Tradition in Late Medieval Germany" (Ph.D. diss., University of Arizona, 1993), 42–79.

[8] In upholding the importance of the *via Gregorii* against the position of Leif Grane and David Steinmetz, Manfred Schulze has poignantly argued: "Wenn sich uns Gregor von Rimini im 15. und beginnenden 16. Jahrhundert als vergessener Autor

Before the question of Luther and late medieval Augustinianism can be answered with greater clarity and higher precision than is now possible, we must first learn far more about late medieval Augustinianism. Even given the advances made in the past twenty years, we still know relatively little about the Augustinian tradition in the later Middle Ages. We now have critical editions of Gregory of Rimini, Hugolino of Orvieto, Johannes von Paltz and Johannes Staupitz. Meanwhile, the *Opera Omnia* of Aegidius Romanus is underway. But, the *Sentences* commentaries of Thomas of Strassburg, Alphonsus Vargas, Dionysius de Burgo, Facinus de Ast, Gerardus de Senis, Johannes Klenkok, Michael de Massa, John of Basel (whom Damasus Trapp called the "gateway to research and study in Augustinian Modern Theology"),[9] Angelus Dobelinus and Augustinus Favaroni remain in manuscripts and early printed editions. If we continue to base our portrayal of late medieval Augustinianism on the magisterial theology of Gregory and Hugolino from the fourteenth century, and Paltz and Staupitz from the fifteenth, we will not achieve a sufficiently historical understanding of Augustinian theology in the later Middle Ages.

---

erwiesen hätte und die Augustintheologie als längst überholt zu dieser Zeit übergegangen worden wäre, dann bestände in der Tat kein Anlass, ernsthaft mit Gregors Bedeutung für Wittenberg zu rechnen. Die *via Gregorii* wäre tatsächlich ein Schreibfehler in den Statuten." Schulze, "Via Gregorii," 125. It remains incomprehensible how Christopher Ocker, seemingly referring to this passage, could claim that Schulze "has shown that the *via Gregorii* had suffered a kind of chronological lapse. Gregory, at the end of the fifteenth century, was a rediscovered theologian. He had been forgotten." Ocker, "Augustinianism in Fourteenth-Century Theology," *Augustinian Studies* 18 (1987): 81–106; 84 and 84, n. 14 (endnote, found on 98). Cf. "Der 'Doctor modernus' Gregor von Rimini wird noch im Jahre 1517 der Tübinger Schule zum herausfordernden Gegner." Schulze, 100. Adolar Zumkeller concluded his study of the Erfurt Augustinians with an investigation of the "Luther question" and affirmed: "Die Frage jedoch, ob und in welchem Umfang Martin Luther von den genannten Autoren in seiner Lehre Anregung empfing oder gar beeinflusst wurde, bleibt auch heute noch offen und wird vielleicht niemals mit voller Sicherheit beantwortet werden können." Zumkeller, *Erbsünde, Gnade, Rechtfertigung und Verdienst nach der Lehre der Erfurter Augustinertheologen des Spätmittelalters*, (Würzburg, 1984): 481–482. In his final conclusion, Zumkeller summarized his findings: "Von Johannes Nathin (d. 1529), der seit 1493 den Universitätslehrstuhl der Augustiner innehatte und ihr Generalstudium leitete, ist nicht bekannt, welche Art Theologie er vertreten hat, da Schriften von ihm nicht überliefert sind . . . Ob sich Martin Luther in den Jahren seiner theologischen Ausbildung mit Schriften von Augustinertheologen näher befasst hat, ist unbekannt. Doch dürften ihm als Studenten an einem Generalstudium des Augustinerordens Namen wie Gregor von Rimini, Hugolin von Orvieto und Simon von Cascia schon frühzeitig begegnet sein." *Ibid.*, 503.

[9] Damasus Trapp, "Augustinian Theology of the 14th Century. Notes on Editions, Marginalia, Opinions and Book-Lore." *Augustiniana* 6 (1956): 146–274; 249.

Yet this is only the beginning. The *Sentences* commentaries of the Order's university *magistri* tell only a small portion of what was "Augustinian" theology. The Biblical scholarship of the Order is essentially *terra incognita*. The sources, however, are abundant. Augustine of Ancona's lectures on the Pauline and canonical epistles come to mind, as well as his lectures on Matthew.[10] The lectures on the Apocalypse of Augustinus Favaroni, Johannes Zachariae and Berthold of Regensburg also offer ample material for future study,[11] as do the Gospel commentaries of Zachariae, Michael de Massa, and Simon Fidati of Cascia.[12] In addition, exegetical handbooks, such as Antonius Rampegolus' *Figurae Bibliorum* and *Biblia Aurea*, and the *Distinctiones sive concordantiae historiales Veteris et Novi Testamenti* of Bindus of Siena should not be overlooked.[13] Before Luther's relationship to his historical context can be charted with more precise coordinates than it has been to date, we have much work to do on the context itself.

---

[10] Augustinus de Ancona, *Lectura in epistolas canonicas*, (see Adolar Zumkeller, *Manuskripte von Werken der Autoren des Augustiner-Eremitenordens in mitteleuropäischen Bibliotheken*, (Würzburg, 1966), 69, nr. 124; this work is extant in forty manuscripts); *idem, Lectura in epistolas Pauli*, (Zumkeller, *Manuskripte*, 77, nr. 140); *idem, Lectura in Evangelium Matthaei*, (Zumkeller, *Manuskripte*, 73, nr. 133, also extant in forty manuscripts).

[11] Augustinus Favaroni, *Lectura super Apocalypsim*, (see Zumkeller, *Manuskripte*, 182, nr. 154); Johannes Zachariae, *Commentarius super librum Apocalypsis*, (see Zumkeller, *Manuskripte*, 280, nr. 623, and Zumkeller, *Leben, Schriftum und Lehrrichtung des Erfurter Universitätsprofessors Johannes Zachariae, O.S.A. (d. 1428)*, (Würzburg, 1984). Zumkeller has also published portions of Zachariae's work on the Apocalypse in the appendix to *Erbsünde*, 544–567); Bertholdus de Ratisbona (d. 1437), *Lectura super Apocalypsim*, (see Zumkeller, *Manuskripte*, 93, nr. 190).

[12] Johannes Zachariae, *Collecta super Mattheum, Marcum et Lucam*, (see Zumkeller, *Manuskripte*, 281, nr. 625); Michael de Massa, *Expositio super Evangelium Matthaei*, (Zumkeller, *Manuskripte*, 331, nr. 694); *idem, Expositio super Evangelium Lucae*, (Zumkeller, *Manuskripte*, 331, nr. 693); Simon Fidati de Cascia, *De gestis Domini Salvatoris*, also known as, *Expositio super totum corpus Evangeliorum*, (see Zumkeller, *Manuskripte*, 359, nr. 778, and M.G. McNeil, *Simone Fidati and his* De gestis Domini Salvatoris, Washington, D.C., 1950). Of equal importance for the Augustinians' biblical scholarship are Jacques Legrand's *Expositio in Psalmos*, (Zumkeller, *Manuskripte*, 206, nr. 430), Johannes Klenkok's *Super librum Actuum Apostolorum*, (Zumkeller, *Manuskripte*, 246, nr. 521), Johannes Merkelin's *Expositio super epistolas dominicales*, (Zumkeller, *Manuskripte*, 253, nr. 544), and Jacobus Perez of Valencia's *Commentarii in Psalmos*, (see Wilfrid Werbeck, *Jacobus Perez von Valencia: Untersuchungen zu seinem Psalmenkommentar*, Tübingen, 1959).

[13] Antonius Rampegolus, *Figurae Bibliorum*, (Zumkeller, *Manuskripte*, 65, nr. 117) extant in thirty-eight manuscripts and numerous printed editions; see Eric Leland Saak, "The *Figurae Bibliorum* of Antonius Rampegolus: MS Uppsala C 162," in *Via Augustini. Augustine in the Later Middle Ages, Renaissance, and Reformation. Essays in Honor of Damasus Trapp, O.S.A.*, ed. Heiko A. Oberman and Frank A. James, III, in cooperation with Eric Leland Saak, SMRT 48, (Leiden, 1991), 19–41; Rampegolus, *Biblia Aurea* (Zumkeller, 62, nr. 115, extant in fifty-five manuscripts); Bindus de Senis, *Distinctiones sive concordantiae historiales Veteris et Novi Testamenti*, is extant in eighty-one manuscripts (see Zumkeller, *Manuskripte*, 96, nr. 202).

This is particularly true regarding the reception of the historical Augustine in the later Middle Ages, exemplified by the type of erudition that yielded the Amerbach edition of the Church Father's *Opera Omnia*. In this light, we leave behind the end of the Augustinian Renaissance and turn to its beginnings, when the symphony of Augustine's heritage still resonated in complex counter-point.

I. *Perspectives*

The historian who seeks to chart the reception of Augustine in the later Middle Ages is faced with an ominous task. The parameters for such an endeavor encompass the totality of late medieval intellectual history—from theology and philosophy to humanism and political theory. Ten years after Petrarch turned to Augustine on Mt. Ventoux and adopted the *gloriosissimus Pater* as the guide for the *Secretum*,[14] the bishop of Avignon, Fernandus de Hispania, praised Augustine in a sermon, referring to him as another Abraham.[15] Augustine's paternity in the later Middle Ages shaped the language of vernacular religious literature;[16] the philosophical discussions of

---

[14] Petrarca, *Secretum*, Proemio, *Opere di Francesco Petrarca*, ed. Emilio Bigi, Milan, 1979, 520; cf. Petrarca, *Rerum Familiarium Libri XXIV*, VIII [IV, 1], *Ad Dyonisium de Burgo Sancti Sepulcri*, *Opere*, 730–742. On Petrarch, see U. Mariani, *Il Petrarca e gli Agostiniani*. Storia e letteratura 12 (Rome, 1959), and P. Courcelle, "Petrarque entre saint-Augustin et les Augustins du 14ᵉ siècle," *Studi petrarcheschi* 7 (1961): 51–71. See also P.O. Kristeller, "Augustine and the Early Renaissance," in Kristeller, *Studies in Renaissance Thought and Letters*, (Rome, 1956): 335–372, and William Bouwsma, "The Two Faces of Humanism: Stoicism and Augustinianism in Renaissance Thought," in *Itinerarium Italicum. The Profile of the Italian Renaissance in the Mirror of its European Transformations*, ed. H.A. Oberman, with Thomas A. Brady, Jr., SMRT 14, (Leiden, 1975), 3–60.

[15] ". . . [Augustinus est] gloriosus Christi confessor velut alter Abraham. . . ." This sermon is embedded in Jordan of Quedlinburg's *Opus Dan (Sermones de Sanctis)* as sermo 150 (ed. Strassburg, 1484; without foliation). It appears in the midst of a series of Jordan's sermons on Augustine (sermones 129–151). The rubric reads: "Sermo de sancto Augustino, factus a magistro Fernando de Hispania persona saeculari et episcopo in Avinione, praesentibus omnibus cardinalibus, anno domini Mccclij." Josef Kürzinger has also pointed to a manuscript of this sermon, Munich, MS Clm. 18223, which gives the same rubric on fol. 233v; see J. Kürzinger, *Alfonsus Vargas Toletanus und seine theologische Einleitungslehre*, Münster, 1930, 98–99. This sermon will be published together with Jordan's *Opus Dan* in, *Jordani de Quedlinburg Opera Omnia*, eds. D.N. Pryds and E.L. Saak, in preparation with Brepols, *Corpus Christianorum, Continuatio Medievalis*. Cf. "Sancti Augustini commendationes diversorum doctorum: Augustinus est alter magnus Abraham . . .", Simon de Bruna, OESA (d. 1448), *Collectanea*, Brünn, UB, MS A. 87 (IV. Z. e. 11), fol. 24v; as cited by Zumkeller, *Manuskripte*, 357, nr. 776.

[16] Margot Schmidt, "Die Suche bei Augustinus im Spiegelbild der deutschen Literatur des Mittelalters," in *Scientia Augustiniana*, ed. C.P. Mayer and W. Eckermann (Würzburg, 1975), 214–233.

divine illumination,[17] divine knowledge,[18] and fruition;[19] and the political doctrines of hierocratic theory,[20] just war,[21] and the dominion of grace.[22] Theologically, no one denied the weight of Augustine's authority. Thus, the Franciscan Adam Wodeham argued Augustine against the Dominican Robert Holcot in the early fourteenth century,[23] and in the later fifteenth, Wendelin Steinbach countered Gregory of Rimini's position on the *auxilium speciale* by claiming that he did not understand Augustine,[24] a bold position to take against one who today is considered to have been the best scholar of Augustine in the entire Middle Ages.[25] The question was not whether one accepted or rejected Augustine, but how Augustine was to be interpreted. The universal influence and acclamation of Augustine rendered him, as Abraham, the "father of multitudes".

---

[17] See Gordon Leff, "Augustinismus im Mittelalter," in *Theologische Realenzyklopädie* IV: 699–717; 700–712.

[18] M.J.F.M. Hoenen, *Marsilius of Inghen. Divine Knowledge in Late Medieval Thought*, SHCT 50, (Leiden, 1993).

[19] William J. Courtenay, "Between Despair and Love: Some Late Medieval Modifications of Augustine's Teaching on Fruition and Psychic States," in *Augustine, the Harvest, and Theology*, 5–19.

[20] M.J. Wilks, *The Problem of Sovereignty in the later Middle Ages. The Papal Monarchy with Augustinus Triumphus and the Publicists*, (Cambridge, 1963).

[21] Anthony Black, *Political Thought in Europe, 1250–1450*, (Cambridge, 1992), 90.

[22] William J. Courtenay, *Schools and Scholars in Fourteenth Century England*, (Princeton, 1987), 309. For Augustine's influence on political thought in general, see H.X. Arquillière, *L'Augustinisme politique*, (Paris, 1934; 2nd ed. Paris, 1955). For artistic representation of Augustine in the later Middle Ages, see J. and P. Courcelle, *Iconographie de s. Augustin. Les cycles du XIVᵉ siècle*, (Paris, 1965); *Iconographie de s. Augustin. Les cycles du XVᵉ siècle*, (Paris, 1969).

[23] See William J. Courtenay, *Adam Wodeham. An Introduction to his Life and Writings*, SMRT 21 (Leiden, 1978), 101–103, n. 225. Courtenay presents substantial portions of Wodeham's and Holcot's texts, in which Wodeham counters the Dominican with reference to Augustine's *De libero arbitrio*, *De fide ad Petrum* (Ps.-Aug.), and *De bono virginitatis*. Courtenay notes: "The work of Augustine that Wodeham knew as *De bono virginitatis* appears in Migne as *De sancta virginitate* (*PL* 40,426). This work is not excerpted in Gratian's *Decretum* nor in Lombard's *Sentences*. The accuracy with which Wodeham locates this passage in the work indicates that he had first-hand knowledge of this Augustinian text." *Ibid.*, 103. A general study of Wodeham's Augustinianism would be most welcomed!

[24] Manuel Santos-Noya notes that in his Hebrew lectures Steinbach claimed: ". . . dass die Lehre vom 'auxilium speciale' keine solide Basis in der Tradition hat und dass Gregor sich nicht nur zu unrecht auf die Lehre der Kirchenväter beruft, sondern dass er—was noch viel gravierender ist—seinen Augustin missversteht und ihm eine falsche Lehre unterstellt." Manuel Santos-Noya, *Die Sünden- und Gnadenlehre des Gregor von Rimini*, (Frankfurt am Main-New York, 1990), 117. On Steinbach's relationship to late medieval Augustinianism and particularly to the *via Gregorii*, see H.A. Oberman, *Werden und Wertung*, 118–140.

[25] See Damasus Trapp, "Augustinian Theology," 181.

Yet against the general background of Augustine's heritage, scholars have discerned a renewed Augustinianism in the later Middle Ages. As Damasus Trapp phrased it:

> What happened in the Early, in the High and in the Late Middle Ages may, who knows, be pressed into the following, somewhat daring formula: Early scholasticism had both an Augustine and an Augustinianism of its own; Aristotelic Thomism had an Augustine, *but no Augustinianism*; late scholasticism rediscovered Augustine with an Augustinianism of its own! It might be true that the great crisis came when formulas of Augustinianism shifted their accents, and drifted away from the context of the original Augustine.[26]

Other scholars have gone beyond Trapp's suggestive sketch by arguing for an identifiable Augustinian Renaissance, comprised of various combinations of an antipelagian Augustinian theology, a more complete and critical knowledge of Augustine's *oeuvre*, and the theology of the Augustinian Order.[27] This research has been both intensified and made more complex by the debate over the relationship between late medieval Augustinianism and Luther. The result, in addition to the monumental critical editions of select Augustinian theologians, has been a quagmire of concepts and terms. Should the label "Augustinian" be applied to a theological Augustinianism, the renewed campaign *contra pelagianos modernos* beginning with Thomas Bradwardine;[28] to a philosophical Augustinianism of illumination under the influence of Bonaventure and Henry of Ghent; to a political Augustinianism

---

[26] Damasus Trapp, "Harvest of Medieval Theology [Notes on Heiko A. Oberman's book, *The Harvest of Medieval Theology*]," *Augustinianum* 5 (1965): 147–151; 150.

[27] The term, "Augustinian Renaissance" is that of Heiko A. Oberman; see Oberman, "'Tuus sum, salvum me fac!' Augustinréveil zwischen Renaissance und Reformation," in *Scientia Augustiniana*, 349–394; and *Werden und Wertung*, 82–140. Oberman's view of the Augustinian Renaissance should not be equated with two other interpretations of late medieval Augustinianism, namely Damasus Trapp's understanding of the *Schola Augustiniana Moderna* and Adolar Zumkeller's conception of the *Augustinerschule*. While the conceptions these three labels designate overlap to an extent, they are not identical. For Trapp's definition of the *Schola Augustiniana Moderna*, see note 30 below; for Zumkeller's interpretation of the *Augustinerschule*, see A. Zumkeller, "Die Augustinerschule des Mittelalters: Vertreter und Philosophisch-Theologische Lehre," *Analecta Augustiniana* 27 (1964): 167–262; A. Zumkeller, "Augustinerschule," *Lexikon des Mittelalters*, 1:1222–1223; and most recently, A. Zumkeller, *Erbsünde, Gnade, Rechtfertigung und Verdienst*. These three terms are often conflated and confused. Even Oberman apparently identified his understanding of the Augustinian Renaissance with the *Schola Augustiniana Moderna*; see *Werden und Wertung*, 130, n. 172.

[28] See Heiko A. Oberman, *Archbishop Thomas Bradwardine. A Fourteenth Century Augustinian*, (Utrecht, 1958).

which can be traced from Giles of Rome and Augustine of Ancona
to Richard Fitzralph and John Wycliff; to the theology of the Augustinian School throughout the later Middle Ages; or to some combination of all the above? As David Steinmetz put it, "it all depends on
what you mean by 'Augustinian.'"[29]

William Courtenay has given a degree of order to the melting-pot
of definitions by making the clear distinction between the new Augustinianism—doctrinally understood, encompassing theology, philosophy
and political theory—and the Augustinian School. The members of
the Augustinian Order may or may not have been Augustinian, and
there certainly were some theologians who unmistakably were Augustinian (such as Bradwardine) although they did not belong to the
OESA.[30] Yet more precision is needed. As an adjective the term
"Augustinian" can aptly be used to describe trends in late medieval
theology, philosophy and political theory. Problems occur, however,
when such descriptions become the basis for definitions of a historical, abstract substantive "Augustinianism". For the sake of clarity
we should distinguish not only a new Augustinianism—doctrinally
understood—from the theology of the Augustinian School, but also
the Augustinian School and doctrinal Augustinianism from the knowl-

---

[29] Steinmetz, *Luther and Staupitz*, 15. William Courtenay has noted that: ". . . Augustinianism may be, like nominalism, one of the most ill-defined and confusing of
labels." Courtenay, *Schools and Scholars*, 307. Cf. note 27 above.

[30] Courtenay, *Schools and Scholars*, 305–324; esp. 310–311. Courtenay asserts: "It
would also be helpful if we did not use the term 'Augustinianism' to describe the
thought of theologians who belonged to the mendicant order known as the Augustinian hermits or Austin Friars, as Adolar Zumkeller, Damasus Trapp, and others
have done." *Ibid.*, 310. Courtenay is correct to list Zumkeller here, but Trapp never
made such an association; in fact, he argued the opposite: "Augustinianism should
not be looked at as belonging to the exclusive domain of any one group of scholars." Trapp, "A Round-Table Discussion of a Parisian OCist-Team and OESA-
Team about A.D. 1350," *Recherches de théologie ancienne et médiévale* 51 (1984): 208.
Trapp was concerned with the historico-critical attitude of 14th-century theologians
toward citing sources in general and with the same attitude within the *Schola Augustiniana Moderna* in particular. He did not equate the *Schola Augustiniana Moderna* with
"Augustinianism", but rather with the historical frame of mind, combined with a
cognitio rei particularis, evident among the Augustinian theologians beginning with Gregory of Rimini, the "first Augustinian of Augustine"; see Trapp, "Augustinian Theology," 147–153. Moreover, the *Schola Augustiniana Moderna* was very short-lived for
Trapp: "The death knell of the *Schola Modernorum* rang when the schism destroyed
the scholastic standards of Paris by subordinating the academic world, its institutions and its magisterial dignities, to political expediency . . . Some of the *Moderni*
were still copied, but the school was at an end." Trapp, "Hiltalinger's Augustinian
Quotations," in *Via Augustini*, 189–220; 198–199, (originally published in *Augustiniana*
4 (1954): 412–449).

edge and use of Augustine's works. Thus, what is called for, to para-phrase Trapp, is a shift away from the varying accents on the definition of Augustinianism and a drift back towards historical descriptions of the reception of the "original Augustine", divorced from *a priori* doc-trinal concepts of what that entailed. No doubt political, philosophi-cal and especially theological "Augustinianism" contributed to the renewed study of Augustine's works,[31] but one important conduit for the reception of Augustine has not been given its due: the significa-tion of the term "Augustinian" not as a doctrinal adjective, but as the historical noun.

II. *The* Religio Augustini

In 1343, the same year Gregory of Rimini began lecturing on the *Sentences* in Paris, Gregory's confrère Jordan of Quedlinburg presented the Parisian Augustinians with the autograph copy of his *Collectanea Sancti Augustini.*[32] In this work Jordan collected a number of sermons ascribed to Augustine, including the first compilation of the *Sermones ad fratres in Heremo, vitae* of Augustine and Monica, a chronology of Augustine's life, various legends about Augustine, and a series of *auc-toritates* from Possidius to the Victorines praising the Bishop of Hippo.[33] In the fourth sermon, *De Prudentia*, Augustine refers to his foundation of a monastery on the outskirts of Hippo.[34] On the margin, in a different hand we read: "Note against the detractors of our Order, how Augustine was the leader and father of the hermits."[35] The precise date of this marginal cannot be determined, but it most likely is a

---

[31] Thus, for example, there is evidence that Bradwardine's anti-pelagianism influ-enced Gregory of Rimini; see Courtenay, *Schools and Scholars*, 323.

[32] Paris, Bibliothèque d'Arsenal, MS 251, 104 fols.

[33] See Rudolphus Arbesmann and Winfridus Hümpfner, eds., *Jordani de Saxonia, Liber Vitasfratrum*, (New York, 1943): xxiv–xxix; (hereafter cited as VF). Jordan's *Collectanea* will be published as volume I of his *Opera Omnia* (see above, n. 15). Cf. Rudolph Arbesmann, "The 'Vita Aurelii Augustini Hipponensis Episcopi' in Cod. Laurent. Plut. 90 Sup. 48," *Traditio* 18 (1962): 319–355.

[34] "Non enim credebam episcopari, ideo secure parveni cum karissimis amicis meis . . . et dei gratia me coadiuvante favoratus non modicum a praedicto sene Valerio, in heremo segregata a gentibus multo labore fatigatus, aedificare coepi monasterium et cum longiori anxietate congregavi in unum servos dei . . ." Jordan, *Collectanea, Ser-mones Sancti Augustini ad fratres suos in heremo*, sermo quartus *De Prudentia*, Paris, Biblio-thèque d'Arsenal, MS 251, fol. 7va [cf. *PL* 40, 1242]; see also VF 1, 7 (23, 37–42).

[35] "Nota contra detractores ordinis nostri qualiter fuit dux et pater heremitarum." Paris, Bibliothèque d'Arsenal, MS 251, fol. 7va.

reference to the Augustinian Canons. From 1327 to the end of the fifteenth century there was bitter dispute between the Canons and the Hermits over which were most authentically Augustine's true heirs.[36] Although Jordan began work on his *Collectanea* while a student at Paris (1319–1322) before the outbreak of the controversy, his compilation of Augustiniana provided documentation that the hermits were the genuine *Ordo Sancti Augustini*. Fourteen years later Jordan had completed the most comprehensive defense and explication of the Augustinian way of life in the Middle Ages, the *Liber Vitasfratrum*.

The *Liber Vitasfratrum* is an extensive commentary on the Order's Rule and Constitutions, illustrated with numerous *exempla* from the lives of the *patres* of old and the *fratres* of modern times. Only the hermits could claim Augustine as genuinely their own, whose combination of the active and contemplative lives formed not merely the *vita perfecta*, but the *vita perfectissima*. Augustine, for Jordan, was the lord and head of all doctors of the church; he was the *sapiens architector ecclesiae*, having restored the foundation of the apostolic life after the time of the apostles.[37] The true heirs of Augustine were to be the *imitatores Patris nostri Augustini*. Only the hermits were the followers of the historical Augustine. Only the hermits lived the *religio Augustini*.[38]

Jordan's praise of his Order's founder was echoed by followers of the *religio Augustini* throughout the later Middle Ages. The late fourteenth-century member of the Order, Augustinus Novellus de Padua, claimed Augustine's works exceeded those of all other authors in richness, order, and eloquence.[39] A contemporary, Simon of Cremona

---

[36] See Kaspar Elm, "Elias, Paulus von Theben und Augustinus als Ordensgründer. Ein Beitrag zur Geschichtsschreibung und Geschichtsdeutung der Eremiten-und Bettelorden des 13. Jahrhunderts," in *Geschichtsschreibung und Geschichtsbewusstsein im späten Mittelalter*, ed. Hans Patze. Vorträge und Forschungen 31, (Sigmaringen, 1987), 371–397; idem, *"Augustinus Canonicus-Augustinus Eremita*: A Quattrocento Cause Célèbre," in *Christianity and the Renaissance. Image and Religious Imagination in the Quattrocentro*, ed. Timothy Verdon and John Henderson, (New York, 1990), 83–107. See also Balbino Rano, "Las dos Primeras Obras Conocidas sobre el Origen de la Orden Agustiniana," *Analecta Augustiniana* 45 (1982): 331–376.

[37] "Beatissimus Augustinus dominus et caput est omnium doctorum. Nam sicut lux inter corpora habet locum primum, sic et hic inter omnes doctores obtinet principatum. Hic est sanctissimus Augustinus, qui tam sapiens architector ecclesiae fundamentum post sanctissimos apostolos construxit et reperavit." Jordan, sermo de Sancto Augustino, *Opus Dan*, sermo 130A (ed. Strassburg, 1484). Cf. VF III, 3 (330, 3–332, 54).

[38] See Saak, "Religio Augustini," 85–148.

[39] ". . . [Augustinus] omnes formae scriptores, qui de rebus sanctis sive in ipsis gentilium sive in nostris litteris ediderint, ubertate, ordine et elegantia superavit." Augustinus Novellus de Padua, *Sermo ad clerum in honorem S. Augustini*, Basel, UB, MS A.N. IV. 13, fol. 223r.

(d. 1390)—the *recollector Hugolini*[40]—uniformly began each of his sermons with a quotation from Augustine, the *lux doctorum*.[41] And the later fifteenth-century General of the Order, Ambrosius de Cora (d. 1485), not only repeated and expanded Jordan's arguments for the primacy of the OESA as the only true heirs of the historical Augustine, but also claimed that the hermits were the first *fratres* to have preached the Gospel to the people.[42]

Singing Augustine's praises was certainly not unique to members of the *Ordo Eremitarum Sancti Augustini*. Yet such hyperbole assumed additional shades of meaning in the writings of the friars. It was not just Augustine who was lauded, but Augustine as the historical founder of the Order. Whereas the Franciscans looked to St. Francis and the Dominicans to St. Dominic, the OESA stood in continuous historical succession to St. Augustine, the source of the Augustinians' mythic community.[43] For the Augustinian hermits, "being" an Augustinian was based not on adherence to given theological or philosophical

---

[40] See Trapp, "Augustinian Theology," 255–263.

[41] Simon of Cremona, *Opus epistolarum dominicalium*, Tübingen, UB, MS Mc 329: E.g.: ". . . quia ut ait lux doctorum Augustinus de trinitate . . .," (fol. 1r); ". . . doctorum lux Augustinus libro de sancta virginitate capitulo 42 . . ." (fol. 7r); ". . . lux doctorum Augustinus in sermone . . ." (fol. 211v); ". . . lux doctorum Augustinus libro de oratione dominica . . ." (fol. 222r). Simon's sermons are extant in thirty-two manuscripts and were printed in Reutlingen in 1484; see Zumkeller, *Manuskripte*, 366–368, nr. 787. Zumkeller gives the title as *Sermones super epistolas dominicales*; in the Tübingen MS Simon refers to his work as ". . . opus epistolarum dominicalium totius anni . . .," fol. 1r. The appellation of Augustine as the *lux doctorum* is seen already in a hymn on Augustine from the later thirteenth century: "Salve lux et dux doctorum/malleus haereticorum/conterens perfidiam." E.J. Mone, *Lateinische Hymnen des Mittelalters aus Handschriften herausgegeben und erklärt*, 3 vols., (Freiburg, 1853–1855), III, 205, nr. 815; as cited by Dorothee Hansen, *Das Bild des Ordenslehrers und die Allegorie des Wissens. Ein gemaltes Programm der Augustiner*, (Berlin, 1995), 82.

[42] Ambrosius de Cora, *Defensorium Ordinis fratrum heremitarum sancti Augustini*, (Rome, 1481), 499–616; "Ubi nota, quod primi fratres, qui praedicaverunt evangelium populo, fuerunt fratres heremitarum Sancti Augustini." Ambrosius de Cora, *Chronica sacratissimi Ordinis fratrum heremitarum sancti Augustini*, (ed. Rome, 1481), 742. See also Balbino Rano, "San Agustin y su Orden en Algunos Sermones de Agustinos del Primer Siglo (1244–1344)," *Analecta Augustiniana* 53 (1990): 7–93.

[43] Regarding the historical continuity within the Order from the time of Augustine, see Saak, "Religio Augustini," 98–117; for the Order as a mythic community, see *ibid.*, 128–133. The term "mythic community" bears similarities to Brian Stock's "textual communities"; see Stock, *The Implications of Literacy. Written Language and Models of Interpretation in the Eleventh and Twelfth Centuries*, (Princeton, 1983); *idem*, *Listening For The Text. On the Uses of the Past*, (Baltimore, 1990). The difference is that the center around which the community is formed is a particular myth rather than a particular text. In the case of the Augustinians, their myth was Augustine's historical foundation of the Order. To this extent, a "mythic community" also resembles Renaissance civic myths: see, for example, Donald Weinstein, *Savonarola and Florence. Prophecy and Patriotism in the Renaissance*, (Princeton, 1970); Edward Muir, *Civic Ritual in Renaissance*

doctrines, but on living the religious life in imitation of Augustine, on following the *religio Augustini*.

Yet being an ardent follower of Augustine's religion did not in and of itself make one an Augustinian scholar. Jordan is a case in point. In his *Expositio Orationis Dominicae*, which originated as ten lectures held in the Order's *studium* at Erfurt in 1327 when he lectured *ordinarie* on the Gospel of Matthew, Jordan cited Augustine more than twice as often as any other non-Biblical authority.[44] Jordan's Augustinian citations, however, are thoroughly traditional, lacking the precision and erudition that was the hallmark of the new scholarship.[45] Indeed, as William Courtenay has noted, whereas the Dominican Nicolas Trevet composed the first commentary on *De civitate dei*, followed by John Baconthorp, Thomas Waleys and the Franciscan John Ridevall, and whereas commentaries on *De trinitate* are known to have come from the pens of Baconthorp and Richard Fitzralph, and whereas Ridevall also wrote a commentary on the *Confessiones*, the late medieval Augustinians "appear to be the only mendicant Order not to have produced a commentary on a work of St. Augustine."[46]

While this fact may cause surprise, two points should be noted. First, writing a commentary on a work of Augustine *per se* does not indicate a singular knowledge of Augustine's *oeuvre* any more than a eulogy on Augustine indicates a special affinity. *De civitate dei*, *De trinitate* and the *Confessiones* were all standard fare throughout the Middle Ages. This is not to say that such commentaries are insignificant or unworthy of study.[47] We must not, however, equate commentary with

---

Venice, (Princeton, 1981); and Richard Trexler, *Public Life in Renaissance Florence*, (New York, 1980).

[44] Jordan cited Augustine forty-nine times; the next most frequently cited author is Chrysostomus with eighteen references. See Saak, "Religio Augustini," 150–419 for an edition of Jordan's *Expositio*.

[45] A similar knowledge of Augustine is evident in the writings of the Augustinian lector, Antonius Rampegolus; see Saak, "The *Figurae Bibliorum* of Antonius Rampegolus," 38.

[46] Courtenay, *Schools and Scholars*, 319–320. Fitzralph's *Glosulae super De trinitate*, however, is not extant. Courtenay is referring to the English Austin Friars; the Augustinian Alexander of San Elpidio (d. 1326) did compose a commentary on *De civitate dei*; see Zumkeller, "Die Augustinerschule," 172, (Courtenay erroneously gives this same reference for Trevet's commentary, 319).

[47] See Beryl Smalley, *English Friars and Antiquity in the Early Fourteenth Century*, (Oxford, 1960): 58–65, 88–100, 121–132. These commentaries, however, were not concerned with Augustine scholarship *per se*, but rather with classical antiquity. Regarding the commentaries on *De civitate dei*, Smalley notes that Trevet's commentary, "gives the pagan background to St. Augustine's polemic. Trevet provided the equipment needed by students whose education in the classics was too narrow to follow their author . . .

a profound level of scholarship. Second, even if no Austin Friar composed a commentary on a work of Augustine, Augustinians such as Gregory of Rimini, Alfonsus Vargas, John Klenkok, Hugolino of Orvieto and John of Basel give evidence of an Augustinian scholarship unparalleled in the later Middle Ages. Moreover, the pinnacle of Augustine scholarship in the later Middle Ages, the *Milleloquium Sancti Augustini*, was compiled by the Augustinian Bartholomew of Urbino. If the renaissance of Augustine was first and foremost a more rigorous erudition regarding the reception of Augustine's *oeuvre*, then the Augustinian revival was the achievement of members of the Augustinian Order, the followers of the *religio Augustini*.

III. *The Renaissance of Augustine Scholarship*

In 1956 Damasus Trapp published a pioneering article on fourteenth-century Augustinian theology.[48] Focusing on the knowledge and use of Augustine evident in *Sentences* commentaries, Trapp argued that the *Schola Augustiniana Moderna* was characterized by a historico-critical, as opposed to a logico-critical, attitude toward citing Augustine.[49] The "happy quoters" were no longer satisfied with the stock Augustine quotations culled from Lombard, Canon Law, and *florilegia*, but went directly to the original source. Trapp placed this return to Augustine within the general fourteenth-century historical frame of mind. The call *ad fontes* characterized not only Italian humanism, but the modern Augustinian school as well.[50] Unfortunately Trapp's announced larger work, for which this article served as a preliminary study,[51] never appeared, and with the notable exception of Richard

---

Trevet thought he was adding just one more apparatus to the patristic text." (62–63). Waley's commentary surpassed that of Trevet, while still in the same mode. Waleys, however, only commented on books 1–10. In the later Middle Ages his commentary circulated together with Trevet's on books 11–22. Ridevall's commentary, on the other hand, extant in only two manuscripts, had a different flavor to an extent. He was interested "in the *mens Augustini*. Waleys tended to ignore the writer except as a gateway to antiquity; his references to St. Augustine's purpose are perfunctory. Ridevall does not lose sight of the polemical purpose of *De Civitate Dei* and brings out the relationship between the allusions and the polemic." (126).

[48] "Augustinian Theology," (as in note 9 above).

[49] For Trapp's understanding of the *Schola Augustiniana Moderna*, see note 30 above.

[50] For the relationship between humanism and the historical attitude of late medieval theologians, see Damasus Trapp, "Hiltalinger's Augustinian Quotations," 195. For the relationship between humanism and the Augustinian Hermits, see R. Arbesmann, *Der Augustiner-Eremitenorden und der Beginn der humanistischen Bewegung*, (Würzburg, 1965).

[51] See Trapp, "Augustinian Theology," 147.

Wetzel's work on Johannes von Staupitz's reception of Augustine,[52] the detailed research into the actual knowledge and use of Augustine in the later Middle Ages epitomized by Trapp has not been pursued. Meanwhile the debates have continued over the influence of Augustinian themes. Yet if we are to delineate the historical contours of Augustine's reception, it is precisely to the lines of research set forth by Trapp that we must return.

Long before "marginal analysis" became a modern trend in historical research, Trapp looked to the "margins" to investigate the core of late medieval Augustinianism. He found the fourteenth-century theologians' historical mentality not so much in their texts themselves, as in their manuscripts' marginalia. Whereas in the text, authorities were cited by referring to the anonymous *quidam*, in the margins specific names and references were given. This was the first level in a three-stage evolution in quoting technique. The second was the development of the quotational inset. A quotational inset was a space left in the text column itself, in which the specific reference and quotation were placed, often written with different ink. This quoting scheme, according to Trapp, was "a highly complicated equivalent to our modern footnote."[53] At times, however, scribes jumbled the text and the quotational inset yielding an incomprehensible reading, or they simply left the space blank. This lead to the third stage, when the *quidam* was abandoned altogether and the specific references were given as part of the text.[54]

The emphasis on precise quotation is seen especially regarding the works of Augustine. John of Basel (d. 1392), for example, gave two chapter references for *De trinitate, De civitate dei, De libero arbitrio* and *De genesi ad litteram*, in addition to showing his familiarity with other divisions. Thus, in the tenth of his *Decem Responsiones*, John cited the

---

[52] Richard Wetzel, "*Staupitz Augustinianus*: An Account of the Reception of Augustine in his Tübingen Sermons," in *Via Augustini*, 72–115. Two additional studies should be noted in this context: Christoph Peter Burger has given a list of Augustine citations in Gregory of Rimini's *Sentences* commentary for 2 Sent. dist. 26–29, comparing them with Lombard; Christoph Peter Burger, "Der Augustinerschüler gegen die modernen Pelagianer: Das 'auxilium speciale dei' in der Gnadenlehre Gregors von Rimini," in *Gregor von Rimini. Werk und Wirkung*, 195–240; 230–240; and Walter Simon has investigated a possible source of Gregory's Augustine reception in his article, "Eine neue Quelle zur Augustinrezeption Gregors?" in *Gregor von Rimini. Werk und Wirkung*, 301–310.

[53] Trapp, "Augustinian Theology," 154. On the authenticity of the marginalia, see *ibid.*, 153–154.

[54] Trapp, "Augustinian Theology," 153–154.

fourth book of *De trinitate*, "chapter 52 *de parvis* and 20 *de magnis*; or according to other books, chapter 21 *de magnis* and 27 and 28 *de parvis*. In addition, book 15 of *De trinitate*, chapter 17 *de magnis* and 51 and 52 *de parvis*."[55] John often gave evidence of his personal acquaintance with the original texts by adding the precise reference for indirect citations found in Lombard,[56] by pointing to the occasional mistakes found in the *Milleloquium*,[57] and by citing Augustinian texts not found in source collections.[58] Although John's quotations of Augustine had "nothing to do with an Augustinian's love for the founder of his Order,"[59] his erudition epitomized the renaissance of Augustine, which Trapp sees as having been initiated by Gregory of Rimini.[60] Furthermore, the historico-critical attitude toward citing Augustine found among the fourteenth-century Augustinians, "produced the gigantic compilation of the *Milleloquium S. Augustini*."[61]

The *Milleloquium Sancti Augustini* is unquestionably the high point of Augustine scholarship before the Amerbach edition. Completed by 1345, the *Milleloquium*, compiled by Bartholomew of Urbino, consists of approximately 15,000 passages from Augustine's works, arranged alphabetically in 1081 entries.[62] Although John of Basel's correction

---

[55] "... capitulo 52 de parvis et 20 de magnis; vel secundum alios libros 21 de magnis et 27 et 28 de parvis. Item 15 De Trinitate capitulo 17 de magnis et 51 et 52 de parvis." Trapp, "Hiltalinger's Augustinian Quotations," 210–211.

[56] Trapp, "Hiltalinger's Augustinian Quotations," 215–217.

[57] *Ibid.*, 214f.

[58] *Ibid.*, 211. John's older confrère, Johannes Klenkok (d. 1374) did likewise; see Trapp, "Notes on John Klenkok, O.S.A. (d. 1374)," *Augustinianum* 4 (1964): 358–404. For example, in 2 Sent. dist. 30 Klenkok wrote: "Declarat Augustinus libro De baptismo parvulorum ut allegat Magister Augustinum; sed non est ibi sed in libro De nuptiis et concupiscentia..." *Ibid.*, 393. Trapp notes: "Klenkok shows his love for St. Augustine by improving upon the Augustinian source-apparatus of his Lombardus-copy; Klenkok's Lombardus-copy comes close to the perfection of MS Erfurt Amplon. 108, a manuscript which served the Quaracchi editors." *Ibid.*, 403.

[59] Trapp, "Hiltalinger's Augustinian Quotations," 211.

[60] "Thomas of Strassburg marks the turning point in Augustinian Modern theology. I call him the 'last Augustinian of Aegidius' and Gregory the 'first Augustinian of Augustine'. The two terms are not mutually exclusive. Aegidianism is old-fashioned Augustinianism coupled with the *cognitio universalis*, the Gregorian Augustinianism is 'Modern', is better acquainted with *all* the books of Augustine not only with his major works, and goes hand in hand with the *cognitio rei particularis*." Trapp, "Augustinian Theology," 181.

[61] Trapp, "Augustinian Theology," 264.

[62] Bartholomew dedicated the work to Denis of Modena: "Reverendo autem patri, fratri Dionysio de Mutina, sacrae paginae professori, et nunc Priori generali meo...," as quoted by Rudolph Arbesmann, "The Question of the Authorship of the *Milleloquium Veritatis Sancti Augustini*," *Analecta Augustiniana* 43 (1980): 165–186; 166. Denis was elected Prior General at the General Chapter of Milan in 1343 and died two

of the *Milleloquium* points to its lack of absolute perfection,[63] Bartholomew strove for precision. He was careful to present only passages he claimed to have seen himself[64] and gave the precise citation, or apologized for not being able to do so.[65] He verified the authenticity of Augustine's works with reference to the *Retractationes*, giving specific references, incipits and explicits. At times he offered variant readings of texts and expressed his doubt concerning the authenticity of some of the works ascribed to Augustine.[66] In addition, Bartholomew is credited with having discovered Augustine's *De Musica*, a work for which Coluccio Salutati was still searching in 1396.[67] The *Milleloquium* is not a mere collection of Augustinian *dicta*, but a critical piece of scholarship carried out by one whose "knowledge of St. Augustine's writings [was] probably unmatched in his time."[68]

Bartholomew's *Milleloquium* gives ample evidence of Trapp's description of the historico-critical attitude toward citing sources. The question that must be asked is to what extent the *Milleloquium* is a product of the historical frame of mind Trapp has identified among the university theologians? Bartholomew displays a knowledge of Augustine equal to that of his Order's *magistri*. The *Milleloquium*, however, stemmed not from a university milieu, but from the "other side" of the Augustinian School, the hitherto neglected network of the non-university *studia*.[69] Bartholomew never ascended to the *magisterium*. The known details of his life are few, but regarding his career

---

years later; see Arbesmann, *Der Augustinereremitenorden und der Beginn der humanistischen Bewegung*, 38. In the same dedicatory letter, however, Bartholomew indicated that he began work on the *Milleloquium* much earlier while he was lector in Bologna, beginning in 1321: "... sub cuius magisterio apud Bononiam compilavi...." Arbesmann, "The Question of the Authorship," 166. Arbesmann estimates the number of excerpts to be approximately 15,000 and the number of alphabetically arranged entries to be "about one thousand." *Ibid.*, 165. In the Tabula of the Lyon 1555 edition, there are 1081 entries (Arbesmann used the Brescia edition of 1734). Scholarship still awaits a critical edition of the *Milleloquium*.

[63] See note 57 above.

[64] "Disquirentis tamen animadvertat ingenium, mihi facile non fuisse multa volumina revoluendo flores eligere, cum non in eodem loco et tempore libros omnes habuerim, et nihil nisi quod in originali proprio vidi, hic rescripserim." Bartholomew of Urbino, letter to Clement VI, *Milleloquium S. Augustini*, (ed. Lyon, 1555), fol. iiv.

[65] Arbesmann, "The Question of the Authorship," 167.

[66] *Ibid.*, 168–169. On the Ps-Augustinian works in the Middle Ages, see M. de Kroon, "Pseudo-Augustin im Mittelalter. Entwurf eines Forschungsberichts," *Augustiniana* 22 (1972): 511–530.

[67] Arbesmann, "The Question of the Authorship," 170; see also below, n. 138.

[68] *Ibid.*, 171.

[69] See Saak, "Religio Augustini," 421–460.

we can only say with certainty that he was lector in Bologna, beginning in 1321.[70] Confessing himself as *pauper in scripturarum campo* in
the dedicatory letter to Pope Clement VI, Bartholomew affirms that
he compiled the *Milleloquium*, a work *magis utilis quam subtilis*, as an
exercise. He did so as an outsider of the Order's theological establishment.[71] Hence, perhaps the greatest achievement of Augustine
scholarship in the later Middle Ages was made independently from
the historical attitude found among the university theologians. Moreover, even though Bartholomew divided Augustine's works into those
designed to affirm the truth and those intended to combat heresy,
there is no evidence that suggests the *Milleloquium* was compiled as
an Augustinian defense against the "modern pelagians".[72] Neither the
upsurge of antipelagianism nor the university historico-critical attitude yielded the *Milleloquium*. If Gregory of Rimini can be seen as
the initiator of a new Augustinianism, we must recognize that the
historical revival of Augustine scholarship had more than one source.
Accordingly, we should acknowledge the contributions of *both* sides
of the Augustinian School. The years 1343–1345 marked not only
Gregory's *Sentences* commentary, but also the completion of the *Milleloquium* and Jordan of Quedlinburg's presentation of the *Collectanea*.
Further research may prove that the most important context for the
reception of Augustine in the later Middle Ages was not a renewed
theological Augustinianism, but the historical, existential emphasis on
living the Augustinian life in imitation of the Bishop of Hippo, the

---

[70] Zumkeller, "Dic Augustinerschule," 206; *Lexikon für Theologie und Kirke*, 2:14–15;
New Catholic Encyclopedia, II, 1134–1135.

[71] "Sed ego mendicus et pauper in scripturarum campo, palaestram mei studii
exercendo, cum caream ordine tribunatus, velut gregalis alienigena insignia gero
alienaque verba compilando transcribo et in paucioribus viam autumans magis fore
tutam, caeteris non spretis, sed pretermissis, Patris Nostri Augustini libros potius
percurrendo quam subtiliter studendo, perlegi verbaque egregia eligendo, in sub-
scriptum opus excerpsi: non ignarus me plures habiturum reprehensores, cum talis
compilatio magis sit utilis quam subtilis, sed quamvis inefficax videatur esse studium
quod ingenii caret effectu, tamen haec verba tamquam fundamenta in montibus
sanctis, meae sufficiunt facultati." Bartholomew of Urbino, letter to Clement VI,
Milleloquium, (ed. Lyon, 1555), fol. iiv.

[72] "Quia in Epistola huic compilationi praemissa, promisi omnium librorum Augustini, quos habui, nomina sive titulos in fine describere, nunc promissum servare
volens, occurrit cordi ipsorum librorum distinctionem ponere hoc modo . . . Et ideo
eius libri primo dupliciter distinguntur, quia primo sunt libri veritatis approbativi;
secundo sunt libri falsitatis destructivi, qui omnium errorum debellant falcitatem, ut
sunt libri contra haereticos principaliter editi." Bartholomew of Urbino, Index librorum, *Milleloquium*, (ed. Lyon, 1555), col. 2395. Cf. Arbesmann, "The Question of
the Authorship," 167.

religio Augustini. Both the *magistri* in the universities, and the *lectores* in the Order's schools effected a revival of Augustine.

Whereas Gregory, Jordan, and Bartholomew represent three independent sources of the reception of Augustine, a brief case study of a fourth will allow us to see how Augustine was actually used. Thus we turn to the Augustinian Alfonsus Vargas, who began reading the *Sentences* at Paris in 1344, and whom Trapp called the Order's first literary historian.[73]

IV. *Alfonsus Vargas*

Alfonsus Vargas read the *Sentences* at Paris during the academic year 1344/45, directly after Gregory of Rimini, and became a *magister* in 1347. He later became the Archbishop of Seville and died in 1366.[74] Only the first book of his commentary on the *Sentences* is extant.[75] Although this work enjoyed considerable influence throughout the 14th and 15th centuries, Alfonsus unfortunately has been the focus of only a single monograph, published in 1930.[76]

Alfonsus is of central importance for understanding Augustine's reception in the later Middle Ages because he gives evidence of the new Augustine scholarship independent from Gregory of Rimini. Adolar Zumkeller pointed to Gregory's relative lack of influence on Alfonsus, calling Alfonsus "the last great adherent to Aegidianism."[77] Trapp, on the other hand, placed Alfonsus among the "Augustinians of Augustine" since Alfonsus cited Augustine better than did the Aegidians. Moreover, Trapp has argued that Alfonsus actually invented the technique of the inset quotation, later referred to as the *stylus Alfonsi.*[78] If Gregory of Rimini deserves credit for having initiated a

---

[73] Trapp, "Augustinian Theology," 265.

[74] See Adolar Zumkeller, "Die Augustinerschule des Mittelalters," 224–225; Trapp, "Augustinian Theology," 213–222.

[75] Trapp, "Augustinian Theology," 213–214.

[76] J. Kürzinger, *Alfonsus Vargas Toletanus und seine theologische Einleitungslehre,* Münster, 1930. On Alfonsus' later influence, see Trapp, "Augustinian Theology," 215; Zumkeller notes: "Sein Sentenzenkommentar ist an Informationen über die vorausgehenden und zeitgenössischen Theologen so reich, dass er im 15. Jahrhundert bisweilen wie eine Art theologiegeschichtlicher Enzyklopädie Verwendung fand." Zumkeller, "Die Augustinerschule," 224.

[77] "Er ist vielmehr der letzte grosse Vertreter des Agidianismus." Zumkeller, "Die Augustinerschule," 224.

[78] Trapp, "Augustinian Theology," 219–220.

new Augustine scholarship, Alfonsus should have equal recognition.

In what follows, I will analyze Alfonsus' references to Augustine in the Prologue and distinctions 1 and 41 of his *Sentences* commentary. Yet one must do so with circumspection. As Berndt Hamm has noted with respect to the Augustine citations of the late 15th- early 16th-century Augustinian Johannes von Paltz, a mere count of citations is insufficient for determining a specific adherence to Augustine.[79] Thus, Alfonsus' references will be compared with those of Aegidius, Ockham, and Gregory to place Alfonsus' knowledge of Augustine within a continuum as demarcated by a representative of the "older" Augustinianism, a "non-Augustinian", and the "best Augustine scholar" of the Middle Ages. In addition, the Augustine citations of these authors will be compared with their citations of Aristotle in order to analyze the relative extent to which their arguments were constructed in Augustinian or Aristotelian terms.[80]

A. *Augustinian Cognition: Alfonsus'* Prologue

Commentaries on Lombard's *Sentences* began with the Prologue, in which scholars set forth their positions on the nature and characteristics of theology and theological knowledge. Alfonsus devoted ten questions to the Prologue. Although he followed Aegidius in characterizing theology as affective knowledge,[81] Alfonsus' argumentation bears an Augustinian stamp to a far greater degree than did his Order's first Parisian *magister*.

In the eleven questions of his Prologue, Aegidius cited Augustine

---

[79] Berndt Hamm, *Frömmigkeitstheologie am Anfang des 16. Jahrhunderts. Studien zu Johannes von Paltz und seinem Umkreis*, BhTh 65, (Tubingen, 1982), 313–319.

[80] I have included all references to Augustine, whether they are substantial quotations or simple references such as: "secundum Augustinum." I have done so to determine the frequency of appeals to Augustine within Alfonsus' argumentation. Thus I have used "citation" and "reference" as synonymous, which may or may not include actual quotation. It is not the simple number of citations with which I am concerned here, but rather with the comparison. Whereas abstract citation counting yields little information, a comparative study can illustrate the relative reliance on Augustine by scholars treating the same text of Lombard in the same academic context.

[81] See Alfonsus Vargas, 1 Sent., Prol. q. 10 art. 2, *In Primum Sententiarum*, (ed. Venice, 1490; reprint 1952), col. 129–131 (all further references are to this edition). On the affective nature of theology among the Augustinians, see Zumkeller, "Die Augustinerschule," 187; Agostino Trapè, "Scuola Teologica e Spiritualia nell'Ordine Agostiniano," in *Sanctus Augustinus Vitae Spiritualis Magister*. 2 vols., (Rome, 1959), 2:5–75.

sixteen times.[82] The bulk of the citations are to *De trinitate*, the only work of Augustine appearing in Lombard's Prologue. In addition, Aegidius cited *De doctrina christiana* and the pseudo-Augustinian *De disciplina christiana*.[83] This compares to his fifty-eight citations of Aristotle. Alfonsus, on the other hand, cited Augustine 111 times in his lengthy Prologue,[84] and Aristotle 141 times.[85] Of these 111 citations, 71 give specific references. Moreover, Alfonsus cited a far greater number of Augustine's works than did Aegidius. As with Aegidius, citations to *De trinitate* dominate, but we also find references to the *Retractationes*, *De genesi ad litteram, Tractatus in evangelium Iohannis*, the *Epistolae, Sermones, De doctrina christiana, De diversis quaestionibus, De libero arbitrio* and *Contra academicos*. Here we see clearly illustrated one of the defining characteristics of the new Augustinian scholarship—an increase in breadth regarding citations of Augustine's *oeuvre*.

We find a similar range of Augustinian citations in Gregory's Prologue.[86] However, whereas Gregory made reference to Augustine 78 times, in 158 instances he called on the authority of Aristotle, which yields an "Augustine/Aristotle ratio" closer to that of Aegidius than Alfonsus. Yet Ockham was even more "Aristotelian". Citing only *De trinitate* and the *Retractationes*, Ockham referred to Augustine a mere 29 times, while appealing to Aristotle on 210 occasions.[87]

To analyze the qualitative, rather than the quantitative, nature of

---

[82] Aegidius divided his Prologue into four parts, corresponding to the material, formal, efficient and final causes of theology; Aegidius Romanus, *In Primum Sententiarum*, (ed. Venice, 1521; reprint, Frankfurt, 1968), fol. 1vb–9ra.

[83] Aegidius also cites a work as Augustine's under the title, *De laude charitatis*. Alfonsus too cites a *De laude charitatis* as Augustine's (Prol. q. 9, col. 119, 25–29). I have not identified this work. Alfonsus later cites *De laude charitatis* of Hugh of St. Victor (dist. 1 q. 3 art. 3 & 4, col. 167, 8–12). This quotation is found in Hugh's treatise of that name (*PL* 176, 973A–B). Neither Alfonsus' nor Aegidius' quotation of the *De laude charitatis* ascribed to Augustine is in Hugh's work, nor have I found their quoted passages in the PS.AUG *De substantia dilectionis* (*PL* 40, 843–848), the PS.AUG *De diligendo deo* (*PL* 40, 847–864), Augustine's *Tractatus in epistolam Iohannis*, or PS.AUG (= Prosper Aquitanus) *Sententiae ex operibus Augustini delibatae* (*PL* 45, 1859–1898; *PL* 51, 427–496B).

[84] Alfonsus' Prologue consists of 137 columns out of a total 658 in the 1952 reprint of the 1490 edition.

[85] When only those citations that enter into Alfonsus' own arguments are considered the Augustine to Aristotle ratio is 75:87.

[86] *Gregorii Ariminensis OESA Lectura Super Primum et Secundum Sententiarum*, ed. D.A. Trapp *et al.*, SuR 6–12, (Berlin, 1978–1987), tom. I, 1–186.

[87] William of Ockham, *Scriptum in librum primum Sententiarum. Ordinatio*, ed. G. Gàl, S. Brown, G. Etzkorn and F. Kelly. St. Bonaventure, New York, 1967–1979 (*Opera Theologica*, v. 1–4): I, 3–370.

Alfonsus' use of Augustine, I turn to a specific theme—cognition.[88] Alfonsus' treatment of cognition was thoroughly Augustinian, although distinct from the "philosophical Augustinianism" of 13th-century theories of illumination. He treated the various types of cognition, or *notitia*, in the first question of his Prologue and began by clarifying his understanding of the habit of knowledge (*de habitu scientifico*). Knowledge, in this light, can be understood in two ways; in a general sense (*communiter proprie*), which is both equated with and distinct from faith, but not from wisdom, and in a specific sense (*magis proprie*), which distinguishes knowledge from wisdom. In the specific sense knowledge concerns the cognition of the temporal world whereas wisdom is the cognition of the eternal. The authorities for his distinctions were Augustine's *De trinitate* and *Retractationes*.[89] He then proceeded to define *notitia*.

In the later Middle Ages, theologians customarily divided cognition into intuitive and abstractive modes (*notitia intuitiva/abstractiva*). This Alfonsus did as well. Katherine Tachau has noted that: "The term intuition, found in Augustine, had been employed to translate Alhazen's hypothesis of a perceptual act whereby the *ultimum sentiens* scrutinizes the intentions it has received."[90] Although "intuition" is present

---

[88] What follows is not a thorough treatment of Alfonsus' epistemology, but rather an illustration of his "Augustinianism".

[89] "Distinguo primo de habitu scientifico, quia potest accipi communiter proprie et magis proprie. Communiter quidem accipitur pro notitia mentis clara vel aenigmatica cum adhesione firma, et sic fides potest dici scientia, sicut loquitur beatus Augustinus quinque decimo *De trinitate* capitulo secundo trecesimo de parvulis, dicens: 'absit ut scire nos negemus quid testimonio didicimus antiquorum.' [AUG de trin. 15, 12, 21; *PL* 42, 1075] Proprie autem accipitur pro notitia mentis, quacumque firma ratione comprehensa, et sic distinguitur a fide, non tamen a sapientia, sic loquitur beatus Augustinus primo *Retractationum* capitulo quarto decimo dicens: 'proprie quippe cum loquimur illud solum scire didicimus quid mentis firma ratione comprehendimus.' [AUG retract. 1, 14, 3; *PL* 32, 607] Scientia igitur proprie dicta est notitia mentis scibilis infallibilis firma ratione comprehensa, quia notitia mentis non convenit cum ceteris virtutibus intellectualibus, quia scibilis infallibilis distinguitur ab opinione, prudentia et arte, quae possunt esse de contingentibus, quia firma ratione comprehensa distinguitur ab intellectu principiorum et fide. Magis proprie vero accipitur pro notitia mentis rerum temporalium firma ratione comprehensa, et sic scientia distinguitur a sapientia. Sic loquitur beatus Augustinus duo decimo *De trinitate* capitulo finali dicens quod: 'haec est sapientiae et scientiae recta distinctio, ut ad sapientiam pertineat aeternarum rerum cognitio intellectualis; ad scientiam vero temporalium rerum cognitio rationalis.' [AUG de trin. 12, 15, 25; *PL* 42, 1012] Scientia igitur sic sumpta est notitia mentis scibilis infallibilis non aeterni, sed temporalis firma ratione comprehensa." Alfonsus Vargas, Prol. q. 1, art. 1, (col. 5, 44–69).

[90] K. Tachau, *Vision and Certitude in the Age of Ockham. Optics, Epistemology and The Foundations of Semantics, 1250–1345*. Studien und Texte zur Geistesgeschichte des Mittelalters 22, (Leiden, 1988), 69.

in the works of Roger Bacon and Richardus de Mediavilla, Duns
Scotus was credited with the invention of the distinction regarding
the modes of cognition. Moreover, ". . . virtually everyone who employed the terminology to the mid-point of the fourteenth century
took Scotus's definition as his starting point."[91] Alfonsus was one of
the exceptions. He took as his point of departure Book 11, chapter
4 (de parvulis) of Augustine's De trinitate.[92]

While Tachau approaches intuition from the philosophical perspective, intuition was actually first and foremost a theological concept,
at least for the Augustinians. The Augustinian Henry of Friemar
(d. 1340) equated the visio dei with intuitive knowledge,[93] and Gregory
of Rimini defined intuition based on 1 Corinthians 13 as the type of
knowledge that is facies ad faciem, commenting that this was common
practice.[94] Alfonsus followed suit: "Intuitive cognition is the cognition
of a thing in itself, actually present; such is the 'face to face cognition'
(cognitio facialis) about which the Apostle spoke in 1 Corinthians 13."[95]

---

[91] Tachau, Vision and Certitude, 70.

[92] Alfonsus, Prol. q. 1 art. 1 (col. 6, 11–12).

[93] "Et quia secundum Augustinum cordis munditia sequitur donum intellectus [AUG
de serm. dom., 1,4 11 (PL 34, 1235; CChr 35.10, 214–217) and 2, 11, 38 (PL 34,
1286; CChr 25.129, 855–856)] quia sicut munditia pupillae facit ad claritatem visus,
ita munditia cordis facit ad claritatem cordis divinae visionis. Quae quidem cognitio
sit intuitiva tunc pertinet ad donum intellectus prout perfecte habetur in patria; si
autem illa cognitio dei sit specularis et imperfecta, tunc pertinet ad donum intellectus
prout habetur in via. Et propter differentiam istam dicit Apostolus: 'videmus nunc
per speculum et in aenigmate,' scilicet in praesenti vita ubi deum cognoscimus per
speculum creaturarum, 'tunc autem' scilicet in vita beata, ipsum videbimus 'facie ad
faciem.' Haec est intuitive et sine medio obscuritatis." Henricus de Frimaria, Expositio
Orationis Dominicae, Basel, UB, MS A.X. 124, fol. 185v. On Henry see Clemens
Stroick, Heinrich von Friemar. Leben, Werke, philosophisch-theologische Stellung in der Scholastik.
Freiburger Theologische Studien 58, (Freiburg, 1954).

[94] "Has tamen sic nominare magis videtur dicto Apostoli, ex quo doctores
sumpserunt huiusmodi distinctionem notitiae, scilicet 1 Ad Corinthios 13, ubi ait:
'Videmus nunc per speculum in aenigmate, tunc autem facie ad faciem.' Quod
autem Apostolus dicit 'videre facie ad faciem', omnes doctores dicunt 'videre intuitive.' . . . Itaque in hac visione faciali, quam doctores vocant intuitivam, videtur res
immediate in se ipsa; in visione vero speculari, quam moderni vocant abstractivam,
non videtur res ipsa in se immediate, sed tantum mediante sua imagine quae immediate videtur. . . . In hoc ergo praecise videtur consistere differentia horum modorum
cognoscendi, scilicet intuitive et abstractive . . ." Gregory of Rimini, 1 Sent. dist. 3,
q. 3 art. 1 (tom. I, 390, 32–392, 2). The editors give no reference for "doctores" or
"moderni". Gregory supported his position with reference to Augustine, De trinitate
15, 9 and 23, and De genesi ad litteram 12, 10 (de magnis).

[95] "Notitia intuitiva est cognitio rei in seipsa actualiter et principaliter existens;
qualis est cognitio facialis, de qua loquitur Apostolus prima ad Corinthios 13: 'videmus
nunc per speculum et in aenigmate; tunc autem facie ad faciem.'" Alfonsus Vargas,
Prol. q. 1, art. 1, (col. 6, 3–7).

For Alfonsus, intuitive cognition was a mode of cognition defined by the theological doctrine of the *visio dei*, and he supported his position with reference to Augustine.[96]

Alfonsus, however did not limit his treatment to intuitive and abstractive cognition. Going beyond the common treatment of the time, he distinguished not two, but four types of *notitia: notitia intuitiva, abstractativa, superintuitiva* and *discursiva* or *deductiva*.[97] For each of his definitions he referred to Augustine. Thus, abstractive cognition, "is the cognition of a thing in its created representation; [it is] how we know things not present through their species, as blessed Augustine taught throughout book 11 of *De trinitate*;"[98] *notitia superintuitiva* "is the cognition of a thing in that in which its being is more perfectly present and known than in itself; such is the cognition of creatures in the Word, as blessed Augustine taught in the fourth book, chapter five of *De genesi ad litteram*;"[99] and discursive or deductive cognition "is the cognition of a thing through discursive reason, deduced from the cognition of another. Thus we are able to know God in some way from creation, as blessed Augustine taught in the fifteenth book of

---

[96] Alfonsus continued the above cited passage as follows: "Et quod ista diffinitio sit convertibilis patet, quia omnis cognitio rei in seipsa est intuitiva et omnis intuitiva est cognitio rei in seipsa; quod patet in notitia intuitiva sensitiva, quia non potest haberi sine actuali praesentia obiecti dictente beato Augustino 11 de trinitate 4 de parvulis [AUG de trin. 11, 24; *PL* 42, 987]." Alfonsus, Prol. q. 1, art. 1, (col. 6, 7–11).

[97] Alfonsus, Prol. q. 1, art. 1, (col. 6, 1–3). Tachau has described Alfonsus' definition of intuition as "an idiosyncratic variation of what he believed to be the 'common opinion'. In addition to intuition and abstraction, which he described traditionally but classed novelly as 'enigmatic vision' . . . he also posited discursive or deductive and superintuitive cognitions." Tachau, *Vision and Certitude*, 371. For his understanding of *notitia discursiva* Alfonsus could have drawn from Scotus; see Scotus, Lectura I dist. 3 pars 1, q. 1–2 (*Opera Omnia* XVI, 257, 14–16) and Ordinatio I dist. 3 pars 1, q. 1–2 (*Opera Omnia* III, 23, 1–5). Scotus or Ockham could have been Alfonsus' source for *notitia superintuitiva*. Although neither Scotus nor Ockham use the precise term *superintuitiva*, Scotus discusses *notitia supernaturalis* in terms very similar to Alfonsus' definition; see Scotus, Ordinatio Prol. pars 1 q. 1 (*Opera Omnia* I, 38, 15–20), and Ockham discusses *cognitio supernaturalis*; see Ockham, Sent. Prol. q. 7 (*Opera Theologica* I, 197, 23–198,4).

[98] "Notitia vero abstractiva est cognitio rei in eius repraesentativo creato, qualiter cognoscimus res absentes per earum species, sicut docet beatus Augustinus 11 de trinitate per totum [*PL* 42, 983–998]." Alfonsus, Prol. q. 1, art. 1, (col. 9, 20–23).

[99] "Notitia vero superintuitiva est cognitio rei in eo in quo perfectius habet esse et cognosci quam in seipsa; qualis est cognitio creaturarum in verbo, sicut docet beatus Augustinus 4 super Genesim ad litteram c. 5 [AUG de gen. ad lit. 4, 22, 39; *PL* 34, 312]." Alfonsus, Prol. q. 1 art. 1, (col. 12, 29–32). Scotus also discussed *cognoscere in Verbo*, Ordinatio Prol. pars 1 q. 1 (*Opera Omnia* I, 147–148).

De trinitate, chapter 2 *de magnis* or 3 *de parvulis.*"[100] Alfonsus' treatment
of cognition in the first article of the first question of his Prologue
was thoroughly Augustinian. Aristotle was cited a mere five times,
and only twice in support of Alfonsus' own arguments; Augustine
was cited 29 times, 19 of which form the foundation of Alfonsus'
argumentation.

Yet Alfonsus' Augustinian doctrine of cognition was in no way a
continuation of the thirteenth-century "philosophical Augustinianism".
The doctrine of illumination is entirely absent from his discussion.
Alfonsus is in frequent dialogue with Ockham, Roddington and
Aureolus, but Henry of Ghent appears in the text of Alfonsus' Prologue only three times;[101] in each case Alfonsus makes his opposition
clear with such responses as "ista tamen solutio est nulla,"[102] and
"nec illa fuit intentio Augustini."[103] Alfonsus presented a thoroughly
Augustinian doctrine of cognition within the framework of fourteenth-
century theology. He offers evidence that Augustine's influence on
late medieval epistemology cannot be limited to the continuation of
the doctrine of divine illumination. It was not the neoplatonic Augustine that provided Alfonsus with the source of his doctrine of cognition, but the Church Father; in arguing against the *opinio communis* that
notitia can only be divided into intuitive and abstractive modes, Alfonsus
objected that if this were so, the knowledge of creation in the Word
would be lost, "which is against the truth of faith and the teaching
of blessed Augustine."[104] Alfonsus endeavored to expound Augustine's
teaching, which he associated with the catholic faith. Not only quan-
titatively, but qualitatively Alfonsus appropriated Augustine anew.

B. *Fruition*

The doctrine of fruition, discussed by scholars in the first distinction
of their *Sentences* commentaries, offers a good test case to analyze the

---

[100] "Notitia vero discursiva sive deductiva est cognitio rei per discursum rationis
ex alterius cognitione deducta; sic deum ex creaturis aliqualiter cognoscere possimus,
sicut docet beatus Augustinus 15 de trinitate c. 2 de magnis vel 3 de parvulis [AUG
de trin. 15, 2, 3; *PL* 42, 1058]." Alfonsus, Prol. q. 1 art. 1, (col. 14, 37–42).

[101] Cols. 40, 110, and 125.

[102] Alfonsus, Prol., q. 8 art. 3 & 4, (col. 110, 33–34).

[103] Alfonsus, Prol. q. 9 art. 3 & 4, (col. 126, 10).

[104] "Ad primum istorum dico, quod antecedens non est verum; aliter periret notitia
creaturarum in verbo, quod est contra veritatem fidei et doctrinam beati Augustini."
Alfonsus, Prol. q. 1 art. 1, (col. 16, 3–5).

relative reliance on Augustine. By its very nature the distinction was "Augustinian". Thus, William Courtenay has discussed the Augustinian elements in Ockham's doctrine of "enjoyment" and has argued that Augustine's broad heritage "should warn us against seeing a single current of Augustinianism re-emerging in the late Middle Ages."[105] By focusing on the documented use of Augustine against the common Augustinian background we can, therefore, discern the degree of adherence to Augustine in ways a doctrinal treatment does not allow.

In his commentary on the first distinction of the *Sentences*, Aegidius cited Augustine 47 times. This compares to his 28 citations of Aristotle, which at first glance seems to present a case for Aegidius' Augustinianism. If, however, we focus on his citations that enter into his own arguments, we find that Augustine and Aristotle were both cited 14 times. In framing his responses Aegidius relied equally on the two authorities. Once again, citations of *De trinitate* are most numerous, followed by *De doctrina christiana*, *De diversis quaestionibus*, and the *Confessiones*.

The contrast with Alfonsus is notable. Alfonsus cited Augustine 169 times, drawing from *De trinitate*, *De civitate dei*, *De doctrina christiana*, *De diversis quaestionibus*, *De libero arbitrio*, *De verbis domini*, the *Confessiones*, the *Enchiridion*, *De genesi ad litteram*, and the *Retractationes*. Of these 169 references, 122 are found in Alfonsus' own arguments. Aristotle, on the other hand, is cited only 49 times in total and 28 times in Alfonsus' argumentation.

Once again, Alfonsus' knowledge and use of Augustine matches that of Gregory. Gregory cited Augustine 164 times. In addition to the works cited by Alfonsus, Gregory appealed to *De baptismo parvulorum*, *Contra Iulianum*, *De spiritu et littera* and the pseudo-Augustinian *De vera innocentia* (= Prosper Aquitanus, *Sententiae*, as in note 83 above). Aristotle appeared in Gregory's text 62 times, twice as often as the 30 references to the Philosopher in distinction one of Ockham's commentary. The "Augustinian" aspects of Ockham's doctrine of fruition, however, are not supported by his Augustine scholarship. Of Ockham's 22 references to Augustine, two are from *De civitate dei*, two from *De doctrina christiana* (via Lombard), and one from the *Retractationes*, with the remainder coming from *De trinitate*. Even with regard to such an "Augustinian" doctrine as fruition, Ockham called more often on

---

[105] William J. Courtenay, "Between Despair and Love," 19.

392 ERIC LELAND SAAK

the authority of Aristotle than on that of the Church Father.

Alfonsus gave evidence of his knowledge of Augustine not only by citing a large variety of Augsutine's works. He also filled in the reference of Lombard's indirect citations.[106] For example, whereas Lombard simply referred to *De doctrina christiana* in distinction 1, chapter 2, 5, Alfonsus quoted the same text, but gave precise chapter reference,[107] and whereas Lombard gave reference to book ten of *De trinitate* in the third chapter, Alfonsus, quoting a larger portion of the text than Lombard, cited the passage as 10 *De trinitate* chapter 10 *de magnis* or 33 *de parvulis*.[108] The latter reference points to the bi-serial system of citation in Alfonsus that we previously noted as well in the works of John of Basel.[109] As John, Alfonsus regularly gave two chapter references for *De trinitate*. We find the same method occasionally employed for *De genesi ad litteram*[110] and *De doctrina christiana*,[111] the latter of which was not cited bi-serially by John. Gregory, it should be noted, only gave evidence of bi-serial citation for *De genesi ad litteram*, and this rarely.[112] This testifies to Alfonsus' erudition and indicates the lack of standardization of Augustine's works; in the later Middle Ages there was no universal chapter divison. Alfonsus makes explicit reference to this fact when he cited the *Enchiridion* in the first article of his sixth question giving reference to chapter 73, "vel 115 secundum aliam quotationem."[113]

Throughout distinction one Alfonsus put his Augustine scholarship to work in combating opponents, such as his fellow countryman

---

[106] Above we pointed to John of Basel and Johannes Klenkok having done likewise; see above, notes 56 and 58.

[107] Lombardus 1, dist. 1, c. 2, 5 (52, and 56, 24–25); cf. Alfonsus, col. 205, 63–65. Lombard's reference is to c. 22 of *De doctrina christiana* (*PL* 34, 26; CChr 32, 16); Alfonsus cited this text as "primo de doctrina christiana capitulo 26." The difference in chapter reference does not stand against Alfonsus' erudition since there was no standardized enumeration of chapters for Augustine's works in the late Middle Ages.

[108] Lombard, 1 dist. 1 c. 3, 10 (60, 30–31); Alfonsus, col. 163, 21–25. The reference is AUG de trin. 10, 10, 13 (*PL* 42, 981).

[109] See above, note 55.

[110] E.g., Alfonsus, col. 247, 38.

[111] E.g., Alfonsus, col. 261, 11.

[112] In his Prologue, Gregory only once cited *De genesi ad litteram* with the designation *de parvis* [Greg. 1 Sent. Prol. q. 2 art. 2 (tom. I, 73, 9)]; in 1 Sent. dist. 3 q. 3 art. 1 we find a citation to the same work with the reference *de magnis* (tom. I, 391, 26–27). Scotus also cited *De trinitate* bi-serially; see, for example, Scotus, Lectura I dist. 3 pars 1 q. 3 (*Opera Omnia* XVI, 282–283).

[113] Alfonsus, col. 217, 10. Alfonsus quotes AUG enchir. 105 (*PL* 40, 281). Cf. above, note 55.

Fernandus[114] and Alfonsus of Portugal.[115] In both cases his argument centered on the proper interpretation of Augustine. In two other instances it is not only the proper interpretation, but the knowledge of Augustine with which Alfonsus clinches his argument. In responding to the position of Adam Wodeham that love and cognition were to be equated based on book 9, chapter 4 of *De trinitate*,[116] Alfonsus pointed out that Augustine had argued the opposite, but in a passage left out of Wodeham's citation.[117] Alfonsus finished his rebuttal with proof texts from *De trinitate* 9, 5 and *De libero arbitrio* chapter 36.[118] In the third article of his seventh question, Alfonsus contradicted the position of Scotus that each divine person has knowledge formally in himself, not in the other persons or in the trinity, based on *De trinitate* 15, by affirming: ". . . the statement is not found in the entire book, by Augustine or by anyone else . . . therefore I conclude that Augustine was poorly used."[119]

In the case of Alfonsus, Augustine was not simply a proof text to support his positions, but was the foundation for theological argument. He agrees with a position "because that is the intention of blessed Augustine."[120] Indeed, Augustine's teaching explicates that of Christ. After quoting Augustine, Alfonsus commented, "This is explicitly the meaning of the savior,"[121] and he rejects an argument "because then the position of Christ and of blessed Augustine would be meaningless."[122]

---

[114] Alfonsus, col. 170, 61–172, 19. This Fernandus has not been identified by Trapp, "Augustinian Theology," 221. Kürzinger, however, claims that he is the same Magister Fernandus of the *Sermo de Sancto Augustino* mentioned above, note 15.

[115] Alfonsus, col. 177, 56–179, 8.

[116] Alfonsus presented Wodeham's position on col. 183, 40–43, citing AUG de trin. 9, 4, 4 (*PL* 42, 963).

[117] ". . . cuius oppositum asserit Augustinus in auctoritate illa dicens quod 'non potest ei inesse sine memoria et intelligentia,' [cf. AUG de trin. 9, 4, 5–6; *PL* 42, 963–964] licet ista verba dimittantur in auctoritate allegata." Alfonsus, dist. 1, q. 4, art. 3 and 4, (col. 185, 51–54).

[118] Alfonsus, col. 185, 54–68.

[119] ". . . in toto libro non invenitur dictum ab Augustino nec ab aliquo . . . ex quo concludo quod minus bene allegatur Augustinus." Alfonsus, col. 266, 15–19. Alfonsus reported Scotus' opinion on col. 265, 65–68. The passage in question is one Scotus later deleted from his work; see Scotus, Ordinatio I dist. 1, pars 1 q. 2 art. 1 (*Opera Omnia* II, 28, 6–22). The Augustine reference is to *De trinitate* 15,7 (*PL* 42, 1065–1066).

[120] "quia illa est intentio beati Augustini." Alfonsus, dist. 1 q. 5 art. 4, ad argumenta principalia, (col. 216, 20).

[121] "haec est expresse sententia salvatoris," Alfonsus, dist. 1 q. 6 art. 2, (col. 219, 54).

[122] ". . . quia tunc ratio Christi et beati Augustini esset nulla." Alfonsus, dist. 1 q. 7 art. 2, (col. 261, 48).

C. Predestination

The doctrine of predestination, treated in distinction 41 of the *Sentences*, would seem to offer the best theme for determining a theologian's adherence to or distance from Augustine. Somewhat surprisingly, all our authors treated this distinction rather briefly. A possible explanation could be that predestination *per se* was not as compelling a theme as the relationship between grace and merit. At least this seems to be Gregory's reasoning when he states that he will give further proof of his position in distinction 26 of book 2.[123] Unfortunately, Alfonsus' commentary on book 2 of the *Sentences* is not extant.

Of our three test cases, this is the only one where Aegidius appears more "Augustinian" than Alfonsus. Aegidius cited Augustine 20 times, as compared to Alfonsus' 13 references. Only fourteen other appeals to authority are found in Aegidius' text. Four of these appeals are to Aristotle, three each to Damascenus, Dionysius, and Anselm, and one to Origin. Alfonsus did not cite Aristotle at all, but referred five times to Lombard, twice to the *Glossa* and Ambrose respectively, and once to Anselm. Aegidius drew most frequently from *De praedestinatione sanctorum*, while also giving reference to the *Retractationes*, *De diversis quaestionibus*, and *De civitate dei*. Only the citation to *De civitate dei* is given specific reference.[124] Alfonsus was consistent in giving book and chapter reference for his citations, which he took from *De genesi ad litteram*, *De trinitate*, *Enchiridion*, *De diversis quaestionibus*, the *Retractationes*, *De praedestinatione sanctorum* and *De praedestinatione contra pelagianos* (Ps.-Aug, *Hypomnesticon*).[125]

Gregory appears the most Augustinian of all. Even if he left his more complete treatment of grace and merit for later, in distinction 41 Gregory referred to Augustine 78 times, drawing from all the

---

[123] "Multae aliae auctoritates possent adduci ad ostendendum quod ad nullum bonum actum agit homo vel coagit, nisi ad coagendum moveatur et iuvetur a deo. Sed istae pro nunc sufficiant, quia in secundo distinctione 26 prolixius istud probabitur." Gregory, I Sent. dist. 41 (tom. III, 331, 9–12); cf. Gregory, 2 Sent. dist. 26–28 q. 1 & 2 (tom. VI, 22–114).

[124] Aegidius, 1 Sent. dist. 41 q. 2 art. 2, f. 217 p.

[125] Alfonsus' citation of the PS.AUG *Hypomnesticon* should not be seen as detracting from his knowledge of the historical Augustine. In distinction 41, Gregory also cited this work as authentic, as well as the PS.AUG *De fide ad Petrum*. Both *De fide ad Petrum* and the *Hypomnesticon* were excerpted by Bartholomew of Urbino as Augustine's in the section, "Praedestinatio," of the *Milleloquium* (*Milleloquium*, Lyon, 1555, col. 1795–1803).

works cited by Alfonsus except *De genesi ad litteram*, and adding others to the list.[126] Aristotle is cited only once. Ockham, on the other hand, cited Augustine only once, and this in quoting Scotus.[127] Yet this was one greater than the number of his references to Aristotle. Ockham devoted his time to discussing the positions of St. Thomas and Scotus, without bringing in classical or patristic authority.

Even if Alfonsus' Augustinian citations in distinction 41 do not match those of distinction 1 and the Prologue in quantity, he did adhere to an Augustinian position on predestination. After setting forth the arguments pro and con for the question, "Utrum omnis praedestinatus ab aeterno fuerit praedestinatus,"[128] Alfonsus advanced four suppositions in the first article of the question: first, "that God does nothing unknowingly;" second, "that in the knowledge of God, nothing is known whereby God would begin to know something *de novo*;" third, "that whatever God does, he does willingly;" and fourth, "that God is able to will nothing with a new, accidental will." Each of these propositions, Alfonsus based on the authority of Augustine.[129] Alfonsus then proceeded to refute the position of his confrère Thomas of Strassburg (d. 1357), the only interlocuter to make an appearance. Thomas had argued that the cause of predestination was God's fore-knowledge of the *viator*'s use of free will in the act of believing.[130] Appealing to Augustine,[131] Alfonsus forcefully argued that "God does not predestine anyone from eternity on account of the act of faith

---

[126] The works cited by Gregory and not by Alfonsus are: *Ad Simplicianum*, *De fide ad Petrum* (PS.AUG), *De gratia et libero arbitrio*, *De vera innocentia* (PS.AUG), *Epistola ad Sixtum*, and *De correctione et gratia* (*De corruptione et gratia*).

[127] Ockham, 1 Sent. dist. 41 (*Opera Theologica* IV, 603, 17–604, 3).

[128] Col. 626, 6–8.

[129] "Haec est prima suppositio: quod deus nihil facit ignorans, et haec nulli theologorum aut philosophorum est dubia, et ponit eam beatus Augustinus 5 super Genesim ad litteram c. 18 [AUG de gen. ad lit. 5, 18, 36; *PL* 34, 334]. Secunda est, quod nihil novi fit in scientia dei ut de novo aliquid incipiat scire; et hanc etiam ponit beatus Augustinus 4 de trinitate c. 6 et c. 27 [cf. AUG de trin. 4, 1, 3 (*PL* 42, 888)] et in multis aliis locis [cf. AUG de trin. 15, 25 (*PL* 42, 1078)]. Tertio est, quod deus non nisi volens facit quicquid facit; et hanc etiam ponit Augustinus Enchiridion c. 7 [AUG enchir. 107; *PL* 40, 276–277]. Quarta est, quod deus nihil potest velle voluntate nova accidente; et hanc ponit 5 de trinitate c. 37 et libro 15 c. 59 [AUG de trin. 5, 16, 17 (*PL* 42, 922); cf. AUG de trin. 15, 25 (*PL* 42, 1078)]." Alfonsus, dist. 40 and 41, art. 1, (col. 626, 29–37).

[130] See Alfonsus, col. 627, 22–628, 9; cf. Thomas de Argentina, *Commentaria in IV libros Sententiarum*, 1 Sent. dist. 41 art. 2 (ed. Venice 1564; reprint Ridgewood, 1965), fol. 112va–113ra. On Thomas, see Joseph L. Shannon, *Good Works and Predestination According to Thomas of Strassburg*, O.S.A., (Baltimore, 1940).

[131] Alfonsus, col. 628, 17–18; the reference is AUG retract. 1, 13, 8 (*PL* 32, 605).

which He foresees,"[132] nor "on account of future good works which
He foresees,"[133] nor "on account of the good use of free will."[134] Rather, "whomever God predestines, He predestines mercifully only by
grace," without preceeding merit.[135]

There is no evidence, however, that Alfonsus' firm Augustinian
position on predestination *ante praevisa merita*, i.e., *sola gratia* was advanced to combat a renewed Pelagianism. In the ninth question of
his Prologue, Alfonsus argued that the meritorious love of God is
not in the power of the will before the infusion of the habit of love,
for otherwise, "we would be able to merit eternal life *ex puris naturalibus*, which is the error of Pelagius."[136] Yet he did not identify the
error pelagii with any contemporary challenge. In all of distinction 41
the issue of—and even word—Pelagianism is absent, aside from the
one citation of (Ps-)Augustine's *De praedestinatione contra pelagianos*.[137] Alfonsus was not involved in a campaign against the *pelagiani moderni*.
In distinction 41 he sought to explicate Augustine's teaching on predestination and to correct the position of Thomas of Strassburg. He
wanted to make sure his fellow Augustinians realized that even Thomas
could deviate from the authentic teaching of Augustine, the founder
of his Order.

From the above case study four observations can be made. First,
the new Augustine scholarship is clearly illustrated. Both Gregory
and Alfonsus cited Augustine far more frequently, far more specifically, and from a far greater number of Augustine's works than did
Aegidius, not to mention Ockham.

Second, if Gregory is hailed as the first representative of a new

---

[132] ". . . deus non praedestinavit aliquem ab aeterno propter actum credendi in
eum quae praevidit ipse finaliter habiturum." Alfonsus, col. 628, 14–16.
[133] ". . . deus non praedestinavit aliquem ab aeterno propter actum credendi in
eum quae praescivit ipsum finaliter habiturum; igitur nec propter aliqua bona operatio
futura quae praescivit ipsum finaliter facturum." Alfonsus, col. 628, 28–31.
[134] ". . . deus non praedestinavit aliquem (cod. aliquam) ab aeterno propter
bonum usum liberi arbitrii, in quo cognovit ipsum finaliter duraturum." Alfonsus,
col. 629, 35–37.
[135] ". . . quemcumque deus praedestinavit, gratis solum et miserabiliter praedestinavit . . . ecce nulla merita praecedunt pro quibus eligatur; sed sola gratia praedesti-
nantis est, ex qua vocatur aliquis et salvatur." Alfonsus, col. 629, 62–630, 2.
[136] ". . . sed constat quod dilectio dei meritoria ante infusionem habitus charitatis
non est in potestate voluntatis, aliter ex puris naturalibus possemus mereri vitam
aeternam, quod est error pelagii." Alfonsus, Prol. q. 9 art. 2, (col. 118, 51–54). Alfonsus mentions the *error pelagii* only one other time in his entire work, 1 Sent. d. 17
q. 1 art. 1 (col. 426, 45).
[137] Alfonsus, col. 630, 56–61. Alfonsus quotes PS.AUG hyp. 6, 13 (*PL* 45, 1664).

Augustinianism, Alfonsus must share the accolade. Alfonsus' knowledge and use of Augustine matched Gregory's. Alfonsus' erudition cannot be attributed simply to his having listened to Gregory's lectures for one year. Alfonsus gives further evidence of his Augustine scholarship in the third distinction of book one where he quoted Augustine's *De Musica*, a work not cited by Gregory.[138] Alfonsus gives independent testimony to the new Augustine scholarship in the later Middle Ages.

Third, in addition to an increased knowledge and use of Augustine, we also notice a greater reliance on Augustine in comparison with Aristotle. Gregory and Alfonsus not only appealed to Augustine's authority more often than did Aegidius and Ockham, but also framed their argumentation in more Augustinian terms. This is especially evident in Alfonsus, whose "Augustine/Aristotle ratio" in his Prologue was more Augustinian than Gregory's. For Alfonsus, Augustine's doctrine was virtually synonymous with Christian doctrine.

Finally, the case of Alfonsus should warn against associating a rebirth of Augustinianism with a particular philosophical or theological position. His Augustinian treatment of knowledge in his Prologue points to the broad nature of Augustine's influence in late medieval intellectual history. William Courtenay's caution against identifying a single strain of Augustinianism reemerging in the later Middle Ages is well taken when Augustinianism is defined doctrinally, but this should not obscure the identifiable resurgence of Augustine scholarship that merits the label renaissance. Ockham's knowledge and use of Augustine in distinction 1 comes nowhere near the level of scholarship of Gregory and Alfonsus. Moreover, Alfonsus' Augustine scholarship had nothing to do with combating a renewed Pelagianism. The case of Alfonsus makes clear that the "Augustinian" campaign *contra pelagianos modernos*, so evident in Gregory and Thomas Bradwardine, was not a *causa sine qua non* of Augustine's reception in the later Middle Ages.

V. *Points of Departure*

In 1490, as Johannes Amerbach was beginning work on Augustine's *Opera Omnia*, the Augustinian Thomas of Spilembergo issued an edition of Alfonsus' *In Primum Sententiarum*. In his introduction Thomas

---

[138] Alfonsus, 1 Sent. dist. 3 q. 2 art. 2 (col. 315, 55–64). Cf. note 67 above. *De Musica* may not have been as rare as Arbesmann thought. James of Viterbo cited *De*

exhorted: ". . . believe the Augustinian religion, printed in [this] book of Alfonsus."[139] Over a century after Jordan of Quedlinburg instructed his fellow brothers to follow the *religio Augustini*, the *religio Augustini* was considered to encompass, at least in part, the academic theology of the Order.

The attempt to chart the theology of late medieval Augustinianism has centered around the examination of *Sentences* commentaries of the Augustinian *magistri*. Little attention has been paid to the teaching in the schools not associated with a university. Yet before a friar received his doctorate in theology, indeed before he was granted permission to lecture on the *Sentences* at a university, he had spent at least five years studying the texts of Aristotle, the *Sentences* and the Bible. This period of study often took place within the Order's non-university *studia*. The instruction in these *studia* should not be seen as only preparatory to higher degrees, or categorized simply as "spiritual teaching". In fact, these *studia* trained the preachers and priests of the Order. In the early fourteenth century there were three universities to which an Augustinian friar could be sent—Paris, Oxford and Cambridge; there were thirty-two additional *studia generalia*.[140] Few friars reached the pinnacle of the Augustinian educational system; the majority of the Order's preachers and teachers, those who did not become masters, were more representative of the theology operative within the Order than were its *magistri* at the universities.[141] And as we have seen, the "other side" of the Augustinian school contributed to the renaissance of Augustine scholarship, evidenced by the *Milleloquium*. If our endeavor is to understand the reception of Augustine in the later Middle Ages, we cannot limit our sights to the university context.

Musica in the twelfth question of his first *Quodlibet*; Jacobi de Viterbio, O.E.S.A., *Disputatio Prima de Quolibet*, ed. Eelcko Ypma, (Würzburg, 1968), 172, 529 and 173, 558–562, and a copy of the work was in the Augustinians' library in Paris; see Zumkeller, "Die Augustinerschule," 171. That Alfonsus went directly to the source is clear; whereas James of Viterbo simply referred to *De Musica* VI, Alfonsus quoted the text of AUG de mus. 6, 8 (*PL* 32, 1167–1168) and 6, 10 (*PL* 32, 1169).

[139] ". . . credite Augustiane religioni in Codice Alphonsi Ispalensis imprimendo." Thomas' introductory epistle is printed at the beginning of the 1490 edition and 1952 reprint preceeding column one.

[140] For a listing of the Order's *studia generalia*, see David Gutierrez, *Geschichte des Augustinerordens*. Vol. I/I, *Die Augustiner im Mittelalter, 1256–1356*, (Würzburg, 1985): 70f.; originally published as *Los Agustinos en la edad media 1256–1356* (Historia de la Orden de San Agustin I/I) (Rome, 1980).

[141] See Saak, "Religio Augustini," 421–460.

Yet to achieve an historical understanding of Augustine's reception, we must extend our field of research beyond the members of the OESA. As Trapp noted:

> Augustinianism should not be looked at as belonging to the exclusive domain of any one group of scholars: they all loved Augustine in the 14th century, the Augustinian Hermits, the Cistercians, the Dominicans, the Franciscans and their libraries, well stocked with Augustine, witness to the fact.[142]

Unfortunately, modern scholarship on the knowledge and use of Augustine among "non-Augustinians" is even further behind. Until we have thorough studies on Scotus' or Ockham's use of Augustine, for example, we will not have an adequate base for determining Augustine's reception. If the influence of Augustine can be viewed as a continuous "thought field", our task is to determine the relative strength and weakness of that field both within and outside the Augustinian Order.

To this end, research needs to shift from a doctrinal approach to late medieval Augustinianism to a source-critical approach. To be sure, political, philosophical and especially theological Augustinianism contributed to the renaissance of Augustine scholarship. However, only by an analysis of the knowledge and use of Augustine's works evidenced in the texts and margins of late medieval manuscripts can we chart Augustine's influence more accurately and historically than by appeals to parallel doctrines. We must refrain from defining "Augustinianism" doctrinally, and seek to trace the empirically identifiable reliance on the Church Father. In other words, as stated above, we must return to the program of research as outlined and pursued by Damasus Trapp, even if we come to reject some of his conclusions. Finally, such an approach will guard against interpreting Augustine's medieval heritage in light of the early Reformation debates. Luther's interpretation of and relationship to late medieval Augustinianism helps us to understand Luther, not the earlier Augustinian tradition in the fourteenth and fifteenth centuries. Alfonsus Vargas stands as witness that neither the antipelagian Augustine, nor the neoplatonic Augustine was the only authentic Augustine of the late medieval scholars who effected a revival of the Church Father.

---

[142] Trapp, "A Round-Table Discussion," 208.

It is impossible in a single chapter to present Augustine's influence in all its variety and complexity. I certainly have no pretensions of having done so. Rather, I hope to have offered a stimulus for future research and to have demarcated some of the directions that research might take and others that it should avoid. The challenge before us is clear: contemporary scholars must initiate a new "Augustinian Renaissance"—a renewal of research investigating the heritage of the late medieval *lux doctorum et dux heremitarum*. Only with much continued work in the sources—and most of all in the manuscripts—will we be in a position to evaluate more historically and with more precision than is now possible the reception of Augustine in the later Middle Ages.

Works Cited

Manuscripts

Basel, UB, MS A.N. IV. 13.
Basel, UB, MS A.X. 124.
Paris, Bibliothèque d'Arsenal, MS 251.
Tübingen, UB, MS Mc 329.

Printed Sources

Aegidius Romanus, *In Primum Sententiarum*. Venice, 1521. Reprint. Frankfurt, 1968.
Alfonsus Vargas, *In Primum Sententiarum*. Venice, 1490. Reprint. New York, 1952.
Ambrosius de Cora, *Defensorium Ordinis fratrum heremitarum sancti Augustini*. Rome, 1481.
—, *Chronica sacratissimi Ordinis fratrum heremitarum sancti Augustini*. Rome, 1481.
Augustinus, Aurelius, *Opera Omnia*. PL 32–47.
Bartholomaeus de Urbino, *Milleloquium S. Augustini*. Lyon, 1555.
Gregorius Ariminesis, *Lectura Super Primum et Secundum Sententiarum*. 7 vols., ed. A. Damasus Trapp, *et al.* Berlin, 1978–1987.
Jacobus de Viterbio, O.E.S.A., *Disputatio Prima de Quolibet*, ed. Eelcko Ypma. Würzburg, 1968.
Johannes Duns Scotus, *Lectura Oxoniensis* (*Opera Omnia*, v. XVI–XVII, ed. C. Balić et socii. Civitas Vaticana, 1960–1966).
—, *Ordinatio* (*Opera Omnia*, v. I–IV, ed. C. Balić et socii. Civitas Vaticana, 1950–1963).
Jordanus de Quedlinburg, *Liber Vitasfratrum*, ed. Winfridus Hümpfner and Rudolph Arbesmann. Cassiciacum 1. New York, 1943.
—, *Opus Dan.* Strassburg, 1484.
Lombardus, Petrus, *Sententiae in IV Libris Distinctae*, ed. P.P. Collegii S. Bonaventuare. Quaracchi, 1971, 1981.

Petrarca, *Opere di Francesco Petrarca*, ed. Emilio Bigi. Milan, 1979.
Thomas de Argentina, *Commentaria in IV libros Sententiarum*. Venice, 1564. Reprint. Ridgewood, 1965.
William of Ockham, *Scriptum in librum primum Sententiarum. Ordinatio*, ed. G. Gàl, S. Brown, G. Etzkorn and F. Kelly. St. Bonaventure, New York, 1967–1979 (*Opera Theologica*, v. 1–4).

Secondary Literature

Arbesmann, Rudolph, "The 'Vita Aurelii Augustini Hipponensis Episcopi' in Cod. Laurent. Plut. 90 Sup. 48." *Traditio* 18 (1962): 319–355.
—, *Der Augustiner-Eremitenorden und der Beginn der humanistischen Bewegung.* Würzburg, 1965.
—, "The Question of the Authorship of the *Milleloquium Veritatis Sancti Augustini.*" *Analecta Augustiniana* 43 (1980): 165–186.
Arquillière, H.X., *L'Augustinisme politique.* Paris, 1934. 2nd ed. Paris, 1955.
Black, Anthony, *Political Thought in Europe, 1250-1450.* Cambridge, 1992.
Bouwsma, William, "The Two Faces of Humanism: Stoicism and Augustinianism in Renaissance Thought." In *Itinerarium Italicum. The Profile of the Italian Renaissance in the Mirror of its European Transformations*, ed. H.A. Oberman, with Thomas A. Brady, Jr., 3–60. SMRT 14. Leiden, 1975.
Burger, Christoph Peter, "Der Augustinerschüler gegen die modernen Pelagianer: Das 'auxilium speciale dei' in der Gnadenlehre Gregors von Rimini." In *Gregor von Rimini. Werk und Wirkung bis zur Reformation*, ed. Heiko A. Oberman, 195–240. SuR 20. Berlin-New York, 1981.
Courcelle, P., "Petrarque entre saint-Augustin et les Augustins du 14ᵉ siècle." *Studi petrarcheschi* 7 (1961): 51–71.
Courcelle, J. and P., *Iconographie de s. Augustin. Les cycles du XIVᵉ siècle.* Paris, 1965.
—, *Iconographie de s. Augustin. Les cycles du XVᵉ siècle.* Paris, 1969.
Courtenay, William J., *Adam Wodeham. An Introduction to his Life and Writings.* SMRT 21. Leiden, 1978.
—, *Schools and Scholars in Fourteenth Century England.* Princeton, 1987.
—, "Between Despair and Love: Some Late Medieval Modifications of Augustine's Teaching on Fruition and Psychic States." In *Augustine, the Harvest, and Theology (1300–1650). Essays Dedicated to Heiko Augustinus Oberman in Honor of his Sixtieth Birthday*, ed. Kenneth Hagen, 5–19. Leiden, 1990.
Elm, Kaspar, "Elias, Paulus von Theben und Augustinus als Ordensgründer. Ein Beitrag zur Geschichtsschreibung und Geschichtsdeutung der Eremiten-und Bettelorden des 13. Jahrhunderts." In *Geschichtsschreibung und Geschichtsbewusstsein im späten Mittelalter*, ed. Hans Patze, 371–397. Vorträge und Forschungen 31. Sigmaringen, 1987.
—, "*Augustinus Canonicus-Augustinus Eremita*: A Quattrocento Cause Célèbre." In *Christianity and the Renaissance. Image and Religious Imagination in the Quattrocentro*, ed. Timothy Verdon and John Henderson, 83–107. New York, 1990.
Gutierrez, David, *Geschichte des Augustinerordens.* Vol. I/I, *Die Augustiner im Mittelalter, 1256–1356.* Würzburg, 1985. Originally published as, *Los Agustinos en la edad media 1256–1356.* Historia de la Orden de San Agustin I/I. Rome, 1980.

Hamm, Berndt, *Frömmigkeitstheologie am Anfang des 16. Jahrhunderts. Studien zu Johannes von Paltz und seinem Umkreis.* BhTh 65. Tübingen, 1982.

—, "Hieronymus—Begeisterung und Augustinismus vor der Reformation. Beobachtungen zur Beziehung zwischen Humanismus und Frömmigkeits-theologie (am Beispiel Nürnbergs)." In *Augustine, the Harvest, and Theology (1300–1650). Essays Dedicated to Heiko Augustinus Oberman in Honor of his Sixtieth Birthday*, ed. Kenneth Hagen, 127–233. Leiden, 1990.

Hansen, Dorothee, *Das Bild des Ordenslehrers und die Allegorie des Wissens. Ein gemaltes Programm der Augustiner.* Berlin, 1995.

Hoenen, M.J.F.M., *Marsilius of Inghen. Divine Knowledge in Late Medieval Thought.* SHCT 50. Leiden, 1993.

Kristeller, P.O., "Augustine and the Early Renaissance." In Kristeller, *Studies in Renaissance Thought and Letters*, 335–372. Rome, 1956.

Kroon, M. de, "Pseudo-Augustin im Mittelalter. Entwurf eines Forschungs-berichts." *Augustiniana* 22 (1972): 511–530.

Kürzinger, J., *Alfonsus Vargas Toletanus und seine theologische Einleitungslehre.* Münster, 1930.

Leff, Gordon, "Augustinismus im Mittelalter." In *Theologische Realenzyklopädie* IV: 699–717.

Lohse, Bernhard, "Zum Wittenberger Augustinismus. Augustins Schrift De Spiritu et Littera in der Auslegung bei Staupitz, Luther und Karlstadt." In *Augustine, the Harvest, and Theology (1300–1650). Essays Dedicated to Heiko Augustinus Oberman in Honor of his Sixtieth Birthday*, ed. Kenneth Hagen, 89–108. Leiden, 1990.

Mariani, U., *Il Petrarca e gli Agostiniani.* Storia e letteratura 12. Rome, 1959.

Mone, E.J., *Lateinische Hymnen des Mittelalters aus Handschriften herausgegeben und erklärt*, 3 vols. Freiburg, 1853–55.

Muir, Edward, *Civic Ritual in Renaissance Venice.* Princeton, 1981.

McNeil, M.G., *Simone Fidati and his De gestis Domini Salvatoris.* Washington, D.C., 1950.

Oberman, Heiko A., *Archbishop Thomas Bradwardine. A Fourteenth Century Augus-tinian.* Utrecht, 1958.

— "'Tuus sum, salvum me fac!' Augustinréveil zwischen Renaissance und Reformation." In *Scientia Augustiniana*, ed. C.P. Mayer and W. Eckermann, 349–393. Würzburg, 1975.

—, *Werden und Wertung der Reformation. Vom Wegestreit zum Glaubenskampf.* Tübin-gen, 1977. 2nd ed. Tübingen, 1979. Translated by Denis Martin as, *Masters of the Reformation.* Cambridge, 1981.

—, ed., *Gregor von Rimini. Werk und Wirkung bis zur Reformation.* SuR 20. Berlin-New York, 1981.

—, "Headwaters of the Reformation: *Initia Lutheri—Initia Reformationis.*" In H.A. Oberman, *The Dawn of the Reformation. Essays in Late Medieval and Early Reformation Thought*, 39–83. Edinburgh, 1986. Originally published in *Luther and the Dawn of the Modern Era: Papers for the Fourth International Con-gress for Luther Research*, ed. H.A. Oberman, 40–88. SHCT 8. Leiden, 1974.

Ocker, Christopher, "Augustinianism in Fourteenth-Century Theology." *Augus-tinian Studies* 18 (1987): 81–106.

Rano, Balbino, "Las dos Primeras Obras Conocidas sobre el Origen de la Orden Agustiniana." *Analecta Augustiniana* 45 (1982): 331–376.

—, "San Agustin y su Orden en Algunos Sermones de Agustinos del Primer Siglo (1244–1344)." *Analecta Augustiniana* 53 (1990): 7–93.

Saak, Eric Leland, "The *Figurae Bibliorum* of Antonius Rampegolus: MS Uppsala C 162." In *Via Augustini. Augustine in the Later Middle Ages, Renaissance, and Reformation. Essays in Honor of Damasus Trapp, O.S.A.*, ed. Heiko A. Oberman and Frank A. James, III, in cooperation with Eric Leland Saak, 19–41. SMRT 48. Leiden, 1991.

—, "Religio Augustini: Jordan of Quedlinburg and the Augustinian Tradition in Late Medieval Germany." Ph.D. diss., University of Arizona, 1993.

Santos-Noya, Manuel, *Die Sunden-und Gnadenlehre des Gregor von Rimini*. Frankfurt am Main-New York, 1990.

Schmidt, Margot, "Die Suche bei Augustinus im Spiegelbild der deutschen Literatur des Mittelalters." In *Scientia Augustiniana*, ed. C.P. Mayer and W. Eckermann, 214–233. Würzburg, 1975.

Schulze, Manfred, "Via Gregorii in Forschung und Quellen." In *Gregor von Rimini. Werk und Wirkung bis zur Reformation*, ed. H.A. Oberman, 1–126. SuR 20. Berlin-New York, 1981.

Shannon, Joseph L., *Good Works and Predestination According to Thomas of Strassburg, O.S.A.* Baltimore, 1940.

Simon, Walter, "Eine neue Quelle zur Augustinrezeption Gregors?" In *Gregor von Rimini. Werk und Wirkung bis zur Reformation*, ed. H.A. Oberman, 301–310. SuR 20. Berlin-New York, 1981.

Smalley, Beryl, *English Friars and Antiquity in the Early Fourteenth Century*. Oxford, 1960.

Smits, Luchesius, *Saint Augustin dans l'oeuvre de Jean Calvin. I: Étude de critique littéraire*. Assen, 1957.

Steinmetz, David C., *Luther and Staupitz. An Essay in the Intellectual Origins of the Protestant Reformation*. Duke Monographs in Medieval and Renaissance Studies 4. Durham, N.C., 1980.

Stock, Brian, *The Implications of Literacy. Written Language and Models of Interpretation in the Eleventh and Twelfth Centuries*. Princeton, 1983.

—, *Listening For The Text. On the Uses of the Past*. Baltimore, 1990.

Stroick, Clemens, *Heinrich von Friemar. Leben, Werke, philosophisch-theologische Stellung in der Scholastik*. Freiburger Theologische Studien 58. Freiburg, 1954.

Tachau, Katherine, *Vision and Certitude in the Age of Ockham. Optics, Epistemology and The Foundations of Semantics, 1250–1345*. Studien und Texte zur Geistesgeschichte des Mittelalters 22. Leiden, 1988.

Trapè, Agostino, "Scuola Teologica e Spiritualia nell'Ordine Agostiniano." In *Sanctus Augustinus Vitae Spiritualis Magister*. 2 Vols., 2: 5–75. Rome, 1959.

Trapp, Damasus, "Augustinian Theology of the 14th Century. Notes on Editions, Marginalia, Opinions and Book-Lore." *Augustiniana* 6 (1956): 146–274.

—, "Notes on John Klenkok, O.S.A. (d. 1374)." *Augustinianum* 4 (1964): 358–404.

—, "Harvest of Medieval Theology [Notes on Heiko A. Oberman's book, *The Harvest of Medieval Theology*]," *Augustinianum* 5 (1965): 147–151.

—, "A Round-Table Discussion of a Parisian OCist-Team and OESA-Team about A.D. 1350," *Recherches de théologie ancienne et médiévale* 51 (1984): 208.

—, "Hiltalinger's Augustinian Quotations." In *Via Augustini. Augustine in the*

Later Middle Ages, Renaissance and Reformation. Essays in Honor of Damasus Trapp, O.S.A., eds. Heiko A. Oberman and Frank A. James III, in cooperation with Eric Leland Saak, 189–220. SMRT 48. Leiden, 1991. Originally published in *Augustiniana* 4 (1954): 412–449.

Trexler, Richard, *Public Life in Renaissance Florence*. New York, 1980.

Weinstein, Donald, *Savonarola and Florence. Prophecy and Patriotism in the Renaissance*. Princeton, 1970.

Werbeck, Wilfrid, *Jacobus Perez von Valencia: Untersuchungen zu seinem Psalmenkommentar*. Tübingen, 1959.

Wetzel, Richard, "*Staupitz Augustinianus*: An Account of the Reception of Augustine in his Tübingen Sermons." In *Via Augustini. Augustine in the Later Middle Ages, Renaissance and Reformation. Essays in Honor of Damasus Trapp, O.S.A.*, eds. Heiko A. Oberman and Frank A. James III, in cooperation with Eric Leland Saak, 72–115. SMRT 48. Leiden, 1991.

Wilks, M.J., *The Problem of Sovereignty in the later Middle Ages. The Papal Monarchy with Augustinus Triumphus and the Publicists*. Cambridge, 1963.

Zumkeller, Adolar, "Die Augustinerschule des Mittelalters: Vertreter und Philosophisch-Theologische Lehre." *Analecta Augustiniana* 27 (1964): 167–262.

—, *Manuskripte von Werken der Autoren des Augustiner-Eremitenordens in mitteleuropäischen Bibliotheken*. Würzburg, 1966.

—, *Erbsünde, Gnade, Rechtfertigung und Verdienst nach der Lehre der Erfurter Augustinertheologen des Spätmittelalters*. Würzburg, 1984.

—, *Leben, Schriftum und Lehrrichtung des Erfurter Universitätsprofessors Johannes Zachariae, O.S.A. (d. 1428)*. Würzburg, 1984.

MEMORES PRISTINAE PERFECTIONIS
THE IMPORTANCE OF THE CHURCH FATHERS
FOR *DEVOTIO MODERNA*

Nikolaus Staubach

I. *The Old and the New Devotion*

Around the year 1334 the Dominican Heinrich Seuse (Henry Suso) published a work which was to rouse his contemporaries (*moderni temporis personae; moderni*) from their sleep like the ringing of an alarm clock, and lead them back to the ancient Christian church's devotion and love of God (*fervor devotionis; amor divinus*): it was the *Horologium Sapientiae*.[1] Half a century later, in 1384, died the man who took Suso's concern for a reawakening of the ancient piety more seriously than any other, and who enabled it to reach its goal in a powerful religious movement of reform. This was Geert Grote, the founder of the "Devotio moderna". Like Suso, Grote too was most profoundly perturbed by the state of the church of his day. The collapse in the monasteries of loyalty to the Rule and of discipline, the neglect of duty and the immorality of the secular clergy—together with the indifference of the laity to religion—seemed to him to be a far-reaching threat to Christian society which he felt obliged to counter, out of concern for the salvation of his own soul and for that of his fellow human beings. In consequence of his conversion, which had been prompted by a crisis in his personal life, he had abandoned all

---

[1] Cf. Heinrich Seuse's *Horologium Sapientiae*, ed. Pius Künzle (*Spicilegium Friburgense* 23) Fribourg/Switzerland 1977, Prologus pp. 363ff.; on the time when the work came into existence *op. cit.* pp. 19ff.; on the terms *devotio, devotus, moderni, moderna tempora* see the references in the index pp. 663 and 675. Suso (Seuse) of course was not the creator of the term *devotio moderna* but he did promote it (to some extent *e contrario*) and did influence the movement of *devoti* strongly; cf. L.A.M. Goossens, *De meditatie in de eerste tijd van de Moderne Devotie*, Haarlem-Antwerp 1952, p. 23; Magnus Ditsche, "Zur Herkunft und Bedeutung des Begriffes Devotio Moderna" in *Historisches Jahrbuch* 79, 1960, pp. 124–145, pp. 134ff.; S.P. Wolfs, "Zum Thema: Seuse und die Niederlande" in *Heinrich Seuse. Studien zum 600. Todestag 1366–1966*, ed. Ephrem M. Filthaut, Cologne 1966, pp. 397–408, pp. 400ff.; Künzle, *op. cit.* pp. 284ff.; N. Staubach, "Von der persönlichen Erfahrung zur Gemeinschaftsliteratur: Entstehungs- und Rezeptionsbedingungen geistlicher Reformtexte im Spätmittelalter" in *Ons Geestelijk Erf* 68, 1994, pp. 200–228.

secular interests and ambitions in order to call his fellow-countrymen
from then onwards—whether clergy, members of orders and laity—
to repentance and religious renewal by preaching and writing.[2] As is
well-known, his missionary activity was so successful that the communities founded by his disciples—houses for the Brothers and Sisters of the Common Life and the foundations for the Augustinian
Canons (*Regulierenkloosters*) of the Windesheim Congregation—spread
quickly over what is now the Netherlands and Belgium, and also
northwestern and southern Germany right into Switzerland.[3]

Although this movement, already designated as *Devotio moderna* by
contemporaries, has its roots entirely in the semi-religiosity and the
Orders of the Middle Ages, and is part of the context of the efforts
at reform and observance in the 14th and 15th centuries,[4] it was
often regarded in less recent research as a branch of Christian humanism, and as preparing the way for the Reformation: its characteristic,
epoch-making spiritual achievements were said to be the promotion
of a lay piety, independent of the imparting of salvation by the official
church, through reading the Bible in the vernacular, emphasis on
religious inwardness instead of righteousness through works and the

---

[2] Karl Grube, *Gerhard Groot und seine Stiftungen*, Cologne 1883; K.C.L.M. de Beer,
Studie over de spiritualiteit van Geert Groote, Brussels-Nijmegen 1938; Jacob van Ginneken,
Geert Groote's levensbeeld naar de oudste gegevens bewerkt, Amsterdam 1942; Theodore
P. van Zijl, *Geert Groote, Ascetic and Reformer* (1340–1384), Washington D.C. 1963;
Georgette Epiney-Burgard, *Gérard Grote et les débuts de la Dévotion moderne*, Wiesbaden
1970.

[3] J.G.R. Acquoy, *Het klooster te Windesheim en zijn invloed*, 3 volumes, Utrecht 1875–
1880; Ernst Barnikol, *Studien zur Geschichte der Brüder vom gemeinsamen Leben*, Tübingen
1917; C. van der Wansem, *Het ontstaan en de geschiedenis der Broederschap van het Gemene
Leven tot 1400*, Louvain 1958; Irene Crusius, *Die Brüder vom gemeinsamen Leben in
Deutschland*, typewritten (thesis), Göttingen 1961; Gerhard Rehm, *Die Schwestern vom
gemeinsamen Leben im nordwestlichen Deutschland*, Berlin 1985; *Monasticon Windeshemense*,
ed. W. Kohl—E. Persoons—A.G. Weiler, Parts 1–4 (*Archief- en Bibliotheekwezen in
Belgie*, supplementary issue 16) Brussels 1976–84; *Monasticon Fratrum Vitae Communis*,
ed. W. Leesch—E. Persoons—A.G. Weiler, Parts 1–2 (*Archief- en Bibliotheekwezen in
Belgie*, supplementary issue 18) Brussels 1977 and 1979.

[4] R.R. Post, *The Modern Devotion*, Leiden 1968; Kaspar Elm, "Die Bruderschaft
vom gemeinsamen Leben. Eine geistliche Lebensform zwischen Kloster und Welt,
Mittelalter und Neuzeit" in *Ons Geestelijk Erf* 59, 1985, pp. 470–496; Wilhelm Kohl,
"Die Windesheimer Kongregation" in *Reformbemühungen und Observanzbestrebungen im
spätmittelalterlichen Ordenswesen*, ed. K. Elm, Berlin, 1989. pp. 83–106.—On the spiritual profile of the Devotio moderna in the context of the history of the devotional
life from the fourteenth century to the sixteenth century inclusive, cf. especially
Stephanus Axters, *Geschiedenis van de vroomheid in de Nederlanden*, volume 3, *De moderne
Devotie*, Antwerp 1956, and also the exhibition catalogue, *Moderne Devotie, figuren en
facetten*, Nijmegen 1984.

observance of ceremony, rejection of scholastic dialectics and speculation in favour of a practical Christianity in one's personal life.[5] This
controversy about the spiritual orientation of the "Devotio moderna"
is entirely relevant to the question of the "reception" of the literature
of the Church Fathers which we are to deal with here. Was the attitude of the *devoti* to the early Christian period characterized by a
critical distance from the church of their day, or did they move in
the context of medieval tradition? Was there a careful re-examination
and purging of the Patristic writings—such as Erasmus attempted—
or were they taken over unquestioningly as an authoritative store of
tradition? How do the Church Fathers rate in comparison with the
Bible and especially the New Testament? And, when all is said, is it
legitimate to deal with the "Devotio moderna" as a new epoch of its

---

[5] Carl Ullmann, *Reformatoren vor der Reformation*, 2 volumes, Hamburg 1841–42,
second edition Gotha 1866; G.H.M. Delprat, *Verhandeling over de broederschap van
G. Groote*, 2nd edition, Arnheim 1856; G. Bonet-Maury, *Gérard de Groote, un précurseur
de la Réforme au quatorzième siècle*, Paris 1878; Paul Mestwerdt, *Die Anfänge des Erasmus.
Humanismus und "Devotio moderna"*, Leipzig 1917; Albert Hyma, *The Christian Renaissance. A History of the "Devotio moderna"*, Grand Rapids, Mich. 1924, 2nd edition, Hamden, Connecticut 1965; Justus Hashagen, "Die Devotio moderna in ihrer Einwirkung
auf Humanismus, Reformation, Gegenreformation und spätere Richtungen" in *Zeitschrift für Kirchengeschichte* 55, 1936, pp. 523–531; Rudolf Kekow, *Luther und die Devotio
moderna*, thesis, Hamburg 1937; Lewis W. Spitz, *The Religious Renaissance of the German
Humanists*, Cambridge, Mass. 1963; W. Lourdaux, *Moderne Devotie en christelijk humanisme.
De geschiedenis van Sint-Maarten te Leuven van 1433 tot het einde der XVI^{de} eeuw*, Louvain
1967.—Since the fundamental revision of the earlier research by Post (as in note 4)
a kind of compromising attitude has established itself in this matter; cf. for instance
W. Lourdaux, "Dévotion moderne et humanisme chrétien" in *The Late Middle Ages
and the Dawn of Humanism outside Italy*, ed. G. Verbeke, IJsewijn, Louvain-The
Hague 1972, pp. 57–77; J. IJsewijn, "The Coming of Humanism to the Low Countries" in *Itinerarium Italicum*, dedicated to P.O. Kristeller, ed. H.A. Oberman—Th.A.
Brady Jr., Leiden 1975, pp. 193–301, especially pp. 208f., 224ff.; Léon E. Halkin,
"La 'Devotio moderna' et l'humanisme" in *Réforme et humanisme*. Actes du IVème col-
loque, Montpellier 1975, pp. 103–112; Heiko A. Oberman, *Spätscholastik und Refor-
mation*, volume 2: *Werden und Wertung der Reformation*, Tübingen 1977, pp. 56–71;
Emile Brouette—Reinhold Mokrosch, "Devotio moderna" in *Theologische Realenzyklopädie*
volume 8, Berlin-New York 1981, pp. 605–616, pp. 609ff.; Georgette Epiney-Burgard,
"Die Wege der Bildung in der Devotio Moderna" in *Lebenslehren und Weltentwürfe im
Übergang vom Mittelalter zur Neuzeit*, ed. H. Boockmann—B. Moeller—K. Stackmann,
Göttingen 1989, pp. 181–200; R.Th.M. van Dijk, "Die Frage einer nördlichen Variante der Devotio moderna: Zur Interferenz zwischen den spätmittelalterlichen Reformbewegungen" in *Wessel Gansfort (1419–1489) and Northern Humanism*, ed. F. Akkerman—
G.C. Huisman—A.J. Vanderjagt, Leiden-New York-Cologne 1993, pp. 157–169;
N. Staubach, "Christianam sectam arripe. Devotio moderna und Humanismus zwischen Zirkelbildung und gesellschaftlicher Integration" in *Europäische Sozietätsbewegung
und demokratische Tradition*, ed. K. Garber—H. Wismann, 2 vols., Tübingen 1996,
vol. 1, pp. 112–167.

own in the history of the "reception" and evaluation of the Church Fathers (*patres*)?

The importance of the *patres* for the "Devotio moderna" is comprehensible and demonstrable only in the framework of their programme for spiritual reform. As for numerous religious movements of earlier centuries the *vita apostolica* of the ancient church was the obligatory ideal for Grote and his followers, by which a Christian renewal had to be guided.[6] Even if their own age was regarded as particularly far-removed from that ideal, it was nevertheless known that the dialectical process of religious decline and reform had been a decisive factor in church history from its very beginnings. Thus Grote admonished the prioress of a nunnery to see that the vow of poverty was observed, using a quotation from Cassian's *Collationes* to remind her of the historical origin of monasticism and the hermits in the early days of the church: after many Christians had abandoned the apostolic ideal for life in the community of goods, those who had not yet forgotten the original state of perfection (*memores pristinae perfectionis*), and had left their towns, would have striven for it on their own behalf alone.[7]

To revive the *memoria pristinae perfectionis* and keep it alive was also the concern of Grote and his pupils. This "remembering", of course, could be attained only in writings that had been passed down. Consequently, systematic efforts to procure literature and create libraries, together with programmes for selected reading and reading techniques, were part of the characteristic profile of the "Devotio moderna" from the start.[8] Here the criterion for the scope and limitations of the way literature was received was the reforming purpose of aligning the will and acts of individuals and the community with the example of

---

[6] Cf. M.-H. Vicaire, *L'imitation des apôtres. Moines, chanoines et mendiants IVᵉ-XIIIᵉ siècles*, Paris 1963; Gordon Leff, "The Apostolic Ideal in Later Medieval Ecclesiology" in *The Journal of Theological Studies*, New Series 18, 1967, pp. 58–82.

[7] *Gerardi Magni Epistolae*, ed. W. Mulder, Antwerp 1933, Epist. 45, p. 178; cf. *Iohannis Cassiani Opera*, Pars II, ed. M. Petschenig (*CSEL* 13) Vienna 1886, Conlatio 18, 5, pp. 510f.—On Cassian see Maria Elisabeth Brunert, *Das Ideal der Wüstenaskese und seine Rezeption in Gallien bis zum Ende des 6. Jahrhunderts*, Münster 1994, pp. 129ff.

[8] W. Lourdaux, "Het boekenbezit en het boekengebruik bij de Moderne Devoten" in *Studies over het boekenbezit en boekengebruik in de Nederlanden vóór 1600* (Archief- en Bibliotheekwezen in Belgie, supplementary issue 11) Brussels 1974, pp. 247–325; A.J. Geurts, "Boek en tekst bij de Moderne Devoten" in *Ons Geestelijk Erf* 59, 1985, pp. 249–259; N. Staubach, "Pragmatische Schriftlichkeit im Bereich der Devotio moderna" in *Frühmittelalterliche Studien* 25, 1991, pp. 418–461; *idem*, "Der Codex als Ware. Wirtschaftliche Aspekte der Handschriftenproduktion im Bereich der Devotio moderna" in *Der Codex im Gebrauch*, ed. H. Keller—Ch. Meier (in the press).

Jesus' life and the apostles. Hugh of St. Victor had already drawn up a series of principles for those readers of the *sacrae scripturae* for whom moral instruction and perfection had to be more important than erudition and scholarly study, and the *devoti* were able to associate themselves with him in this and carry on his teaching. Thus in the *Didascalicon* we read:

> How Scripture is to be read for the correction of morals. Those who seek information on virtues and the way to live in sacred eloquence must rather read these books which commend contempt for this world and kindle the soul to love of their creator, and teach the right way of living, and show just how virtues can be acquired and vices set aside . . . this knowledge indeed is furnished in two ways, namely by example and by teaching; by example when we read the acts of the saints, by doctrine when we learn their sayings which are relevant for our instruction . . . for a Christian philosopher reading must be exhortation—not study—and it must nourish good desires, not kill them off.[9]

Hugh illustrates this rule by offering the example of a devout man who has devoted himself to reading the Bible with increasing zeal and finally has also traced out the secrets of its most difficult books until, totally overtaxed, he collapses. He is then warned in a vision to give up his excessive study of the Bible and devote his attention instead to simpler edifying reading—the legends of the martyrs and the lives of the Fathers:

> Things finally changed since he had begun to read the scriptures for the upbuilding of his life, not knowing how to use discrimination as his guide, he found they led him into error. But at length by the divine compassion he was counselled through a revelation not to apply himself further to studying the scriptures, but to accustom himself to dwell on the lives of the holy Fathers and the triumphs of the martyrs, and other such things that have been written down with an unadorned pen; and being thus brought back to his former condition . . . he deserved to receive the grace of inner peace.[10]

---

[9] *Quomodo sit legenda scriptura ad correctionem morum. Qui virtutum notitiam et formam vivendi in sacro quaerit eloquio, hos libros magis legere debet, qui huius mundi contemptum suadent et animum ad amorem conditoris sui accendunt rectumque vivendi tramitem docent qualiterque virtutes acquiri et vitia declinari possint ostendunt . . . Haec vero scientia duobus modis comparatur, videlicet exemplo et doctrina; exemplo, quando sanctorum facta legimus, doctrina, quando eorum dicta ad disciplinam nostram pertinentia discimus . . . Christiano philosopho lectio exhortatio debet esse, non occupatio, et bona desideria pascere, non necare.*—Hugonis de Sancto Victore Didascalicon, ed. Charles H. Buttimer, Washington D.C. 1939, V 7, pp. 105f.

[10] *Verso siquidem eventu in contrarium qui legere scripturas ad aedificationem vitae suae coeperat, quia discretionis moderamine uti non novit, easdem nunc occasionem erroris habebat. Sed miseratione*

The definition—relevant to such a selection—of the overall scope of
the *sacrae scripturae* is no less important than the criteria for selecting
a functional reading that would be subordinated to the purpose of
moral edification: as is well known Hugh includes in the *sacrae scripturae*
the Old and New Testaments and adds to the latter the Fathers
(*patres*), i.e. the sources of canonical law and the literature of the
Church Fathers alongside the Gospels, Epistles, Revelation and Acts:

> All of Holy Scripture is contained in the two Testaments, i.e. in the
> Old and the New. Each of them is divided into three orders. The Old
> Testament contains the Law, the Prophets and the Writings (Hagiog-
> rapha); and the New contains the Gospel, the Apostles and the Fa-
> thers ... In the third part (of the New Testament) the decretals, which
> we call "canons" (i.e. "rules") have first place, then the writings of the
> holy Fathers and Doctors of the Church: Jerome, Augustine, Gregory,
> Ambrose, Isidore, Origen, Bede and many other orthodox [writers]
> that are so many that they cannot be numbered.[11]

With the inclusion of the *patres* Hugh's comprehensive exposition of
the term *scriptura divina* reflects a practice of "reception" which was
also not questioned by those of the "Devotio moderna". Thus they
do not generally assume any difference in rank between the church
writers of the Patristic period and those of the Middle Ages and
their own day in terms of age and authority, and they hardly pay
any heed to the gap separating the *patres* from the biblical writers.
Rather, the spiritual benefit of a text—in other words its capacity for
arousing devotion and stimulating moral actions—was what determined the value placed on it. The guiding principle motivating reception of the Fathers by those following the "Devotio Moderna"
was to have the entire church tradition freely at their disposal, and
to select deliberately the material appropriate to their own concern
for reform.

---

*divina tandem per revelationem admonitus est, ne amplius harum scripturarum studio incumberet,
sed sanctorum patrum vitam et martyrum triumphos aliasque tales simplici stylo dictatas frequentare
consuesceret, sicque in brevi ad statum pristinum reductus ... internae quietis gratiam accipere
meruit.—Ibid.* (p. 106).

[11] *Omnis divina scriptura in duobus testamentis continetur, in veteri videlicet et novo. Utrumque
testamentum tribus ordinibus distinguitur. Vetus testamentum continet legem, prophetas, hagiographos,
novum autem evangelium, apostolos, patres ... In tertio ordine (novi testamenti) primum locum
habent decretalia, quos canones id est regulares appellamus, deinde sanctorum patrum et doctorum
ecclesiae scripta: Hieronymi, Augustini, Gregorii, Ambrosii, Isidori, Origenis, Bedae et aliorum
multorum orthodoxorum, quae tam infinita sunt ut numerari non possint ... op. cit.* IV 2,
pp. 71f.

II. *Quantum ad bonam vitam, pauca sufficerent . . .*

The first and best example of the tension between the tradition as a whole and the injunction to make a selection was Grote himself. Thanks to his all-round scholarly education he was able to take up a stance in relation to the most varied contemporary problems of Christian morality and life-style in treatises and letters which are impressive in offering us the entire theological, legal and philosophical learning of his age.[12] In places these writings—on luxury, voluntary poverty, marriage, celibacy, schism and simony, the instruction of novices and meditation—consist, almost without any gaps, of biblical passages, canonical and Patristic authorities and quotations from ancient literature, pre-eminently of a popular philosophical nature. Contemporaries were not wrong in seeing in them compilations put together from "the genuine writings of the saints" (*ex authenticis dictis sanctorum*)[13] or "in line with canon law and the statutes of the Fathers" (*secundum iura canonica ac patrum statuta*).[14] On the other hand, Grote's modern biographers have reconstructed a detailed, comprehensive survey of the sources he used and from which he quoted, embracing the most important ecclesiastical writers from the Patristic period to the fourteenth century inclusive.[15] Except for later and contemporary authors—Seuse, Eckhart, Ruysbroeck—this list corresponds very exactly with the catalogue of authorities which Grote himself provided in a statement to certify his orthodoxy; here besides the Bible and Church Law he mentions specifically the writings of the following "holy Doctors and Fathers" as the basis for his teaching: Ambrose, Augustine, Gregory, Jerome, Chrysostom, Dionysius, Bernard, Bede, Isidore, Hugh (Hugo) and Richard, "whose books together with those of other saints I esteem and try to obtain more than earthly possessions".[16]

---

[12] Cf. J.G.J. Tiecke, *De werken van Geert Groote*, Utrecht-Nijmegen 1941.

[13] Thomas à Kempis (Thomas van Kempen) *Dialogus noviciorum* II 13 in his *Opera omnia*, ed. M.J. Pohl, 7 volumes, Freiburg im Breisgau 1902–1922, vol. 7, p. 66.

[14] Petrus Horn, *Vita Magistri Gerardi Magni*, ed. W.J. Kühler, in *Nederlandsch Archief voor Kerkgeschiedenis*, N.S. 6. 1909, pp. 325–370, cap. 15, p. 370.

[15] Cf. Beer (as in note 2), pp. 248–289; Epiney-Burgard (as in note 2), pp. 57–103.

[16] *Ambrosii, Augustini, Gregorii, Iheronimi, Crisostomi, Dionisii, Bernardi, Bede, Ysidori, Hugonis et Ricardi, quorum libros una cum sanctorum aliorum libris pro terrenis habeo et quero.*—Geert Grote, Epist. 57 (*Protestacio . . . super epistolis, dictis, predicacionibus et sermocinacionibus eius*)

Grote's remarkable biblical, patristic and legal erudition does not reveal such a clear spiritual character as would place this close follower of scholasticism in the ranks of the radical religious reformers. It is true that he mostly did not content himself with borrowing arguments and quotations from theological *summae* or legal collections but used the original texts as far as possible and was therefore during his life on the look-out for books—which he bought or borrowed everywhere, and of which he had copies made for himself.[17]

But his legacy to *Devotio moderna*, which he called into being, lay more in a deliberate intellectual self-limitation—a programme of reading limited to the amendment of morals (*correctio morum*), such as Hugh of St. Victor had outlined—than in his encyclopaedic thirst for knowledge and his diligence as a collector. The contradiction between universal erudition and a modest pragmatic approach to devotional edification, between the cult of books and scepticism about them, already struck Grote's contemporaries and compelled the Master—as Thomas à Kempis reports—to make this statement:

> On one occasion a certain man connected with him by friendship asked him: Dearest master, what do all these books do that you have and have been carrying about with you so long? He answered: As far as a good life is concerned, few things are sufficient; but to teach others and defend the truth we ought to have all these things so that those who by chance don't believe me may place credence in the authorities of the saints.[18]

While Grote believed he had to equip and justify himself in his role as a teacher with the collected authority of the Church Fathers, considerably more modest material sufficed him for the practice of his own spiritual life. A reading plan entitled *De sacris libris studendis*

---

ed. Mulder (as in note 7), p. 214; cf. Thomas à Kempis, *Dialogus noviciorum* II 18, ed. Pohl (as in note 13), volume 7, p. 86.

[17] Cf. for instance his well-known admission to Ruysbroeck: "I have always coveted books-extremely so" (*semper sum . . . avarus et peravarus librorum*); Epist. 24, ed. Mulder (cf. note 7) p. 108; Thomas à Kempis, *Dialogus noviciorum* II 13, ed. Pohl (cf. note 13) vol. 7, p. 65. Numerous requests for books and orders for manuscripts in his correspondence confirm this statement, e.g. Epist. 7, *op. cit.* pp. 15f.; Epist. 12, p. 41; Epist. 13, pp. 43ff. On this see Lourdaux (cf. note 8) pp. 251–265.

[18] *Interrogavit aliquando eum vir quidam amicabiliter sibi coniunctus: Carissime magister, quid facient omnes libri isti, quos habetis et vobiscum tam longe fertis? Respondit ille: Quantum ad bonam vitam, pauca sufficerent; sed ad instructionem aliorum et propter veritatis defensionem oportet nos haec omnia habere, ut qui forte mihi non credunt, auctoritatibus sanctorum acquiescant.—* Thomas à Kempis, *Ex chronica . . . quae domum nostram non concernunt*, cap. 3, ed. Pohl (cf. note 13), vol. 7, p. 484.

("On sacred books to be studied"), which he had copied for future personal use after his conversion, has come down to us. This programme of (spiritual) exercises reveals a constant striving for limitation to what was most essential, with only those titles and categories being taken into account which had a direct relation to spiritual experience. In doubtful instances the moral purpose is expressly addressed:

> Let the basis of study and mirror of life be first the Gospel of Christ because there we find Christ's life; then the lives and the *Collationes* of the Fathers; then Paul's and the canonical Epistles and the Acts of the Apostles; then devotional books such as Bernard's and Anselm's *Meditationes, Horologium,* Bernard's *De Conscientia,* Augustine's *Soliloquia* and similar books. Also the Legends and anthologies of the Saints. The Fathers' moral teachings such as Gregory's *Pastorale,* St. Augustine's *De Opere monachali,* Gregory on *Job* and the like; the Holy Fathers' Homilies on the Gospels and those of the four Doctors; the holy Fathers' interpretations and postills on Paul's Epistles, because they are contained in the church's ordinances; study of the books of Solomon's Proverbs and Ecclesiastes and Ecclesiasticus, because they are contained in the church's lectionaries and ordinances—"I will pray with the spirit, but I will pray with the mind also" [1 Cor. 14:15]; study and comprehension of the Psalter because the Psalms are contained in the ecclesia of the holy Fathers: "I will sing praise with the spirit, but I will sing praise with the mind too" [1 Cor. 14:15]; study of the historical books of Moses, Joshua, Judges and Kings, of the Prophets, and the Fathers' expositions of these. As to the way to go through the *Decreta,* you should know the Institutes of the ancestors and of the church, not to ingest them fully but to run through them, lest you turn devotion into disobedience through ignorance of the law; so that you may see the fruits of the early church and may know those of whom you must beware and those of whom you must warn others to beware.[19]

In contrast to a catalogue of the sources used and quoted by Geert Grote, this private reading list reveals a clear programme of reform which was to become constitutive for the spirit of the *Devotio Moderna*: the supreme and exclusive aim of study was conversion to a way of life—*forma vivendi*—corresponding to the ideal life of the apostles. This was promoted by *exemplum* and *doctrina*—precept and example—i.e., in the words of Hugh of St. Victor, through knowledge of the deeds of the Saints and of their ascetic teachings. Correspondingly the Gospel as the life of Christ—*vita Christi*—and the lives and conversations of the monastic Fathers headed the list, followed by the letters and

---

[19] *Radix studii tui et speculum vitae sint primo Evangelium Christi, quia ibi est vita Christi.*

"deeds" of the Apostles. This idea attributes a twofold position to the old and new doctors of the church. They appear first of all as the authors of popular edifying, devotional books and basic moral treatises (*libri devoti; instructiones patrum ad mores*) and then in their capacity as exegetes of the Bible. Of course, what was involved here was not, for instance, a theological study of Patristic and scholastic commentaries but a deliberate opening up of those texts of the New and Old Testaments, in their various categories, which any Christian, and therefore laypeople too, might come across in the liturgy of the church and in their own prayers. Grote therefore justified the need for a proper understanding of Scripture with the frankly programmatic quotation (1 Cor. 14:15) from Paul: *Orabo spiritu, orabo et mente; psallam spiritu, psallam et mente* — "I will pray with the spirit, but I will pray with the mind also; I will sing praise with the spirit, but I will sing praise with the mind also".[20] The same call for internalized access to the liturgical texts of the church later led Grote to translate the Book of Hours into the vernacular and provide glosses on difficult verses in the Psalms.[21] Finally, study for its own sake was to be devoted just as little to church law as to biblical exegesis; it was to be noted only as far as necessary in order to keep effort towards a new Devotion in harmony with the laws and traditions of the church.

In Grote's programme of reading, the *sancti patres* are addressed as a great, amorphous, collective body representing the authority and

---

Deinde vitae et collationes patrum. Deinde epistulae Pauli et canonicae et Actus apostolorum. Deinde libri devoti ut Meditationes Bernardi et Anselmi, Horologium, de Conscientia Bernardi, Soliloquia Augustini et consimiles libri. Item Legenda et Flores sanctorum. Instructiones patrum ad mores sicut Pastorale Gregorii, de Opere monachali beati Augustini, Gregorius super Iob et similia. Homiliae evangeliorum sanctorum patrum et quattuor doctorum, intellectus sanctorum patrum et postillae super Epistulas Pauli, quia continentur in capitulis ecclesiae. Studium in libris Salomonis Parabolarum et Ecclesiastes et Ecclesiastici, quia continentur in ecclesia in lectionibus et capitulis: Orabo spiritu, orabo et mente. Studium et intellectus Psalterii, quia continentur in ecclesia sanctorum patrum: Psallam spiritu, psallam et mente. Librorum Mosaicorum studium historiarum, Iosue, Iudicum et Regum prophetarum, et expositiones patrum in his. De modo transcurrendi Decreta propter scire instituta maiorum et ecclesiae, non ad incorporandum, sed transcurrere: ne ignorantia iuris pietatem vertas in inoboedientiam, ut videas grossos ecclesiae primitivae fructus, ut scias a quibus debes cavere et a quibus monere cavendum.—Thomas à Kempis, *Dialogus noviciorum* II 18, ed. Pohl (cf. note 13), vol. 7, pp. 97f.

[20] I Cor. 14:15. The quotation is adduced later to justify prayer books and Psalters in the vernacular; cf. *De libris teutonicalibus*, ed. Hyma (cf. note 71) p. 67.

[21] Cf. N. van Wijk. *Het Getijdenboek van Geert Grote*, Leiden 1940; B. van den Berg, "Geert Grote's psalmvertaling" in *Nederlandse Taal- en Letterkunde* 61, 1942, pp. 259–314; R. van Dijk, "Het Getijdenboek van Geert Grote. Terugblik en vooruitzicht" in *Ons Geestelijk Erf* 64, 1990, pp. 156–194; Margaret Wesseling, "The Rhetoric of Meditation. Variations on Geert Grote's Translation of the Penitential Psalms found

enduring validity of the doctrine of the ancient church. Only a few are specifically named, such as Augustine, Gregory and Bernard. Otherwise only the *quattuor doctores*, the "four Doctors" stand out as a special group. Nevertheless we know that Grote specially valued and venerated two among all the Church Fathers—Augustine and Bernard—not only as teachers but also as holy patrons.[22] Faced with death, he trusted himself to them for safe guidance and it was noted as a special grace that he was called away on the eve of the Feast of St. Bernard—*speciali devotione sancto Bernardo affectatus*—"aspiring to special devotion to St. Bernard".[23] Not least he valued Bernard's style, his *gravitas* and the *flores Bernardini*; but even more he valued his capacity for appropriating the thoughts of Augustine and other more ancient Church Fathers by as it were organic assimilation—a mediating function which he missed among the *novi et moderni doctores*, the new, present-day Doctors: "thus St. Bernard . . . appropriated the teachings of the teachers who went before him, with not a few of which he made himself familiar, and disseminated them to others" (*sic beatus Bernardus . . . doctorum eum precedentium doctrinas, quarum non paucas pervagavit, sibi attraxit et aliis effluxit*).[24] Thus Grote thought himself capable of making a genuine judgment on authenticity in the case of this author and in the end rightly denied Bernard's authorship of *De conscientia*, which still appears as a work of Bernard's in his reading plan.[25]

---

in Manuscripts of the 15th and 16th Centuries in the Royal Library, Den Haag" in *Ons Geestelijk Erf* 67, 1993, pp. 94–130.

[22] Cf. for instance Georgette Epiney-Burgard, "Saint-Augustin et la 'vie commune' dans la Dévotion moderne" in *Medioevo* 9, 1983, pp. 61–75; Heinrich Gleumes, "Gerhard Groot und die Windesheimer als Verehrer des hl. Bernhard von Clairvaux" in *Zeitschrift für Aszese und Mystik* 10, 1935, pp. 90–112; J. van Mierlo, "De hl. Bernardus in de middelnederlandse letterkunde" in *Ons Geestelijk Erf* 27, 1953, pp. 231–258: E. Mikkers. "S. Bernardus en de Moderne Devotie" in *Cîteaux in de Nederlanden*, vol. 4, Westmalle 1953, pp. 149–186; Carine Lingier, "Over de verspreiding van Sint-Bernardus' liturgische sermoenen in het Middelnederlands" in *Ons Geestelijk Erf* 64, 1990, pp. 18–40; Ulrich Köpf, "Die Rezeptions- und Wirkungsgeschichte Bernhards von Clairvaux. Forschungsstand und Forschungsaufgaben" in *Bernhard von Clairvaux. Rezeption und Wirkung im Mittelalter und in der Neuzeit*, ed. K. Elm, Wiesbaden 1994, pp. 5–65.

[23] Thomas à Kempis, *Dialogus noviciorum* II 16, ed. Pohl (cf. note 13) vol. 7, pp. 79, 82. In a celestial vision, Heinrich Mande, the Windesheim canon, saw Geert Grote alongside St. Augustine: Johannes Busch, *Chronicon Windeshemense und Liber de reformatione monasteriorum*, ed. Karl Grube (*Geschichtsquellen der Provinz Sachsen* 19) Halle 1886, p. 127.

[24] Geert Grote, Epist. 8, ed. Mulder (cf. note 7) pp. 17f.

[25] *Ibid.* (p. 18). On the likewise pseudepigraphical *Meditationes Bernardi* see below, note 39.

Like his personal veneration of Augustine and Bernard, Grote's programme of spiritual readings and exercises also became standard for his followers and for the whole *Devotio moderna* movement. Thus it is no accident that the movement's reception of the Church Fathers likewise exhibits the contrast between a widely applied provision of literature and a functionally restricted, selective reading technique. In investigation of the significance of the Fathers for the "Devotio moderna" as a movement of reform we have to distinguish both aspects of reception—the extensive accumulation of texts and their intensive evaluation and appropriation.

III. *Extensive reception of patristic literature—building up the libraries of the "Devotio moderna"*

The libraries of the communities of the "Devotio moderna"—that is, of the houses of the Brethren of the Common Life and the Windesheim monasteries—were the places where Patristic literature was, outwardly, "received". A variety of motives worked together to make the building up of libraries the most important task in the renewal of the apostolic Common Life (*vita communis*), namely Grote's and the Carthusians' love of books (the latter were esteemed as models because of their faithfulness to their Rule),[26] the consciousness of having to rescue and safeguard the ancient foundations of Christian piety which were threatened with oblivion, and finally the decision in favour of a particular writer's work—*opus scriptoris*—as the most appropriate form of manual activity. Hence it was characteristic of the self-understanding of the *devoti* that Grote's collection of books was regarded as the institutional core of the House in Deventer[27] and

---

[26] Cf. for instance Paul Lehmann, "Bücherliebe und Bücherpflege bei den Karthäusern" in his *Erforschung des Mittelalters*, vol. 3, Stuttgart 1960, pp. 121–142 (first published in 1924); H.J.J. Scholtens "Iets over de aanleg van boekerijen bij de Kartuizers" in *Huldeboek Bonaventura Kruitwagen aangeboden*, The Hague 1949, pp. 372–388; J.P. Gumbert, *Die Utrechter Kartäuser und ihre Bücher im frühen fünfzehnten Jahrhundert*, Leiden 1974; W. Lourdaux, "Kartuizers—Moderne Devoten. Een probleem van afhankelijkheid" in *Ons Geestelijk Erf* 37, 1963, pp. 402–418; Heinrich Rüthing, "Zum Einfluß der Kartäuserstatuten auf die Windesheimer Konstitutionen" in *Ons Geestelijk Erf* 59, 1985, pp. 197–210; Gerhard Achten, "Kartäuser und Devotio moderna. Kleiner Beitrag zur Geschichte der spätmittelalterlichen Mystik" in *Die Geschichte des Kartäuserordens*, vol. 2 (*Analecta Cartusiana* 125) Salzburg-Lewiston, N.Y. 1992, pp. 154–181.

[27] Cf. Rudolf Dier van Muiden, "Scriptum de magistro Gherardo Grote, domino

that Thomas à Kempis impressed the following exhortation on his novices:

> The books by the Doctors are the treasuries of clerks (i.e. clergy)...
> for a clerk without holy books is like a soldier without weapons...
> Likewise a monastery and congregation of clerks without holy books
> is like a kitchen without pots, a table without foods, a well without
> waters....[28]

Johannes Busch, the chronicler, gives an impressive balance-sheet of the writing activities in the early years of the Windesheim monastery,[29] distinguishing three great projects of work, the accomplishing of which was to document the zeal for reform and ascetic achievement of the founding generation:

a) Provision of the liturgical manuscripts needed for the choral services, in a uniform edition which was made obligatory for all the communities of the congregation:—more than thirty-five large volumes (*ultra triginta quinque magna volumina*).[30]

b) Preparation of a text of the Vulgate in which the effort was made to come as close as possible to the original version by St. Jerome:

> They emended with total faithfulness the Old and New Testament
> according to the most ancient and correct copies following the author-
> ity of the ancients rather than the common practice of the moderns.[31]

c) Building up a library of authentic texts "of the four Doctors of the Church and other orthodox Fathers":

> They likewise restored most faithfully all the sermons, homilies, books
> and treatises of the four Doctors of the Church and of other orthodox

---

Florencio et multis aliis devotis fratribus" in Gerhard Dumbar (ed.), *Analecta seu vetera aliquot scripta inedita*, vol. 1, Deventer 1719, pp. 1–113, pp. 9 and 11.

[28] *Libri doctorum thesauri sunt clericorum ... Nam clericus sine sacris libris quasi miles sine armis ... Similiter claustrum et congregatio clericorum sine sacris libris quasi coquina sine ollis, mensa sine cibis, puteus sine aquis ...*—Thomas à Kempis, *Doctrinale iuvenum*, cap. 3 and 7, ed. Pohl (cf. note 13) vol. 4, pp. 184 and 189.

[29] Johannes Busch, *Chronicon Windeshemense*, ed. Grube (cf. note 23) pp. 310–313; V. Becker (ed.), "Eene onbekende kronijk van het klooster te Windesheim" in *Bijdragen en Mededelingen van het Historisch Genootschap* 10, 1887, pp. 376–445, pp. 402–405.

[30] Grube (cf. note 23) pp. 310f. and 313.

[31] *Corpus tocius biblie veteris ac novi testamenti iuxta exemplariorum antiquorum magis correctorum tenorem integra fide emendantes et corrigentes veterumque auctoritatem plus quam modernorum usum communem imitantes.—Ibid.* (pp. 311f.)

Fathers to the initial state of the source as many as they were able to get from the more error-free copies collected everywhere. . . . We saw . . . more than a hundred large and noteworthy codices of the orthodox Doctors, written up in good script and on parchment for our libraries by these people themselves.[32]

Of course one will not place too high a value on the efforts of the Windesheim brethren at textual criticism, which Busch highlighted with pardonable pride; Grote himself had also at times tried his hand at philological problems and had even been commended as a second Jerome because of his decided aversion to *codices incorrecti*—codices with errors in them.[33] Nevertheless the stock of books attested by Busch for the Windesheim library is remarkable, particularly in regard to both its range and its composition.[34] After the *quatuor patres*, his list cites first of all Bernard and then further authors, in approximately chronological sequence, from Chrysostom and Origen down to Geert Grote—who is thus presented as the last of the orthodox Fathers (*patres orthodoxi*). Almost all the genres of spiritual literature are represented, except scholastic theology and writings on canon law, therefore also exegetical writings, church history and hagiography. Neither John of Genoa's *Catholicon* nor Petrarch's *De vita solitaria* nor Pseudo-Basil's (Peter Damian's) thematically related work is missing. The devotional texts that were particularly popular among the *devoti* are indeed present, but they by no means predominate. Alongside the anonymous *Vitas patrum, Speculum beate virginis* and *Speculum virginum*, mention is also made of *Collationes* and *Instituta patrum, Horologium,*

---

[32] *Simili modo omnes sermones, omelias libros et tractatus quatuor ecclesie doctorum aliorumque patrum orthodoxorum ad primam sui fontis originem, quantum in exemplaribus emendacioribus e diverso collectis habere potuerunt, fidelissime reduxerunt . . . Vidimus . . . ultra centum codices magnos et notabiles doctorum orthodoxorum per ipsos pro libraria nostra in bona litera et pergameno conscriptos.—Ibid.* (pp. 312f.)

[33] Thomas à Kempis, *Dialogus noviciorum* II 13, ed. Pohl (cf. note 13) vol. 7, p. 66. See above in note 25.—Cf. also N. Greitemann, *De Windesheimsche Vulgaatrevisie in de vijftiende eeuw,* Hilversum 1937.

[34] Only the first version of Busch's *Chronicon Windeshemense* has a (select) list of the authors and works in the library at Windesheim. See Becker (cf. note 29) p. 402: . . . "But who will tell how many books large and small . . . were written by our brothers for the library? Therefore let us present to the public . . . at least some of them in confirmation of the extremely great concern of our earlier brothers for sacred literature. And first of all regarding the books of our father Augustine . . ." *Pro libraria autem fratres nostri quot et quantos libros magnos et parvos . . . conscripserunt, quis enarrabit? Ad comprobandam ergo priorum fratrum nostrorum maximam scripturarum sanctarum diligentiam aliqua saltem e pluribus nostre interim memorie occurrentia in medium proferamus. Et primo de libris patris nostri Augustini . . .*

Profectus religiosorum and *Speculum monachorum* without any indication of authorship. The series of authors' names may explain the broad concept of "literature of the Fathers" which Busch attests as having been determinative in the building up of the library at Windesheim: Augustine, Gregory, Ambrose, Jerome, Bernard, Guerricus, Chrysostom, Origen, Hilary of Poitiers, Prosper of Aquitaine, Cyprian, Leo, Eusebius of Emesa, Bede, Hugh of St. Victor, Richard of St. Victor, Pseudo-Dionysius, Isidore, Thomas Aquinas, Bonaventure, Pseudo-Basil, Petrarch and Grote.[35]

Undoubtedly the more or less extensive libraries of other communities of *devoti* were essentially also collections of Patristic texts, similar to the Windesheim library. Although not a few residual elements and archival or literary testimonies tell us about these stocks of books, systematic research on the library concerns of the "Devotio moderna" is still just beginning.[36] We shall be able to reconstruct a picture of a standard library of the *devoti*—that is, what we may call the "Patrologia devota"—only when there is systematic collection and evaluation of the contemporary library catalogues, lists of donations and historiographic evidences, inventories related to the secularization of the monasteries, auction catalogues and references to the provenance of the acquired manuscripts. Such an attempt at synthesis appears meaningful because the reconstruction of actual individual libraries

---

[35] Becker (cf. note 29) pp. 402-404. The title "Speculum monachorum" relates here to the first part—usually called the "Formula novitiorum" of *De exterioris et interioris hominis compositione*, by David of Augsburg. The second and third parts of this work is called "Profectus religiosorum"; cf. Marcel Viller, "Le Speculum monachorum et la 'Dévotion moderne'" in *Revue d'Ascétique et Mystique* 3, 1922, pp. 45-56; Kurt Ruh, "David von Augsburg" in *Die deutsche Literatur des Mittelalters. Verfasserlexikon*, vol. 2, Berlin-New York 1980, columns 47-58. Both titles are to be found paired elsewhere, cf. Thomas à Kempis, *Dialogus noviciorum* IV 8 ed. Pohl (cf. note 13) vol. 7, p. 281: "Gerhard Zerbolt of Zutphen before the end of his life like a newly converted began to read again the *Speculum monachorum* and *Profectus religiosorum*, in which he took great pains to bring out again the spirit of devotion and renew the initial ardour." *(ante finem vitae suae quasi noviter conversus Speculum monachorum et Profectus religiosorum iterum legere coepit, in quibus spiritum devotionis studuit recolligere et ad primitivum fervorem se innovare.)*—On Petrarch cf. K.A.E. Enenkel, "Der andere Petrarca: Francesco Petrarcas *De vita solitaria* and the *devotio moderna*" in *Quaerendo* 17, 1987, pp. 137-147.

[36] On the present state of research see M. Haverals, "De scriptoria en de bibliotheken van de Windesheimers in de Zuidelijke Nederlanden" in *Ons Geestelijk Erf* 59, 1985, pp. 260-270; Staubach, *Der Codex als Ware* (cf. note 8) note 13. E. Persoons ("Het intellectuele leven in het klooster Bethlehem in de 15de eeuw" in *Archief- en Bibliotheekwezen in Belgie* 43, 1972, pp. 47-84, 44; 1973, pp. 85-143) uses the example of the books possessed by the Bethlehem monastery in Herent to give a sketch of a standard library of the *devoti*.

on the basis of tradition has good prospects only in very few instances. Moreover, as such, a well-documented monastery library cannot be reckoned to be a representative reflection of the joint interests
and principles of the *devoti* for that reason alone, because its growth
has generally been conditioned not merely by efforts to copy and
acquire volumes methodically but also by chance acquisitions. Finally, as opposed to older views, we have to note once again that
the collection of religious literature and not its dissemination was the
real concern of the reform movement of the *devoti*. That collection
can to some extent be understood as a highly extended network of
book clubs and reading circles. The notable attempts of the *devoti* to
lay hold on numerous individual library stocks synoptically and link
them up by means of trans-regional catalogues prove this, and also
illustrate the huge scope of an accumulation of books carried out
systematically for more than a century: the catalogue of an entire
library of *scriptores ecclesiastici* of the Rooklooster, dated around 1535,
has come down to us with thousands of names of authors and titles
of works, just as the Bendictine abbot Johannes Trithemius had compiled them four decades previously, to a degree of completeness hitherto unknown.[37]

IV. *Intensive reception of Patristic literature—planned reading, excerpts, translations*

We certainly must not equate the extensive reception of the Church
Fathers in the libraries of the "Devotio moderna" with the spiritual

---

[37] Cf. Willem de Vreese, "Een catalogus der handschriften in Nederlandsche
kloosters uit het jaar 1487" in his *Over handschriften en handschriftenkunde. Tien codicologische
studien*, ed. P.J.H. Vermeeren, Zwolle 1962, pp. 71–84 (first published in 1913);
J. van Mierlo, "Een katalogus van handschriften in Nederlandsche bibliotheken uit
1487" in *Ons Geestelijk Erf* 2, 1928, pp. 275–303; also "De anonymi uit den katalogus
van handschriften van Rooklooster" in *Ons Geestelijk Erf* 4, 1930, pp. 84–102, 316–
357; Paul Lehmann, "Alte Vorläufer des Gesamtkatalogs" in his *Erforschung des Mittelalters*, vol. 4, Stuttgart 1961, pp. 172–183 (first published in 1937); Lourdaux, *Boekenbezit*
(cf. note 8) pp. 299–325; Hermann Knaus, "Ein rheinischer Gesamtkatalog des 15.
Jahrhunderts" in *Gutenberg-Jahrbuch* 1976, pp. 509–519; Pieter F.J. Obbema, "The
Rookloster Register Evaluated" in *Quaerendo* 7, 1977, pp. 326–353; A. Gruis, "Fragment d'un catalogue ancien de Groenendael ayant servi à la composition du répertoire collectif de Rougecloître" in *Varia Codicologica. Essays presented to G.I. Lieftinck*,
vol. 1, Amsterdam 1972, pp. 75–86; W. Lourdaux—M. Haverals, *Bibliotheca Vallis
S. Martini in Lovanio. Bijdrage tot de studie van het geestesleven in de Nederlanden (15de–18de
eeuw)* vol. 2, Louvain 1982, pp. 44–84; R.H. and M.A. Rouse, "Bibliography before
print: The Medieval *De viris illustribus*" in *The Role of the Book in Medieval Culture*, ed.

and intellectual education of the *devoti*. For the maxim of their programme of religious reform was not extensive study of the sources
but intensive appropriation of a few texts. Geert Grote explained
this intensive process of reception with the graphic figure of the in-
take of food, digestion and transformation into the substance of one's
own body.[38] Florens Radewijns, despite his scholarly training, was
just as convinced as his teacher Grote that a few simple books were
adequate as an introduction to the spiritual life:

> Master Florentius used to read books with simple subject-matter such
> as the Meditations of St. Bernard or the like. Although he was a Master
> of Arts at [the University of] Prague he nevertheless did not busy him-
> self with lofty or difficult writings but with those that could instil the
> fear of God and humility.[39]

Radewijns therefore made the following recommendation to Henricus
Balveren, the canon at Windesheim:

> I advise you to have around you the *Speculum monachorum* or *Speculum
> Bernardi*, in accordance with which you can order everything you do;
> and also to become acquainted with this book so thoroughly that you
> will know instantly in all your activities how you must comport your-
> self or in what respects you have behaved badly.[40]

P. Ganz, Turnhout 1986, pp. 133–153, reprinted in their *Authentic Witnesses. Approaches to Medieval Texts and Manuscripts*, Notre Dame, Indiana 1991, pp. 469–494.

[38] Geert Grote, Epist. 8, ed. Mulder (cf. note 7) pp. 17f.

[39] *Dominus Florencius solebat legere libros de simplici materia, ut puta Mediationes beati Bernardi
vel similes. Quamvis esset magister in artibus Pragensibus, non tamen occupavit se cum altis sive
difficilibus scripturis, sed cum hiis que poterant incutere timorem Dei et humilitatem.*—Dier van
Muiden, ed. Dumbar (cf. note 27), p. 51. On the pseudo-Bernardine *Meditationes
piissimae* (Migne Patrologia Latina 184, columns 485–508) see M. van Woerkum,
"Het libellus 'Omnes, inquit, artes'. Een rapiarium van Florentius Radewijns" in
Ons Geestelijk Erf 25, 1951, pp. 113–158 and 225–268, pp. 226f. A "Speculum monachorum" is attested as a further favourite book of Radewijns; cf. Thomas à Kempis,
Dialogus noviciorum III 24, ed. Pohl (cf. note 13) vol. 7, p. 178: "Understanding of the
sacred writings shone brilliantly in him like some heavenly beam . . . Yet he possessed simple and moral books and particularly the *Speculum monachorum* and some
moral exercises against vices with which he taught himself and his fellow-soldiers in
the knighthood of Christ to triumph over the efforts of the devil." *(Intellectus sanctarum
scripturarum velut quidam caelestis radius in eo luculenter resplenduit . . . Habebat tamen apud se
simplices et morales libros et praecipue Speculum monachorum et quaedam virtutum exercitia contra
vitia, quibus se suosque commilitones in Christi militia docuit contra diabolica temptamenta
triumphare.)*—On the identification of the *Speculum monachorum* see notes 35 and 40.

[40] *Consulo tibi quod habeas circa te Speculum monachorum aut Speculum Bernardi secundum
quod omnes actus tuos potes ordinare, quem librum etiam ita discas exterius quod in omnibus
operibus tuis leviter occurrat quomodo te debes habere aut in quo te male habuisti.*—Thomas à
Kempis, *Dialogus noviciorum* III 29, *in loc.* p. 197. Cf. Dier van Muiden, *op. cit.* p. 50;

Of course such simple advice was far from satisfying for the imparting of edifying devotional literature from the treasury of the Fathers' writings. Rather, a complete system was developed, for the appropriation and internalizing of spiritual subject-matter by means of an ascetic method that became characteristic of the reform of the individual and the community on the part of the *devoti*. Pre-eminently this system of reception embraced three teaching techniques that were important for private and collective reading:

1. Selection of the reading matter in terms of suitability and the compilation of reading plans;
2. Instructions for preserving and working on what had been read (and heard) through excerpts in private florilegia (anthologies or *rapiaria*) or memoranda, and repeated meditation;
3. Translation into the vernacular.

First and foremost Florens Radewijns, the first rector of the house of the Brethren at Deventer, and his pupil Gerhard Zerbolt of Zutphen provided the basis for the programme of spiritual exercises of the "Devotio moderna", both in theory and in practice: their treatises not only formulate the principles and rules for effective reading for the amendment of behaviour—*ad correctionem morum*—but themselves are also really Patristic florilegia and examples for the correct use of the literature of the Fathers, using numerous quotations from the older ascetic monastic tradition.[41]

1. *Planned reading*

In their criteria for selecting readings Radewijns and Zerbolt conjoin arguments from Cassian, Augustine, William of St. Thierry and Hugh

---

Johannes Busch, *Chronicon Windeshemense*, ed. Grube (cf. note 23) p. 111.—Viller (cf. note 35) p. 49 sees the *Speculum monachorum aut Speculum Bernardi* as variant titles for a single work; van Woerkum (cf. note 39) pp. 227f. is probably right in seeing in it a recommendation of two different writings. We should then have to relate the *Speculum monachorum* to David of Augsburg's treatise for Novices (see above, note 35) while the *Speculum Bernardi* might mean the "Speculum" of Arnulf de Boeriis (Migne *PL* 184, columns 1175–1178). Both "Specula" are also mentioned alongside each other in other circumstances, see below in notes 48, 49 and 59.

[41] Florens Radewijns, *Tractatulus devotus* ("Multum valet"), ed. Goossens (cf. note 1) pp. 213–254; and his "Omnes, inquit, artes", ed. M. van Woerkum, *Het libellus "Omnes, inquit, artes", een rapiarium van Florentius Radewijns*, thesis, Louvain 1950, 3 vols.; Gerhard Zerbolt of Zutphen, *De reformatione virium animae* and *De spiritualibus ascensionibus*, in *Maxima bibliotheca veterum patrum*, ed. Margarinus de la Bigne, vol. 26, Lyon 1677, pp. 235–258 and 258–289.

of St. Victor in a new, logical scheme; the reading (*lectio*) is not to be carried on for its own sake but must serve the moral and ascetic purpose of purity of heart (*puritas cordis*) and lead on to the higher level of exercises in meditation (*meditatio*) and sacred communication (*oratio*). Hence it must be neither too extensive nor too demanding but must limit itself to such texts as address the feelings rather than the intellect and thus move one to act morally. Zerbolt writes:

> There should not be so much concern for the books of commentators but you should rather direct all the diligence and purposefulness of your heart towards the correction of vices... And if indeed it pleases you to devote some work to reading the scriptures, because it is at any rate of sufficient advantage to you as a Christian philosopher, the reading must be admonition and not a preoccupation, and it should not be reflexion aimed at learning more of what has been written but rather that you may be kindled by what you read into purity of heart.[42]

And in another place we read:

> Whence you must attend rather to reading those writings which kindle your emotions more towards spiritual progress and ascent than to the things that enlighten the mind and sharpen curiosity in difficult and curious matters such as subjects on which disputes are held... And so let reading not keep us too absorbed in it but direct us beyond itself to pious meditations and spiritual communications and let these lead us beyond themselves by their sweetness and joyous nature into actions.[43]

---

[42] *Non tam laborandum est erga libros commentatorum, sed potius omnem industriam et intentionem cordis debes dirigere erga emendationem vitiorum... Et si quidem laborem aliquem lectioni scripturarum adhibere libuerit, quod utique satis expedit tibi tanquam Christiano philosopho, lectio debet esse admonitio, non occupatio, nec expendes multum ut scripturam addiscas, sed potius ut per lectionem ad puritatem cordis inflammeris.*—Gerhard Zerbolt, *De reformatione virium animae* (cf. note 41) cap. 14, p. 242. Here the following are quoted: Cassian, "De institutis coenobiorum" V 34 in *Iohannis Cassiani Opera*, Pars I, ed. M. Petschenig (*CSEL* 17) Vienna 1888, p. 107, and Hugh of St. Victor, *Didascalicon* V 7, ed. Buttimer (cf. note 9) p. 106. Cf. Florens Radewijns, *Tractatulus devotus* (cf. note 41) cap. 7, pp. 218ff.: *de lectione et sex considerandis circa lectionem*, where preeminently the argument follows Augustine, *De doctrina christiana* I 43f. and William of St. Thierry, *Epistola ad Fratres de Monte Dei*, cap. 56 (ed. M.-M. Davy, *Un traité de la vie solitaire*, Paris 1940, p. 105).

[43] *Unde illarum scripturarum lectionibus magis debes incumbere, quae tuum affectum magis inflammant ad spiritualem profectum et ascensum, quam quae in rebus difficilibus et curiosis illuminant intellectum et acuunt curiositatem, sicut sunt materiae disputabiles... Itaque lectio non nos retineat in se occupatos, sed ulterius dirigat ad devotas meditationes et spirituales orationes, et illae sua dulcedine et affectione dirigant ulterius in opus.*—Gerhard Zerbolt, *De spiritualibus ascensionibus* (cf. note 41) cap. 44, p. 276. Cf. William of St. Thierry, *Epistola ad Fratres de Monte Dei*, cap. 56, ed. Davy (cf. note 42) p. 105: "From the sequence of readings a frame of mind is to be derived, and prayerful communication created, which may interrupt the reading but may not be so much a hindrance by interrupting as immediately restorative of a clearer mind, so that the point of the reading will be grasped." (*Hauriendum est de lectionis serie affectus et formanda oratio, quae lectionem interrumpat*

The texts which correspond most to these conditions are the *libri mo-rales et devoti*—"pious and moral books".[44] The fundamental principle of the need for regulation of the spiritual life demanded that their selection should not be left to chance. Detailed reading-lists were particularly indispensable for readings at table and for the education of novices. On the other hand, Geert Grote, who was self-taught, had given himself a private rule of life in his *Conclusa et proposita* and part of it was also the personal reading plan already discussed—*De sacris libris studendis*. As far as I can see it has so far gone unnoticed that he may have been stimulated by the recommendations for readings for novices in Humbert de Romanis' tractate on ministries.[45] At all events Grote's examples set a precedent among the *devoti*. Thus Radewijns compiled a plan for Henricus Balveren's life which also included the instructions for reading already quoted. It is also attested that he likewise committed his own resolutions to writing: "He also wrote down certain points by which he sought to govern his actions" (*Scripsit etiam quedam puncta secundum que actus suos volebat moderare*).[46] There is much to be said for the idea that the *Propositum cuiusdam Canonici*, which has been handed down anonymously, should be linked with this personal rule of life of Florens Radewijns, or

---

nec tam impediat interrumpendo quam puriorem continuo animum ad intelligentiam lectionis restituat.)

[44] Gerhard Zerbolt, *De reformatione virium animae* (cf. note 41) cap. 15, p. 242; Florens Radewijns, *Tractatulus devotus* (cf. note 41) cap. 7, p. 220.

[45] Cf. Hubertus de Romanis, "Instructiones de officiis ordinis", cap. 5, 18, in his *Opera de vita regulari*, ed. J.J. Berthier, vol. 2, Rome 1889, p. 230: "Likewise they are to be instructed by him (the master of the novices) about study so that they neglect secular knowledge and go over wholly to matters of divine knowledge and among these things from the start pay more care to useful and straightforward things than to the more subtle and obscure things—and may especially have leisure for those that are more useful for moral instruction and inspiration and for strengthening themselves, such as are Hugh's book *De Disciplina*, the *De Claustro animae*, St. Bernard's *Meditationes*, Anselm's *Meditationes* and *Orationes*, Augustine's *Confessions*, his *Abbreviata* and *Florigerus*, the *Collationes* and *Vitae* and *Dicta* of the Fathers, the *Passiones et Legendae Sanctorum*, *Epistola ad Fratres de Monte Dei D. Bernardi*, *De gradibus superbiae*, *De diligendo Deo*, the *liber Balaam*, *Tractatus de vitiis et virtutibus*, and the like."

(*Item instruendi sunt ab ipso*—sc. magistro novitiorum—*circa studium, quod saecularibus scientiis neglectis se totos transferant ad divinas, et inter illas a principio magis vacent utilibus et planis quam subtilioribus et obscurioribus, et praecipue illis quae utiliores sunt ad informationem et inflammationem et corroborationem ipsorum, ut sunt liber Hugonis De Disciplina, liber De Claustro animae, Meditationes beati Bernardi, Meditationes et Orationes Anselmi, liber Confessionum Augustini, Abbreviata et Florigerus ejusdem, Collationes et Vitae et Dicta Patrum, Passiones et Legendae Sanctorum, Epistola ad Fratres de Monte Dei D. Bernardi, De gradibus superbiae, liber De diligendo Deo, liber Balaam, Tractatus de vitiis et virtutibus, et similia.*)

[46] Dier van Muiden, ed. Dumbar (cf. note 27) p. 51.

even identified with it.[47] However that may be it is noteworthy that
that *Propositum* contains a reading-list which plainly refers to Grote's
De sacris libris studendis:

> I shall study the Holy Gospel, because the life of Christ is there, the
> Epistles of Paul, the Canonical Epistles, and the books of the four
> Doctors, also religious books, namely Bernard's *Meditations, the Speculum
> monachorum*, Bernard's *Speculum*, Bernard's *Letters to the Monks of Mons
> Dei*, the *Profectus Religiosorum*, The *Horologium aeternae sapientiae*, the *Instituta
> sanctorum Patrum*, the *Collationes Patrum*, Augustine's *Soliloquium*, Gregory's
> *Moralia* and his Homilies and other devout books.[48]

The list has become even more well-ordered than Geert Grote's: the
New Testament and its exposition by the *libri quatuor doctorum* come
directly together, then come the *libri devoti* in the narrower sense.
They too constitute two groups: first come those either written anonymously by Bernard or falsely attributed to him, viz. the devotional
treatises of William of St. Thierry (Epistola ad Fratres de Monte
Dei), David of Augsburg (Speculum monachorum, Profectus religiosorum), Arnulf de Boeriis (Speculum Bernardi)[49] and Heinrich Seuse
(Horologium); then the *libri devoti* of the Patristic period, the writings
of the ancient Fathers (Instituta and Collaciones Patrum),[50] Augustine and Gregory. The reading programme, despite its conciseness,
clearly shows the range of interests of the modern devoti: the *libri
morales et devoti* predominate while dogmatics and exegesis fall almost
entirely into the background, as the respectful but nevertheless very
wholesale mention of the *libri quatuor doctorum* demonstrates.

Later and much more detailed reading lists present this picture
more precisely and confirm it. Towards the end of the fifteenth century

---

[47] "Propositum cuiusdam Canonici" in *Collationes Brugenses* 14, 1909, pp. 5–21; on
this M. van Woerkum, "Florentius Radewijns, leven, geschriften, persoonlijkheid en
ideen" in *Ons Geestelijk Erf* 24, 1950, pp. 337–364, p. 350.

[48] *Studium meum erit Evangelium sanctum, quia ibi est vita Christi, Epistole Pauli, Epistole
canonice, et libri quatuor doctorum, et libri devoti, videlicet meditaciones Bernardi, Speculum
monachorum, Speculum Bernardi, Epistole Bernardi ad Fratres de Monte Dei, Profectus religiosorum,
Horologium eterne sapientie, instituta sanctorum Patrum, Collaciones Patrum, Soliloquium Augustini,
Moralia Gregorii, Omelie Gregorii et ceteri libri devoti*. "Propositum" (as in note 47) pp. 8f.
There follows a dismissal of ancient literature: "And I shall altogether shun the
moral books of the heathen and the poets because they are fictions and are vain."
(*Et morales libros gentilium et poetarum omnino vitabo, quia fabulae et vani sunt.*) Geert Grote
himself was as is well-known less strict on this point and considered the *libri morales*
of the heathen to be relatively useful, cf. Thomas à Kempis, *Dialogus noviciorum* II
18, ed. Pohl (cf. note 13) vol. 7, pp. 91f.

[49] See above, note 40.

[50] Cassian's *Collationes* and *Instituta coenobiorum* are probably meant.

Johannes Mombaer (Mauburnus) drew up a *Tabula librorum praecipue legendorum* which divided all the reading matter suitable for a *devotus* into three categories—*studium morale, studium devotionale* and *studium intellectuale*.[51] Although these categories are not expressly allotted to specific ages and educational stages, they do represent a threefold model of promotion and development: the moral studies lay the foundation for the religious life, while devotional studies are meant to strengthen it, to reinforce spiritual *élan* and to fan the flame of pious ardour (*fervor*). Intellectual studies follow as a third stage in this programme, not because they constitute the highest stage of perfection, but because they are full of problems and dangerous, and call for a consolidated and experienced personality with sound judgment. Jan Brugman, the Franciscan, had already lamented the ruin of his order through novices' inadequate training in observance, and—after they had made their profession—their immediate contempt for the *libri devotionales*, so that they could plunge into the study of law and the theology of the *Sentences*:

> . . . young brothers (unhappily) abandon the source of living water, holy communication and devotion . . . nor are they instructed in the writings of the Order, viz. the statements of the rule . . . Likewise I dare to say that observance must suffer ruin to the extent that after making their profession the young men of this kind despise devotional books, such as *Vita Jesu, Profectus religiosorum, Speculum novitiorum, Stimulus amoris, Beatus vir, Homo quidam, Qui sequitur me, Audiam quid loquatur, Regnum Dei, Renovamini, Speculum monachorum, Horologium, Soliloquium Gerlaci, Manuale Augustini, Meditationes eiusdem, Meditationes Bernardi, Quatuor exercitia Bonaventurae, Arbor crucifixi eiusdem*. But as soon as they have been weaned from the breast of the teacher of novices . . . they fly wingless to the stars . . . by studying ordinances, the law, the *Sentences* and all sorts of ostentatious things, so that they may appear as holy clerks and be called such though they are ill-founded in the basic learning.[52]

---

[51] Reprinted with explanatory information in Pierre Debongnie, *Jean Mombaer de Bruxelles, abbé de Livry. Ses écrits et ses réformes*, Louvain-Toulouse 1922, pp. 319–331.

[52] . . . *fratres iuvenes derelinquunt (proh dolor) fontem aquae vivae sanctae orationis et devotionis* . . ., *immo nec instruuntur in scriptis ordinis, ut pote in regulae declarationibus* . . . *Item audeo dicere quod necesse est observantiam ruinam pati eatenus, quia iuvenes huiusmodi statim post professionem spernunt libros devotionales ut pote: Vitam Jesu, Profectum religiosorum, Speculum novitiorum, Stimulum amoris, Beatus vir, Homo quidam, Qui sequitur me, Audiam quid loquatur, Regnum Dei, Renovamini, Speculum monachorum, Horologium, Soliloquium Gerlaci, Manuale Augustini, Meditationes eiusdem, Meditationes Bernardi, Quatuor exercitia Bonaventurae, Arbor crucifixi eiusdem. Sed* . . . *statim cum ablactati fuerint ab uberibus magistri novitiorum* . . . *sine alis ad astra volant* . . . *studendo leges, iura, sententias et pompatica quaevis, ut appareant tantum et vocentur clerici voce tantum, non fundati in praemissis.*—Jan Brugman, *Speculum imperfectionis*, ed.

The restrictive comments Mombaer linked with his hints on reading for *studium intellectuale* prove that he thought along the same lines as Brugman: while the Bible and commentaries of the Church Fathers on the Psalms, Augustine's *De doctrina christiana* and Eusebius' *Ecclesiastical History*, the works of the *sancti patres* Dionysius the (Pseudo-) Areopagite, Origen, Lactantius and Ambrose, together with the theological manuals of Peter Lombard, Hugh of St. Victor (*De sacramentis, Didascalicon*), Bonaventure (*Breviloquium*, Commentary on the *Sentences*) and Alexander of Hales are unreservedly recommended, on other authors the comment is that "you should read the others in such a way that you rather judge them than follow them" (*Ceteras sic lege, ut magis iudices quam sequaris*). Texts on ecclesiastical law were to be read only so that the novices should not be ignorant where the need arises (*ne ignorentur in casibus necessariis*), and contemporary authors such as Petrarch, Giovanni Pico della Mirandola or Reuchlin were not so much to be read as glanced through (*non tam legendi quam percurrendi*).[53]

If we now examine the contents of the first two study-divisions the distinction between them really turns out to be very arbitrary. It is true that the *morale studium*, with commentaries on the rule and treatises for novices, relates to those beginning the monastic life but most of the texts would also be suitable for advanced readers: *Speculum Bernardi; Speculum monachorum; Epistola ad Fratres de Monte Dei; Sermones beati Bernardi; Profectus religiosorum; Vitae, collationes et instituta Patrum; Legendae et flores sanctorum; Climacus; Gregorii Moralia; omnia opuscula Iacobi et Dionysii Carthusiensis*; and—from the ranks of the *devoti* themselves Zerbolt's two treatises, *De reformatione virium anime* and *De spiritualibus ascensionibus*, Johannes of Schoonhoven's *Epistolae in Emsteyn* and the *devota opuscula Thomae Kempis*.[54]

F.A.H. van den Homberg, *Leven en werk van Jan Brugman O.F.M.*, Groningen 1967, pp. 118–138, cap. 5, p. 121f.—The works mentioned are: Ludolf of Saxony, *Vita Christi*; David of Augsburg, *De exterioris et interioris hominis compositione* (*Speculum novitiorum, Profectus religiosorum*); James of Milan, *Stimulus amoris*; Gerhard Zerbolt of Zutphen, *De spiritualibus ascensionibus* and *De reformatione virium animae* (*Beatus vir, Homo quidam*); Thomas à Kempis, *De imitatione* Christi, Books I, III and II (*Qui sequitur me, Audiam quid loquatur, Regnum Dei*) and also the *Libellus spiritualis exercitii* (*Renovamini*); Arnulf de Boeriis, *Speculum monachorum*; Suso, *Horologium*; Gerlach Peters, *Soliloquium*; Pseudo-Augustine, *Manuale* and *Meditationes*; Pseudo-Bernard, *Meditationes*; Bonaventura, *Soliloquium* (*Quatuor exercitia*) and also *Lignum vitae* (*Arbor crucifixi*). The large proportion of authors and writings from the *Devotio moderna* is striking: Gerhard Zerbolt, Thomas à Kempis, Gerlach Peters.

[53] Debongnie (cf. note 51) pp. 328ff.
[54] *Op. cit.* pp. 320ff.

Thus it may be said that the significance of the second canon of readings consists in showing that life in a monastery, even after profession, should be devoted pre-eminently to devotional books—*libri devoti*. Accordingly *devotionale studium* is to be regarded as the centre of the religious life (*vita religiosa*). Among its authors were Ludolf of Saxony (*Vita Christi*), Seuse (*Horologium*), Schoonhoven (*De passione Domini*), Augustine (*Soliloquia, Confessiones* among others), Pseudo-Bernard (*Meditationes, De conscientia, Cantica*), (Pseudo-) Anselm (*Meditationes*), Bonaventure with the *Stimulus maior* (*De triplici via* or James of Milan's *Stimulus amoris?*), with *De quatuor exercitiis* (*Soliloquium*), and also *cum omnibus devotionalibus*, Thomas (*De dilectione Dei*) and, highlighted in the final position, Jean Gerson, "with nearly all his smaller works in which he mingles speculative with devotional matters" (*cum omnibus ferme opusculis, ubi speculativa miscet devotis*).[55]

Johannes Mombaer's programme of study, despite its impressive range, has great consistency and is without exception uniform in its colouring: the *libri devoti* of the high and later Middle Ages—often anonymous or pseudepigraphcial writings—indicate its tone, whereas Patristic theology is almost wholly lacking except for a few biblical commentaries and Gregory's *Moralia*. Even Augustine is represented only by a handful of titles; Mombaer mentions the *Rule*, the *Confessions*, the *Enarrationes in Psalmos, De doctrina christiana*; also the *Spuria: Manuale, Soliloquia, Suspiria* and *Meditationes*, the genuineness of which, however, he already regarded as doubtful.[56] Only the *Vitae, Collationes et Instituta Patrum* from the older literature maintain their place as an essential of the canon of devotional education. On the other hand, the "modern" devotional texts of a Zerbolt, a Schoonhoven and Thomas à Kempis are included in the reading programme—as is Gerson, the all-round author who in the eyes of the *devoti* had already attained to the rank of a Father of the Church as a result of his spiritual affinity to them and his vigorous support for their cause.

The fact that despite their rich content Mombaer's recommendations for reading the texts were fundamentally restrictive, and sought to guide towards a strict and narrow ascetic monastic ideal of virtue, becomes clear when we consider their agreement with the restorative educational ideas of a Johannes Brugman. Comparison with the reading plan—datable to around 1525—from the Martinstal monas-

---

[55] *Ibid.* pp. 325ff.
[56] *Op. cit.* pp. 65, 251, note 1.

tery in Louvain may show how far they had become representative of the spiritual climate of the *Devotio moderna* at the beginning of the sixteenth century.[57] This list is in two divisions and is related expressly to novices (Part 1) and professing brothers (Part 2). Thus a section here corresponding to Mombaer's *studium intellectuale* is missing. Instead, a final comment refers to the study of biblical theology as a task for the advanced and, along the lines of Zerbolt's rules for reading, also warns against overtaxing oneself with difficult and problematic matters.[58] As with Mombaer, the first part of the list includes commentaries on the rule and other devotionally edifying literature such as the *Speculum monachorum, Speculum beati Bernardi, Horologium* and the *Profectus religiosorum*, and, finally, the *Imitatio Christi* and other works of Thomas à Kempis.[59] In the second part individual titles and collective references to the works of specific authors alternate. Recommended are:

> "St. Bernard's works; some works of St. Anselm; all St. Gregory's works; some devotional works of Hugh of St. Victor; all the small works of St. Bonaventure; all the works of Gerson" and finally, in a group of four,

---

[57] Brussels Manuscript K.B. 11915–19, folio 67v–70r. On this see Lourdaux, *Moderne Devotie* (cf. note 5) pp. 180f.

[58] Folio 69v–70r: "And all those studies are to be passed on to them, which can shape and lead the mind of the newly converted towards true humility, holy penitence and perfect fear of God or certainly keep it in exercises on the virtues mentioned and other virtues. If then they are rooted in the steady desire to make progress, let them be admitted to studies of the sacred writings of each Testament and to the other Doctors in accordance with what seems to be advantageous. For they should not be admitted to handling books dealing with deep and doubtful matters unless there is reasonable cause because those whose understanding is inadequate are very easily led astray in these matters. Moreover, even if they do understand well, better advice will nevertheless be given by the saints to *devoti* and solitaries to study books which rather kindle the emotions and teach them to eradicate vices and implant virtues, than books that enlighten the intellect and give information about many things that are doubtful and problematic." (*Et universalia sunt eis tradenda studia, que mentem noviter conversi ad veram humilitatem, sanctam compunctionem et perfectum Dei timorem informare ac inducere possint vel certe in exercitiis predictarum et aliarum virtutum conservare. Deinde constanter in proficiendi desiderio radicati ad studia sacre scripture utriusque testamenti admittantur et ad alios doctores secundum quod expedire videbitur. Non enim videntur admittendi ad libros de profundis materiis et dubiis tractantes nisi causa subsit rationabilis, quia parum intelligentes in his facillime decipiuntur. Preterea dato quod bene intelligerent, a sanctis tamen magis consulitur devotis et abstractis ut studeant libros qui magis inflammant affectum et docent vicia exstirpare et virtutes inserere quam libros qui intellectum illuminant et de multis dubiis et quaestionibus informant.*)—On the contrast between *inflammare affectum* and *illuminare intellectum* see above, note 43.

[59] *Speculum monachorum* here is certainly not David of Augsburg's treatise for novices, as it is quoted as *liber de disciplina noviciorum qui incipit: Primo considerare.* Cf. above, notes 35 and 40.

"some works of St. Augustine ... St. Jerome ... St. Ambrose ... St. John Chrysostom" (*opera beati Bernardi; aliqua opera beati Anselmi; omnia opera beati Gregorii; quedam opera devota Hugonis de S. Victore; omnia parva opuscula sancti Bonaventure; omnia opera Gersonis ... quedam opera beati Augustini ... beati Ieronimi ... beati Ambrosii ... beati Iohannis Crisostomi*).

Thomas à Kempis also appears here—with, moreover, the *Dialogus noviciorum* and the addition "all the other works of brother Thomas à Kempis which are available" (*omnia alia opera fratris Thome Kempis que haberi possunt*). Apart from this the authors of the *Devotio moderna* are represented by Zerbolt (*De reformatione, De spiritualibus ascensionibus*), Schoonhoven (*Epistola in Eemsteyn*) and Johannes Mombaer (*quedam ex Rosetis*); and we find another contemporary in Johannes Nyder (*Opuscula de oculo morali ac de morali lepra*). Finally, alongside Ludolf's *Vita Jesu Christi* and the obligatory writings of the ancient Fathers (*Vitas Patrum, Verba Seniorum, Collationes Patrum*) the lives and histories of Orders from the High Middle Ages are also taken into account (*Liber de initio Ordinis Cisterciensium; Vitae fratrum praedicatorum; Vitae sanctorum Bernardi, Francisci, Dominici ac similium sanctorum*). Altogether, we get a picture similar to that for Mombaer: medieval devotional literature predominates, together with a high proportion of writings by the modern *devoti* and other contemporaries (Gerson, Nyder), while the Church Fathers, though they are indeed cited, are not mentioned along with specific works. Hence we may suppose that these generalizing references were less important for the reading that was actually done than the recommendation of specific individual works.

Accordingly, if Patristic literature did not play a dominant part in the private study of the *devoti*, it was nevertheless set before them in the broadest of selections, though certainly in very fragmentary form. The catalogue of table readings from the monastery of Zevenborren, which may have come into existence about the same time as the Martinstal list, offers such a rich provision of accurately described textual passages traceable by means of book classifications and page references, that it is possible to reconstruct from it the principal stock of the monastery library.[60] The following authors from the patristic

---

[60] Brussels MSS K.B. II 1038, folios 91v–94v, 121r–202v and II 7602, folios 89v–120r. On this see Albert Derolez, "A late medieval reading-list of the priory of Zevenborren near Brussels" in *Studia varia Bruxellensia ad orbem Graeco-Latinum pertinentia*, ed. R. de Smet—H. Melaerts—C. Saerens, Louvain 1990, pp. 21–27; and his "A Reconstruction of the Library of the Priory of Zevenborren at the End of the Middle Ages" in *Miscellanea Martin Wittek*, ed. A. Raman—E. Manning, Louvain-Paris 1993, pp. 113–126.

period are represented—often repeatedly and in numerous works—
in this reading list: Cyprian, Lactantius, Leo the Great, Ambrose,
Jerome, Augustine, Sulpicius Severus, Prosper of Aquitaine, John
Cassian, Julian Pomerius, Caesarius of Arles, Boethius, Cassiodorus,
Gregory of Tours, Gregory the Great, Isidore and Bede; and from
among the Greeks Origen, Eusebius of Caesarea, Athanasius, Didymus the Blind, Basil the Great, Gregory of Nazianzus, John Chrysostom, Ephraem Syrus, John Climacus, John of Damascus.

Be that as it may, the practical significance of the Zevenborren
catalogue of table readings should not be overrated. For the number
of readings recorded for individual days is so large that even in a
cycle of several years the entire material could probably not be
mastered. Nevertheless it may be counted as a noteworthy testimony
to the effort to make an extremely rich library stock really serviceable over an appropriately wide range. Elsewhere similar efforts at
development led to the creation of library catalogues which in their
systematizing approach were already taking readers' needs into account
and were thus also fulfilling the function of a plan of spiritual reading: the most interesting example for this is certainly the catalogue
of the Carthusian library at Erfurt which is similarly annotated.[61]

2. *The making of extracts*

Intensive reception of spiritual literature among the *devoti* did not
take place only by way of hearing and reading. Rather, the manual
work involved in writing books was valued so highly not least because it called for detailed involvement with the text in question—no
matter whether this had to be reproduced for commercial purposes
(*pro pretio*) or for their own library (*pro domo*—for the *"house"*). In the
case of the production of manuscript books the result for the writers

---

[61] *Mittelalterliche Bibliothekskataloge Deutschlands und der Schweiz*, vol. 2, ed. P. Lehmann,
Munich 1928, pp. 221–592; on p. 242 of this the fundamental idea for organizing
a library is stated: "All books arranged in their [proper] order and according to
their nature serve the purposes of sacred theology in accordance with its four senses . . .
and sacred theology itself is like some spiritual house for the pious mind, in which
it ought to dwell during its travels in this place of exile so that it may happily be
able to reach the heavenly Jerusalem." (*omnes libri ordine suo et qualitate sua subordinate
deserviunt sacre theologie secundum eius quatuor sensus et . . . ipsa sacra theologia est comparative
quedam spiritualis domus devote mentis, quam inhabitare debet in huius exilii peregrinacione ut
celestem Jherusalem feliciter possit attingere.*) On this cf. J. de Ghellinck, "Les catalogues
des bibliothèques médiévales chez les chartreux et un guide de lectures spirituelles"
in *Revue d'Ascétique et de Mystique* 25, 1949, pp. 284–298.

was always a spiritual yield too (or so at least it was thought), in that
they became attentive to edifying statements and ideas (*notabilia puncta*)
which they could record in their private anthologies—*florilegia* or
rapiaria—once they had completed their load of work.[62] This process
of making excerpts was, however, intended to supplement not only
the work of writing but also the reading (and listening) and to make
these things an enduring acquisition. On this Zerbolt remarked:

> You must therefore turn your reading as directly as possible to purity,
> and always extract something from the reading which is suitable for
> your purpose, stays in your memory, and urges you to make progress,
> so that you may be a pure creature accustomed to ruminate.[63]

Contemporaries had already described the literary achievements of a
Radewijns or Zerbolt as the making of excerpts and had seen their
treatises clearly as a kind of model *rapiaria*:

> He himself (i.e. Radewijns) gathered together from the sayings of the
> Doctors a little book which begins "All skills . . .", from which, as people
> say, Master Gerhard Zerbolt took the opportunity or the material for
> composing those two treatises.[64]

But while their compilations were built up very systematically, a completely different, unregulated kind of *rapiarium* came into existence as

---

[62] Cf. Johannes Trithemius, *De laude scriptorum*, ed. Klaus Arnold (*Mainfränkische Hefte* 60) Würzburg 1973, cap. 10, p. 74.

[63] *Debes igitur, ut immediatius lectionem ad puritatem referas, semper aliquid de lectione extrahere, quod tuo proposito conveniat, quod memoriam occupet, quod te ad proficiendum admoneat, ut sis animal mundum quod consuevit ruminare.*—Gerhard Zerbolt, *De spiritualibus ascensionibus* (cf. note 41) cap. 44, p. 276; cf. his *De reformatione virium animae* (cf. note 41) cap. 15, p. 242.

[64] *Collegit ipse* (i.e. Radewijns) *ex dictis doctorum libellum qui incipit "Omnes, inquit, artes", ex quo, ut fertur, dominus Gherardus Serbolt occasionem sive materiam accepit componendi illos duos tractatus . . .*—Dier van Muiden, ed. Dumbar (cf. note 27) p. 50; cf. Thomas à Kempis, *Dialogus noviciorum* III 14, ed. Pohl (cf. note 13) vol. 7, p. 150: "He (Radewijns) compiled some notable devotional passages of the sacred writings for the consolation of the brethren and the exercise of the inner life" (. . . *de scripturis sanctis aliqua devota notabilia ad consolationem fratrum et exercitationem internorum compilavit*— sc. Radewijns); *ibid.* IV 8, p. 275: "For he (Zerbolt) was very learned in the sacred writings, even extracting from abstruse opinions of the Doctors various kinds of fragrances against the sicknesses of vices, for the healing of faintnesses of the soul, as is evident from two little books he published, one of which begins *Homo quidam* (a certain man) and the other is entitled *Beatus vir* (Blessed <is the> man)" (*Erat enim studiosus valde in scripturis sanctis* (sc. Zerbolt), *trahens etiam ex abditis sententiis doctorum varias aromatum species contra vitiorum morbos, ad sanandum animarum languores, sicut praecipue patet in duobus libellis ab eo editis, quorum unus incipit Homo quidam et alius Beatus vir intitulatur.*)

a result of the spontaneous, step-by-step recording of the gleanings from their reading—a volume suited only for personal use, of which the chances of survival after the death of its owner were bound to be very small indeed.[65] The fact that one could also deliberately turn this random, individual use of *rapiaria*, with its loose association of individual *puncta*, into a principle of literary production is demonstrated by Thomas à Kempis' mosaic-work treatises—most impressively in his *Imitatio Christi*.[66] However, one thing is common to every kind of technique for *rapiaria*: the appropriation of texts that have been read, heard or written down does not extend over relatively long passages or the whole context of the work, but lays hold only on individual sentences or short sections which correspond particularly well to the needs of the *devotus*. Under these conditions, reception of Patristic literature can only involve a collection of moral maxims and *sententiae, dicta* and *exempla* that is guided by subjective feelings and relates to specific detailed situations. The popularity among the *devoti* of the writings by the ancient Desert Fathers may well rest not least on the fact that in their episodic and aphoristic structure they matched this selection method. Moreover, the almost arbitrary control of the readers over their texts was certainly felt not as a problem, but simply as a precondition for emotional identification with the tradition which was able to eliminate completely the historical distance from the early Christian period. The freedom to make excerpts in dealing with the original work constituted a concession to the interests of the individual reader which were narrowed down and controlled by reading lists and study plans. In an example from the early period of the "Devotio moderna" Johannes Busch illustrates the fact that it was possible to utilize the original texts for *florilegia* of a very different kind, from the standpoint of personal spiritual use:[67]

> Our venerable Fathers and masters of virtue do not always obtain the
> same graces of inner edification from what they read or write, but
> each of them is filled by the Lord with a special grace in accordance

---

[65] Cf. van Woerkum (cf. note 39) pp. 123ff.; Th. Mertens, "Rapiarium", in *Dictionnaire de spiritualité ascétique et mystique* 13, Paris 1988, columns 114–119; also his "Het rapiarium" in *Moderne Devotie, figuren en facetten* (cf. note 4) pp. 153–157; and his "Lezen met de pen. Ontwikkelingen in het laatmiddeleeuws geestelijk proza" in *De studie van de Middelnederlandse letterkunde: stand en toekomst*, ed. F.P. van Oostrom—F. Willaert, Hilversum 1989, pp. 187–200.

[66] Cf. Staubach (cf. note 1) pp. 223f.

[67] Johannes Busch, *Chronicon Windeshemense*, ed. Grube (cf. note 23) pp. 95f.

with his spiritual temperament and character. Thus Johannes Huesden, our Prior, made for himself a stock of comprehensive excerpts for devotional use from St. Bernard's sermons on the Song of Solomon, amounting to nearly half the whole text. Brother John of Kempen likewise wanted to make extracts from that work for devotional exercises. However, he did not select what the Prior had collected, but just what those excerpts did not have: for on the basis of his own experience he was convinced that these texts moved him more, and were more serviceable for his spiritual progress.

3. Translation

The most important precondition for the intensive internalizing of a document is to understand its wording. If the desire was to facilitate access to the sources of religious renewal for the "laity" too, then it was necessary to strive for translations from the Latin into the vernacular. With this in mind, Geert Grote translated parts of the church office, and his *Getijdenboek* (Book of Hours) became perhaps the most successful document of the *Devotio moderna*:

> He translated the Hours of the Blessed Virgin together with certain other Hours from Latin into the Germanic language [Dutch] so that simple and unlearned laypeople might have them in their mother tongue for their use in praying on holy days, so that when the faithful read these or heard them read by other devout persons they might the more easily keep themselves from many vanities and idle conversations and progress in the love and praise of God aided by their sacred readings.[68]

Grote's undertaking was by no means revolutionary but matched a need of the age which had been recognized by others before him, as the extensive activity in translation in the *Bijbelvertaler van 1360* (Bible Translator of 1360) demonstrates.[69] Nor was there anything more

---

[68] *Transtulit horas beatae virginis cum quibusdam aliis horis de Latino in linguam Teutonicalem, ut simplices et indocti laici haberent in lingua materna, quibus se occuparent sacris diebus orando, quatenus dum fideles haec legerent aut ab aliis devotis audirent legere, facilius a multis vanitatibus et otiosis sermonibus abstinerent atque in Dei amore et laudibus divinis sacris lectionibus adiuti proficerent.*—Thomas à Kempis, *Ex chronica . . . quae domum nostram non concernunt*, cap. 3, ed. Pohl (cf. note 13) vol. 7, p. 484; cf. Dier van Muiden, ed. Dumbar (cf. note 27) p. 6; Petrus Horn, *Vita Magistri Gerardi*, ed. Kühler (cf. note 14) cap. 7, p. 349. See also above, note 21.

[69] C.G.N. de Vooys, "Iets over middeleeuwse bijbelvertalingen" in *Theologisch Tijdschrift* 37, 1903, pp. 111–158; C.C. de Bruin. "Bespiegelingen over de 'Bijbelvertaler van 1360'. Zijn milieu, werk en persoon" in *Nederlands Archief voor Kerkgeschiedenis*,

novel, of course, in ecclesiastical and theological reservations about—
and resistance to—increasing "reception" of spiritual literature in the
vernacular.[70] The success of Grote's missionary activity and the spread
of his movement nevertheless increased considerably the need for
religious reading-matter for the "laity" and at the same time it
intensified the controversy about its legitimacy. This question was of
personal-existential significance for the *devoti*, particularly because the
concept of "laity" had been defined solely in terms of linguistic competence (*simplices, illiterati*) and not of secular life-style (*personae saeculares*):
thus for the church to prohibit religious literature in the vernacular
would have cut off the numerous members of devout communities,
the Sisters of the Common Life and the lay brethren in monasteries
and houses of the Brethren from their spiritual nourishment. This
explains why the theological and canon law treatises that were now
produced in defence of lay reading were at once translated into the
vernacular and edited as excerpts and even *collationes*: for after all it
was of great concern for the "laity" to know the extent and the limitations of the reading freedom they were allowed.[71] The fundamental

---

New Series 48, 1967–68, pp. 39–59; 49, 1968–69, pp. 134–154; 50, 1969–70, pp.
11–27; 51, 1970–71, pp. 16–41; and his "De moderne devotie en de verspreiding
van de volkstaalbijbel" in *Ons Geestelijk Erf* 59, 1985, pp. 344–356.

[70] Cf. Klaus Schreiner, "Laienbildung als Herausforderung für Kirche und Gesellschaft" in *Zeitschrift für historische Forschung* 11, 1984, pp. 257–354; Josef Klapper, *Im
Kampf um die deutsche Bibel. Zwei Traktate des 14. Jahrhunderts*, Breslau 1922; F. Löser—
Ch. Stöllinger-Löser, "Verteidigung der Laienbibel. Zwei programmatische Vorreden
des österreichischen Bibelübersetzers der ersten Hälfte des 14. Jahrhunderts" in *Überlieferungsgeschichtliche Editionen und Studien zur deutschen Literatur des Mittelalters. Kurt Ruh
zum 75. Geburtstag*, ed. K. Kunze *et al.*, Tübingen 1989, pp. 245–313.—The *Bijbelvertaler*
("Bible translator") was already aware of instances of resistance to his work; see his
prologue to the Pentateuch in the *Corpus S. Scripturae Neerlandicae Medii Aevi*, Series
maior, Tomus I: Vetus Testamentum, Pars prima, ed. C.C. de Bruin, Leiden 1977,
p. 3: "This work ... will be greatly envied among the clergy ... for some (holy)
clerks are angry that the mysteries of the Scriptures should be opened up to the
common people and do not want to know that Christ's apostles wrote down and
preached their teaching in every tongue and language." (*Dit werc. ... sal sijn seer
benijdt onder die clergie ... Want enighen clerken tornt dat men die heymelijcheit der Scriftueren
den ghemeynen volke onthynden soude, ende en willen niet weten dat Cristus apostelen in allen
tonghen ende spraken haer leringhe beschreven ende predicten den volke.*)

[71] Cf. A. Hyma, "The 'De libris teutonicalibus' by Gerard Zerbolt of Zutphen"
in *Nederlandsch Archief voor Kerkgeschiedenis*, New series 17, 1924, pp. 42–70; and his
"Het traktaat 'Super modo vivendi devotorum hominum simul commorantium' door
Gerard Zerbolt van Zutphen" in *Archief voor de Geschiedenis van het Aartsbisdom Utrecht*
52, 1926, pp. 1–100; C.J. Jellouschek, "Ein mittelalterliches Gutachten über das
Lesen der Bibel und sonstiger religiöser Bücher in der Volkssprache" in *Aus der
Geisteswelt des Mittelalters. Studien und Texte M. Grabmann gewidmet*, 2nd half-volume,

rule was the limitation that the *libri teutonicales*—books in German, Dutch etc.—should agree in style and content with the tradition of the doctors of the church and that only simple, easily understood subjects which were relevant to the moral life should be dealt with—"such as are the lives and acts of the saints, the sufferings and triumphs of the martyrs, and other teachings on vices and virtues, exposing plainly and openly the glory of the saints and misery of the damned, and other such things" (*sicut sunt vitae et gesta sanctorum, passiones et triumphi martyrum aliaeque doctrinae de vitiis et virtutibus, de sanctorum gloria ac damnatorum miseria hisque similibus plane et aperte pertractantes*).[72] By way of justification it was pointed out that the laity had limited mental capacity, and Hugh's example of the dangers of over-demanding Bible study was quoted. Accordingly both some books of the Old and New Testaments and extensive sections of the Church Fathers' writings were unsuitable for reading by the laity—the Prophets, Paul's letters and Revelation were mentioned as examples, also Augustine's writings *Super Genesim, De trinitate, De civitate dei* and *Contra Faustum*.[74] A look at translations of the Church Fathers which were used or produced and disseminated in the "Devotio moderna" shows that these principles really did determine how reception took place. Three focal points stand out here: Augustine, Cassian and the *Vitae patrum*, and also Gregory the Great.

In line with the selection criteria among the *devoti*, the pseudo-Augustinian devotional writings from the late twelfth century came into consideration for translation into the vernacular to a greater degree than the genuine writings of Augustine himself. Thus there are Middle Dutch versions of the *Manuale* (2 versions), the *Soliloquia* and the *Speculum peccatoris*, though judging from the number of known

---

Münster 1935, pp. 1181–1199; C.G.N. de Vooys, "De dietse tekst van het traktaat 'De libris teutonicalibus' in *Nederlandsch Archief voor Kerkgeschiedenis*, New Series, 4, 1906, pp. 113–134; J. Deschamps, "Middelnederlandse vertalingen van Super modo vivendi (7 de hoofdstuk) en De libris teutonicalibus van Gerard Zerbolt van Zutphen" in *Koninklijke Zuidnederlandse Maatschappij voor Taal- en Letterkunde en Geschiedenis. Handelingen* 14, 1960, pp. 67–108; 15, 1961, pp. 175–220; Volker Honemann, "Zu Interpretation und Überlieferung des Traktats 'De libris teutonicalibus'" in *Miscellanea Neerlandica. Opstellen voor J. Deschamps*, ed. E. Cockx-Indesteege—F. Hendrickx, vol. 3, Louvain 1987, pp. 113–124; also his "Der Laie als Leser" in *Laienfrömmigkeit im späten Mittelalter*, ed. K. Schreiner, Munich 1992, pp. 241–251.

[72] Hyma, "De libris teutonicalibus" (as in note 71) 1961, p. 46.
[73] Deschamps (cf. note 71) 1961, pp. 211f. Cf. above, note 10.
[74] Deschamps *op. cit.* p. 193.

manuscripts the dissemination of these must have varied greatly. Also translated were sermons and prayers handed down under Augustine's name, such as a selection from the *Sermones ad fratres in eremo* and the *Psalter*.[75] Finally, a revealing and representative testimony to the reception in the "Devotio moderna" of the Church Fathers in the vernacular is the *Eerste Collatieboek* of Dirc van Herxen, which contains a systematic arrangement of numerous texts of Augustine and *Exempla* from the *Vitae patrum* and other collections, together with excerpts from Chrysostom, Jerome, Gregory, Bede, Bernard, Seuse and David of Augsburg.[76]

Two Middle Dutch translations of John Cassian's *Collationes patrum* are known. The first comes from the *Bijbelvertaler van 1360* and was intended for a citizen of Brussels who acquired it in 1382. However, it has been handed down only fragmentarily in copies made by the *devoti* of the fifteenth century, and thus it documents a tradition of reading by the religious laity with which Geert Grote's movement could associate itself. There is much better testimony for the Northern Dutch translation, made in the sphere of the *Devotio moderna*, of which 26 manuscripts have been preserved.[77] The first Middle Dutch translations of the *Vitae patrum* also go back to the *Bijbelvertaler—Der vader boek* (*Vitae patrum* Part II and extracts from Part I) and the *Verba seniorum* (Parts V and VI). They too were copied in the communities of the *devoti*.[78] However, alongside this, they made efforts for new

---

[75] Kurt Ruh, "Augustinus" in *Die deutsche Literatur des Mittelalters. Verfasserlexikon*, vol. 1, Berlin-New York 1978, columns 531–543; Willem de Vreese, "Sint Augustinus in het Middelnederlandsch uit de Bibliotheca Neerlandica Manuscripta" in his *Over handschriften en handschriftenkunde* (cf. note 37) pp. 85–115 (first published in 1930).

[76] J. Deschamps, *Middelnederlandse handschriften uit Europese en Amerikaanse bibliotheken. Catalogus*. Brussels 1970, no. 90, pp. 248ff. Cf. A.M.J. van Buuren, "'Wat materien gheliken op sonnendage ende hoechtijde te lesen'. Het Middelnederlandse collatieboek van Dirc van Herxen" in *Boeken voor de eeuwigheid. Middelnederlands geestelijk proza*, ed. Th. Mertens *et al.*, Amsterdam 1993, pp. 245–263.

[77] Klaus Klein, "Johannes Cassianus" in *Die deutsche Literatur des Mittelalters. Verfasserlexikon*, vol. 4, Berlin-New York 1983, columns 567–570; Deschamps (cf. note 76) nos. 74–75, pp. 209–213.

[78] Deschamps (cf. note 76) nos. 56 and 58, pp. 170ff. and 174ff.—On the reception of the *Vitas patrum* in late Middle Ages, cf. Columba M. Battle, *Die "Adhortationes sanctorum patrum" ("Verba seniorum") im lateinischen Mittelalter* (*Beiträge zur Geschichte des alten Mönchtums und des Benediktinerordens* 31) Münster 1972; K. Klein, "Frühchristliche Eremiten im Spätmittelalter und in der Reformationszeit. Zu Überlieferung und Rezeption der deutschen 'Vitaspatrum'-Prosa" in *Literatur und Laienbildung im Spätmittelalter und in der Reformationszeit*, ed. L. Grenzmann—K. Stackmann, Stuttgart 1984, pp. 686–695; and his *Die Vitaspatrum. Überlieferungsgeschichtliche Untersuchungen zu den Prosaübersetzungen im deutschen Mittelalter*, thesis, Würzburg 1985; K. Kunze—

translations of their own. A codex written in the monastery of
Vredendaal near Utrecht in 1417 contains a second Middle Dutch
version of the *Historia monachorum in Aegypto* (= *Vitae patrum* Part II)
and the first translation of the *Historia Lausiaca* (= *Vitae patrum* Part
VIII).[79] And the remarkable thing about this provenance is that Wermbold van Buscop († 1413), the founder of the monastery, had put
himself forward as a promoter and apologist of reading for the religious laity. Wermbold was a close friend of Florens Radewijns and
protected and specially looked after the Sisters of the Common Life—
which gave him the honorary title of a "father to all the devout
sisters in Holland" (*communis pater devotarum in Hollandia*).[80] As rector of
various convents in Utrecht and its environs he had to offer resistance in 1394 to the attacks of Eylard Schoeneveld, the Inquisitor,
who censured the *devoti* for (among other things) their practice of
table readings and prayers in the vernacular. It is said that in this
conflict Wermbold tried to arm the sisters through the translation of
legal material for their defence.[81] It is therefore easy to connect him
not only with the justificatory treatise *De libris teutonicalibus* which is
usually ascribed to Zerbolt,[82] but also with the Vredendaal translation of the *Vitae patrum*. At all events, Thomas à Kempis explicitly

U. Williams—Ph. Kaiser, "Information und innere Formung. Zur Rezeption der
'Vitaspatrum'" in *Wissensorganisierende und wissensvermittelnde Literatur im Mittelalter.
Perspektiven ihrer Erforschung*, ed. N.R. Wolf, Wiesbaden 1987, pp. 123–142.

[79] Deschamps (cf. note 76) no. 57, pp. 173f.

[80] Dier van Muiden, ed. Dumbar (cf. note 27) pp. 29f.; cf. Thomas à Kempis,
Dialogus noviciorum III 27, ed. Pohl (cf. note 13) vol. 7, p. 187; Michael Schoengen,
Monasticon Batavum, part 1, Amsterdam 1941, pp. 183f.

[81] Dier van Muiden, *ibid.*: "At that time Master Eylard was inquisitor into heretical irregularities; he greatly troubled the devout sisters in Utrecht but Masters
Florencius and Wermbold resisted him." (*Tunc temporis fuit magister Eylardus inquisitor
heretice pravitatis, qui multum molestabat devotas sorores in Traiecto, sed dominus Florencius et
dominus Werenboldus resistebant ei.*) Cf. Paul Fredericq (ed.), *Corpus documentorum haereticae
pravitatis neerlandicae*, vol. 2, Ghent-The Hague 1896, no. 106ff. pp. 153ff.; no. 114,
pp. 181ff., especially p. 184, "For they have some material produced—though not
adequately—for the defence of their position against the inquisitors and translated
into vernacular by their own Rector and priest [Wermbold]—an ill-advised man—
with quotations and allegations." (*Habent enim quasdam informationes pro defensione status
sui contra inquisitores . . . satis tamen impertinenter pro eis factas et per praetactum presbyterum,
ipsarum gubernatorem* (i.e. Wermbold), *in vulgari malo utentem consilio cum auctoritatibus et
allegationibus translatas.*)

[82] A. Hyma, "Is Gerard Zerbolt of Zutphen the author of the 'Super modo
vivendi'?" in *Nederlandsch Archief voor Kerkgeschiedenis*, New Series 16, 1921, pp. 107–
128; J. van Rooij, *Gerard Zerbolt van Zutphen*, vol. 1: Leven en geschriften, Nijmegen-
Utrecht-Antwerp 1936, pp. 47ff.

confirms that Wermbold had theological interests and also translated Latin devotional literature into the vernacular:

> He caused many books of sacred theology to be copied down and for the use of the lay faithful . . . he translated certain sayings of the saints into Dutch.[83]

Of course it does seem questionable whether we may argue from the expression Thomas uses here—*dicta sanctorum*—to a specific work or genre, viz. a collection of *dicta*, as Deschamps has suggested.[84] If we wished to do that, we should need to have in mind a new translation of the *Verba seniorum* (= *Vitae patrum* Parts V and VI) as having come into existence in the circles of the *devoti*, with Wermbold as its possible author.[85]

The Middle Dutch reception of Gregory exhibits a two-phase model similar to that of Cassian and the *Vitae patrum*. Thus the *devoti* copied a collection of the *Homiliae in evangelia*, arranged in liturgical sequence, which had been translated in 1380 by the "Bijbelvertaler" ("Bible translator"). Numerous manuscripts of this copy were distributed.[86] But in addition the "Devotio moderna" also produced new translations here, as Dirc van Herxen's vernacular books of *Collationes* prove.[87] There is also a translation of Gregory's *Dialogi* dated 1388 and made by the "Bijbelvertaler", which was copied a few years after it came into existence in the monastery of Rooklooster. Probably at the beginning of the fifteenth century a new translation was then undertaken in the northern Netherlands; only a few manuscripts (4–5) of both versions have been handed down.[88] Once again Dirc van Herxen and numerous other excerpts testify to the existence of yet more—independent—translations. Finally, a version of Gregory's *Moralia* in

---

[83] *Plures sacrae theologiae libros fecit conscribi et pro utilitate fidelium laicorum . . . quaedam sanctorum dicta Teutonicis verbis transposuit.*—Thomas à Kempis, *Ex chronica . . . quae domum nostrum non concernunt*, cap. 19, ed. Pohl (cf. note 13) vol. 7, p. 509.

[84] Deschamps (cf. note 76), pp. 176f. Here as usual, however, we must probably understand *dicta sanctorum* simply as "texts of the Church Fathers".

[85] Thus Deschamps, *ibid.*

[86] Kurt Ruh, "Gregor der Große" in *Die deutsche Literatur des Mittelalters. Verfasserlexikon*, vol. 3, Berlin-New York 1981, columns 233–244; Deschamps (cf. note 76) no. 91, pp. 251ff.

[87] Deschamps *op. cit.* no. 90, pp. 248ff.

[88] *Op. cit.* nos. 60 and 61, pp. 177–182. Cf. Martta Jaatinen, "Dialogi Gregorii nach der Handschrift Theol. germ. 11 der Stadtbibliothek Lübeck" in *Bulletin de la Société Néophilologique de Helsinki* 53, 1952, pp. 82–115; J. Deschamps, "Die mittelniederländischen Übersetzungen der Dialoge Gregors des Großen", *ibid.* pp. 466–470.

Middle Dutch has so far been known only in a single manuscript from the Harlem monastery of St. Margaret.[89]

It goes without saying that only a fragment of the vernacular "reception" of the Church Fathers in the "Devotio moderna" can be noted by the mention of identifiable translations. Innumerable brief quotations in *rapiaria*, treatises, *Collationes* and other genres make it clear that the appropriation of the Patristic heritage through their own language was frequently not a literary undertaking but a spontaneous act. It often happens that not the individual Latin work or its sections constituted the item to be made available, but the collected exegetical authority of the Fathers, of which it was possible for a learned clerk to make free use as he required. Thus in his translation of the Book of Hours Geert Grote had already made glosses on obscure passages in the Psalms along the lines of Patristic exegesis.[90] Something similar is reported of Johannes Scutken, the Windesheim canon, who as librarian in charge of the *libri teutonici* made special efforts for the instruction of the "laity" who did not know Latin. He commented on Gospel *pericopae*, and on the Psalms, in accordance with the exegesis of the Fathers, translated them into the vernacular and where necessary was also able to explain impromptu the texts for table reading in the lay brothers' refectory:

> For our lay brothers he also wrote down certain books, translating them himself from Latin into German, namely the Gospels through the year and the Psalms, with his glosses from the *dicta* of the saints which he himself had collected, and certain other similar things. For he was the librarian of the Dutch books here which he allowed literate lay brothers to read. For more or less a dozen years he himself, indeed, was in the habit of reading almost daily to the lay brothers in the refectory at dinner and supper, expounding difficult passages that cropped up, without books, because he was a good catholic, full of the Holy Scriptures and inspired by the Holy Spirit.[91]

---

[89] Ruh (cf. note 86) column 236.

[90] See above in notes 21 and 68.

[91] *Quosdam eciam libros, videlicet evangelia per annum et psalterium, singula cum suis glosis ex dictis sanctorum per ipsum collectis, et alia quedam similia ex latino vertens in teutonicum manu propria . . . pro laicis nostris conscripsit. Librarius enim hic erat librorum teutonicorum, quos laycis legere scientibus concessit ad legendum. Ipse vero per annos plus minus duodecim singulis pene diebus laycis in refectorio ad prandium et ad cenam legere consuevit, passus occurrentes ad intelligendum difficiles sine libris exponens, quia bonus fuit catholicus sanctis scripturis plenus, spiritu sancto afflatus.*—Johannes Busch, *Chronicon Windeshemense* ed. Grube (cf. note 23) p. 192. Cf. on this J. Deschamps, "De verspreiding van Johan Scutkens vertaling van het Nieuwe Testament en de oudtestamentische perikopen" in *Nederlands Archief voor Kerkgeschiedenis*

V. *Erasmus and the* devoti: *a* querelle des humanistes et modernes

In the history of biblical philology and reception of the Church Fathers the year 1516 is significant as a turning-point. With his editions of the New Testament and the works of Jerome, Erasmus of Rotterdam was able to make available almost simultaneously two monumental witnesses to his own long work, from which he rightly expected a decisive stimulus for the renewal of theology and Christian life.[92] The date at which they appeared could not have been more favourably chosen. Interest in the original Greek text of the New Testament had increased considerably, not least as a result of Lorenzo Valla's

---

56, 1975, pp. 158–179; and his *Catalogus* (cf. note 76) no. 52, pp. 159ff.; W.C.M. Wüstefeld, *Middeleeuwse boeken van het Catharijneconvent*, Zwolle-Utrecht 1993, no. 21, p. 49.

[92] Cf. R.J. Schoeck, *Erasmus of Europe. The prince of humanists 1501–1536*, Edinburgh 1993, pp. 165ff. and 175ff.; Cornelis Augustijn, *Erasmus. His Life, Works and Influence*, Toronto-Buffalo-London 1991, pp. 89ff.; Leon E. Halkin, *Erasmus von Rotterdam. Eine Biographie*, Zürich 1989, pp. 123ff; Margaret Mann Phillips, *Erasmus and the Northern Renaissance*, Rev. Ed. Woodbridge, Suffolk 1981, pp. 55ff.; Jerry H. Bentley, *Humanists and Holy Writ. New Testament Scholarship in the Renaissance*, Princeton, N.J. 1983; August Bludau, *Die beiden ersten Erasmus-Ausgaben des Neuen Testaments und ihre Gegner*, Freiburg im Breisgau 1902; Rudolf Pfeiffer, "Erasmus und die Einheit der klassischen und christlichen Renaissance" in *Historisches Jahrbuch* 74, 1955, pp. 175–188, reprinted in his *Ausgewählte Schriften*, ed. W. Bühler, Munich 1960, pp. 208–221; Jacques Etienne, *Spiritualisme érasmien et théologiens louvanistes*, Louvain-Gembloux 1956; Denys Gorce, "La patristique dans la réforme d'Erasme" in *Festgabe J. Lortz*, ed. E. Iserloh—P. Manns, vol. 1: *Reformation—Schicksal und Auftrag*, Baden-Baden 1958, pp. 233–276; Joseph Coppens, "Les idées réformistes d'Erasme dans les préfaces aux Paraphrases du Nouveau Testament" in *Scrinium Lovaniense. Mélanges historiques Etienne van Cauwenbergh*, Louvain 1961, pp. 344–371; August Buck, "Der Rückgriff des Renaissance-Humanismus auf die Patristik" in *Festschrift W. von Wartburg*, ed. K. Baldinger, Tübingen, 1968, pp. 153–175; Jean Hadot, "Le Nouveau Testament d'Erasme" in *Colloquium Erasmianum*, Mons 1968, pp. 59–67; A. Rabil, *Erasmus and the New Testament. The Mind of a Christian Humanist*, San Antonio 1972; also "Erasmus's Paraphrases of the New Testament" in *Essays on the Works of Erasmus*, ed. R.L. de Molen, New Haven-London 1978, pp. 145–161; Gerhard B. Winkler, *Erasmus von Rotterdam und die Einleitungsschriften zum Neuen Testament*, Münster 1973; Heinz Holeczek, *Humanistische Bibelphilologie als Reformproblem bei Erasmus von Rotterdam, Thomas More und William Tyndale*, Leiden 1975; Marjorie O'Rourke Boyle, *Erasmus on Language and Method in Theology*, Toronto-Buffalo 1977; Friedhelm Krüger, *Humanistische Evangelienauslegung. Desiderius Erasmus von Rotterdam als Ausleger der Evangelien in seinen Paraphrasen*, Tübingen 1986; Henk Jan de Jonge, "Novum Testamentum a nobis versum: The Essence of Erasmus' Edition of the New Testament" in *The Journal of Theological Studies*, N.S. 35, 1984, pp. 394–413; also his "Wann ist Erasmus' Übersetzung des neuen Testaments entstanden?" in *Erasmus of Rotterdam. The Man and the Scholar. Proceedings of the Symposium Rotterdam 1986*, ed. J. Sperna Weiland—W.Th.M. Frijhoff, Leiden-Cologne 1988, pp. 151–157; J. den Boeft, "'Illic aureum quoddam ire flumen': Erasmus' Enthusiasm for the Patres", *ibid.* pp. 172–181; John C. Olin, "Erasmus and Saint Jerome: an Appraisal of the Bond, *ibid.* pp. 182–186. Cf. also J. den Boeft, pp. 537–572 *infra*.

critical notes on the translation of the Vulgate, which Erasmus himself had made accessible to the public a decade previously.[93] As early
as 1512 Faber Stapulensis in Paris published an edition of Paul's
epistles with a commentary. This edition, besides the Vulgate, contained a new Latin translation from the Greek,[94] and in Spain a
polyglot Bible was in preparation (that Erasmus' publisher anxiously
kept in view). This was intended to offer the user, among other things,
a parallel version of the New Testament in Greek and Latin.[95] At
this juncture, Erasmus' edition with the Greek text, his own Latin
translation and critical philological apparatus became the first to meet
all the needs of the moment. But with his Jerome too, Erasmus mani-
festly hit upon an extremely favourable moment for publication. For
the popularity of that saint in the late Middle Ages, after rising steadily
over a relatively long period, had reached its absolute high water-
mark precisely in the decade from 1510 to 1520.[96] The reason for
this popularity was doubtless the wealth of sides to the figure of Jerome,
which likewise made him attractive to a variety of spiritual movements of the age: while his writings commended the Church Father
on account of his classical education, linguistic knowledge and cultivated style as the leading figure of a Christian humanism, the picture of his personality, which had been overgrown with legend, revealed the initiator of the ascetic, contemplative monastic life. Thus
for Geert Grote too and for the modern *devoti*, Jerome was a particularly esteemed model—as a translator of the Bible and creator of the
Vulgate, as a teacher of virtue and as the relentless foe of heretics.[97]

---

[93] Jacques Chomarat, "Les Annotations de Valla, celles d'Erasme et la grammaire"
in *Histoire de l'exégèse au XVIᵉ siècle*, ed. O. Fatio—P. Fraenkel, Geneva 1978, pp.
202–228; Christopher S. Celenza, "Renaissance Humanism and the New Testament: Lorenzo Valla's Annotations to the Vulgate" in *The Journal of Medieval and
Renaissance Studies* 24, 1994, pp. 33–52; Bentley (cf. note 92) pp. 32ff.

[94] Bludau (cf. note 92) pp. 63ff.

[95] Bentley (cf. note 92) pp. 70ff.; den Boeft, p. 561ff., *infra*.

[96] Eugene F. Rice Jr., *Saint Jerome in the Renaissance*, Baltimore-London 1985; Renate
Jungblut, *Hieronymus. Darstellung und Verehrung eines Kirchenvaters*, thesis, Tübingen 1967;
Peter G. Bietenholz, "Erasmus von Rotterdam und der Kult des heiligen Hieronymus"
in *Poesis et Pictura. Festschrift D. Wuttke*, ed. St. Füssel—J. Knape, Baden-Baden 1989,
pp. 191–221; Berndt Hamm, "Hieronymus-Begeisterung und Augustinismus vor der
Reformation" in *Augustine, the Harvest, and Theology (1300–1650). Essays dedicated to
H.A. Oberman*, ed. K. Hagen, Leiden-Cologne 1990, pp. 127–235; Hans-Peter Hasse,
"Ambrosius Blarer liest Hieronymus" in *Auctoritas Patrum. Zur Rezeption der Kirchenväter
im 15. und 16. Jahrhundert*, ed. L. Grane—A. Schindler—M. Wriedt, Mainz 1993,
pp. 33–53.

[97] Epiney-Burgard (cf. note 2) pp. 68f.; cf. note 33 above.

Not a few Brotherhoods chose him as their eponymous patron, and now and then the Brothers of the Common Life were also called simply *Hieronymiani*—perhaps for that very reason.[98]

Thus, given that Erasmus' turning of his attention programmatically to study of the Bible and the Church Fathers fits apparently seamlessly into the picture of the interests of his own day, we do have to enquire into the originality and innovative achievement of his theological involvement on the eve of the Reformation. Is the view represented by older research correct, that the high value he placed on Holy Scripture and the authors of the early church came from the spiritual milieu of the "Devotio moderna" in which he was brought up and spent his years as a monk? Is it perhaps possible to relate his work on the text of the New Testament to the revision of the Vulgate done by those from Windesheim? Can we compare his plea for promotion of Bible-reading in all classes of the Christian people with the efforts made by Zerbolt or Wermbold? The questions relate to the well-known controversy on whether we ought to deal with the "Devotio moderna" as "*humanisme chrétien*" or as the "Northern Renaissance".[99] In reply to this it is enough to contrast the motives and aims of Erasmus' biblical and Patristic philology with the programme of spiritual studies and reform of the *devoti*. It is even simpler to observe the divergence between the educational ideals of the humanists and those of the *devoti* in actual historical conflict between them. For in the conflict with Erasmus and his followers the modern *devoti* did not show themselves to be at all so "modern" and contemporary as their name may still at times subliminally suggest.

---

[98] *Moderne Devotie, figuren en facetten* (cf. note 4), pp. 136f. The monastic Houses in Cambrai, Ghent, Gheraardsbergen, Hulsbergen, Herford and Magdeburg held a Hieronymian advowson. "Hieronymiani" was not a collective designation for the Brothers of the Common Life, as has been repeatedly asserted in the literature, but solely a locally limited description in each case for the members of a particular "Hieronymian" House. The misunderstanding probably goes back to Allen (cf. note 112) volume 2, p. 210 and vol. 3, p. 91 note; he clearly misunderstood and illegitimately generalized remarks by L. Schulze, "Brüder des gemeinsamen Lebens" in *Realencyklopädie für protestantische Theologie und Kirche*, vol. 3, Leipzig³ 1897, pp. 472–507, pp. 486f. and Zöckler "Hieronymiten", *ibid.* vol. 8, Leipzig³ 1900, pp. 40f. On the further genealogy of this error cf. J. Uttenweiler, "Zur Stellung des hl. Hieronymus im Mittelalter" in *Benediktinische Monatsschrift* 2, 1920, pp. 522–541, pp. 533f.; Alfons Auer, *Die vollkommene Frömmigkeit des Christen. Nach dem Enchiridion militis Christiani des Erasmus von Rotterdam*, Düsseldorf 1954, pp. 34f.; Buck (cf. note 92) p. 171 note 80; Rice (cf. note 96) p. 116; Olin (cf. note 92) p. 182; Fidel Rädle, "Erasmus als Lehrer" in *Lebenslehren und Weltentwürfe* (cf. note 5) pp. 214–232, p. 222.

[99] See above, note 5.

Clear similarities, but also serious divergences, reveal themselves between Erasmus and the *devoti* in their attitude to biblical and Patristic tradition. Common to both sides is the aim to implement in practice the "work of restoration" (*opus restaurationis*) in humanity which was initiated by Christ, through the acceptance of his Word and through discipleship. Any study of the Holy Scriptures must therefore not lead to the mere acquisition of knowledge, but must contribute to the moral improvement of individuals and the transformation of their lives. Erasmus, as is well known, uses the term *philosophia Christi* to describe this task. In complete agreement with the Fathers of the "Devotio moderna" he characterizes this as a personal-existential process which should not so much exercise the intellect as mobilize the emotions:

> This kind of philosophy is located more truly in the emotions than in syllogisms, it is life rather than disputation, it is inspiration more than learning, transformation rather than reasoning . . . For what else is the philosophy of Christ, which he himself calls regeneration, than the restauration of a disposition that has a sound foundation?[100]

Even in his recommendations for study-techniques Erasmus shows his indebtedness to the *devoti*: if reading is to change people, it must be digested and internalized in their physical beings. The criterion for such growth is the gradual conquest of vice. The appropriate form of spiritual exchanges of ideas was, he would say, not conflict (*conflictatio*) but discussion (*collatio*); theological disputation had to approximate to that. But reading could also take the form of what might be called dialogue, through inserted prayers, petitions and gratitude, in order to take stronger hold on the readers and support their progress.[101]

Despite these agreements, we must not overlook the fact that for Erasmus the evaluation and use made of biblical and church tradition in the reform programme of the *devoti* had become altogether obsolete. We can perhaps best outline his new perspective from the

---

[100] *Hoc philosophiae genus in affectibus situm verius quam in syllogismis vita magis est quam disputatio, afflatus potius quam eruditio, transformatio magis quam ratio . . . quid autem aliud est Christi philosophia, quam ipse renascentiam vocat, quam instauratio bene conditae naturae?*— Erasmus, *Paraclesis* in his *Ausgewählte Werke*, ed. Hajo Holborn, Munich 1933, pp. 144f. Cf. *Methodus ibid.* p. 154: *professio theologica magis constat affectibus quam argutiis.*

[101] Erasmus, *Methodus*, ed. Holborn (cf. note 100), p. 151; *Ratio seu Methodus, op. cit.* p. 180.

concept of the *philosophia Christi*. It was a concept completely familiar to the *devoti* also: Seuse had recommended Arsenius the Desert Father and preceptor of monks as teacher of "Christian Philosophy",[102] and Zerbolt, with his rules for reading—like Hugh of St. Victor whom he quotes here—had recourse to the "Christian philosopher" (*philosophus christianus*).[103] Thus what was meant by this *philosophia Christi* was the ascetic life-style of the ancient monks who in their lack of needs and their community of goods were reminiscent of the Pythagoreans and other pagan sects.[104] To the *devoti* they represented that primary perfection (*pristina perfectio*) towards which one had to strive by means of moral spiritual exercises (*exercitia spiritualia*) such as reading, meditation and prayer. Imitation of the models for living to be found in the *Vita Jesu* and the *Vitae patrum* led to perfection: the writings were needed only in so far as they passed on examples and rules for virtue. As the Bible was to a great extent obscure and difficult, only in parts was it suitable for devout reading and it was always to be interpreted and understood in the light of the Fathers' commentaries.[105]

---

[102] Seuse, *Horologium* II 3, ed. Künzle (cf. note 1), pp. 546f.

[103] See above, note 42 and note 9.

[104] See for example Gerhard Zerbolt, *Super modo vivendi*, ed. Hyma (cf. note 71), pp. 38f.; W. Moll, "Geert Groote's sermoen voor Palmzondag over de vrijwillige armoede" in *Studien en Bijdragen op het Gebied der Historische Theologie* 2, 1872, pp. 425–469, pp. 468f.—Cf. J. Leclercq, "Pour l'histoire de l'expression 'philosophie chrétienne'" in *Mélanges de Science Religieuse* 9, 1952, pp. 221–226; Paul Rabbow, *Seelenführung. Methoden der Exerzitien in der Antike*, Munich 1954; Pierre Hadot, *Exercices spirituels et philosophie antique*, Paris 1981, pp. 59–74.

[105] Cf. Thomas à Kempis, *Dialogus noviciorum* III 29, ed. Pohl (cf. note 13) vol. 7, p. 199: "Your conscience is good and your reasoning right when you do nothing except in accordance with Holy Scripture and understand it as the saints understood it . . ." (*Tunc conscientia est bona et ratio tua recta, quando nihil agis nisi secundum sacram scripturam et intellegis eam sicut sancti intellexerunt . . .*); and p. 206: "There is not a lot to be gained from much study unless the person studying improves his life . . . for the devil knows many things from Scripture and yet they do not do him any good" (*Parum prodest multum studere, nisi quis studeat vitam suam emendare . . . nam diabolus multa scit de scripturis et tamen nihil ei prodest*); likewise in III 23, pp. 175f.: "A certain Jew who had become a Christian . . . was anxious to discuss the ancient patriarchs and prophets with him . . . (Florentius) spoke to him nicely persuading him to hold a sincere faith in Christ and persevere in good works but he was unwilling to fan the flames of questions about the law that had no bearing on salvation and about the family-trees of the ancients—not because he did not know, but because these things did not contribute to devotional edification". (*Vir quidam ex Iudaeis ad fidem christianam conversus . . . cupiebat cum ipso de antiquis patriarchis et prophetis disserere . . . (Florentius) humane et caritative cum eo egit fidem sinceram in Christo suadens tenere ac operibus bonis insudare, de quaestionibus vero legis ad salutem non pertinentibus et genealogiis veterum nihil ventilare voluit, non quia ignorabat, sed quia aedificationem non importabant.*)—On the basis of his personal experience in his period in Windesheim as a novice Johannes Busch was convinced

It was even conceivable that one could dispense with it, like the
Desert Fathers, who lived holy lives even without books:

> And thus a man must not seek high and curious things or questions in
> the Scriptures for their own sake; because all Holy Scripture is about
> virtues; and should a man have virtues and keep them unspoiled, he
> would not—as Augustine and Chrysostom say—need Scripture for its
> own sake, because many have lived holy lives in the desert places with-
> out books.[106]

Erasmus had a wholly different idea. He did not wish to separate
theology from the way people lived, as the *devoti* did, but explicitly
called for their integration.[107] At the same time he set his face against
monopolization of the Christian ideal of virtue by the church Orders
and communities.[108] This explains the new version of the concept of
philosophia Christi, which was now more strongly emphasized by analogy with the ancient philosophical schools, and which in addition
loses its exclusive reference to the status of the religious: the community of all the baptized was to be understood as a *secta* or *factio Christi*—
a "Christ party"—constituted by a direct link to the teaching of their
charismatic founder and achieving unity of knowledge and moral
conduct, learning and living.[109] The secular model of the philosophi-

---

that extensive reading of the Bible could lead to a crisis in one's spiritual life, cf.
Liber de reformatione monasteriorum, ed. Grube (cf. note 23) pp. 708ff., esp. p. 709: "Not
all are required to know and do and strive to research into the deep things of God
and Holy Scripture, but it is enough for them to live well, believe well and have the
good will to do the will of God." (*Non requiritur ab omnibus, quod profunda Dei et scripture
sancte sciant et faciant et investigare laborarent, sed sufficit eis ut bene vivant, bene credant et
bonam habeant voluntatem Dei facere voluntatem*).

[106] *Et sic homo non debet querere alia, curiosa aut questiones in scripturis, saltem propter se;
quia tota sacra scriptura est propter virtutes; et si homo haberet virtutes et inconcusse servaret, non
indigeret scriptura quantum ad se, ut dicunt Augustinus et Crysostomus, quia multi sine codicibus
sancte vixerunt in solitudinibus.*—Radewijns, *Tractatulus devotus*, ed. Goossens (cf. note 41)
cap. 7, p. 219. Cf. Augustine, *De doctrina christiana* I 43: "And so a man supported
by faith and hope and love and holding to these things without wavering does not
need scriptures except to instruct others. Therefore many live alone in desert places
without books through these three." (*Homo itaque fide et spe et caritate subnixus eaque
inconcusse retinens non indiget scripturis nisi ad alios instruendos. Itaque multi per haec tria etiam
in solitudine sine codicibus vivunt.*)

[107] Cf. Augustijn (cf. note 92) p. 102.

[108] Erasmus, *Enchiridion militis Chistiani*, ed. Holborn (cf. note 100) pp. 17ff.

[109] Erasmus, *Paraclesis*, ed. Holborn (cf. note 100) pp. 140ff., cf. *Enchiridion*,
p. 110: "Lay hold on the Christian school . . . Christ alone, who is the sole model
for right feeling and blessed living, is enough for you (. . . *Christianam sectam arripe . . .
unus Christus tibi satis sit, unicus auctor et recte sentiendi et beate vivendi*). See also *Ratio seu
Methodus, ibid.* pp. 178ff.

cal schools enabled Erasmus to explain his ideas on a renewal of Christian society. First of all, everyone who belonged to the *secta Christi* must know the words of their master, as the Pythagoreans knew Pythagoras' teaching or the Peripatetics the teaching of Aristotle. Hence all other revealed writings and those of the church's tradition fell behind the gospels. In reality, of course, the simple message of Christ, which might be accessible to anyone, had been distorted as a result of being debased in transmission, and had been shoved entirely into the background by the fruitless speculations and dialectical subtleties of scholastic theology. The progressive increase in linguistic barbarism since the end of the ancient days of the church had played an essential part in this process of decline: the "ancient theologians" were infinitely superior to the "modern" ones. Hence, instead of resigning oneself to the incomprehensibility of the Bible, or seeking refuge in ignorant and misleading commentators, one must test the tradition and restore the texts in their genuine form. Everyone will then be able to read them and be his or her own theologian, and therefore a true *philosophus Christi*.[110]

Erasmus' programme for a reform of the text of the New Testament contained so much critical force that it was impossible for almost any sphere of ecclesiastical tradition to remain untroubled. The simultaneous publication of the New Testament and Jerome made that evident at a single blow. It was not by chance that Erasmus opened the long series of his editions of Patristic works with this Church Father, and thus so to speak protected the flanks of his New Testament; for the figure of Jerome was to him both a way of justifying himself and a subject for controversy—as a humanist, monk, translator and commentator of Holy Scripture he must have seemed to Erasmus to be his *alter ego*, colleague, and rival, patron and challenger all at once. Jerome represented a better age of the church, though one which was related to his own day in its task of criticizing what had been handed down. Thus in his prolegomena and scholia to the New Testament and to the *Opera S. Hieronymi* Erasmus frequently had the opportunity to lament the decline of genuine texts and point to its maleficent effects for theology and the Christian life. In this connexion, his experiences of his own age and life made him sensitive to the faulty developments of the past, as his presentation of

---

[110] Erasmus, *Paraclesis*, ed. Holborn (cf. note 100) pp. 142ff.; *Methodus, ibid.* pp. 160f.

Jerome's entry into the monastic life perhaps shows. Even back in those days many had been only nominal Christians—the clergy had let themselves be made captive by worldly interests and had yielded to the tendency to thirst for power, while only monasticism still constituted a haven of Christian piety and freedom.

> Whence it was inevitable that most of those who professed Christ were Christians more in name than in their lives . . . therefore, having weighed everything up he embraced monasticism because, lest any one should be misled in this, monasticism was very different then from what we see wrapped up in solemn ceremonies today; rather, it was those who were the freest in spirit who took monastic vows.[111]

The actual criticism of the process by which the church passed on the text was more explosive than such general laments about decadence. With unheard-of daring Erasmus with his annotation and translation of the New Testament was bold enough to demonstrate that the Vulgate version—the foundation of theology, liturgy and spiritual life—was altogether inadequate and defective. Not least, therefore, this was bound to call forth contradiction because it seemed to show contempt for the authority of Jerome and denigrate his achievement. Erasmus protected himself in advance from such reproaches by declaring that the edition of the New Testament which Jerome had prepared was lost and certainly not identical to the Vulgate. The most diverse versions of the gospels and Pauline and other epistles were quoted, he claimed, by the Church fathers, but not the Vulgate, which had to be regarded as a late product of scribal stupidity and arbitrariness.[112] But in addition to this Erasmus also called in prin-

---

[111] *Unde fieri necesse erat, ut qui Christum profitebantur plerique titulo magis quam vita, essent Christiani . . . Pensitatis igitur omnibus ac circumspectis monachi placuit institutum, quod, ne quis in hoc erret, id temporis longe diversum erat ab hoc quod hodie videmus caerimoniis obstrictum, immo quibus maxime libertas erat cordi, hi monachi professionem suscipiebant.* Erasmus, *Hieronymi Vita* in *S. Hieronymi Stridonensis Opera omnia*, Frankfurt am Main-Leipzig 1684, vol. 1, fol. BB 5r. Cf. also the new edition of the *Collected Works of Erasmus*, vol. 61: *Patristic Scholarship. The Edition of St. Jerome*, ed. J.F. Brady—J.C. Olin, Toronto 1992.

[112] Erasmus, *Apologia*, ed. Holborn (cf. note 100) pp. 165ff.; and "Capita argumentorum contra morosos quosdam et indoctos" in *D. Erasmi Opera omnia*, ed. Joannes Clericus, 10 volumes, Leiden 1703–1706, vol. 6, fol. ** 5v–*** 4r. Cf. also epist. no. 843 in *Opus Epistolarum Des. Erasmi Roterodami*, ed. P.S. Allen, 12 volumes, Oxford 1906–1958, vol. 3, p. 313: "He takes this translation of the New Testament which we commonly use to be Jerome's although it is certainly neither Cyprian's nor Hilary's nor Augustine's nor Jerome's, as the latter has different readings, far less the translation he affirms he corrected, as there are things in this of which he does not approve, not only as to the words but also as to the meaning." (. . . *as sumit hanc*

ciple for the freedom to check the sacred texts repeatedly for genuineness, and to be able to correct them where appropriate. For even
a Jerome had not been infallible:

> What if Jerome alone neither could nor did restore everything? What
> if likewise he either emended or translated something wrongly? . . .
> However good and learned he was, he was a man and could mislead
> and be misled. As I believe, many things escaped him; many caused
> him to err.[113]

Finally, Erasmus asserted that he was not concerned to do away
with the Vulgate; it could continue to be used in church and school.
But those who wanted to make use of the new translation for reading at home would certainly arrive at a better understanding of the
text—an argument which was nothing if not cryptic, and bore witness less to modesty than to setting a low value on church services
as opposed to private piety.[114]

Erasmus did not see the process of debasing the text of the Bible—
such as he believed he had perceived in the Vulgate—as an isolated
phenomenon but in the context of a general spiritual and linguistic
and cultural decline in the western church since the age of the Fathers.
A progressive loss of the original transmission and of the freedom of
the Christian life, and the continual increase in laws and ceremo-
nies, forged and falsely attributed documents, together with scholastic literature in the form of *summae*, treatises and commentaries were,
with the barbarizing of language, the essential characteristics of this

---

*Novi Testamenti interpretationem qua vulgo utimur, esse Hieronymi, cum eam constet nec esse
Cypriani nec Hilarii nec Augustini nec Hieronymi cum is diversa legat, multo minus eam quam
emendasse se testatur, cum in hac deprehendantur quae ille damnat, non solum quo ad verba verum
etiam quo ad sensus.*) Similarly *op. cit.* no. 860, p. 381.

[113] *Quid, quod Hieronymus unus omnia nec restituit nec potuit restituere? Quid, si idem quaedam
perperam vel emendavit vel transtulit? . . . Quamlibet vir pius, quamlibet eruditus, homo erat et
falli potuit et fallere. Multa, ut opinor, illum fugerunt, multa fefellerunt.*—Erasmus, *Ratio seu
Methodus*, ed. Holborn (cf. note 100), pp. 182f.; cf. *Methodus, ibid.* p. 152.

[114] Erasmus, *Apologia*, ed. Holborn (cf. note 100) pp. 165 and 168.—Erasmus sees
no contradiction between his ideal that every artisan and farmer should be able to
read the Bible and ambitions to produce the New Testament in a more sophisticated
and elegant Latin. The widest possible dissemination of that text calls for different
translations—in the vernacular and likewise in a language cultivated people can
tolerate. Cf. Erasmus *Capita argumentorum*, ed. Clericus (cf. note 112) fol. ** 6r, and
Opus Epistolarum, ed. Allen (cf. note 112) vol. 3, no. 843, p. 313: "Because if we look
after the interests of ignorant and simple people in simple language why should we
not also look after the interests of the learned in elegant language?" (*Quod si imperitis
ac simplicibus consulitur simplicitate sermonis, cur non consulamus et eruditis mundicia sermonis?*).
On this see Augustijn (cf. note 92) pp. 94 and 104f.

decline.[115] Jerome's catalogue of sacred writers taught him about the wealth of spiritual life in the ancient church, and the notion of the value and scope of lost Patristic literature filled him with bitterness against recent theology, which had asserted itself at that literature's expense:

> Oh, what a truly deplorable sacrifice, if it did any good to lament! . . . How the bishops and theologians have slept, who allowed us to forget so many luminaries of the world, so many marks of our faith, leaders and standard-bearers, eminent in letters, illustrious in eloquence, commended by the holiness of their lives, and some also distinguished by their martyrdom, so that this shabby clan of writers could replace them— makers of petty "sentences", "summae", "treatises" and "specula" the recollection of whom—Oh, ever-living God!—sickens noble and well-born minds.[116]

For Erasmus, however, the refusal to "receive" was no less lamentable than the total loss of the tradition. Using Jerome as an example, he shows that a great deal of injustice had been done even to those authors whose works had been preserved: they had been distorted and fragmented so that they were scarcely in better case than if they had been completely forgotten.[117] The "four Doctors of the church" did indeed appear to enjoy special prestige, but the schematic treatment of this selection—a selection determined by the fact that there are four gospel writers and four senses of Scripture—was a clear proof of complacency and lack of judgment. And therefore little even of them was really read—at most writings misleadingly attributed to them.[118]

Erasmus had to take issue with the problem of the forged and faked transmission of texts, especially in regard to the apocryphal *Vita Hieronymi* and the three letters on the death and miracles of that saint. As these writings enjoyed great popularity—even, among others, in the circles of the modern *devoti*—the question was, whether their edifying purpose could justify fabrication. Erasmus did not wish to

---

[115] Erasmus, Dedication of his edition of Jerome to William Warham, in *Opus Epistolarum*, ed. Allen (cf. note 112) vol. 2, pp. 211–221.

[116] *O jacturam vere deplorandam, si quid proficeretur complorationibus! . . . Quam dormitatum est ab episcopis ac theologis, qui tot orbis lumina, tot insignes fidei nostrae proceres et antesignanos, literis eximios, eloquentia illustres, vitae sanctimonia commendatos, aliquot et martyrio claros, intercidere passi sunt, ut hoc sordidum scriptorum genus succederet sententiariorum, summulariorum, fasciculariorum, speculariorum et, o Deum immortalem! quorum vel recordatio nauseam moveat generosis ac bene natis ingeniis.*—S. *Hieronymi Opera omnia* (cf. note 111) vol. 1, p. 196.

[117] Erasmus, Dedication to Warham (cf. note 115) pp. 213ff.

[118] Erasmus, *Hieronymi Vita* (cf. note 111) fol. CC 2r.

contest this as a matter of principle, but he did plead on behalf of priority for historical truth—fictional hagiography could be tolerated at best if it presented not recondite forms of asceticism but a picture of pure, early Christian piety in line with the Gospel.[119]

Erasmus left no doubt about the high value he placed on the Church Fathers, the "theologians of old" (*veteres theologi*): they made use of good literature (*bonae litterae*)—that classical education which Christianity was able to inherit as the fruit of the culture of the ancient world. But, above all, they opened up the message of Christ with their commentaries because of their direct proximity to its source. In comparison with the thin trickles of modern theologians (*recentiores, neoterici*) they were a "golden river"—they led directly to the haven of the Gospel, whereas the moderns struggle and float in the crags of scholastic doctrines and questions of ecclesiastical law.[120] The contrast to the reception practised by the modern *devoti* is unmistakable: Erasmus restricts the concept of "Church Fathers" to the Greek and Latin writers of the first few Christian centuries and clearly excludes even the authors of the early Middle Ages—Gregory, Isidore and Bede. Thus in his introductory writings on the New Testament he repeatedly mentions Origen, Basil, Chrysostom, Augustine, Ambrose and Jerome, and also Gregory of Nazianzus, Athanasius, Cyril, Cyprian and Hilary of Poitiers as *veteres theologi*.[121] His programme of publications focused on this list and largely followed it: editions and translations of Cyprian, Arnobius, Hilary, Ambrose, Augustine, John Chrysostom, Irenaeus and Origen continued the work of restoring the textual transmission which had begun with the text of Jerome. With his notes and Paraphrases on the New Testament, however,

---

[119] *Op. cit.* fol. BB 4r.—On the dissemination of the *Hieronymus-Briefe* see Erika Bauer, "Hieronymus-Briefe" in *Die deutsche Literatur des Mittelalters. Verfasserlexikon*, vol. 3, Berlin-New York 1981, columns 1233–1238; also her "Die sogenannten 'Hieronymus-Briefe' und ihre volkssprachliche Überlieferung" in *Historia et Spiritualitas Cartusiensis. Colloquii quarti internationalis Acta*, Destelbergen 1983, pp. 21–33; also her "Zur Geschichte der 'Hieronymus-Briefe'" in *Festschrift Walter Haug und Burghart Wachinger*, vol. 1, Tübingen 1992, pp. 305–321.

[120] Erasmus, *Methodus*, ed. Holborn (cf. note 100) pp. 154f.; *Apologia*, p. 165; *Ratio seu Methodus*, pp. 189f., 304f.

[121] E.g. Erasmus, *Methodus*, ed. Holborn (cf. note 100), pp. 154, 156, 160; *Ratio seu Methodus*, pp. 187, 189, 295f.—The ambivalent relation of Erasmus to the medieval tradition of exegesis—he openly despises it and tacitly uses it—was already criticized by his contemporaries; cf. H.J. de Jonge, "Erasmus und die Glossa Ordinaria zum Neuen Testament" in *Nederlands Archief voor Kerkgeschiedenis*, New Series 56, 1975–76, pp. 51–77.

Erasmus had also ranged himself to an extent in the circle of those
veteres theologi, in order to do justice, like them, to a lasting commitment to the fundamental text of the *philosophia Christi*.[122]

The development of Erasmus' programme of theological renewal
was overlaid by the dynamics of Luther's Reformation, and was partly
strengthened and partly neutralized by it—as happens with the
modifying effects of a variety of currents. The direct effect of Erasmus'
programme on his contemporaries was both an exciting and a confusing historical drama in which the reaction of the modern *devoti* represents no more than one episode. In many respects they were close
to Erasmus's stance—in their focus on *pristina perfectio* together with
their distance at the same time from scholastic theology, in their
emphasis on private devotion nourished by the "sacrament of the
Word"[123] and not least in a certain critical philological attitude towards their texts. On the other hand the radical "humanistic" rejection of the Middle Ages in the church was altogether alien to them.
For they were indebted to a monastic tradition (which, despite repeated periods of decline and reform, led from Cassian by way of
Bernard right down to their own day in unbroken continuity) for
ascetic techniques, for the organization of the religious life of their
community, and for spiritual reading-matter. They must therefore
have felt that they too were the target of Erasmus' criticism of the
church and of the transmission of texts, even when they were not in
fact the declared aim of that criticism. Nevertheless there were not a
few among the *devoti* who secretly approved of his work of reform or
even sought to support it actively. Perhaps the most important among
them was Martin Lips, the Augustinian canon from the Windesheim
monastery of Martinstal in Louvain—a competent scholar, though
his name has remained well-known more through the fame of his

---

[122] On the *Paraphrases* cf. Coppens (cf. note 92); Rabil, *Paraphrases* (cf. note 92);
Krüger (cf. note 92).

[123] On this cf. Thomas à Kempis, *Dialogus noviciorum* IV 8, ed. Pohl (cf. note 13)
vol. 7, p. 278: "The sacred writings are the lights of our souls; we can do without
them no less in this pilgrimage than the sacraments of the church" (*libri sacri sunt
animarum nostrarum lumina, quibus non minus in hace peregrinatione carere possumus quam ecclesiae
sacramentis*). Also his *De imitatione Christi* IV 11, vol. 2, p. 122: "The one table is that
of the holy altar which has the holy bread, that is, the precious Body of Christ; the
other is that of God's law which holds the holy teaching". (. . . *Una mensa est sacri
altaris habens panem sanctum id est corpus Christi pretiosum, altera est divinae legis continens
doctrinam sanctam*).

great-nephew Justus Lipsius than through his own works. His correspondence with Erasmus and with *devoti* of like mind offers us a vivid insight into the memorable controversy between "modern piety" and "Christian humanism" in the early sixteenth century.[124]

An opportunity arose for Lips to come into contact with the humanist—already long respected—in the context of the controversies about the edition of the New Testament. When towards the end of 1517 he obtained a collection of critical notes on that edition which the English theologian Edward Lee—probably out of injured pride—had produced against Erasmus, he made a copy of it and sent it to the victim of the attack, who was staying in Louvain. Erasmus reacted with some irritation and made it clear that such criticism was immaterial to him, and he recommended spending time and effort rather on profitable things such as the study of Jerome.[125] Nevertheless this was the start of a lasting literary exchange (*commercium litterarium*). For Lips, who felt himself called to be the defender of Erasmus' name everywhere (*Erasmiani nominis ubique defensor*),[126] continued to keep the master informed about all hostile machinations and Erasmus learned to value his services so much that finally he even counselled him to cultivate contacts with opponents like Lee on purpose, so that he could remain constantly informed.[127] Lips' ticklish situation became even more of a problem because there were considerable reservations against Erasmus both in his Martinstal community and in other Windesheim monasteries. He was regarded as a vehement foe of monasticism, a forerunner and promoter of Luther, and was reproached for having entered the field of theology as a *rhetor* and *poeta* without authorization.[128] There was resistance not least to his absolutizing of the Gospel as the only authentic way in which Christ communicated himself, and insistence on the customary position that the Bible was only an aid in the pursuit of virtue and

---

[124] Adalbert Horawitz, "Erasmus von Rotterdam und Martinus Lipsius. Ein Beitrag zur Gelehrtengeschichte Belgiens" in *Sitzungsberichte der kaiserlichen Akademie der Wissenschaften*, Phil.-Hist. Cl. vol. 100, 2, Vienna 1882, pp. 665–799; Lourdaux, *Moderne Devotie* (cf. note 5) pp. 149ff., 182ff., 293ff.

[125] *Opus Epistolarum*, ed. Allen (cf. note 112) vol. 3, no. 750, pp. 184ff. Cf. Bludau (cf. note 92) pp. 86ff.

[126] Allen (cf. note 112) vol. 3, p. 185.

[127] *Opus Epistolarum*, ed. Allen (cf. note 112) vol. 3, no. 912, p. 471; vol. 4, no. 1056, p. 154; cf. Horawitz (cf. note 124) p. 684.

[128] *Opus Epistolarum*, ed. Allen (cf. note 112) vol. 3, no. 922, p. 498; vol. 7, no. 1837, p. 86; cf. Horawitz (cf. note 124) p. 681.

perfection, encoded against the varied capacity of human beings to understand it and certainly not accessible or of use to anyone in all its parts.[129] Lips gave highly detailed reports on the opinions and statements of those *devoti* who were opposed to Erasmus, nor was he afraid to purloin a manuscript now and then from their cells in order to thwart their publishing plans by making them prematurely known.[130] He also complained so vigorously about his brethren's hostility to education and the oppressive atmosphere of the monastery that Erasmus repeatedly warned him to persevere patiently in the way of life he had once chosen and seek consolation in study of the writings of the Fathers.[131]

Not all the *devoti* were ill-disposed to the new humanistic theology to the same extent. Many esteemed Lips precisely because of his connexion with Erasmus and considered him an initiate with whom they sought to correspond—in the highly complimentary fashion of the admired models—on literary questions, plans for work and the

---

[129] See above, note 105. Among the *devoti* Erasmus' main opponent was Nicolaus van Winghe from Martinstal who himself came into prominence with a translation of the Bible into the vernacular and set forth his view of the relative value of Holy Scripture in the preface to it and in a programmatic treatise of his own; cf. P. van Herreweghen, "De Leuvense bijbelvertaler Nicolaus van Winghe. Zijn leven en zijn werk" in *Ons Geestelijk Erf* 23, 1949, pp. 5–38, 150–167, 268–314, 357–395; Lourdaux, *Moderne Devotie* (cf. note 5) pp. 208ff.

[130] *Opus epistolarum*, ed. Allen (cf. note 112) vol. 7, no. 1837, p. 87: "The subprior says that he who passed on to you Winghe's book should be condemned as a thief, as Augustine says in his Rule" (*Subprior dicit eum qui tibi librum Winghii prodidit, furti iudicio condemnandum, ut Augustinus habet in regula.*) Cf. *op. cit.* vol. 9, no. 2566, p. 372: "I also found in his [i.e. Nicolaus van Winghe's] cell writings in which he indicates why both I and others who are supporting you are not studying your writings rightly" (*Inveni et literas in cellula eius, quibus docet quare et ego et caeteri tibi faventes non recto animo versemur in scriptis tuis . . .*).

[131] Admonitions to stay in one's chosen station: *Opus Epistolarum*, ed. Allen (cf. note 112) vol. 3, no. 901, p. 442; vol. 4, no. 1070, p. 193; recommendation of patristic studies: vol. 3, no. 750, pp. 186f.; no. 807, p. 261; no. 843, p. 330; vol. 4, nos. 1048 and 1049, pp. 136f.; complaint about the "freedom of the new gospel" and secularization of the Leonhard monastery in Basel: vol. 6, no. 1547, pp. 23f.: "Nowadays the world is full of vagrants and deceivers with whom the freedom of the new gospel floods us . . . Here is some news for you: we have here a college of regulars of St. Leonard's. Around the Feast of the Purification everyone including the Prior took off their monk's habit together. However, those who wish to do so still live there in different clothes. The civil authority gives sixty florins apiece—a little more to the Prior. Nor is anyone surprised at these things, and I fear the same thing is going to be happening all over." (*Mundus nunc plenus est erronibus et impostoribus, quos nobis offundit novi Evangelii libertas . . . Accipe rem novam: Est hic collegium regularium sancti Leonardi. Sub Purificationem omnes simul cum Priore exuerunt habitum. Vivunt tamen ibi qui volunt, mutata veste. Magistratus dat singulis florenos sexaginta, Priori paulo plus. Neque quisquam haec miratur, et metuo idem passim futurum . . .*)

exchange of books. Some of his fellow-monks at Louvain even asked him to guide them in the line of study imparted by Erasmus. Lips truthfully replied that he had received from his master only the advice "to read Jerome and the other ancient and genuine authors", and sighed with mock modesty over the sad state of the age in which the "sons of St. Augustine were hoping to find no teacher other than just him"![132]

With his sarcastic and self-critical witticism Lips was indicating that the figure of Augustine signified the point of reference for a desirable integration of monastic study and the humanistic *philosophia Christi*. Already at the start of his correspondence he had tried to interest Erasmus in Augustine, but the humanist left him in no doubt that he placed a higher value on the Greeks and also on Latin Fathers such as Jerome, Ambrose, Hilary and Cyprian.[133] Clearly Erasmus saw in the preference of the *devoti* for Augustine a relatively superficial acknowledgement of the patron of their order, which was an unpleasant reminder to him of his past as a monk, and so he finally remonstrated with Lips as follows:

> If you want to be seen as really Augustinian you should imitate his study and his life. If Augustine were alive he would be quicker to recognize me than to recognize many who pride themselves in the most stupid way on his name.[134]

But Lips did not give up. He was insistent in pointing out to Erasmus that he could help his work of theological renewal which was so controversial to a break-through with an edition of Augustine: those who still looked sceptically on the project on Jerome could be won over if they also saw "their Augustine" restored with such a display of learning:

> There are nevertheless some ... who, like me, have faith and hope that you will yet consider "our" Augustine (as we put it) worthy of your pen. If you were able to do it (for I don't doubt you are willing)

---

[132] *Opus Epistolarum*, ed. Allen (cf. note 112) vol. 3, no. 922, pp. 498ff.; cf. Horawitz (cf. note 124) pp. 681ff.—Lips had followers and correspondents in the ten-Troon monastery in Grobbendonk above all: Jacobus Cortebeeck, Jacobus Thomas, Godefridus van Brecht and Ludovicus Roelants; see Lourdaux, *Moderne Devotie* (cf. note 5) pp. 218f. and 301f.

[133] *Opus Epistolarum*, ed. Allen (cf. note 112) vol. 3, no. 898, p. 438. Cf. Charles Béné, *Erasme et Saint Augustin*, Geneva 1969.

[134] *Si vis valde Augustinianus videri, studium ac vitam illius imitare. Si viveret Augustinus, citius cognosceret me quam multos, qui titulo illius stultissime gloriantur.*—*Opus Epistolarum*, ed. Allen (cf. note 112) vol. 3, no. 899, p. 440.

you would see here and there those who on account of your restoration of Jerome do not agree with you (for not everyone is charmed by Jerome's style)—I say you would see them most devoted to you were you to devote your efforts to Augustine, whose sharp mind they admire. Some even reckon you are wrong not to do this for so great a doctor of the holy church—you who have thus honoured so many pagan writers . . .[135]

As a result of a similar request from the Prior of Agnietenberg who visited Erasmus in Louvain in the summer of 1520, the latter learned that Lips' reproduction of the expectations of the *devoti* had not been wide of the mark.[136] He still showed himself unwilling, but just a few months later (December 1520) he informed Lips in a letter, as if in an aside, "I am busy restoring Augustine" (*versor in restituendo Augustino*).[137] The wishes of Froben, his publisher, who wanted to continue his project for a comprehensive edition of the *quatuor doctores* with Augustine, were probably decisive for his change of mind.[138] At all events, Lips had now found his life's work which made it possible for him to pursue humanistic studies as spiritual exercises (*exercitia devota*).[139] First of all as a collaborator of Erasmus and later on his own account he worked for decades on examining critically the transmission of texts of Augustine, and on philological commentaries on them. While it might be difficult to estimate his share in Erasmus' edition of 1528/29, he is named and appreciated as the responsible reviser in the new edition organized by Froben in 1543 and even the epoch-making edition of Augustine by the theologians of Louvain, which appeared under the imprint of Plantin in 1576/77, still relied on his materials in extensive sections.[140]

---

[135] *Sunt autem nonnulli . . . qui mecum confidunt et sperant, quod tandem nostrum (ut loquimur) Augustinum tuo dignum iudicabis obelo. Si id . . . praestare posses (velle enim te non ambigo), videres passim eos qui ob Hieronymum a te restitutum tibi non accedunt (non enim phrasi Hieronymiana omnes delectantur)—videres, inquam, eos ob operam Augustino impensam, cuius suspiciunt acumen, tibi deditissimos. Alii nefas etiam ducunt te hoc non prestitisse tanto sanctae Ecclesiae doctori, qui tot ethnicis id exhibuisti honoris . . .—op. cit.* no. 922, p. 499.

[136] *Ibid.* vol. 4, no. 1140, p. 338.

[137] *Ibid.* no. 1174, p. 425.

[138] J. de Ghellinck, *Patristique et Moyen Age*, vol. 3, Brussels-Paris 1948, pp. 378ff.

[139] The canon regular Augustinus Dodo from St. Leonhard's in Basel, a scholar who was a member of the Devotio moderna, had already played a considerable part in the preparation of Amerbach's edition of Augustine (1506); cf. Ghellinck (cf. note 138) p. 374; Beat M. von Scarpatetti, *Die Kirche und das Augustiner-Chorherrenstift St. Leonhard in Basel*, Basle-Stuttgart 1974, pp. 326ff.

[140] Ghellinck (cf. note 138) p. 397 note 5; Lourdaux, *Moderne Devotie* (cf. note 5) pp. 234, 239ff.

We have to ask, finally, how far the critical, philological studies of Lips and his successors in Louvain actually influenced and changed the spirit of the communities of *devoti*. In research there has been a tendency at times to overemphasise this influence because of an unquestioning conviction about the value of the new direction taken by the humanists.[141] The traditions of the *devoti* had really resisted unscathed the spell of Erasmus and his disciples. The brief but highly interesting correspondence conducted by Martin Lips with Wilhelm of Gheershoven in 1525/26 illustrates this.[142]

Gheershoven was a canon in Groenendaal and clearly belonged to those supporters of the new humanistic direction for life and study who saw their model in Lips. In order to establish contact with him, Gheershoven used a stereotyped motif in the correspondence of humanists and pretended he wanted books. Referring to a general library catalogue of the *devoti* which was clearly both in Groenendaal and in the Rookloster, he asked Lips for help in procuring a collection of sermons by Petrus Chrysologus which was shown there as being at Louvain.[143] A lively exchange developed at once out of the enquiry because Lips in turn asked for manuscripts of Augustine from Groenendaal.[144] In return Gheershoven used this request as an opportunity to reveal in a personal confession his inward alienation from the monastic life. The codices Lips desired would always be at his disposal and for as long as he wanted, as in any case they were not needed in Groenendaal and would scarcely be missed: the monastery library was rich in manuscripts of Augustine, and it was said that the young Erasmus had once been most zealous in ferreting out these very texts when he paid a visit here, studying them and even taking them with him to his cell even through the night, while the canons had simply been astonished and indeed exhilarated at such enthusiasm for study; and even at present Augustine unfortunately

---

[141] Thus especially Lourdaux, *Moderne Devotie* (cf. note 5).

[142] Summary in Lourdaux, *Moderne Devotie* (cf. note 5), pp. 300f.; Reprint of letters in Horawitz (cf. note 124). On Gheershoven cf. Luc Versluys, "Enkele aspecten over Groenendaal ten tijde der Hervorming" in *Zoniën* 7, 1983, pp. 54–62. Gheershoven was librarian in Groenendaal; see *Obituaire du monastère de Groenendael*, ed. Marc Dykmans, Brussels 1940, pp. 145f. with note 5.

[143] Horawitz (cf. note 124) pp. 773–775. Cf. Obbema (cf. note 37) p. 338. The book should be *in bibliotheca facultatis (ut vocant) artium academiae nostrae Lovaniensis* ("so-called faculty of arts library of our university of Louvain"); on this see A. van Hove, *La bibliothèque de la faculté des arts de l'Université de Louvain au milieu du XVe siècle*, in *Mélanges d'histoire offerts à Ch. Moeller*, vol. 1, Louvain 1914, pp. 602–625.

[144] Horawitz (cf. note 124) pp. 775f.

met with no greater interest among them than at that time. On the other hand an entirely different kind of literature was highly esteemed and indispensable to the brothers: *Vitae patrum, Legenda aurea* (the Golden Legend)—which would be better called the Bronze (*aerea*) Legend, *Liber apum, Profectus religiosorum* and the writings of Thomas à Kempis. They were welcome to this kind of edification which, however, meant so little to himself that he would gladly give up the entire mass of lumber for a single letter from the hand of a scholar such as Lips![145]

The candour of this letter surprised Lips and disquieted him. From his own experience he knew the annoyances which could come the way of someone living in a monastery if his excessively critical or progressive comments became known.[146] He therefore urgently counselled Gheershoven to keep his convictions to himself and tell them only to brethren who were of like mind or wanted to be instructed. He had moreover reservations in the matter, and attempted to tone down somewhat the radicalism of his admirer: the favourite writings of the *devoti* which Gheershoven so despised must be neither spurned nor valued too highly; rather it was a matter of noting carefully the correct order of priority for the texts: just as the Old Testament must come after the New Testament so too one had to give those other books a lower standing than the works of the ancient doctors of the church.[147] They would of course become injurious when they blocked the way to the Church Fathers and would be more serviceable to superstition than to piety, just as holding fast to the law had prevented the Jews from attaining to the truth of the Gospel.

> I do think they (i.e. these books) should be not naughtily or impudently rejected or condemned but judiciously subordinated to those that are more wholesome. For as we subordinate the books of the Old Testament to those which Christ, the author of the new covenant, communicated to us, so too we subordinate these and other books of the same character to these outstanding works by famous men . . . But if you ask what in general I think of all the books of this kind, then I would boldly say that, just as that magisterial law which did not serve the teaching of the Gospel is recognized to have been harmful to the

---

[145] *Ibid.* pp. 776f.—On the Erasmus anecdote cf. Béné (cf. note 133) pp. 64ff.

[146] Lips had written to an enthusiastic supporter of Luther's a well-intentioned and sympathetic letter which became known through an indiscretion, so that he was compromised in the eyes of his fellow-monks. The long letter of justification to his prior—in which he tries to deny his real attitude using all the resources of sophistry and dissimulation—bears witness to the awkward situation in which he found himself.

[147] Horawitz (cf. note 124) pp. 778f.

Jews, so too these books unless they were a sort of stepping-stone to the writings of the ancient Doctors of the church make their zealous readers more superstitious than devout.[148]

With the model of a hierarchy of texts, Lips produced a happy compromise in the controversy between humanists and the modern *devoti* which had been brought about by the Reformation: neither radical reduction to the origins nor indiscriminate reception of the continuous tradition was to be determinative for the study of the *libri sacri*. The remarkable feature in this compromise, which regarded and justified the new as leading back to the old, was the fact that it corresponded entirely to the basic concept of the "Devotio moderna". Seuse had already seen the novel teaching of piety in his *Horologium* as pointing the way to the "ancient piety" and had emphasized its congruity with the Bible and the Church Fathers.[149] The dialectic between old and new was described even more impressively by Geert Grote. In his *Sermo de focariis* he describes Christian preaching as a process which, starting from the Word of God, extends through the Bible and the Church Fathers, legal scholars and "modern theologians" right up to the current preaching of the Word, and must likewise be led back again into a *regressio* (backward movement) through these traditional authorities to the divine authority in order to remain in the truth and not be overlaid by human dogma—as in the case of the Jews:

> We must understand the traditions of lawyers and human ordinances and decisions of modern theologians to the extent that they are in accord with the spirit of the holy Fathers and their opinions. And we

---

[148] ... *Non maliciose aut procaciter obiiciendos aut contemnendos (sc. libellos istos), sed prudenter salubrioribus posthabendos censeo. Ut enim veteris Instrumenti libros postponimus iis quos Christus, sanctae novitatis autor, nobis tradidit, ita et hos et alios eiusdem farinae libellos egregiis illis clarorum virorum monumentis posthabemus ... At si roges, quid in totum de istiusmodi libellis sentiam, audacter dixerim: Quemadmodum lex illa imperiosa, quae evangelicae doctrinae non famulabatur, Iudaeis noxia fuisse noscitur, sic et libelli isti, nisi gradus quidam fuerint ad veterum sanctae ecclesiae doctorum scripta, potius superstitiosos reddent sui studiosos quam pios.*—Ibid. (p. 779).

[149] Cf. e.g. Suso, *Horologium*, ed. Künzle (cf. note 1), Prologus, pp. 365f.: "I have set forth in simple style the truths of the Fathers or things experienced which are most certainly attested as true according to Holy Scripture, as I received them from the Lord, by saying of set purpose nothing beyond these truths." (*Veritates quidem patrum vel ea quae comperta sunt certissima attestatione rerum secundum sacrae scripturae sensum, prout accepi a Domino, simplici stilo posui, extra eas a proposito nihil dicendo.*)—*Op. cit.* p. 370: "so that there would be nothing in these things which would be at odds with the Fathers" (... *ut nihil in his esset, quod a dictis sanctorum patrum discreparet.*)

must filter the opinions of the saints back and forth into the canonical writings of each Testament in such a way that we are able to rise through the curtain of the holy writ to the divine light and the divine laws, discerning more clearly the same spirit and the same truth in the writings of both the Old and the New Testament... lest we make ineffective the commands of God and transgress them because of the traditions of men and of our elders, and are condemned in our purblindness, as the Jews have been.[150]

Here the theological scheme of Dionysius the (Pseudo)-Areopagite enabled Grote to have for church tradition an understanding which saw a return to the *fons et origo* implied in each stage of its development. Thus renewal of *pristina perfectio* is not a revolutionary act of liberation from the tradition, but the continuous process of "receiving" it, testing it and going thoroughly into it right back to its starting-point above and beyond history. Thus the "Devotio moderna" was a genuine "catholic" reform, among the unquestionable presuppositions of which is the legitimacy of the Middle Ages, regardless of all the church's criticism.

Transl. James C.G. Greig

Bibliography

Gerhard Achten, "Kartäuser und Devotio moderna. Kleiner Beitrag zur Geschichte der spätmittelalterlichen Mystik" in *Die Geschichte des Kartäuserordens*, vol. 2 (Analecta Cartusiana 125) Salzburg-Lewiston, N.Y., 1992, pp. 154–181.

J.G.R. Acquoy, *Het klooster te Windesheim en zijn invloed*, 3 vols., Utrecht 1875–1880.

Opus Epistolarum Des. Erasmi Roterodami, ed. P.S. Allen, 12 vols., Oxford 1906–1958.

Johannes Trithemius, *De laude scriptorum*, ed. Klaus Arnold (Mainfränkische Hefte 60) Würzburg 1973.

Alfons Auer, *Die vollkommene Frömmigkeit des Christen. Nach dem Enchiridion militis Christiani des Erasmus von Rotterdam*, Düsseldorf 1954.

---

[150] *Sic iurisperitorum traditiones et constitutiones hominum et determinationes modernorum theologorum moderare et intellegere debemus, prout spiritui sanctorum patrum et eorum sententiis congruant. Atque sanctorum sententias debemus in canonicas scripturas utriusque Testamenti sic refundere et infundere, ut eundem spiritum et eandem veritatem in utriusque scripturis Veteris et Novi Testamenti clarius perspicientes per sacrarum scripturarum velamina ad divinum radium et ad divinas leges Altissimi valeamus ascendere... ne cum damnatione nostra more Iudaeorum nimium excaecati irrita faciamus et transgrediamur mandata Dei propter traditiones hominum et seniorum.—Sermo Magistri Gerardi magni, dicti Groot, de Focariis*, ed. J. Clarisse, in *Archief voor Kerkelijke Geschiedenis, inzonderheid van Nederland*, vol. 1, Leiden 1829, pp. 364–379, p. 369.

Cornelis Augustijn, *Erasmus. His Life, Works and Influence*, Toronto-Buffalo-London 1991.

Stephanus Axters, *Geschiedenis van de vroomheid in de Nederlanden*, vol. 3: *De Moderne Devotie*, Antwerp 1956.

Ernst Barnikol, *Studien zur Geschichte der Brüder vom gemeinsamen Leben*, Tübingen 1917.

Columba M. Battle, *Die "Adhortationes sanctorum patrum" ("Verba seniorum") im lateinischen Mittelalter (Beiträge zur Geschichte des alten Mönchtums und des Benediktinerordens* 31) Münster 1972.

Erika Bauer, "Zur Geschichte der 'Hieronymus-Briefe'" in *Festschrift Walter Haug und Burghart Wachinger*, vol. 1, Tübingen 1992 pp. 305–321.

—, "'Hieronymus-Briefe'" in *Die deutsche Literatur des Mittelalters. Verfasserlexikon*, vol. 3, Berlin-New York 1981, cols. 1233–1238.

—, "Die sogenannten 'Hieronymus-Briefe' und ihre volkssprachliche Überlieferung" in *Historia et Spiritualitas Cartusiensis. Colloquii quarti internationalis Acta*, Destelbergen 1983, pp. 21–33.

V. Becker (ed.), "Eene onbekende kronijk van het klooster te Windesheim" in *Bijdragen en Mededelingen van het Historisch Genootschap* 10, 1887, pp. 376–445.

K.C.L.M. de Beer, *Studie over de spiritualiteit van Geert Groote*, Brussels-Nijmegen 1938.

Charles Béné, *Erasme et Saint Augustin*, Geneva 1969.

Jerry H. Bentley, *The Humanists and Holy Writ. New Testament Scholarship in the Renaissance*, Princeton, N.J. 1983.

B. van den Berg, "Geert Grotes's psalmvertaling" in *Nederlandse Taal- en Letterkunde* 61, 1942, pp. 259–314.

Humbertus de Romanis, *Opera de vita regulari*, ed. J.J. Berthier, vol. 2, Rome 1889.

Peter G. Bietenholz, "Erasmus von Rotterdam und der Kult des heiligen Hieronymus" in *Poesis et Pictura. Feschrift D. Wittke*, ed. St. Flüssel—J. Knape, Baden-Baden 1989 pp. 191–221.

August Bludau, *Die beiden ersten Erasmus-Ausgaben des Neuen Testaments und ihre Gegner*, Freiburg im Breisgau 1902.

Gerhard Zerbolt of Zutphen, "De reformatione virium animae" in *Maxima bibliotheca veterum patrum*, ed. Margarinus de la Bigne, vol. 26, Lyon 1677, pp. 235–258.

—, "De spiritualibus ascensionibus" in *Maxima bibliotheca veterum patrum*, ed. Margarinus de la Bigne, vol. 26, Lyon 1677, pp. 258–289.

J. den Boeft, "'Illic aureum quoddam ire flumen': Erasmus' Enthusiasm for the Patres" in *Erasmus of Rotterdam. The Man and the Scholar. Proceedings of the Symposium Rotterdam 1986*, ed. J. Sperna Weiland—W.Th.M. Frijhoff, Leiden-Cologne 1988, pp. 172–181.

G. Bonet-Maury, *Gérard Grote, un précurseur de la Réforme au quatorzième siècle*, Paris 1878.

Collected Works of Erasmus, vol. 61: *Patristic Scholarship. The Edition of St. Jerome*, ed. J.F. Brady—J.C. Olin, Toronto 1992.

Emile Brouette—Reinhold Mokrosch, "Devotio moderna" in *Theologische Realenzyklopädie*, vol. 8, Berlin-New York 1981, pp. 605–616.

C.C. de Bruin, "Bespiegelingen over de 'Bibelvertaler van 1360'. Zijn milieu, werk en persoon" in *Nederlands Archief voor Kerkgeschiedenis*, New Series

48, 1967–68, pp. 39–59; 49, 1968–69, pp. 135–154; 50, 1969–70, pp. 11–27; 51, 1970–71, pp. 16–41.

C.C. de Bruin, "De moderne devotie en de verspreiding van de volkstaalbijbel" in *Ons Geestelijk Erf* 59, 1985, pp. 344–356.

Maria Elisabeth Brunert, *Das Ideal der Wüstenaskese und seine Rezeption in Gallien bis zum Ende des 6. Jahrhunderts*, Münster 1994.

August Buck, "Der Rückgriff des Renaissance-Humanismus auf die Patristik" in *Festschrift W. von Wartburg*, ed. K. Baldinger, Tübingen 1968, pp. 153–175.

Hugonis de Sancto Victore Didascalicon, ed. Charles H. Buttimer, Washington, D.C. 1939.

A.M.J. van Buuren, "'Wat materien gheliken op sonnendage ende hoechtijde te lesen'. Het Middelnederlandse collatieboek van Dirc van Herxen" in *Boeken voor de eeuwigheid. Middelnederlands geestelijk proza*, ed. Th. Mertens *et al.*, Amsterdam 1993, pp. 245–263.

Christopher S. Celenza, "Renaissance Humanism and the New Testament: Lorenzo Valla's annotations to the Vulgate" in *Journal of Medieval and Renaissance Studies* 24, 1994, pp. 33–52.

Jacques Chomarat, "Les Annotations de Valla, celles d'Erasme et la grammaire" in *Histoire de l'exégèse au XVIe siècle*, ed. O. Fatio—P. Fraenkel, Geneva 1978, pp. 202–228.

"Sermo Magistri Gerardi Magni, dicti Groot, de Focariis", ed. J. Clarisse, in *Archief voor Kerkelijke Geschiedenis, inzonderheid van Nederland*, vol. 1, Leiden 1829, pp. 364–379.

"Erasmus von Rotterdam, Capita argumentorum contra morosos quosdam et indoctos" in *D. Erasmi Opera omnia*, ed. Joannes Clericus, 10 volumes, Leiden 1703–1706, vol. 6, fol. ** 5 verso–*** 4 recto.

Joseph Coppens, "Les idées réformistes d'Erasme dans les préfaces aux Paraphrases du Nouveau Testament" in *Scrinium Lovaniense. Mélanges historiques Etienne van Cauwenbergh*, Louvain 1961, pp. 344–371.

Irene Crusius, *Die Brüder vom gemeinsamen Leben in Deutschland*, thesis in typescript, Göttingen 1961.

M.-M. Davy, *Un traité de la vie solitaire*, Paris 1940.

Pierre Debongnie, *Jean Mombaer de Bruxelles, abbé de Livry. Ses écrits et ses réformes*, Louvain-Toulouse 1922.

G.H.M. Delprat, *Verhandeling over de broederschap van G. Groote*, second edition, Arnhem 1856.

Albert Derolez, "A late Medieval Reading-List of the priory of Zevenborren near Brussels" in *Studia varia Bruxellensia ad orbem Greco-Latinum pertinentia*, ed. R. De Smet—H. Melaerts—C. Saerens, Louvain 1990, pp. 21–27.

—, "A Reconstruction of the Library of Zevenborren at the End of the Middle Ages" in *Miscellanea Martin Wittek*, ed. A. Raman—E. Manning, Louvain-Paris 1993, pp. 113–126.

J. Deschamps, *Middelnederlandse handschriften uit Europese en Amerikaanse bibliotheken*. Catalogue, Brussels 1970.

—, "Die mittelniederländischen Übersetzungen der Dialoge Gregors des Großen" in *Bulletin de la Société néophilologique de Helsinki* 53, 1952, pp. 466–470.

—, "De verspreiding van Johan Scutkens vertaling van het Nieuwe Testament en de oudtestamentische perikopen" in *Nederlands Archief voor Kerkgeschiedenis* 56, 1975, pp. 158–179.

—, "Middelnederlandse vertalingen van Super modo vivendi (7de hoofdstuk) en De libris teutonicalibus van Gerhard Zerbolt van Zutphen" in *Koninklijke Zuidnederlandse Maatschappij voor Taal- en Letterkunde en Geschiedenis*. Handelingen 14, 1960, pp. 67–108; 15, 1961, pp. 175–220.

Moderne Devotie, figuren en facetten, Nijmegen 1984.

R.Th.M. van Dijk, "Die Frage einer nördlichen Variante der Devotio moderna: Zur Interferenz zwischen den spätmittelalterlichen Reformbewegungen" in *Wessel Gansfort (1419–1489) and Northern Humanism*, ed. F. Akkerman—G.C. Huisman—A.J. Vanderjagt, Leiden-New York-Cologne 1993, pp. 157–169.

—, "Het Getijdenboek van Geert Grote. Terugblik en vooruitzicht" in *Ons Geestelijk Erf* 64, 1990, pp. 156–194.

Magnus Ditsche, "Zur Herkunft und Bedeutung des Begriffes Devotio Moderna" in *Historisches Jahrbuch* 79, 1960, pp. 124–145.

Rudolf Dier van Muiden, "Scriptum de magistro Gherardo Grote, domino Florencio et multis aliis devotis fratribus" in Gerhard Dumbar (ed.), *Analecta seu vetera aliquot scripta inedita*, vol. 1, Deventer 1719.

Obituaire du monastère de Groenendael, ed. Marc Dykmans, Brussels 1940.

Kaspar Elm, "Die Bruderschaft vom gemeinsamen Leben. Eine geistliche Lebensform zwischen Kloster und Welt, Mittelalter und Neuzeit" in *Ons Geestelijk Erf*, 59, 1985, pp. 470–496.

K.A.E. Enenkel, "Der andere Petrarca: Francesco Petrarcas '*De vita solitaria*' und die *devotio moderna*" in *Quaerendo* 17, 1987, pp. 137–147.

Georgette Epiney-Burgard, "Saint Augustin et la 'vie commune' dans la Dévotion Moderne" in *Medioevo* 9, 1983, pp. 61–75.

—, *Gérard Grote et les débuts de la Dévotion moderne*, Wiesbaden 1970.

—, "Die Wege der Bildung in der Devotio Moderna" in *Lebenslehren und Weltentwürfe im Übergang vom Mittelalter zur Neuzeit*, ed. H. Boockmann—B. Moeller—K. Stackmann, Göttingen 1989, pp. 181–200.

Jacques Etienne, *Spiritualisme érasmien et théologiens louvanistes*, Louvain-Gembloux 1956.

Paul Fredericq (ed.), *Corpus documentorum haereticae pravitatis Neerlandicae*, vol. 2, Ghent-The Hague 1896.

A.J. Geurts, "Boek en tekst bij de Moderne Devoten" in *Ons Geestelijk Erf* 59, 1985, pp. 249–259.

J. de Ghellinck, "Les catalogues des bibliothèques médiévales chez les chartreux et un guide de lectures spirituelles" in *Revue d'Ascétique et de Mystique* 25, 1949, pp. 284–298.

—, *Patristique et Moyen Age*, vol. 3, Brussels-Paris 1948.

Jacob van Ginneken, *Geert Groote's levensbeeld naar de oudste gegevens bewerkt*, Amsterdam 1942.

Heinrich Gleumes, "Gerhard Groot und die Windesheimer als Verehrer des hl. Bernhard von Clairvaux" in *Zeitschrift für Askese und Mystik* 10, 1935, pp. 90–112.

L.A.M. Goossens, *De meditatie in de eerste tijd van de Moderne Devotie*, Haarlem-Antwerp 1952.

Denys Gorce, "La patristique dans la réforme d'Erasme" in *Festgabe J. Lortz*, ed. E. Iserloh—P. Manns, vol. 1: Reformation—Schicksal und Auftrag, Baden-Baden 1958, pp. 233–276.

N. Greitemann, *De Windesheimsche Vulgaatrevisie in de vijftiende eeuw*, Hilversum 1937.

Johannes Busch, *Chronicon Windeshemense und Liber de reformatione monasteriorum*, ed. Karl Grube (*Geschichtsquellen der Provinz Sachsen* 19) Halle 1886.

Karl Grube, *Gerhard Groot und seine Stiftungen*, Cologne 1883.

A. Gruis, "Fragment d'un catalogue ancien de Groenendael ayant servi à la composition du répertoire collectif de Rougecloître" in *Varia codicologica. Essays presented to G.I. Lieftinck*, vol. 1, Amsterdam 1972, pp. 75–86.

J.P. Gumbert, *Die Utrechter Kartäuser und ihre Bücher im frühen fünfzehnten Jahrhundert*, Leiden 1974.

Jean Hadot, "Le Nouveau Testament d'Erasme" in *Colloquium Erasmianum*, Mons 1968, pp. 59–67.

Pierre Hadot, *Exercices spirituels et philosophie antique*, Paris 1981.

Léon E. Halkin, "La 'Devotio moderna' et l'humanisme" in *Réforme et humanisme. Actes du IVième colloque*, Montpellier 1975, pp. 103–112.

—, *Erasmus von Rotterdam. Eine Biographie*, Zürich 1989.

Berndt Hamm, "Hieronymus-Begeisterung und Augustinismus vor der Reformation" in *Augustine, the Harvest, and Theology* (1300–1650). *Essays dedicated to H.A. Oberman*, ed. K. Hagen, Leiden-Cologne 1990, pp. 127–235.

Justus Hashagen, "Die Devotio moderna in ihrer Einwirkung auf Humanismus, Reformation, Gegenreformation und spätere Richtungen" in *Zeitschrift für Kirchengeschichte* 55, 1936, pp. 523–531.

Hans-Peter Hasse, "Ambrosius Blarer liest Hieronymus" in *Auctoritas Patrum. Zur Rezeption der Kirchenväter im 15. und 16. Jahrhundert*, ed. L. Grane—A. Schindler—M. Wriedt, Mainz 1993, pp. 33–53.

M. Haverals, "De scriptoria in de bibliotheken van de Windesheimers in de Zuidelijke Nederlanden" in *Ons Geestelijk Erf* 59, 1985, pp. 260–270.

P. van Herreweghen, "De Leuvense bijbelvertaler Nicolaus van Winghe. Zijn leven en zijn werk" in *Ons Geestelijk Erf* 23, 1949, pp. 5–38, 150–167, 268–314, 357–395.

S. Hieronymi Stridonensis Opera omnia, Frankfurt am Main-Leipzig 1684.

Erasmus, Ausgewählte Werke, ed. Hajo Holborn, Munich 1933.

Heinz Holeczek, *Humanistische Bibelphilologie als Reformproblem bei Erasmus von Rotterdam, Thomas More und William Tyndale*, Leiden 1975.

F.A.H. van den Homberg, *Leven en werk van Jan Brugman O.F.M.*, Groningen 1967.

Volker Honemann, "Zu Interpretation und Überlieferung des Traktats 'De libris teutonicalibus'" in *Miscellanea Neerlandica. Opstellen voor J. Deschamps*, ed. E. Cockx-Indesteege—F. Hendrickx, vol. 3, Louvain 1987, pp. 113–124.

—, "Der Laie als Leser" in *Laienfrömmigkeit im späten Mittelalter*, ed. K. Schreiner, Munich 1992, pp. 241–251.

Adalbert Horawitz, "Erasmus von Rotterdam und Martinus Lipsius. Ein Beitrag zur Gelehrtengeschichte Belgiens" in *Sitzungsberichte der kaiserlichen Akademie der Wissenschaften*, Phil.-Hist. Cl., vol. 100, 2, Vienna 1882.

A. van Hove, "La bibliothèque de la faculté des arts de l'Université de

Louvain au milieu du XVe siècle" in *Mélanges d'histoire offerts à Ch. Moeller*, vol. 1, Louvain 1914, pp. 602–625.

Albert Hyma, *The Christian Renaissance. A history of the "Devotio moderna"*, Grand Rapids, Mich. 1924, 2nd edition, Hamden, Connecticut 1965.

—, "Is Gerard Zerbolt of Zutphen the author of the 'Super modo vivendi'?" in *Nederlandsch Archief voor Kerkgeschiedenis*, New Series 16, 1921, pp. 107–128.

—, "The 'De libris teutonicalibus' by Gerard Zerbolt of Zutphen" in *Nederlandsch Archief voor Kerkgeschiedenis*, New Series 17, 1924, pp. 42–70.

—, "Het traktaat 'Super modo vivendi devotorum hominum simul commorantium' door Gerard Zerbolt van Zutphen" in *Archief voor de Geschiedenis van het Aartsbisdom Utrecht* 52, 1926, pp. 1–100.

J. IJsewijn, "The Coming of Humanism to the Low Countries" in *Itinerarium Italicum, dedicated to P.O. Kristeller*, ed. H.A. Oberman—Th. A. Brady Jr., Leiden 1975, pp. 193–301.

Martta Jaatinen, "Dialogi Gregorii nach der Handschrift Theol. germ. 11 der Stadtbibliothek Lübeck" in *Bulletin de la Société néophilologique de Helsinki* 53, 1952, pp. 82–115.

C.J. Jellouschek, "Ein mittelalterliches Gutachten über das Lesen der Bibel und sonstiger religiöser Bücher in der Volkssprache" in *Aus der Geisteswelt des Mittelalters. Studien und Texte M. Grabmann gewidmet*, 2nd half-volume, Münster 1935, pp. 1181–1199.

Henk Jan de Jonge, "Erasmus und die Glossa Ordinaria zum Neuen Testament" in *Nederlands Archief voor Kerkgeschiedenis*, New Series 56, 1975–76, pp. 51–77.

—, "Wann ist Erasmus' Übersetzung des Neuen Testaments entstanden?" in *Erasmus of Rotterdam. The Man and the Scholar. Proceedings of the Symposium Rotterdam 1986*, ed. J. Sperna Weiland—W.Th.M. Frijhoff, Leiden-Cologne 1988, pp. 151–157.

—, "Novum Testamentum a nobis versum: The Essence of Erasmus' Edition of the New Testament" in *The Journal of Theological Studies*, New Series 35, 1984, pp. 394–413.

Renate Jungblut, *Hieronymus. Darstellung und Verehrung eines Kirchenvaters*, thesis, Tübingen 1967.

Rudolf Kekow, *Luther und die Devotio moderna*, thesis, Hamburg 1937.

Josef Klapper, *Im Kampf um die deutsche Bibel. Zwei Traktate des 14. Jahrhunderts*, Breslau 1922.

Klaus Klein, "Johannes Cassianus" in *Die deutsche Literatur des Mittelalters. Verfasserlexikon*, vol. 4, Berlin-New York 1983, columns 567–570.

—, "Frühchristliche Eremiten im Spätmittelalter und in der Reformationszeit. Zu Überlieferung und Rezeption der deutschen 'Vitaspatrum'-Prosa" in *Literatur und Laienbildung im Spätmittelalter und in der Reformationszeit*, ed. L. Grenzmann—K. Stackmann, Stuttgart 1984, pp. 686–695.

—, *Die Vitaspatrum. Überlieferungsgeschichtliche Untersuchungen zu den Prosaübersetzungen im deutschen Mittelalter*, thesis, Würzburg 1985.

Hermann Knaus, "Ein rheinischer Gesamtkatalog des 15. Jahrhunderts" in *Gutenberg-Jahrbuch* 1976, pp. 509–519.

Ulrich Köpf, "Die Rezeptions- und Wirkungsgeschichte Bernhards von Clairvaux. Forschungsstand und Forschungsaufgaben" in *Bernhard von Clairvaux.*

Rezeption und Wirkung im Mittelalter und in der Neuzeit, ed. K. Elm, Wiesbaden 1994, pp. 5–65.

Monasticon Windeshemense, ed. W. Kohl—E. Persoons—A.G. Weiler, parts 1–4 (*Archief-en Bibliotheekwezen in Belgie*, extra number 16) Brussels 1976–1984.

Wilhelm Kohl, "Die Windesheimer Kongregation" in *Reformbemühungen und Observanzbestrebungen im spätmittelalterlichen Ordenswesen*, ed. K. Elm, Berlin 1989, pp. 83–106.

Friedhelm Krüger, *Humanistische Evangelienauslegung. Desiderius Erasmus von Rotterdam als Ausleger der Evangelien in seinen Paraphrasen*, Tübingen 1986.

Petrus Horn, *Vita Magistri Gerardi Magni*, ed. W.J. Kühler in *Nederlandsch Archief voor Kerkgeschiedenis*, New Series 6, 1909, pp. 325–370.

Heinrich Seuses Horologium Sapientiae, ed. Pius Künzle (*Spicilegium Friburgense* 23) Fribourg, Switzerland 1977.

K. Kunze—U. Williams—Ph. Kaiser, "Information und innere Formung. Zur Rezeption der 'Vitaspatrum'" in *Wissensorganisierende und wissensvermittelnde Literatur im Mittelalter. Perspektiven ihrer Erforschung*, ed. N.R. Wolf, Wiesbaden 1987, pp. 123–142.

J. Leclercq, "Pour l'histoire de l'expression 'philosophie chrétienne'" in *Mélanges de Science Religieuse* 9, 1952, pp. 221–226.

Monasticon Fratrum Vitae Communis, ed. W. Leesch—E. Persoons—A.G. Weiler, parts 1–2 (*Archief-en Bibliotheekwezen in Belgie*, extra number 18) Brussels 1977 and 1979.

Gordon Leff, "The Apostolic Ideal in Later Medieval Ecclesiology" in *Journal of Theological Studies*, New Series 18, 1967, pp. 58–82.

Mittelalterliche Bibliothekskataloge Deutschlands und der Schweiz, vol. 2, ed. P. Lehmann, Munich 1928.

Paul Lehmann, "Bücherliebe und Bücherpflege bei den Karthäusern" in his *Erforschung des Mittelalters*, vol. 3, Stuttgart 1960, pp. 121–142 (first published 1924).

—, "Alte Vorläufer des Gesamtkatalogs" in his *Erforschung des Mittelalters*, vol. 4, Stuttgart 1961, pp. 172–183 (first published 1937).

Carine Lingier, "Over de verspreiding van Sint-Bernardus' liturgische sermoenen in het Middelnederlands" in *Ons Geestelijk Erf* 64, 1990, pp. 18–40.

F. Löser—Ch. Stöllinger-Löser, "Verteidigung der Laienbibel. Zwei programmatische Vorreden des österreichischen Bibelübersetzers der ersten Hälfte des 14. Jahrhunderts" in *Überlieferungsgeschichtliche Editionen und Studien zur deutschen Literatur des Mittelalters. Kurt Ruh zum 75. Geburtstag*, ed. K. Kunze et al. Tübingen 1989, pp. 245–313.

W. Lourdaux, "Het boekenbezit en het boekengebruik bij de Moderne Devoten" in *Studies over het boekenbezit en boekengebruik in de Nederlanden vóór 1600* (*Archief-en Bibliotheekwezen in Belgie*, extra number 11) Brussels 1974, pp. 247–325.

—, *Moderne Devotie en christelijk humanisme. De geschiedenis van Sint-Maarten te Leuven van 1433 tot het einde der XVI^{de} eeuw*, Louvain 1967.

—, "Dévotion moderne et humanisme chrétien" in *The Late Middle Ages and the Dawn of Humanism outside Italy*, ed. G. Verbeke—J. IJsewijn, Louvain-The Hague 1972, pp. 57–77.

—, "Kartuizers—Moderne Devoten. Een probleem van afhankelijkheid" in *Ons Geestelijk Erf* 37, 1963, pp. 402–418.

W. Lourdaux—M. Haverals, *Bibliotheca Vallis S. Martini in Lovanio. Bijdrage tot de studie van het geestesleven in de Nederlanden (15de-18de eeuw)*, vol. 2, Louvain 1982.

Margaret Mann Phillips, *Erasmus and the Northern Renaissance*, Rev. Ed., Woodbridge, Suffolk 1981.

Th. Mertens, "Lezen met de pen. Ontwikkelingen in het laatmiddeleeuws geestelijk proza" in *De studie van de Middelnederlandse letterkunde: stand en toekomst*, ed. F.P. van Oostrom—F. Willaert, Hilversum 1989, pp. 187-200.

—, "Rapiarium" in *Dictionnaire de spiritualité ascétique et mystique* 13, Paris 1988, columns 114-119.

Paul Mestwerdt, *Die Anfänge des Erasmus. Humanismus und "Devotio moderna"*, Leipzig 1917.

J. van Mierlo, "De anonymi uit den katalogus van handschriften van Rooklooster" in *Ons Geestelijk Erf* 4, 1930, pp. 84-102, 316-357.

—, "De hl. Bernardus in de middelnederlandse letterkunde" in *Ons Geestelijk Erf* 27, 1953, pp. 231-258.

—, "Een katalogus van handschriften in Nederlandsche bibliotheken uit 1487" in *Ons Geestelijk Erf* 2, 1928, pp. 275-303.

E. Mikkers, "S. Bernardus en de Moderne Devotie" in *Cîteaux in de Nederlanden*, vol. 4, Westmalle 1953, pp. 149-186.

W. Moll, "Geert Grote's sermoen voor Palmzondag over de vrijwillige armoede" in *Studien en Bijdragen op het Gebied der Historische Theologie* 2, 1872, pp. 425-469.

Gerardi Magni Epistolae, ed. W. Mulder, Antwerp 1933.

Pieter F.J. Obbema, "The Rooklooster Register Evaluated" in *Quaerendo* 7, 1977, pp. 326-353.

Heiko A. Oberman, *Spätscholastik und Reformation*, vol. 2: *Werden und Wertung der Reformation*, Tübingen 1977.

John C. Olin, "Erasmus and Saint-Jerome: an Appraisal of the Bond" in *Erasmus of Rotterdam. The Man and the Scholar. Proceedings of the Symposium Rotterdam 1986*, ed. J. Sperna Weiland—W.Th.M. Frijhoff, Leiden-Cologne 1988, pp. 182-186.

Marjorie O'Rourke Boyle, *Erasmus on Language and Method in Theology*, Toronto-Buffalo 1977.

E. Persoons, "Het intellectuele leven in het klooster Bethlehem in de 15de eeuw" in *Archief-en Bibliotheekwezen in Belgie* 43, 1972, pp. 47-84; 44, 1973, pp. 85-143.

Iohannis Cassiani Opera, Pars I, ed. M. Petschenig (*CSEL* 17) Vienna 1888.

—, *Pars II*, ed. M. Petschenig (*CSEL* 13) Vienna 1886.

Rudolf Pfeiffer, "Erasmus und die Einheit der klassischen und der christlichen Renaissance" in *Historisches Jahrbuch* 74, 1955, pp. 175-188, reprinted in his *Ausgewählte Schriften*, ed. W. Bühler, Munich 1960, pp. 208-221.

Thomas à Kempis, *Opera omnia*, ed. M.J. Pohl, 7 vols., Freiburg im Breisgau 1902-1922.

R.R. Post, *The Modern Devotion*, Leiden 1968.

"Propositum cuiusdam canonici" in *Collationes Brugenses* 14, 1909, pp. 5-21.

Paul Rabbow, *Seelenführung. Methoden der Exerzitien in der Antike*, Munich 1954.

A. Rabil, *Erasmus and the New Testament. The Mind of a Christian Humanist*, San Antonio 1972.

—, "Erasmus's Paraphrases of the New Testament" in *Essays on the Works of Erasmus*, ed. R.L. de Molen, New Haven-London 1978, pp. 145–161.

Fidel Rädle, "Erasmus als Lehrer" in *Lebenslehren und Weltentwürfe im Übergang vom Mittelalter zur Neuzeit*, ed. H. Boockmann—B. Moeller—K. Stackmann, Göttingen 1989, pp. 214–232.

Gerhard Rehm, *Die Schwestern vom gemeinsamen Leben im nordwestlichen Deutschland*, Berlin 1985.

Eugene F. Rice Jr., *Saint Jerome in the Renaissance*, Baltimore-London 1985.

J. van Rooij, *Gerhard Zerbolt van Zutphen*, vol. 1: Leven en Geschriften, Nijmegen-Utrecht-Antwerp 1936.

R.H. and M.A. Rouse, "Bibliography before print: The medieval *De viris illustribus*" in *The Role of the Book in Medieval Culture*, ed. P. Ganz, Turnhout 1986, pp. 133–153; reprinted in their *Authentic Witnesses. Approaches to Medieval Texts and Manuscripts*, Notre Dame, Indiana 1991, pp. 469–494.

Heinrich Rüthing, "Zum Einfluß der Kartäuserstatuten auf die Windesheimer Konstitutionen" in *Ons Geestelijk Erf* 59, 1985, pp. 197–210.

Kurt Ruh, "Augustinus" in *Die deutsche Literatur des Mittelalters. Verfasserlexikon*, vol. 1, Berlin-New York 1978, columns 531–543.

—, "David von Augsburg" in *Die deutsche Literatur des Mittelalters. Verfasserlexikon*, vol. 2, Berlin-New York 1980, columns 47–58.

—, "Gregor der Große" in *Die deutsche Literatur des Mittelalters. Verfasserlexikon*, vol. 3, Berlin-New York 1981, columns 233–244.

Beat M. von Scarpatetti, *Die Kirche und das Augustiner-Chorherrenstift St. Leonhard in Basel*, Basel-Stuttgart 1974.

R.J. Schoeck, *Erasmus of Europe. The Prince of Humanists 1501–1536*, Edinburgh 1993.

Michael Schoengen, *Monasticon Batavum*, Part 1, Amsterdam 1941.

H.J.J. Scholtens, "Iets over de aanleg van boekerijen bij de Kartuizers" in *Huldeboek Bonaventura Kruitwagen aangeboden*, The Hague 1949, pp. 372–388.

Klaus Schreiner, "Laienbildung als Herausforderung für Kirche und Gesellschaft" in *Zeitschrift für historische Forschung* 11, 1984, pp. 257–354.

L. Schulze, "Brüder des gemeinsamen Lebens" in *Realencyklopädie für protestantische Theologie und Kirche*, vol. 3, Leipzig³ 1897, pp. 472–507.

Lewis W. Spitz, *The Religious Renaissance of the German Humanists*, Cambridge, Mass. 1963.

N. Staubach, "Christianam sectam arripe. Devotio moderna und Humanismus zwischen Zirkelbildung und gesellschaftlicher Integration" in *Europäische Sozietätsbewegung und demokratische Tradition*, ed. K. Garber—H. Wismann, 2 vols., Tübingen, 1996, vol. 1, pp. 112–167.

—, "Pragmatische Schriftlichkeit im Bereich der Devotio moderna" in *Frühmittelalterliche Studien* 25, 1991, pp. 418–461.

—, "Der Codex als Ware. Wirtschaftliche Aspekte der Handschriftenproduktion im Bereich der Devotio moderna" in *Der Codex im Gebrauch*, ed. H. Keller—Ch. Meier (printing).

—, "Von der persönlichen Erfahrung zur Gemeinschaftsliteratur: Entstehungs- und Rezeptionsbedingungen geistlicher Reformtexte im Spätmittelalter" in *Ons Geestelijk Erf* 68, 1994, pp. 200–228.

J.G.J. Tiecke, *De werken van Geert Groote*, Utrecht-Nijmegen 1941.

Carl Ullmann, *Reformatoren vor der Reformation*, 2 vols., Hamburg 1841–42, 2nd edition Gotha 1866.

J. Uttenweiler, "Zur Stellung des hl. Hieronymus im Mittelalter" in *Benediktinische Monatsschrift* 2, 1920, pp. 522–541.

J. Van Engen, *Devotio moderna: Basic Writings*, New York 1988.

Luc Versluys, "Enkele aspecten over Groenendaal ten tijde der Hervorming" in *Zoniën* 7, 1983, pp. 54–62.

M.-H. Vicaire, *L'imitation des apôtres. Moines, chanoines et mendiants IVᵉ–XIIIᵉ siècles*, Paris 1963.

Marcel Viller, "Le speculum monachorum et la 'Dévotion moderne' in *Revue d'Ascétique et Mystique* 3, 1922, pp. 45–56.

C.G.N. de Vooys, "Iets over middeleeuwse bijbelvertalingen" in *Theologisch Tijdschrift* 37, 1903, pp. 111–158.

—, "De dietse tekst van het traktaat 'De libris teutonicalibus'" in *Nederlandsch Archief voor Kerkgeschiedenis*, New Series 4, 1906, pp. 113–134.

Willem de Vreese, "Sint Augustinus in het Middelnederlandsch uit de Bibliotheca Neerlandica Manuscripta", in his *Over handschriften en handschriftenkunde. Tien codicologische studien*, ed. P.J.H. Vermeeren, Zwolle 1962, pp. 85–115 (first published 1930).

—, "Een catalogus der handschriften in Nederlandsche kloosters uit het jaar 1487" in his *Over handschriften en handschriftenkunde. Tien codicologische studien*, ed. P.J.H. Vermeeren, Zwolle 1962, pp. 71–84 (first published 1913).

C. van der Wansem, *Het ontstaan en de geschiedenis der Broederschap van het Gemene Leven tot 1400*, Louvain 1958.

Margaret Wesseling, "The Rhetoric of Meditation. Variations on Geert Grote's Translation of the Penitential Psalms found in the Manuscripts of the 15th and 16th Centuries in the Royal Library, Den Haag" in *Ons Geestelijk Erf* 67, 1993, pp. 94–130.

N. van Wijk, *Het Getijdenboek van Geert Grote*, Leiden 1940.

Gerhard B. Winkler, *Erasmus von Rotterdam und die Einleitungsschriften zum Neuen Testament*, Münster 1973.

M. van Woerkum, "Florentius Radewijns: leven, geschriften, persoonlijkheid en ideen" in *Ons Geestelijk Erf* 24, 1950, pp. 337–364.

—, "Het libellus 'Omnes, inquit, artes'—Een rapiarium van Florentius Radewijns" in *Ons Geestelijk Erf* 25, 1951, pp. 113–158, 225–268.

—, *Het libellus "Omnes, inquit, artes", een rapiarium van Florentius Radewijns*, thesis, Louvain 1950, 3 vols.

S.P. Wolfs, "Zum Thema: Seuse und die Niederlande" in *Heinrich Seuse. Studien zum 600. Todestag 1366–1966*, ed. Ephrem M. Filthaut, Cologne 1966, pp. 397–408.

W.C.M. Wüstefeld, *Middeleeuwse boeken van het Catharijneconvent*, Zwolle-Utrecht 1993.

Theodore P. van Zijl, *Gerhard Groote, Ascetic and Reformer (1340–1384)*, Washington, D.C. 1963.

Zöckler, "Hieronymiten" in *Realencyklopädie für protestantische Theologie und Kirche*, vol. 8, Leipzig³ 1900, pp. 40f.